Silent Mystery and
Detective Movies

ALSO BY KEN WLASCHIN AND FROM MCFARLAND

The Silent Cinema in Song, 1896–1929: An Illustrated History and Catalog of Songs Inspired by the Movies and Stars, with a List of Recordings (2009)

Encyclopedia of American Opera (2006)

Gian Carlo Menotti on Screen: Opera, Dance and Choral Works on Film, Television and Video (1999)

Silent Mystery and Detective Movies

A Comprehensive Filmography

KEN WLASCHIN

McFarland & Company, Inc., Publishers
Jefferson, North Carolina, and London

LIBRARY OF CONGRESS CATALOGUING-IN-PUBLICATION DATA

Wlaschin, Ken.
Silent mystery and detective movies : a comprehensive
filmography / Ken Wlaschin.
p.   cm.
Includes bibliographical references and index.

ISBN 978-0-7864-4350-5
softcover : 50# alkaline paper ∞

1. Silent films—Catalogs.   2. Detective and mystery films—Catalogs.
I. Title.
PN1995.75W53   2009   791.43'655 — dc22   2009011891

British Library cataloguing data are available

©2009 Ken Wlaschin. All rights reserved

*No part of this book may be reproduced or transmitted in any form
or by any means, electronic or mechanical, including photocopying
or recording, or by any information storage and retrieval system,
without permission in writing from the publisher.*

On the cover: Jeff Tarrant (Hugh Allan) tracks down
criminals behind a series of fires in *The Fire Detective* (1929)

Manufactured in the United States of America

*McFarland & Company, Inc., Publishers
Box 611, Jefferson, North Carolina 28640
www.mcfarlandpub.com*

Contents

Introduction 1

The Films 3

*Appendix: Authors Whose Stories Were
Filmed in the Silent Era* 249
Bibliography 265
Index 269

Introduction

The popular cinema of the silent era is not as well known as it deserves to be. Standard histories of the cinema tend to emphasize "quality" films and major directors, skipping over "entertainment" genres like detective and mystery movies. And yet these films were among the most popular of the silent era with large audiences around the world.

It is not always easy to find information about these films. Silent cinema enthusiasts may be aware of early American and British Sherlock Holmes movies but are less likely to know of the Danish and German versions. They may know America's Boston Blackie films but are less likely to know European series detectives like Nick Carter, Nat Pinkerton and Miss Nobody.

Silent Mystery and Detective Movies is a comprehensive encyclopedic guide to the famous and the little-known mystery and detective films of the silent cinema, a signpost to a vast and relatively unexplored territory. Most of the films in the guide are American and English but there are also many from Australia, Austria, Canada, Czechoslovakia, Denmark, France, Germany, Hungary, India, Italy, Japan, the Netherlands, Russia and Spain.

There are entries on series, serials, detectives, villains and rogues (there were quite a few) and more than 1500 films. Thrill-a-minute cliffhanger serials are included as they often feature detectives, but most western and espionage films are excluded as they belong to separate genres. There are also illustrations showing scenes from the films, postcards portraits of stars, posters advertising the movies and, when available, the DVD and VHS covers of the films that are on video.

Mystery and detective fiction authors whose work was filmed in the silent era are described in an appendix with cross-references to their movies and illustrations of some of their books.

The book has been designed as a user-friendly guide with entries in alphabetical order and many cross-references. Information about archival prints and DVDs and videos of films is included, though, sadly, fewer than ten percent of these films seem to have survived. I have seen most of the surviving films and, by and large, they are still enjoyable to view. Some are even masterpieces. As I also collect detective fiction and write mysteries (three have been published), I have a lot of empathy for the genre.

Note: Famous sleuths, villains and rogues have entries by last name, e.g., "Holmes, Sherlock." Entries on series and novels that were filmed more than once have an omnibus entry as well as a regular direct entry for each of them.

The Films

Aa mujô—Dai ippen: Hôrô no maki

1923 Japanese film (Shochiku/5 reels) based on Victor Hugo's novel *Les Misérables*. Hiroshi Masakuni played the relentless detective Javert pursuing Masao Inoue as Jean Valjean, Akio Isono was little Gervais, Yukichi Iwata was Thénardier and Hosaku Yoshida was Monsignor Myriel. Daisuke Itô wrote the screenplay and Kiyohiko Ushihara directed. See *Les Misérables* for other films based on the novel.

The Abbey Grange

1922 British film (Stoll/2 reels), an episode in the *Further Adventures of Sherlock Holmes* series based on a story by Sir Arthur Conan Doyle. Sherlock Holmes solves the murder of Sir Eustace Brackenstall. Eille Norwood portrays Holmes with Hubert Willis as Dr. Watson, Madame D'Esterre as Mrs. Hudson, Teddy Arundell, Lawford Davidson, Madeleine Seymour, Leslie Stiles and Madge Tree. Alfred H. Moise was the cinematographer and George Ridgewell wrote the adaptation and directed. Print survives at BFI archive.

Die Abenteurer G.m.b.H. (Adventurers Inc.)

1928 German film (Orplid Film/6 reels) based on Agatha Christie's 1922 novel *The Secret Adversary* which introduced private detectives Tommy and "Tuppence" Beresford. It has a complicated plot with a disappearing client, numerous disguises and a good deal of historical intrigue including the sinking of the *Lusitania*. The villain, as with most Christie plots, is the last person we would have suspected. Scriptwriter Jane Bess changed the names of the detecting duo to Pierre and Lucienne for unexplainable reasons. They're played by Carlo Aldini and Hilda Bayley with a supporting cast including Eve Gray, Eberhard Leithoff, Elfriede Borodin and Hans Mierendorff. Fred Sauer directed.

The Ace of Hearts

1921 American film (Goldwyn/6 reels) based on a story by Gouverneur Morris probably inspired by Edgar Wallace's *The Four Just Men*. Members of a bomb-throwing secret society plan to kill off people they don't like and select the assassins by drawing cards; the person drawing the Ace of Hearts does the dirty deed. Forrest (John Bowers), who loves society member Lilith (Leatrice Joy), "wins" the draw but refuses to explode the bomb when he

Dangerous Lon Chaney is a disillusioned bomber in *The Ace of Hearts*.

finds innocent people will be killed. The society votes to get rid of him but disillusioned member Farralone (Lon Chaney) uses the bomb to blow up the society itself. Ruth Wightman wrote the screenplay and Wallace Worsley directed.

The Ace of Scotland Yard

1929 American serial (Universal/ten 2-reel chapters), the sequel to *Blake of Scotland Yard* describing further adventures of retired Scotland Yard detective Angus Blake. This time Blake (Cranford Kent) does battle with the Queen of Diamonds (Grace Cunard) as she attempts to steal a valuable ring. Lord Blanton (Herbert Prior), the father of Blake's fiancée Lady Diana (Florence Allen), has acquired the famous "Love Ring" stolen long ago from a palace in the Gobi Desert. Prince Darius (Albert Prisco), a descendent of the family that originally owned the ring, has sworn to recover it and has enlisted the aid of the master criminal Queen of Diamonds.

The serial, written by Harold M. Atkinson and directed by Ray Taylor, was released in silent and sound versions. The chapter titles, in order of release, were *The Fatal Circlet, A Cry in the Night, The Dungeon of Doom, The Depths of Limehouse, Menace of the Mummy, Dead or Alive, Shadows of Fear, The Baited Trap, A Battle of Wits* and *The Final Judgment*.

The Ace of Spades

1925 American serial (Universal/fifteen 2-reel chapters) Villains attempt to terrify their opponents by sending Ace of Spades death cards as warnings while they seek a lost survey map. The map, showing mineral deposits, dates back to the Louisiana Purchase but the film is mainly set in 1889 during the Oklahoma land rush. William Desmond and Mary McAllister are the hero and hero but William P. De Vaul got to play Napoleon and John Herdman was Thomas Jefferson. Isadore Bernstein and William Lord Wright wrote the semi-historical screenplay and Henry McRae directed. The episodes are titled *The Fatal Card, No Greater Love, Whirling Waters, Fires of Sacrifice, Thundering Hoofs, Flung from the Sky, Trail of Terror, Lariat of Death, Fingers of Fate, Road to Ruin, Chasm of Peril, The Avalanche, The Fury of Fate, Chasm of Courage* and *A Deal of Destiny*.

The Acid Test

1924 British film (Stoll/2 reels) based on a story by Austin Philips, an episode in the series *Thrilling Stories from the Strand*. Eric Bransby Williams, Betty Fare, Eric Hardin and Hal Martin star under the direction of Sinclair Hill.

The Acquittal

1923 American film (Universal/7 reels) based on the 1920 play *The Acquittal* by Rita Weiman. The adopted sons of a millionaire love the same woman and this causes a lot of bad feelings. When the father is killed, one son is put on trial for the murder while the other, a district attorney, is the prosecutor. The accused son is proven innocent and then breaks down and confesses he really did it. With Norman Kerry, Richard Travers, Claire Windsor and Barbara Bedford. Raymond L. Schrock made the adaptation of the play, Jules Furthman wrote the screenplay and Clarence Brown directed.

Acquitted

1916 American film (Triangle/5 reels) based on Mary Roberts Rinehart's 1907 mystery story "Acquitted." Bookkeeper John Carter (Wilfred Lucas) is accused of murdering a cashier and appears guilty when interrogated by police detectives James O'Shea and F. A. Turner. A reporter (Elmer Clifton), who loves Carter's daughter (Bessie Love), investigates and proves the night watchman was the killer. Carter is freed but his boss (Sam De Grasse) won't give him his job back. When Carter tries to kill himself, the boss relents. Paul Powell directed and Roy Somerville wrote the screenplay.

The Active Life of Dolly of the Dailies

1914 American serial (Edison/twelve 1-reel episodes) starring Mary Fuller as a newspaper reporter in the big city who has to act as an investigating detective in many episodes, including one titled *Dolly Plays Detective*. Because of this she often finds herself in danger. The supporting cast included Gladys Hulette, Charles Ogle and Miriam Nesbitt. Walter Edwin directed and Acton Davies wrote the screenplays. The episodes, in order of release, were *The Perfect Truth, The Ghost of Mother Eve, An Affair of Dress, Putting One over, The Chinese Fan, On the Heights, The End of the Umbrella, A Tight Squeeze, A Terror of the Night, Dolly Plays Detective, Dolly at the Helm* and *The Last Assignment*.

The Adventure of the Actress's Jewels

1914 American comedy (Edison/1 reel) in the series *Octavius, Amateur Detective* about an amateur detective who bumbles his way through various adventures and solves crimes through pure luck. Herbert Yost (using the name Barry O'Moore) played Octavius. In this adventure Octavius investigates the theft of jewelry from an actress. Frederic Arnold Kummer wrote the screenplay and Charles M. Seay directed.

The Adventure of the Alarm Clock

1914 American comedy (Edison/1 reel) in the series *Octavius, Amateur Detective* about an amateur detective who stumbles his way through cases that he solves by wildly good luck. Herbert Yost (using the name Barry O'Moore) played Octavius. In this adventure Octavius has problems with an alarm clock. Frederic Arnold Kummer wrote the screenplay and Charles M. Seay directed.

The Adventure of the Ambassador's Disappearance

1912 American film (Vitagraph/1 reel), one of eight films featuring detective Lambert Chase. Modeled on Sherlock Holmes, Chase was created for the Vitagraph Studio by writer B. R. Brooker and actor Maurice Costello who portrayed him in all the films. Charles Eldridge played the Ambassador, Earle Williams was Walter Cross, Robert Gaillard and Barney Reed were the thieves and Rosemary Theby was the nurse. B. R. Brooker wrote the screenplay and Costello directed. See Chase, Lambert for the other films.

Demure Bessie Love is the daughter of a murder suspect in *Acquitted*.

Mary Fuller is an investigative reporter in the Edison serial *The Active Life of Dollie of the Dailies*.

The Adventure of the Copper Beeches

1912 Anglo-French film (Franco British Film Company–Éclair/2 reels), an episode in the *Sherlock Holmes* series based on a story by Sir Arthur Conan Doyle. Sherlock Holmes solves a mystery involving a woman who takes a post as governess at a place called Copper Beeches. George Treville played Sherlock Holmes with M. Moyse as Dr. Watson and British actors in the supporting roles. Treville also directed in collaboration with Conan Doyle. This film survives and is on video. See Holmes, Sherlock for other films.

The Adventure of the Counterfeit Bills

1912 American film (Vitagraph/1 reel), one of eight films featuring detective Lambert Chase. Modeled on Sherlock Holmes, Chase was created for the Vitagraph Studio by writer B. R. Brooker and actor Maurice Costello who portrayed him in all the films. The supporting cast included Tefft Johnson, L. Rogers Lytton, Charles Eldridge and Edna Holland. B. R. Brooker wrote the screenplay and Costello directed. See Chase, Lambert for the other films.

The Adventure of the Counterfeit Money

1914 American comedy (Edison/1 reel) in the series *Octavius, Amateur Detective* about an amateur detective who bumbles his way through cases which he solves by pure good luck. Herbert Yost (as Barry O'Moore) played Octavius. In this adventure Octavius decides to investigate counterfeit money. Frederic Arnold Kummer wrote the screenplay and Charles M. Seay directed.

The Adventure of the Extra Baby

1914 American comedy (Edison/1 reel) in the series *Octavius, Amateur Detective* about an amateur detective who bumbles his way through investigations. Herbert Yost (using the name Barry O'Moore) played Octavius. In this adventure Octavius investigates and finds there is one baby too many. Frederic Arnold Kummer wrote the screenplay and Charles M. Seay directed.

The Adventure of the Hasty Elopement

1914 American comedy (Edison/1 reel) in the series *Octavius, Amateur Detective* about an amateur detective who bumbles his way through various adventures. Herbert Yost (as Barry O'Moore) played Octavius. In this adventure Octavius buys a car and decides to investigate car thefts. His car is stolen by a woman rushing to get married, he steals a car to chase her and the police chase after them both. Frederic Arnold Kummer wrote the screenplay and Charles M. Seay directed. Film is on DVD.

The Adventure of the Italian Model

1912 American film (Vitagraph/1 reel), one of eight films featuring detective Lambert Chase. Modeled on Sherlock Holmes, Chase was created for the Vitagraph Studio by writer B. R. Brooker and actor Maurice Costello who portrayed him in all the films. Leah Baird played the model, Rose Tapley was the model's mother, James Morrison was the artist, and George Cooper was the killer. B. R. Brooker wrote the screenplay and Van Dyke Brooke directed. See Chase, Lambert for the other films.

The Adventure of the Lost Wife

1914 American comedy (Edison/1 reel) in the series *Octavius, Amateur Detective* about an amateur detective who bumbles his way through various adventures. Herbert Yost (as Barry O'Moore) played Octavius. In this adventure Octavius investigates a missing wife. Frederic Arnold Kummer wrote the screenplay and Charles M. Seay directed.

The Adventure of the Missing Legacy

1914 American comedy (Edison/1 reel) in the series *Octavius, Amateur Detective* about an amateur detective who and various adventures. Herbert Yost played Octavius. In this adventure Octavius investigates a missing legacy. Frederic Arnold Kummer wrote the screenplay and Charles M. Seay directed.

The Adventure of the Retired Army Colonel

1912 American film (Vitagraph/1 reel), one of eight films featuring detective Lambert Chase. Modeled on Sherlock Holmes, Chase was created for the Vitagraph Studio by writer

B. R. Brooker and actor Maurice Costello who portrayed him in all the films. Van Dyke Brooke played the retired army colonel, Robert Gaillard was the police constable and Edward Thomas was the chief of police. B. R. Brooker wrote the screenplay and Van Dyke Brooke directed. See Chase, Lambert for the other films.

The Adventure of the Smuggled Diamonds

1914 American comedy (Edison/1 reel) in the series *Octavius, Amateur Detective* about an amateur detective who bumbles his way through adventures. Herbert Yost (as Barry O'Moore) played Octavius. In this adventure he investigates diamond smuggling. Frederic Arnold Kummer wrote the screenplay and Charles M. Seay directed.

The Adventure of the Stolen Slipper

1914 American comedy (Edison/1 reel) in the series *Octavius, Amateur Detective* about an inept amateur detective. Herbert Yost (as Barry O'Moore) played Octavius. In this adventure Octavius investigates the theft of a slipper. Frederic Arnold Kummer wrote the screenplay and Charles M. Seay directed.

The Adventure of the Thumb Print

1912 American film (Vitagraph/1 reel), one of eight films featuring detective Lambert Chase. Modeled on Sherlock Holmes, Chase was created for the Vitagraph Studio by writer B. R. Brooker and actor Maurice Costello who portrayed him in all the films. The supporting cast included Van Dyke Brooke, Rose Tapley and George Cooper. B. R. Brooker wrote the screenplay and Van Dyke Brooks directed. See Chase, Lambert for other films.

The Adventure of the Wrong Santa Claus

1914 American comedy (Edison/1 reel) in the series *Octavius, Amateur Detective* about an amateur detective who bumbles his way through adventures. Herbert Yost (as Barry O'Moore) played Octavius. In this adventure Octavius is asked to play Santa Claus for a family and buys a Santa Claus costume for the occasion. Unfortunately they already have one and it is donned by a burglar who knocks out Octavius and robs the family. Octavius pursues him. Frederic Arnold Kummer wrote the screenplay and Charles M. Seay directed. Film is on DVD.

The Adventure of the Yellow Curl Papers

1915 American film (IMP-Universal/2 reels) based on the story "The Adventure of the Yellow Curl Papers" by Hugh C. Weir. Violet Mersereau and William Garwood starred while Clem Easton wrote the screenplay and directed. Weir was the creator of the pioneer female detective Madelyn Mack.

The Adventures of Dorcas Dene, Detective

1919 British film series (Life Dramas/four 2-reel episodes) based on stories by George R. Sims. Dorcas Dene is an actress who has became a detective to earn money after her husband is blinded. She is gifted at disguise. The series starred Winifred Rose as Dorcas Dene and Tom Radford as her husband Paul. The episodes are titled *The Blackmailer, A Well-Planned West End Jewel Robbery, An Insurance Fraud* and *A Murder in Limehouse*. Frank Carlton directed them. See also *Dene, Dorcas*.

The Adventures of Joe Fock

(Dobrodružství Joe Focka)

1918 Czechoslovakian comedy (Weteb/2 reels) featuring detective Joe Fock. This was the first of a proposed ten-film series but it is now lost and its plot is unknown. Václav Binovec directed, Vladimír Novotný wrote the screenplay and Alois Jalovec was the cinematographer. Vladimír Novotný and Joe Novotný headed the cast that included Hana Jenčiková, František Pelíšek, Josef Smetana and Luigi Hofman.

The Adventures of Kathlyn

1913 American serial (Selig/thirteen 2-reel chapters) based on a novel by Harold MacGrath. This was the first true serial and it cre-

Pundita (Goldie Colwell, right) seizes Kathlyn (Kathlyn Williams) in a tense moment in the Selig serial *The Adventures of Kathlyn.*

ated the format for the mystery/suspense serial with continued-next-week endings to each chapter and a powerful villain out to destroy the heroine. MacGrath, one of the most popular genre writers of the era, deserves a lot of credit for helping create the serial vogue in collaboration with screenplay writer Gilson Willets, director Francis J. Grandon and star Kathlyn Williams. The story revolves around Williams' adventures in India fighting the villainous Umballah (Charles Clary) and many of the more dangerous animals in the Selig Zoo. The episodes were titled *The Unwelcome Throne, The Two Ordeals, The Temple of the Lion, The Royal Slave, A Colonel in Chains, Three Bags of Silver, The Garden of Brides, The Cruel Crown, The Spellbound Multitude, The Warrior Maid, The Forged Parchment, The King's Will* and *The Court of Death.*

The Adventures of Lieutenant Petrosino

1912 American film (Feature Photoplay/4 reels) based on the life of Italian-American detective Joseph Petrosino. Petrosino's investigates the murder of a banker by the Black Hand Society. He traces the crime to a ragpicker but is knocked out while pursuing him. When Black Hand members flee to Sicily, Petrosino follows but is killed by a Black Hand assassin in Palermo. He is brought home and hailed as a martyr. Sidney M. Goldin directed. The 1960 film *Pay or Die* starring Ernest Borgnine was also based on Petrosino's life.

The Adventures of P. C. Sharpe

1911 British series (Cricks and Martin/two 1-reel films) about a police constable who turns detective to track down counterfeiters and kidnappers. He gets a bit knocked around while do it. In *The Adventures of P. C. Sharpe* he disguises himself to follow a counterfeiter and gets thrown down a well. In *The Adventures of P. C. Sharpe: The Stolen Child*, he follows a crooked governess and gets tied to a railroad track. A. E. Colby directed both films.

The Adventures of Ruth

1919 American serial (Pathé/fifteen 2-reel

Ruth (Ruth Roland) turns detective in the Pathé serial *The Adventures of Ruth.*

chapters). Ruth (Ruth Roland) turns detective to find a lost peacock fan which has an important secret. She also has to locate a stolen painting, solve a forgery, catch bank robbers, disentangle a mistaken identity, carry out instructions on thirteen keys and keep from getting killed. The supporting cast includes Herbert Heyes, Thomas Lingham, Charles Bennett and Helen Case. Gilson Willets wrote the imaginative screenplay and George Marshall directed. The episodes are *The Wrong Countess, The Celestial Maiden, The Bewitching Spy, The Bank Robbery, The Border Fury, The Substitute Messenger, The Harem Model, The Cellar Gangsters, The Forged Check, The Trap, The Vault of Terror, Within Hollow Walls, The Fighting Chance* and *The Key to Victor.*

The Adventures of Sherlock Holmes

1921 British series (Stoll/fifteen 2-reel episodes and a 5-reel feature) starring Eille Norwood as Holmes, Hubert Willis as Dr. Watson, Arthur Bell as Inspector Lastrade and Madame d'Esterre as Mrs. Hudson. Maurice Elvey directed the films from screenplays by William J. Elliott based on the Doyle stories. Norwood, who modeled himself on Sidney Paget's illustrations of Holmes, had great success in the role and played him again on stage and cinema. The films are *The Beryl Coronet, A Case of Identity, The Copper Beaches, The Devil's Foot, The Dying Detective, The Empty House, The Hound of the Baskervilles* (5 reels), *The Man with the Twisted Lip, The Noble Bachelor, The Priory School, The Red-Headed League, The Resident Patient, A Scandal in Bohemia, The Solitary Cyclist, The Tiger of San Pedro* and *The Yellow Face.* These films survive at the BFI film archive and some are on video. See Holmes, Sherlock for other films.

The Adventures of Sherlock Holmes; or, Held for a Ransom

1905 American film (Vitagraph/1 reel) with Maurice Costello portraying the great detective Sherlock Holmes and H. Kyrle Bellew playing Dr. Watson. J. Stuart Blackton directed and Theodore A. Liebler, Jr., wrote the screenplay. See also Holmes, Sherlock.

Maurice Costello played Sherlock Holmes in a 1905 American film.

The Affair at the Novelty Theatre

1924 British film (Stoll/2 reels), an episode in the *Old Man in the Corner* series based on a story by Baroness Orczy. An armchair detective known as the Old Man in the Corner solves crimes while sitting in a tea shop and tells the solutions to a young woman journalist named Mary Hatley. In this episode he solves the mystery surrounding the theft of a pearl necklace from an actress at the Novelty Theater. Rolf Leslie played the Old Man and Renée Wakefield was Mary Hatley with supporting cast of Phyllis Lyton, Moore Marriott, Walter Tennyson and Charles Vane, D. P. Cooper was the cinematographer and Hugh Croise wrote the adaptation and directed.

An Affair of Three Nations

1915 American film (5 reels) based on the story "An Affair of Three Nations" by John Thomas McIntyre in *Ashton-Kirk: Secret Agent.* Detective Ashton-Kirk is asked by Stella Morse (Louise Rutter) to find who is threatening her uncle Dr. Morse (Sheldon Lewis). Morse has a copy of a secret treaty between Russia and the United States made during the Russo-Japanese War. Morse is killed despite the detective's protection but he is still able to deliver the treaty to the American government. See Ashton-Kirk for other films.

L'Affaire des bijoux (The Jewel Affair)

1908 French film (Éclair/1 reel), an episode in the *Nick Carter, le roi des détectives* series about the master detective Nick Carter. It was distributed in America *The Great Jewel Affair*. In this episode Carter investigates the theft of valuable jewels. Pierre Bressol played Nick Carter and Victorin Jassett wrote and directed the film.

L'Affaire d'Orcival

1914 French film (Éclair/3 reels) based on Émile Gaboriau's 1867 novel *Le Crime d'Orcival* (The Orcival Crime) featuring the French detective Monsieur Lecoq. A countess is found murdered in the village of Orcival and the count has disappeared. Lecoq investigates. Gérard Bourgeois wrote and directed the film starring Henry Roussell, Henry Gouget, Jules Mondos and Fernande Van Doren. *The Mystery of Orcival* is based on the same book.

L'Affaire du train 24
(The Case of Train 24)

1921 French serial (Pathé Frères/eight 2-reel episodes) based on André Bencey's novel *L' affaire du train 24* adapted by J. Mandemant and directed by Gaston Leprieur. André Muzillac (Adolphe Cande) flees to South America after defrauding his employer and leaves a pregnant fiancée behind. He returns 25 years later as a rich married banker and hires his son Jacques as an assistant. When Muzillac is murdered, Jacques is the top suspect. Detective William Baluchet (Georges Mauloy) proves that the murderer is an old accomplice. The cast included Jeanne Brindeau, Philippe Damorés and Eugénie Nau. The episodes were *Fautes de jeunesse, L'Ombre du passe, Baluchet opère lui-meme, A la recherche de l'inconnu, Le Rapide do Bordeaux, Contre-enquête, Une Lueur dans les tenèbres* and *Baluchet triomphe*. See also Baluchet, William.

After Dark

1924 British film (Stoll/2 reels) based on story by Bertram Atkey, an episode in the series *Thrilling Stories from the Strand*. With Eric Bransby Williams, Joyce Dearsley, Gertrude Sterroll and John Hamilton. Thomas Bentley directed.

Alias Jimmy Valentine

The character of Jimmy Valentine originated in O Henry's 1909 story *A Retrieved Reformation* which was then transformed by Paul Armstrong into the 1910 Broadway play *Alias Jimmy Valentine*. Valentine, a master safecracker, has reformed and now lives honestly in a small town. A detective, who has been chasing him for a year, arrives on the day a little girl gets locked in a bank vault. If Valentine opens the safe the detective will know that he is the safecracker and send him back to prison. He opens the safe all the same and waits to be arrested but the detective tells him he is not the man he was seeking. The story was filmed three times in the silent era (see below).

Alias Jimmy Valentine

1915 American film (World/5 reels) starring Robert Warwick as Jimmy Valentine,

Robert Warwick plays cracksman Jimmy Valentine in the 1915 film *Alias Jimmy Valentine*.

Robert Cummings as Detective Doyle, Ruth Shepley as Valentine's sweetheart Rose, Fred Truesdell as her father, Alec B. Francis as Bill Avery; John Hines as Red Joclyn, David Flanagan as Cotton and John Boone was Blinkey Davis. Maurice Tourneur directed. The film survives in archives and is on video.

Alias Jimmy Valentine

1920 American film (Metro/5 reels) starring Bert Lytell as Jimmy Valentine, Wilton Taylor as Detective Doyle, Vola Vale as his sweetheart Rose, Eugene Pallette as "Red" Jocelyn. Marc Robbins as Bill Avery, Robert Dunbar as Lt. Governor Fay, Winter Hall as William Lane and James Farley as Cotton. Edmund Mortimer directed, Finis Fox wrote the screenplay and Sol Polito was the cinematographer.

Alias Jimmy Valentine

1928 American film (MGM/8 reels) starring William Haines as Valentine, Lionel Barrymore as Detective Doyle, Leila Hyams as Rose, Karl Dane as Swede, Tully Marshall as Avery and Evelyn Mills as Rose's little sister. A. P. Younger wrote the screenplay and Jack Conway directed. The film is silent but it has a music soundtrack.

Alias Ladyfingers

1921 American film (Metro/6 reels) based on the 1920 mystery novel *Ladyfingers* by Jackson Gregory. Ladyfingers is gentleman thief Robert Ashe (Bert Lytell), an orphan raised by a safecracker who has becomes the best cracksman in the business. He has fallen in love with Enid (Ora Carew), the ward of wealthy Mrs. Stetherill (Edythe Chapman), and thinks his chances of winning her are poor. While attending a charity ball at Mrs. Stetherill's house a string of pearls disappears and the police suspect him. However, the pearls are returned and Mrs. Stetherill learns that Ladyfingers is her grandson, the son of a disowned daughter. He decides to reform so he can marry Enid. Lenore J. Coffee wrote the screenplay and Bayard Veiller directed.

Bert Lytell is gentleman thief Robert Ashe in the Metro film *Alias Ladyfingers*.

Alias Mary Brown

1918 American film (Triangle/5 reels) Dick Browning (Casson Ferguson) has been cheated of his inheritance by crooked financiers so he decides to steal from them in return. He dresses as society woman Mary Brown and joins a gang that includes Betty (Pauline Starke). After two successful thefts, he is double-crossed by a gang member but is able to escape with Betty. They decide it is time to go straight. E. Magnus Ingleton wrote the screenplay and H. D'Elba directed.

Alias the Lone Wolf

1927 American film (Columbia/7 reels) based on the 1921 novel *Alias the Lone Wolf* by Louis Joseph Vance. Eve de Montalais (Lois Wilson) asks Michael Lanyard (Bert Lytell) to help her smuggle jewels into the US after he thwarts a gang's plan to steal them on a ship. When Eve discovers Lanyard is The Lone Wolf, she gives the jewels to a crook pretending to be a customs agent. Lanyard declares the jewels to real customs officials who arrest the gang. Eve learns that Lanyard is actually a Secret Service agent. Dorothy Howell and Edward H. Griffith wrote the screenplay and Griffith directed. (For other films with this character see *The Lone Wolf*.)

Alias the Night Wind

1923 American film (Fox/5 reels) based on the novel *Alias the Night Wind* by Varick Vanardy (pseudonym of Frederic Van Rensselaer Dey) published in *The Cavalier* magazine in 1913. Bing Howard (William Russell) is called the Night Wind by the police because he is a fugitive from justice who seems able to vanish at will. He is very strong and has a tendency to thrown policeman around He is being chased by Clifford Rushton (Donald MacDonald), the detective who framed him for a robbery. When Rushton fails, the head of the detective bureau turns the case over to Katherine Maxwell (Maude Wayne) whose brother was sent to prison on the same evidence that convicted Howard. Katherine, known as Lady Kate, falls in love with the Night Wind and becomes convinced that Rushton is the real criminal. Robert

N. Lee wrote the screenplay and Joseph Franz directed. Dey wrote three other novels featuring the Night Wind but they were not filmed.

The Alibi

1916 American film (Vitagraph/5 reels) based on the 1916 mystery novel *The Alibi* by George Allan England published in *All Story Weekly*. Enid (Betty Howe) hires a detective to help free Arthur Mansfield (James Morrison) who was falsely imprisoned for murder after an embezzlement scheme went wrong. The detective proves Mansfield's innocence and the real murderer commits suicide. George H. Plympton wrote the screenplay and Paul Scardon directed.

The Alibi

1917 American film (Monmouth/2 reels), an episode in the serial *Jimmy Dale Alias the Grey Seal*) based on stories by Frank L Packard. Socialite Jimmy Dale, secretly the crime fighter known as The Grey Seal, is an urban Robin Hood. In this episode he has problems with an alibi. Mildred Considine wrote the screenplay and McRae Webster directed.

William Russell, who plays the super strong Night Wind, throws policeman around with ease in the film *Alias the Night Wind* (also shown on a book cover).

Alibi

1929 American film (UA-Feature Productions/10 reels) based on the 1927 play *Nightstick* by John Griffith Wray, J. C. Nugent and Elaine S. Carrington. Detective's daughter Joan Manning (Eleanor Griffiths) marries gangster Chick Williams (Chester Morris) thinking he has reformed. He hasn't. He uses her for an alibi when he commits a robbery and kills a policeman. When the police plant a spy in his gang, he kills him as well but this time there is no alibi. Roland West directed and wrote the screenplay with C. Gardner Sullivan.

All the Winners

1920 British film (Samuelson/6 reels) based on the English mystery novel *Wicked* by Arthur Applin who wrote the screenplay. A rich sportsman (Owen Nares) is blackmailed by a clever woman who wants him to force his daughter to marry a criminal. The cast included Maudie Dunham, Sam Livesey, Maidie Hope and Ena Beaumont. Geoffrey H. Malins directed.

All the World's a Stage

1917 British film (5 reels) based on a novel by Herbert Everett. Eve Balfour stars as Lavender Lawn, a woman framed for the murder of her producer mentor by the jealous actress who actually shot him. After many complications she marries a fisherman who is secretly the son of a rich man and gets her name cleared. The supporting cast included Esme Beringer, James Lindsay, Judd Green and Leslie Howard Gordon. Leslie Howard Gordon wrote the screenplay and Harold Weston directed.

Alone in London

1915 British film (Turner Films/4 reels) based on a play by Robert Buchanan and Harriet Jay. A really old-fashioned murder mystery made by Americans Lawrence Trimble (director) and Florence Turner (star) during their cinematic sojourn in England. It even includes a girl being tied to the lock gates of a canal by a nefarious villain. The plot revolves around an attempt to turn a good man into a thief. The supporting cast included Henry Edwards, Edward Lingard, James Lindsay and Amy Lorraine.

Florence Turner stars in the old-fashioned British murder mystery *Alone in London.*

The Alster Case

1915 American film (Essanay/5 reels) based on a 1914 novel by Rufus Gillmore. Pri-

Bryant Washburn plays a double game in *The Alster Case.*

vate detective Trask (John H. Cossar) is hired by George Swan (Bryant Washburn) to investigate the murder of wealthy spinster Cornelia Alster (Louise Crolius). Clues lead him to suspect Beatrice (Ruth Stonehouse) and Linda (Betty Scott), the wards of the spinster, whom she had caught with men in their rooms the night before her murder. Trask exonerates them and proves Swan himself killed Alster to save the girls' reputation. *Variety* said the story was interesting with a good surprise ending but didn't have enough stars for a feature. J. Charles Haydon directed.

The Amateur Detective

1907 American film (Kalem/half reel), one of the earliest detective films made by the Kalem studio which began to specialize in the genre. Frank Marion wrote the screenplay and Sidney Olcott directed.

The Amateur Detective

1914 American comedy (Thanhauser/2 reels). Cook Jane (Carey L. Hastings) convinces her policeman sweetheart Pat (Ernest C. Warde) that he is another Sherlock Holmes and they think they have discovered a Black Hand plot when they find mysterious signs on a wall. They are actually messages from Jack (Harris Gordon) to his sweetheart (Muriel Ostriche) but he pretends to be a detective to solve the case. Carroll Fleming directed.

The Amateur Detective

1925 American comedy (Fox/2 reels) based on Richard Harding Davis's short story *The Amateur* and starring Earle Foxe as newspaperman who fancies himself an amateur detective. The film was publicized as the eighth episode in the *Adventures of Van Bibber* series. Robert P. Kerr directed.

Der Amateur-Detektiv

(The Amateur Detective)

1910 German film (Deutsche Bioscop/1 reel). No plot information available.

Der Amateur-Detektiv

(The Amateur Detective)

1915 German film (Deutsche Bioscop/2 reels). No plot information available.

The Amazing Impostor

1919 American film (American Film Co./5 reels) based on a story by Joseph Franklin Poland. Joan Hope (Mary Miles Minter) is a naïve romantic who agrees to switch identities with the Russian Countess of Crex (Margaret Shelby) not knowing she is a jewel thief. After Joan ends up in possession of a diamond necklace the countess stole, she is pursued by detective Kent Standish (Allan Forrest), a gang of jewel thieves and Bolshevik agents. All ends well after some hectic chases. Frank Howard Clark wrote the screenplay and Lloyd Ingraham directed.

Mary Miles Minter switches identities with a jewel thief in *The Amazing Imposter.*

Amazing Lovers

1921 American film (Jans Film Service/6 reels) based on a story by Charles A. Logue who wrote the screenplay. French Secret Service agent Yvonne La Rue (Diana Allen) goes undercover and infiltrates a French counterfeiting ring. She is sent to America by the gang where she meets the banker masterminding the scheme. After the French gangleader kills the banker during a row, she arrests the whole gang. With Marc MacDermott, Eugene Strong and E. J. Ratcliffe. B. A. Rolfe directed.

The Amazing Partnership

1921 British film (Stoll/5 reels) based on the novel *The Amazing Partnership* by E. Phillips Oppenheim. Detective Grace Burton (Gladys Mason) forms a partnership with reporter Pryde (Milton Rosmer) to investigate the theft of valuable jewels they discover are hidden in a Chinese idol. The supporting cast included Arthur Walcott, Temple Bell, Teddy Arundell and Harry J. North. George Ridgwell directed and Charles Barnett wrote the screenplay.

Les Amours de Rocambole

1923 French film (SEC/6 reels) featuring the villainous anti-hero Rocambole created by Pierre Alexis Ponson Du Terrail. Rocambole (Maurice Thorèze) and Sir William (Albert Decoeur) lead a gang known as the Valets de Coeur. They are paid six million to separate the Marquise van Hope (Germaine Fontanes) from her husband but are foiled by her friend Baccara (Claude Mereille). Rocambole ends up killing Sir William and is caught by the police. Charles Maudru wrote the screenplay and directed. See also Rocambole.

Angel Esquire

1919 British film (Gaumont/7 reels) based on the 1908 novel *Angel Esquire* by Edgar Wallace. Angel, a millionaire gambler with a bizarre sense of humor, decides to leave his fortune to whoever can discover the combination of his safe. This creates a lot of problems (and a good deal of danger) for those trying to figure it out. Aurele Sydney starred as Jimmy, Gertrude McCoy was Kathleen, Dick Webb was Angel and W.T. Ellwanger was Spedding. George Pearson wrote the screenplay and W. P. Kellino directed.

Anna the Adventuress

1920 British film (Hepworth/6 reels)

Alma Taylor is double trouble in *Anna the Adventuress.*

based on a 1904 novel by E. Phillips Oppenheim. Anna (Alma Taylor), a cabaret dancer whose husband has betrayed her, decides to get revenge by inventing an imaginary twin sister named Annabel who can shoot him and then disappear. She carries it off but there are many twists and turns before fade-out as with all Oppenheim mysteries. The cast included Gerald Ames, Jean Cadell, James Carew and Ronald Colman. Blanche McIntosh wrote the screenplay and Cecil M. Hepworth directed.

Another Man's Shoes

1922 American film (Universal/5 reels) based on Victor Bridges' mystery novel *Another Man's Shoes*. When businessman Stuart Granger (Herbert Rawlinson) learns that a gang is out to kill him, he persuades his look-alike cousin Jack (Rawlinson in a double role) to impersonate him Jack survives assassination attempts and falls in love with gang leader Mercia (Barbara Bedford). After the real Stuart is found and killed, Mercia is happy to learn of Jack's real identity. Jack Conway directed and novelist Victor Bridges wrote the screenplay with Raymond L. Schrock and Arthur F. Statter. (The 1916 film *The Phantom Buccaneer* is based on the same novel.)

Apartment 29

1917 American film (Vitagraph/5 reels) based on a story by Edward J. Montagne who also wrote the screenplay. Critic Stanley Ormsby (Earle Williams) trashes a play by Bobby Davis (Denton Vane) as being improbable so Davis devises a scheme to change his mind. Ormsby is tricked into finding an apparently dead woman in front of Apartment 29 where he has gone for an interview. He carries her inside and finds her dead husband. The police accuse him of the murders but he escapes and Davis agrees to hide him in a girl's trunk. The girl (Ethel Grey Terry) confesses she is the murderess and the police track them down. Davis then reveals he hired actors to fake this "improbable" murder story. Ormsby is convinced and rewrites his review. Paul Scardon directed.

The Ape

1928 American film (Collwyn Pictures/5 reels). This mystery is so mysterious that even the *Variety* reviewer couldn't figure out what it was about though it was supposedly based on a an actual police record. It has lots of shadowy figures and fights in the dark but no noticeable plot. Gladys Walton, Ruth Stonehouse, Basil Wilson and Bradley Barker were the baffled actors and B. C. Rule directed.

Arabia: The Equine Detective

1913 American film (Selig/2 reels) starring a horse named Arabia as a detective. Oscar Eagle directed and Chris Lane wrote the screenplay. The film's poster is impressive but there is not much information about the film which has not survived. Arabia seems to been a genuine movie star as he was featured in two other films for Selig, *Arabia and the Baby* and *Arabia Takes the Health Cure*. Selig was noted for the use of animals in its films and had its own zoo.

Arabia the horse plays a four-legged sleuth in *Arabia: The Equine Detective*.

The Argyle Case

1917 American film (Selznick/6 reels) based on the 1912 play *The Argyle Case* by Harriet Ford and Harvey J. O'Higgins written with help from detective William J. Burns. Detective Asche Kayton (Robert Warwick) investigates the murder of millionaire banker John Argyle (Frank McGlynn). Argyle's adopted daughter Mary (Elaine Hammerstein) and son Bruce (Arthur Albertson) are the chief suspects. Kayton, who uses modern scientific methods, discovers a woman's fingerprints at the crime scene. After finding her and analyzing several clues, he proves the killer was the boss of a counterfeiting organization Argyle was going to expose. Ralph W. Ince directed and Frederic Chapin wrote the screenplay.

Elaine Hammerstein is a chief suspect in *The Argyle Case.*

Armadale

1916 American film (Gaumont/3 reels) based on the 1864 novel *Armadale* by Wilkie Collins, his third great mystery novel after *The Woman in White* and *The Moonstone*. It revolves around the suspenseful stories of two men both named Allan Armadale, one of whom has inherited the Armadale estate. There is also the beautiful but evil Lydia Gwilt. Richard Garrick directed a cast headed by Alexander Gaden, Iva Shepard, John E. Mackin, Henry W. Pemberton, Lucille Taft, Harry Chira and Kathleen Butler.

The Armored Car (Pancéřové auto)

1929 Czechoslovakian film (Molas Film/6 reels). Banker Sam Hamilton (Hans Mierendorff) starts using an armored car belonging to Nick Houlton (Jan W. Speerger) after he suffers several robberies and hires racing champion Charley Allan (Carlo Aldini) to drive. When the banker's daughter Bessy (Zet Molas) is kidnapped, Allan turns detective to find her. He discovers Houlton is behind the robberies and rescues Bessy. Zet Molas wrote the screenplay and Rolf Randolf directed, and Georg Muschner.

Arsène Lupin

1909 French film (Éclair/1 reel) based on the 1907 French collection *Arsène Lupin; Gentleman-Cambrioleur* (Arsène Lupin, Gentleman Burglar) by Maurice Leblanc about the French master thief Arsène Lupin. Lupin seems to delight in stealing appears to be uncatchable. George Treville played Lupin with support from Harry Baur and Jules Mondos. Michel Carré directed. See Lupin, Arsène for listing of other films.

Arsène Lupin

1916 British film (Jury/7 reels) based on the 1908 French play *Arsène Lupin* by Francis de Croisset and Maurice Leblanc. French gentleman thief Arsène Lupin (Gerald Ames) pretends to be a duke so he can stealing art and jewelry from wealthy neighbor Gournay-Martin (Douglas Munro). The great detective Inspector Guerchard (Kenelm Foss) is hired to investigate as Lupin gets involved with lovely fellow thief Savia (Manora Thew). They get away, however, and decide to go straight. George Loane Tucker directed and Kenelm Foss wrote the screenplay. See Lupin, Arsène for other films.

Arsène Lupin

1917 American film (Vitagraph/5 reels) based on the 1908 French play *Arsène Lupin* by Francis de Croisset and Maurice Leblanc. French master thief Arsène Lupin (Earle Williams) poses as a duke, gets engaged to a wealthy man's daughter and begins stealing his valuables. Detective Guerchard is hired to investigate and causes problems while Lupin is falling in love with fellow thief Sonia (Ethel Gray Terry). They escape with the help of Lupin's assistant Victoire (Julia Swayne Gordon) and decide to reform. Paul Scardon directed the film, Garfield Thompson wrote the screenplay and Robert A. Stuart was the cinematographer. See Lupin, Arsène for other films.

Arsène Lupin contra Sherlock Holmes

1910 German series (Vitascope/five 2-reel episodes) starring Paul Otto as Arsène Lupin and Viggo Larsen as Sherlock Holmes. Larsen wrote and directed these films in which Holmes defeats French master criminal Arsène Lupin in the final episode. The series was distributed in England as well as Germany. The episodes, with English and German titles, are *Arsène Lupin (Die Alte Sekretar)*, *The Blue Diamond (Der Blaue Diamant)*, *The Two Rembrandts (Die Falschen Rembrandts)*, *The Escape (Die Flught)* and *The End of Arsène Lupin (Arsène Lupin ende)*. (See Lupin, Arsène and Holmes, Sherlock for other films.)

Arsène Lupin contre Ganimard

1914 French film starring Georges Tréville as Arsène Lupin. The French gentleman thief nearly meets his match in a battle of wits with Sureté inspector Justin Ganimard. Michel Carré directed. See Lupin, Arsène for his other films.

Arsène Lupin contre Herlock Sholmes
(Chairo no-Onna)

1927 Japanese film (6 reels) based on a story in the 1908 collection *Arsène Lupin contre Herlock Sholmes* by Maurice Leblanc in which Lupin defeats the great English detective (name disguised for copyright reasons). Mitsuaki Mimami portrayed the French master thief Arsène Lupin for the second time with Shozo Nanbu as Herlock Sholmes. Genjiro Saegusa directed. See Lupin, Arsène for other films.

Arsène Lupin's Last Adventure
(Arsène Lupin utolsó kalandja)

1921 Hungarian serial (Studio Mobil/six 2-reel chapters) about the final adventure of the French master thief Arsène Lupin. With Gusztav Partos, Mara Jankovsky, Aniko Urmosfy, Lajos Gellert, Odon Bardi and Lajos Gardony Pal Foro wrote the screenplay and Paul Fejos directed. See Lupin, Arsène for other films.

Ashi ni sawatta onna (The Woman Who Touched the Legs)

1926 Japanese film (Nikkatsu/6 reels) known in English as *The Woman Who Touched*

French master thief Arsène Lupin made his first appearance in print in 1905 and was on screen by 1909. Earle Williams played him in the 1917 American film.

the Legs. A detective arrests a pretty young woman who has bewitched a writer and stolen his wallet. She turn out to be a famous pickpocket and she bewitches him as well. Koji Shima played the detective opposite Yôko Umemura and Tokihiko Okada. Yutaka Abe directed from a screenplay by Hajime Masuda. Abe's comedy was one of the earliest Japanese films to feature a detective; he had just returned from working in Hollywood and was considered the most "western" director working in Japan. The film was remade twice in the sound era, by Kon Ichikawa in 1952 and by Yasuzo Masumura in 1960.

Ashton-Kirk

Ashton-Kirk, a Philadelphia detective who specializes in mysteries involving ancient documents, was the creation of John Thomas McIntyre. His adventures were related in *Ashton-Kirk, Investigator* (1910), *Ashton-Kirk: Special Detective* (1912), *Ashton-Kirk: Secret Agent* (1912) and *Ashton-Kirk: Criminologist* (1918). Stories from these books were the basis of three feature films produced by Gold Rooster-Pathé in 1915: *An Affair of Nations, The House of Fear* and *The Menace of the Mute*, Arnold Daly took on the role of Ashton-Kirk following his success playing Craig Kennedy in *The Exploits of Elaine*. The Ashton-Kirk films were probably Daly's idea as he produced and co-directed them with Ashley Miller.

Asphalt

1929 German film (UFA/8 reels). Berlin policeman Albert Holk (Gustav Fröhlich) attempts to arrest jewel thief Elsa Kramer (Betty Amann) but she seduces him instead in this German Expressionist variation of the Carmen story. She even convinces him this was her first theft but after he asks her to marry him she reveals her truly lurid criminal past. Joe May directed and wrote the screenplay with Hans Székely and Rolf Vanloo while the cinematographer Günther Rittau helped them create a visual masterpiece. Film is on DVD with orchestral score.

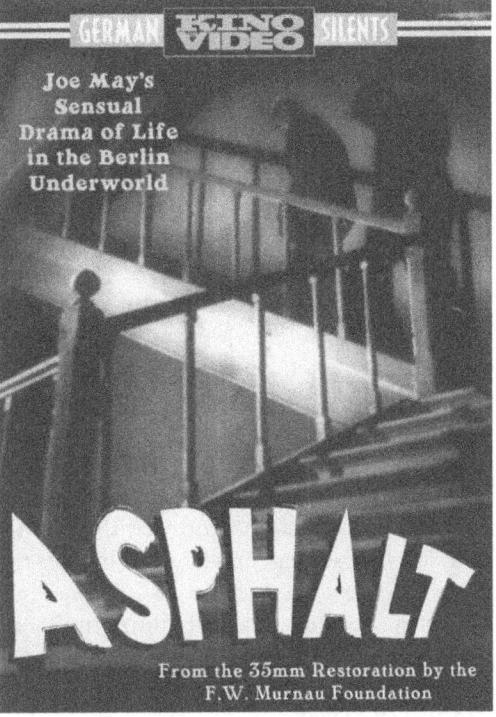

Asphalt is the story of a jewel thief and a policeman in 1920s Berlin.

At Bay

1915 American film (Pathé-Gold Rooster/5 reels) based on 1913 mystery play *At Bay* by George Scarborough. Aline Graham (Florence Reed) is tricked into the marrying crook Joe Hunter (Lyster Chambers) so gambling boss Judson Flagg (De Witt C. Jennings) can blackmail her district attorney father. Flagg arranges a meeting with Aline recorded on concealed cameras. During a struggle, Aline stabs Flagg with a paper cutter and later thinks she killed him. However, the film shows Flagg died of heart failure before he was stabbed. Ouida Bergère wrote the screenplay and George Fitzmaurice directed.

At It Again

1913 American comedy (Keystone/1 reel), the first film in the second *Two Sleuths* series produced and directed by Mack Sennett and starring Sennett and Fred Mace. They played comic detectives who bumbled their way through ten cases.

At the Mercy of Tiberius

1920 British/American film (Sunrise Pictures/6 reels) based on Augusta Jane Evans Wilson's 1887 mystery novel *At the Mercy of Tiberius*. Beryl is accused of murdering her grandfather after she has gone to see him to get money for her mother. As she believes her brother did it, she refuses to testify and is arrested. Later her brother tells what really happened. The general was struck and killed by a lightning bolt while they were arguing. A photograph imprinted on a window when the lightning struck proves his story is true. Peggy Hyland played Beryl, Campbell Gullan was her grandfather and Van Dycke was her brother. Fred Le Roy Granville directed and British producer G. B. Samuelson produced the film in America. It was released in England in as *At the Mercy of Tiberius* and in the USA as *The Price of Silence*. (The novel was also filmed in 1916 as *God's Witness*.)

At the Villa Rose

1920 British film (Stoll/7 reels) based on a novel by A.E.W. Mason and masterfully directed by Maurice Elvey. Inspector Hanaud (Teddy Arundell) is asked to investigate a murder in which a young woman is accused of murdering her wealthy employer in a Riviera mansion and running away. She is innocent, of course, but the clever villain is able to make her seem guilty. Hanaud uncovers the truth, that the murder was the result of a jewel robbery gone wrong. Manora Thew plays Celia Harland, Langhorn Burton is Harry Weathermill, Norman Page is Julius Ricardo, Joan Beverly is Adele Rossignol, Eva Westlake is Mme. Dauvray and Kate Gurney is Helene. Sinclair Hill wrote the screenplay and Paul Burger was the cinematographer. A print of this film survives at the BFI film archive.

Das Auge des Götzen (The Eye of the Idol)

1915 German film (May Film/4 reels) featuring the "American" detective Joe Deebs as played by Heinrich Schroth. This was a film in the long-running Deeb series created by producer Joe May. There were over thirty Deebs films with the detective portrayed by six different actors. See Deebs, Joe for other films.

Aurora Floyd

The "sensation" novel *Aurora Floyd*, written in 1863 by Mary Elizabeth Braddon, was filmed three times in the silent era. As in Braddon's more famous novel *Lady Audley's Secret*, the plot revolves around the unintentional bigamy of a woman (Aurora Floyd) and the murder of a first husband (John Conyers) whom she believed had died earlier. Aurora is suspected of the murder but her second husband (John Mellish) believes she is innocent. For details about the films see entries below and *Her Bitter Lesson*.

Aurora Floyd

1912 American film (Thanhouser/2 reels) based on Mary Elizabeth Bradden's 1863 novel *Aurora Floyd*. Aurora Floyd is suspected of the murder of her first husband whom she mistakenly believed had died earlier but her second husband believes she is innocent. Florence La Badie stars as Aurora Floyd with Harry Benham as Aurora's second husband, David Thompson as her first husband and Justus D. Barnes as Aurora's father. Theodore Marston directed.

Aurora Floyd

1915 American film (Biograph/4 reels) based on Mary Elizabeth Bradden's 1863 novel *Aurora Floyd*. Aurora Floyd is suspected of the murder of a first husband whom she mistakenly believed had died earlier but her second husband thinks she is innocent. Louise Vale plays Aurora Floyd with support from Franklin Ritchie, Jack Drumier, Alan Hale and Laura La Varnie.

The Avenging Arrow

1921 American serial (Pathé/fifteen 2-reel chapters). Anita (Ruth Roland) turns detective to find out why her female ancestors were killed on their 21st birthday, all shot by arrows. An arrow aimed at her misses, however, so she joins forces with Ralph Troy (Edward Hearn) to investigate the mystery. Jack Cunningham wrote the screenplay and W.S. Van Dyke and

Ruth Roland turns detective in *The Avenging Arrow*.

William Bowman directed. The episodes are *Vow of Mystery, The Enemy Strikes, The Hand of Treachery, A Life in Jeopardy, The Message Stone, The Midnight Attack, The Double Game, The Strange Pact, The Auction Block, Outwitted, Dangerous Waters, House of Treachery, On Perilous Grounds, Shifting Sands* and *The Toll of the Desert*.

The Avenging Conscience: Thou Shalt Not Kill

1914 American film (Majestic Motion Picture Co./8 reels) based on Edgar Allan Poe's story "The Tell-Tale Heart" and poem "Annabel Lee." A Poe enthusiast (Henry B. Walthall) wants to marry his sweetheart (Blanche Sweet) but his jealous uncle (Spottiswoode Aitken) objects. He gets angry, kills the uncle in a fit of pique and hides the body in a fireplace. A detective (Ralph Lewis) becomes suspicious, starts investigating and makes the young man so nervous he hangs himself. The

Henry Walthall is the protagonist of a Poe tale in *The Avenging Conscience*.

detective cuts him down but it is too late so the sweetheart kills herself as well. Then the young man wakes up and realizes he has been dreaming a Poe tale. He makes up with his uncle and marries his sweetheart. D. W. Griffith wrote and directed this criminous fantasy splendidly filmed by G. W. Bitzer. On DVD.

The Avenging Shadow

1928 American film (Pathé/5 reels). Grey Boy, a Great Dane, starred as police dog detective Klondike in *The Avenging Shadow*. Bank clerk James Hamilton (Ray Hailer) is falsely accused of stealing a factory payroll and sent to prison though the real crook is Brooks, a warden at the prison. Klondike pursues Brooks (LeRoy Mason) and eventually gets a confession from him that frees Hamilton. Bennett Cohen wrote the screenplay and Ray Taylor directed.

Babette

1917 American film (Vitagraph/5 reels) based on the 1916 novel *Babette* by Frank Berkeley Smith. Detective Guinard (William Dunn) recognizes gentleman thief Raveau (Marc MacDermott) at a party celebrating Raveau's marriage to Babette (Peggy Hyland). He tries to arrest him but Raveau escapes with his bride and turns from stealing to painting. When his paintings don't sell and Babette gets pregnant, he takes up gambling and stealing again. He is observed by Guinard and about to be arrested when his victim refuses to charge him. It seems Raveau had once saved the man's gambler wife from committing suicide. A. Van Buren Powell wrote the screenplay and Charles J. Brabin directed.

Baby Sherlock

1912 American comedy (Powers Picture Plays/1 reel). Little Margaret (Baby Early Gorman) is the child detective. She finds the evidence that leads to the capture of the tramps who robbed Grandfather Dobbs (Charles Manley Farmer). Harry C. Mathews directed.

Bachelor Brides

1926 American film (PDC-De Mille Pictures/6 reels) based on the 1925 play *Bachelor Brides* by Charles Horace Malcolm. A spoof of the mystery film with double duplicities all round. English aristocrat Percy Ashfield (Rod La Rocque) is about to marry American Mary Bowing (Elinor Fair) in a Scottish castle when the family pearls are stolen. A woman then claims Percy is her child's father by a secret marriage, a doctor says she is an escaped inmate of an insane asylum and a Scotland Yard inspector claims he has been sent to protect the pearls. Finally a real detective turns up and explains that the other three visitors are jewel thieves and that he substituted fake pearls for the real ones, which are safe. Garrett Fort and C. Gardner Sullivan wrote the screenplay and William K. Howard directed.

Back to Liberty

1927 American film (Excellent Pictures/6 reels) based on a story by Arthur Hoerl who wrote the screenplay. Tom Devon (Edmund Breese) heads an organization of gentlemen crooks that includes Rudolph Gambier (Jean Del Val) and Jimmy Stevens (George Walsh). Both are interested in Devon's daughter Gloria (Dorothy Hall) who doesn't know her father is a crook. Devon wants them to stop seeing her and is killed by Gambier during an argument. Stevens is convicted to the murder but Gloria, convinced of his innocence, masquerades as a thief and tricks Gambier into a confession Bernard McEveety directed.

Baffles, Gentleman Burglar

1914 American comedy (Keystone/2 reels). Slapstick parody of E. W. Hornung's famous gentleman thief Raffles starring Ford Sterling, Chester Conklin and Alice Davenport.

Balaoo

1913 French film (Éclair/2 reels) based on Gaston Leroux's 1912 novel *Balaoo* about an ape that is trained to kill people. A newspaper reporter investigates and discovers the secret in time to save the life of a judge and his daughter. Lucien Bataille played Balaoo, Henri Gouget was Dr. Coriolis, Madeleine Grandjean was Madeleine and Camille Bardou was the poacher Victorin Jasset directed and wrote the screenplay. (The novel was filmed again in 1927 as *The Wizard*.)

Baluchet, William

William Baluchet, the French "king of detectives," was the creation of "André Bencey" in a mysterious paperback novel titled *William Baluchet, roi des détectives*. No copies of this book or any other books by this author have ever been traced but the character had such appeal that it became the basis of two French detective serials, *William Baluchet, roi des détectives,* and *L'Affaire du train 24.*

The Bandbox

1919 American film (Pathé/Dietrich-Beck/6 reels) based on the 1912 mystery novel *The Bandbox* by Louis Joseph Vance. Actress Alison Landis (Gretchen Hartman) hides a pearl necklace in a hat box to avoid paying duty when her ocean liner lands. The box is accidentally switched with an identical one belonging to Eleanor Searle (Doris Kenyon) who gets trailed by a crook (Walter McEwen) to a deserted island. She has to fight him for her life but is saved by her father (also played by Walter McEwen). Roy Somerville wrote the screenplay and R. William Neill directed.

Les Bandits en noirs (The Bandits in Black)

1908 French film (Éclair/1 reel), an episode in the *Nick Carter, le roi des détectives* series about the master detective Nick Carter. It was distributed in America as *Nick Carter and the Black-Coated Thieves*. In this episode Carter investigates a criminal gang that dresses in black. Pierre Bressol played Nick Carter and Victorin Jassett wrote and directed the film.

The Banker's Double

1915 American film (Edison/1 reel), one of five films in the *Felix Boyd* series revolving around a fictional private detective created by Scott Campbell. Boyd was a tough street fighter like Nick Carter with the smarts of Sherlock Holmes. Robert Conness starred as Boyd with support from Bigelow Cooper. Langdon West directed. (See Boyd, Felix for other films.)

La Banque ténébreuse (The Shadowy Bank)

1914 French film (Eclectic/2 reels), an episode in a popular tongue-in-cheek comedy series about an "American" detective named Nick Winter. It was shown in America as *The House of Mystery* but failed to impress the *Variety* reviewer who didn't realize it was meant to be funny though he did note that the audience laughed uproariously as its absurdities. Georges Vinter played Nick. See Winter, Nick for other films.

Der Bär von Baskerville (The Baskerville Bear)

1915 German film (PAGU/6 reels) featuring Harry Piel as an "American" detective. It featured a famous stunt in which he drives a car over the edge of a cliff. The film survives in an archive and was screened at the Pordenone Silent Film Festival in 1990.

Barcelona and Its Mysteries (Barcelona y sus misterios)

1915 Spanish serial (Hispano Films/eight 2-reel chapters). American serials were very popular in Spain at this period and this serial was reportedly inspired by *The Exploits of Elaine*. The plot seems more like *The Count of Monte Cristo*. Joaquín Carrasco starred, Antonio Altadill wrote the screenplay and Alberto Marro directed.

The Barnes Murder Case see The Conspirators

Barrabas

1919 French serial (Gaumont/12 episodes) directed by Louis Feuillade and written by him in collaboration with Maurice Level. It describes the activities of an international association of criminals headed by the mysterious Barrabas and fronted by banker Rudolph Strelitz. The gang members sport the tattoo B.R.A.S. The cast, headed by Gaston Michel as the villainous Strelitz, includes Edouard Mathé, Blanche Montel, Fernand Herrmann, Georges Biscot, Violette Jyl, Jeanne Rollette and Lyne Stanka. The episodes were *La Maîtresse du juif errant*, *La Justice des hommes*, *La Villa des glycines*, *Le Stigmate*, *Noëlle Maupré*, *La Fille du condamné*, *Les Ailes de Satan*, *Le Manoir mystérieux*, *L'Otage*, *L'Oubliette*, *Le Revenant* and *Justice*.

The Bat

1926 American film (United Artists/9 reels) based on the 1920 play *The Bat* by Mary Roberts Rinehart and Avery Hopwood derived from Rinehart's 1908 novel *The Circular Staircase*. Wealthy spinster Cornelia (Emily Fitzroy) receives threatening notes from a criminal known as The Bat at the Long Island mansion she has rented for the summer. Detectives Moletti (Tullio Carminati) and Anderson (Eddie Gribbon) come to protect her but are unable to prevent murders, including that of a banker. It seems $200,000 from a bank robbery is hidden in the mansion and the Bat wants it. Cornelia's niece Dale (Jewel Carmen) and boyfriend Brooks (Jack Pickford) are suspects while maid Lizzie (Louise Fazenda) suspects everyone and screams at everything. Roland West directed from a screenplay by Julien Josephson. The play, one of the most popular mystery dramas ever staged, is still being presented by high school drama groups. On video.

A Bear Escape　　24

Jewel Carmen is a suspect in *The Bat*.

A Bear Escape

1913 American comedy (Keystone/1 reel), a film in the *Two Sleuths* series produced and directed by Mack Sennett and starring Sennett and Fred Mace. They play comic detectives.

Beauty and the Rogue

1918 American film (Mutual/5 reels) based on a story Arthur Berthelet. Reform-minded Roberta (Mary Miles Minter) get her wealthy father to hire "Slippery" Bill Dorgan, a thief just as out of prison as his gardener and this gives him the chance to steal her jewels. Richard Van Stone, who fancies Roberta, buys one of the jewels from Slippery Bill and presents it to her a gift. He is arrested for the robbery by Detective Callahan (Clarence Burton but Roberta get kidnapped by one of Bill's criminal friends when he learns of her wealth. Bill feels remorse, rescues Roberta and returns the jewels. Elizabeth Mahoney wrote the screenplay and Henry King directed.

The Bedroom Window

1924 American film (Paramount/7 reels) based on a story by Clara Beranger who wrote the screenplay. Mystery novelist Matilda Jones (Ethel Wales) investigates the murder of her brother-in-law. His daughter (and her favorite niece) Ruth (May McAvoy) is engaged to Robert Delano (Ricardo Cortez) who discovered the body and is now the chief suspect. Matilda and her alter ego, fictional detective Rufus Rome, unravel the mystery and pin the murder on the family lawyer. William De Mille directed.

Before Midnight

1925 American film (Banner Productions/ 5 reels). Detective J. Dallas Durand (Alan Roscoe) forces Helene (Barbara Bedford) to watch suspected emerald smuggler Tom Galloway (William Russell). Galloway offers Durand a big bribe to keep quiet when he is found with an emerald. Durand accepts and Galloway reveals that he is the head of the detective agency for which Durand works. He fires Durand and helps Helene. Jules Furthman wrote the screenplay and John Adolfi directed.

Behind Masks

1921 American film (Paramount/5 reels) based on the 1908 mystery novel *Jeanne of the*

Dorothy Dalton is an orphaned heiress in *Behind Masks*.

Marshes by Edward Phillips Oppenheim. A typically complicated Oppenheim plot with many twists and turns. Orphaned heiress Jeanne Mesurier (Dorothy Dalton) is the ward of card sharp Madame Ena Delore (Julia Swayne Gordon). While visiting the estate of Cecil Bourne (Kempton Greene), Delore swindles guests at card games. Cecil helps Delore rob Ronald Engleton (Lewis Broughton) who is hidden in a smuggler's cave under the house. Jeanne discovers what is going on and follows the crooks to the cave. She is locked in but finds an opening to the sea and swims out. The crooks are foiled. Katherine Stuart wrote the screenplay and Frank Reicher directed.

Behind the Curtain

1924 American film (Universal/5 reels). Wealthy George Belmont (Charles Clary) blames his mistress Laura (Winifred Bryson) when his son Hugh (Johnny Harron) elopes with her sister Sylvia (Lucille Ricksen). When George is found dead, Laura and a criminal friend are blames and convicted on circumstantial evidence. The District Attorney (Clarence Geldert) then discovers that fake spiritualist Gregorius (Eric Mayne) was the killer. Emil Forest and Harvey Gates wrote the screenplay and Chester M. Franklin directed.

The Beloved Rogue

1927 American film (United Artists/10 reels). Poet-thief-vagabond-rogue François Villon (John Barrymore), who enjoys stealing food from the rich and passing it to the poor, makes a joke about the Duke of Burgundy (Lawson Butt) and is banished from Paris by King Louis XI (Conrad Veidt). After he falls in love with Charlotte (Marceline Day), who is to be forced into marriage with one of the Duke's men, he gains the king's confidence by revealing schemes against him hatched by the Duke. He and Charlotte are kidnapped by the Duke but rescued by the king. Paul Bern wrote the screenplay and Alan Crosland directed.

Below the Deadline

1920 American film (Ascher Productions/5 reels) based on a story by Arthur Henry Gooden who wrote the screenplay. Police detective Joe Donovan (J. B. Warner) sets out to prove that crooked wharfmaster Buck Elliot (Bert Sprotte) and his gang killed a policeman. Elliot's wife Alice (Lillian Biron), unaware of his criminal activities, provides him with an alibi but is later shown evidence of his criminal life. Donovan and his police team foil a train robbery but Eliot escapes. Donovan tracks him down and Elliot is killed J. P. McGowan directed.

Belphégor

1927 French serial (Société des Cinéromans/four 4-reel episodes) by Arthur Bernède based on the novel *Belphégor* serialized in *Le Petit Parisien* in 1927 and published in four volumes. Belphégor is a supposed ghost haunting the Louvre and seeking the lost treasure of French kings hidden under the museum. Its nemesis is Chantecoq, the King of Detectives, who investigates its activities in partnership with journalist Jacques Bellegarde. The ghost turns out to be villainous Simone Desroches, the mistress of Bellegard. The serial starred René Navarre as Chantecoq, Lucien Dalsace as Bellegarde and Emire Vautier as Deroches. Bernède wrote the screenplay and Henri Desfontaines directed. This was a conscious attempt by Bernède, the co-creator of *Judex,* to create a character that would rival *Fantômas* and *Judex.*

Beresford, Tuppence and Tommy

Young married private detectives Tommy and Prudence "Tuppence" Beresford, the creations of Agatha Christie, founded Blunt's Brilliant Detectives after working together in British intelligence during World War I. Their eccentric behavior and light-hearted approach to solving crimes makes them similar to the "Honeymoon Detectives" Richard and Grace Duvall. Some of their cases even parody the work of other famous detectives The Beresfords were featured in five books but inspired only one film in the silent era, the German picture *Die Abenteurer G.m.b.H.*

The Beryl Coronet

1912 Anglo-French film (Franco British Film Company–Éclair/2 reels), an episode in the *Sherlock Holmes* series based on a story by

Sir Arthur Conan Doyle. Sherlock Holmes solves a mystery involving the theft of a beryl coronet. George Treville played Sherlock Holmes with M. Moyse as Dr. Watson and British actors in the supporting roles. Treville also directed in collaboration with Conan Doyle. See Holmes, Sherlock for other films.

The Beryl Coronet

1921 British film (Stoll/2 reels), an episode in the *Adventures of Sherlock Holmes* series based on a story by Sir Arthur Conan Doyle. Holmes proves that a man did not steal a valuable beryl coronet even though he was apparently seen doing the deed. Eille Norwood portrays Sherlock Holmes with Hubert Willis as Dr. Watson. William J. Elliot wrote the script and Maurice Elvey directed. A print of this film survives at the BFI archive.

Bess the Detectress

1914 American comedy series (Universal-Joker/2 reels) starring Bess Meredyth and directed by Allen Curtis. The supporting cast included William Wolbert, Jack Dillon and Phil Dunham. The films, in the order of their release, are listed below. Meredyth (1890–1969/ nee: Helen MacGlashan) was also a successful screenwriter and adapted many mysteries for the movies including *Charlie Chan at the Opera* and *The Unsuspected*.

Bess the Detectress in Tick, Tick, Tick

1914 (July 1) American comedy (Univeral-Joker/1 reel), second film in the *Bess the Detectress* series starring Bess Meredyth as Bess. The supporting cast included William Wolbert, Jack Dillon and Phil Dunham. Allen Curtis directed.

Bess the Detectress or the Dog Watch

1914 (July 8) American comedy (Univeral-Joker/1 reel), third episode in the *Bess the Detectress* series starring Bess Meredyth as Bess. The supporting cast included William Wolbert, Jack Dillon and Phil Dunham. Allen Curtis directed.

Bess the Detectress or the Old Mill at Midnight

1914 (June 6) American comedy (Univeral-Joker/1 reel), first film in the *Bess the Detectress* series starring Bess Meredyth as Bess. The supporting cast included William Wolbert, Jack Dillon and Phil Dunham. Allen Curtis directed.

Betsy's Burglar

1917 American comedy (Triangle/5 reels). Betsy (Constance Talmadge), dreams of becoming a detective while working as a maid in an apartment house. She thinks she has an opportunity when Harry (Kenneth Harlan) rents a room. He persuades her to help him steal a box of jewels in the possession of the lawyer Jasper (Joseph Singleton) who lives across the hall. He says the jewels are his and the box has a will in his favor hidden by the crooked lawyer. Surprisingly this turns out to be true and after a kidnapping and other misadventures, the real thieves are arrested. Frank E. Woods wrote the screenplay and Paul Powell directed.

Constance Talmadge dreams of being a detective in *Betsy's Burglar*.

Beware of Blondes

1928 American film (Columbia/6 reels) based on a story by George C. Hull. Jewelry store clerk Jeffrey Black (Matt Moore) prevents

Matt Moore is wary of jewel thieves in *Beware of Blondes*.

a robbery and is rewarded with a holiday in Hawaii. He is asked to transport a valuable emerald and is warned against a thief called Blonde Mary (Hazel Howell). On the boat he meets a blonde named Mary (Dorothy Revier) and is naturally suspicious. This Mary, however, is a detective sent to protect the emerald. She ensures it arrives safely and arrests the real Blonde Mary. Harvey Thew wrote the screenplay and George B. Seitz directed.

A Bid for Fortune

1917 English film (Unity-Super/4 reels) based on Guy Boothby's *A Bid for Fortune* about the villainous Dr. Nikola. The evil doctor attempts to gain the secrets of life and death by obtaining a Tibetan cane that will allow entry into a mysterious monastery in Tibet. He steals the cane from an English collector and is able to get into the monastery and steal its treasure but the secrets elude him. A. Harding Steerman starred as Dr Nikola Violet Graham played Phyllis Wetherall and Sydney Vautier was Dick Hattras. Sidney Morgan directed. See also Nikola, Dr.

The Big City

1928 American film (MGM/7 reels) based on a story by Tod Browning. Master criminal Chuck Collins (Lon Chaney) is not pleased when a rival gang robs the patrons of his cabaret run by a Texas Guinan clone named Tennessee (Virginia Pearson). He tricks them into passing the items to members of his gang with the help of Helen (Betty Compson) who has a costume shop where jewels are hidden in plain sight. Her naive employee Sunshine (Marceline Day) persuades them to go straight. Waldemar Young wrote the screenplay and Browning directed.

Big Town Ideas

1921 American film (Fox/5 reels) based on a story by John Montague who also wrote the screenplay. Small town waitress Fan Tilden (Eileen Percy) thinks a man (Kenneth Gibson) being sent to prison as a bond thief is innocent so she turns detective to prove it. She helps him escape from prison, catches the real crooks and gets the man a pardon. Carl Harbaugh directed.

The Billionaire Lord

1915 American film (American Commercial Film/4 reel). Amateur detective Tom, who will conceal evidence for a dollar, creates problems for his sister Mary. He learns that visiting Lord Wallingford is a fake billionaire but Wallingford pays him off so Tom introduces him to his sister. She refuses to give him money for the truth about Wallingford so Tom gets money from him and Mary's fiancé who fight. When Wallingford hires thugs, Tom tells Mary about it without payment. All finally ends well. La Verne Barber wrote and directed this odd film.

Billy the Detective

1912 American comedy (Solax/1 reel) starring comic Billy Quirk. This film was one episode of Quirk's *Billy* series in which he portrayed many types of characters, including even a burglar. He played a detective again in the four-film 1914 Solax series *Burstup Holmes, Detective*.

Billy Quirk is a comic detective in *Billy the Detective.*

Binks the Hawkshaw

1913 American comedy (IMP/1 reel), an episode in the *Binks* series starring George De Forrest. "Hawkshaw" began to be used as a term for a detective following the success of a detective named Hawkshaw in Tom Taylor's 1863 play *The Ticket of Leave Man.*

The Bishop's Candlesticks

1913 American film (IMP/2 reels) film based on an episode in Victor Hugo's novel *Les Misérables.* This film concentrates on Valjean's theft of the bishop's candlesticks, Detective Javert's pursuit of him for the crime and the bishop's forgiveness saying the candlesticks were a gift. With Frank Smith and William Shay. Herbert Brenon directed. (See *Les Misérables.*)

The Black Bag

1922 American film (Universal/5 reels) based on Louis Joseph Vance's 1908 novel *The Black Bag.* Billy Kirkwood (Herbert Rawlinson) becomes involved with Dorothy Calender (Virginia Valli) who he thinks has stolen a diamond necklace. He recovers the necklace from a gang of thieves and then learns Dorothy stole her own necklace to raise money for her brother. George Hively wrote the screenplay and Stuart Paton directed.

The Black Bird

1926 American film (MGM/7 reels). The Bishop, a cripple who runs a rescue mission in London's Limehouse district, and the Blackbird, a criminal well known to the police, are actually the same person (both played by Lon Chaney). The Blackbird is competing with rival West End Bertie (Owen Moore) for the favors of beautiful Fifi (Renée Adorée). Both try to steal a diamond necklace for Fifi but the Black-

Owen Moore has to compete with the Black Bird (Lon Chaney) for the favors of Fifi (Renée Adorée) in this Tod Browning crime film.

bird runs into difficulties and has to shoot a Scotland Yard detective to escape. He goes into hiding as the Bishop but this time his joints stay locked and he becomes a real cripple. Tod Browning directed and wrote the screenplay with Waldemar Young.

The Black Book

1929 American serial (Pathé/ten 2-reel chapters) starring Allene Ray as detective Dora Drake. She gets support from Ted Bradley (Walter Miller) when she battles a criminal gang for a black book with a secret code describing a platinum deposit. The supporting cast included Frank Lackteen, Edith London, Willie Fung and Marie Mosquini. Joseph Anthony Roach wrote the screenplay and Spencer G. Bennet directed. The episodes were *The Secret of the Vault, The Death Rail, A Shot in the Night, The Dagger Sign, The Flaming Trap, The Black Dam, The Fatal Hour, The Mystery Mill, The Assassin Strikes* and *Out of the Shadows*.

The Black Box

1915 American serial (Universal/fifteen 2-reel chapters) based on a story by E. Phillips Oppenheim which he turned into the novel *The Black Box*. Herbert Rawlinson plays Herbert Quest, a kind of scientific Sherlock Holmes who invents gadgets to help solve crimes, including a cell phone equivalent he calls a "pocket wireless." When someone asks if Quest is a detective, he is told "you could call him that, in the same way you could call Napoleon a soldier." Quest battles a master criminal as he tries to discover the secret of the black box while working in with Anna Little. The supporting cast included Laura Oakley, William Worthington, Helen Wright and Beatrice Van. Otis Turner wrote the screenplay and directed the film. The episodes were *An Apartment House Mystery, The Hidden Hands, The Pocket Wireless, An Old Grudge, On the Rack, The Unseen Terror, The House of Mystery, The Inherited Sin, Lost in London, The Ship of Horror, A Desert Vengeance, Neath Iron Wheels, Tongues of Flame, A Bolt from the Blue* and *The Black Box*.

Herbert Rawlinson and Anna Little star in the serial *The Black Box.*

The Black Gate

1919 American film (Vitagraph/5 reels) based on a story by Hilliard Booth. Allan Bowen is killed while attempting to rape Vera Hampton (Ruth Clifford) and wealthy Wade DeForrest (Harry Spingler) is charged with his murder. Wade's despondent friend Shaler (Earle Williams) says he will confess to the killing if Wade's mother (Clarissa Selwyn) will pay his brother $100,000 when he enters the death chamber nicknamed "the black gate." She agrees but when Shaler's ex-lover Vera visits him and they reconcile, he backs out of the agreement. In the end Wade confesses that he actually did kill Bowen. Lucien Hubbard wrote the screenplay and Theodore Marston directed.

Black Paradise

1926 American film (Fox/5 reels). Detective Graham (Edmund Lowe) is pursuing criminal James Callahan (Leslie Fenton) at sea when he is shanghaied and taken as a prisoner to the South Sea island where Callahan lives with his girl Sylvia (Madge Bellamy). He is forced work on a sulfur train but eventually escapes and rescues Sylvia from an attack. The island volcano explodes and everyone is killed except Graham and Sylvia. L. G. Rigby wrote the unbelievable screenplay and R. William Neill directed.

The Black Pearl

1928 American film (Trem Carr-Rayart/6 reels) based on the 1912 novel *The Black Pearl* by Nancy Mann Waddel Woodrow. This is one of many clones of *The Moonstone*. A black pearl that was taken from an Indian idol carries a curse. Silas Lathrop (Thomas Curran), who inherited it, receives threatening notes and is eventually murdered. Others in his family also die but eventually a detective solves the mystery. The film starred Lila Lee, Ray Hallor and Carlton Stockdale. Arthur Hoerl wrote the screenplay and Scott Pembroke directed.

Black Peter

1922 British film (Stoll/2 reels), an episode in the *Further Adventures of Sherlock Holmes* series based on a story by Sir Arthur Conan Doyle. Sherlock Holmes solves the murder of a retire sea captain known as Black Peter Eille Norwood portrays Holmes with Hubert Willis as Dr. Watson. George Ridgewell wrote the adaptation and directed. A print survives at the BFI archive.

Black Roses

1921 American film (Robertson-Cole/6 reels). Japanese architect Yoda (Sessue Hayakawa) is framed for the murder of a gangster boss and Yoda's wife (Tsura Aoki) is kidnapped by the gang. He escapes from prison, pretends to be a rich aristocrat and tricks the gang into leading him to his wife. He frees her and proves his innocence. Myrtle Stedman and Henry Hebert were the main gang members. Richard Schayer wrote the screenplay and Colin Campbell directed.

The Black Secret

1919 American serial (Pathé/fifteen 2-reel episodes) based on the story "In Secret" by

Pearl White battles baddies in the Pathé serial *The Black Secret*.

Robert W. Chambers. Pearl White battles a nasty gang as she attempts to learn the "black secret" while escaping gas attacks and acid baths. The supporting cast included Walter McGrail, Wallace McCutcheon and Marjorie Milton. Bertram Millhauser wrote the screenplay and George B. Seitz directed. The episodes were *The Great Secret, Marked for Death, The Gas Chamber, Below the Water Line, The Acid Bath, The Unknown, The Betrayal, A Crippled Hand, Webs of Deceit, The Inn of Dread, The Death Studio, The Chance Trail, Wings of Mystery, The Hidden Way* and *The Secret Host*.

The Black Sheep of the Family

1916 American film (Universal/5 reels). Esther Saunders (Francelia Billington) marries detective Elwood Collins (Gilmore Hammond) on condition he stop pursuing her brother Bert (Paul Byron). She and former sweetheart Kenneth Carmont (Jack Holt) hide Bert on the night that Kenneth's father is murdered but Kenneth refuses to say where he was to protect her. After he is convicted of the murder, Esther finally reveals the truth and the real killer confesses. Frank Wiltermood and Jay Hunt wrote the screenplay and Jay Hunt directed.

A Black Sherlock Holmes

1918 American black cast comedy (Ebony Film Company/2 reels) starring Sam Robinson as the detective. R.W. Phillips directed this satire with a large cast that included Walter Brogsdale, Robert Duree, Samuel 'Sambo' Jacks, Yvonne Junior, Julia Mason and Rudolph Tatum. The Ebony Film Company of Chicago, which produced sixteen black cast comedies in the late 1910s, was a white-owned company whose advertisements in *Motion Picture World* said "Colored people are funny." Black newspapers like the *Chicago Defender* campaigned to prevent Ebony films like this from being screened.

The Black Triangle

This was the first chapter of a five-reel European detective serial released in America in 1914 without further identification. *Variety* relished its clichés: "A detective takes it upon himself to rescue a young girl who has been kidnapped by a desperate gang. He goes through the various trials which these wonderful men have to endure. His task takes him to mysterious houses in which he falls into pits and wells, always escaping without a scratch."

Blackbirds

1915 American film (Paramount/5 reels) based on the 1913 play *Blackbirds* by Harry James Smith. Detective Hawke Jr. (Raymond Hatton) sets out to capture the smuggler gang known as The Blackbirds. Gang leader Bechel (George Gebhardt) orders Leonie (Laura Hope Crews) to become friendly with the wealthy Crocker family and replace a valuable rug with a fake one. Leonie, however, has become involved with jewel thief Trask (Thomas Meighan) and they decide to reform. Hawke overhears their plan, follows them to the Blackbirds hideout and arrests the whole gang while allowing the reformed couple to escape. Margaret Turnbull wrote the screenplay and J. P. McGowan directed.

Blackie, Boston

Boston Blackie, one of the most famous fictional safecrackers, was created by Jack Boyle. He made his first appearance in print in *American Magazine* in 1914 and his first appearance on screen in 1918 in *Boston Blackie's Little Pal*. The only book about him is the story collection *Boston Blackie* (1919). Most of his fame comes from his movies, ten in the silent era and a famous sound series starring Chester Morris. Boston Blackie, who got his name because he was born in Boston and has piercing black eyes, lives in San Francisco where his slogan was later said to be "Enemy to those who make him an enemy, friend to those who have no friend." See *Blackie's Redemption, Boston Blackie, Boston Blackie's Little Pal, Crooked Alley, The Face in the Fog, Missing Millions, The Poppy Girl's Husband, The Return of Boston Blackie, The Silk Lined Burglar, Through the Dark*.

Blackie's Redemption

1919 American film (Metro/5 reels) based on Jack Boyle's stories "Boston Blackie's Mary" and "Fred the Count" published in *Red Book*

Magazine. Cracksman Boston Blackie (Bert Lytell) is sent to jail for twenty years after Fred the Count (Henry Kolker) plants stolen jewelry on him. The Count fancies Blackie's fiancée Mary (Alice Lake) but she rejects him and Blackie escapes from prison and returns to her. The prison warden tracks him down but lets him go when Blackie refuses to kill him when he could. Blackie then frames the Count who goes to prison. John Ince directed and Finis Fox wrote the screenplay. See also Blackie, Boston.

The Blackmailer

1919 British film (Life Dramas/2 reels), an episode in the series *The Adventures of Dorcas Dene, Detective*. Dene is an actress who become a detective to earn money after her husband is blinded. Winifred Rose plays Dene and Tom Radford is her husband. George Sims wrote the screenplay and Frank Carlton directed.

Blake, Sexton

The seemingly immortal master detective Sexton Blake, created by Harry Blyth in 1893, is the British equivalent of American detective Nick Carter, a pulp hero with impressive longevity. He is the protagonist of more stories and novels than any other detective in fiction, over 4000 already by numerous authors and they continue to be published. His first appearance was in the story "The Missing Millionaire" in *The Halfpenny Marvel* on December 20, 1893. He began as a clone of Sherlock Holmes and even moved to Baker Street with his boy assistant Tinker. He has changed a lot since his beginnings, however, and has kept up with modern times. His silent screen career, which began in 1909, was quite large and includes three different series but all the films featuring him were British. See *The Dorrington Diamonds, The Further Exploits of Sexton Blake, Sexton Blake* (1909 film), *Sexton Blake* (1910 series), *Sexton Blake* (1913 series), *Sexton Blake* (1928 series), *Sexton Blake vs. Baron Kettler*.

Blake of Scotland Yard

1927 American serial (Universal/twelve 2-reel chapters) starring Hayden Stevenson as retired Scotland Yard detective Angus Blake. He is persuaded by Lady Diana Blanton (Gloria Grey) to come out of retirement and capture The Spider (Albert Hart), a criminal mastermind who wants to steal a secret formula from Diana's father (Herbert Prior). He succeeds with the help of a mysterious woman in white (Grace Cunard). The serial, written by William Lord Wright and directed by Robert F. Hill, was a huge success and led to a 1929 sequel, *The Ace of Scotland Yard*, in which Blake fights another master criminal. The chapters were *The Castle of Fear, The Spider's Web, The Vanishing Heiress, The Room Without a Door, Shots in the Dark, Ambushed, The Secret of the Coin, Into the Web, The Baited Trap, The Lady in White, The Closing Web* and *The Final Reckoning*.

Blake the Lawbreaker

1928 British film (British Filmcraft/2 reels), one of a six-film series featuring master detective *Sexton Blake* played by Langhorne Burton with Mickey Brantford as his assistant Tinker. The supporting cast included Fred Raynham, Thelma Murray, Philip Desborough and Leslie Perrins. George J. Banfield produced, George A. Cooper directed and G. H. Teed wrote the screenplay.

Blau-weisse Steine (Blue-White Stone)

1913 German film (Imperator/4 reels) distributed in America by Midgar Features as *Diamonds of Destiny*. Detective Sharp pursues a gang of diamond and even jumps off a bridge to continue the pursuit on water. He eventually falls in love with a woman in the gang but then she kills herself for love of him. *The New York Times* reviewed this film quite favorably when it opened in New York in 1914.

Bleak House

Inspector Bucket the Detective, the first great detective in English literature, was created by Charles Dickens for his 1852 novel *Bleak House*. He is honest, middle-aged, running to stoutness, tenacious and unforgettable. The plot of the novel is almost too complex to put on film, involving among other things the blackmailing of Lady Dedlock, but two attempts were made in the silent cinema era by concentrating on Bucket's investigation of a murder (See entries below.)

Bleak House

1920 British feature (Ideal Films/7 reels) directed by Maurice Elvey. Clifford Heatherley played Inspector Bucket with Constance Collier as the blackmailed Lady Dedlock, Berta Gellardi is Esther, E Vivian Reynolds is Tulkinghorne and Norman Page is Guppy. William J. Elliot wrote the adaptation.

Constance Collier is blackmailed Lady Dedlock in *Bleak House* (1920).

Bleak House

1922 British film (Master Films/3 reels) made for the *Tense Moments from Great Plays* series. Inspector Bucket was played by Harry J. Worth with Sybil Thorndike as Lady Dedlock, Betty Doyle as Esther and Stacey Gaunt as Sir Leicester Dedlock. Frank Miller wrote the adaptation and H. B Parkinson directed.

The Blind Adventure

1918 American film (Vitagraph/5 reels) based on the novel *The Agony Column* by mystery writer Earl Derr Biggers serialized in *The Saturday Evening Post* in 1916. Geoffrey West (Edward Earle) sees American Marion Larned (Betty Howe) reading the agony column of personal ads in a London newspaper and inserts an ad asking to meet her. She says he must write her a letter proving he is interesting. He writes a letter describing the justified murder of an army captain and says he did it. She promises to protect him but is called home by her father when war begins. He joins her on the boat and confesses he made the story up to prove he was interesting. But did he? George H. Plympton wrote the screenplay and Wesley H. Ruggles directed.

The Blind Detective

1910 French Film (Le Lion/1 reel). A blind man can still detect as this film shows. A government official is attacked and robbed and an innocent passerby is accused of the crime. An old blind man, who overheard the real thieves dividing up the loot, identifies them by their voices.

The Blind Goddess

1926 American film (Paramount/8 reels) based on Arthur Chesney Train's novel *The Blind Goddess*. New York politician Big Bill Devens (Ernest Torrence) is killed and his ex-wife Eileen (Louise Dresser) is the chief suspect. District Attorney Hugh Dillon (Jack Holt) resigns to defend her when he learns that Eileen is the mother of his fiancée Moira (Esther Ralston). His investigation turns up a dictaphone recording in which the dying Devens says he was shot by his partner Kelling (Richard Tucker). Gertrude Orr wrote the screenplay and Victor Fleming directed.

Blind Man's Eyes

1919 American film (MGM/5 reels) based on the 1916 novel *The Blind Man's Eyes* by William Briggs MacHarg and Edwin Balmer. Hugh Overton (Bert Lytell) escapes from prison in order to prove he did not kill crooked financier Matthew Latrone (Joseph Kilgour). Latrone, who is actually still alive, sends a man to kill Hugh on a train but he goes to the wrong compartment and nearly kills blind lawyer Basil Santoine (Frank Currier). Santoine suspects Overton of the attack but invites him to his house to investigate. Overton goes knowing Santoine has a confession that could prove his innocence and falls in love with Santoine's daughter Harriet (Naomi Childers), "the blind man's eyes." When Latrone breaks in to the house and tries to steal the incriminating confession, he is killed in a struggle with Overton. June Mathis wrote the screenplay and John Ince directed.

Blood and Soul (Chi to rei)

1923 Japanese film (Nikkatsu/4 reels) by Kenji Mizoguchi based on the 1819 novella *Das Fräulein von Scudéry* by E. T. A. Hoffman. *Mademoiselle De Scudery* is one of the earliest detective tales. A clever society woman acts as a detective to solve a murder mystery that baffles the police of 17th century Paris. It turns out that a goldsmith with a split personality kills people who commission works from him so he can reclaim them. Kokuseki Ohizumi adapted the story and gave it a Japanese setting and Mizoguchi shot it in a German expressionist style. The actors were Chiyoko Eguchi, Harue Ichikawa, Yutaka Mimasu, Komei Minami and Yoneko Sakai.

The Blue Carbuncle

1923 British film (Stoll/2 reels), an episode in the *Last Adventures of Sherlock Holmes* series based on a story by Sir Arthur Conan Doyle. Sherlock Holmes solves the mystery of a blue carbuncle found in a goose. Eille Norwood portrays Holmes with Hubert Willis as Dr. Watson and a supporting cast including Alec Hunter, Gordon Hopkirk, Mary Mackintosh and Sebastian Smith. Alfred Moise was the cinematographer and George Ridgewell wrote the adaptation and directed. Print survives at BFI archive.

Blue Mountains Mystery

1921 Australian film (Southern Cross Pictures/6 reels). A murder mystery set in the Blue Mountains and involving members of Australian high society. Majorie Osborne headed the cast that included Bernice Vere, Vivian Edwards, John Faulkner, Billy Williams and Redmond Barry. Raymond Longford directed and Arthur Higgins was cinematographer. Australian critics praised the film's direction, photography and scenic effects.

The Blue Pearl

1920 American film (L. Lawrence Weber Photo Dramas/6 reels) based on the 1918 play *The Blue Pearl* by Anne Crawford Flexner. Thurston (D. J. Flanagan) sells a stolen blue pearl to Webb (Lumsden Hare) who gives it to his mistress Sybil (Florence Billings). She wears it to a party given by Webb and his wife Laura (Edith Hallor). When it is stolen police detective Richard Drake (Jack Halliday) investigates and finds that Laura stole the pearl to use as evidence in a divorce suit against her unfaithful husband. Emma Bell Clifton wrote the screenplay and George Irving directed.

Bobby als Detektiv (Bobby as Detective)

1908 German film (1 reel) about a boy who decides to be a detective. A print of this film survives in an archive.

Bobby Bumps and the Detective Story

1916 American animated comedy (J. R. Bray Studios/1 reel) written and directed by Earl Hurd. The popular Bobby Bumps series consisted of more than fifty films describing Bobby's comical adventures including one titled *Bobby Bumps and the Speckled Death*.

Bobby the Boy Scout or the Boy Detective

1909 British film (Clarendon/525 feet). Boy Scout Bobby proves to be a better detective than the police. After a burglary he discovers footprints, follows them to the burglar's shack, locks the crooks inside and brings the police. Percy Stow directed.

The Boomerang

1913 American film (Kay-Bee Pictures/3 reels) based on a novel by mystery writer William Hamilton Osborne. The son-in-law of a millionaire meatpacker investigates the criminal activities of his father-in-law's business and proves it is selling spoiled meat. Charles Ray, Louise Glaum and Gertrude Claire starred, C. Gardner Sullivan wrote the screenplay and Thomas H. Ince directed.

The Boomerang

1919 American film (Pioneer/7 reels) based on a novel by William Hamilton Osborne

The son-in-law of a millionaire meatpacker investigates the activities of his father-in-law's business and proves it is selling spoiled meat. With Henry B. Walthall, Nina Byron and Melbourne McDowell. Bertram Bracken directed the screenplay.

Boots

1919 American film (Paramount/5 reels) based on a story by Martha Pittman and S.E.V. Taylor. Boots (Dorothy Gish) is a romance-reading maid at a London hotel that has a secret tunnel which terrorists plan to use in a plot to blow up world leaders. Madame De Valdee (Fontine LaRue), the terrorist's leader, is staying at the hotel awaiting the right moment but Scotland Yard detective Everett White (Richard Barthelmess), pretending to be a student, is also there watching. Boots falls in love with the supposed student but gets jealous of his attentions to De Valdee and, in a fit of pique, buries her romance books in the hotel cellar. She discovers the tunnel, uncovers the plot and wins the detective. M. M. Stearns wrote the screenplay and Elmer Clifton directed.

Borrowed Finery

1925 American film (Tiffany/7 reels) based on a story by George Bronson Howard who also wrote the screenplay. Model Sheila Conroy (Louise Lorraine) is hired by society crook Harlan (Lou Tellegen) who she thinks is a government agent. Her job is to get evidence that Mrs. Bordon (Hedda Hopper) has smuggled a jewel into the country. Genuine government agent Channing Maynard (Ward Crane) sorts it out and exposes Harlan's scheme. Oscar Apfel directed.

The Boscombe Valley Mystery

1922 British film (Stoll/2 reels), an episode in the *Further Adventures of Sherlock Holmes* series based on a story by Sir Arthur Conan Doyle. Sherlock Holmes proves that a man did not murder his father and uncovers the real killer. Eille Norwood portrays Holmes with Hubert Willis as Dr. Watson. George Ridgewell wrote the adaptation and directed. A print survives at the BFI archive.

Boston Blackie

1923 American film (Fox/5 reels) based on Jack Boyle's story "The Water Cross" in *Cosmopolitan*. Boston Blackie (William Russell) tells prison warden Benton (Frank Brownlee) he will have him fired for using water torture on prisoners. Prison officers take Blackie to Benton to be tortured but meanwhile Blackie's sweetheart Mary (Eva Novak) has appealed to the governor. A reprieve arrives in time to save Blackie and Benton is sacked. Scott Dunlap directed and Paul Schofield wrote the screenplay. See also Blackie, Boston.

Lou Tellegen is a society crook in *Borrowed Finery*.

Boston Blackie (William Russell) confronts the warden (Frank Brownlee) *in Boston Blackie* (1923).

Boston Blackie's Little Pal

1918 American film (Metro/5 reels) based on Jack Boyle's story "The Baby and the Burglar" in *Red Book Magazine*. Safecracker Boston Blackie (Bert Lytell) and accomplice Mary (Rhea Mitchell) get acquainted with little pal Martin (Joel Jacobs) while stealing jewels from his parents' house. Blackie eventually gets his little pal's parents to reconcile. E. Mason Hopper directed and Albert S. Le Vino wrote the screenplay. See also Blackie, Boston.

La Boucle énigmatique

(The Enigmatic Ring)

1920 French film (Pathé-Consortium-Cinéma/3 reels), an episode in a popular tongue-in-cheek comedy series about an "American" detective named Nick Winter. In this episode Nick (Georges Vinter) looks for the second half of a mysterious ring that will reveal the location of a treasure. Maurice Maitre directed.

Bound and Gagged

1919 American serial (Pathé/ten 2-reel chapters). This is a spoof of the mystery serial satirizing the conventions of the genre but following the format most seriously. Director George B. Seitz plays the impeccable hero Archibald A. Barlow who has to protect the beautiful Princess Istra, played by Marguerite Courtot. The supporting cast includes Frank Redman as the villain plus Harry Semels, Nellie Burt, John Reinhardt and Tom Goodwin. Frank Leon Smith wrote the lighthearted screenplay. The chapters are *The Wager, Overboard, Help! Help!, An Unwilling Princess, Held for Ransom, Out Again, In Again, The Fatal Error, Arrested, A Harmless Princess* and *Hopley Takes the Liberty*.

The Boy Detective

1908 American film (Biograph/497 feet) based on the newspaper serial *Swipsey* and intended to be the start of a series. Boy newspaper vendor Swipsey learns about plans for a kidnapping a rich man's daughter and foils it by dressing in her clothes and taking her place in her carriage. He captures the abductors by

A newsboy turns into a juvenile Sherlock Holmes in *The Boy Detective*.

frightening them a gun but later reveals to the audience that it was really just a cigarette container. Swipsey was played by an unidentified young woman and Robert Harron was the messenger boy. Wallace McCutcheon wrote and directed the film photographed by G. W. Bitzer. On DVD.

Boyd, Felix

Felix Boyd, a private detective created by Scott Campbell (pseudonym of Frederick W. Davis), made his first appearance in *The Popular Magazine* in 1904. Boyd is a mixture of Nick Carter and Sherlock Holmes, a tough street fighter with a fine mind, and was featured in more than sixty stories in *The Popular Magazine*, *Magnet* and *New Magnet*. His arch-enemy is a criminal genius known as the Big Finger. The Boyd stories, set in New York City, were collected in five books beginning with *Below the Dead-Line* in 1906. Five of Boyd's cases were filmed by Edison in 1914 and 1915 with Robert Conness and Yale Boss in the lead roles under the direction of Langdon West. See *The Case of the Vanished Bonds*, *The Man Who Vanished*, *Dickson's Diamonds*, *The Banker's Double* and *An Unpaid Ransom*.

The Branded Four

1920 American serial (Select/fifteen 2-reel chapters). Criminologist A. B. C. Drake (Ben Wilson) helps Marion Leonard (Neva Gerber) solve the mystery of the "branded four." It seems four babies were branded at birth by eccentric Dr. Scraggs (Joseph W. Girard). The brands are secret marks that will become visible when they reach adulthood and reveal the hiding place of a treasure in gold. Unfortunately a lost diary is needed to decode the message. Marion, one of the four, is now twenty-one and would like to get the gold but Scraggs' evil lawyer (William Dyer) covets it as well so there is much villainous work afoot. Hope Loring wrote the bizarre screenplay and Duke Worne directed. The episodes are *A Strange Legacy*, *The Devil's Trap*, *Flames of Revenge*, *The Blade of Death*, *Fate's Pawn*, *The Hidden Cave*, *Shanghaied*, *Mutiny*, *The House of Doom*, *The Ray of Destruction*, *Buried Alive*, *Lost to the World*, *The Valley of Death*, *From the Sky* and *Sands of Torment*.

The Brass Bowl

1914 American feature (Edison/4 reels) based on Louis Joseph Vance's 1907 novel about a detective who looks exactly like thief he is trying to catch. Dan (Ben Wilson) has to capture the thief who seems to be his double (Wilson plays both roles). The supporting cast included Gertrude McCoy, Harry Bates, Clem Easton, Edwin O'Connor and Charles Sutton.

The Brass Bowl

1924 American feature (Fox/6 reels). based on Louis Joseph Vance's 1907 novel about a detective who looks exactly like thief he is trying to catch. Dan (Edmund Lowe) discovers Sylvia (Claire Adams) attempting to open his safe. She mistakes him for the famous thief Anisty, who is Dan's double. When the real Anisty (Edmund Lowe again) turns up, there is a lot of confusion. Anisty is captured but escapes and poses as Dan who finally tricks him and sends him to prison. Jerome Storm directed and Thomas Dixon, Jr., wrote the screenplay.

The Brass Bullet

1918 American serial (Universal/eighteen 2-reel chapters) based on Frank R. Adams' 1918 mystery novel *Pleasure Island*. Jack (Jack Mulhall) escapes from a sanitarium to which he was wrongly committed so he can save Rosalind (Juanita Hansen) from her evil uncle Gilbert (Joseph W. Girard). Gilbert wants gold hidden on Paradise Island to which Rosalind is the heir. A mysterious Mystery Man (Hallam Cooley) is also involved. Walter Woods wrote the screenplay and Ben F. Wilson directed. The episodes are *A Flying Start*, *The Muffled Man*, *The Mysterious Murder*, *Smoked Out*, *The Mock Bride*, *A Dangerous Honeymoon*, *Pleasure Island*, *The Magnetic Bug*, *The Room of Flame*, *A New Peril*, *Evil Waters*, *Caught by Wireless*, *$500 Reward*, *On Trial for His Life*, *In the Shadow*, *The Noose*, *The Avenger* and *The Amazing Confession*. The novel was also filmed as *Haunted Island*.

The Brass Check

1918 American film (Metro/5 reels) based on the 1916 story "The Brass Check" by George Allan England in *All-Story Weekly*. Richard Trevor (Francis X. Bushman) takes on the role of detective replacing the real detective that Edith Everett (Beverly Bayne) hired to help her brother Henry (Frank Joyner). Henry has been incarcerated in an asylum by an evil trust for refusing to hand over a valuable invention. Trevor solves the mystery, frees the brother and wins Edith. William S. Davis directed and June Mathis wrote the screenplay.

Francis X Bushman pretends to be a detective in *The Brass Check*.

The Breaker

1916 American film (Essanay/5 reels) based on the story "The Breaker" by Arthur Stringer published in *The Saturday Evening Post* in 1916. Salesman John Widder (Bryant Washburn) is tricked into hiding counterfeit money by Piazzia (Ernest Maupain). After Piazza is sent to prison, police hire Widden's neighbor Alice (Nell Craig) to act as a detective and find out what happened to the phony money. she soon realizes his innocence and gets him to hand over the money. Fred E. Wright wrote the screenplay and directed. Several real Chicago detectives were hired to add authenticity to the film.

The Breaking Point

1924 American film (Paramount/7 reels) based on the 1922 novel *The Breaking Point* by Mary Roberts Rinehart. Judson Clark (Matt Moore) believes he has killed the husband of the woman (Nita Naldi) he loves and flees into a blizzard. He survives but loses his memory and is believed dead until an actress recognizes him. After many complications, the real killer confesses, Clark regains his memory and wins the woman he loves and it stops snowing. The women in his life include also include Patsy Ruth Miller and Edythe Chaplin. Edfrid Bingham and Julie Herne wrote the screenplay and Herbert Brenon directed.

A Bride for a Knight

1923 American comedy (Renown Pictures/5 reels). Jimmy Poe (Henry Hull) inhales so much gas in a dentist's chair that he imagines he's a famous detective. His sweetheart Jean (Mary Thurman) is mystified but he begins sleuthing anyway and actually captures a gang of crooks in the act of robbing Jean's uncle (William H. Tooker). Then he runs out of gas.

The Bride's Silence

1917 American film (Mutual/5 reels). A woman stabs Nathan Standish (Henry A. Barrows) and Nathan's sister Sylvia (Gail Kane) hides the knife. Bobbins the butler (Robert Klein) is arrested but Sylvia says nothing. Detective Bull Ziegler (James Lee Farley) thinks Bobbins is innocent and suspects Sylvia who is married to attorney Paul Wagner (Lewis J. Cody). When she is caught trying to help Bobbins, she has a mental breakdown. Ziegler is ready to arrest her for murder when a telegram arrives saying Sylvia's cousin confessed that she killed Nathan to avenge betrayal by him. Sylvia knew this but kept it secret to protect the family name.

The Brighton Mystery

1924 British film (Stoll/2 reels), an episode in the *Old Man in the Corner* series based on a story by Baroness Orczy. An armchair detective known as the Old Man in the Corner solves crimes while sitting in a tea shop and tells the solutions to a journalist. Rolf Leslie played the Old Man and Renée Wakefield was journalist Mary Hatley. D. P. Cooper was the cinematographer and Hugh Croise wrote the adaptation and directed.

Britain's Secret Treaty

1914 British film (Davidson/3 reels), one of seven films in a series featuring master detective Sexton Blake written and directed by Charles Raymond. Philip Kay played Blake with Lewis Carlton as his assistant Tinker. A German count exposes Blake masquerading as a war minister and hangs him over Beachy Head with a bomb. Based on Andrew Murray's story *The Case of the German Admiral*. (See Blake, Sexton for other films and background.)

The Broken Coin

1915 American serial (Universal/twenty-two 2-reel chapters) based on a story by Emerson Hough. Reporter Kitty Gray (Grace Cunard) sets out to solve the mystery of a two-part coin after she buys one part in an antique store. She learns that it holds the secret of a treasure and decides to go to the Balkan country where the King (Harry Schumm) has the other half. She soon finds herself in big trouble as evil Count Frederick (Francis Ford) also wants the coin, the treasure and the throne. The supporting cast included Francis Ford's younger brother John just starting in the movies, Eddie Polo and Ernest Shields. Grace Cunard wrote the screenplay and Francis Ford directed. The episodes were *The Broken Coin, The Satan of the Sands, When the Throne Rocked, The Face at the Window, The Underground Foe, A Startling Discovery, Between Two Fires, The Prison in the Palace, Room 22, Cornered, The Clash of Arms, A Cry in the Dark, War, On the Battle Field, The Deluge, Kitty in Danger, The Castaways, The Underground City, The Sacred Fire, Danger on the High Seas, A Timely Rescue* and *An American Queen*.

The Bromley Case

1920 American Film (Arrow Film/5 reels) starring Glen White as Tex, a famous criminologist. Tex has to find who killed wealthy John Bromley Sr. (Clarence Heritage) and robbed his safe. Bromley's son (Wallace Ray)

Glen White stars as detective Tex in *The Bromley Case*.

and a gambler (Walter Lewis) to whom he owed money had broken into the house on the night of the murder but Tex clears them. Suspicion moves to a second son (Joseph Striker) and then to a woman of easy virtue (Mabel Bardine). Tex finally proves that the butler (William Cavanaugh) did it while attempting to take money from the safe. David Wall wrote and directed the film for the *Tex, Elucidator of Mysteries* series.

Francis Ford and Grace Cunard star in the serial *The Broken Coin*.

The Bronze Bell

1921 American film (Paramount/6 reels) based on Louis Joseph Vance's 1909 novel *The Bronze Bell*. David Amber (Courtenay Foote) looks exactly like East Indian prince Har Dyal Rutton (Foote again) who is living incognito in America. When the prince is assassinated, Amber is asked to go to India and pretend to be the prince in order to quell a rebellion. Fanatics learn of the deception and abduct Amber's girlfriend Sophia (Doris May). She is taken to the Temple of the Bronze Bell along with Amber but British troops arrive to save them in the nick of time.

Brooding Eyes

1926 American film (Banner Productions/6 reels) based on the 1921 novel *The Man with the Brooding Eyes* by John Goodwin (pseudonym of Sidney Gowing). Lionel Barrymore has a triple role in this complicated mystery set in London. He begins as Slim Jim Carey, the head of a gang specializing in forgeries and swindles. In reality he is Lord Tallbois, an aristocrat who was thrown out by his family but is now the heir of the estate. When he is reported dead, his daughter Joan (Ruth Clifford) becomes the heir but Carey's gang sets out to take it away from her. Barrymore, who is not dead, spies on them through the eyes of a portrait of himself on the mantel and returns disguised as a tramp. He foils their scheme but is killed for real this time. Mary Alice Scully and Pierre Gendron wrote the screen play and Edward J. Le Saint directed.

The Bruce Partington Plans

1922 British film (Still/2 reels), an episode in the *Further Adventures of Sherlock Holmes* series based on a story by Sir Arthur Conan Doyle. Sherlock Holmes solves the mystery of the disappearance of secret plans. Eille Norwood portrays Holmes with Hubert Willis as Dr. Watson. George Ridgewell wrote the adaptation and directed. A print survives at the BFI archive.

Bucket, Inspector

Inspector Bucket of the Detective, the first great detective in English literature, was created by Charles Dickens for his 1852 novel *Bleak House*. He is honest, middle-aged, running to stoutness, tenacious and unforgettable. The plot of the novel is almost too complex to put on film, involving among other things the blackmailing of Lady Dedlock, but two attempts were made in the silent cinema era by concentrating on Bucket's investigation of a murder. See *Bleak House* for details.

Bulldog Drummond

1922 English film (Hollandia/6 reels) based on H. C. McNeile's play and novel *Bulldog Drummond*. Drummond (Carlyle Blackwell) learns that a crooked nursing home is run by his arch-enemy Carl Peterson (Horace de Vere) as a way of stealing money from wealthy patients. Drummond puts a stop to that with help from Evelyn Greeley and Gerald Dean. Oscar Apfel directed and C. B. Doxat-Pratt wrote the screenplay. See Drummond, Bulldog for other films and background.

Bulldog Drummond's Third Round

1925 English film (Astra-National/7 reels) based on H. C. McNeile's 1925 novel *The Third Round*. Drummond (Jack Buchanan) learns that his arch-enemy Carl Peterson (Allan Jeaves) is behind a scheme to kidnap a scientist who has discovered how to manufacture diamonds. The supporting cast included Betty Faire and Juliette Compton. Sidney Morgan directed and wrote the screenplay. See Drummond, Bulldog for other films and background.

A Bundle of Trouble

1917 American comedy (Nestor/2 reels) starring Lee Moran as bungling Detective Potts. Eddie Lyons plays his friend while Edith Roberts and Harry Nolan provide support. Karl R. Coolidge wrote the script and Louis Chaudet directed the fourth film in the *Detective Potts* series.

Bungling Bill, Detective

1916 American comedy (Vogue Motion Picture Company/2 reels) starring Paddy McGuire. This was one of a series featuring former circus clown McGuire as Bungling Bill in different occupations, including that of burglar and doctor. The supporting cast included Jack Gaines, Merta Sterling, Jack Connolly and Louise Owen. Robert Dillon wrote and directed.

The Burglar and the Lady

1914 American film (Blaché-Warners/5 reels). Boxing champion "Gentleman Jim" Corbett portrayed a Raffles-like gentleman thief in this movie about a poor man forced to become a cracksman to support his ailing mother. A detective pursues him until he finally decides to go straight. Corbett has a double role in the film disguising himself as the detective when not cracking safes as the burglar. He has a clergyman brother who gets him to reform. With Claire Whitney, Fraunie Fraunholz and James O'Neill. Langdon McCormick wrote the script and Herbert Blaché directed.

Burning Up Broadway

1928 American film (Sterling Pictures/6 reels) based on a story by Norman Houston New York chorus girl Floss (Helen Costello) is introduced to out-of-town visitor Bob (Robert Frazer) by her friend Harry (Ernest Hilliard) and they quickly run into trouble with bootlegger Spike (Sam Hardy). When they are kidnapped by the bootlegger's gang, Harry rides to the rescue with a police posse as a shipment of liquor is unloaded. Floss and Harry, it turns out, are really undercover detectives out to capture a gang of rum runners. Frances Guihan wrote the screenplay and Phil Rosen directed.

Burns, William J.

Detective William J. Burns (1860–1932), who created the William J. Burns International Detective Agency and headed the Bureau of Investigation (predecessor of the FBI) from 1921 to 1924, appeared in a number of early films based on his cases. They included the 1913 Kalem short *Exposure of the Land Swindlers* and the 1914 Dramascope feature *$5,000,000 Coun-*

Detective William J. Burns with Mayor Thompson.

terfeiting Plot. He was an advisor on *The Argyle Case* (1917).

Burnt Fingers

1927 American film (Pathé/6 reels). Café dancer Anne Cabell (Eileen Percy) is caught searching the apartment of her dancing partner Stockmar (Ivan Doline) while looking for love letters and Stockmar is shot by an unknown person. She gets away but is tracked down by the police and arrested. Lord Cumberly (Wilfred Lucas) of the British Foreign Office proves that Stockmar was a spy for a unfriendly country and was killed by another spy. Maurice Campbell directed and wrote the screenplay with G. Marion Burton.

Burstup Holmes, Detective

1913 American comedy series made for the Solax studio starring Billy Quirk as an Sherlock Holmes clone. He was featured in four films: *Burstup Holmes Detective, Burstup Holmes Murder Case, The Case of the Missing Girl* and *The Mystery of the Lost Cat*, all directed by Alice Guy Blaché. Quirk had starred earlier in a Solax comedy titled *Billy the Detective*.

Burstup Holmes Detective

1913 American comedy (Solax/2 reels)

starring comic Billy Quirk and directed by Alice Guy Blaché. Quirk plays a bumbling detective who models himself on Sherlock Holmes. The supporting cast included Blanche Cornwall and Darwin Karr.

Burstup Holmes Murder Case

1913 American comedy (Solax/2 reels) starring comic Billy Quirk and directed by Alice Guy Blaché. He plays a bumbling detective modeled on Sherlock Holmes and is hired by Blanche Cornwall to find her husband (Darwin Karr). She thinks has been murdered but he has really just slipped out to play poker. Burstup misses all the clues and Cornwall ends up having to find him herself.

By Whose Hand?

1916 American film (World-Equitable/5 reels). This is a "lady or the tiger" type mystery with the identity of the murderer still up in the air at the end of the film as the audience has to decide who dunnit. Simon Baird is carrying $5000 when he is killed. David (James Ryley), who needed $5000 to marry Helen (Muriel Ostriche), is arrested the next day with that exact sum. But Edith (Edna Wallace Hopper) says she killed Simon because he had wronged her and gave David the money. David says this is not true, that he did it. The judge can't decide who is telling the truth and asks the audience to decide. Channing Pollock and Rennold Wolf wrote the screenplay and James Durkin directed.

By Whose Hand?

1927 American film (Columbia/6 reels) based on a story by Marion Orth who wrote the screenplay. A detective is sent undercover to trap a jewel thief and entertainer Peg Hewlett (Eugenia Gilbert) is the prime suspect. Among those attending a party at which jewels are stolen are smart set members Van Suydam Smith (Ricardo Cortez), "Society Charlie" Mortimer (William Scott) and Mr. Sidney (J. Thornton Baston). Smith, who is the undercover detective, and Sidney, who is an insurance agent, expose Mortimer as the criminal. Walter Lang directed.

Cabaret

1927 American film (Paramount/7 reels) based on a story by Owen Davis. Detective Tom Westcott (Tom Moore) loves nightclub entertainer Gloria Trask (Gilda Gray) but gangster Sam Roberts (Charles Byer) has a hold over her through her brother Andy (Jack Egan). When Andy shoots Roberts in self-defense, Gloria helps him escape and Westcott gets Roberts' girlfriend Blanche (Mona Palma) to reveal what really happened. Becky Gardiner wrote the screenplay and Robert G. Vignola directed.

The Café L'Egypte

1924 British film (Stoll/2 reels), an episode in *The Further Mysteries of Fu Manchu* series based on a story by Sax Rohmer Harry Agar Lyons plays Dr. Fu Manchu, Fred Paul is Nayland Smith and Humberston Wright is Dr. Petrie. Fred Paul directed and wrote the screenplay and Frank Canham was the cinematographer.

Calamity Ann, Detective

1913 American comedy (American Film/1 reel) starring Louise Lester as the detective. This was the first episode in a series of twelve comedies starring Lester filmed in 1912–1914. Lester wrote the scripts and Alan Dwan directed with supporting casts that included J. Warren Kerrigan and Jack Richardson. Allan Dwan directed.

Calínez and Gedeón Detectives

(Calínez y Gedeón Detectives)

1916 Spanish film (Studio Films/3 reels) directed by Domènec Ceret and written by Alfredo Fontanals & Juan Solá Mestres. The cast included José Alfonso, Domènec Ceret, Pilar España, Josep Font, Dolores Mas and José Uvall.

Calvert's Valley

1922 American film (Fox/5 reels) based on Margaret Prescott Montague's novel *In Calvert's Valley*. James Calvert (Philo McCullough) is pushed off a cliff and an old woman (Lulu Warrenton) says his drunken companion Page Emlyn (Jack Gilbert) did it. He is arrested but Calvert's former sweetheart Hester (Sylvia Breamer) believes it was suicide. After more questioning the old woman admits that her halfwit son was the killer. Jules Furthman wrote the screenplay and Jack Dillon directed.

Camillo Emulates Sherlock Holmes
(Camillo emulo di Sherlok Holmes)

1921 Italian comedy (Caesar Film/987 meters). Italian comic Camillo De Riso stars as Camillo who has dreams of becoming a detective. He gets support from Myriel, Ermnia Cigoli and Alberto Albertini. De Riso directed and Alfredo Manzi wrote the screenplay.

Captain of His Soul

1918 American film (Triangle/5 reels). Ebenezer Boyce (Walt Whitman) hands over control of his factory to Martin (Jack Richardson) at the suggestion of his sons Horace (William Desmond) and Henry (Charles Gunn) and dies shortly later. When Martin is found murdered, the brothers suspect each other and Henry publicly accuses Horace. At that point Martin's mistress Annette De Searcy (Claire McDowell) confesses that she killed Martin in self-defense. Lillian Ducey wrote the screenplay and Gilbert P. Hamilton directed.

The Cardboard Box

1923 British film (Stoll/2 reels), an episode in the *Last Adventures of Sherlock Holmes* series based on a story by Sir Arthur Conan Doyle. Sherlock Holmes solves the mystery of a pair of human ears sent to a woman in a cardboard box. Eille Norwood portrays Holmes with Hubert Willis as Dr. Watson. Alfred Moise was the cinematographer and George Ridgewell wrote the adaptation and directed. Print survives at BFI archive.

Carter, Nick

American detective Nick Carter has had more fictional adventures than any other American detective and series of films featuring his adventures have been made in France, Germany and America. He is said to be immensely strong, incredibly clever, a master of disguise and a veritable encyclopedia of arcane knowledge. Carter was the creation of dime

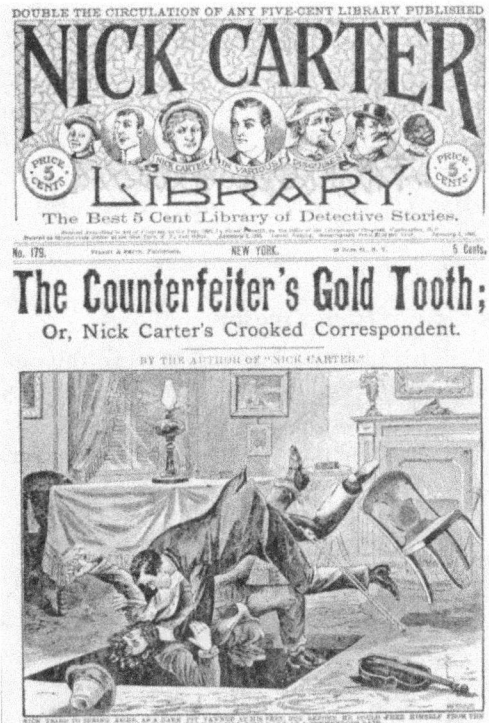

Nick Carter has had more fictional adventures than any other American detective since his creation in 1886 and was on screen on 1908.

novelist John Russell Coryell and his first case appeared in the *New York Weekly* in 1886. Later stories (and they still continue) were written by dozens of authors including the prolific Frederic Van Rensselaer Dey who churned out over a thousand. Carter had his own magazine by 1896, the *Nick Carter Library*, and was being featured in movies by 1908. For his films See *Nick Carter, Nick Carter le roi des détectives* and *Les Nouveaux Exploits de Nick Carter*.

The Carter Case

1919 American serial (Oliver Films/fifteen 2-reel chapters) based on Craig Kennedy stories by Arthur B. Reeve. Anita Carter (Marguerite Marsh) asks scientific detective Craig Kennedy (Herbert Rawlinson) to investigate the murder of her father, factory owner Shelby Carter (Donald Hall), and the theft of his secret formulas. Master criminal Avion (Joseph Marba), who killed her father, is now seeking to murder her. Reeve and John W. Grey wrote the screenplay and Donald McKenzie and William G Haddock directed. The supporting cast included Ethel Grey Terry as Cleo Clark, William Pike as Walter Jameson and Kempton Greene as Rance Dixon. The chapters have "scientific" titles like *The Vacuum Room, The Air Terror, The Wireless Detective, The Nervagraph, The Silent Shot, The Camera Trap* and *The X-Ray Detective*.

A Case of High Treason

1911 American film (Edison/1 reel) based on the story "The Under Man" by mystery writer Thomas Hanshew. Starring Herbert Prior with James Gordon, Laura Sawyer, Charles Sutton and Richard Ridgely.

Herbert Prior stars in the 1911 mystery film *The Case of High Treason*.

A Case of Identity

1921 British film (Stoll/2 reels), an episode in the *Adventures of Sherlock Holmes* series based on a story by Sir Arthur Conan Doyle. Sherlock Holmes solves a mystery involving a missing bridegroom. Eille Norwood portrays Holmes with Hubert Willis as Dr. Watson. William J. Elliot wrote the script and Maurice Elvey directed. A print of this film survives at the BFI archive.

The Case of the Missing Girl

1913 American comedy (Solax/2 reels) starring comic Billy Quirk as detective Burstup Holmes. He is really awful as an investigator but he thinks of himself as the equivalent of Sherlock Holmes. The supporting cast included Blanche Cornwall and Darwin Karr. Alice Guy Blaché directed.

The Case of the Vanished Bonds

1914 American film (Edison/1 reel), one of five films in the *Felix Boyd* series based on a private detective created by Scott Campbell. Boyd was a tough street fighter like Nick Carter with a brilliant mind like Sherlock Holmes. Robert Conness starred in the series with support from Yale Boss, Bigelow Cooper and Richard Neil. Langdon West directed. (See Boyd, Felix for list of other films.)

The Cat and the Canary

1927 American film (Universal/8 reels) based on the 1922 play *The Cat and the Canary* by John Willard. The most famous of the old dark house mystery movies does not have a real detective but bumbling Paul Jones (Creighton

Laura La Plante has inheritance problems in *The Cat and the Canary* (sheet music).

Hale) does his best as he tries to find out what is going on and protect cousin Annabelle (Laura La Plante) from a mysterious criminal. La Plante is the canary who has inherited an eccentric millionaire's estate (at midnight, no less) if she can prove she is not insane; otherwise the money goes to an unnamed someone else (guess who the bad guy will be). La Plante has a long night ahead of her as some of the other guests are as weird as the house. Paul Leni directed in a nicely scary manner, Alfred Cohn wrote a clever screenplay and cinematographer Gilbert Warrenton has a grand time with the frightening sets by Charles D. Hall. On DVD.

The Catspaw

1916 American film (Edison/5 reels) Based on the 1911 novel *Catspaw* by mystery writer William Hamilton Osborne. Thief Kittredge St. John (Marc MacDermott) hires a look-alike double who will be seen in public during a robbery. The plan works so well that Kittredge's sweetheart/partner Roxane Bellairs (Miriam Nesbitt) is fooled. When she sees the double with another woman, she becomes jealous and tells the police about his thefts. At the trial Kittredge manages to put the blame on the double and escape with Roxane. James Harris and Brad Sutton play the investigating detectives. George A. Wright directed.

Caught, a Detective Story

1908 American film (Vitagraph/560 feet). No other details available.

Caught in the Fog

1928 American film (Warner Bros./7 reels) based on a story by Jerome Kingston. Incompetent detectives Ryan (Mack Swain) and Riley (Hugh Herbert) go to a houseboat to investigate a jewel robbery and get fogged in. No wonder. Wealthy Bob Vicker (Conrad Nagel) had gone there to retrieve his mother's jewels and found the boat full of thieves pretending to be something else. The girl (May McAvoy) pretends to be the maid, her crook partner (Charles Gerrard) pretends to be the cook and an elderly couple (Emil Chautard and Ruth Cherrington) pretend to be guests of his mother. Not to be outdone Bob pretends to be the butler. After a long night of comings and going, the detectives arrest everyone but the girl as Bob has fallen for her. Charles R. Condon wrote the screenplay and Howard Bretherton directed.

Caught with the Goods

1911 American comedy (Biograph/1 reel), a film in the *Two Sleuths* series produced and directed by Mack Sennett and starring Sennett and Fred Mace. They play comic detectives who involved with John T. Dillon, William Bechtel and Kate Toncray. George Hennessy wrote the screenplay.

The Cavern Spider

1924 British film (Stoll/2 reels) based on story by L. J. Beeston, an episode in the series *Thrilling Stories from the Strand*. With Jameson Thomas, Freddy Fraynham, Winifred Izard and Ian Wilson. Thomas Bentley directed.

Chains of Evidence

1920 American film (Hallmark Pictures/5 reels) based on a story by Leon D. Britton. Judge Sturgis (Edmund Breese) is murdered and radium is stolen from his safe. The principal suspect is Dick (Wallace Ray), the son of Mrs. Sturgis (Marie Shotwell) by a previous marriage. He had been unjustly imprisoned by the judge and is now involved with the judge's daughter Edith (Anna Lehr). An old cobbler (Edward Elkas) tells Detective Simms (James F. Cullen) that he witnessed the murder carried out by the criminal Brownlow gang as vengeance. J. Clarkson Miller wrote the screenplay and Dallas M. Fitzgerald directed.

Chairo no-Onna see Arsène Lupin contre Herlock Sholmes

Champion of Lost Causes

1925 American film (Fox/5 reels) based on the short story "Champion of Lost Causes" by Max Brand published in *Flynn's Magazine* in 1924. During a visit to a gambling resort run by a man named Zanten (Walter McGrail), the journalist Loring (Edmund Lowe) meets a man who is later murdered. Peter Charles (Alec Francis), the father of the woman he loves (Barbara Bedford), is accused of the murder but

Loring believes he is innocent and decides to investigate. He asks Zanten for help but this leads to his being attacked by a gang of thugs. It turns out that Zanten himself was the murderer. Thomas Dixon, Jr., wrote the screenplay and Chester Bennett directed.

Chan, Charlie

Charlie Chan, the creation of Earl Derr Biggers, has become the most famous Chinese detective in the movies though he was never portrayed on screen by a Chinese actor. Chan, who works for the Honolulu police department, made his first appearance in print in 1925 in the novel *The House Without a Key* and his first appearance on screen in the 1926 Pathé serial based on that book. His appearances in the silent cinema did not show him at his best. He was played by Japanese actor George Kuwa in *The House Without a Key* in 1926 and by Japanese actor Sojin in *The Chinese Parrot* in 1928. Chan's real movie fame began in the 1930s when he was played by Swedish-born Warner Oland and Missouri-born Sidney Toler. Who would have thought that there weren't Chinese actors capable of playing the role!.

Charles Augustus Milverton

1922 British film (Stoll/2 reels), an episode in the *Further Adventures of Sherlock Holmes* series based on a story by Sir Arthur Conan Doyle. Sherlock Holmes witnesses the murder a blackmailer but will not tell the police what he saw. Eille Norwood portrays Holmes with Hubert Willis as Dr. Watson. George Ridgewell wrote the adaptation and directed. A print survives at the BFI archive.

Charles Peace, King of Criminals

1914 British film (British & Colonial/2 reels) about the famous Victorian burglar villain, a favorite subject of penny dreadfuls and the protagonist of two famous 1905 British films. This film, directed by Ernest G. Batley and starring Jeff Barlow as Charles Peace, shows Peace carrying out burglaries and escaping by using disguises. He is eventually caught and executed. Batley made his films with his wife Ethyle as co-director. See also *Life of Charles Peace*.

Chase, Lambert

Lambert Chase is an American detective modeled on Sherlock Holmes created by Maurice Costello and B. R. Brooker for the Vitagraph Studio. He was portrayed by Maurice Costello in a series of eight 1-reel films shot in 1912 and 1913 and directed by Costello and Van Dyke Brooks. See *The Adventure of the Ambassador's Disappearance*, *The Adventure of the Counterfeit Bills*, *The Adventure of the Italian Model*, *The Adventure of the Retired Army Colonel*, *The Adventure of the Thumb Print*, *The Mystery of the Stolen Child*, *The Mystery of the Stolen Jewels*, and *On the Pupil of His Eye*.

Chauncey Proves a Good Detective

1908 British film (Crescent Film/750 feet) starring William Kolle as Chauncey. The film was distributed in America with this title but the original British title is unknown.

Cheating Cheaters

1919 American film (Select Pictures/5 reels) based on a play by Max Marchin about an undercover woman detective. The Brockton and Palmer gangs, who have set up households

Clara Kimball Young is an undercover detective in *Cheating Cheaters* (1919).

next to each other in a fashionable neighborhood to facilitate robbing rich neighbors, join forces when they learn the truth about each other. Then they learn that one of their number is a detective in disguise sent to trap them. They abandon their robbery plans and the woman detective decides to lets them go free because she has fallen in love with a gang member. Clara Kimball Young played Detective Ferris who disguises herself as gang member Ruth Brockton to infiltrate the gang with Jack Holt playing Tom Palmer, the crook she fancies. The cast included Anna Q. Nilsson, Frederick Burton and Tully Marshall. Kathryn Stuart wrote the screenplay and Allan Dwan directed.

Cheating Cheaters

1927 American film (Universal/6 reels) based on a play by Max Marchin about an undercover woman detective. Betty Compson plays the double role of undercover detective and fake gang member in this second film version of the play described above. This time she is a minor criminal who the police have forced to turn detective. Kenneth Harlan is the guy she loves and the supporting cast includes Sylvia Ashton, Erwin Connelly and Maude Turner Gordon. Charles A. Logue wrote the screenplay and Edward Laemmle directed.

Chelsea 7750

1913 American film (Famous Players/4 reels). Kate Kirby (Laura Sawyer), daughter of crippled detective Kirby (Henry E. Dixey), turns detective to aid her father. She is kidnapped by a gang of counterfeiters headed by the villainous Professor Grimble (House Peters) whose son had been sent to prison by her father. Kate is able to use a telephone to send her father a Morse code message. She escapes and Grimble is killed in an explosion. J. Searle Dawley wrote and directed the film, the first in the *Kate Kirby* series.

Chéri-Bibi

Chéri-Bibi is the anti-hero of three novels by French mystery writer Gaston Leroux. In the first novel, serialized in *Le Matin* in 1913, he is falsely convicted of murdering his boss and sent to Devil's Island while his rival Maxime marries his love Cécily. He escapes, finds Maxime dead on his shipwrecked yacht and swaps faces with him with the help of a surgeon. He returns to France only to find that police have discovered that Maxime was the real murderer. He is arrested in his new identity and sent back to Devil's Island. The character was immensely popular in France and was featured in three silent films. See below and *La Nouvelle Aurore*.

Chéri-Bibi

1913 French film (3 reels) based on Gaston Leroux's novel *Chéri-Bibi* about a man who escapes from Devil's Island after being falsely convicted of murdering his boss. Meanwhile the real murderer has married his love Cécily. René Navarre starred as Chéri-Bibi with Josette Andriot as Cécily. Gérard Bourgeois directed.

Chéri-Bibi

1914 French film (Eclair/4 reels) based on Gaston Leroux's novel *Chéri-Bibi* about a man who escapes from Devil's Island after being falsely convicted of murdering his boss. Meanwhile the real murderer has married his love Cécily. Émile Keppens starred as Chéri-Bibi with Marise Dauvray as Cécily. Charles Krauss directed and wrote the screenplay.

Detective Kate Kirby (Laura Sawyer) and her father (Henry E. Dixey) prepare a mechanical spy in *Chelsea 7750*.

Le Cheveu d'or (The Hair of Gold)

1912 French film (Eclipse/2 reels). "Nat Pinkerton of the Pinkerton Detective Agency" is asked by an inventor's daughter to investigate the theft of plans for a new machine. Her sweetheart, the inventor's assistant, is accused of the crime but the daughter knows they were taken by family friend Bronson. Pinkerton gets him to confess and return the designs. Pierre Bressol played Pinkerton and directed the film. A print of this film survives in an archive.

The Chinatown Mystery

1928 American serial (Syndicate/ten 2-reel chapters). Strongman Joe Masters (Joe Bonomo) battles the evil Sphinx (Francis Ford) to get a secret formula and save the life of Sally Warren (Ruth Hiatt) who has it. Ford wrote the screenplay and J. P. McGowan directed. The chapters are titled *The Chinatown Mystery, The Clutching Claw, The Devil's Dice, The Mysterious, Galloping Fury, The Depth of Danger, The Invisible Hand, The Wreck, Broken Jade* and *The Thirteenth Hour*.

The Chinese Parrot

1928 American film (Universal/7 reels) based on Earl Derr Biggers' 1926 novel *The Chinese Parrot*. Detective Charlie Chan (Sojin) is hired by Sally Philimore (Marian Nixon) to handle the sale of a pearl necklace to Philip Madden (Hobart Bosworth). Madden is kidnapped and the necklace stolen but Chan solves both crimes with the help of a Chinese parrot. J. Grubb Alexander wrote the screenplay and Paul Leni directed the film in what was called a "stylized manner."

Chicago May, the Modern Adventuress

1909 British film (Anglo-American Films/985 feet) Chicago May was a real person, an Irish folk heroine rogue whose amazing real-life adventures were explored by the Irish writer Nuala O'Faolain. In the 26 scenes in the film May leaves Ireland for America, become a card sharp, earns money as a prostitute, joins a gang, robs a bank, kidnaps a woman, breaks out of jail and generally behaves in a most unladylike manner.

The Chronicles of Cleek

1913–1914 American serial (Edison/thirteen 1-reel episodes) based on stories by Thomas W. Hanshew and featuring Ben Wilson as Hamilton Cleek and Robert Brower as Detective Narkom. Cleek, known as the "man of forty faces," dons multiple disguises, solves all types of baffling crimes (including the theft of a Stradivarius) and constantly outwits Detective Narkom. George A Lessey and Ben Wilson directed the films written and produced by Hanshew. The episodes were titled *The Vanishing Cracksman, The Mystery of the Dover Express, The Mystery of the Talking Wire, The Mystery of the Ladder of Light, The Mystery of the Laughing Death, The Mystery of the Silver Snare, The Mystery of the Amsterdam Diamonds, The Mystery of the Fadeless Tints, The Mystery of the Lost Stradivarius, The Mystery of the Octagonal Room, The Mystery of the Glass Tubes, The Mystery of the Sealed Art Gallery* and *The Heritage of Hamilton Cleek*.

Cleek (Ben Wilson, second from left) catches the villains in *The Chronicles of Cleek*.

The Cinema Murder

1919 American film (Paramount/6 reels) based on E. Phillips Oppenheim's 1917 novel *The Cinema Murder*. Elizabeth (Marion Davies) is fired from a movie after rehearsing a murder scene. The film's backer, financier Sylvanus Power (Anders Randolf), has arranged it as he wants to make her his mistress. He pays for her to go to England to study drama and while there she witnesses a fight between the Romilly brothers in which Philip supposedly kills his brother. Elizabeth falls in love with Philip and persuades Power to back a play by Philip. It makes her a star but Power gets jealous and tries to get Philip arrested for killing his brother. But then, surprise, the brother turns up alive; it was just acting to attract her attention. George D. Baker directed, Frances Marion wrote the screenplay and Hal Rosson was the cinematographer.

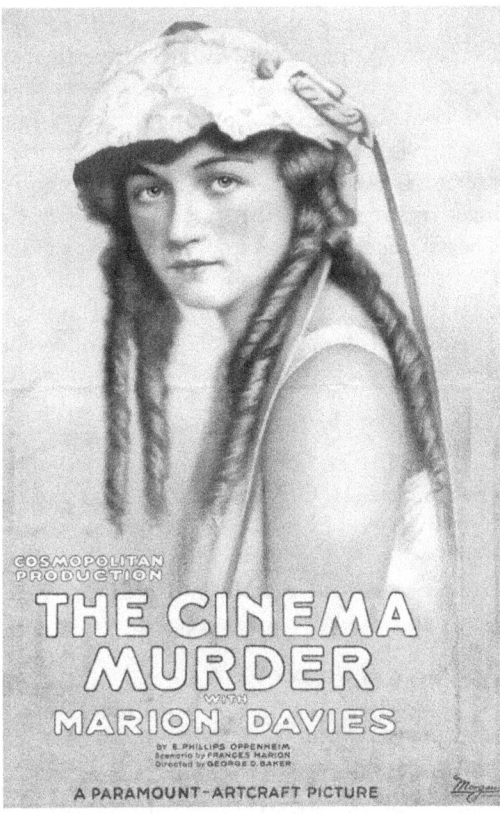

Marion Davies is involved in a murder in *The Cinema Murder*.

The Circular Staircase

1915 American film (Selig/5 reels) based on Mary Roberts Rinehart's 1908 novel *The Circular Staircase*. Aunt Ray (Eugenie Besserer) has rented banker Paul Armstrong's mansion for the summer and is visited there by Halsey (Guy Oliver), his sister Gertrude (Stella Razeto) and her fiancé Jack (William Howard). When the banker's son Arnold (Clyde Benson) is found dead at the foot of the circular staircase and Jack disappears, an investigation begins. Detective Jamieson (Fred Huntly) learns that a large sum of money has disappeared from Armstrong's bank and may be hidden in the mansion. Edward J. Le Saint directed.

Circumstantial Evidence

1920 American Film (Arrow Film/5 reels) starring Glen White as Tex, a famous criminologist. Tex tells how he began his career solving crimes. He was arrested for murder on circumstantial evidence because he tried to protect a victim's wife and was sent to prison. After he is pardoned, he discovers that the real killer was the wife he tried protect. He decides to become a detective with the intention of clearing innocent suspects. The supporting cast included Leo Delaney, Jane McAlpin, Alfred Warman and David Wall. Tom Collins wrote the screenplay and directed the film, part of the *Tex, Elucidator of Mysteries* series.

City of Silent Men

1921 American film (Paramount/6 reels) based on John A. Moroso's 1913 novel *The Quarry*. Jim Montgomery (Thomas Meighan) is framed for murder and sent to prison for life. His cellmate (Paul Everton) helps him escape to attend his mother's funeral. Afterwards he goes to California, gets a job with a company and marries the owner's daughter Molly (Lois Wilson) who believes in his innocence. Detective Mike Kearney (George MacQuarrie) finds Jim in California but decides to let him go after he learns that the real killer has made a death-bed confession. Frank Condon wrote the screenplay and Tom Forman directed.

The City Gone Wild

1927 American film (Paramount/6 reels) based on a story by Jules and Charles Furthman with screenplay by Jules. District attorney Franklin Ames investigates a gang war, discovers that that the secret boss of crime is the father of his fiancée Nada (Marietta Millner) and is killed before he can expose him. Criminal lawyer John Phelan (Thomas Meighan), who also loves Nada, takes over as district attorney to avenge his friend. Gang moll Snuggles (Louise Brooks) confesses to the murder. James Cruze directed.

Cleek, Hamilton

Hamilton Cleek, the creation of Thomas W. Hanshew, began as a crook the police knew only as the "man of forty faces" though he later turned detective. Like most early pulp rogues he is a master of disguise but Cleek is different. He can change his appearance without makeup as he has the ability to contort his face into any shape. His nemesis is Detective Narkom who is always on his trail though always a step behind. The first Cleek stories were told in *The Man of Forty Faces* series in *People's Ideal Fiction Magazine* in 1910 followed by the *Cleek of Scotland Yard* series in *Cassell's Saturday Journal* in 1912. His adventures were filmed by Edison in 1913 as *The Chronicles of Cleek*.

The Closed Door

1915 American film (Kalem/2 reels, the only surviving episode of the serial *The Girl Detective*. Marin Sais stars as a society girl who works with the police and is able to help them solve crimes because of her society connections. The supporting cast includes Paul Hurst and Ollie Kirby. Hamilton Smith wrote the screenplay, Knute Olaf Rahm was cinematographer and James W. Horne directed.

The Closing Net

1915 American film (Pathé/5 reels) based on the 1912 novel *The Closing Net* by Henry C. Rowland serialized in *The Saturday Evening Post*. Frank Clamart (Howard Estabrook) joins a gang of robbers led by Chu Chu (Arthur Albro). When they attempt to rob a mansion, Frank is shot and wounded by the owner and then identified by a birthmark as his long lost half brother. Frank agrees to reform but when Chu Chu steals the family jewels, Frank becomes the main suspect. To clear his name he tricks Chu Chu and gets the gems back. Chu Chu tries again and is killed. George B. Seitz wrote the screenplay and Edward José directed.

Le Club des suicides (The Suicide Club)

1909 French film (Éclair/1 reel), an episode in the *Les Nouveaux Exploits de Nick Carter* series about the master detective Nick Carter. It was loosely based on a story by Robert Louis Stevenson and distributed in America as *Nick Carter and the Suicide Club*. Carter prevents a journalist from being tricked into committing suicide. Pierre Bressol played Nick Carter and Victorin Jassett wrote and directed the film. See also *The Suicide Club*.

The Clue

1915 American film (Paramount/5 reels). Detective Williams (Billy Elmer) investigates the murder of Russian Alexis (Page Peters) who had come to America planning to marry Eve (Gertrude Keller). He finds a coin nearby that incriminates Guy (Edward Mackey) who is loved by Eve's friend Christine (Blanche Sweet). The real killer turns out to be Japanese spy Nogi (Sessue Hayakawa) who was trying to retrieve a secret Japanese map from Alexis. Margaret Turnbull wrote the screenplay and James Neill directed.

The Clue of the Cigar Band

1915 British film (Big Ben/4 reels). A customs officer (H. O. Martinek) traps a gang of cigar smugglers by pretending to be a blind seaman and saves a girl (Ivy Montford) they had compromised. L. C. MacBean wrote the screenplay and H. O. Martinek directed.

The Clue of the New Pin

1929 British film (British Lion/7 reels) based on the 1923 novel *The Clue of the New Pin* by Edgar Wallace. A wealthy recluse is found dead in a locked vault with the key beside him. In his will he leaves everything to his ward (Benita Hume) so she becomes the chief suspect. The real killer then tries to bump her off. The cast members included Donald Calthrop, Kim Peacock, Caleb Porter and John Gielgud. Kathleen Hayden wrote the screenplay and Arthur Maude directed. This was a silent film but there was a later a sound-on-disc version.

The Clue of the Oak Leaf

1926 British film (FHC Productions/2 reels), an episode in the series *Inscrutable Drew, Investigator* featuring Henry Ainley as private detective Victor Drew. In this episode Drew and his assistant Dracos follows the clue of an oak leaf. The cast includes Bertram Burleigh, Molly Wynn, H. Agary Lyson, Harry Davo and Cameron Carr. Elliot Stannard wrote the screenplay and A. E. Coleby directed.

The Clue of the Pigtail

1923 British film (Stoll/2 reels), an episode in the *Mystery of Fu Manchu* series based on a story by Sax Rohmer. Harry Agar Lyons plays Dr. Fu Manchu, Fred Paul is Nayland Smith and Humberston Wright is Dr. Petrie. A. E. Colby directed, Frank Wilson wrote the screenplay with Colby and D. P. Cooper was the cinematographer.

The Clue of the Second Goblet

1928 British film (British Filmcraft/2 reels), one of a six-film series featuring master detective Sexton Blake played by Langhorne Burton with Mickey Brantford as his assistant Tinker. The supporting cast included Fred Raynham, Gabrielle Morton and Leslie Perrins. George J. Banfield produced, George A Cooper directed and G. H Teed wrote the screenplay. (See Blake, Sexton for background on detective and list of other films in which he appears.)

La Collana dei quattro millione
(The Million Dollar Necklace)

Italian film (Cines/1 reel) starring comedian Raymond Frau as Kri Kri distributed in France as *Le Détective improvisé*. Kri Kri turns detective to obtain the reward for finding a stolen necklace. He has an imitation made and through it tricks the thieve into revealing himself.

The College Boys Special

1917 American film (Kalem/1reel), an episode in the series *A Daughter of Daring* starring Helen Gibson. This was a railway adventure series in which Gibson solved mysteries, fought villains and demonstrated her stunting ability. In this episode college boy Bob Cotter (L.T. Whitlock) and his chums, known for their fondness for playing pranks, head for Lone Point for a camping holiday. Helen, the telegraph operator and station agent at Lone Point, is warned of their coming and is on the lookout for trouble. Scott Sidney directed. Print survives at the BFI.

Come to My House

1927 American film (Fox/6 reels) based on the 1927 novel *Come to My House* by Arthur Somers Roche. Social butterfly Joan Century (Olive Borden) is engaged to wealthy Murtaugh Pell (Cornelius Keefe) but foolishly accepts a midnight dinner invitation from handsome Floyd Benning (Antonio Moreno). She is seen entering his house by a blackmailer who says he will tell Pell unless she pays him off. Benning offers to take care of the blackmailer who is subsequently found dead. Benning is arrested but refuses to explain anything. Joan finally confesses to save his life though it ruins her reputation and hopes of marriage. Marion Orth wrote the screenplay and Alfred E. Green directed.

Comment Nick Winter connut les courses (Why Nick Winter Went to the Races)

1910 French film (Pathé/1 reel), an episode in a popular tongue-in-cheek comedy series about an "American" detective named Nick Winter. In this episode Nick has to go to a racetrack. Georges Vinter played Nick and Paul Garbagni wrote the screenplay and directed. (A print of this film survives in an archive.) See Winter, Nick for other films.

The Confidence Man

1924 American film (Paramount/8 reels) based on the 1925 novel *The Confidence Man* by Laurie York Erskine. Crooks Dan Corvan

Virginia Valli reforms a crook in *The Confidence Man*.

(Thomas Meighan) and Larry Maddox (Laurence Wheat) make many friends in Fairfield, Florida, while setting up a scheme to swindle tightfisted Godfred Queritt (Charles Dow Clark) with phony oil stock. Local beauty Margaret Leland (Virginia Valli) has such faith in Corvan that it drives him to go straight. Paul Sloane wrote the screenplay and Victor Heerman directed.

The Conspiracy

1914 American film (Paramount/5 reels) based on the 1912 play *The Conspiracy* by Robert B. Baker and John Emerson. Mystery writer Clavering (John Emerson) decides to try his hand at real detective work and find the killer of white slaver Pedro Alvarez. He asks for help from Margaret Holt (Lois Meredith), the sister of the district attorney, who had been kidnapped by Alvarez's gang. After escaping she worked for Alvarez as a typist while looking for evidence of his crimes. When he caught and attacked her, she killed him. Clavering arranges for the arrest of the gang and proves Margaret had justifiably defended herself. Allan Dwan directed.

The Conspirators

1924 British film (Stoll/5 reels/released in America as *The Barnes Murder Case*) based on the 1907 novel *Conspirators* by E. Phillips Oppenheim. Blackmail leads to murder as a father kills a blackmailer to protect this son's reputation. Unfortunately an innocent woman is accused of the crime. Moore Marriott is Barnes and Morris, David Hawthorne is Herbert and Betty Faire is Louise in this mystery The supporting cast included Fred Rains, Edward O'Neill and Margaret Hoppe. Sinclair Hill wrote the screenplay and directed the film.

Convict 993

1918 American film (Pathé/5 reels) based on a story by Wallace C. Clifton who wrote the screenplay. Irene Castle plays Roslyn, an uncover Secret Service detective who traps a gang of jewel thieves by masquerading as jewel thief. She has been put in prison and, as Convict 993, becomes friends with fellow convict Neva (Helen Chadwick). After she breaks out of prison and Neva is released, Roslyn is forced to help her and gang leader Dan (Warner Oland) rob guests at a reception. She does so and then turns the gang into the police. William Parke directed.

The Copper Beeches

1921 British film (Stoll/2 reels), an episode in the *Adventures of Sherlock Holmes* series based on a story by Sir Arthur Conan Doyle. Sherlock Holmes solves a mystery involving a woman who takes a post as governess at a place called Copper Beeches. Eille Norwood portrays Holmes with Hubert Willis as Dr. Watson. William J. Elliot wrote the script and Maurice Elvey directed. A print of this film survives at the BFI archive.

The Copper Cylinder

1926 British film (FHC Productions/2 reels), an episode in the series *Inscrutable Drew, Investigator* featuring Henry Ainley as private detective Victor Drew. In this episode Drew and his assistant Dracos investigate a mysterious copper cylinder. Philip Valentine plays Abdul. Elliot Stannard wrote the screenplay and A. E. Coleby directed.

A Corn-Fed Sleuth

1923 American comedy (Century Film/2 reels) written and directed by Albert Herman with Jack Earle playing the corny sleuth.

A Cottage on Dartmoor

1929 British film (BIF/8 reels) based on a story by Herbert C. Price and written and directed by Anthony Asquith. A recently restored and re-evaluated thriller with one of the great razor scenes of the cinema. A prisoner escapes form Dartmoor Prison vowing revenge. He was formerly a barber who attacked a customer with an open razor for stealing the affections of his manicurist girlfriend. Uno Henning played the jealous barber, Norah Baring was the manicurist, and Hans Adalbert Schlettow was the man she preferred. The outstanding (and quite eerie) cinematography is by Stanley Rodwell. The film has been restored by the BFI and is on DVD.

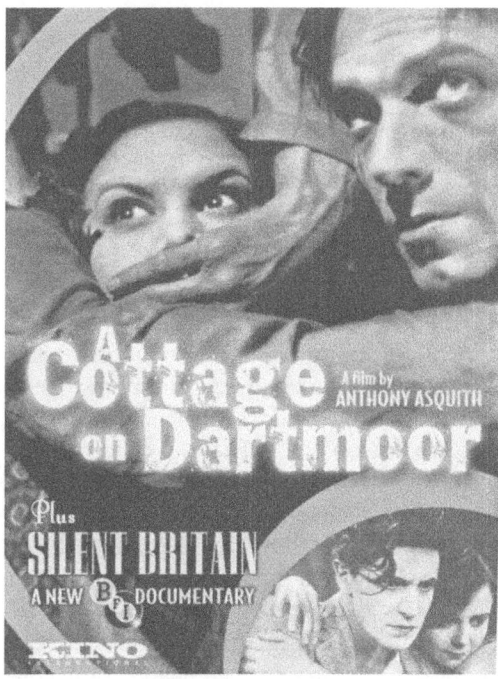

A prisoner escapes from Dartmoor in the classic *A Cottage in Dartmoor.*

The Coughing Horror

1924 British film (Stoll/2 reels), an episode in the *Further Mysteries of Fu Manchu* series based on a story by Sax Rohmer. Nayland Smith (Fred Paul) investigates a series of murders and meets a servant of Dr Fu Manchu (Harry Agar Lyons) known as the "Coughing Horror." Fred Paul directed and wrote the screenplay and Frank Canham was the cinematographer. Print survives at BFI film archive.

The Council of Three

1909 British film (London Cinematograph/1 reel), one of three films in a series titled *Sexton Blake* featuring master detective Sexton Blake. He was played by C. Douglas Carlile under the direction of S. Wormald. Blake poses as a gang's messenger to rescue a kidnapped girl.

Counterfeit

1919 American film (Paramount/5 reels) based on a story by Robert Baker. Virginia Griswold (Elsie Ferguson), who works for the Secret Service, sets out to catch a gang of counterfeiters by taking up a position in Newport society. She discovers that wealthy Mrs. Palmer (Helene Montrose) is involved with criminal Vincent Cortez (Charles Gerard) who gives her counterfeit bills to pass. Virginia steals the bills from Palmer's safe but is observed by Stuart Kent (David Powell) who has fallen in love with her but now thinks she is a crook. Virginia learns that a luxurious yacht is being used as headquarters by the counterfeiters and leads a raid by detectives. The gang is rounded up, Virginia earns a reward and Kent learns her real identity. Ouida Bergère wrote the screenplay and George Fitzmaurice directed.

The Counterfeiters

1905 American film (Lubin/700 feet/20 scenes). A detective disguises himself as an old woman to spy on a gang of counterfeiters. The gang members are arrested and sent to prison but are able escape. They are tracked down and caught by the detective and police.

The Counterfeiters

1914 British film (Davidson/3 reels), one of seven films in a series written and directed by Charles Raymond. Harry Lorraine played the famous detective Sexton Blake with Bert Rex as his assistant Tinker. A counterfeit gang using an old mill as their base capture Blake and tie him to the waterwheel. (See Blake, Sexton for the other films and background.)

Cousins of Sherlock Holmes

1913 American comedy (Solax/1 reel). A Sherlock Holmes parody starring Fraunie Fraunholz as both Fraunie and Spike.

The Cowboy Cavalier

1928 American film (Action Pictures/5 reels). A woman (Olive Hasbrouck) sees her uncle killed and the shock causes her to lose her memory. The murderer kidnaps her and tries to force her to confess to the killing. A cowboy detective (Buddy Roosevelt) investigates and discovers that the woman's cousin, who expected to inherit his uncle's ranch, hired the killer. He tracks him down and rescues the woman who then recovers her memory. Frank L. Inghram wrote the screenplay and Richard Thorpe directed.

Cragmire Tower

1924 British film (Stoll/2 reels), an episode in the *Further Mysteries of Fu Manchu* series based on a story by Sax Rohmer. Nayland Smith (Fred Paul) and Dr. Petrie (Humberston Wright) are tricked into going to Cragmire Tower where they are nearly killed. Fred Paul directed and wrote the screenplay and Frank Canham was the cinematographer. Print survives at BFI film archive.

Crime and Punishment

1866 novel by Russian novelist Fyodor Dostoevsky which features one of the most memorable detectives in literary fiction. Inspector Porfiry relentlessly interrogates university student Raskolnikov whom he suspects of killing a pawnbroker and her sister. The detective not only gets a confession, he gets repentance while Raskolnikov falls in love with streetwalker Sonia. The novel was filmed five times in the silent era, in Russia, Hungary, Germany and the USA. See below and Raskolnikov.

Crime and Punishment
(Prestuplenie i nakazanie)

1913 Russian film (2 reels) based on Fyodor Dostoevsky's 1866 novel *Crime and Punishment*. Pavel Orlenev and Ivan Vronsky have the main roles and Vronsky directed.

Crime and Punishment

1917 American film (Arrow Film/5 reels) based on Fyodor Dostoevsky's 1866 novel *Crime and Punishment*. In this revised version of the novel set in America, Raskolnikov is forced to flee Russia because of his radical ideas. He ends up in New York City where the plot of the novel takes place somewhat transformed. Derwent Hall Caine played Raskolnikov, Marguerite Courtot was Sonia and Robert Cummings was the inspector. Charles Taylor wrote the screenplay and Lawrence B. McGill directed the film.

Crime and Punishment
(Paper Parinam)

1924 Indian film (Madan Theatres/6 reels) based on Fyodor Dostoevsky's 1866 novel *Crime and Punishment*. The main roles are played by Probodh Bose, Nirmalendu Lahiri and Prabhadevi.

The Criminal Path

1914 American film (Ramo Films/4 reels). Detective Bob Darrell (Stuart Holmes) suspects that Mary (Edith Hallor), the daughter of criminal Jim Jepson (H. Jeffries), is involved in a plan to rob a bank. She is arrested with her father and both are sent to prison. When she is released she is helped by the Rev. John Horton (Jack Hopkins) but threatened by Richard Blair (Will S. Davis), Horton's brother-in-law. When Blair is killed, Darrell thinks Mary did it but her father, who has escaped from prison, confesses to the crime. Will S. Davis wrote the screenplay and directed.

Stuart Holmes is the detective in *The Criminal Path*.

Stewart Rome is the police inspector in *The Crimson Circle* (1929).

The Crimson Circle

1922 British film (Kinema Club/5 reels) based on a 1922 novel by Edgar Wallace A police inspector investigates a blackmail gang known as the Crimson Circle He gets assistance from a young woman who has been arrested and could be a member of the Crimson Circle. The leader of the gang turns out to be a detective. Fred Groves plays the police inspector with Madge Stuart as the young woman in trouble. The other cast members were Clifton Boyne, Lawford Davidson, Eva Moore, Rex Davis, Mary Odette and Victor McLaglen. Patrick Mannock wrote the screenplay and George Ridgwell directed.

The Crimson Circle

1929 British film (BIFD/6 reels) with screenplay by Edgar Wallace based on a 1922 novel by Edgar Wallace A police inspector investigates a blackmail gang known as the Crimson Circle and gets help from a young woman who could be a member of the gang. Stewart Rome played the police inspector with Lya Mara as the young woman. The cast members included John Castle, Louis Lerch Albert Steinruck and Hans Marow. Friedrich Zelnick directed. There were silent and sound-on-disc versions.

The Crimson Flash

1927 American serial (Pathé/ten 2-reel episodes) about a Secret Service detective (Cullen Landis) who goes undercover and pretends to be an importer so he can catch a gang of smugglers. The gang is headed by a master criminal known only as The Ghost. The Crimson Flash is a famous ruby which is being smuggled. The episodes were titled *A Shot in the Night, The Ghost Takes a Hand, When Thieves Fall Out, Decoyed, Held in Bondage, Checkmate, The Shadow of the Menace, Into the Trap, The Flaming Menace* and *The End of the Trail*.

The Crimson Runner

1925 American Film (PDC-Hunt Stromberg/6 reels) based on a story by Harvey Gates who also wrote the screenplay. Bianca (Priscilla Dean), who is known as the Crimson Runner, leads a gang of daring thieves who steal from the rich of Vienna to aid the poor. Count Meinhard (Ward Crane) falls in love with Bianca and shields her from police and eventually kills the evil police chief (Alan Hale) who had caused her father's death. Tom Forman directed.

The Crimson Stain Mystery

1916 American serial (Consolidated-Metro/sixteen 2-reel chapters) based on a story by Albert Payson Terhune. An ambitious detective (Maurice Costello) sets out to find the leader of a group of killers who have small crimson stains in their eyes. He become involved with a woman (Ethel Grandin) whose doctor father (Thomas J. McGrane) had attempted to create super-people but instead created monsters. T. Hayes Hunter directed. The episodes were *The Brand of Satan, In the Demon's Spell, The Broken Spell, The Mysterious Disappearance, The Figure in Black, The Phantom Image, The Devil's Symphony, In the Shadow of Death, The Haunting Spectre, The Infernal Fiend, The Tortured Soul, The Restless Spirit, Despoiling Brutes, The Bloodhound, The Human Tiger* and *The Unmasking*.

Crooked Alley

1923 American film (Universal/5 reels) based on Jack Boyle's story "The Daughter of Crooked Alley." Boston Blackie (Thomas Carrigan) seeks revenge on a judge who refused to arrange a pardon for a dying friend. He persuades the friend's daughter (Laura La Plante) to vamp and then spurn the judge's son. The plot fails when the pair fall in love for real. Robert F. Hill directed and Adrian Johnson wrote the screenplay. See also Blackie, Boston.

The Crooked Man

1923 British film (Stoll/2 reels), an episode in the *Last Adventures of Sherlock Holmes* series based on a story by Sir Arthur Conan Doyle. Sherlock Holmes solves the mystery of the "murder" of an army office by his wife. Eille Norwood portrays Holmes with Hubert Willis as Dr. Watson. Alfred Moise was the cinematographer and George Ridgewell wrote the adaptation and directed. Print survives at BFI archive.

A Crooked Romance

1917 American film (Pathé/5 reels). Detective Gifford Cannon (William Parke, Jr.) arrests thief Mary Flynn (Gladys Hulette) and her father (Paul Clerget). She falls in love with him but is able to escape. Because of her love she decides to reform and they finally get together. Will M. Ritchey and Marc Edmund Jones wrote the screenplay and William Parke directed.

Crooked Streets

1920 American film (Paramount/5 reels based on Samuel Merwin's short story "Dinner at Eight." American and British secret service detectives working undercover meet in Shanghai while investigating opium smuggling. American Gail (Ethel Clayton) is secretary to Professor Griswald (Clyde Fillmore) who has come to China to buy antique vases in which he plans to secrete opium. Gail is rescued from a kidnapping attempt by British tourist Rupert (Jack Holt) who then arrests Griswald and reveals his secret identity. She admits she is investigating the same crime. Edith Kennedy wrote the screenplay and Paul Powell directed.

Cuff, Sergeant

Sergeant Cuff was one of the first important detectives in English literature with an important role in Wilkie Collins' 1868 novel *The Moonstone* which was filmed four times in the silent era. Considered the finest police detective in England at the time, he is called to investigate the theft of a giant yellow diamond after another detective is unable to solve the crime. He is not impressive to look at being extremely lean, quite elderly and sharp-faced but he solves crimes by perseverance and determination. He comes to a wrong conclusion at first but then comes back with the correct one.

The Curse of Ravenscroft

1926 British film (FHC Productions/2 reels), an episode in the series *Inscrutable Drew, Investigator* featuring Henry Ainley as private detective Victor Drew. In this episode he investigates the mysterious deaths of members of the Ravenscroft family. Forbes Alexander plays Lord Ravenscroft. Elliot Stannard wrote the screenplay and A. E. Coleby directed.

The Cry of the Night Hawk

1923 British film (Stoll/2 reels), an episode

in the *Mystery of Fu Manchu* series based on a story by Sax Rohmer. Nayland Smith (Fred Paul) investigates a series of murders and escapes a trap laid for him by Fu Manchu (Harry Agar Lyons). A. E. Colby directed, Frank Wilson wrote the screenplay with Colby and D. P. Cooper was the cinematographer. Print survives at BFI film archive.

Cynthia-of-the-Minute

1920 American film (Gibraltar Pictures/6 reels) based on Louis Joseph Vance's 1911 mystery novel *Cynthia-of-the-Minute*. Cynthia (Leah Baird) accompanies Madame Savarin (Mathilde Brundage) and her valuable jewels on a sea voyage. As her father was a wireless expert who taught her code, she is able to learn of a plot to sink the ship and steal the jewels. She sounds the alarm and rescues her boyfriend Bruce (Hugh Thompson) by swimming to his rescue with the jewels strapped to her back. Star Leah Baird wrote the screenplay and Perry N. Vekroff directed.

Police receive telegraphic messages from Cynthia on a troubled liner in *Cynthia of the Minute*.

The Cypher Message

1913 American film (Selig/1 reel) written by Wallace Clifton about a society thief and his maid accomplice who steal diamonds and the detective who sets a trap for them. The poster shows the detective urging Miss Kent who is wearing a pearl necklace to "Give him every chance to steal them." The actors were Lafe McKee, Adele Lane, Barney Furey, Al W. Filson, Frank Newburg, Lillian Leighton and Madeline Pardee. Francis J. Grandon directed.

Dale, Jimmie

Jimmie Dale, a New York thief and rogue with three separate identities, was featured in the 1917 serial *Jimmy Dale Alias the Grey Seal*. He was created by Frank L Packard for *People's Magazine* and his adventures were later published as *The Adventures of Jimmie Dale*. He is best known as the Gray Seal, a fun-loving safecracker who thumbs his nose at the police by leaving a gray seal marker at crime scenes. He is also sometimes a petty criminal known as Larry the Bat. When not engaged in criminal activity, he enjoys life as playboy Jimmie Dale. He is pressured into crime fighting by the Tocsin, otherwise known as Marie La Salle.

Die Dame im Koffer (The Woman in the Trunk)

1921 German film (Kassandra Film/5 reels), one of the episodes in the *Joe Jenkins, Detektiv* series. Georg H. Schnell played Joe Jenkins and the supporting cast included Margit Barnay, Paul Bildt, Gerda Frey, Gert Sascha and Fred Selva-Goebe. Paul Rosenhayn wrote the screenplay and Emil Albes directed.

The Dancing Men

1923 British film (Stoll/2 reels), an episode in the *Last Adventures of Sherlock Holmes* series based on a story by Sir Arthur Conan Doyle. Sherlock Holmes solves the mystery of a message containing drawings of little dancing men. Eille Norwood portrays Holmes with Hubert Willis as Dr. Watson. Alfred Moise was the cinematographer and George Ridgewell wrote the adaptation and directed. Print survives at BFI archive.

The Danger Girl

1926 American film (Metropolitan Pictures/6 reels) based on the 1926 novel *The Bride* by George Middleton. Marie Duquesne (Priscilla Dean) persuades the eccentric Travers brothers Wilson (John Bowers) and Mortimer (Arthur Hoyt) to let her stay overnight in their house to escape an unwanted marriage. They agree even though police have warned them that thieves are planning to steal their jewel collection. The next morning James the butler (Gustav von Seyffertitz) calls the police saying he is suspicious because of seeing her walking around during the night. A policeman takes her away but she returns that night and arrests the butler as he is stealing the jewels. She is actually an undercover detective. Finis Fox wrote the screenplay and Edward Dillon directed.

Dangerous Lies

1921 British film (Famous Players-Lasky British/7 reels) based on a mystery story by E. Phillips Oppenheim set in Monte Carlo. Mary Glynne played Joan Farrant, David Powell was Sir Henry Bond and the supporting cast included Minna Grey, Arthur M. Cullin, Ernest A Douglas and Clifford Grey. Paul Powell directed, Mary O'Connor wrote the screenplay and Alfred Hitchcock stared to learn the movie business by writing the intertitles.

Dangerous Traffic

1926 American film (Goodwill Pictures/5 reels). Newspaper reporter Ned (Francis X. Bushman, Jr.) turns detective to investigate the activities of a gang of smugglers after his friend Tom (Jack Perrin) is wounded by them. He is helped by Helen (Mildred Harris) whose brother was killed by he smugglers. Bennett Cohn wrote the screenplay and directed.

Dark Stairways

1924 American film (Universal/5 reels) based on a story by Marion Orth. Sheldon Polk (Herbert Rawlinson) is robbed while delivering a loan to Frank Farnsworth (Hayden Stevenson) and framed for the robbery. He escapes from prison via a dirigible and proves that Farnsworth is the real criminal. G. Rigby wrote the screenplay and Robert F. Hill directed.

A Daughter of Daring

1917 American series (Kalem/eleven 1-reel episodes) starring Helen Gibson. This was a railway adventure series in which Gibson solved mysteries, fought villains, demonstrated derring-do and worked with railroad detectives. The supporting casts included Gladys Blue, Lloyd Whitlock, George Routh and George A. Williams. Edward W. Matlack and Herman A Blackman wrote the scripts and James Davis, Scott Sidney and Walter Morton directed. The episodes were *In the Path of Peril*, *The Registered Pouch*, *The Borrowed Engine*, *The Mystery of the Burning Freight*, *The Lone Point Feud*, *The College Boys Special*, *The Munitions Plot*, *The Railroad Smugglers*, *A Race to the Drawbridge*, *The Detective's Danger* and *The Deserted Engine*. Two episodes survive, *The College Boys Special* and *The Deserted Engine*.

A Daughter of the Law

1921 American film (Universal/5 reels) based on the story "The Black Cap" by Wadsworth Camp first published in *Collier's* on 24 January 1920. Nora Hayes (Carmel Myers), daughter of police inspector Hayes (Charles Arling) and the sweetheart of detective Jim Garth (Jack O'Brien) tries to extricate her brother Eddie (Joe Bennett) from the clutches of gangster George Stacey (Fred Kohler). She is captured by the gang but rescued by Garth. They are sent to jail because of her testimony but escape and capture her with Garth. She frees them both by using a container of vitriol and the gang is sent back to prison. Harvey Gates wrote the screenplay and Jack Conway directed.

The Dazzling Miss Davison

1917 American film (Mutual-Frank Powell Productions/5 reels) based on the 1908 novel *The Dazzling Miss Davison* by Florence Warden. Rachel (Marjorie Rambeau) is the dazzling Miss Davison who claims to be a designer but may be a thief. Socialite Gerard Buckland (Robert Elliott) thinks she's a crook because he saw her receive a diamond necklace from a suspicious-looking older man (Fred Williams). She even entertains people at a party given by the wealthy Van Santens by picking pockets. All gets explained when Davison exposes the Van Santens as international crooks preying on the rich and reveals that the mysterious old man is her bureau chief. It seems Rachel is actually "the best woman detective in New York." Frank Powell directed.

A Dead Certainty

1918 British film (Broadwest/5 reels) based on the 1900 novel *A Dead Certainty* by Nat Gould. Crime at the racetrack. A man refuses to fix a race despite the efforts of his sweetheart's wicked uncle to persuade him to do it. Gregory Scott starred as Arthur Dunbar, Poppy Wyndham was Pat Stone, Cameron Carr was Henry Stone, Harry Royston was Martin Mills and Mary Masters was Mrs. Woodruff. Patrick L. Mannock wrote the screenplay and George Dewhurst directed.

The Dead Secret

1913 American film (Monopol/2 reels) based on the 1873 novel *The Dead Secret* by Wilkie Collins. The secret has to do with the Cornish mansion Porthgenna. Rosamund, the heir to the mansion, decides to turn detective to find out what forgotten crime lies in the past. Marion Leonard played a double role through the use of double exposure portraying Rosamund and the strong-minded actress at the core of the secret. Stanner E.V. Taylor directed.

A Dear Liar

1925 British film (Stoll/2 reels) based on a story by Edgar Wallace, an episode in the second series of *Thrilling Stories from the Strand*. The cast included Eileen Dennes, James Knight, Edward O'Neilla and John Colin. Hugh Croise wrote the screenplay and Fred Leroy Granville directed.

Deebs, Joe

Joe Deebs was one of the most famous screen detectives of the German silent cinema, the suave crime-solving star of at least thirty films. He made his first appearance in 1914 under the patronage of Joe May, who had earlier helped created the Stuart Webbs detective series, and his production company filmed twenty-three Joe Deebs adventures. Deebs, like most of the "American" movie detectives of the German cinema, had an Anglo-Saxon name and was modeled on Nick Carter. After May stopped making Deebs films, the mantle was picked up by Projektions-AG Union (PAGU), a company headed by Paul Davidson. Deebs was portrayed by six different actors through the years though Max Landa is the one most identified with him. The following listing by actor is incomplete but shows the range of films..

Max Landa starred in at least eight Deebs films produced by Joe May who wrote and directed them for May Film. They included *Das Gesetz der Mine, Der Geheimsekretär* and *Sein schwierigster Fall* in 1915; *Die Gespensteruhr* in 1916; *Der Onyxknopf, Das Klima von Vancour* and *Die Kaukasierin* in 1917; and *Sein bester Freund* in 1918.

Harry Liedtke starred in at least three films written, produced and directed by Joe May. They included *Das Rätselhafte Inserat* and *Wie ich Detektiv wurde* in 1916 and *Das Geheimnis der leeren Wasserflasche* in 1917.

Heinrich Schroth starred in at least eight Deebs films written and directed by Harry Piel for May Film. They included *Diplomaten, Die Ratte* and *Das Rollende Hotel* in 1918; and *Das Auge des Götzen, Der Blaue Drachen, Die Krone von Palma, Der Muff* and *Die Närrische Fabrik* in 1919.

Carl Augen starred in at least four Deebs films produced by the PAGU company. They included *Der heulende Wolf* and *Die Pantherbraut* in 1919; and *Kaliber fünf Komma zwei* and *Tamburin und Castagnetten* in 1920.

Ferdinand von Alten starred in at least three Deebs films produced by the PAGU company: *Gentlemen-Gaune* in 1920 and *Das Geheimnis der Mumie* and *Das Handicap der Liebe* in 1921.

Curt Goetz starred in at least two Deebs films produced by the PAGU company in 1920:

Carl Augen as detective Deebs in *Der heulende Wolf* (*The Howling Wolf*).

Die Dame in Schwarz and *Das Skelett des Herrn Markutius*.

Dene, Dorcas

Dorcas Dene, the creation of George R. Sims, was one of the first and most successful fictional female detectives. Her cases were filmed in England in 1919 as *The Adventures of Dorcas Dene, Detective*. Dorcas is an actress who becomes a detective to earn money after her husband is blinded and she turns out to be very good at the job. Her adventures were first related in stories published as *Dorcas Dene, Detective* (1897) *and Dorcas Dene, Detective. Second Series* (1898).

The Desert of the Lost

1927 American film (Action Pictures/5 reels) based on a story by Walter J. Coburn. Detective Murray (Edward Cecil) follows fugitive Jim Drake (Wally Wales) to Mexico after Drake shoots a man in self-defense. Drake makes friends with Dolores (Peggy Montgomery) whose father (William J. Dyer) is trying to get her to marry a Chinese bandit so he can learn about a secret gold mine. Drake defends Dolores from her father, discovers the location of the gold mine and arranges the capture of the bandit gang. Detective Murray finds Drake and tells him the charges against him have been dropped. Frank L. Inghram wrote the screenplay and Richard Thorpe directed.

The Deserted Engine

1917 American film (Kalem/1reel), an episode in the series *A Daughter of Daring* starring Helen Gibson. This was a railway adventure series in which Gibson solved mysteries, fought villains and demonstrated stunting ability. In this episode Helen, the telegraph operator and station agent at Lone Point, has to solve the mystery of a deserted engine. Scott Sidney directed. Print survives at the BFI.

The Destroying Angel

1915 American film (Edison/4 reels) based on 1912 mystery novel by Louis Joseph Vance. Actress Mary (Mabel Trunnelle) becomes known as the destroying angel after her first husband dies in an auto accident and second husband Hugh (Marc McDermott) goes West and is reported dead. Jealous theatrical manager Max (Walter Craven) kills one of her admirers, her millionaire fiancé dies in a boating accident and admirer Drummond disappears. Hugh returns alive to save Mary from Max. Richard Ridgely wrote the screenplay and directed. The novel was filmed a second time in 1923.

The Destroying Angel

1923 American film (Associated Exhibitors/6 reels) based on a1912 mystery novel by Louis Joseph Vance. A woman who becomes known as a "destroying angel" because of the mysterious deaths, murders and disappearances of her husbands and admirers. Leah Baird plays Mary, the destroying angel, with John Bowers as her savior Hugh, Ford Sterling as Max and Noah Beery as Drummond. Leah Baird wrote the screenplay and W. S Van Dyke directed.

Ein Detektiv-Duell (A Detective Duel)

1917 German film (Egede Nissen Film Company/5 reels) featuring a female detective known as Miss Clever. It was one of a series of ten films about the woman detective starring Norwegian actress Ada Egede-Nissen (using the screen name of "Ada Van Ehlers") It was written by Rudolf Baron and Else Cressin and directed by Georg Alexander who took the male lead in the film. See *Miss Clever* for other films in the series.

Das Detecktivduell—Harry Hill contra Sherlock Holmes (The Detective Duel)

1920 German film (Valy Arnheim/6 reels). Fictional German detective Harry Hill, portrayed by Valy Arnheim in a dozen films made between 1919 and 1927, battles Sherlock Holmes in this movie, the only Harry Hill film that has survived. It was written, produced and directed by Arnheim himself with Marga Lindt playing his girlfriend.

Le Détective

1906 French film (Pathé/1 reel). A family hires a detective after their daughter is kidnapped by apaches who demand a ransom. The detective is captured by the apaches but escapes with the girl from an isolated cabin in the woods.

The Detective

1917 American film (Sparkle-General Film/2 reels) starring Kate Price and Billy Ruge.

The Detective

1923 American film (Vitagraph/2 reels) written and directed by John P. Smith.

Détective Amateur (Amateur Detective)

1909 French film (Pathé Frères/390 feet), a comedy.

Detective and Matchmaker

1914 American film (Vitagraph/1 reel). Comedy featuring William Duncan, George Holt, George Kunkel, Jane Novak, Margaret Gibson and George Stanley. L. D. Paxton wrote the screenplay and Ulysses Danis directed.

The Detective and the Jewel Trick

1911 British film (Hepworth/1 reel) directed by Lewin Fitzhamon. A thief poses as a woman to steal some jewels but is tricked by a clever detective who uses a similar ruse.

Detective Barock Holmes and His Hound

1909) French comedy (Gaumont/1 reel) distributed in America with this title. French title unknown.

Detective Blinn

1915 American film (American Film/2 reels) starring Ed Coxen with George Field, Winifred Greenwood, John Steppling and Beatrice Van. L. B. Hawes wrote the screenplay and Henry Otto directed.

Detective Bonzo and the Black Hand Gang

1925 British animated film (New Era/1 reel). Bonzo, a cartoon puppy dog, foils the Black Hand Gang in a plot to kidnap a jockey. This was the 12th in a 26-film series, the most popular British animation series of the silent era. Bonzo was the creation of artist George Ernest Studdy and originally appeared in the magazine The Sketch. This was his only adventures as a detective.

Detective Burton's Triumph

1914 American film (Reliance-Mutual/1 reel) starring Eugene Pallette, Sam De Grasse and Billie West.

Detective Craig's Coup

1914 American film (Eclectic/5 reels) loosely based on Tom Taylor's play *The Ticket-*

Francis Carlyle was the sleuth in *Detective Craig's Coup*.

of-Leave Man. Police Detective Craig (Francis Carlyle) knows that master criminal James Dalton (Charles Arling) is behind a counterfeit ring but is unable to prove it because Dalton uses innocent people to pass money. One of them is high-living Bob Brierly (Jack Standing) who gets caught and sent to prison. When he gets out, Dalton tries to use him for a bank robbery scheme but Brierly sends a warning to Craig who is working undercover. The counterfeiter and his gang are intercepted, chased and killed when their boat blows up. Donald MacKenzie directed and George B. Seitz wrote the screenplay.

Detective Dan Cupid

1914 American comedy (Nestor/1 reel). No other information available.

Detective Daring and the Thames Coiners

1914 British film (Daring Films/3 reels). Detective Daring (Harry Lorraine) captures a gang of counterfeiters and proves that suspect (Will Discombe) is innocent. The real crooks were Flash Harry (Claude Winn), Spider (Bert Berry) and Barney (Arthur Mavity). Sydney Northcote directed and Harold Brett wrote the screenplay.

Detective Dervieux

1912 French series (Gaumont/3 reels each) created by Louis Feuillade with René Navarre portraying detective Jean Dervieux. The series began with *Le Proscrit* in May 1912 and was followed by *La Oubliette* (the only film in the series that has survived) and *La Course aux millions* in 1912. This series, which ended in 1913 with *Le Guet-Apens* and *L'Ecrin du Radjah*, was virtually a dress rehearsal for Feuillade's serial masterpiece *Fantômas* which also starred Navarre.

Detective Dorothy

1912 American comedy (Essanay/1 reel) starring Frances Osman as Detective Dorothy and Bryant Washburn as the supposed murderer she is pursuing.

Detective Dot

1913 American comedy (Lubin/1 reel) starring Frences Ne Moyer as Detecuve Dot. E.W. Sargent wrote the screenplay and Arthur Hotaling directed. Ne Moyer also acted in the 1913 comedy *The Female Detective*.

Le Détective féminin

1912 French film (Askala/2 reels) about a female detective. No details available.

Detective Ferris

1912 British film (Hepworth/925 feet). Detective Ferris poses as an old woman in order to save a royal prince from a gang of anarchists who plan to kill him. Gilbert Southwell directed.

Detective Finn

1914 British series (Regent Films/two 3-reel films) starring Arthur Finn as Detective Finn. Charles West directed and produced the films in collaboration with Finn (see below).

Detective Finn, or, In the Heart of London

1914 British film (Regent Films/3 reels) distributed in America as *Society Detective*. Detective Finn captures Slippery Kate (Alice Inwood) and Silk Hat Harry (Charles Weston) who are posing as a maid and a police inspector while attempting to steal a diamond.

Detective Finn, and the Foreign Spies

1914 British film (Regent Films/3 reels) distributed in America as *The Foreign Spies*. Detective Finn pretends to be a criminal so he can trap a butler who has stolen an inventor's plans.

Détective Flegmatique
(The Phlegmatic Detective)

1916 French film (SCAGL/1reel) starring Firmin Gémier as phlegmatic detective John Has and Marc Gerard as his Apache opponent.

A Detective for a Day

1912 British comedy (Hepworth/475 feet) directed by Frank Wilson. A waiter (Jack Raymond) who thinks he is a detective mistakes a policeman for a wanted criminal.

Le Detective Gallows contre la bande des XXX (Detective Gallows Fights the XXX Gang)

1912 French film (Pathé Frères/1reel). No other information available.

Detective Hayes

1914 German series (Vitascope/2 reels) distributed in America by the Apex Film Company. The titles shown in America included *Detective Hayes and the Duchess's Diamonds* and *Detective Hayes Sixth Case* (a.k.a. *The Dare-Devil Detective*).

Detective Henry and the Paris Apaches

1911 British film (Natural Colour Kinematograph/1 reel) directed by Theo Frenkel. This film was shot in an experimental early color process.

Il detective innamorato
(The Detective in Love)

1913 Italian film comedy (Savoia Film/1 reel). Detective Trouville is in love with a girl whose father had forbidden suitors. When the father returns unexpectedly, thief Pontrose saves the day by pretending to be the detective and arresting Trouville. After stealing several items he once again escapes.

The Detective in Peril

1910 British film (Hepworth/750 feet) directed by and starring Lewin Fitzhamon. He plays a detective who is captured by criminals and rescued by his dog.

Detective Potts

1915 American comedy series starring Lee Moran as Detective Lee Potts. Moran and Eddie Lyons co-starred in Nestor comedies under the direction of Al Christie from 1912 to 1916. The character of the incompetent detective Lee Potts seems to have been created for the 1915 Universal five-reel feature *Mrs. Plum's Pudding* and continued in the Nestor two-reelers *The Downfall of Potts*, *Potts Bungles Again* and *A Bundle of Trouble*.

Lee Moran played Potts in the Detective Potts series.

The Detective Queen

1914 American film (Sawyer/4 reels) No other information available. Sawyer distributed five films in 1914 but didn't do a very good job of advertising them.

Detective Robert's Peril
(Una telefonata misteriosa)

1912 Italian film (Cines/1 reel) distributed in America as *Detective Robert's Peril*. Detective Roberts gets a phone call about a robbery in progress but it is cut off before he learns the location. He sets a trap and catches the crooks. *The New York Dramatic Mirror* reviewer said "Ordinarily a telephone is not a very inspiring object; but when it is located in the dingy basement of an empty house and is the instrument of apprehending a band of daring criminals, one's interest quickens."

Detective Sharp and the Stolen Miniatures

1912 British film (Martin & Cricks/1 reel). Detective Sharp catches a burglar who stole valuable miniatures by posing as a thief. Charles Calvert directed.

Detective Short

1914 American comedy (Lubin/1 reel). No other information available.

Detective Swift

1914 American film (Eclectic/3 reels). New York Giants baseball star John J. McGraw plays Detective Swift who is investigating of the theft of jewels from a society woman. He discovers learns a gentleman safecracker is the villain and chases him around the world. By a strange coincidence the thief visits the same places that the New York Giants visited on a world tour. Frank McGlynn wrote the screenplay while Louis Gasnier and Donald McKenzie directed.

Detective Yuri see Kishin Yuri keiji

Detectives

1928 American comedy (MGM/7 reels). When jewels are stolen in a luxury hotel, the house detective (Karl Dane) and bellhop (George K. Arthur) compete to find them and win the love of a stenographer (Marceline Day) — and a large reward. The bellhop proves to be a better detective than his rival. Chester M. Franklin directed and wrote the screenplay with Robert Lord.

The Detective's Conscience

1912 American film (Lubin/1 reel) starring Burton King, Adele Lane, Romaine Fielding and W. J Wells.

The Detective's Daughter

1913 Italian film (Dante Feature Sales Corp/4 reels) distributed in America with this title. Italian title unknown but it was written by Vellettieri.

The Detective's Desperate Chance

1912 American film (Pathé/1 reel). No further information available.

The Detective's Dog

1910 British film (Hepworth/675 feet) directed by Lewin Fitzhamon. A detective's dog trails a thief who steals money bags from a train.

The Detective's Dog

1912 American comedy (Solax/1 reel) about a dog detective starring Lee Beggs, Blanche Cornwall, Magda Foy and Darwin Karr.

The Detective's Nursemaid
(Detectivens Barnepige)

1914 Danish film (Nordisk/3 reels) distributed in America as *The Charlotte Street Mystery*. Detective Robert Barker (Robert Schyberg) hires a red-headed nursemaid (Else Frölich) for his children not realizing she is a thief. She and partner (R. Hjort-Clausen) are planning to steal a necklace from his countess neighbor. They succeed by utilizing disguises, drugs and a secret room. Barker gets on the case, finds a red hair at the scene of the crime and realizes who dunnit. The thieves escape on a boat but Barker chases them down and arrests them. Hjalmar Davidsen directed and A. Lumbye wrote the screenplay.

The Detectives of the Italian Bureau

1909 American film (Kalem/800 feet). A nine year old girl is kidnapped by the Black Hand and the detectives of the Italian Bureau set out to find her.

The Detective's Peril

1915 American film (Kalem/1 reel), an episode in *The Hazards of Helen* series. Helen Gibson plays the heroic railroad telegrapher Helen who has to save the life of a railroad detective (and show off her death-defying ability to perform dangerous stunts). James Davis directed.

The Detective's Ruse

1908 British film (Hepworth/300 feet). A detective impersonates an old man in a bath chair so he can catch a burglar. Lewin Fitzhamon directed.

The Detective's Santa Claus

1912 French film (Éclair/1 reel) copyrighted in America with this title. Original French title unknown.

The Detective's Sister

1914 American film (Kalem/2 reels) directed by George Melford and written by

Hamilton Smith. Carlyle Blackwell played the detective with Neva Gerber as his sister.

The Detective's Stratagem

1913 American film (Biograph/1 reel) based on a story by John J. A. Gibney Harry Carey plays detective Keene who has a stratagem for catching criminals Charles H. West and Joseph McDermott. Bank employees Reggie Morris and Claire McDowell are the intended victims.

A Detective's Strategy

1912 American film (Selig/1 reel) based on the story "Thistledown" by Frederick Jackson. Charles Clary headed the cast portraying detective Narrow with support from William McCullough, Lafe McKee, Pat Carson and Mack Barnes. Lem B. Parker directed.

The Detective's Trap

1913 American film (Kalem/1 reel) featuring two detectives with James Vincent as detective Harry Graham and James B. Ross as detective Briton. The supporting cast included Irene Boyle as Helen and Charlotte Courtot as her mother.

A Detective's Trip Around the World
(Tour du monde d'un policier)

1906 French film (Pathé Frères/1 reel) distributed in America as *A Detective's Trip Around the World*. A detective chases a criminal around the world and gets involved in dangerous situations in several countries. Gaston Velle directed the film with Charles Lépine as his cinematographer.

The Detectress

1919 American comedy (Bulls Eye/2 reels). Lizzie (Gale Henry), who considers herself a "detectress" in training, sees a thief (Eddie Baker) rob an inventor (Hap H. Ward) of a secret formula. She goes to retrieve it and, with the help of a policeman (Milburn Moranti), finally does so. The formula turns out to be for eyeglasses that will enable "the eaters of chop suey to see what's in it." Then Lizzie wakes up and discovers it was all a dream. Bruno C. Becker directed. Henry also starred as Baffles in the *Lady Baffles and Detective Duck* series.

Les Dévaliseurs de banque
(The Bank Burglars)

1908 French film (Éclair/1 reel), an episode in the *Nick Carter, le roi des détectives* series about the master detective Nick Carter. It was distributed in America as *The Bankers*. In this episode Carter investigates a bank robbery. Pierre Bressol played Nick Carter and Victorin Jassett wrote and directed the film.

The Devil Stone

1917 American film (Artcraft/5 reels). Criminologist Robert Judson (Hobart Bosworth) is hired by Guy Sterling (Wallace Reid) to find who killed fishery owner Silas Martin (Tully Marshall). He learns Martin had married Breton fisherwoman Marcia Manot (Geraldine Farrar) to get an emerald she found. The emerald, stolen from a church, is cursed and will serve the devil until it is restored. Martin had attempted to steal the stone from Marcia and she hit him on the head with a candlestick during the struggle. When Judson discovers this, Marcia pleads self-defense and returns the emerald to the church. Jeanie MacPherson wrote the screenplay and Cecil B. DeMille directed.

The Devil to Pay

1920 American film (Pathé/6 reels) based on the 1918 novel *The Devil to Pay* by Frances Nimmo Greene. District attorney Cullen Grant (Roy Stewart) sets out to prove that financial bigwig Brent Warren is the real murderer following the hanging of his employee George Roan (Joseph J. Dowling) for the crime. His star witness turns out to be the supposedly dead employee. Warren kills himself. Jack Cunningham wrote the screenplay and Ernest C. Warde directed.

The Devil's Foot

1921 British film (Stoll/2 reels), an episode in the *Adventures of Sherlock Holmes* series based on a story by Sir Arthur Conan Doyle. Sherlock Holmes solves a mystery involving the strange death of three people at a table. Eille

Norwood portrays Holmes with Hubert Willis as Dr. Watson. William J. Elliot wrote the script and Maurice Elvey directed. A print of this film survives at the BFI archive.

The Diamond from the Sky

1915 American serial (American/thirty 2-reel chapters) Mystery and murder surround the dangerous diamond from the sky (it originally came from a meteorite) as competing factions attempt to find and claim the stone and battle its gypsy owner Esther (Lottie Pickford). It's hard to distinguish the good guys from the villains but the other stars include Irving Cumming, William Russell, Charlotte Burton as a femme fatale and William Tedmarsh as a hunchback. Jacques Jaccard and Roy L. McCardell wrote the screenplay and Jaccard and William Desmond Taylor directed. The episodes were *A Heritage of Hate, Eye for an Eye, The Silent Witness, The Prodigal's Progress, For the Sake of a False Friend, The Queen of Love and Beauty, The Fox and the Pig, A Mind in the Past, A Runaway Match, Old Foes with New Faces, Over the Hills and Far Away, To the Highest Bidder, The Man in the Mask, For Love and Money, Desperate Chances, The Path of Peril, King of Diamonds and Queen of Hearts, Charm Against Harm, Fire Fury and Confusion, The Soul Stranglers, The Lion's Bride, The Rose in the Dust, The Double Cross, The Mad Millionaire, A House of Cards, The Garden of the Gods, Mine Own People, The Falling Aeroplane, A Deal with Destiny* and *The American Earl*. This was the biggest film made by the American "Flying A" company of Santa Barbara, California. A four-episode sequel was made in 1916 prosaically titled *The Sequel to The Diamond from the Sky*.

The stars of *The Diamond in the Sky serial* shown in publicity postcards: Lottie Pickford, William Russell, Irving Cummings and Charlotte Burton.

The Diamond Man

1924 British film (Davidson/6 reels) based

on a *News of the World* serial by Edgar Wallace. Orphan Audrey Bedford (Mary Odette) takes the blame for her half-sister's gem theft and later exposes her crooked husband. Arthur Wontner played Lacy Marshall, Gertrude McCoy was Lacy's wife Julia, Reginald Fox was Captain Dick Shannon and Philip Hewland was Henry Torrington. Eliot Stannard wrote the screenplay and A. H. Rooke directed.

The Diamond Master

1914 American film (Éclair American/3 reels) based on a mystery novel by Jacques Futrelle. A detective (Edward Roseman) helps Doris (Belle Adair) fight villains who want to steal her father's invention that turns dust into diamonds. Alec B. Francis plays her boyfriend and J. Gunnis Davis was diamond expert Czenki.

The Diamond Master

1929 American serial (Universal/ten 2-reel chapters) based on a mystery novel by Jacques Futrelle. Detective Mark Van Cortland Wynne (Hayden Stevenson) helps Doris (Louise Lorraine) fight villains who want to steal her father's invention that turns dust into diamonds. Jack Nelson directed. The chapters are titled *The Secret of the Night, The Diamond of Death, The Tunnel of Terror, Trapped, The Diamond Machine, The Wolf Pack, The Death Trap, Into the Flames, The Last Stand* and *The Reckoning*.

The Diamond Mystery

1913 American film (Vitagraph/2 reels). This was publicized as "The most exciting detective story ever shown, the contest story of the *Motion Picture Story Magazine*, an absorbing plot with splendid acting, realistic and thrilling." Courtenay Foote played the detective heading a cast featuring Charles Kent, Mary Maurice, Leah Baird, Herbert Barry and Earle Williams. Charles Kent directed.

The Diamond Queen

1921 American serial (Universal/eighteen 2-reel chapters) based on a mystery novel by Jacques Futrelle. Detective Bruce Weston (George Chesebro) helps Doris (Eileen Sedgewich) fight villains who want to steal her

Courtenay Foote is the detective in *The Diamond Mystery*.

father's invention, a machine that turns dust into diamonds. For some unexplained reason she has to spend a lot of time in Africa. George W. Pyper wrote the screenplay and Ed Kull directed. The chapters are titled *Vow of Vengeance, Plunge of Doom, Perils of the Jungle, Fires of Hates, Tide of Destiny, The Colossal Game, An Amazing Ultimatum, In Merciless Clutches, A Race with Rogues, The Betrayal, In Torture's Grip, The Kidnapping, Weird Walls, The Plunge, The Decoy, The Dip of Death, The hand of Fate* and *The Hour of Reckoning*. The novel was also filmed as *The Diamond Master*.

The Diamond Runners

1916 American film (Signal Film-Mutual/5 reels). Secret Service detective Hudson (Leo D. Maloney) is on the track of diamond smuggler Helen (Helen Holmes) in South Africa. She has hidden the gems in bouquets of roses and smuggled them on board a ship headed for America. The detective and the smuggler fall in love and she decides to reform and betray her boss (Paul Hurst). J. P. McGowan wrote the screenplay and directed. McGowan and Holmes are best known for their *Hazards of Helen* films.

Diamonds of Destiny see Blau-weisse Steine

Dice of Destiny

1920 American film (Pathé/5 reels) based on Frank A. Moroso's novel *The People Against Nancy Preston*. Detective James Tierney (Claude Payton) is warned by ex-convict Jimmy Doyle (H. B. Warner) that he will kill him if he tries to arrest him again. He plans to go straight for love of Nancy Preston (Lillian Rich) but is double-crossed and sent back to prison. He escapes and rescues Nancy from his betrayer Dave Monteith (Howard Davis) but Monteith is killed and Doyle is the chief suspect. He hides out with Nancy but Tierney tracks him down. After Doyle saves Tierney's life and word arrives that the real killer has been found, Tierny lets him go free. Fred Myton wrote the screenplay and Henry King directed. The novel was filmed again in 1925 as *The People vs. Nancy Preston*.

Dickson's Diamonds

1914 American film (Edison/1 reel), one of five films in the Felix Boyd series based on a fictional private detective created by Scott Campbell. Boyd was a tough street fighter like Nick Carter with a brilliant mind like Sherlock Holmes. Robert Conness starred with support from Carleton King and Richard Neil. Langdon West directed. (See Boyd, Felix for list of other films.)

A Dime Novel Detective

1909 American comedy (Lubin/820 feet). A man models himself on dime novel detectives like Nick Carter and Old Sleuth.

Diplomaten (Diplomats)

1915 German film (May Film/4 reels) featuring the "American" detective Joe Deebs as played by Heinrich Schroth. This was a film in the long-running Deebs series created by producer Joe May in 1914. The supporting cast included Max Rubeck. Harry Piel directed and wrote the screenplay with Harry Hutter. See Deebs, Joe for other films.

The Disappearance of Lady Frances Carfax

1923 British film (Stoll/2 reels), an episode in the *Last Adventures of Sherlock Holmes* series based on a story by Sir Arthur Conan Doyle. Sherlock Holmes rescues a woman threatened by a pair of criminals. Eille Norwood portrays Holmes with Hubert Willis as Dr. Watson. Alfred Moise was the cinematographer and George Ridgewell wrote the adaptation and directed. Print survives at BFI archive.

Do Detectives Think?

1927 American comedy (Hal Roach Studios/2 reels). Stan Laurel and Oliver Hardy star as the totally inept detectives Ferdinand Finkleberry and Sherlock Pinkham. They have

Laurel and Hardy are incompetent detectives in *Do Detectives Think?*

been asked to guard Judge Fozzle (James Finlayson) because an escaped convict known as the Tipton Slasher (Noah Young) has threatened to kill him. Frank Brownlee plays the incompetent head of the detective agency that employs Laurel and Hardy and Viola Richard is the judge's wife. Hal Roach wrote the screenplay and Fred Guiol directed the film. On video.

Dr. Brian Pellie and the Bank Robbery

1911 British film (Clarendon/1 reel) in the *Dr. Brian Pellie* series. Master criminal Dr. Pellie takes a bank manager prisoner and then impersonates him so he can rob his bank. Wilfred Noy directed. See also Pellie, Dr. Brian.

Dr. Brian Pellie and the Baronet's Bride

1911 British film (Clarendon/1 reel) in the *Dr. Brian Pellie* series. Master criminal Dr. Pellie kidnaps the bride of a millionaire for ransom but is foiled after she sets his yacht on fire. Wilfred Noy directed. See also Pellie, Dr. Brian.

Dr. Brian Pellie and the Secret Despatch

1912 British film (Clarendon/1 reel) in the *Dr. Brian Pellie* series. Master criminal Dr. Pellie is captured after a dangerous rooftop struggle and pursuit on a tram. Wilfred Noy directed. See also Pellie, Dr. Brian.

Dr. Brian Pellie and the Spanish Grandee

1912 British film (Clarendon/1 reel) in the *Dr. Brian Pellie* series. Master criminal Dr. Pellie and his gang take a duchess and her friends prisoner so they can impersonate them and gain entry to a fancy ball. Wilfred Noy directed. See also Pellie, Dr. Brian.

Dr. Brian Pellie and the Wedding Gifts

1913 British film (Clarendon/1 reel) in the *Dr. Brian Pellie* series. Master criminal Dr Brian Pellie impersonates a policeman so he can rob a millionaire's daughter of her wedding presents. She foils him by sending an SOS message via pigeon to her fiancé. Wilfred Noy directed. See also Pellie, Dr. Brian.

Dr. Brian Pellie Escapes from Prison

1912 British film (Clarendon/1 reel) in the *Dr. Brian Pellie* series. Master criminal Dr. Pellie escapes from jail by impersonating the prison chaplain but is pursued by police on bicycles. Wilfred Noy directed. See also Pellie, Dr. Brian.

Dr. Brian Pellie, Thief and Coiner

1910 British film (Clarendon/1 reel) in the *Dr. Brian Pellie* series. Master criminal Dr. Pellie hypnotizes a rich heiress on a train but is foiled by a child who informs the police. Wilfred Noy directed. See also Pellie, Dr. Brian.

Dr. Fu Manchu

Sax Rohmer's Dr. Fu Manchu is the most sinister Oriental villain in film and fiction, the would-be emperor of the world. He made his first appearance in print in 1912 in *The Storyteller* magazine and the stories of his mad dreams came out in book form in 1913 as *The Mystery of Dr. Fu-Manchu* (he later lost his hyphen). He reached the screen in 1923 in a British series with Harry Agar Lyons as Fu Manchu battling his arch-enemy, Scotland Yard detective Sir Dennis Nayland Smith and his cohort Dr. Petrie. Films about Fu Manchu became even more popular in the sound era with some of the screen's great actor-villains portraying him including Boris Karloff and Christopher Lee. See *The Mystery of Dr. Fu Manchu* (series), *Further Mysteries of Dr. Fu Manchu* (series) and *The Mysterious Dr. Fu Manchu*.

Dr. Gar El Hama

Dr. Gar El Hama is an Oriental master criminal who was featured in a Danish film series produced by Nordisk in the 1910s. His nationality is never explained nor how he got into the medical or crime business but he is plenty evil. He was created by Eduard Schnedler-Sorensen and Ludwig Landmann who made his first two films. The five *Dr. Gar el Hama* films, memorable for their location filming and spectacular action scenes, were all set in England. See below for films.

Dr. Gar el Hama

1911 Danish film (Nordisk/2 reels). Also known as *Bedraget i doden* and shown in America as *A Dead Man's Child*. Dr. Gar el Hama (Aage Hertel) is hired by moneylender James

Pendleton (Otto Lagoni) to help him gain a fortune. He drugs heiress Lady Edith (Edith Buemann) so she appears dead and is put in a tomb. He then steals her "corpse" and takes it to Pendleton in Istanbul. Edith's fiancé Baron Sternberg (Henry Seeman) becomes suspicious and hires Detective Newton (Einar Zangenberg) to find her. Gar el Hama tries to kill the baron when he arrives in Istanbul but Newton foils him. Pendleton and Gar el Hama escape on the Orient Express but Newton catches them, flings Gar el Hama off the train and arrests Pendleton. Ludwig Landmann wrote the screenplay and Eduard Schnedler-Sorensen directed. This film survives and was well received when it was shown at the Pordenone Silent Film Festival in 2006.

Dr. Gar el Hama II

1912 Danish film (Nordisk/2 reels) released in America as *Dr. Gar el Hama Escapes*. The evil doctor is found unconscious by the side of the railroad tracks and nearly captured by Sherlock Holmes collaborator Dr. Watson (Robert Schyberg). He returns to evildoing but is hunted down by Watson after further adventures. Ludwig Landmann wrote the screenplay and Eduard Schnedler-Sorensen directed.

Dr. Gar el Hama III and Dr. Gar el Hama IV

1914 Danish films (Nordisk/each 2 reels). These two films seem to have been released together in America as a feature titled *Adventures of Gar El Hama*. Gar El Hama escapes from prison and kidnaps the daughter of a rich man and takes her to his island headquarters where he demands ransom. Her sweetheart, a naval lieutenant, tracks his down and raids the island but the gang escapes through secret tunnels. The girl is recaptured and her sweetheart taken prisoner and tortured. They are rescued by sailors and Gar El Hama is sent back to prison. *Variety* thought the film was quite entertaining and was impressed by the actor playing Gar El Hama.

Dr. Gar el Hama V

1916 Danish film (Nordisk/2 reels) More adventures of the crooked doctor directed by Robert Dinesen.

Dr. Jekyll and Mr. Hyde

Robert Louis Stevenson's created one of the most terrifying villains of fiction in his 1886 novella *The Strange Case of Dr. Jekyll and Mr. Hyde*. He is particularly terrifying because he shows, as Pogo once put it, that the villain is us. Jekyll believes that everyone contains good and evil personalities and he proves it by creating a drug that separates the two. Jekyll is a good man but his alter ego Hyde is totally bad and eventually a murderer. The only way Jekyll can rid the world of Hyde is by killing himself. Stevenson's creation has fascinated filmmakers and actors since the earliest days of cinema so there were seven silent films about him (none oddly from England). The stories and the names of the characters vary widely. See below plus *Der Januskopf* and *A Modern Jekyll and Hyde*.

Dr. Jekyll and Mr. Hyde

1908 American film (Selig/1 reel) based on Robert Louis Stevenson's 1886 novella *The Strange Case of Dr. Jekyll and Mr. Hyde*. Hobart Bosworth portrays Jekyll-Hyde and is quite nasty to Betty Harte. Otis Turner directed and George F. Fish wrote the scenario.

Dr. Jekyll and Mr. Hyde; or, A Strange Case (Den Skæbnesvangre opfindelse)

1910 Danish film (Nordisk/1 reel) based on Robert Louis Stevenson's 1886 novella *The Strange Case of Dr. Jekyll and Mr. Hyde*. Alwin Neuss stars as Jekyll-Hyde. August Blom wrote and directed the film distributed in America by the Great Northern Film Company.

Dr. Jekyll and Mr. Hyde

1912 American film (Thanhouser/1 reel) based on Robert Louis Stevenson's 1886 novella *The Strange Case of Dr. Jekyll and Mr. Hyde*. James Cruze stars as Jekyll-Hyde with Florence La Badie as Jekyll's sweetheart Marie and a supporting cast that included Marguerite Snow and Harry Benham. Lucius Henderson directed.

Dr. Jekyll and Mr. Hyde

1913 American film (Imp/2 reels) based on Robert Louis Stevenson's 1886 novella *The

King Baggot played the double role in the 1913 *Dr. Jekyll and Mr. Hyde.*

John Barrymore played the doctor and his evil double in *Dr. Jekyll and Mr. Hyde* (1920).

Strange Case of Dr. Jekyll and Mr. Hyde. King Baggot plays Jekyll-Hyde with Jane Gail as Jekyll's sweetheart Alice. Matt Snyder played Alice's father, Howard Crampton was Dr. Lanyon and William Sorelle was the attorney Utterson. Herbert Brenon wrote the screenplay and directed the film. This film is on video.

Dr. Jekyll and Mr. Hyde

1920 American film (Paramount/7 reels) based on Robert Louis Stevenson's 1886 novella *The Strange Case of Dr. Jekyll and Mr. Hyde.* John Barrymore stars as Jekyll-Hyde and gives one of his finest performances. Jekyll discovers a drug that separates the good from the evil in a person and decides to live both roles. Jekyll loves Millicent (Martha Mansfield), the daughter of Sir George Carew (Brandon Hurst) while Hyde amuses himself with dance hall girl Gina (Nita Naldi). When Hyde kills Sir George, Jekyll decides there is only one solution to the problem and kills himself. Clara S. Beranger wrote the screenplay, John S. Robertson directed the film and Roy Overbaugh photographed it. The film is on video.

Dr. Jekyll and Mr. Hyde

1920 American film (Pioneer/5 reels) loosely based on Robert Louis Stevenson's 1886 novella *The Strange Case of Dr. Jekyll and Mr. Hyde.* Sheldon Lewis stars as Jekyll-Hyde. Jekyll, who lives in modern New York, is a radical free-thinking atheist. He discovers a drug that can separate the good from the evil in a person and when he takes it he becomes a frenzied wild man with a lust to be wicked. His behavior causes Jekyll's sweetheart Bernice (Gladys Field) to break their engagement. Hyde goes on a murderous spree and is caught and jailed. He is about to be executed when he wakes up as Jekyll and finds it was just a dream. He decides to reform and renounces his atheistic ways. Charles J. Hayden wrote and directed the film produced by Louis B. Mayer. Some critics considered this the worst movie ever made about the story.

Dr. Mabuse, der Spieler
(Dr. Mabuse the Gambler)

1922 German film (Decla-Bishop/30 reels/two parts) based on the 1920 novel *Dr. Mabuse, der Spieler* by Norbert Jacques. Thea von Harbou wrote the screenplay and Fritz Lang, directed what is considered one of the silent screen's masterpieces Police detective Norbert Von Wenk (Bernhard Goetzke) sets out to stop the mad genius Dr. Mabuse (Rudolf Klein-Rogge) from taking control of Berlin. Mabuse's latest victim is the young millionaire Edgar Hull (Paul Richter) whom Mabuse has hypnotized into losing heavily in a card game. Danish actress Aud Egede Nissen played cabaret dancer Cara Carozza, Gertrude Welcker was Countess Dusy Told and Alfred Abel was Count Told. *Dr. Mabuse*, which is in two parts, was originally screened as two films: Part One is *The Gambler*, Part Two is *King of Crime*.

Fritz Lang's criminal masterpiece *Dr. Mabuse the Gambler* is on DVD.

Dr. Nikola

1909 Danish serial (Nordisk/three 1-reel chapters) based on Guy Boothby's *A Bid for Fortune* about the villainous Dr. Nikola and starring August Blom as Dr. Nikola. The three films tell a continuous story. In *Dr. Nikola I*, the villainous doctor learns about a Tibetan cane that will give him unlimited power and access to a treasure in a monastery. In *Dr. Nikola II* he steals the cane from an English collector and in *Dr Nikola III* he is able to get into the monastery and steal the treasure. The films were distributed in America by Great Northern Films.

Dr. Sin Fang

1928 British serial (Paul & Brooks/six 2-reel chapters) starring H. Agar Lyons as the Chinese master criminal Dr. Sin Fang and his battles with his nemesis Naval Lt. John Byrne (Fred Paul). Patrick K. Heale wrote the screenplays and Fred Paul directed. The episodes are titled *The Scarred Face, The Zone of Death, The Light on the Wall, The Living Death, The Torture Cage* and *Under the Tide*. Lyons had portrayed Fu Manchu in two series that were the inspiration for this imitation.

The Dog Detective

1906 British film (Norwood/730 feet). A dog tracks down bank robbers and saves his master's life. Harold Hough directed. This film was distributed in America and is on DVD.

The Dog Detective
(Le Chien du détective)

1909 French film (Gaumont/1 reel) distributed in America as *The Dog Detective*. After a man is kidnapped for ransom, the police send out a special trained dog to find him. This "dog detective" tracks the man to an abandoned warehouse, unties the ropes that bind him and brings him a gun to hold the kidnappers until the police arrive.

The Dog Detective
(Le Chien du détective)

1912 French film (ACAD/one) about a dog trained to behave like a detective and help solve crimes. Distributed in America as *The Dog Detective*.

Dog Detective

1926 American serial (Chesterfield/twelve 2-reel chapters) starring Alaskan wolfhound Fearless as a canine detective. He tracks baddies, catches and fights them and jumps out of danger when threatened. He works with detective humans, of course, mainly co-star Joe Rock. Also in the cast were Grace Cunard, Bruce Gordon and Jack Mower. Rock produced and directed the series for Ernest Van Pelt productions. The episodes were titled *A String of Diamonds, The Love Fighter, The Wolf, Detective K-9, A Dumb Romeo, Fangs of Vengeance, The Silent Trailer, Dog Scents, Dog of Dogs, The Thief, His Pal* and *Almost Human*. The serial has not survived but a 1926 short *Fangs of Vengeance* starring Fearless is on DVD.

Dog Detectives

Dogs were behaving like detectives in the earliest days of cinema solving crimes and rescuing people as in *Rescued by Rover*. Other early dog detective films include *The Detective's Dog, The Dog Detective,* and *Tracked by the Police Dog*. By the 1920s dogs had become major stars and were starring in feature films, often in detective-like roles. Dog stars promoted as detectives in the 1920s include Fearless as "Detective K-9" in *Dog Detective* and Peter the Great as "The Great Dog Detective" in *The Sign of the Claw*. Other dogs behaving like detectives include Dynamite in *The Four-Footed Ranger*, Flame in *The Law's Lash*, Flash in *Shadows of Night*, Grey Boy in *The Avenging Shadow*, Ranger in *Dog Justice* and Rin Tin Tin in *Rinty of the Desert*.

Dog Justice

1928 American film (FBO/6 reels). Dog detective Ranger, a German Shepherd, helps Northwest Mounted Police trooper Jimmie O'Neill (Edward Hearn) find the man who murdered a mine owner. Ethel Hill wrote the screenplay and Jerome Storm directed. Ranger starred in seventeen films at the end of the 1920s, usually helping to track down villains.

Dolly Plays Detective

1914 American film (Edison/2 reels) with Mary Fuller as Dolly and supporting cast of Yale Boss and Duncan McRae. Walter Edwin directed.

Don Q

Don Q, the creation of Hesketh Prichard and his mother Kate, is an aristocratic Spanish rogue, a hard-boiled nineteenth century Robin Hood who kidnaps the rich for ransom but never harms the poor. He took to the hills after being framed for a murder but eventually proves his innocence. He was popular with filmmakers in England and America in the silent era (see below). Don Q made his first appearance in 1898 in *Badminton Magazine* and his stories were collected in several book including *Don Q in the Sierra, The Chronicles of Don Q* and *Don Q's Love Story*. The Douglas Fairbanks film about Don Q makes him the son of Zorro, a geographical and chronological impossibility, but who needs logic in swashbuckling.

Don Q

1912 British film series (B&C/three 1-reel episodes) based on the serial by Hesketh Prichard published in *Pearson's Magazine* in England. Charles Raymond played the rogue-like Don Q having adventures in Spain. The supporting casts include Ivy Martinek and H.O. Martinek who also directed. Harold Brett wrote the screenplays. The films were *Don Q and the Artist, Don Q— How He Outwitted Don Lewis,* and *Don Q— How He Treated the Parole of Gevil Hay* (see below).

Don Q. and the Artist

1912 British film (B & C/1 reel), an episode in the series *Don Q* with Charles Raymond as Don Q. In this episode he becomes involved with an artist. Harold Brett wrote the screenplay and H.O. Martinek directed.

Don Q—How He Outwitted Don Luis

1912 British film (B & C/1 reel), an episode in the series *Don Q* with Charles Raymond playing Don Q. In this episode he is warned by Isabella (Ivy Martinek) about an assassination plot and tricks the assassin by a switch in glasses. Harold Brett wrote the screenplay and H.O. Martinek directed.

Don Q—How He Treated the Parole of Gevil Hay

1912 British film (B & C/1 reel), an episode

in the series *Don Q* with Charles Raymond as Don Q. In this episode he tests the honor of his English prisoner Gevil Hay (H. O. Martinek) by arranging his escape. Harold Brett wrote the screenplay and H.O. Martinek directed.

Don Q, Son of Zorro

1925 American film (UA-Elton/11 reels) based on the 1909 novel *Don Q's Love Story* by Hesketh and Kate Prichard. Zorro's son Don César de Vega (Douglas Fairbanks), as much of a rogue as his father, leaves California and goes to Spain to complete his studies. He falls in love with Dolores (Mary Astor) but jealous rival Don Sebastian (Donald Crisp) frames him for the murder of a visiting Austrian archduke (Warner Oland). Don Q fakes his own death to gain time to uncover the real assassin and, with the help of his father (Fairbanks in a double role), clears his name. Don Q wields a whip rather than a sword and is pretty good at it. Lotta Woods wrote the screenplay and Donald Crisp directed. On DVD.

Dope

1924 Australian film (Australasian Picture Productions/5 reels) about opium smuggling in Australia and a man who thinks he killed a man in a brawl. Gordon Collingridge and Lorraine Esmond starred, Con Drew wrote the screenplay, Lacey Percival was cinematographer and Dunstan Webb directed.

Douglas Fairbanks in the poster for *Don Q, Son of Zorro.*

Production still from the 1924 Australian film *Dope*.

The Dorrington Diamonds

1922 British film (Screen Plays/4 reels) written and directed by Jack Denton with Douglas Payne as master detective Sexton Blake and George Bellamy as Tinker. Percy Nash produced. (See Blake, Sexton for background and a list of his films.)

Le Dossier 33 (Dossier 33)

1920 French film (Série Nick Winter/3 reels), a late episode in a popular tongue-in-cheek comedy series about an "American" detective named Nick Winter. In this episode Nick (Georges Vinter) investigates the disappearance of an important diplomatic dossier. He discovers the document was taken by the diplomat's daughter (Denise Weill) who had been hypnotized by a spy.

A Double Identity

1915 American film (Kalem/2 reels), an episode in the detective series *Mysteries of the Grand Hotel*. Marin Sais and True Boardman are the detectives in this story about the mysterious theft of diamonds in a grand hotel. The woman detective solves the crime after peeking through a keyhole as the thief hides the diamonds. He had taken connecting rooms, one as his real self, the other in another identify, and committed the robbery in disguise. Hamilton Smith wrote the screenplay and James W. Horne directed. The story was supposedly based on a robbery at the Hotel Jefferson in St. Louis.

Doubling with Danger

1936 American film (FBO/5 reels). Master detective Dick Forsythe (Richard Talmadge) lets his eccentric partner Avery McCade (Fred Kelsey) be the detective guarding Elwood Haver (Joseph Girard) while he works incognito. Haver has secret papers belonging to a murdered inventor and Forsythe needs anonymity to investigates the murder. He finally catches the criminal and rescues Haver's daughter (Ena Gregory) when she is kidnapped. Scott R. Dunlap directed and Grover Jones wrote the screenplay.

The Downfall of Potts

1915 American comedy (Nestor/2 reels) starring Lee Moran as bungling Detective Potts. Eddie Lyons plays his friend Eddie while Victoria Forde and Harry Rattenberry provide support. Al Christie directed and Bennett Cohen wrote the script. Second film in the *Detective Potts* series.

Les Dragées soporifiques
(The Sleeping Pills)

1909 French film (Éclair/1 reel), an episode in the *Les Nouveaux Exploits de Nick Carter* series about the master detective Nick Carter released in America as *The Sleeping Pills*. In this episode Carter has to avoid being drugged (dragées are sugared almonds). Pierre Bressol played Nick Carter and Victorin Jassett wrote and directed the film.

The Dragnet

1928 American film (Paramount/6 reels) based on a story by Oliver H. P. Garrett. An ultra-tough police detective nicknamed "Two-Gun" Nolan (George Bancroft) attempts to rid his city of the gangs that are exploiting it. He is successful until crime boss "Dapper Frank" Trent (William Powell) tricks him into thinking he has shot his own partner. He begins to drink heavily and resigns from the police. Trent's girlfriend the Magpie (Evelyn Brent), who fancies Nolan, lets him know what really happened. Nolan sobers up and goes after Trent who is killed in a shootout. Josef von Sternberg directed and Jules Furthman wrote the screenplay.

Une Drame en express (A Fast Drama)

1906 French film (Pathé/1 reel). An apache dressed like a gentleman follows a woman into a first-class compartment on a train, chloroforms her, steals her money and throws her off the train. Peasants find her on the tracks, learns what has happened and inform the police. Detectives arrest the criminal at the next station and the woman identifies him.

The Drum

1924 British film (Stoll/2 reels) based on a story by F. Britten Austin, an episode in the series *Thrilling Stories from the Strand*. Two men set out to kill each other. The actors included James Carew, Jameston Thomas and Molly Johnson. Sinclair Hill directed.

Drummond, Bulldog

Captain Hugh "Bulldog" Drummond was the creation of H. C. McNeile writing as "Sapper" and made his first appearance in the 1920 novel *Bulldog Drummond*. He is a bit of a racist and intensely patriotic so his books have never been as popular in America as they are in England but his adventures are action-packed and full of thrills. His major opponent is the evil genius Carl Peterson who has dreams of ruling the world. Drummond's two silent films were made in England but America moviegoers did not discover Drummond in the sound era when actors like Ronald Colman and Walter Pidgeon made him more acceptable to American tastes. See *Bulldog Drummond* and *Bulldog Drummond's Third Round*.

Duds

1920 American film (Goldwyn/5 reels) based on the novel *Duds* by Henry C. Rowland serialized in *The Saturday Evening Post*. Captain Plunkett (Tom Moore) is sent to head off jewel thieves seeking the Sultana diamond. He meets Patricia Melton (Christine May) who claims to be a French secret agent also sent to guard the diamond. Plunkett falls in love with Olga Karakoff (Naomi Childers) but suspects her father may be working with the smugglers. When Patricia finds that the diamond is in a locket worn by Olga, she kidnaps her to get the gem. Plunkett rescues her and recovers the diamond. Harvey Thew wrote the screenplay and Thomas Mills directed.

Dull Care

1919 American comedy (Vitagraph/2 reels) written and directed by Larry Semon who stars as a detective named Larry. William Hauber is the chief crook, Frank Alexander is the police chief, Lucille Carlisle is the police chief's wife and Oliver Hardy plays a janitor.

The Dummy

1917 American feature film (Paramount/5 reels) based on the 1914 play *The Dummy* by Harvey J. O'Higgins and Harriet Ford. Young Barney Cook (Jack Pickford) is hired by detective Babbings (Frank Losee) to pretend to be

Jack Pickford is hired as a detective in *The Dummy*.

the deaf-mute son of a rich family and let himself get kidnapped. The gang has kidnapped the daughter of a wealthy family and Babbings hopes to find their hiding place with this ruse. It works but there are nasty complications and Barney has to rescue the little girl himself. Eve Unsell wrote the screenplay and Francis J. Grandon directed. The film was remade as a sound picture in 1929.

Dupin, C. Auguste

Edgar Allan Poe created C. Austin Dupin, the first significant detective in fiction and the model for most later fictional detectives. He is arrogantly intellectual and believes he can solve any crime with his mental abilities. He was featured in three stories. "The Murders in the Rue Morgue" (1841), "The Mystery of Marie Roget" (1842) and "The Purloined Letter" (1944). Only one was filmed in the silent era, *The Murders in the Rue Morgue*.

Duvall, Richard and Grace

The "Honeymoon Detectives" Richard and Grace Duvall were created by Frederic

Arnold Kummer under the pseudonym Arnold Fredericks. They were the hero and heroine of five serials published in magazines in the 1910s and two of their adventures were filmed. They meet and marry in 1912 in the first serial, *The Honeymooning Detectives*, filmed by Metro after it was published as the novel *One Million Francs*. The same year World made a film of their second adventure, *The Ivory Snuff Box*. The pair were also featured in a novel set in the movie world, *The Film of Fear* published in *All-Story Weekly* in 1917, but it was not filmed.

The Dying Detective

1921 British film (Stoll/2 reels), an episode in the *Adventures of Sherlock Holmes* series based on a story by Sir Arthur Conan Doyle. Sherlock Holmes pretends to be dying so he can trick a doctor into confessing to a murder. Eille Norwood portrays Holmes with Hubert Willis as Dr. Watson. William J. Elliot wrote the script and Maurice Elvey directed. A print of this film survives at the BFI archive.

Easy Pickings

1927 American film (First National Pictures/6 reels) based on the 1929 mystery play *Easy Pickings* by Paul A. Cruger. Burglar Mary Ryan (Anna Q. Nilsson) is caught by lawyer Stewart (Philo McCullough) and forced to pretend to be the deceased Dolores for an inheritance scam. Stewart had killed Simeon Van Horne in order to gain control of half of his estate which will be divided between Dolores, who no one knows is dead, and Peter Van Horne (Kenneth Harlan). Detective Billy Bevan) and others are subject to hoaxes and other spooky goings-on while Stewart is being frightened into a confession. Louis Stevens wrote the screenplay and George Archainbaud directed.

813

1920 American film (Robertson-Cole/6 reels) based on the story collection *813* about the French gentleman thief Arsène Lupin. Lupin (Wedgwood Nowell) is trying to obtain secret papers held by Robert Castleback (Ralph Lewis) which could affect the political situation in Europe. He prefers they go to France but Baron Ribeira (Wallace Beery) wants them for Germany. When Castleback is found murdered with Lupin's card on him, the police think he is the killer. Lupin impersonates a police detective and investigates the case himself. He dodges traps set for him, gets involved with Genevieve (Laura La Plante) and helps police catch the real criminal. Scott Sidney and Charles Christie directed, W. Scott Darling wrote the screenplay and Anton Nagy was the cinematographer. (See Lupin, Arsène for details about the character and a listing of the other films in which he appeared.)

813

1923 Japanese film (5 reels) based on the story collection *813* about the French master thief Arsène Lupin. The story revolves around Lupin's his efforts to obtain secret diplomatic papers. Mitsuaki Mimami portrayed Lupin and Kenji Mizoguchi directed. (See Lupin, Arsène for details about the character and a listing of the other films in which he appeared.)

Les Empreintes (The Fingerprints)

1908 French film (Éclair/1 reel), an episode in the *Nick Carter, le roi des détectives* series about the master detective Nick Carter. It was distributed in America as *The Fingerprint Clue*. In this episode Carter solves a crime with the help of fingerprints. Pierre Bressol played Nick Carter and Victorin Jassett wrote and directed the film.

The Empty House

1921 British film (Stoll/2 reels), an episode in the *Adventures of Sherlock Holmes* series based on a story by Sir Arthur Conan Doyle. Sherlock Holmes foils an attempt to kill him and proves the man guilty of a previous murder. Eille Norwood portrays Holmes with Hubert Willis as Dr. Watson. William J. Elliot wrote the script and Maurice Elvey directed. A print of this film survives at the BFI archive.

Empty Pockets

1918 American film (First National/6 reels) based on Rupert Hughes novel *Empty Pockets*. Millionaire Merrithew (Malcolm Williams) is found murdered with strands of auburn hair clutched in his hand. The red hairs implicates four women: Merrithew's mistress, a millionaire's daughter, a cabaret dancer and a society woman's daughter. Investigator Clinton Worthing (Bert Lytell) has to sort it out with suspects Barbara Castleton, Peggy Betts, Ketty Galanta and Susanne Willa. George Edwards Hall wrote the screenplay and Herbert Brenon directed.

En danger (In Danger)

1909 French film (Éclair/1 reel), an episode in the *Les Nouveaux Exploits de Nick Carter* series about the master detective Nick Carter In this episode Carter has to avoid being killed himself. Pierre Bressol played Nick Carter and Victorin Jassett wrote and directed the film. Distributed in America as *Nick Carter in Danger*.

Encore Nick Winter (Nick Winter Again)

1913 French film (Pathé/1 reel), an episode in a popular tongue-in-cheek comedy series about an "American" detective named Nick Winter. In this episode Nick Georges Vinter played Nick. (A print of this film survives in an archive.) See Winter, Nick for other films.

The Engineer's Thumb

1923 British film (Stoll/2 reels), an episode in the *Last Adventures of Sherlock Holmes* series based on a story by Sir Arthur Conan Doyle. Sherlock Holmes solves a mystery involving a master forger. Eille Norwood portrays Holmes with Hubert Willis as Dr. Watson. Alfred Moise was the cinematographer and George Ridgewell wrote the adaptation and directed. Print survives at BFI archive.

Erzgauner (The Cunning Rogue)

1921 German film (Althoff Film/2 reels), an episode in the four-film *Nick Carter* series featuring master detective Nick Carter. It was released in English-speaking countries as *The Cunning Rogue*. Bruno Eichgrün played Nick Carter and wrote and directed the film.

The Eternal Law

1910 American film (Lesobra/2 reels) directed by L. Brainherd. Detectives arrest the wrong man but it gets sorted out in the end.

L'Évasion de forçat de Croze (The Escape of the Convict de Cruze)

1913 French film (Gaumont/2 reels) written and directed by Léonce Perret. The criminal Baron de Croze (Perret) has escaped from prison and reconstituted his White Gloves gang using a bank in Marseilles as front. Inspector Necker, known as Main de fer (Iron Hand). is soon on his trail, learns about the bank and arrests everyone in it. Only the baron's secretary/mistress (Suzanne Grandais) escapes and she flees to the baron's yacht. Iron Hand follows them and the desperate baron sets the boat on fire. See also *Main de Fer*.

L'Évasion de Vidocq (Vidocq's Escape)

1910 French film (Pathé/1 reel) based on the *Memoirs* of François-Eugène Vidocq, the French criminal who reformed and became the first official police detective. Harry Baur portrays Vidocq with support from Andrée Marly. George Denola directed.

Every Thief Leaves a Clew

1913 American film (Essanay/2 reels). Police detective Powers (E. H. Calvert), who claims Sherlock Holmes is a friend, investigates the robbery of $50,000. He is baffled until his wife makes him think about a shirt with violet dots and he examines the cloth under a magnifying glass.

Detective Powers examines a clue under a magnifying glass in *Every Thief Leaves a Clew.*

The Evidence of the Film

1913 American film (Thanhauser/1 reel). A messenger boy is accused of stealing bonds but the supposed crime happened while a movie was being shot in the street. Film of what really happened is presented as evidence in the court. Marie Eline played the boy, Florence La Badie was his sister, William Garwood was the broker and Riley Chamberlin was the clerk. Lawrence Marston directed.

The Exiles

1923 American feature film (Fox/5 reels) based on the 1894 book *The Exiles and Other Stories* by Richard Harding Davis. Nightclub singer Alice Carroll (Betty Bouton) is discovered with the dead body of the club owner and is presumed guilty of his murder. She flees to Tangiers but she is tracked down by district attorney Henry Holcombe (John Gilbert) who knows she is innocent. He rescues Alice from the clutches of gambling den owner Wilhelm von Linke (John Webb Dillon) and takes her back to the States. Edmund Mortimer directed and Fred Jackson wrote the screenplay.

Expiation

1922 British film (Stoll/5 reels) based on the 1887 novel *Expiation* by E. Phillips Oppenheim. Ivy Close starred with support from Fred Raynham, Lionelle Howard, Malcolm Tod and Fred Rains. Sinclair Hill wrote the screenplay and directed.

The Exploits of Elaine

1914 American serial (Star-Pathé/fourteen 2-reel chapters) based on Arthur B. Reeve's novel *The Exploits of Elaine* which inspired three serials in the silent era. In this one Detective Craig Kennedy (Arnold Daly) and Elaine Dodge (Pearl White) fight the villainous Clutching Hand (Sheldon Lewis). The Hand killed Elaine's father because he had papers that would have revealed the Hand's secret hideout and he now menaces Elaine. Kennedy's "scientific" tools in the serial include a portable lie

Ivy Close was the star of the British film *Expiation*.

Detective Craig Kennedy (Arnold Daly) and Elaine Dodge (Pearl White) decide to go after the villainous Clutching Hand in the serial *The Exploits of Elaine*.

detector and a device for spying through keyholes. Journalist Walter Jameson (Creighton Hale in the first three episodes, then Raymond Owens) acts as Kennedy's Watson describing his adventures. Louis Gasnier and George B. Seitz directed, Charles L. Goddard and Seitz wrote the screenplay and Joseph Dubray was cinematographer, The chapters were titled *The Clutching Hand, The Twilight Sleep, The Vanishing Jewels, The Frozen Safe, The Poisoned Room, The Vampire, The Double Trap, The Hidden Voice, The Death Ray, The Life Current, The Hour of Three, The Blood Crystals, The Devil Worshippers* and *The Reckoning*. See also *The New Exploits of Elaine, Barcelona y sus misterios* and *The Romance of Elaine*.

The Exploits of Three-Fingered Kate

1909 British film (British & Colonial/1 reel), an episode in the *Three-Fingered Kate* series. Jewel thief Three-Fingered Kate escapes detection by Detective Sheerluck by switching clothes with a black woman at a public bath.

Exposure of the Land Swindlers

1913 American film (Kalem/2 reels). William J. Burns of the National Detective Agency stars in this drama based on a real case he solved. Giving him support are Kalem repertory players Alice Joyce, Guy Coombs, Henry Hallam, Miriam Cooper, Kenean Buel, Hal Clements and Stuart Holmes. Kenean Buel directed. Burns was considered the greatest sleuth of his time.

The Exquisite Thief

1919 American film (Universal/6 reels) based on the story "Raggedy Ann" by Charles W. Tyler published in the magazine *Detective Stories*. Jewel thief Blue Jean Billie (Priscilla Dean) knocks out detective Wood (Milton Ross) and robs the guests at the engagement party of Algernon Smythe (Thurston Hall) and Muriel Vanderflip (Jean Calhoun).The detective and Smythe pursue her but she tricks them and makes them prisoners. She learns that Smythe is a famous crook known as "English Harry" and she falls in love with him. They return the jewels and go straight. Tod Browning directed and Harvey Gates wrote the screenplay.

The Eyes of Mystery

1918 American film (Metro/5 reels) based on the 1917 story "The House in the Mist" by Octavus Roy Cohen published in *People's Magazine*. Detective Jack Carrington (Bradley Barker) is sent to investigate the kidnapping of Carma (Edith Storey). The kidnapper is supposedly Carma's renegade father Roger but he's actually an imposter (Harry S. Northrup) who has taken over the family estate. Carrington succeeds in rescuing Carma with the help of her uncle (Frank Andrews). June Mathis wrote the screenplay and Tod Browning directed.

The Face in the Dark

1918 American film (Goldwyn/6 reels) based on Irvin S. Cobb's story "The Web." Jane Ridgeway (Mae Marsh) sets out to prove that her sweetheart Richard (Niles Welch) did not rob a bank but she discovers that her father (Alec B. Francis), a former Secret Service agent, is now working with thieves and a master criminal known as the Face in the Dark. She confronts him but he escapes with the thieves who lead him to the hiding place of the Face in the Dark. He is followed by the police who arrest the crooks and congratulate him on his undercover detective work. Tom Bret wrote the screenplay and Hobart Henley directed.

The Face in the Fog

1922 American film (Paramount/7 reels) based on Jack Boyle's story "The Face in the Fog" in *Cosmopolitan*. Cracksman Boston Blackie (Lionel Barrymore) has accidentally acquired the Romanov jewels which Russian Grand Duchess Tatiana (Seena Owen) brought to America. Revolutionaries try to steal them from Blackie who gives paste copies to the American government and returns the real jewels to the Duchess. Alan Crosland directed while John Lynch and Jack Boyle wrote the screenplay. See also Blackie, Boston.

Face to Face

1922 American film (Playgoers Pictures/5 reels). Burglar Bert (William Kendall) shoots his reflection in a mirror at the same time that John Weston (Richard Stewart) shoots himself.

Bert is accused of the murder but schoolgirl Helen (Marguerite Marsh) turns detective and gets evidence clearing him. Weston's assistant had kept the suicide secret to hide his theft of Weston's money. Harry Grossman wrote and directed the film.

The False Faces

1919 American film (Paramount-Artcraft/7 reels) based on the 1918 novel *The False Faces: Further Adventures from the History of the Lone Wolf* by Louis Joseph Vance. Reformed thief Michael Lanyard (Henry B. Walthall), Known as the Lone Wolf, is commissioned by Scotland Yard detective Thackeray to take secret information to America by ship. German agent Karl Ekstrom (Lon Chaney) gets a German submarine to torpedo the boat but Lanyard and American agent Cecilia Brooke (Mary Anderson) escape and deliver the document. Irvin V. Willat wrote the screenplay and directed. (For other films featuring this character see *The Lone Wolf*.)

The Family Stain

1915 American film (Fox/6 reels) based on Émile Gaboriau's novel *L'Affaire Lerouge*. Detectives Tabaret and Lecoq investigate the murder of the widow Lerouge in a small town. They learn that Lerouge, when she was a nursemaid years before, was paid by Cameron to switch his wife's baby with that of his mistress Madam Gerdy. Cameron's son Albert is arrested for the murder but Tabaret learns that the switch never took place. Suspicion falls on Gerdy's son Noel and he confesses. The film stars Einar Linden, Walter Miller, Frederick Perry, Stephen Grattan, Carey Lee, Dixie Compton, Helen Tiffany and Carl Gerard. Will S. Davis directed and wrote the screenplay with Joseph H. Trant. *Variety* thought it was excellent and "opened up a new lane for feature film literature." See also Lecoq, Monsieur.

Fangs of Vengeance

1926 American film (Chesterfield/1 reel) stars the Alaskan Wolfhound Fearless who was promoted as a dog detective in the 1926 series *Dog Detective*. It's on DVD.

Fantômas

The French surrealistic supervillain Fantômas and his archenemy Detective Juve were created on paper by Marcel Allain and Pierre Souvestre in 1911. They were brought to the screen in 1913 and 1914 in five popular French serials written and directed by Louis Feuillade and photographed by Guérin. René Navarre portrayed Fantômas, Bréon played Detective Juve, George Melchior was journalist Fandor and Renée Carl was Fantômas's lover Lady Beltham. The films are close adaptations of the novels and as entertaining today as they

Henry B. Walthall is the Lone Wolf fighting evil Lon Chaney with help from Mary Anderson in *The False Faces*.

These posters for the *Fantômas* French serials are famous, especially the one in which a gigantic Fantômas surveys Paris.

were in their time; prints survive and the films are on DVD. An American serial based on the character was filmed in 1920. The five serials, which tell a continuing story with the same characters are, in the order of their production: *Fantômas à l'Ombre de la guillotine, Juve Contre Fantômas, Le Mort qui tue, Fantômas contre Fantômas* and *Le Faux Magistrat, Fantômas à l'Ombre de la guillotine* (*Fantômas Under the Shadow of the Guillotine*).

Fantômas

1920 American serial (Fox/twenty 2-reel chapters) based on the 1911 French novel *Fantômas*. Fantômas (Edward Roseman) vows revenge after police reject his request for an amnesty. After he kidnaps Prof. Harrington (Lionel Adams), his arch-enemy Detective Dixon (John Willard) sets out to track him down with help from Harrington's daughter Ruth (Edna Murphy) and her fiancé Jack (Johnnie Walker). Eve Balfour shows up as the Woman in Black, Rena Parker as the Countess and Irving Brooks as the Duke. Edward Sedgwick directed and co-wrote the screenplay with George Eshenfelder. The chapters were titled *On the Stroke of Nine, The Million Dollar Reward, The Triple Peril, Blades of Terror, Heights of Horror, The Altar of Sacrifice, Flames of Destruction, At Death's Door, The Haunted Hotel, The Fatal Card, The Phantom Sword, The Danger Signal, On the Count of Three, The Blazing Train, The Sacred Necklace, The Phantom Shadow, The Price of Fang Wu, Double-Crossed, The Hawk's Prey* and *The Hell Ship*.

Fantômas à l'Ombre de la guillotine
(Fantômas Under the Shadow of the Guillotine)

1913 French serial (Gaumont/54 minutes in three 1-reel chapters) based on the 1911 novel *Fantômas* and written and directed by Louis Feuillade. This is the first serial in the Fantômas series. René Navarre plays super villain Fantômas who is seen in three disguises in this film; as Dr. Chalek when he robs a princess in a hotel, as a bellhop when he escapes from the hotel and a man called Gurn with a deadly secret. Detective Juve (Bréon) and journalist Fandor (George Melchior) investigate the disappearance of Lord Beltham and Juve finds the peer's corpse in a trunk in Gurn's apartment. Gurn is put in jail but freed through a scheme devised by Lady Beltham (Renée Carl) who has become Fantômas's lover. She arranges for actor Volgran (Vobert), who is portraying Fantômas in a stage play, to replace him in jail. Guérin was the cinematographer. On DVD.

Fantômas contre Fantômas
(Fantômas vs. Fantômas)

1914 French serial (Gaumont/59 minutes in four 1-reel chapters) written and directed by Louis Feuillade and based on the 1911 novel *Le Policier apache*. This is the first serial in the Fantômas series. Fantômas and his arch-enemies Detective Jove and reporter Fandor imitate each other in this complex narrative in which they constantly changing disguises making one unsure who is really who. Lady Beltham returns as the wife of a prince, gets her jewels stolen by Fantômas and collects money for turning him in to the police (he steals if from her). Juve captures Fantômas's gang at the end but the master criminal slips away once more. René Navarre plays Fantômas, Bréon is Detective Juve, George Melchior is Fandor and Renée Carl is Fantômas's lover Lady Beltham. Guérin was the cinematographer. On DVD. See *Fantômas*.

The Fatal Ring

1917 American serial (Astra-Path/twenty 2-reel chapters) based on a story by Frederick J. Jackson. Violet Standish (Pearl White) has a violet diamond ring that makes it wearer invisible. Competing villains attempt to steal it including the evil Richard Carlslake (Warner Oland) and the treacherous High Priestess of the Sacred Order (Ruby Hoffman). She gets help from former adversary Nicholas Knox (Earle Fox) in thrilling episodes with titles like *The Crushing Wall, Rays of Death, The Dice of Death* and *The Dagger Duel*. Bertram Mill-

Pearl White has a ring that makes the wearer invisible in *The Fatal Ring*.

hauser wrote the screenplay and George B. Seitz directed.

Le Faux Magistrat (The False Magistrate)

1914 French serial (Gaumont/70 minutes in four 1-reel chapters) written and directed by Louis Feuillade based on the 1912 Fantômas novel *Le Magistrat cambrioleur*. This is the fifth and final serial in the Fantômas series. Fantômas escapes from prison in Belgium with the help of Detective Juve (in disguise) who plans to follow him back to France and capture the rest of his gang. Their hideout is an abandoned railroad car in the town of Saint-Calais southwest of Paris. A marquis is robbed and murdered and his wife blackmailed as Fantômas searches for gems that keeps disappearing (they reappear when a church bell with a crook hung inside is rung for a funeral). Juve unmasks Fantômas when he disguises himself as judge by disguising himself as Fantômas. René Navarre plays Fantômas, Bréon is Detective Juve, George Melchior is Fandor and Renée Carl is Lady Beltham. Guérin was the cinematographer. On DVD. See *Fantômas*.

Les Faux-Monnayeurs (The Counterfeiters)

1908 French film (Éclair/1 reel), an episode in the *Nick Carter, le roi des détectives* series about the master detective Nick Carter. It was distributed in America as *The False Coiners*. In this episode Carter investigates a bank robbery. Pierre Bressol played Nick Carter and Victorin Jassett wrote and directed the film. A print of this film survives in the AFI collection at the Library of Congress.

Feet of Clay

1917 American film (General Film/4 reels) based on the story "Feet of Clay" by William Morton. When Scotland Yard detective Brandsby Mordant (Barney Fury) tries to rescue his nephew from a gang, it boomerangs on him and he ends up in prison. He escapes and vows revenge on his betrayers Glenister (Charles Elder), Armstrong (Carl McInroy) and Gassner (Frank Erlanger). He tracks them to San Francisco where he find that Gassner has been killed and Glenister's daughter Dorothy (Margaret Landis) has been kidnapped. He rescues her and she persuades him to drop his plans for revenge. A Scotland Yard detective locates Mordant but Dorothy convinces him Mordant is innocent. Harry Harvey directed and Luther Morton wrote the screenplay.

The Female Detective

1913 American comedy (Lubin/1 reel) starring Mae Hotely as the detective. She gets support from Tommy Atkins, Frances Ne Moyer and George Reehm. Jerold T. Hevener directed.

The Female Sleuth

1909 French film (Pathé Frères/604 feet). No other details available.

The Fiery Hand

1923 British film (Stoll/2 reels), an episode in the *Mystery of Fu Manchu* series based on a story by Sax Rohmer. Nayland Smith (Fred Paul) and Dr. Petrie investigate the mystery of a haunted house and are captured by Dr. Fu Manchu (Harry Agar Lyons) who tortures Smith. A. E. Colby directed, Frank Wilson wrote the screenplay with Colby and D. P. Cooper was the cinematographer. Print survives at BFI film archive.

Fifty Candles

1921 American film (W.W. Hodkinson/5 reels) based on the novel *Fifty Candles* by mystery writer Earl Derr Biggers, the creator of Charlie Chan. Henry Drew (William Carroll) is murdered with an unusual Chinese dagger and Ralph (Edward Burns), who owns it and loves Drew's secretary Mary (Marjorie Daw), is accused of the crime. However, investigators eventually discover that Drew's indentured servant Hung Chin Chung (Bertram Grassby) has harbored resentment for many year and he eventually confesses. Irvin V. Willat directed.

The Fight for Millions

1913 American feature film (Blaché Features/4 reels). Detective Delaney (Barney Gilmore) is hired by an heiress (Marian Swayne) to investigate the kidnapping of her banker father. Her fiancé (Darwin Karr) is the chief suspect but Delaney pins it on Italian gang leader Sorenti (Joseph Levering) after arranging his own kidnapping. Herbert Blaché directed.

Fighting Snub Reilly

1924 British film (Stoll/2 reels) based on story by Edgar Wallace, an episode in the series *Thrilling Stories from the Strand*. With David Hawthorne, Ena Evans, Fred Raynham and Dallas Cairns. Andrew P. Wilson directed.

File No. 113

1915 American film (Biograph/2 reels) based on Émile Gaboriau's novel *Le Dossier No 113*. Detective Lecoq dons multiple disguises to solve a blackmail case, a bank robbery and other crimes. The actors were Ivan Christy, Jack Drumier, Louise Vale, Alan Hale, Gretchen Hartman, William Jefferson, Laura La Varnie and Franklin Ritchie. The novel was also filmed as *Thou Shalt Not Steal*.

The Film Detective (Il film rivelatore)

1914 Italian film (Pasquali/4 reels) distributed in America as *The Film Detective*. A film is the detective that reveals the truth in this Italian movie which gives it characters English names in the American release print. Jack Dangerfield/Count De Lys (Gustavo Serena) fritters away his fortune so a creditor arrange for him to marry wealthy heiress Mary Delmar/Maria Desmar (Maria Jacobini). Jealous suitor Lord Lytton/Count Metzberg (Nello Carotenuto) causes problems and Jack has to go to work He joins a film company and his first job involves hunting lions in Africa. Lytton and the creditor shoot Jack while he is on location in the jungle but a cinematographer films the attempted murder (Jack is only wounded). The evil duo are shown in their true colors and arrested. Umberto Paradisi directed. *Variety* thought it was a pretty good film.

The Final Problem

1923 British film (Stoll/2 reels), an episode in the *Last Adventures of Sherlock Holmes* series based on a story by Sir Arthur Conan Doyle. Sherlock Holmes meets the arch-criminal Professor Moriarty with disastrous results. Eille Norwood portrays Holmes with Hubert Willis as Dr. Watson. Alfred Moise was the cinematographer and George Ridgewell wrote the adaptation and directed. Print survives at BFI archive.

Find the Woman

1922 American film (Cosmopolitan-Paramount/6 reels) based on the 1921 novel *Find the Woman* by Arthur Somers Roche. Sophie Carey (Alma Rubens) is trying to steal blackmail letters from the office of blackmailer Maurice Beiner (Arthur Donaldson) when she meets would-be actress Clancy Deane (Eileen Huban) on a fire escape. Beiner is found murdered and both are suspects. Judge Walbrough (George MacQuarrie) is knocked out by the murderer and fingerprints prove that Don Carey (Henry Sedley) was the killer. Doty Hobart wrote the screenplay and Tom Terriss directed.

Finger Prints

1914 American film (Essanay/3 reels). Detective Richard Neal (Francis X. Bushman) saves his sweetheart (Gerda Holmes) who had been kidnapped and retrieves a valuable stolen scarab.

Finger Prints

1923 American movie (Hyperion/5 reels). Violet Palmer stars as the daughter of a banker who is killed before he can give her a diamond necklace. Her boyfriend turns detective to investigate the murder and theft. Alton Floyd wrote the screenplay and Joseph Levering directed.

Finger Prints

1927 American film (Warner Bros./7 reels) based on the short story "Finger Prints" by Arthur Somers Roche. The old dark house story gets the slapstick treatment in this story about a mansion where a crook had hidden his ill-gotten gains. Undercover detective Dora (Louise Fazenda) knows where the secret buttons are hidden as she tricks a gang trying to find the loot while holding the crook's daugh-

Louise Fazenda is an undercover detective in *Finger Prints*.

Detective Jeff Tarrant (Hugh Allan) has to track down criminals behind a series of fires in *The Fire Detective*.

ter Jacqueline (Helene Costello). George Nichols plays another undercover dick, Myrna Loy gets to be vamp the guys and Franklin Pangborn is the not-very-dangerous Bandoline Kid. Graham Baker wrote the screenplay and Lloyd Bacon directed.

The Fire Detective

1929 American serial (Pathé/ten 2-reel chapters) based on a story by Frank Leon Smith. Fire detective Jeff Tarrant (Hugh Allan) sets out to track down the criminals behind a series of disastrous fires. His sweetheart Gladys (Gladys McConnell) is constantly in peril and a senator, an attorney and a convict are all involved. The other cast members are Leo D. Maloney as the fire chief, Frank Lackteen, John Cossar, Larry Steers, Bruce Gordon and Carlton S. King. George Arthur Gray wrote the screenplay and Spencer G. Bennet and Thomas L. Storey directed. The film begins with an episode titled *The Arson Trail*.

The First Law

1918 American film (Pathé/5 reels) based on Gilson Willets' novel *The First Law*. Norma Webb (Irene Castle) shoots her evil husband when he attacks her and runs away but a detective (Edward J. Connelly) learns about it and blackmails her when she marries a second time. When he demands secret information about her wealthy second husband (Antonio Moreno), she tells him what happened. They follow the detective to his home and see him kill her first husband who had only been wounded when she shot him before. The detective is arrested. Roy Sommerville wrote the screenplay and Lawrence McGill directed.

$500 Reward

1911 American comedy (Biograph/1 reel), a film in the *Two Sleuths* series produced and directed by Mack Sennett and starring Sennett and Fred Mace. They play comic detectives attempting to earn a $500 reward.

$5,000,000 Counterfeiting Plot

1914 American feature film (Dramascope/6 reels) starring detective William J. Burns (1860–1932) who created the William J. Burns International Detective Agency and headed the Bureau of Investigation (predecessor of the FBI) from 1921 to 1924. The film, based on one of Burns' cases, tells how he and agent Florence Castle uncovered a counterfeiting ring headed by James Long. In an epilogue, Sir Arthur Conan Doyle congratulates Burns on his detective work. George G. Nathan wrote the screenplay and Bertram Harrison directed. The supporting cast includes Charles E. Graham, Glen White, Joseph Sullivan and Jack Sharkey. Burns introduced the film at the New York premiere.

$5,000 Reward

1918 American film (Bluebird Photoplays/5 reels) based on the story "My Arcadian Wife" by mystery writer Charles Wesley Sanders first published in *All-Story Magazine*. Dick Arlington (Franklyn Farnum) quarrels with his uncle Henry (William Lloyd) who is later found murdered. As Dick is the number one suspect, he flees to the country where he marries Margaret (Gloria Hope) who believes in his innocence. She turns detective to find the real killer and gets a confession from the family lawyer F. McGrew Willis wrote the screenplay and Douglas Gerrard directed.

The Flaming Clue

1920 American film (Vitagraph/5 reels) base on the story "Detective Jim" by Frederic Van Rensselaer Dey (Dey wrote Nick Carter stories so this may be an adaptation of one of them). Detective Cornell (Harry T. Morey) tracks a counterfeiting gang to a country boarding house run by Mrs. Quail (Eleanor Barry) and her daughter Betty (Lucy Fox). They don't know that their boarder Aaron Prine (Sidney Dalbrook) is the counterfeiter boss and that there is a secret passage in their cellar leading to the counterfeiters' hideout. Cornell becomes a boarder and woos Betty fall but Prine is suspicious. Cornell finally gets his evidence and sends out word but gets trapped with Betty in the cellar. The police arrive in time to rescue them and catch the counterfeiters. William B. Courtney wrote the screenplay and Edwin L. Hollywood directed.

The Flashlight

1917 American film (Bluebird Photoplays/5 reels) based on Albert M. Treynore's story "The Flashlight" in *All-Story Magazine*. Photographer Jack Lane (William Stowell) is camping in the mountains when he hears a gun shot and finds that his automatic flash camera has taken a picture of a woman running with a shotgun. He goes to a nearby cabin to see what happened and finds the owner dead. The police arrive and arrest him for the murder but he escapes. He meets up with Delice Brixton (Dorothy Phillips), the woman in the photograph, but both think the other is the killer. Lane is recaptured and tried but the dead man's brother (Lon Chaney) tells the court he killed his brother in self defense. Ida May Park wrote the screenplay and directed.

The Floor Above

1914 American film (Mutual/4 reels) based on the story "The Tragedy of Charlecot Mansions" by E. Phillips Oppenheim in the 1914 collection *The Amazing Partnership*. English detectives Grace Burton (Estelle Coffin) and Stephen Pryde (Henry Walthall) plan to marry but he is afraid to tell her he has inherited wealth and a title. Her sister Stella (Dorothy Gish) is accused of murder when a dead man is found in her flat but Grace and Stephen believe her innocent. The dead man frequently visited a woman on the floor above Stella and the detectives discover that he and a rival mistakenly entered Stella's flat on the night of the murder where one killed the other. James Kirkwood directed the film supervised by D. W. Griffith;.

Flying Colors

1917 American film (Triangle/5 reels) based on a story by R. Cecil Smith. Former college pole vaulter Brent Brewster (William Desmond) goes to work for a detective agency and finds a use for his pole vaulting skills. He is hired by family friend Craig Lansing (J. Barney Sherry) to investigate jewel robberies in

Poughkeepsie. While working undercover at a party, he recognizes English thief Captain Drake (Jack Livingston). When he gets proof of Drake's thievery, he has to pole vault though a window to prevent his escape. John Lynch wrote the screenplay and Frank Borzage directed.

The Flying Squad

1929 British film (British Lion/7 reels) based on the novel *The Flying Squad* by Edgar Wallace. A detective pretends to be a Jew who was murdered and is able to get the killer to confess. John Longden played Inspector John Bradley, Donald Calthrop was Sederman, Dorothy Bartlam was Ann Perryman and Laurence Ireland was Ronnie Perryman, Kathleen Hayden wrote the screenplay and Arthur Maude directed.

Foolish Monte Carlo

1922 American film (Wid Gunning/5 reels) based on Carlton Dawe's novel *The Black Spider*. An audacious thief in Monte Carlo always leaves his calling card, a drawing of a black spider, at the scene of the robbery. Reggie Cosway (Sam Livesey) accuses Archie Lowndes (Robert Corbins) of the latest theft but Angela Brentwood (Mary Clare) defends him saying she took the necklace as a prank. Cosway accuses her of being the spider but then the real thief is apprehended — her fiancé Beauvais. William Humphrey directed and wrote the screenplay with George Edwardes-Hall.

For the Defense

1922 American film (Paramount/5 reels) based on Elmer Rice's novel *For the Defense*. Anne Woodstock (Ethel Clayton) is hypnotized by her Hindu physician Kasimir (Bertram Grassby) in his office but doesn't remember it when she leaves for Europe the next day. Kasimir is found murdered and his assistant Jennie (ZaSu Pitts) is accused of the crime as her pin was found next to the body. Anne remembers that she was in the office that night and returns from her trip to insist she must be the guilty person. Jennie then confesses that she killed Kasimir out of jealousy of Anne. Beulah Marie Dix wrote the screenplay and Paul Powell directed.

The Forger

1928 British film (British Lion/7 reels) based on a *Daily Mail* serial by Edgar Wallace who wrote the screenplay. A doctor helps a criminal frame a woman for forgery. Lillian Rich starred with support from Sam Livesey as Inspector Rouper, Sam Nigel Barrie, Winter Hall and Ivo Dawson. G. B. Samuelson directed.

The Four-Footed Ranger

1928 American film (Universal/5 reels) starring German shepherd Dynamite as a canine detective. He helps Texas Ranger Jack Dunne (Edmund Cobb) catch a gang of cattle rustlers led by Francis Ford. Cromwell Kent and Paul M. Bryan wrote the screenplay and Stuart Paton directed.

The Four Just Men

1921 British film (Stoll/5 reels) based on a novel by Edgar Wallace. The four just men are Manfred, Thery, Poiccart and Gonsalez. Their first work of "justice" is a plan to assassinate a government minister unless he changes his mind about a law they don't like. They send threats and even say when he will be killed unless the cooperates. Scotland Yard Inspector Falmouth investigates but is unable to solve the crime in time. Cecil Humphreys played Manfred, Charles Croker-King was Thery, Owen Roughwood was Poiccart, George Bellamy was Gonsalez. Teddy Arundell was Inspector Falmouth, C. Tilson-Chowne was the minister and Robert Vallis was Billy Marks. George Ridgewell wrote and directed the film.

Four Thirteen

1914 American film (Vitagraph/3 reels). A Secret Service detective (Harry Morey) captures a diamond smuggling gang with the help of a jeweler's daughter (Anita Stewart) Donald Buchanan wrote the screenplay and Ralph Ince directed.

The Fourteenth Man

1920 American film (Paramount/5 reels) based on the 1903 play *The Man from Blankley's* by F. Anstey (pseudonym of Thomas Anstey Guthrie). Detective Jenks (Robert Mi-lash) follows Captain Douglas Gordon (Robert Warwick) from Scotland to New York after he wounds another officer. To dodge Jenks he agrees to substitute for Deacon (James Marsh) in a charity boxing match. Deacon turns out to be a burglar but Gordon prevents him from robbing a safe. Jenks catches him at last but only to inform him that he is heir to a fortune. He is now able to marry heiress Marjory (Bebe Daniels). Walter Woods wrote the screenplay and Joseph Henabery directed. Anstey's play was filmed again in 1930 and 1934.

The Frame Up

1923 American film (Premium Picture Productions/5 reels). A Secret Service detective (Jack Livingston) goes undercover and pretends to be a crook so he can investigate a gang of railroad thieves. Harry Moody directed.

Die Frau mit den Millionarden
(The Woman with Millions)

1920 German film (May Film/9 reels), the sixth episode in the big budget German series *Herrin der Welt* (Mistress of the World) based on a novel by Karl Figdor. Mia May stars as Maud Gregaards-Fergusson who has found the lost treasure of the Queen of Sheba and become the richest woman in the world. The cast includes Michael Bohnen, Hans Mierendorff and Henry Sze. Richard Hutter wrote the screenplay and Uwe Jens Krafft directed.

Frauen, die Ehe brechen
(Women and the Marriage Break)

1921 German film (Althoff Film/2 reels), an episode in the four-film German *Nick Carter* series featuring master detective Nick Carter. It was released in English-speaking countries as *Women and the Marriage Break*. Bruno Eichgrün played Nick Carter and wrote and directed the film.

Free Lips

1928 American film (First Division/6 reels) based on a story by Raymond Wells. Anne Baldridge (June Marlowe), a hostess at the Free Lips Nightclub, may have shot and killed a misbehaving drunk but her boss Bill Dugan (Frank Hagney) says he did it. He is tried and convicted but then the murder weapon turns up and reveals the real killer. With Olin Francis as Detective Kelly and Jane Novak as Flossie. Wallace MacDonald directed and Jack Kelly wrote the screenplay.

Die Freundin des gelben Mannes
(The Yellow Man's Friend)

1919 German film (May Film/9 reels), the first episode in the big budget German series *Herrin der Welt* (Mistress of the World). It was based on a novel by Karl Figdor and distributed in America in 1922 in a five-reel version as *The Dragon's Claw*. Mia May stars as Maud Gregaards who goes to China seeking to find the key to the lost treasure of the Queen of Sheba and some thrilling adventure. She finds it in spades and is soon involved in awe-inspiring chases, earthquakes and plane crashes along with her sidekick Madsen (Michael Bohnen). Ruth Goetz wrote the screenplay and Joseph Klein & Joe May directed. (In the version shown in America the main characters were renamed: Maud became Helen and Madsen became Benson.)

Fritzchen als Sherlock Holmes in Germany (Fritzchen as Sherlock Holmes in Germany)

1911 German comedy (1 reel). Fritzchen wants to be a detective so he emulates Sherlock Holmes.

From Now On

1920 American film (Fox/5 reels) based on the 1919 *From Now On* by Frank L. Packard. Dave Henderson (George Walsh) is cheated of $100,000 by racetrack tout Martin Tydeman (J. A. Marcus) but is able to steal it back. After he has hidden it, he is caught and sent to prison When he gets out, Tydeman and police wait for him to try to retrieve the money. After he falls in love with Teresa (Regina Quinn) and nearly loses the money to another thief, he decides to reform and return the loot. Raoul Walsh wrote the screenplay and directed.

The Fungi Cellars

1923 British film (Stoll/2 reels), an episode

in the *Mystery of Fu Manchu* series based on a story by Sax Rohmer. Dr. Fu Manchu (Harry Agar Lyons) creates a deadly poisonous mushroom. A. E. Colby directed, Frank Wilson wrote the screenplay with Colby and D. P. Cooper was the cinematographer. Print survives at BFI film archive.

The Further Adventures of Sherlock Holmes

1922 British series (Stoll/fifteen 2-reel films) starring Eille Norwood as Holmes and Hubert Willis as Dr. Watson, Arthur Bell as Inspector Lastrade and Madame d'Esterre as Mrs. Hudson. The films were directed by George Ridgewell with screenplays by Patrick L Mannock and Geoffrey H. Malins based on the Doyle stories. The films are *The Abbey Grange, Black Peter, The Boscombe Valley Mystery, The Bruce Partington Plans, Charles Augustus Milverton, The Greek Interpreter, The Golden Pince-Nez, The Musgrave Ritual, The Naval Treaty, The Norwood Builder, The Red Circle, The Reigate Squires, The Second Stain, The Six Napoleons* and *The Stockbroker's Clerk*. All of these films survive at the BFI film archive.

The Further Adventures of Stingaree

1917 American serial (Kalem/fifteen 2-reel episodes). Stingaree is a Robin Hood-like Australian bandit created by E. W. Hornung. He is actually an Englishman named Irving Randolph who was cheated out of his fortune by a villainous brother. He was portrayed in two Kalem serials (this is the second) by True Boardman with Marin Sais as the woman who loves him, Paul Hurst as his friend and partner Howie and William Brunton as his nasty brother Robert. James W. Horne directed. Joseph F. Poland wrote the screenplay and Paul C Hurst directed. In this serial Stingaree is back living in London where he learns that he is penniless because his wastrel brother spent his fortune while he was away. He is persuaded to return to Australia by his old partner Howie who advises him police have a warrant for his arrest. The episodes are *The Fugitive Passenger, A Model Marauder, A Double Deception, An Eye for an Eye, Mark of Stingaree, Through Fire and Water, An Order of the Court, Tracking of Stingaree, A Bushranger's Strategy, Poisoned Cup, Arrayed with the Enemy, The Jackaroo, At the Sign of the Kangaroo, The Stranger at Dumcriff* and *A Champion of the Law*. See also *Stingaree*.

The Further Adventures of Terence O'Rourke

1915 American series (Universal/three 2-reel episodes) based on mystery writer Louis Joseph Vance's stories about the roguish Irish adventurer Terence O'Rourke. The episodes are titled *Terence O'Rourke, The King and the Man* and *A Captain of Villainy*. See *Terence O'Rourke, Gentleman Adventurer* for further information and other films.

The Further Exploits of Sexton Blake: The Mystery of the SS Olympic

1919 British film (Gaumont/5 reels) written, directed and produced by Harry Lorraine with Douglas Payne as the master detective Sexton Blake and Neil Warrington as Tinker. Blake saves the daughter of s scientist who has been murdered for his secret formula. (See Blake, Sexton for other films.)

The Further Mysteries of Dr. Fu Manchu

1924 British series (Stoll/eight 2-reel episodes) based on the original stories. Harry Agar Lyons returned as Fu Manchu in this second series with Fred Paul again as detective Nayland Smith, Humberston Wright as Dr Petrie and Dorinea Shirley as Karamaneh. Paul directed the films and wrote the screenplays with Frank Canham as cinematographer. The supporting cast included Frank Wilson, Dorinea Shirley, Fred Morgan, Johnny Butt and Harry Rignold. The films in the series, many of which survive at the BFI Film Archive, are *The Café L'Egypte, The Coughing Horror, Cragmire Tower, The Golden Pomegranates, The Green Mist, Greywater Park, Karamaneh* and *The Midnight Summons*. See *Dr. Fu Manchu* for other films.

A Game of Graft

1922 American film (Garsson Productions/2 reels), one of four films in a *Nick Carter* series featuring the famous detective Nick Carter. In this one he battles graft. Carter was played by Edmund Lowe under the direction of Alexander Hall. With Diana Allen and Henry Sedley.

The Game of Liberty

1916 British film (London Film/6 reels) based on the 1916 mystery novel *The Game of Liberty* by E. Phillips Oppenheim. Distributed in America as *Under Suspicion*. English aristocrat Paul Walmsley (Gerald Ames) falls in love with Laura Cowie (Eva Parker) the daughter of a counterfeiter who steals a valuable necklace. Bert Wynne played Inspector Cullen, and Douglas was Munro was Joseph H. Parker. George Loane Tucker directed.

The Game of Three

1915 American film (Sterling Camera and Film Co./5 reels) based on a story by Leon Wagner who wrote the screenplay. Detective O'Bryan (Barney Gilmore) shoots and wounds his wayward son Jim (Roy Gahris) after he steals a diamond necklace in partnership with adventuress Mazie King (Lillian Niederaur). Jim hides out with Molly (Violet Stuart) and Tom Ryan (John Sharkey), who earlier helped him, and slips to the necklace into her pocket. The police and the detective track him down and arrest Molly because she has the necklace. Jim gives into guilt and admits that he was the thief.

The Gangsters and the Girl

1914 American film (Kay-Bee/2 reels) based on a story by Richard V. Spencer. Charles Ray plays an undercover detective in this hyperactive melodrama about a woman kidnapped by gangsters. Ray is able to join the gang and becomes involved with gangster Alma Rubens but he I sable to reform her. The film featured location shooting in Venice (California), a rooftop gun battle and a good car chase. The supporting cast included Elizabeth Burbridge, Arthur Jarret and Margaret Thomson. Scott Sidney directed from a screenplay by J. G. Hawks.

Charles Ray plays an undercover detective in *The Gangsters and the Girl*.

Gas, Oil and Water

1922 American film (Charles Ray Productions-First National/5 reels). Secret Service detective George Oliver Watson (Charles Ray) goes undercover to catch a gang of smugglers. He opens a gas station on the Mexican border and becomes involved with Susie (Charlotte Pierce, the daughter of a hotelier. He finds the villains and arrests two of them but the third kidnaps Susie and escapes in a car. After a wild pursuit, he rescues her as the evildoer's car crashes and explodes. Richard Andres wrote the screenplay and Charles Ray directed.

Das Gasthaus von Chicago
(The Chicago Inn)

1921 German film (Althoff Film/2 reels), an episode in the four-film *Nick Carter* series featuring master detective Nick Carter. It was released in English-speaking countries as *The Chicago Inn*. Bruno Eichgrün played Nick Carter and wrote and directed the film.

The Gate Crasher

1928 American film (Universal/6 reels) based on a story by Jack Foley and William

James Craft. Dick Henshaw (Glenn Tryon) is only a bill poster but he is taking a correspondence course on how to become a detective. He gets involved in a car accident with Broadway star Mara Di Leon (Patsy Ruth Miller) and later learns that her jewels have been stolen. He sets out to find them for her, proves that the thieves were her maid and press agent and recovers the gems. Carl Krusada wrote the screenplay and William James Craft directed.

Das Geheimnis der Breifmarke
(The Mystery of the Stamp)

1917 German film (Egede Nissen Film Company/5 reels) featuring a female detective known as Miss Clever. It was one of a series of ten films about the woman detective starring Norwegian actress Ada Egede-Nissen using the screen name of "Ada Van Ehlers." It was written by Rudolf Baron and Else Cressin and directed by Georg Alexander who took the male lead in the film. See *Miss Clever* for other films in the series.

Das Geheimnis der Mumie
(The Mystery of the Mummy)

1920 German film (PAGU/5 reels) featuring the "American" detective Joe Deebs played by Ferdinand von Alten. This was a late film in the long-running Deebs series created by producer Joe May. After May stopped making Deebs films, the mantle was picked up by Projektions-AG Union (PAGU). Paul Rosenhayn wrote the screenplay with Josef Coböken and Victor Janson directed. The cast included Aud Egede Nissen, Magnus Stifter. Julia Serda and Hannes Sturm. See Deebs, Joe for other films.

Das Geheimnis von Chateau Richmond
(The Mystery of Castle Richmond)

1913 German film (Midgar Features-Karl Werner Film /4 reels). This film in the German *Miss Nobody* detective series was released in America in 1914 without indication of nationality or cast so it was reviewed as an American picture. Senta Eichstaedt, who played Miss Nobody, was renamed Grace Carter in the American titles. She is hired to investigate a strange man who has inherited Richmond Castle and soon discovers that he is under threat from a secret society. She helps him outwit them by dressing in his clothes and leading the gang on a wild goose chase. The police capture the gang and all ends well. Rudolf Del Zopp wrote the German screenplay and Willy Zeyn directed. See *Miss Nobody* for other films.

Der Geheimnisvolle Klub
(The Mysterious Club)

1913 German film (Richard Eichberg-Film/4 reels) loosely based on the story *The Suicide Club* by Robert Louis Stevenson. A man is tricked into a requirement that he kill himself. Fred Sauer, Ilse Bois and Joseph Delmont starred and Joseph Demont directed. See also *The Suicide Club*.

Die Geheimnisvolle Villa
(The Mysterious Villa)

1914 German film (Continental Kunstfilm/4 reels) distributed in America as *Trapped by Camera* and featuring the "American" detective Stuart Webbs. This was the first film in the long-running Webbs series. Detective Webbs (Ernst Reicher) investigates mysterious noises made by phantoms in the basement and walls of a professor's house. He discovers that the noises are being made by a criminal gang looking for secret military plans. Webb traps them through the use of a hidden camera. The supporting cast included Sabine Impekoven and Julius Falkenstein. Joe May directed, Ernst Reicher wrote the screenplay and Max Fassbender was the cinematographer. See Webbs, Stuart for other films.

Der Geheimsekretär
(The Confidential Secretary)

1915 German film (May Film/4 reels) featuring the "American" detective Joe Deebs as played by Max Landa. This was a film in the long-running Deebs series created by producer Joe May who wrote and directed it. There were over thirty Deebs films with the detective portrayed by six different actors. See Deebs, Joe for other films.

Der Geisterspuk im Hause des Professors
(The Ghost in the Professor's House)

1914 German film (Continental Kunstfilm/4 reels) featuring the "American" detective Stuart Webbs played by Ernst Reicher. This was third film in the long-running Webbs series. He is asked to investigate a series of mysterious break-ins in a professor's office. Joe May directed, Ernst Reicher wrote the screenplay and Max Fassbender was the cinematographer. (Print survives in film archive) See Webbs, Stuart for other films.

The Gentleman Burglar

1909 American film (Edison/1 reel) loosely based on *Arsène Lupin, gentleman-cambrioleur* (Arsène Lupin, Gentleman Burglar) by Maurice Leblanc about the French master thief. William Ranous played the suave thief and Edwin S. Porter directed.

Die Geschichte der Maud Gregaards
(The Story of Maud Gregaards)

1919 German film (May Film/9 reels), the second episode in the big budget German series *Herrin der Welt* (*Mistress of the World*). It was based on a novel by Karl Figdor and distributed in America in 1922 in a five-reel version as *The Race for Life*. Mia May stars as Maud Gregaards who goes to China seeking to find the lost treasure of the Queen of Sheba and become the richest woman in the world. She is involved in chases, earthquakes and plane crashes along with sidekick Michael Bohnen. The supporting cast includes Hans Mierendorff as her arch-enemy Baron Murphy and Henry Sze as Dr. Kien-Lung. Richard Hutter wrote the screenplay and Joe May directed. (In the version shown in America the main characters were renamed and Maud became Helen Nielsen.)

Das Gesetz der Mine
(The Law of the Mine)

1915 German film (May Film/4 reels) featuring the "American" detective Joe Deebs as played by Max Landa. This was an early film in the long-running Deebs series created by producer Joe May in 1914 who also wrote and directed it. The supporting cast included Ellen Richter and Lewis Brody. See Deebs, Joe for other films.

Der Gestreifte Domino
(The Striped Domino)

1915 German film (Adolf Gartner-Stuart Webbs Film Company/4 reels) featuring the "American" detective Stuart Webbs played by Ernst Reicher. This was an early film in the long-running Webbs series which continued until 1926. The supporting actors included Emmerich Hanus and Ludwig Trautmann, Ernst Reicher wrote the screenplay and Adolf Gartner directed. (Print survives in a film archive.) See Webbs, Stuart for other films.

Get-Rich-Quick Wallingford

1916 Australian film (J. C. Williamson/5 reels) based on George Randolph Chester's novel *Get-Rich-Quick Wallingford*. Con men J. Rufus Wallingford (Fred Niblo) and Blackie Daw (Henry Carson Clarke) arrive in a small town and get rich quick selling shares in a carpet tack company. Enid Bennett played Fanny with Eddie Lamb, Pirie Bush and Sydney Stirling in supporting roles. Fred Niblo also directed. See also Wallingford, J. Rufus.

Get-Rich-Quick Wallingford

1921 American film (Cosmopolitan Productions/7 reels) based on the 1910 play by George M. Cohan and the novel by George Randolph Chester. Con men J. Rufus Wallingford (Sam Hardy) and Blackie Daw (Norman Kerry) arrive in a small town posing as businessmen looking for investments. With the town's money they build a factory to produce carpet tacks. Stockholders suspect a fraud but there is an offer of a buyout when carpet tacks become a hot-selling item. Wallingford marries his stenographer Fannie (Doris Kenyon) and Blackie weds Dorothy (Billie Dove). Luther Reed wrote the screenplay and Frank Borzage directed. See also Wallingford, J. Rufus.

Getting Evidence, Showing the Trials and Tribulations of a Private Detective

1906 American film (Edison/1 reel) photographed and directed by Edwin S. Porter. A jealous husband hires private detective Hawkshaw to get evidence that his wife is being un-

A Girl at Bay

faithful. The detective trails the wife but an accident prevents him from getting a photo.

A Girl at Bay

1919 American film (Vitagraph/5 reels) based on the story "Hunt the Woman" by mystery writer Joseph Gollomb. Mary Allen (Corinne Griffith) is shown holding a bloodstained knife next to the body of Robert Craigin. She later marries his brother Bruce (Walter Miller). Detective Hooker (Walter Horton) and criminal psychologist Francis Galt (Harry Davenport) believe Mary killed Craigin and Galt devises a psychological trap for her. It convinces her new husband of her guilt but it causes Thomas Gray (Denton Vane) to confess to the killing. He says he was avenging his wife's honor and that Mary fainted before it happened. Katherine S. Reed wrote the screenplay and Tom Mills directed. The psychologist Galt, nicknamed Goldfish, was featured in three novels by Gollomb.

The Girl by the Roadside

1917 American film (Bluebird/5 reels) based on the novel *The Girl by the Roadside* by Varick Vanardy (Frederic Van Rensselaer Dey). Judith Ralston (Violet Mersereau) doesn't know that her brother Budd (Cecil Owen) and wife Vera (Ann Andrews) are counterfeiters. They leave her in a small Virginia town where she meets Boone Pendleton (Allen Edwards). Detective Fayban (Robert F. Hill) is tracking Budd and Vera and is suspicious of Judith. When she is asked by brother Budd to return to their house and destroy papers, Fayban follows. Budd gets there first and is persuaded to reform by Judith and then escape. John C. Brownell wrote the screenplay and Theodore Marston directed. The novel was filmed a second time as *The Girl in the Rain*.

The Girl Detective

1915 American serial (Kalem/seventeen 2-reel episodes) about a society girl who works with the police and is able to help them solve crimes because of her society connection. Ruth Roland played the detective in the first seven films, Cleo Ridgeley took over the role for Episodes 8 to 14 and Marin Sais was the detec-

Ruth Roland in the detective in the Kalem serial *The Girl Detective*.

tive in Episodes 15 to 17. Hamilton Smith wrote the scripts, Knute Olaf Rahmn was the cinematographer and James W. Horne directed the series shot in California. The supporting players included Edward Clisbee, Robert Gray, Frank Jonasson, James W. Horne, Paul Hurst, Anna Lingham, William H. West The first episode, *The Affair of the Deserted House*, was released January 27, 1915. The other episodes, in alphabetical order, were *The Apartment House Mystery, The Closed Door, The Diamond Broker, The Disappearance of Harry Warrington, Following the Clue, Jared Fairfax's Millions, Mike Donegal's Escape, The Mystery of the Tea Dansant, Old Isaacson's Diamonds, Scotty Weed's Alibi, The Tattooed Hand, The Thumb Prints on the Safe* and *The Writing on the Wall*. A print of *The Closed Door* survives.

The Girl Detective

1916 American film (Selig/1 reel) starring Robyn Adair as the Girl Detective with a supporting cast including Leo D. Maloney, Ed Brady, Virginia Kirtley and Eugenie Ford. Burton L. King directed and William Alfred Corey wrote the screenplay.

The Girl Detective's Ruse

1913 American film (Thanhouser/1 reel) starring Marguerite Snow as a detective who impersonates a counterfeiter. She is picked up by a gang member as she leaves the prison dressed in prison garb and taken to the counterfeiters' headquarters. She is unveiled as a spy when the woman's husband arrives but is able to escape as the police arrive and arrest the gang.

The Girl from Chicago

1927 American film (Warner Bros./6 reels) based on the short story "Business Is Best" by Arthur Somers Roche. Mary Carlton (Myrna Loy) poses as a Chicago gunmoll to infiltrate the Chicago underground and get evidence to prove that her imprisoned brother Bob (Carroll Nye) is innocent of a crime. She suspects gangsters Handsome Joe (Conrad Nagel) and ("Big Steve" Drummond (William Russell) of being involved and eventually learns that Drummond is the guilty one and Handsome Joe is an undercover detective. After a gun battle, Drummond and his gang are arrested and Bob is freed. Graham Baker wrote the screenplay and Ray Enright directed.

The Girl from Havana

1929 American film (Fox/6 reels). Woman detective Lola Lane (Joan Anders) goes undercover as a chorus girl to catch a gang of jewel thieves. She sails with a musical comedy troupe (the Roxyettes) to Havana and gets evidence on the gang but before she falls in love with one of the gang members (Paul Page). It works out, however, as he is also undercover seeking the gangster who killed his father Benjamin Stoloff and Edwin Burke directed and John Stone wrote the screenplay with intertitles by Edwin Burke (the film was released in both silent and sound versions).

The Girl in the Rain

1920 American feature film (Universal/5 reels) based on the novel *The Girl by the Roadside* by Varick Vanardy (Frederic Van Rensselaer Dey). Judith (Anne Cornwall) goes to a country hotel with brother Walter (Lloyd Bacon) and his wife Vera (Jessalyn Van Trump) who are suspected of stealing bonds. Detectives arrest Walter and Vera while Vera is out riding. She falls from her horse and aided by Boone Pendleton (James Liddy). When the detectives come after Judith, she escapes and helps her brother and his wife break out of jail. The detectives catch up with them at Boone's estate but let them go when they learn that Walter is returning the bonds and that this a was a first offence Boone and Judith get together. Doris Schroeder wrote the screenplay and Rollin Sturgeon directed. The novel was filmed earlier as *The Girl by the Roadside*.

The Girl in the Web

1920 American film (Pathé/6 reels) based on the 1918 mystery novel *Miss Maitland, Private Secretary* by Geraldine Bonner. A detective investigating a theft suspects Esther Maitland (Blanche Sweet) of robbing the safe of her wealthy employer Mrs. Janney (Adele Farrington). When Mrs. Janney's grandchild is kidnapped, she is suspected of that crime, too.

Blanche Sweet is suspected of being a thief in *The Girl in the Web.*

Only neighbor Dick Ferguson (Nigel Barrie) believes in her innocence. They eventually discover that the kidnapper is the detective hired to investigate the robbery which was committed by Ferguson's servant. Waldemar Young wrote the screenplay and Robert Thornby directed.

The Girl on the Stairs

1924 American film (Peninsula Studios/7 reels) based on Winston Bouve's story "The Girl on the Stairs" in *Ainslee's Magazine*. Dora Sinclair (Patsy Ruth Miller) goes to the home of her married ex-lover Dick Wakefield (Freeman Wood) while sleepwalking. He is found dead the next day and she is accused of his murder. At her trial she is hypnotized and is able to recall what happened that night. She tells the jury she saw jealous José Sarmento (Bertram Grassby) kill Wakefield for flirting with his wife. Sarmento confesses and Dora is freed. William Worthington directed and Elmer Harris wrote the screenplay.

The Gloria Scott

1923 British film (Stoll/2 reels), an episode in the *Last Adventures of Sherlock Holmes* series based on a story by Sir Arthur Conan Doyle. Sherlock Holmes solves a mystery involving a mutiny on a convict ship. Eille Norwood portrays Holmes with Hubert Willis as Dr. Watson. Alfred Moise was the cinematographer and George Ridgewell wrote the adaptation and directed. Print survives at BFI archive.

God's Witness

1915 American film (Thanhouser/4 reels) based on Augusta Jane Evans Wilson's 1887 mystery novel *At the Mercy of Tiberius*. Beryl is accused of murdering her grandfather after she has gone to see him to get money for her mother. As she believes her brother did it, she refuses to testify and is arrested. Later her brother comes forward and tells what really happened. The general was struck by a lightning bolt while they were arguing and fell dead. A photograph imprinted on a window when the lightning struck proves his story is true. Florence La Badie played Beryl, Arthur Bauer played her grandfather and Morris Foster was her brother. Eugene W. Moore directed. The novel was filmed again in 1920 as *At the Mercy of Tiberius*.

The Golden Fleece

1918 American film (Triangle/5 reels) based on the story "Golden Fleece" by Frederick Irving Anderson. Jack Curtis plays Detective Bainge who uses naïve country inventor Jason (Joe Bennett) to trap crooked promoter Regelman (Harvey Clark). After much confusion the scheme works out and Jason returns to the country with his sweetheart Rose (Peggy Pearce) to settle down. The film was directed by Gilbert P. Hamilton an written by George Elwood Jenks.

The Golden Pince-Nez

1922 British film (Stoll/2 reels), an episode in the *Further Adventures of Sherlock Holmes* series based on a story by Sir Arthur Conan Doyle. Sherlock Holmes solves the mystery of the golden pince-nez. Eille Norwood portrays Holmes with Hubert Willis as Dr. Watson. George Ridgewell wrote the adaptation and directed. A print survives at the BFI archive.

The Golden Pomegranates

1924 British film (Stoll/2 reels), an episode in the *Further Mysteries of Fu Manchu* series based on a story by Sax Rohmer. Inspector Weymouth (Frank Wilson) joins Nayland Smith (Fred Paul) and Dr. Petrie (Humberston Wright) in their battle with Dr. Fu Manchu Nayland Smith (Fred Paul) solves the mystery of the chest with the golden pomegranates. Fred Paul directed and wrote the screenplay and Frank Canham was the cinematographer. Print survives at BFI film archive.

The Golden Web

1920 American film (Garrick Pictures/5 reels) based on E. Phillips Oppenheim's 1910 mystery novel *The Golden Web* about the stolen deed to a valuable mine. Milton Rosmer played Sterling Deans, Ena Beaumont was Winifred Rowan, Victor Robson was Sinclair and Nina Munro was Rosalie. Milton Rosmer wrote the screenplay and Geoffrey Malins directed. The novel was filmed a second time in 1926.

The Golden Web

1926 American film (Gotham Productions/5 reels) based on E. Phillips Oppenheim's 1910 mystery novel *The Golden Web*. Mine owner Roland Deane (Huntly Gordon) sends John Rowan (Jay Hunt) to meet with Dave Sinclair (Boris Karloff) after the deed of sale is stolen. When Sinclair is murdered, Rowan is arrested. His daughter Ruth (Lillian Rich) is sure her father is innocent and investigates with help from Deane. She finds the missing deed in Sinclair's coat. Partner George Sisk (Lawford Davidson) is arrested when he tries to steal the deed and he then confesses to the murder. James Bell Smith wrote the screenplay and Walter Lang directed.

The Gorilla

1927 American film (First National/8 reels) based on *The Gorilla, a Mystery Comedy* by Ralph Spence. The detectives in this mystery are incompetent but Garrity (Charlie Murray) and Mulligan (Fred Kelsey) eventually stumble through to a solution with help from another sleuth. Cyrus Townsend (Claude Gillingwater) is murdered in his mansion and circumstances are similar to those of other murders believed to have been perpetrated by a gorilla. Townsend's daughter Alice (Alice Day) is worried because her sweetheart Arthur Marsden (Gaston Glass) is the main suspect. Alice and her friend Stevens (Walter Pidgeon) begin to investigate as strange lights and odd noises multiply when Garrity and Mulligan show up. The detectives find the gorilla and get a false confession from a sailor but it is up to Marsden (who is really an undercover detective) to discover the real killer. Al Cohn, Henry McCarty and James T. O'Donohoe wrote the screenplay and Alfred Santell directed.

Graft

1915 American serial (Universal/twenty 2-reel episodes) based on stories in the collection *The Crack o' Doom* by mystery writer Anna Katherine Green, Louis Joseph Vance, A. M. Williamson and other writers. Each episode is based on a different story as revised by scriptwriters Joe Brandt, Hugh Weir and Walter Woods but all describe the efforts of the Larnigan brothers to investigate graft in various industries. Hobart Henley and Harry Carey played the Larnigans and the large supporting cast included Jane Novak, Eddie Polo, Richard Stanton, Nanine Wright and Jack Connolly. Richard Stanton and George Lessey directed. The episodes were titled *Liquor and the Law, The Tenement House Evil, The Traction Grab, The Power of the People, Grinding Life Down, The Railroad Monopoly, America Saved from War, Old King Coal, The Insurance Swindlers, The Harbor Transportation Trust, The Illegal Bucket Shops, The Milk Battle, The Powder Trust and the War, The Iron Ring, The Patent Medicine Danger, The Pirates of Finance, Queen of the Prophets, The Hidden City of Crime, The Photo Badger Game* and *The Final Conquest*.

Grant, Police Reporter

1916–1917 American series (Kalem/twenty-nine 1-reel episodes) starring George Larkin as police reporter Grant who investigates and solves crimes like a detective. They usually fea-

Detectives Garrity (Charlie Murray) and Mulligan (Fred Kelsey) are incompetent but funny in *The Gorilla* (sheet music cover).

tured daredevil acrobatic stunts including climbing walls and leaping from roofs. Robert Welles Ritchie wrote the series directed by Robert Ellis and the supporting cast included Ollie Kirkby Arthur Albertson, Cyril Courtney, Betty Dial, T. Justin Down and others. The series began in October 1916 with the episode titled *The Code Letter* and ended in November 1917 with *Sign of the Scarf*. The other episodes, in alphabetical order, are: *The Black Circle, A Deal in Bonds, The House of Three Deuces, The House of Secrets, In the Web of the Spider, The Man from Yukon, The Man with the Limp, The Menace, The Mirror of Fear, The Missing Financier, The Missing Heiress, A Mission of State, The Mystery of Room 422, The Net of Intrigue, The Pencil Clue, The Rogue's Pawn, The Screened Vault, The Secret of the Borgias, Sign of the Scarf, The Wizard's Plot, The Tiger's Claw, The Trail of Graft, The Trunk Mystery, The Trap, The Vanishing Bishop, The Veiled Thunderbolt, The Violet Ray, Winged Diamonds*.

The Gray Ghost

1917 American serial (Universal/sixteen 2-reel chapter) based on Arthur Somers Roche's 1916 novel *Loot*. The Gray Ghost (Harry Carter) steals a $2 million dollar necklace and becomes involved with Morn Light (Priscilla Dean), Lady Gwendolyn (Gertrude Astor), Wade Hildreth (Emory Johnson) and Marco (Eddie Polo). The episodes are *The Bank Mystery, The Mysterious Message, The Warning, The Fight, Plunder, The House of Mystery, Caught in the Web, The Double Floor, The Pearl Necklace, Shadows, The Flaming Meteor, The Poisoned Ring, The Tightening Snare, At Bay, The Duel* and *From Out of the Past*. Stuart Paton directed. The novel was filmed again in 1919 as *Loot*.

The Gray Mask

1915 American film (World Film/5 reels) based on the 1915 story "The Gray Mask" by Charles Wadsworth Camp first published in *Collier's*. Police detective Jim Garth (Edwin Arden) disguises himself with a gray mask in order to join the Hennions gang and find the murderer of a detective who had been investigating the gang. Nora (Barbara Tennant), the former lover of that detective, has also infiltrated the gang looking for the killer. Garth foils a plot to steal a secret formula, arrests the murderer and wins the love of Nora. Charles Wadsworth Camp wrote the screenplay and Frank Crane directed.

The Great Bradley Mystery

1917 American film (Apollo Pictures/5 reels). Bradley (Edward Ellis) tries various dirty tricks to win Mary (Alma Hanlon) from his partner Collier (Edward Earle) including ruining his reputation and sending a telegram saying he has been killed. Mary marries Bradley but he is found dead soon after. The father of a woman Bradley seduced is arrested but Collier returns and explains what happened. Bradley accidentally shot himself with his own gun while threatening Collier. Richard Ridgley directed and Edward Ellis wrote the screenplay.

The Great Cheque Fraud

1915 British film (Davidson/3 reels), one of seven films featuring the famous detective Sexton Blake in a series written and directed by Charles Raymond. Blake saves Tinker after escaping from a fire by using an overhead cable. Philip Kay played Blake with Lewis Carlton as his assistant Tinker. (See Blake, Sexton for other films.)

The Great Detective

1915 American comedy film (Lubin/2 reels) starring D. L. Don as a great detective who sports a very large moustache. The supporting cast included George Egan, Florence Williams Patsy De Forest and James Cassady. Edwin McKim directed.

The Great Detective

1916 American comedy (Kalem/2 reels) starring Bud Duncan and Lloyd Hamilton. This was one of a hundred slapstick comedies made for the "Ham and Bud" series. They were the Abbott and Costello of the early silent era (Hamilton was big and tall, Duncan was short) and they parodied most genres. Print survives at the Library of Congress film archive.

Lubin advertised three of its mystery films in the this 1915 ad in *Motion Picture News*.

The Great Diamond Mystery

1924 American film (Fox/5 reels) based on a story by Shannon Fife. Mystery writer Ruth Winton (Shirley Mason) believes that murderers return to the scene of the crime. At least that is what she wrote in her novel *The Great Diamond Mystery*. When her lover Perry (William Collier, Jr.) is arrested and charged with killing diamond merchant Graves (John Cossar), she puts her theory to the test. She rents Graves' house, hires his butler Davis (Hector V. Sarno) and finds Graves' partner Mallison (Philo McCullough) sneaking around the house. In the end the butler gets shot and confesses to the murder. Denison Clift directed and Thomas Dixon, Jr., wrote the screenplay.

The Great Diamond Robbery

1903 American comedy (Selig/100 feet) — Safecrackers get bad information. When they open the safe they are robbing, They find it is full of coal rather than money.

The Great Diamond Robbery

1912 American comedy (Vitagraph/1 reel). Tom Powers and Arthur Rosson play incompetent detectives trying to solve a diamond robbery. Kate Price gives support.

The Great Diamond Robbery

1914 American feature (Playgoers Film Company/6 reels) — Wallace Eddinger stars as detective Dick Brummage in a case involving a Brazilian adventuress (Gail Kane) and the theft of the fabulous Romanoff diamonds. When he proves her guilt, she takes poison. The film was based on a play by Edward M. Alfriend and A. C. Wheeler and directed by Edward A. Morange.

The Great Hansom Cab Mystery

1917 animated cartoon (International Films/1 reel) inspired by Fergus Hume's novel *The Mystery of a Hansom Cab* It was created by director Gregory La Cava for the *Bringing Up Father* series based on a famous comic strip by George McManus.

The Great Jewel Robbery

1908 American film (Lubin/1 reel). A young orphan known as Rags is adopted by a gang of thieves but turns against them when they plan to steal jewels from a woman who helped her. Rags disguises herself as a boy and helps a detective capture the thief after identifying him by a wound on his hand.

The Great Jewel Robbery

1925 American film (Kerman Films/5 reels) Detective Doris Dunbar (Grace Darmond) is investigating a jewel theft when she meets Steve Martindale (Herbert Rawlinson) at the Red Mill Inn. Jewel thief Hooper (Carlton Griffin) slips the stolen jewels into Steve's pocket but Doris is not deceived. Hooper kidnaps them and holds them prisoner at his hideout where they are eventually rescued by police. John Ince directed.

The Great K & A Train Robbery

1926 American western (Fox/5 reels) based on the 1897 novel *The Great K & A Train Robbery* by Paul Leicester Ford. Detective Tom

Gordon (Tom Mix) is sent to investigate a series of robberies at the K & A Railroad. He pretends to be a bandit and boards the train carrying K & A president Cullen and his daughter Madge (Dorothy Dwan). He discovers that Cullen's secretary Burton (Carl Miller) is in league with the bandits and captures the gang. John Stone wrote the screenplay and Lewis Seiler. The film is on DVD.

The Great London Mystery

1920 British serial (Torquay & Paignton Photoplays/twelve 2-reel episodes. The Master Magician (music hall illusionist David Devant) exposes supernatural frauds while confronting fake Oriental magician Ching Fu (Charles Raymond) and his gang. He also has to outwit French vamp Froggie the Vampire (Lola di Liane) and Monkey Man (Lester Gard) and prevent the ravishment of Audrey Malvern (Lady Doris Stapleton). Charles Raymond directed the screenplay he co-wrote with Hope Loring. The episodes are *The Sacred Snake Worshippers, The Vengeance of Ching Fu, The Search for the Will, The Daylight Gold Robbery, The House of Mystery, Echoes of the Past, The Rogue Unmasked, The Fraudulent Spiritualistic Seance, The Living Dead, Her Fortune at Stake, Checkmated* and *The Mystery Resolved*. A print of this serial, shot in Cornwall and London, survives at the BFI film archive.

The Great Mail Robbery

1927 American film (FBO-RC Pictures/7 reels). U.S. Marine detective Howard (Lee Shumway) goes undercover pretending to be a criminal on the run so he can infiltrate a gang robbing gold trains while Marine Lieutenant Macready (Theodore von Eltz) are investigating the thefts. When he learns that gang leader Davis (De Witt Jennings) is about to rob a gold train, he radios Macready who captures the gang. Peter Milne wrote the screenplay and George B. Seitz directed.

The Great Office Mystery

1928 British film (British Filmcraft/2 reels), one of a six-film series featuring master detective Sexton Blake as played by Langhorne Burton with Mickey Brantford as his assistant Tinker. The supporting cast included Fred Raynham, Gabrielle Morton and Ronald Curtis. George J. Banfield produced, Leslie Eveleigh directed and Lewis Jackson wrote the screenplay. (See Blake, Sexton for background on detective and list of other films in which he appears.)

The Great Radium Mystery

1919 American serial (Universal/eighteen 2-reel chapters). Cleo Madison, Eileen Sedgwich and Bob Reeves star in this mystery revolving around the disappearance of a wealthy heir and a vanishing armored car. The chapters were *The Mystic Stone, The Death Trap, The Fatal Ride, The Swing for Life, The Torture Chamber, The Tunnel of Doom, A Flash in the Dark, In the Clutches of the Mad Man, The Roaring Volcano, Creeping Flames, Perils of Doom, Shackled, The Scalding Pit, Hemmed In, The Flaming Arrow, Over the Cataract, The Wheels of Death, Liquid Flame*. Frederick Bennett wrote the screenplay and Robert Broadwell and Robert F. Hill directed.

The Great Ruby

1915 American film (Lubin/5 reels) based on the 1898 play *The Great Ruby* by Cecil Raleigh and Henry Hamilton. Detective James Brett (Ferdinand Tidmarsh) is hired to investigate jewel thefts from Sir John Garnett's wife (Beatrice Morgan). Diamond Gang boss Longman (Howard M. Mitchell) steals her great ruby which is hidden in a chocolate box. Brett chases Longman to a balloon and recovers the jewel when Longman falls to his death. Clay M. Greene wrote the screenplay and Barry O'Neil directed.

The Great Ruby Mystery

1915 American film (Universal-2 reels) starring Herbert Rawlinson as a detective investigating the theft of a ruby. Anna Little, Laura Oakley and William Worthington head the supporting cast while Otis Turner wrote and directed the film.

The Great Universal Mystery

1914 American film (Nestor-Universal/1 reel) has been called the ultimate film mystery.

It was said to have pictured every employee of the Universal film company from studio boss Carl Laemmle and star King Baggot down to the gatekeepers. It was filmed at Universal City in California, Universal offices in New York, Imp Studios in New York and Victor Studios in New Jersey. The mystery is what the movie is about. All prints have been lost and no synopsis exists.

The Great Vacuum Robbery

1915 American comedy (Triangle-Keystone/2 reel). Charles Murray and Slim Summerville play "a pair of dime novel detectives" in this slapstick comedy in which a pair of crooks (Ed Kennedy and Louise Fazenda) take over their office to rob a bank. After knocking them out, the crooks use a vacuum tube to siphon up money from the bank below the office. They take their loot to a hotel where the defective detectives and uniformed police catch up with them and there is a bang-up battle that brings down the building. Dick Jones directed and Hampton Del Ruth wrote the screenplay.

The Greek Interpreter

1922 British film (Stoll/2 reels), an episode in the *Further Adventures of Sherlock Holmes* series based on a story by Sir Arthur Conan Doyle. Sherlock Holmes finds a man with the help of a Greek interpreter. Eille Norwood portrays Holmes with Hubert Willis as Dr. Watson. George Ridgewell wrote the adaptation and directed. Print survives at the BFI archive.

The Green Archer

1925 American serial (Pathé/ten 2-reel episodes) based on Edgar Wallace's 1913 novel *The Green Archer*. A mysterious green archer has begun to make appearances at spooky Bellamy Castle on the Hudson River. It is owned by a millionaire criminal (Burr McIntosh) and has a dungeon where the millionaire keeps a prisoner. Nosy neighbor Valerie (Allene Ray) decides to investigate with the help of a police captain (Walter Miller). Also involved are Frank Lackteen, Dorothy King, Stephen Grattan and William R. Randall. Spencer G. Bennet directed the serial and Frank Leon Smith wrote the screenplay. Three reels of the film survive at the UCLA film archive.

The Green Cloak

1915 American film (George Kleine/5 reels). Ruth McAllister (Irene Fenwick) is accused of murdering visitor Paul Duncan (John Davidson) when he found dead clutching a piece of her green cloak. Her father finds the real murderer by hypnotizing the new maid who has a tattoo on her arm similar to one on Duncan's arm. Both belonged to a Denver gang and the maid had been sent to kill Duncan who had double-crossed the gang. Walter Edwin directed and Owen Davis and Henry K. Webster wrote the screenplay.

The Green Flame

1920 American film (Robert Brunton Productions/5 reels) based on a story by Raymond G. Hill. Frank Markham (J. Warren Kerrigan) goes to work at a New York jewelry store where he meets newspaperwoman Ruth Gardner (Fritzi Brunette). She is investigating jewel robberies with detective Dan Lantry (Jay Morley). Jewelry store manager Roger Imlay (Edwin Wallock) is working with a gang to steal a famous emerald known as the Green Flame. Imray tricks Markam into bringing the stone to the gang headquarters but Markam outsmarts him. Lantry wants to arrest Markham who he thinks he is the gang boss but the store owner reveals that Markham is actually a member of the Jeweler's Protective Association and was hired to watch Imray. Jack Cunningham wrote the screenplay and Ernest C. Warde directed.

The Green God

1918 American film (Vitagraph/5 reels) based on the 1911 mystery novel *The Green God* by Frederic Arnold Kummer. Robert Ashton (George Majeroni) is found dead in his room with the doors bolted from the inside. He had stolen a green Buddha statue for Major Temple (Arthur Donaldson) but wanted $50,000 and Temple's daughter Muriel (Betty Blythe) as payment. Temple refused and said Ashton would not leave the house alive unless he handed over the green god. Muriel had visited

Ashton's room on the night of the murder and Muriel's sweetheart Owen (Harry T. Morey) learned of Muriel's visit and was jealous. Temple, Morgan and Muriel are the prime suspects but are cleared when Temple's servant shamefacedly explains what actually happened. He had peered into Ashton's window and startled him so much that he jumped up, fell down and impaled himself on a sword. Paul Scardon directed and Garfield Thompson wrote the screenplay.

The Green Mist

1924 British film (Stoll/2 reels), an episode in *The Further Mysteries of Fu Manchu* series based on a story by Sax Rohmer Harry Agar Lyons plays Dr. Fu Manchu, Fred Paul is Nayland Smith and Humberston Wright is Dr. Petrie. Fred Paul directed and wrote the screenplay and Frank Canham was the cinematographer.

The Green Terror

1919 British film (Gaumont/6 reels) based on a serial by Edgar Wallace published in the *News of the World*. Mad genius Dr Harden (W. T. Ellwanger) plans to destroy the world's grain crops with a formula he has invented. He kidnaps heiress Olivia Cressell (Heather Thatcher) to get funding for the plot. American detective Beale (Aurele Sydney) rescues the heiress and foils the evildoer's plans. W. P. Kellino directed and G. W. Clifford wrote the screenplay.

The Grell Mystery

1917 American film (Vitagraph/5 reels) based on the 1913 novel *The Grell Mystery* by Frank Froest. Criminologist Heldon Foyle (Earle Williams) and detective Green (Robert Gaillard) investigate the murder of Robert Grell (Denton Vane). Helen Meredith (Miriam Miles) left her fingerprints on the dagger that killed the man who it turns out is not Grell but his look-alike brother. The murderer was the brother's wife. Graham Baker wrote the screenplay and Paul Scardon directed.

The Grey Glove

1928 Australian film (J. C. Williamson Films/6 reels) based on a story by E. V. Timms. An amateur detective (Aubrey Keiner) tries to catch a criminal who leaves a grey glove at the scene of his crimes. Much of the action takes place in an opium den. Val Lassau played the femme fatale who tries to vamp the detective. The supporting cast included James Alexander, William Thornton and Claud Turton. Dunstan Webb directed.

Greywater Park

1924 British film (Stoll/2 reels), an episode in *The Further Mysteries of Fu Manchu* series based on a story by Sax Rohmer Harry Agar Lyons plays Dr. Fu Manchu, Fred Paul is Nayland Smith and Humberston Wright is Dr. Petrie. Fred Paul directed and wrote the screenplay and Frank Canham was the cinematographer.

The Grim Game

1919 American film (Paramount/5 reels) based on a story by mystery writer Arthur B. Reeve who wrote the screenplay with John Grey. Escapist entertainment in the true sense of the word. Harvey Hanford (Harry Houdini) is framed and sent to prison for murdering the guardian of his sweetheart Mary (Ann Forrest). As he has the wondrous gift of being able to escape from places, he immediately escapes and sets out to track down the actual killers. In the meantime they have kidnapped Mary so he has to rescue her as well. While doing this he performs stunts like leaping from plane to plane, jumping from a bridge in handcuffs and escaping from chains, and straitjackets whenever the villains catch him. Irvin Willat directed. Only five minutes of this film survive at Eastman House but they're on DVD.

Grumpy

1923 American film (Paramount/6 reels) based on the 1913 play *Grumpy* by Horace Hodges and Thomas Wigney Percyval. Retired lawyer Andrew Bullivant (Theodore Roberts), known as Grumpy, has to solve the mystery of the theft of a valuable diamond. It was taken from Ernest Heron (Conrad Nagel) who had just arrived at Bullivant's estate to see his daughter Virginia (May McAvoy). Grumpy thinks houseguest Chamberlain Jarvis did it and follows him to London. He frightens him into returning the jewel. Clara Beranger wrote the screenplay and William De Mille directed.

Gryce, Ebenezer

Ebenezer Gryce, one of the first notable detectives in American crime fiction, was the creation of Anna Katherine Green. He made his debut in the novel *The Leavenworth Case* in 1878, returned in *A Strange Disappearance* in 1880 and was featured in a dozen more cases. He is quite astute but he does not have a very exciting personality and is portly, middle-aged and stolid. He seems to been disliked by silent filmmakers as he was cut out of the films based on his cases and his detective work was carried out by others.

Le Guet-apens (The Ambush)

1908 French film (Éclair/1 reel), the first episode in the *Nick Carter, le roi des détectives* series about the master detective Nick Carter. It was distributed in America as *Nick Carter the King of Detectives and the Kidnappers' Plot*. In this episode Carter rescues a doctor who has been kidnapped. Pierre Bressol played Nick Carter and Victorin Jassett wrote and directed the film. A print of this film survives at the BFI film archive.

The Gunsaulus Mystery

1921 American black cast film (Micheaux Films/5 reels) based on the 1913 Leo Frank murder case. A black night watchman at a factory reports finding a murdered white woman and is accused of the murder. With Edward Abra, Evelynn Preer, Lawrence Cheenault and Louise De Bulger. Oscar Micheaux wrote the screenplay and directed. He remade the film with sound in 1935 as Murder in Harlem.

Der Haisschmuck

1917 German film (Egede Nissen Film Company/5 reels) featuring a female detective known as Miss Clever. It was one of a series of ten films about this woman detective starring Norwegian actress Ada Egede-Nissen (using the screen name of "Ada Van Ehlers") It was written by Rudolf Baron and Else Cressin and directed by Georg Alexander who took the male lead in the film. See *Miss Clever* for other films in the series.

Haldane of the Secret Service

1923 American film (Houdini Picture Corp-FBO/6 reels) written and directed by and starring escapologist Harry Houdini. He plays Heath Haldane, an undercover agent infiltrating a gang of counterfeiters who had killed his father. He is able to rescues his sweetheart Adele Ormsby (Gladys Leslie) from the gang but gets capture himself and thrown bound and gagged into a freezing river. He escapes, of course, and gets the gang arrested. Unfortunately he then discovers that Adele's father Edward Ormsby (William Humphrey) is the gang leader of the gang. The film has been preserved by Eastman House and is on DVD.

The Half Million Bribe

1916 American film (Metro/5 reels) based on the 1909 mystery novel *The Red Mouse* by William Hamilton Osborne. Miriam (Marguerite Snow) bribes district attorney William Murgatroyd (Carl Brickert) with half a million dollars so he will acquit her wastrel husband J. Lawrence Challoner (Hamilton Revelle) in a murder trial. Instead he double-crosses her and gets a conviction. When another man confesses to the murder, Challoner is released but the couple now live in poverty as they have no money left. This leads to Challoner reforming himself and becoming a better person. Murgatroyd then tells Miriam that he double-crossed her with the hope that poverty would make her husband a better person. It has and he gives Miriam back the half million. Harry O. Hoyt wrote the screenplay and Edgar Jones directed.

Ham, the Detective

1915 American comedy (Kalem/1 reel). Lloyd Hamilton (Ham) stars as an incompetent detective in this film in the *Ham and Bud* series with Bud Duncan (Bud) adding to the problems.

Hanaud, Inspector

Inspector Gabriel Hanaud is a professional French detective, the creation of A. E. W. Mason. He is middle-aged and rather stout with a nice sense of humor and a kindly manner. In his first appearance in the novel *At the Villa Rose* (1910) he is able to prove that a beautiful young girl did not murder her wealthy employer but was herself a victim. Hanaud reappears in *The House of the Arrow* (1924), *The Prison in the Opal* (1928) and other stories. His only appearance on the silent screen was in the 1920 British film *At the Villa Rose*, but he was featured in five sound films.

The Hand at the Window

1918 American film (Triangle/5 reels) based on the 1918 story "In the Spring" by John A. Moroso first published in *Collier's*. Detective Roderick Moran (Joe King) arrests counterfeiter Tony Brachieri (Francis McDonald) on his wedding days and Tony vows revenge when Moran marries. When Moran does marry the somewhat mysterious Laura Bowers (Margery Wilson), he is nervous but relieved when he learns Tony was killed trying to escape from jail. All the same Moran is nearly killed when he is shot at in his cottage and Tony's fingerprints are found on the window sill. Finally Laura, who is actually a Secret Service agent, tracks down the shooter. It was Tony's wife (Irene Hunt) sworn on her wedding day that she would get revenge, John A. Moroso wrote the screenplay and Raymond Wells directed.

The Hand Print Mystery

1914 American film (Kalem/2 reels). A detective investigates the theft of valuable jewels and is both helped and hindered by the hand prints he finds. He suspects the theft was made by one of the family members so he questions them all. *The New York Dramatic Mirror* thought the story was pretty implausible "yet it is a good mystery film." Alice Joyce played Ruth with Tom Moore as her sweetheart Dick, Marguerite Courtot as Alice's sister Bess, Harry Millarde as her brother Kenneth and James B. Ross as their father. Robert G. Vignola directed.

The Handsome Brute

1925 American film (Columbia/5 reels). Police detective Larry O'Day (William Fairbanks) has lost his job on the Metropolitan police force but he tells his sweetheart Nelly (Virginia Lee Corbin) that he will solve the Brady case on his own. The famous detective John Granger (Lee Shumway) is called to work on the case and O'Day notices his resemblance to a known criminal. He follows Granger, catches him looting a jewelry store and captures him and his accomplices. He is reinstated. Lillian Taft Maize wrote the screenplay and Robert Eddy directed.

Hardrock Dome, the Great Detective

1919 American cartoon series (Bray/1 reel) made by Pat Sullivan. Three episodes about this animated detective modeled on Sherlock Holmes were distributed by Paramount.

The Haunted House

1928 American film (First National/7 reels) based on a play by Owen Davis. Mysteries involving the reading of wills in haunted houses were popular in the silent era with *The Cat and the Canary* leading the pack. In this film the heirs to a fortune go a spooky house (lots of sliding panels and weird noises) for the reading of a strange will and encounter a crazy doctor, a sleepwalker and a sinister handyman. It turns out to have all been staged. With Thelma Todd, Flora Finch, Chester Conklin, Larry Kent and Edmund Breese. Lajos Biró wrote the screenplay and Benjamin Christensen, best known for his Danish film *Witchcraft Through the Ages*, directed.

Haunted Island

1928 American serial (Universal/ten 2-reel chapters) based on Frank R. Adams' 1918 mystery novel *Pleasure Island*. Jerry Fitzjames plays the heroic Jack opposite Helen Foster as heiress Rosalind in this remake of the serial *The Brass Bullet* based on the same novel. The Mystery Man has been transmuted into The Phantom Rider in this version but he is just as mysterious. Al Ferguson portrays evil uncle Gilbert and Grace Cunard has a major role. Robert F. Hill directed. The chapters are titled *A Night of Fear, The Phantom Rider, A Trail of Terror, The Haunted Room, Buried Alive, A Race with Death, Fires of Fury, The Treasure Trap, Un-*

masked and *Uncut Diamonds*. The novel was filmed earlier as *The Brass Bullet*.

The Hawk's Trail

1919/1920 American serial (Burston Films/fifteen 2-reel episodes) starring King Baggot as criminologist Sheldon Steele known as The Hawk. Grace Darmond played Claire Drake, Rhea Mitchell was Jean Drake, Harry Lorraine was Stephen Drake and Iron Dugan, Fred Windemere was Bob Dugan and George Siegmann was Quang Goo Hai. Nan Blair and John B. Clymer wrote the screenplay and W.S. Van Dyke directed. The episodes are titled *False Faces, The Superman, Yellow Shadows, Stained Hands, House of Fear, Room Above, The Bargain, The Phantom Melody, The Lure, The Swoop, One Fatal Step, Tides That Tell, Face to Face, The Substitute* and *The Showdown*.

King Baggot is the criminologist known as the Hawk in *The Hawk's Trail*.

The Hazards of Helen

1914–1916 American series (Kalem/one hundred nineteen 1-reel episodes), the longest running and most popular series of the silent

Helen Holmes as Helen in *A Railroader's Bravery*, an episode of *The Hazards of Helen*.

era. Helen is a heroic railroad telegrapher who has to fight every kind of railroad villain while leaping on to moving trains from cars and horses to save lives. She often works with detectives as in *The Detective's Peril* and *The Mystery of the Rails*. Helen Holmes starred in the first 48 episodes under the direction of J. P. McGowan, and Helen Gibson starred in the other 71 under the direction of James Davis. At least 22 of the 119 episodes survive and a number are on DVD.

Hearts or Diamonds?

1918 American film (William Russell Productions/5 reels) based on the 1915 story "Adrienne Gascoyne" by mystery writer William Hamilton Osborne published in the *Illustrated Sunday Magazine*. Diamond collector Larry Hanrahan (William Russell) saves Adrienne Gascoyne (Charlotte Burton) from thieves when she and her guardian Col. Paul Gascoyne (Howard Davies) are attacked. Hanrahan is later robbed of his jewel collection by a woman wearing Adrienne's scarf and finds the jewels

William Russell is a diamond collector in *Hearts or Diamonds?*

hidden at Gascoyne's house. He is overpowered by thugs before he can escape but Adrienne helps him call police who arrest Gascoyne. She had been the colonel's innocent dupe. William Parker wrote the screenplay and Henry King directed.

Hemlock Hoax, the Detective

1910 American comedy (Lubin/232 feet). A Sherlock Holmes parody.

Her Bitter Lesson

1912 American film (Selig/1 reel) based on Mary Elizabeth Braddon's 1863 novel *Aurora Floyd*. The plot revolves around the unintentional bigamy of a woman (Aurora Floyd) and the murder of a first husband (John Conyers) whom she believed had died earlier. Aurora is suspected of the murder but her second husband (John Mellish) believes she is innocent. Adrienne Kroell played Aurora Floyd and the supporting cast included Maxwell Sargent, Charles Clary, Walter Roberts and Charles Barney. Hardee Kirkland directed. (For other films based on the novel see *Aurora Floyd*.)

Her One Mistake

1918 American film (Fox/5 reels) based on a story by George Scarborough. Detective Scully (Willard Lewis), who put gentleman crook Chicago Charlie (William Scott) in prison, knows how he evilly deceived heiress Harriet Gordon (Gladys Brockwell). When Charles escapes from prison and threatens Harriet, she kills him in self-defense. Scully, who knows what actually happened, reports that he killed the villain. Charles Kenyon wrote the screenplay and Edward J. Le Saint directed.

The Heritage of Hamilton Cleek

1914 American film (Edison/1 reel), an episode in *the Chronicles of Cleek* series written by Thomas W. Hanshew. Ben Wilson plays master criminal Hamilton Cleek, known as the "man of forty faces," and Robert Brower is his nemesis Detective Narko. Harry Beaumont and Gertrude McCoy gives support and George Lessey directed.

Herrin der Welt (Mistress of the World)

1919–1920 German serial (May Film/eight episodes) based on the novel *Herrin der Welt*

German actress Mia May as mistress of the world in *Herrin der Welt*.

by Karl Figdor. Danish adventurer Maud Gregaards (Mia May) goes to China seeking to find the key to the lost treasure of the Queen of Sheba and become so wealthy that she will be mistress of the world. She quickly meets the Hermit of Kuan Fu and the King of the Beggars and gets involved in thrilling chases, earthquakes and plane crashes along with her sidekick, Danish Consul Holger Madsen (Michael Bohnen). After she finds the treasure and becomes rich, she exacts revenge on her enemies, especially Baron Murphy (Hans Mierendorff). The directors and screenplay writers varied by film; the writers were Joe May, Ruth Goetz, Fritz Lang, Richard Hutter and Wilhelm Roellinghoff while the directors were Joe May, Joseph Klein, Uwe Jens Krafft and Karl Gerhardt. This series (eleven and one-half hours in Germany as each episode was feature length) was one of the biggest budgeted spectacles of the German silent cinema, heavily promoted around the world (including America) and apparently quite popular with audiences. The episodes were titled *Die Freundin des gelben Mannes, Die Geschichte der Maud Gregaards, Der Rabbi von Kuan-Fu, Die König Macombe, Die Ophir, die Stadt der Vergangenheit, Die Frau mit den Millionarden, Die Wohltäterin der Menschheit* and *Die Rache der Maud Fergusson*.

In America the serial was distributed in a shortened version, four 5-reel chapters beginning with *The Dragon's Claw* and *The Race for Life*. The main characters were renamed: Maud Gregaards became Helen Nielsen and Danish Consul Madsen became Benson. It opened big way on Broadway at the Rivoli and Rialto and was heavily advertised, but *The New York Times* was not impressed, calling it "infantile fiction, inexpressibly cheap and trashy in its story composition but having great pictorial effects in its scenic elements."

Hey Hey Cowboy

1927 American film (Universal/6 reels) based on a story by Lynn Reynolds. Detective Jimmie Roberts (Hoot Gibson) poses as a hobo to investigate mysterious occurrences that have caused a feud between ranchers. John Evans (Wheeler Oakman), who is engaged to rancher's daughter Emily Decker (Kathleen Key), turns out to be troublemaker and is foiled in his attempt to elope with Emily. Reynolds also wrote the screenplay and directed.

The Hidden Hand

1917 American serial (Pathé/fifteen 2-reel chapters) based on a story by Arthur B. Reeve who wrote the screenplay with Charles W. Goddard The villainous Hidden Hand (Sheldon Lewis who wears a claw-like glove) attempts to get an inheritance for a fake daughter (Arline Pretty) but the real daughter (Doris Kenyon) is inconveniently in the way. She gets help from government official Jack Raysey Mahlon Hamilton) who investigates and learns that Hidden Hand killed her father and forged the fake heiress's papers. James Vincent directed the twelve chapters: *The Gauntlet of Death, Counterfeit Faces, The Island of Dread, The False Locket, The Air-Lock, The Flower of Death, The Fire Trap, Slide for Life, Jets of Flame, Dogs of Death, Trapped by Treachery, Eyes in the Wall, Jaws of the Tiger, The Unmasking* and *The Gift of the Prophecy.*

Sheldon Lewis is the villain in the serial *The Hidden Hand.*

The Hidden Light

1920 American film (Schomer-Ross Productions/6 reels) based on a story by Abraham S. Schomer who also wrote the screenplay and directed. Detective Hayden (Arthur Donaldson) arrests Victor Bailey (Ben Taggart) for attacking blind musician Cynthia Holmes (Dolores Cassinelli) in her home and killing her secretary. Bailey claims he is innocent and Cynthia believes him but he is still sentenced to death. At a recital Cynthia shakes hands with music critic Harry Warren (Henry Sedley) and accuses him of the murder as she recognizes his touch. He tries to flee but detective Hayden captures him and gets a confession.

Hide and Seek Detectives

1918 American comedy (Mack Sennett Comedies/2 reels) starring Ben Turpin with support from Marie Prevost, Heinie Conklin, Tom Kennedy, Paddy McGuire, Al McKinnon and Charles Murray. Mack Sennett and Fred Hibbard wrote the screenplay and Edward F. Cline directed.

Higgs, Harry

Harry Higgs was a tough "American" detective in German films of the 1910s (like the other German film detectives of his era he was given an American name though there was little American about him. He was portrayed on screen by Hans Mierendorff from 1916 to 1919 in a series produced and directed by Rudolf Meinert (who later produced *The Cabinet of Dr. Caligari*). The Harry Higgs films made Mierendorff famous and he is mainly remembered for them. The films included *Der Gast aus der vierten Dimension* (with Curt Bois and Friedrich Kühne), *Der Goldene Pol*, *Nur um 1000 Dollar*, *Die Sterbenden Perlen* (written by E. A, Dupont with Fritz Achterberg and Magda Madeleine) and *Halloh — Hier Harry Higgs, wer dort?*

High Stakes

1918 American film (Triangle/5 reels) based on the 1917 story "High Stakes" by Andrew Soutar first published in *Red Book Magazine*. Gentleman crook Ralph Stanning (J. Barney Sherry) is suspected of stealing jewels but Scotland Yard detective Reginald Culvert (Harvey Clark) can't prove it. When Stanning reforms, marries Marie (Jane Miller) and moves to a small village, Culvert remains suspicious. When jewels belonging to neighbor Lady Alice (Myrtle Rishell) are stolen, Culvert sets out to arrest him. Lady Alice stops him as she has found the jewels which had fallen through a crack in a sofa. Arthur Hoyt directed and Alvin J. Neitz wrote the screenplay.

Hill, Harry

"American" detective Harry Hill, portrayed in German films by Valy Arnheim, was featured in a ten-year series that ran in various formats from 1919 to 1927. Most of the films were written, produced and directed by Arnheim himself and featured Marga Lindt as his girlfriend (she is called Pearl White in one movie). Harry Hill became so popular in Germany in the 1920s that he even inspired a pulp fiction series (*Harry Hill, der Weltmeister der Sensationen*) with plots borrowed from his movies and Arnheim's face on the magazine cover. The only Harry Hill movie that seems to have survived is *Das Detecktivduel* (1920) in which he battles Sherlock Holmes.

Hans Mierendorff played detective Harry Higgs in a German film series.

The other Hill films include *Der Kampf in den Lüften* (1919), *Die Todesfahrt* (1919), *Das Unbewohnte Haus* (1920), *Die Blitzzentrale* (1921), *Die Schmuggler von San Diego* (1921), *Die Hochbahnkatastrophe* (1921), *Der Todesflieger* (1921), *Der Höllenreiter* (1922), *Harry Hill, der Herr der Welt* (1923), *Harry Hills Jagd auf den Tod* (1925) and *Die Piraten der Ostseebäder* (1927).

Hiram Green, Detective

1913 American comedy (Edison/1 reel) directed by Charles M. Seay and written by Monte M. Katterjohn. The actors were Yale Benner, Edna Flugrath, Edward Mack, William Wadsworth and Herbert Yost.

His Darker Self

1924 American comedy film (Albert Gray Productions/5 reels). *The New York Times* headlined its review of this bizarre murder mystery comedy as "The Blackened Sleuth." It was reportedly meant to star Al Jolson in blackface under the direction of D. W. Griffith. Instead it starred Lloyd Hamilton, best known for the Kalem *Ham and Bud* comedy series, as a mystery writer who dons blackface to prove that an old black man is innocent of a murder. As his "darker self" he gets a job at an African-American dance hall run by liquor smuggler Bill Jackson (African-American actor Tom Wilson). He learns Jackson was behind the frame-up and captures him after a motorboat chase. Edna May Sperl played Jackson's sweetheart and Irma Harrison was portrayed as "Darktown's Cleopatra." Arthur Caesar wrote the screenplay and John W. Noble directed.

His Father's Son

1917 American film (Metro/5 reels) based on a story by Channing Pollock and Rennold Wolf. J. Dabney Barron (Lionel Barrymore) goes to work at a detective agency after his father (Charles Eldridge) cuts off his allowance. He is sent undercover as a butler to protect a priceless emerald in the home of John Arden (Frank Currier) and catches Lord Lawrence (Walter Horton) in the act. He also wins the hand of Arden's daughter Betty (Irene Howley). June Mathis wrote the screenplay and George D. Baker directed.

His Hidden Talent

1917 American comedy (Triangle/1 reel) a.k.a. *Detective Story*. Raymond Griffith is the star of this farcical detective story with Vera Reynolds as his sweetheart, James Rowe as his father, Phyllis Daniels as his mother, Mario Bianchi as the crook and Marianne De La Torre as the crook's wife. Reggie Morris directed.

His Last Bow

1923 British film (Stoll/2 reels), an episode in the *Last Adventures of Sherlock Holmes* series based on a story by Sir Arthur Conan Doyle. Sherlock Holmes uncovers the schemes of a German secret agent. Eille Norwood portrays Holmes with Hubert Willis as Dr. Watson. Alfred Moise was the cinematographer and George Ridgewell wrote the adaptation and directed. Print survives at BFI archive.

His Wife's Friend

1919 American film (Paramount-Artcraft/6 reels) based on John Burland Harris's novel *The White Rook*. Lady Marion (Dorothy Dalton) is unhappily married to Sir Robert Grimwood (Warren Cook) whose body is found floating in his lake soon after the arrival of her old suitor John Heritage (Henry Mortimer). She receives a suicide note saying her husband killed himself because of Heritage but it is stolen by Lord Waverly (Richard Neil) who tries to force himself on her. She is rescued by Heritage and Waverly falls to his death over a cliff. Heritage discovers the person behind the deaths was Waverly's servant Ling Foo (Paul Cazeneuve) who was seeking revenge on Sir Robert. Joseph De Grasse directed and R. Cecil Smith wrote the screenplay.

His Wife's Husband

1922 American film (Pyramid/6 reels) based on the 1907 mystery novel *The Mayor's Wife* by Anna Katharine Green. The film has a complicated plot involving double bigamy, the mystery of a husband who did not die, a false suicide note and real blackmail. Olympia (Betty Blythe) marries Brainerd (Arthur Carewe) but leaves after she sees him shot by another woman. She leaves a suicide note and vanishes. Years later she marries rising politician George Packard (Huntley Gordon) who is blackmailed for bigamy by Brainerd who did not die from the gunshot wound. Olympia investigates and finds proof Brainerd was already married when he married her so the real bigamist is Brainerd. Kenneth Webb directed and Dorothy Farnum wrote the screenplay.

The Hocussing of Cigarette

1924 British film (Stoll/2 reels), an episode in the *Old Man in the Corner* series based on a story by Baroness Orczy. An armchair detective known as the Old Man in the Corner solves crimes while sitting in a tea shop and tells the solutions to a young woman journalist. Rolf Leslie played the Old Man and Renée Wakefield was journalist Mary Hatley with supporting cast of Roy Travers, Ena Evans and Frank Perfitt. D. P. Cooper was the cinematographer and Hugh Croise wrote the adaptation and directed.

The Hole in the Wall

1921 film (Metro/6 reels) based on the 1920 play *The Hole in the Wall* by Fred Jackson. Gordon Grant (Allan Forrest) turns detective to investigate the connection between the late medium Madame Mysteria and robberies committed on her clients. He is in love with Jean Oliver (Alice Lake) who is impersonating the Madame to get revenge for being framed. Grant sorts out all the problems and clears Jean of all wrongdoing. June Mathis wrote the screenplay and Maxwell Karger directed.

Holloway's Treasure

1924 British film (Stoll/2 reels) based on a story by Morley Roberts, an episode in the series *Thrilling Stories from the Strand*. The actors included Dallas Cairns, Kathleen Kilfoyle, Jack Trevor and Amy Willard. Sinclair Hill directed.

Holmes, Sherlock

Sherlock Holmes, the creation of Sir Arthur Conan Doyle, is easily the most famous fictional detective and the role model for most that followed him. The cold, hawk-nosed cocaine-snorting violin-playing detective made his first appearance in print in 1887 in the novella *A Study in Scarlet* in *Beetons's Christmas Annual* but his real fame began with the short story *A Scandal in Bohemia* published in *The Strand* in July 1891. Doyle grew tired of Sherlock Holmes after two dozen stories and tried to kill him off but the detective wouldn't stay dead so Doyle had to start writing about him again. The Holmes canon eventually reached 56 stories and 4 novels. The first Sherlock Holmes film, *Sherlock Holmes Baffled*, was made in 1903; it was also the first film about a named detective. There are now more than 200 Holmes films and 75 of them are silent. The Americans made the first two films about Holmes and the Danish made the first series but the British did not begin to put their famous detective on screen until 1912. They made up for lost time in the 1920s when Eille Norwood played Holmes in three series and a feature. Films and film series starring Holmes include *The Adventures of Sherlock Holmes* (1905 film), *The Adventures of Sherlock Holmes* (1921 series), *Arsène Lupin contra Sherlock Holmes*, *Das Detecktivduell*, *The Further Adventures of Sherlock Holmes* (1923 series), *The Hound of the Baskervilles* (1914/1920/1921), *The Last Adventures of Sherlock Holmes* (1923 series), *Sherlock Holmes* (1909/1912/1916/1922), *The Sign of the Four*, *A Study in Scarlet* (1914/1914), *The Valley of Fear*.

Holmes, Sherlock: Parodies and Imitations

The popularity of Sherlock Holmes films led to a large number of satires, parodies, send-ups and imitations in the silent era including one in which Holmes was played by an African-American actor. The finest by far is *Sherlock, Jr.*, a 1924 American comedy starring Buster Keaton. The others are *Baby Sherlock*, *A Black Sherlock Holmes*, *Burstup Holmes*, *Camillo Emulates Sherlock Holmes*, *Cousins of Sherlock Holmes*, *Detective Barock Holmes And His Hound*, *Fritz As Sherlock Holmes*, *Hemlock Hoax the Detective*, *Hardrock Dome the Great Detective*, *Homlock Shermes*, *The Italian Sherlock Holmes, I Will*, *A Midget Sherlock Holmes*, *Miss Sherlock Holmes*, *A Modern Sherlock*, *The Mys-*

tery of the Leaping Fish, A Rival Sherlock Holmes, Sherlock Ambrose, Sherlock Bonehead, The Sherlock Boob, Sherlock Boob, Detective, Sherlock Brown, The Sherlock Holmes Girl, Sherlock Hawkshaw and Company, Sherlock Holmes, Jr., Sherlock Sleuth, Sherlock Jr., Sherluck Jones, Shorty and Sherlock Holmes, A Society Sherlock, A Squeedunk Sherlock Holmes, and Stronger Than Sherlock Holmes.

Homlock Shermes

1913 comedy (Crystal-Universal/1 reel), a Sherlock Holmes parody starring Pearl White before she became a serial queen. Chester Barnett provides support and Phillips Smalley directed.

The Honeymooning Detectives

1915 American film (Metro/5 reels) based on *One Million Francs*, the novelization of the series *The Honeymoon Detectives* by Frederic Arnold Kummer published in *The Cavalier* magazine. The film has a slightly different plot from the novel. Detective Richard Duvall (William Faversham) meets Grace Ellicott (Carlotta De Felice) while she is traveling in India with her wealthy aunt, the Countess D'Estes (Mayme Kelso). Count D'Estes (Henry Bergman) murders the countess when she returns to England so he can gain control of the fortune which Grace will inherit. Duvall becomes aware of the crime and gets a friend (Arthur Morrison) to leave notes for the count signed "Victor Gerard" saying he has proof of the murder and demanding one million dollars to keep quiet. Disguised as Gerard, he collects the million, saves Grace from being poisoned and forces the count to confess. George D. Proctor wrote the screenplay and John W. Noble directed.

The Honorable Member for Outside Left

1925 British film (Stoll/2 reels) based on a story by Sidney Horler, an episode in the second series of *Thrilling Stories From The Strand*. Eric Bransby Williams starred, Hugh Croise wrote the screenplay and Sinclair Hill directed.

The Hope Diamond Mystery

1921 American serial (Kosmik Films/ fifteen 2-reel episodes) starring serial queen Grace Darmond. She has to solve the mystery of the Hope Diamond while battling baddies (including Boris Karloff), fighting fires, recognizing forgeries and avoiding dangerous traps. Charles Goddard and John B. Clymer wrote the screenplay and Stuart Paton directed. The episodes tell the story: *The Hope Diamond Mystery, The Vanishing Hand, The Forged Note, The Jewel of Sita, A Virgin's Love, The House of Terror, Flames of Despair, Yellow Whisperings, The Evil Eye, In the Spider's Web, The Cup of Fear, The Ring of Death, The Lash of Hate, Primitive passions* and *An Island of Destiny*.

The Hornet's Nest

1919 American film (Vitagraph/6 reels) based on the 1917 novel *The Hornet's Nest* by Nancy Mann Waddel Woodrow. Muriel Fletcher (Vola Vale) thinks her guardians Freda (Kathleen Kirkman) and William (Ogden Crane) Whitfield are cheating her and her cousin Fletcher (Brinsley Shaw) of their estate. She gets help from Ashe Colvin (Earle Williams) whose earlier career was ruined by Freda. Ashe hires Fletcher, a burglar known as The Hornet, to rob the Whitefield's safe of documents proving their wrongdoing. James Dayton wrote the screenplay and James Young directed.

Houdini, Harry

American magician and escape artist (1874–1926) was usually cast in an investigative role as an undercover detective or government agent in his films, solving mysteries and crimes while escaping from various types of imprisonment. Three of his movies were written by mystery writer Arthur B. Reeve (*The Master Mystery, The Grim Game, Terror Island*) but Houdini was the true progenitor of his films and even took over writing and directing chores on *The Man from Beyond* and *Haldane of the Secret Service*.

The Hound of the Baskervilles
(Der Hund von Baskerville)

1914 German series (PAGU /four parts) based on the Sherlock Holmes novel *The Hound of the Baskervilles* in which Holmes investigates the death of Sir Charles Baskerville and the mystery of a ghostly hound. Alwin Neuss plays

Sherlock Holmes in the first part and Eugen Burg is Holmes in the segment called *Das Dunkle Schloss* (The Dark Castle). The plot is more or less the same as the novel but there are additions and there is no Watson. Rudolf Meinert directed from a screenplay by Richard Oswald. The supporting cast included Friedrich Kühne, Hanni Weisse, Erwin Fichtner and Andreas Van Horn. A print survives in a Russian film archive.

The Hound of the Baskervilles
(Der Hund von Baskerville: Das Haus ohne Fenster)

1920 German film (4 reels) based on the Sherlock Holmes novel *The Hound of the Baskervilles*. Willy Kaiser-Heyl plays Sherlock Holmes with supporting cast of Erwin Fichtner, Lu Juergens and Ludwig Rex. Willy Zeyn directed and Robert Liebmann wrote the screenplay.

The Hound of the Baskervilles

1921 British film (Stoll/5 reels) based on the A. Conan Doyle novel *The Hound of the Baskervilles*, an episode in the *Adventures of Sherlock Holmes* series with the time moved from the Victorian era to the 1920s. Holmes solves the murder of Sir Charles Baskerville and blocks another murder by the mysterious hound. Eille Norwood plays Sherlock Holmes with Hubert Willis as Dr. Watson, Madame d'Esterre as Mrs. Hudson and Rex McDougall as Sir Henry Baskerville. Maurice Elvey directed and William J. Elliott and Dorothy Westlake wrote the screenplay.

The Hound of the Baskervilles
(Der Hund von Baskerville)

1929 German film (Erda Film/7 reels) based on the Sherlock Holmes novel *The Hound of the Baskervilles*. Carlyle Blackwell plays Sherlock Holmes with George Seroff as Dr. Watson, Alexander Murski as Lord Charles Baskerville, Livio Pavanelli as Sir Henry Baskerville, Betty Bird as Beryl, Fritz Rasp as Stapleton and Alma Taylor. Herbert Juttke wrote the adaptation and Richard Oswald directed. This was the last silent Holmes film.

An Hour Before Dawn

1913 American film (Famous Players/4 reels). Kate Kirby (Laura Sawyer), daughter of crippled detective Kirby (House Peters), has become a detective herself. For this case she has to pretend to be a chorus girl to get information about a suspect. A scientist was found dead in his lab after he threatened to disinherit his son unless he broke up his romance with chorus girl Violet. Kate discovers that Violet is innocent and proves that the scientist caused his own death with a invention gone wrong. J. Searle Dawley wrote and directed the film, the second in the *Kate Kirby* series.

The House of Fear

1915 American film (5 reels). based on the story "The House of Fear" by John Thomas McIntyre in *Ashton-Kirk: Special Detective*. Ashton-Kirk is asked by Grace Camp (Jeanne Eagels) and her brother Charles (Sheldon Lewis) to investigate mysterious goings-on at their house. He learns that their engraver father had forged currency plates for a crook but never delivered them. The crook's aunt Miss Hohenlo (Ina Hammer) and her gang have been breaking into the house to try to find the plates. Ashton-Kirk catches the gang and destroys the forgery. See Ashton-Kirk for other films.

The House of Hate

1918 American serial (Astral-Pathé/20 episodes) based on a story by Arthur B. Reeve and Charles Logue. The villainous Hooded Terror (Paul Panzer) and his gang set out to destroy heiress Pearl Grant (Pearl White) so he can gain control of her family's munitions factory. After her father is murdered, she gets help investigating the situation from scientist Harry Gresham (Antonio Moreno). It takes them twenty exciting episodes to figure it out. Bertram Millhauser wrote the screenplay and George B. Seitz directed. The episodes were *The Hooded Terror, The Tiger's eye, A Woman's Perfidy, The Man from Java, Spies Within, A Living Target, Germ Menace, The Untold Secret, Poisoned Darts, Double Crossed, Haunts of Evil, Flashes in the Dark, Enemy Aliens, Underworld*

Paul Panzer is the Hooded Terror in *House of Hate.*

Alma Taylor battles a crooked uncle in *The House of Marney.*

Allies, the False Signal, The Vial of Death, The Death Switch, At the Pistol's Point, The Hooded Terror Unmasked and *Following Old Glory.*

The House of Marney

1926 British film (Nettlefold/7 reels) based on the 1923 novel *The House of Marney* by John Goodwin (pseudonym of Sidney Gowing). Alma Taylor starred in this mystery as a woman battling a crooked uncle and getting unexpected help from a chivalrous sailor. The uncle is attempting to cheat her of her fortune. The supporting cast included John London, James Carew and Patrick Susands. Harry Hughes wrote the screenplay and Cecil M. Hepworth directed.

The House of Mystery

1920 American Film (Arrow Film/5 reels) starring Glen White as Tex, a famous criminologist. Tex investigates the murder of blackmailer Ellis Gale which involves spiritualism, seances and a fake medium. The supposed spirit giving bad advice turns out to a man in disguise, the murderer of Gale. Alexander Frank wrote the screenplay and Tom Collins directed the film for the *Tex, Elucidator of Mysteries* series.

Glen White stars as the detective Tex in *The House of Mystery.*

House of Peril

1922 British film (Astra/5 reels) based on Marie Belloc Lowndes' 1912 novel *The Chink in the Armour* and its theatrical adaptation by Horace Annesley Vachell. A villainous German couple in Deauville stalk a woman gambler and persuade her to visit a "haunted house." Fay Compton starred, Nelson Ramsey and Irene Tripod played the German couple, Roy Travers helped rescue her, Madeline Seymour played Anna and A. B. Imeson was Count Kenelm Foss directed and wrote the screenplay. Ernest Hemingway said the base novel was "a masterpiece of dread and suspense."

The House of Whispers

1920 American film (Robert Brunton Production/5 reels) based on William Andrew Johnston's novel *The House of Whispers*. Spaulding Nelson (J. Warren Kerrigan) moves into an apartment haunted by weird sounds and discovers it was built as a "house of whispers" by Henry Kent (Myles McCarthy). It is honeycombed with secret passageways and sliding panels. Spaulding is arrested for the murder of an actress in the apartment but escapes down a secret passage and finds Kent, his partner Roldo and Roldo's wife Nettie. She confesses to murdering the actress out of jealousy. Ernest C. Warde directed and Jack Cunningham wrote the screenplay.

The House on the Marsh

1920 British film (London Film/5 reels) based on the 1905 novel *The House by the River* by Florence Warden which was described on the book jacket as "not only a love story, but a rattling good detective story." A mystery about a governess in a house full of secrets who learns that the master of the household and the housekeeper are jewel thieves. Peggy Patterson played Violet Christie, Cecil Humphreys was Gervas Rayner, Harry Welchman was Laurence Reed, Madge Tree was Sarah Gooch and Frank Stanmore was the Reverend Golightly. Fred Paul directed.

The House Without a Key

1926 American serial (Pathé/ten 2-reel chapters) based on a novel by Earl Derr Biggers. Honolulu detective Charlie Chan (George Kuwa) does not have much to do in this film version of his first case and he only gets 12th billing. In the original novel Chan had to solve a murder involving feuding brothers. In the film he is sidelined to a story about a stolen treasure chest with Allene Ray and Walter Miller in the main roles. Spencer G. Bennet directed and Frank Leon Smith wrote the screenplay.

How Sir Andrew Lost His Vote

1911 American film (Edison/1 reel) based on Richard Harding Davis's much anthologized novelette *In the Fog*. A murder mystery unfolds suspensefully as the participants relate various parts of what happened. The suspense keeps an English MP from participating in a crucial vote. Or does it? The cast included Marc McDermott, Charles Ogle, Camille Dalberg, Mabel Trunnelle and William West.

The Hypnotic Detective

1912 American film (Selig/1 reel). Professor Locksley, the Hypnotic Detective (Charles Clary), is hired to investigate the murder of Dr. Pelhem (Frank Weed). Alfred (Harry Lonsdale), the son of widow Morton (Winifred Greenwood), is accused of the crime. Locksley discovers that Pelham faked his death as part of a revenge plot aimed at the widow who had rejected him. Colin Campbell wrote and directed the film which survives at the UCLA film archive.

I Will

1919 English film (Lucky Cat/5 reels). Wally Bosco plays Sherlock Blake in this comedy satirizing the Sherlock Holmes and Sexton Blake detective films. An aristocrat (Guy Newell) woos a socialist's daughter (Ivy Duke) and there is skullduggery afoot. Kenhelm Foss wrote the screenplay and co-directed with Hubert Herrick.

The Iced Bullet

1917 American film (Triangle/5 reels). A would-be screenwriter (William Desmond) falls asleep at the Thomas H. Ince studio and dreams he is New York detective Horace Lee.

He is hired to investigate the shooting of banker Richard Deering (Barney Sherry) in an mountain lodge where he was staying with daughter Evelyn (Margaret Thompson) and friend Donald Greene (Robert McKim). He discovers that a gun was hidden in a bedroom wall and fixed to fire when the temperature reached freezing. Greene arranged it because the banker refused to allow him to marry his daughter. The screenwriter wakes up and is chased off the Ince lot. C. Gardner Sullivan wrote the screenplay and Reginald Barker directed. The film includes a tour of the Ince studios in which see Barker directing this film.

The Illustrious Prince

1919 American film (Haworth Pictures/5 reels) based on the 1910 novel *The Illustrious Prince* by E. Phillips Oppenheim. Japanese Prince Maiyo (Sessue Hayakawa) goes to London seeking revenge against the swindler who ruined his father and caused his death. Count de la Mar (Bertram Grassby) is the criminal and he is found in a taxi killed by the sword the Prince's father used to kill himself. American Penelope Morse (Mabel Ballin) urges the Prince to leave the country before he is arrested but he refuses. Then the Prince's servant Soto (Toyo Fujita) confesses to the crime saying the Count had wronged his daughter. Richard Schayer wrote the screenplay and William Worthington directed.

In Old Tennessee

1912 American film (Imp/2 reels). Woman detective Nell Gwinn (Jane Fearnley)is sent by her bureau chief to locate an illicit still in the Tennessee hills. She goes pretending to be a dressmaker and becomes involved with Jim Howard (King Baggott). He has become a moonshiner to raise money for an operation needed by his crippled brother (Joe Moore). Nell is about to turn him in when she is caught spying and saved by Jim's brother. She gives up detective work and marries Jim. Otis Turner directed.

In the Grip of Spies

1914 British film (Big Ben Union/3 reels). Detective Dick Steele (H. O. Martinek) disguises himself as an Indian sailor so he can stop Chinese cook from stealing naval plans. With Ivy Montford as Kate Halifax. L.C. MacBean wrote the screenplay and Martinek directed.

In the Hollow of Her Hand

1918 American film (Select Pictures/5 reels) based on George Barr McCutcheon's novel *The Hollow of Her Hand*. Sara Wrandall (Myrtle Stedman) learns that her philandering husband was murdered in an inn by an unidentified woman. On her way home from the inn she rescues a woman about to drown herself who she thinks is the murderer. As her husband treated her so badly she takes the woman Hetty (Alice Brady) home as her companion. Sometime later a detective appears and accuses Sarah of killing her husband but Hetty clears her by confessing. She says she was lured to the inn by the husband who attacked her and she killed him defending herself. Charles Maigne directed and wrote the screenplay.

Sessue Hayakawa is a Japanese prince seeking revenge in *The Illustrious Prince*.

Inscrutable Drew, Investigator

1926 British series (FHC Productions/six 2-reel episodes) featuring Henry Ainley as private detective Victor Drew. He solves six mysteries in six episodes: *The Copper Cylinder, The Clue of the Oak Leaf, The Curse of Ravenscroft, The River House Mystery, The Moon Diamond* and *The Locked Door.* Elliot Stannard wrote the screenplays and A. E. Coleby directed. Fragments of two episodes survive at the BFI film archive.

The Inspirations of Harry Larrabee

1917 American film (Fortune Photoplay/4 reels) based on Howard Fielding's story "The Inspirations of Harry Larrabee." Carolyn Vaughn (Margaret Landis) is chloroformed in her apartment and robbed of her jewels by a thief known as The Wolf (Frank Brownlee). Harry Larrabee (Clifford Gray), who lives down the hall, hears the robbery in progress and rescues Carolyn. The jewels are recovered when The Wolf and his accomplice Stettin quarrel and shoot each other. Bertram Bracken directed and Douglas Bronston wrote the screenplay.

An Insurance Fraud

1919 British film (Life Dramas/2 reels), an episode in the series *The Adventures of Dorcas Dene, Detective.* Dene is an actress who become a detective to earn money after her husband is blinded. Winifred Rose plays Dene and Tom Radford is her husband. George Sims wrote the screenplay and Frank Carlton directed.

An Invincible Sleuth (Kri Kri Detective)

1912 Italian comedy (Cines/2 reels) titled *Kri Kri Detective* distributed in America in 1913 as *An Invincible Sleuth.* Kri Kri was a popular Italian series character played by Raymond Frau in dozens of short films.

The Invisible Web

1921 American film (Fidelity/6 reels). A woman detective, a stockbroker, a banker, his femme fatale wife and a blackmailer are the main suspects in a murder investigation and a police commissioner grills them unmercilessly. Beverly C. Rule wrote the screenplay and directed.

The Iron Claw

1916 American serial (Pathé/twenty 2-reel chapters). Pearl White is at her serial thrills best in this much-praised serial with a masked mystery hero as well as a masked villain. The hero is The Laughing Mask (Harry Fraser) who spends a lot of time rescuing Pearl from the evil Legar known as The Iron Claw (Sheldon Lewis). Creighton Hale is also involved. George B. Seitz wrote the screenplay and co-directed with Edward Jose. The chapter titles are *The Vengeance of Legar, The House of Unhappiness, The Cognac Mask, The Name and the Game, The Incorrigible Captive, The Spotted Warning, The Hooded Helper, The Stroke of 12, Arrows of Hate, The Living Dead, The Saving of Dan O'Mara, The Plunge for Life, The Double Resurrection, The Unmasking of Davey, The Vanishing Fakir, The Green-Eyed God, The Cave of Despair* and *The Triumph of the Laughing Mask.*

The Iron Man

1924 American serial (Universal/fifteen 2-reel chapters). The mystery at the core of this film is the kidnapping in Paris of American heiress Arlene (Margaret Morris) and the substitution of a woman who looks like her (Lola Todd) and will be able to claim the inheritance for her gang. Investigating these nefarious goings-on is reporter Paul Breen (Lucien Albertini) who rescues Arlene and accompanies her to America to unmask the imposter. As Albertini was given the role because of his reputation as a daredevil athlete, there are stunts galore including fights on airplane. Strongman Joe Bonomo adds to the intrigue. Arthur Henry Gooden and Swillilam E. Wing wrote the screenplay and Jay Marchant directed. The chapter titles are *Into the Sewers of Paris, The Imposter, The Dynamite Truck, Wings Aflame, The False Trail, The Stolen Passport, False Faces, Shadowed, The Missing Heirloom, Sinister Shadows, The Betrayal, Flames of Fate, The Crisis, Hidden Dangers* and *The Confession.*

The Island of Intrigue

1919 American film (Metro/5 reels) based on the 1918 novel *The Island of Intrigue* by mystery writer Isabel Ostrander. Maida Waring (May Allison) is sent to vacation to an island owned by a friend of her father's but it is actually a kidnapping scheme. Her father is sent ransom notes and, when he doesn't reply, the gang lock her up. She escapes with camper Gilbert Spear (Jack Mower) and her father arrives with police as they are about to be recaptured. A. S. Le Vino and June Mathis wrote the screenplay and Henry Otto directed.

The Italian Sherlock Holmes

1910 American comedy (Yankee Film/1 reel). A Sherlock Holmes satire.

The Ivory Snuff Box

1915 American film (World/5 reels) based on the novel *The Ivory Snuff Box* by Frederic Arnold Kummer published in *The Cavalier* magazine in 1912. Detective Richard Duvall (Holbrook Blinn) is hired by the French government to find an ivory snuff box stolen from the French ambassador to England. Richard goes to London to investigate while his wife Grace (Alma Belwin) puts herself in a sanitarium run by German spy Dr. Hartmann (Norman Trevor). Richard goes to the sanitarium, steals the snuff box and hides it before being caught by Hartmann. Richard, who knew the box contained a secret code, has substituted a phony code. When Hartmann tortures Richard in front of Grace to get the box, she tells him where it is. Hartmann releases them and they take the real code to the French government. Maurice Tourneur directed and E. M. Ingleton wrote the screenplay.

Izzy the Detective

1914 American film (Reliance-Mutual/1 reel), a film in the Izzy comedy series starring comic Max Davidson. The supporting cast included Billie West, Frank Bennett and Richard Cummings.

The Jade Box

1930 American serial (Universal/ten 2-reel chapters) based on a story by Frederick J. Jackson who also wrote the screenplay. Villain Martin Morgan (Francis Ford). steals a jade box containing the secret of invisibility. His daughter Helen (Louise Lorraine) and her fiancé Jack Lamar (Jack Perrin) must get it back or Jack's father will be killed by the Far East cult that originally owned it. They are aided by the mysterious Shadow seen in the episodes "The Shadow Man," "The Haunting Shadow " and "Out of the Shadows." Ray Taylor directed silent and sound versions of the serial.

Die Jagd nach der Hundertpfundnote oder Die Reise um die Welt (The Hunt for the Hundred Pound Note or Travels around the World)

1913 German film (Werner/4 reels) featuring a woman detective known as Miss Nobody, part of a three-film series produced by Karl Werner for his company. Miss Nobody, who was portrayed by Senta Eichstaedt, was famous for her deductive abilities and the films were known for their exciting car chases. Rudolf Del Zopp wrote the screenplay and Willy Zeyn directed. See *Miss Nobody* for the other films in the series.

Jane's Sleuth

1927 American comedy (Century Film/2 reels).This was the eleventh episode in the *What Happened to Jane* comedy series starring Ethlyne Clair as Jane. Sam Newfield directed and Roy Evans wrote the screenplay.

Der Januskopf (The Two-Faced Man)

1920 German film (Lipow Film/7 reels) loosely based on Robert Louis Stevenson's1886 novella *The Strange Case of Dr. Jekyll and Mr. Hyde*. Conrad Veidt stars as the Jekyll-Hyde character. Director F. W. Murnau did not have the rights to the story so he had his screenwriter Hans Janowitz change the names of all the characters (as he had earlier done transmuting Dracula into Nosferatu). Dr. Jekyll became Dr. Warren and Mr. Hyde became Mr. O'Connor. Margarete Schlegel played Grace/Jane, Conrad Magnus Stifter was Warren's friend and Bela Lugosi was Warren's butler. No one was fooled and the film was distributed in England as *Dr. Jekyll and Mr. Hyde*. Unfortunately this is a lost film by this notable director.

Javert, Inspector

The implacable Inspector Javert, the most hated detective in all fiction, was created by Victor Hugo in his 1862 novel *Les Misérables*. The character was based on Eugène François Vidocq, a reformed criminal who became director of the French civil police. In the novel the merciless Javert ("the law doesn't allow me to be merciful") devotes much of his time to tracking down Jean Valjean, a reformed convict who spent 14 years in prison after stealing a loaf of bread. Javert continues to menace Valjean until, confused by Valjean's goodness, he solves his moral dilemma by leaping into the Seine. The novel was filmed eight times in the silent era. See *Les Misérables* for films.

The Jazz Girl

1926 American film (Motion Picture Guild/6 reels) The "jazz girl" is socialite Janet Marsh (Edith Roberts) who turns detective in an attempt to catch rum runners. She teams up with newspaperman Rodney Blake (Gaston Glass) who is on the same mission though both suspect the other of being in the illegal liquor business. After some misadventures they succeed. Bruce Truman wrote the screenplay and Howard Mitchell directed.

La Jeunesse de Vidocq ou comment on devient policier (Vidocq's Youth or How One Becomes a Policeman)

1909 French film (Pathé/1 reel) based on the *Memoirs* of François-Eugène Vidocq, the French criminal who reformed and became the first official police detective. Harry Baur portrays Vidocq with support from Paul Landrin, Paul Lack and Andrée Marly.

The Jewel Thieves Run to Earth by Sexton Blake

1910 British film (London Cinematograph/1 reel), one of three films in a series titled *Sexton Blake* featuring master detective Sexton Blake In this episode he saves a man who has been tied to a clock-operated gun. Blake was played by C. Douglas Carlile under the direction of S. Wormald.

Jimmy Dale Alias the Grey Seal

1917 American serial (Monmouth/sixteen 2-reel episodes) based on stories by Frank L Packard. New York socialite Jimmy Dale (Elmo Lincoln) fights crime and rights wrongs like a modern Robin Hood using three other identities. As the Gray Seal he battles evildoers and as Larry the Bat he learns about crimes through underworld gossip. After Larry's role is discovered, Dale creates drug addict/artist Smarlingue to replace him. Dale gets pressured to do good deeds by Marie La Sale (Edna Hunter) and a mysterious Woman in Black (Doris Mitchell). Mildred Considine wrote the screenplay and McRae Webster directed. The episodes were titled *The Grey Seal, The Stolen Rubies, The Counterfeit Five, The Metzer Murder Mystery, A Fight for Honor, Below the Deadline, The Devil's Work, The Underdog, The Alibi, Two Crooks and a Knave, A Rogue's Defeat, The Man Higher Up, Good for Evil, A Sheep Among Wolves, The Tapped Wires* and *The Victory*. See also Dale, Jimmy.

Joe Jenkins, Detektiv

Joe Jenkins is a tough "American" detective featured in 1920s German films produced by Kassandra Film. Like the other German film detectives of the period, he has an Anglo-Saxon name and is modeled more on Nick Carter than Sherlock Holmes. He was played by Kurt Brenkendort in *Der Pokal der Fürstin* (The Prince's Cup) and by Georg H. Schnell in *Die Dame im Koffer* (The Woman in the Trunk).

Judex

1916 French serial (Gaumont/ 5 hours and 15 minutes in twelve 2-reel chapters) *Judex* was French filmmaker Louis Feuillade's answer to criticism that his great serials Fantômas and *Les Vampires* glorified criminals. Judex is a righteousness hero (his name is Latin for "judge") but he still gets to wear an impressive costume including dark cloak and slouch hat. Like the villains who preceded him, he is a master of disguise, has a secret hideout and is able to appear and disappear at will. The character of Judex was created by Feuillade with co-writer Arthur Bernède and featured in two se-

Judex is a righteous hero in the Louis Feuillade serial.

rials. Judex was portrayed by René Cresté with Louis Leubas as the evil banker Favraux and Musidora as Favraux's equally evil mistress Diana. Judex eventually spares the life of Favraux because of his love for the banker's innocent daughter Jacqueline (Yvette Andreyor). While popular, *Judex* never had the impact of its predecessors though there were remakes of his story in the sound era, including one by Georges Franju. The episodes are titled *L'Ombre mystérieuse, L'Expiation, La Meute fantastique, Le Secret de la tombe, Le Moulin tragique, Le Môme réglisse, La Femme en noir, Les Souterrains du chateau rouge, Lorsque l'enfant paru, Le Coeur de Jacqueline, L'Ondine* and *Le Pardon d'amour*. The serial is on DVD with orchestral score. A sequel was filmed in 1917 with the same cast, *La Nouvelle Mission de Judex*.

Just for Tonight

1918 American film (Goldwyn/5 reels) based on a story by Charles A. Logue. Ted Whitney, Jr. (Tom Moore) is hired by his father to retrieve a stolen stock certificate. He becomes involved with Betty Blake (Lucy Fox), the niece of Major Blackburn (Henry Hallam) whose home has been robbed. Detective Chase (Edwin Sturgis) arrives to investigate disguised as British nobleman Lord Roxenham. Ted bribes the detective to let him play the Lord for one night but it all goes wrong when Lady Roxenham (Ethel Grey Terry) turns up. She goes along with the ruse but Ted later catches her breaking in the Major's safe. It turns out that she and the butler are notorious thieves. J. Clarkson Miller wrote the screenplay and Charles Giblyn directed.

Juve contre Fantômas

(Juve vs. Fantômas)

1913 French serial (Gaumont/59 minutes in four 1-reel chapters) written and directed by Louis Feuillade and based on the 1911 novel *Juve contre Fantômas*. This is the second serial in the Fantômas series. Fantômas disguises himself as the gangster Loupart and uses streetwalker Josephine to help him rob wine merchant Martielle and lure Detective Juve and reporter Fandor to a trap in a warehouse. Lady Beltham comes out of hiding and help Fantômas plots Juve's murder by boa constrictor. This ploy fails (barely) but Juve finally traps him in Lady Beltham's villa which Fantômas blows up in order to escape and (hopefully) destroy his pursuers. René Navarre plays Fantômas, Bréon is Detective Juve, George Melchior is Fandor, Yvette Andreyor is Josephine and Renée Carl is Lady Beltham. Guérin was the cinematographer. On DVD. See also *Fantômas*.

The Kaiser's Spy

1914 British film (Davidson/3 reels), one of seven films in a series written and directed by Charles Raymond. Philip Kay played the famous detective Sexton Blake with Lewis Carlton as his assistant Tinker. Blake discovers a German spy ring composed of bus drivers operating from a tower in Epping Forest. (See Blake, Sexton for the other films and background.)

Der Kampf mit dem Sturmvogel
(The Fight with the Stormbird)

1917 German film (Egede Nissen Film Company/5 reels) featuring a female detective known as Miss Clever. It was one of a series of ten films about the woman detective starring Norwegian actress Ada Egede-Nissen (using the screen name of "Ada Van Ehlers") It was written by Rudolf Baron and Else Cressin and directed by Georg Alexander who took the male lead in the film. See *Miss Clever* for other films in the series.

Karamaneh

1924 British film (Stoll/2 reels), an episode in *The Further Mysteries of Fu Manchu* series based on a story by Sax Rohmer. Dorinea Shirley plays Karamaneh, Harry Agar Lyons is the villainous Dr. Fu Manchu, Fred Paul is detective Nayland Smith and Humberston Wright is Dr. Petrie. Fred Paul directed and wrote the screenplay and Frank Canham was the cinematographer.

Katchem Kate

1912 American comedy (Biograph/1 reel) based on Dell Anderson's story "Cunning Kate." Mabel Normand stars as Kate who thinks she has become a detective because she answered a newspaper ad on how to become one. She has a number of comic misadventures but finally captures a band of anarchists through masquerading as a man.

Kennedy, Craig

Craig Kennedy, regarded in the 1910s as the American equivalent of Sherlock Holmes, was the creation of Arthur B. Reeve. He was a "scientific detective" who employed the latest technical devices of his time including lie detectors, x-rays and sound analyzers. He made his first appearance in *Cosmopolitan* magazine in December 1910 in a story titled "The Case of Helen Bond" collected in the 1912 book *The Silent Bullet*. He made his first screen appearance opposite Pearl White in the Pathé serial *The Exploits of Elaine* in 1915 and returned in two sequels with White, *The New Exploits of Elaine* and *The Romance of Elaine*. Kennedy was featured in two other silent serials, *The Carter Case* and *The Radio Detective*, but they were less popular.

The Kensington Mystery

1924 British film (Stoll/2 reels), an episode in the *Old Man in the Corner* series based on a story by Baroness Orczy. An armchair detective known as the Old Man in the Corner solves crimes while sitting in a tea shop and tells the solutions to a young woman journalist. In this episode he solves the mystery of a missing deed. Rolf Leslie played the Old Man and Renée Wakefield was journalist Mary Hatley with supporting cast of Reginald Fox, Kate Gurney, Dorothy Harris and Elsa Martini. John J. Cox was the cinematographer and Hugh Croise wrote the adaptation and directed. Print survives at BFI archive.

The Kid and the Sleuth

1912 American comedy (Imp-Universal/1 reel) parodying Nick Carter detective films. Messenger boy Red Gallagher (Tom Barry) falls asleep reading a Nick Carter book and dreams he has hired Nick (played by King Baggot). Together they foil the plans of a villain (William Robert Daly) and a villainess (Lucille Young) who have planned horrible things for the heroine (Ethel Grandin). They even have to rescue her from a sawmill where she is about to be cut in half. The film, based on a vaudeville sketch by Tom Barry, was directed by Thomas H. Ince.

The King of Detectives

1902 American film (Biograph/55 feet). After a man is shot on a city street, his woman friend goes through his pockets looking for something. She runs off when a crowd gathers. Robert K. Bonine was the cinematographer. The film was remade in 1903 with added detail.

King, the Detective

1911/1914 American series of five 1-reel films produced by Imp-Universal and written and directed by King Baggot who played King, the Detective. King is a knowledgeable sleuth able to solves crimes by fingerprinting suspects, creating undetectable disguises and outwitting slow-thinking villains. The supporting casts varied in each film (see below).

King, the Detective

1911 American film (Imp-Universal/1 reel). King the detective (King Baggot) catches a murderous chauffeur by tricking him into leaving incriminating fingerprints. Frank W. Smith played the bad driver. Baggot also wrote and directed the film.

King, the Detective and the Opium Smugglers

1912 American film (Imp-Universal/1 reel). King the detective (King Baggot) disguises himself as a fisherman to capture a gang of opium smugglers, gets involved with a girl (Jane Fearnley) but has trouble with jealous Bully (Fred Kelsey) who actually heads the smuggling gang.

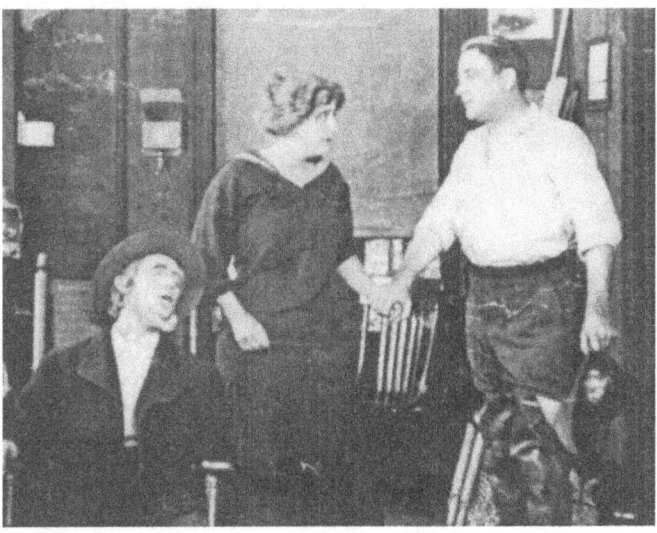

King Baggot, right, in *King the Detective and the Opium Smugglers* with Jane Fearnley.

King, the Detective in the Jarvis Case

1913 American film (Imp-Universal/1 reel). King the detective (King Baggot) proves that an old man pretending to be dead is still alive. A girl (Ethel Grandin) was accused of his murder.

King, the Detective in Formula 879

1914 American film (Imp-Universal/1 reel). King the detective (King Baggot) proves that a chemist did not murder a man with toxic fumes. Baggot played both the chemist and the detective through double exposure.

King, the Detective in the Marine Mystery

1914 American film (Imp-Universal/1 reel). King the detective (King Baggot) proves that a drugged sailor is really a stockbroker and that his twin brother is responsible. David Lithgow played the twins.

Kinkaid, Gambler

1916 American film (Universal/5 reels). Female detective Nellie Gleason (Ruth Stonehouse) follows gambler Jim Kinkaid (R. A. Cavin) to Mexico after he robs real estate millionaire George Arnold (Raymond Whittaker). She then discovers that Arnold is a crook who swindles immigrants and that Kinkaid robbed him to pay back people Arnold had cheated. Nellie decides to let him escape. Fred Myton wrote the screenplay and Raymond Wells directed.

Ruth Stonehouse is the detective in *Kinkaid, Gambler.*

Kirby, Kate

Kate Kirby was a female detective featured in three 1913 American films made by Famous Players. One of the first series to feature a woman detective, it was the creation of writer/director J. Searle Dawley. A virtually forgotten actress named Laura Sawyer played detective Kate Kirby in all three films. Kate learned the trade from her detective father who has been crippled by criminals but is still able to help here. He is played by Henry E. Dixey in *Chelsea 7750* and by House Peters in *An Hour Before Dawn* and *The Port of Doom*.

Kishin Yuri keiji (Detective Yuri)

1924 Japanese film (Shoshiku/6 reels) written and directed by Teinosuke Kinugasa. This is one of the earliest Japanese detective films. Detective fiction did not became popular in Japan until the 1920s but Kinugasa was always ahead of the artistic curve as shown by his 1926 masterpiece *A Page of Madness*. He is best known in the West for winning the grand prize at the Cannes Film Festival in 1954 with *Gate of Hell*.

Die König Macombe (King Macombe)

1919 German film (May Film/9 reels), the fourth episode in the big budget, "thrill-packed" German series *Herrin der Welt* (Mistress of the World) based on a novel by Karl Figdor. Mia May stars as Maud Gregaards who has to cross the cannibal kingdom of King Macombe to reach the lost city of Ophir where the treasure of the Queen of Sheba is hidden. The supporting cast includes Michael Bohnen, Hans Mierendorff and Henry Sze. Richard Hutter wrote the screenplay and Joe May directed.

Ladies Beware

1927 American film (R-C Pictures/5 reels) based on the story "Jack of Diamonds" by Frederick J. Jackson. Jewel thief Jack O'Diamonds (George O'Hara) goes to a party given by Mrs. Ring (Florence Wix) pretending to be a detective. He says he has been sent to prevent the theft of her ruby. A former colleague Jeannie (Nola Luxford), now working as Mrs. Ring's secretary, warns him off but there is yet another thief present. Count Bodevsky (Mario Carillo) steals the gem but Jack steals it back and returns it to Jeannie. Charles Giblyn directed and Enid Hibbard wrote the screenplay.

Lady Audley's Secret

English author Mary Elizabeth Braddon (1813–1915) did not write detective fiction per se (her books were called "sensation novels") but mystery critics Barzun and Taylor pointed out that her novel *Lady Audley's Secret* (1862) has "more detection than is found in many a modern thriller." The detective in *Lady Audley's Secret* is the lady's barrister stepson who unearths her secret: she is a bigamist who shoved her first husband down a well when he turned up not as dead as she thought he was. Our sympathy, however, is with her rather than the priggish barrister. The novel was filmed five times in the silent era (see below).

Lady Audley's Secret

1906 British film (Walterdaw/1 reel).

Lady Audley's Secret

1908 American film (Kalem/1 reel) starring Gene Gauntier as Lady Audley. She also wrote the screenplay.

Lady Audley's Secret

1912 America film (Fox/2 reels) starring Jane Fearnley as Lady Audley with King Baggot as first husband George Talboys, William Welsh as second husband Sir Michael Audley, William E. Shay as stepson Robert Audley, and William R. Daly as Luke Marks. Herbert Brenon directed and wrote the screenplay with Otis Turner.

Lady Audley's Secret

1915 America film (Fox/5 reels) with Theda Bara as Lady Audley, Clifford Bruce as first husband George Talboys, Warner Richmond as second husband Sir Michael Audley and Riley Hatch as Luke Martin. Marshall Farnum directed and Mary Asquith wrote the screenplay.

Lady Audley's Secret

1920 English film (Ideal Films/5 reels) with Margaret Bannerman as Lady Audley. H, Manning Haynes as Robert Audley, Randolph

McLeod as first husband George Talboys, Hubert Willis as second husband Sir Michael Audley, Betty Farquhar as Alysia Audley, William Burchill as Captain Malden and Wallace Bosco as Luke Marks. Jack Denton directed and Eliot Stannard wrote the screenplay.

Lady Baffles and Detective Duck

1915 American comedy series (Powers Picture Plays/twelve 1-reel episodes) in which Raffles-like thief Lady Baffles battles Detective Duck. Gale Henry played Lady Baffles, Max Asher was Detective Duck (who is also an inventor), William Franey was the Chief of Police and Milburn Morante, Lillian Peacock and Arthur Moon lent support. Clarence G. Badger wrote the screenplays based on stories by Gale Henry. Allen Curtis directed. The films were *Lady Baffles and Detective Duck*, *Lady Baffles and Detective Duck in Baffles Aids Cupid*, *Lady Baffles and Detective Duck in Kidnapping the King's Kids*, *Lady Baffles and Detective Duck in Saved by a Scent*, *Lady Baffles and Detective Duck in the 18 Carrot Mystery*, *Lady Baffles and Detective Duck in the Dread Society of the Sacred Sausage*, *Lady Baffles and Detective Duck in the Great Egg Robbery*, *Lady Baffles and Detective Duck in The Lost Roll*, *Lady Baffles and Detective Duck in the Ore Mystery*, *Lady Baffles and Detective Duck in the Signal of the Three Socks*, *Lady Baffles and Detective Duck in the Sign of the Sacred Safety Pin* and *Lady Baffles and Detective Duck in When the Wets Went Dry*.

Lady Candale's Diamonds

1910 British film (London Cinematograph/1 reel), one of three films in a series titled *Sexton Blake* featuring master detective Sexton Blake. Blake follows jewel thieves who have stolen a lady's car as their escape vehicle. Blake was played by C. Douglas Carlile under the direction of S. Wormald.

Lady Raffles

1928 American film (Columbia/ 6 reels) based on a story by Jack Jungmeyer inspired by the tales about the gentleman crook Raffles. Estelle Taylor plays Lady Raffles, a former society crook who is now an undercover Scotland Yard detective. She is mistaken for a maid at a party where Warren Blake (Roland Drew) has a priceless necklace. Jewel thieves Lillian (Lilyan Tashman) and Dick (Ernest Hilliard) realize she is Lady Raffles and try to frame her when their theft fails. Earl Hudson wrote the screenplay and Roy William Neill directed.

The Last Adventures of Sherlock Holmes

1923 British series (Stoll/fifteen 2-reel episodes) starring Eille Norwood as detective Sherlock Holmes, Hubert Willis as Dr. Watson and Madame d'Esterre as Mrs. Hudson. The films were directed by George Ridgewell with screenplays by Patrick L. Mannock and Geoffrey H. Malins based on the original Doyle stories. Alfred Moise was the cinematographer. The films are *The Blue Carbuncle*, *The Cardboard Box*, *The Crooked Man*, *The Dancing Men*, *The Disappearance of Lady Frances Carfax*, *The Engineer's Thumb*, *The Final Problem*, *The Gloria Scott*, *His Last Bow*, *The Mazarin Stone*, *The Missing Three Quarter*, *The Mystery of Thor Bridge*, *Silver Blaze*, *The Speckled Band* and *The Three Students*. All of these films survive at the BFI film archive.

The Last Call

1922 American film (Garsson Productions/2 reels), one of four films in a *Nick Carter* series featuring the famous detective Nick Carter. In this one he battles a criminal gang. Carter was played by Edmund Lowe under the direction of Alexander Hall. With Diana Allen and Henry Sedley. This film survives in an archive.

The Last Hour

1923 American film (Mastodon Films/7 reels) based on the short story "Blind Justice" by Frank R. Adams first published in *Munsey's Magazine*. Steve Cline (Milton Sills) helps forger Reever McCall (Alec Francis) and daughter Saidee (Carmel Myers) escape from the police. Years later corrupt detective William Mallory (Charles Clary), who killed Cline's brother, becomes a political boss and demands Saidee marry him or he will reveal her criminal past. Mallory is killed by McCall to protect his daughter and Cline takes the blame but Reever confesses to save Cline's life. Edward Sloman directed.

The Last of the Mafia

1915 American film (Neutral Film Co./5 reels). An Italian detective is sent to New York to trail two Mafia gangsters and is killed. An Italian merchant's child is kidnapped by the Black Hand and a bombing creates panic. A New York detective eventually rescues the child, captures the Black Hand gang and arranges for the Mafia men to be sent back to Italy. Jack Clark, William Conrad and Catherine Lee played the leading roles in the film written and directed by Sidney M. Goldin.

The Last Witness

1925 British film (Stoll/6 reels) based on the mystery novel *The Last Witness* by F. Britten Austin. Barrister Stephen Brand (Fred Paul) prosecutes his wife Letitia (Isobel Elsom) for killing her lover. She is innocent but how can it be prove. Stella Arbenina played Mrs. Stapleton, Queenie Thomas was Lady Somerville, Aubrey Fitzgerald was Lord "Bunny" Somerville, John F. Hamilton was Eric Norton and Tom Nesbitt was Maurice Tregarthen. Fred Paul directed.

The Lavender Bath Lady

1922 American film (Universal/5 reels) based on a story by Shannon Fife adapted for the screen by mystery writer George Randolph Chester. Shopgirl Mamie Conroy (Gladys Walton) is involved in two kidnappings and is accused of robbery. Detective David Bruce (Edward Burns), who is an undercover detective pretending to be a crook, sorts it all out. King Baggot directed.

Lawful Cheaters

1925 American film (B.P. Schulberg Productions/5 reels). Clara Bow turns amateur detective (with police approval) in this colorful melodrama. She dresses as a boy to infiltrate a gang and is able to recovers stolen bonds and prevent her brothers and boyfriends from becoming crooks. Adele Buffington wrote the screenplay and Frank O'Connor directed.

The Law's Lash

1928 American film (Pathé/5 reels) starring German shepherd Flame as Royal Mounted police dog whose master is killed by a criminal. He proves his worth as a detective by leading the Mounties to the hideout of a gang of villains, uncovering their hiding places and revealing the name of man who killed his master. Noel Mason Smith directed.

Leave It to Me

1920 American film (Fox/5 reels) based on a story by Arthur Jackson. Wealthy but lazy Dick Derrickson (William Russell) buys a detective agency to show his fiancée Madge Earle (Eileen Percy) that he can work. As there are no cases he hires thugs to steal things from his rich friends. One friend hires him to get back love letter he wrote to a vamp but in revenge she kidnaps the friend. Derrickson rescues the friend and recovers all the things stolen by the thugs. Jules Furthman wrote the screenplay and Emmett J. Flynn directed.

The Leavenworth Case

1923 American film (Vitagraph/6 reels) based on the 1878 novel *The Leavenworth Case* by Anna Katherine Green. In the novel detective Ebenezer Gryce solves the crime with the

Harwell (Paul Ducet) covers the detectives with a gun in *The Leavenworth Case.*

help of the lawyer Raymond but in the film Raymond investigates the murder on his own and Gryce does not appear. Eleanor Leavenworth (Seena Owen) is suspected of killing her rich uncle (William Walcott) but other members of the Leavenworth household also come under suspicion, including Mary Leavenworth (Martha Mansfield), Anderson (Wilfred Lytell) and Harwell (Paul Doucet). Eleanor's lawyer lover Raymond (Bradley Barker) investigates and reveals the real killer who falls to his death while trying to escape. Charles Giblyn directed for Whitman Bennett Productions and Eve Stuyvesant wrote the screenplay.

Lecoq, Monsieur

French detective Monsieur Lecoq, the creation of novelist Émile Gaboriau, was detecting before Sherlock Holmes and the great detective jealously called him as a bungler. Lecoq, who is never given a first name, made his initial appearance in 1886 in *L'Affaire Lerouge* (The Widow Lerouge), the first detective novel, as the assistant of detective Tabaret. He returned as the main character in *Monsieur Lecoq* (1869), *Le Dossier No 113* (1867), *Le Crime d'Orcival* (1867), *Les Esclaves de Paris* (1858) and *Le Petit Vieux des Batignolles* (1876). Seven silent films were based on his cases: see *Le Crime d'Orcival, The Family Stain, Le Dossier No 113, Monsieur Lecoq*.

The Leopard Lady

1928 American film (De Mille Pictures/7 reels) Based on the 1928 play *The Leopard Lady* by Edward Childs Carpenter. Leopard trainer Paula (Jacqueline Logan) is hired by police to investigates thefts and murders at a circus. She learns that Caesar (Alan Hale) has an ape trained to be a killer. When the ape almost kills her fiancé, she has Caesar arrested. Beulah Marie Dix wrote the screenplay and Rupert Julian directed.

The Life Mask

1918 American film (Petrova Picture Company/6 reels) based on the 1913 novel *The Life Mask* by Alice Muriel Williamson. Anita Courtland (Olga Petrova) is forced to marry millionaire Woodruffe Clay (Wyndham Standing) to avoid a scandal. He is injured on their wedding night and makes her life miserable while recovering. One morning, after dreaming of poisoning him, she finds him dead and believes she has killed him. She flees to Europe with her nurse Sarah (Lucille La Verne) and takes up with her old love Hugh Shannon (Thomas Holding). Before she can confess her guilt, Sarah says she killed him to free her mistress from a bad marriage. Lillian Case Russell wrote the screenplay and Frank Crane directed.

Life of Charles Peace

1905 British film (Haggar & Sons/1 reel of 770 feet). Charles Peace, the best known of Britain's Victorian villains and a favorite subject of penny dreadfuls, was the protagonist of two famous 1905 British films. This was the first (released in August 1905) and it has been called "the first British fiction film in the real sense of the word." Produced and directed by William Haggar, it consists of ten scenes. Peace disguises himself as a parson to escape capture but is recognized and caught. He is put on a train to Sheffield to stand trial for the murder of Arthur Dyson but leaps from the train. He is recaptured, tried and hanged. The actors were all members of the Haggar family. William's son Walter played Peace, James Haggar was Dyson, Violet Haggar was Mrs. Dyson, Lily Haggar was Peace's accomplice. Sarah Haggar was Peace's mother and Henry Haggar was the policeman. The film survives in the BFI film archive and is on DVD.

Life of Charles Peace

1905 film (Sheffield Photo Company/1 reel of 870 feet). This was the second film about the famous Victorian burglar (released in November 1905). Produced and directed by Charles Mottershaw, it consists of twelve scenes Peace becomes friends with Arthur Dyson and his wife in a suburb of Sheffield. After an argument he shoots Dyson in his garden. He is caught by police while committing a burglary in Manchester but escapes in disguise. He is recaptured and put on a train to Sheffield but leaps off it. Injured, he is unable to hide so is recaptured and tried. Mottershaw had made earlier crime movies including the 1903 films *The Daring Daylight Burglary* and *Robbery of the Mail Coach*.

Life or Honor?

1918 American film (Ivan Film/7 reels) based on a story by Betta Breuil who also wrote the screenplay. Criminologist Martin Cross (Ben Hendricks) is asked to investigate the murder of merchant J. T. Manley. His son James is convicted through the testimony of Manley's valet Aguinaldo (James Morrison). Sidney Holmes (Edward MacKay) tells Cross he saw Aguinaldo commit the murder through the bedroom window of his best friend's wife (Leah Baird) but can't testify without ruining her reputation. Cross gets the superstitious Aguinaldo to confess by using fake ghosts and spirits that accuse him of the crime. Edmund Lawrence directed.

Life's Whirlpool

1917 American film (Metro/5 reels). Detective B. J. Hendrix (Paul Everton) investigates the murder of John Martin (Reginald Carrington). His wife Esther (Ethel Barrymore) is the chief suspect because Martin's sister Ruth (Ricca Allen) accuses her of the murder. The detective finds an old hat outside a window and traces it back to a farmer (Frank Leigh) who had been ruined by Martin. He confesses that he killed Martin Esther is now free to marry an old suitor (Alan Hale). Lionel Barrymore wrote and directed the film.

The Line-Up at Police Headquarters

1914 American film (Nonpareil Feature Film Corp/6 reels). George S. Dougherty, Deputy Commissioner of Police of New York in charge of the Detective Bureau, plays himself in this "authentic" mystery. He allows millionaire James B. Maxwell (Horace Vinton) and daughter Vera (Marian Swayne) to tour police headquarters with assistant Dick Vernon (Joseph Levering). Sometime later Maxwell is robbed of a $50,000 necklace and Dougherty investigates the crime himself with Vernon assisting. He tracks down the criminals, recovers the necklace and handcuffs Vernon to Vera at their wedding. Frank Beal directed.

The Lion Man

1919 American serial (Universal/eighteen 2 reel chapters) based on Randall Parish's novel *The Strange Cast of Cavendish*. Newspaper reporter Stella (Kathleen O'Connor) investigates the apparent murder of millionaire Cavendish (J. Barney Sherry) in a fire and the disappearance of his will. Westcott (Jack Perrin), who is accused of the murder, joins her in the investigation and they are aided in times by a mysterious masked Lion Man (Mack Wright). Karl Coolidge wrote the screenplay and Albert Russell co-directed with Jack Wells. The chapters were titled *Flames of Hate, Rope of Death, Kidnappers, A Devilish Device, In the Lion's Den, House of Horrors, Doomed, Dungeon of Despair, Sold into Slavery, Perilous Plunge, At the Mercy of Monsters, Jaws of Destruction, When Hell Broke Loose, Desperate Deeds, Furnace of Fury, Relentless Renegades, In Cruel Clutches* and *In the Nick of Time*.

The Lion's Mouse

1922 British film (Granger-Binger/6 reels) based on the novel *The Lion's Mouse* by A. M. and C. N. Williamson. A secret society kidnaps a man in an attempt to force his sister to steal plans for them but she refuses and foils them. Mary Odette played the Mouse, Wyndham Standing was Dick Sands, Rex Davis was Justin O'Reilly and Marguerite Marsh was Olga Beverley. Oscar Apfel directed.

Listen Lester

1924 American film (Principal Pictures/6 reels) based on the 1918 play *Listen Lester* by Harry Linsley Cort, G. E. Stoddard and Harold Orlog. Woman detective Miss Pink (Dot Farley) is hired by Colonel Dodge (Alec Francis) to recover incriminating letters from old lover Arbutus Quilty (Louise Fazenda) who is threatening a breach-of-promise suit. Hotel detective Listen Lester (Harry Myers) gets involved with the search and with Dodge's daughter Mary (Eva Novak). In the end Dodge decides it is simpler to marry Miss Quilty as his daughter is marrying Lester. Louise Milestone wrote the screenplay and William A. Seiter directed.

The Little Detective

1908 American film (Vitagraph/half reel). No other information available.

The Little Detective

1915 American film (Lubin/2 reels) based on a story by Ethel D Pitney. The cast included with Margaret Dawson, Mildred Gregory, Louise Huff, Edgar Jones and Joseph Kaufman.

The Little Detective

1915 American comedy (Cub Comedies/1 reels) directed by Milton J. Fahrney with a cast including Goldie Colwell, Louis Fitzroy, Jefferson Osborne, George Ovey and Janet Sully.

Living Lies

1922 American film (Mayflower Photoplay/5 reels) based on Arthur Somers Roche's story "A Scrap of Paper" and his novel *Plunder*. Newspaper reporter Dixon Grant (Edmund Lowe) investigates a syndicate of crooked financiers headed by evil Masterman. Grant gets a copy of an agreement for an illegal deal but Masterman tortures him until he reveals its hiding place. Later Grant and his sweetheart Miss Rowland (Mona Kingsley) get the evidence needed to publicize the crooked deal. Masterman dies when his houseboat hideout is destroyed. Emile Chautard directed.

The Livingston Case

1910 American film (Edison/1 reel) written and directed by Edwin S. Porter. A clever Sherlock Holmes-like detective solves a murder case and reveals the murderer purely through deductive reasoning.

The Locked Door

1926 British film (FHC Productions/2 reels), an episode in the series *Inscrutable Drew, Investigator* featuring Henry Ainley as private detective Victor Drew. In this episode Drew and his assistant Dracos investigate the mystery of a locked door. Howard Elliot Stannard wrote the screenplay and A. E. Coleby directed.

The Lodger

1926 British film (Gainsborough/8 reels) based on the 1913 novel *The Lodger* by Marie Belloc Lowndes. The detective in this Alfred Hitchcock film is a bit of loser as he almost gets an innocent man killed. Ivor Novello is the lodger detective Joe Betts (Malcolm Keen). believes could be the mysterious Avenger who's been strangling women on the back streets of London. He thinks this because he is jealous of Novello who has rented a room in the house where his girlfriend Daisy (June, Lady Interclyde) lives. The detective deceives us, the movie audience, because we accept his suspicions. The lodger is innocent, of course, and goes out late at night because he is trying to capture the Avenger who murdered his sister. The detective's conviction of the lodger's guilt eventually causes a vengeful mob to chase and nearly kill him. He survives only because the real killer is found in the nick of time. Eliot Stannard and Hitchcock wrote the screenplay and Baron Ventimiglia was the cinematographer.

London After Midnight

1927 American film (MGM/7 reels) based on a story by Tod Browning. This Lon Chaney film is essentially a tongue-in-cheek parody of a detective film. Detective Burke (Lon Chaney) is still investigating the suicide of Roger Balfour five years later and thinks one of four suspects murdered him. The four are Balfour's daughter Lucille (Marceline Day), his butler (Percy Williams), his best friend Sir James Hamlin (Henry B. Walthall) and Hamlin's nephew Arthur (Conrad Nagel). Burke finds the killer by hypnotizing each of the suspects. Waldemar Young wrote the screenplay and Tod Browning directed. The film is lost but it has been reconstructed from the script and photos.

The Lone Wolf

The master thief Michael Lanyard, known to police as The Lone Wolf, was the creation of Louis Joseph Vance and made his first appearance in the story "The Lone Wolf" in *Munsey's Magazine* in March 1914. Vance's Lone Wolf stories provided the basis for six silent films and another twenty in the sound era. For descriptions of the films see below plus *Alias the Lone Wolf* and *The False Faces*.

The Lone Wolf

1917 American film (Selznick/8 reels) based on the 1914 novel *The Lone Wolf* by Louis Joseph Vance. Cracksman Burke (Stephen Grattan) teaches young Marcel (Cornish Beck) the safe cracking business. When he become a master thief, he calls himself Michael Lanyard (Bert Lytell) but the Paris police call him "The Lone Wolf." A gang known as the Pack attempt to kill him but he gets away with help from Lucy Shannon (Hazel Dawn), a detective masquerading as a crook. Lucy and Lanyard are pursued to England by the Pack but the Pack members are killed in a plane crash. Lanyard goes straight and marries Lucy. George Edwards-Hall wrote the screenplay and Herbert Brenon directed.

The Lone Wolf

1924 American film (Associated Exhibitors/6 reels) based on the story "The Lone Wolf" by Louis Joseph Vance published in *Munsey's Magazine* in March 1914. Master thief Michael Lanyard (Jack Holt), known as the Lone Wolf, agrees to recover stolen secret plans in exchange for asylum in the United States. Lucy Shannon (Dorothy Dalton), seemingly a member of the gang that stole the plans but actually a Secret Service agent, assists Lanyard in getting the plans back and helps him to escape and deliver the plans. S. E. V. Taylor wrote the screenplay and directed.

The Lone Wolf Returns

1926 American film (Columbia/6 reels) based on the 1923 novel *The Lone Wolf Returns* by Louis Joseph Vance. Master thief Michael Lanyard (Bert Lytell), known as the Lone Wolf, steals a necklace and hides from detectives at a masked ball where he meets Marcia Mayfair (Billie Dove). She doesn't give him away when they are forced to unmask so he replaces jewels he took from her bedroom. Detective Crane (Alphonse Ethier) suspects him when Marcia's jewels are stolen by Morphew (Gustav von Seyffertitz) and his gang but Lanyard traps them. J. Grubb Alexander wrote the screenplay and Ralph Ince directed.

The Lone Wolf (Bert Lytell) with Eve (Billie Dove) in *The Love Wolf* (1926).

The Lone Wolf's Daughter

1919 American film (Parker Reed-Pathé/7 reels) based on a story by Louis Joseph Vance who wrote the screenplay. Michael Lanyard (Bertram Grassby), known as the Lone Wolf, buys a painting which conceals incriminating letters by Princess Sonia (Louise Glaum). He gives them to her, she divorces evil Prince Victor (Edwin Stevens), they marry and have a daughter and then the princess dies. Twenty years later their daughter Sonia (again played by Louise Glaum), who does not know her real identity, is found by Prince Victor who has plans to become dictator of England. Sonia falls in love with Victor's secretary Roger Karslake (Thomas Holding), who is really a Scotland Yard detective, and tells him of Victor's evil plan. Karslake and Lanyard, also working for Scotland Yard and disguised as Victor's Oriental butler, capture the gang. William P. S. Earle directed.

Louise Glaum plays the master thief's daughter in *The Lone Wolf's Daughter*.

Loot

1919 American film (Universal/6 reels). based on Arthur Somers Roche's 1916 novel *Loot*. Crooks led by Pete Fielding (Joseph Girard), known as the Shadow, plan to steal a diamond necklace from Wade Hildreth (Darrell Foss) who is transporting it for Lady Gwendolyn (Gertrude Astor). Actress Morn Light (Ora Carew), who is loved by the Shadow, agrees to help but betrays him in an act of revenge. The Shadow kidnaps them both and robs the jewelry store. Detective Tyron (Arthur Mackey) follows the getaway boat and captures the gang but the Shadow gets away, Violet Clark wrote the screenplay and William C. Dowlan directed. The novel was filmed in 1917 as the serial *The Gray Ghost*.

Lord John's Journal

1915–1916 American serial (Universal/five 3-reel episodes) based on the novelette "Lord John in New York" by Charles N. and Alice M. Williamson in *McClure's Magazine*. Lord John (William Garwood) is a detective novelist who

William Garwood plays a detective novelist in *Lord John's Journal*.

has problems with millionaire Roger Odell (Ogden Crane). He confronts him on an ocean liner and agrees to discover why the previous fiancés of Odell's fiancée Grace Callender (Grace Benham) died mysteriously. After stopping the evil hypnotist Dr. Rameses (Albert MacQuarrie) from stealing a gold mummy from Odell's adopted sister Maida (Stella Razetto), Lord John discovers that Grace's guardian aunt Marian was behind the deaths. She confesses and kills herself. The episodes are *Lord John in New York. The Gray Sisterhood, Three-Fingered Jenny, The Eye of Horus* and *The League of the Future.* Harvey Gates wrote the screenplay and Edward J. Le Saint directed.

Lost at Sea

1926 American film (Tiffany/7 reels) based on Louis Joseph Vance's novel *Mainstream*. The Chief of Detectives (William Walling) investigates the murder of Norman Travers (Lowell Sherman) and finds that Natalie

(Jane Novak) is the prime suspect. Richard Lane (Huntly Gordon) confesses to protect Natalie but the detective discovers that Travers' mistress, cabaret dancer Nita Howard (Natalie Kingston), was the real killer. Esther Shulkin wrote the screenplay and Louis J. Gasnier directed.

The Love Flower

1920 American film (United Artists/7 reels) based on the 1919 story "Black Beach" by Ralph Stock published in *Collier's Weekly*. Vindictive detective Matthew Crane (Anders Randolf), who convicted innocent Bevan (George MacQuarrie) of an earlier killing, believes he has killed again. Bevan flees with daughter Stella (Carol Dempster) to a South Pacific island where she meets and falls in love with Bruce Sanders (Richard Barthelmess). Crane uses Sanders to find Bevan's island but Sanders then tricks him into thinking that Bevan has died so he will quit chasing him. G. W. Bitzer and Paul H. Allen were the cinematographers D. W. Griffith directed. On DVD.

Carol Dempster stars in D.W. Griffith's *The Love Flower* (DVD cover and sheet music cover).

Love Letters

1917 American film (Paramount/5 reels) based on a story by Shannon Fife. Eileen Rodney (Dorothy Dalton) goes to see Raymond Moreland (William Conklin) to try to retrieve love letters she wrote a year ago before she married district attorney John Harland (Thurston Hall). She fails. When Moreland is found murdered the next day, she returns to his apartment to try again fearing the letters will incriminate her. Her husband and the police arrive at the same time and things look bad until Eleanor Dare (Dorcas Matthews), another woman betrayed by Moreland, is revealed to be his murderer. R. William Neill directed and Ella Stuart Carson wrote the screenplay.

Love Without Question

1920 American film (Jans Pictures/7 reels) based on the 1917 novel *The Abandoned Room* by Charles Wadsworth Camp. Katherine (Olive Tell) discovers her guardian Silus Blackburn (Mario Majeroni) murdered in the room where three generations of Blackburns have died. An investigating detective is murdered in the same room and suspicion falls on Silus's grandson Robert (James W. Morrison). On day of Silus's burial, he is found sitting by the fire. It turns out

Silus had a twin brother whom he murdered and Katherine is the brother's daughter. Silus kills himself out of guilt. Violet Clark wrote the screenplay and B. A. Rolfe directed.

Love's Prisoner

1919 American film (Triangle/6 reels) based on a story by E. Magnus Ingleton who also wrote the screen play. Nancy (Olive Thomas) becomes the mysterious thief known as the Bird to support her sisters after her elderly husband dies without leaving her any money. She is helped in her criminal endeavors by aged fence Jonathan Twist (William V. Mong). Detective Jim Garside (Joe King) loves Nancy but suspect she is the Bird and that she killed Twist. It turns out that Twist died of a heart attack. Nancy decides to go straight and marry Jim. Jack Dillon directed.

Lucille Love, Girl of Mystery

1914 American serial (Universal/fifteen 2-reel chapters). Daredevil Lucille Love (Grace Cunard) battles the villainous Hugo (Francis Ford) around the world from China and South Sea islands to Mexico and San Francisco as she attempts to retrieve stolen plans and clear her fiancé's name. Cunard and Ford wrote the screenplay and Ford directed this action-packed ultramystery based on a story by James Keeley. This was the film that made the pair into serial stars.

Lupin, Arsène

Arsène Lupin was a gentleman thief, the prince of French burglars, who delighted in deceiving people and disguising himself. Lupin, the creation of French author Maurice Leblanc, made his first appearance in print in 1905 in the magazine *Je Sais Tout*. His film career began in France in 1909 but soon spread around the world; silent movies about him were produced in six other countries including England, Hungary, Italy, Germany, Japan and the USA. For the films see below and *Arsène Lupin, Arsène Lupin contra Sherlock Holmes, Arsène Lupin contre Ganimard, Arsène Lupin's Last Adventure, Chairo no-Onna, 813, The Gentleman Burglar, Lupin the Gentleman Burglar, The Teeth of the Tiger* and *Le Voleur mondain*.

Lupin the Gentleman Burglar

1914 Italian film (Pasquali/3 reels). This was the American release title of a film shown in Italy as *La redenzione di Raffles* (The Redemption of Raffles) with Ubaldo Maria Del Colle playing Raffles rather than the French master thief Arsène Lupin. Confusing but possible in the silent era simply by altering the intertitles. (See Lupin, Arsène for details about the character and a listing of the other films in which he appeared.)

Luring Lips

1921 American film (Univesal/5 reels) based on the story "The Gossamer Web" by John A. Moroso. Bank teller Dave Martin (Darrel Foss) marries Adele Martin (Edith Roberts), secretary to office manager Frederick Vibart (Ramsey Wallace). He is convicted of stealing $50,000 from the bank and sent to jail. He believe Adele is having an affair with Vibart and rushes to confront them when freed. Adele, however, has simply been luring him until she gained evidence that he stole the money. George Hively wrote the screenplay and King Baggot directed.

Luring Shadows

1920 American film (Catholic Art Association/7 reels) based on a story by Condé B. Pallen and O. E. Goebel who wrote the screenplay together. Bank treasurer J. H. Waring is murdered in his library and securities are missing. The butler is the main suspect but Waring's daughter Florence is also under suspicion. Dr. Barton arranges a séance to find the murderer but it goes wrong and he betrays his own guilt. Joseph Levering directed.

Mabuse, Dr.

The power mad master criminal Dr. Mabuse, the creation of German author Norbert Jacques, was featured in three novels and three films directed by Fritz Lang He was introduced in the 1920 novel *Dr. Mabuse, der Spieler* published in English as *Dr. Mabuse, Master of Mystery*. It provided the basis for Fritz Lang's silent masterpiece *Dr. Mabuse the Gambler*. The made doctor plans to take over the city of Berlin first and eventually gain control of the whole the world. Lang made two other Mabuse films in the sound era and films by other directors featuring Mabuse continue to be made in Germany.

A Macaroni Sleuth

1917 American comedy short (Nestor Film/2 reels) starring Eddie Lyons and Lee Moran who wrote the screenplay together. The supporting cast included Edith Roberts Harry Nolan and Jane Bernoudy Louis Chaudet directed.

Mack, Madelyn

Miss Madelyn Mack was one of the first notable woman detectives in crime fiction. Two of her adventures were filmed by the Kalem studio in 1914 and 1914 with Alice Joyce as Mack. Her adventures were written by Hugh C. Weir and published in book form in 1914 as *Miss Madelyn Mack, Detective* with photos of Joyce in the films. The stories in the book are not the same as the ones filmed so Weir may have created the character for Kalem and written the other stories afterwards. The films were *The Riddle of the Green Umbrella*, which involves a poisoned needle in a college town, and *The Riddle of the Tin Soldier,* which involves the kidnapping of a child.

The Mad Doctor (Šílený lékař)

1920 Czechoslovakian film (Poja Film/5 reels) based on detective stories by Alfons Bohumil Šťastny. Detective Harry Gordon (Jaroslav Hurt) tracks down crazy Dr. John Smith (Karel Železnský) who has been killing people while making weird experiments. Gordon is aided by bank clerk Maud (Laura Železnská) who has fallen in love with a man destined to be the doctor's next victim. Drahoš Železnský directed, K. Sohard wrote the screenplay and Svatopluk Innemann was the cinematographer.

Madame Sphinx

1918 American film (Triangle/5 reels) based on a story by Raymond L. Schrock. Celeste (Alma Rubens) turns detective to investigate the murder of her guardian Henri Du Bois (Frank MacQuarrie). She finds a cuff link near the scene of the crime with a sphinx engraved on it and eventually locates a man (Wallace McDonald) wearing a tie pin with an identical sphinx. She has him arrested but he turns out to be the missing son of her guardian. The real murderer is a suitor she had rejected so she decides to gives up detecting. Lanier Bartlett wrote the screenplay and Thomas N. Heffron directed.

A Madonna of the Cells

1925 British film (Stoll/2 reels) based on a story by Morley Roberts, an episode in the second series of *Thrilling Stories from the Strand*. The cast included Betty Faire, Fred Paul and Moore Mariott. Hugh Croise wrote the screenplay and Fred Paul directed.

The Maelstrom

1917 American film (Vitagraph/5 reels) Based on the 1916 novel *The Maelstrom* by Frank Froest. Jimmie Hallet (Earle Williams) is given an address by as girl he meets in the fog, goes to it, is knocked out and awakes next

Alice Joyce as detective Madelyn Mack recalls the butler and his connection to the riddle.

to dead body. It turns out to be the father of the girl. She is Peggy Greye-Stratton (Dorothy Kelly) and she leads him a merry chase next sending to the house of Gwennie Lyne (Julia Swayne Gordon) where he falls through a trapdoor. He finally discovers she is trying to protect her brother who is in the clutches of a gang head by Ling (Denton Vane) whose henchmen were the murders. Garfield Thompson and Edward J. Montagne wrote the screenplay and Paul Scardon directed.

Main de fer (Iron Hand)

1912–1913 French series written and directed by Léonce Perret and describing the continuing conflicts between Inspector Necker (Émile Keppens), nicknamed Main de Fer (Iron Hand), and various villains played by Léonce Perret. The glamour supporting cast included Yvette Andreyor, Manette Simonet and Suzanne Grandais The three films in the series were *Main de fer*, *Main de fer contre la Bande aux Gant Blancs* and *L'Evasion de forçat de Croze*.

Main de fer (Iron Hand)

1912 French film (Gaumont/2 reels) directed by Léonce Perret. Spy Rizzio (Perrett) plans to steal secret documents from a safe at a villa in Villefranche, the home of Admiral Nyord (Maurice Luguet) and his daughter Yvette (Yvette Andreyor), Inspector Necker (Émile Keppens) known as Main de Fer (Iron Hand) learns of the plan and sets out stop him. Unfortunately he is captured and tied to a train track. He escapes but the robbery succeeds. The secret, documents, however, were spirited away the daughter who flees with them to the admiral's boat. Prints survive in archives.

Main de fer contre la Bande aux Gant Blancs (Iron Hand vs. the White Gloves Gang)

1913 French film (Gaumont/2 reels) written and directed by Léonce Perret. Perret plays Baron de Croze, the leader of a gang of jewel thieves, being pursued by Inspector Necker (Émile Keppens), known as Main de fer. Necker gets chloroformed and captured by the gang but is able to escape with the help of the baron's mistress Nini (Manette Simonet) He taps her phones, learns of gang plans and turns the tables on them. Prints survive in archives.

The Man Behind the Curtain

1916 American film (Vitagraph/5 reels). Edna Hall (Lillian Walker) has to turn detective to clear herself of a murder charge. The wealthy Mrs. Stanhope is killed minutes before she arrives for a job interview and a man behind a curtain drops a dagger at her feet. She flees to another town and eventually gets married. Her husband, it turns out, is Mrs. Stanhope's son and he thinks the woman who visited his mother killed her. To prove her innocence Edna begins investigating the mystery of the man behind the curtain and eventually traps him. Minnie Krakauer wrote the screenplay and Courtlandt J. Van Deusen directed. The *Variety* critic thought Lillian Walker did a good job in the role.

The Man from Beyond

1922 American film (Houdini Picture Corp/7 reels) based on a story by Harry Houdini who stars. He plays a man who has been frozen in a block of Arctic ice for 100 years and brought back to life. Despite the fantasy trappings, Houdini once again sets to work as an investigator. He has to find the missing father of a woman (Nita Naldi) who is the reincarnation of his long-ago love. Naturally he has some thrilling escapes culminating in an amazing rescue of Naldi atop Niagara Falls. Coolidge Streeter wrote the screenplay and Burton King directed. The film has been preserved by the Library of Congress and is on DVD.

The Man from Nowhere

1916 American film (Universal-Red Feather Photoplays/5 reels) based on a novel by Victor Bridges. James Herron (King Baggot) is sent to prison for killing his sister Betty (Irene Hunt) though the real murderer was Dorenzo (Joseph Granby). He becomes a trustee and is sent undercover to expose a card sharp who turns out to be Dorenzo. They have a duel and Dorenzo confesses he killed Betty just before he dies. William H. Clifford wrote the screenplay and Henry Otto directed.

The Man from Painted Post

1917 American film (Artcraft/5 reels) based on the 1916 story "Silver Slippers" by Jackson Gregory published in *Adventure Magazine*. Detective "Fancy Jim" Sherwood (Douglas Fairbanks) is hired to find out who is stealing cattle from a ranch. He goes to the ranch disguised as a dude and discovers that "Bull" Madden (Frank Campeau) is the rustler boss. When Madden kidnaps schoolteacher Jane Forbes (Eileen Percy), Sherwood drops his cover, rescues Jane and arrests Madden. Douglas Fairbanks wrote the screenplay and Joseph Henabery directed.

The Man Hunt

1916 American film (Vitagraph/3 reels) based on the 1907 story "The Man Hunt" by mystery writer Arthur Cheyney Train published in *The Saturday Evening Post* and the collection *Mortmain*. Fellow mystery writer Joseph Gollomb wrote the screenplay and Paul Scardon directed. The cast included James Morrison, Robert Gaillord, Raymond Walburn, Billy Billings, F.A. Turner and Marguerite Blake.

The Man on Watch

1915 American film (Kalem/2 reels), an episode in the detective series *Mysteries of the Grand Hotel*. This episode revolves around the theft of a silver service from the Grand Hotel. The silver was intended for an American. battleship so a navy detective investigates. James W. Horne directed and Hamilton Smith wrote the screenplay.

The Man Who Bought London

1916 British film (Windsor/5 reels) based on a novel by Edgar Wallace who wrote the screenplay. A brother tries to kill his sister so he can inherit the City of London which his billionaire father has just bought. The stars included E. J Arundel, Evelyn Boucher, Roy Travers and Reginald Fox. F. Martin Thornton directed.

The Man Who Changed His Name

1928 British film (British Lion/7 reels) based on a play by Edgar Wallace. The unfaithful wife of a millionaire thinks he is a murderer but it a ruse to prevent her elopement. Stewart Rome played the millionaire and Betty Faire was his wife. Kathleen Hayden wrote the screenplay and A. V. Bramble directed. Remade as a sound film in 1934.

Stewart Rome plays a tricky millionaire in *The Man Who Changed His Name*.

The Man Who Vanished

1914 American film (Edison/1 reel), one of five films in the *Felix Boyd* series based on a private eye created by Scott Campbell. Boyd is a street fighter like Nick Carter with a brilliant mind like Sherlock Holmes. Robert Conness starred with support from Robert Kegerreis, Yale Boss and Bigelow Cooper-. Langdon West directed. (See Boyd, Felix for other films.)

The Man with the Twisted Lip

1921 British film (Stoll/2 reels), an episode in the *Adventures of Sherlock Holmes* series based on a story by Sir Arthur Conan Doyle.

Holmes prove that a beggar with a twisted lip is not a murderer because he is actually that man in disguise. Eille Norwood portrays Holmes with Hubert Willis as Dr. Watson. William J. Elliot wrote the script and Maurice Elvey directed. A print of this film survives at the BFI archive.

A Manhattan Knight

1920 American film (Fox/5 reels) based on Gelett Burgess's novel *Find The Woman*. John Fenton (George Walsh) dodges a police raid by ducking into an apartment where Belle Charmion (Virginia Hammond) is standing over the body of a man who has shot himself. She says he is her brother who he stole jewels from his uncle and was afraid of being captured. They take the brother to his uncle's home to recover and Fenton returns to get the jewels. The family butler, who belongs to an underworld gang, tips off friends who try steal the jewels but Fenton recovers them and all ends well. George A. Beranger directed and wrote the screenplay with Paul H. Sloane.

Der Mann im Keller (The Man in the Cellar)

1914 German film (Continental Kunstfilm/4 reels) featuring the "American" detective Stuart Webbs played by Ernst Reicher. This was the second film in the long-running Webbs series. In this one he starts off by investigating mysterious sounds from a cellar and ends up trapping a gang of war criminals. He has to wear three different disguises to do it. Joe May directed, Ernst Reicher wrote the screenplay and Max Fassbender was the cinematographer. Print survives in a film archive. See Webbs, Joe for other films.

The Mark of Cain

1917 American film (Pathé/5 reels) based on a story by Carolyn Wells. Kane Langdon (Antonio Moreno) is accused of murdering Trowbridge (J. H. Gilmour) but Trowbridge's daughter Alice (Mrs. Vernon Castle) is convinced of his innocence. They begin to investigate and discover that Judge Hoyt (John Sainpolis) killed him after forging his will. The judge breaks down and confesses. George Fitzmaurice directed and Philip Bartholomae wrote the screenplay.

The Mark of the Frog

1928 American serial (Pathé/ten 2-reel chapters) based on Edgar Wallace's 1925 novel *The Fellowship of the Frog* with screenplay adaptation by Wallace. The masked and villainous Frog has built a crime empire in New York City with a million dollars from a robbery, his followers branded with the mark of the Frog. Then, after twenty years, his former partner returns for his share of the loot and heroic Donald Reed sets out to unmask the Frog while enjoying the company of Margaret Morris. Arch B. Heath directed. The chapters are titled *The Gas Attack, Decoyed, The Jail Delivery, Triple Vengeance, The Enemy Within, Cross Fire, Framed, A Life at Stake, A Race with Death* and *Paying the Penalty*.

La Maschera che sanguina (The Mask that Bleeds)

1914 Italian film (Pasquali Films/3 reels). Two clever detectives investigate the kidnapping of a banker and track down the gang responsible. Pier Angelo Mazzalotti directed the cast headed by Alberto O. Capozzi, Giuseppe Majone Diaz, Suzanne De Labroy and Leo Ragusi.

The Master Cracksman

1914 American film (Progress Motion Picture Co./6 reels) based on the play *The Master Cracksman* by Harry Carey who wrote the screenplay and directed. Detective Dan McRae (Herbert Russell) is hired by gem merchant Peter J. Martin (E. A. Locke) to protect a valuable diamond at a party. He is knocked out by the master thief Gentleman Joe (Harry Carey) who impersonates him at the event. Things go wrong, however, and Martin's nephew Robert Kendall (Louis Morrell) ends up stealing the diamond and killing Martin. Joe sees this happen and intervenes when Martin's son Harold is charged with the murder. He gets him to confess and returns the diamond to the detective. The film was re-issued by Alliance in 1915 as *The Martin Mystery* and by Excel Pictures in 1920 as *The Square Shooter*.

The Master Crook

1913/1914 British series (British & Colonial/three 3-reel films) about an eccentric master criminal known as the Master Crook who seems to get into a lot of difficulties while committing his robberies. In his final adventure he even has to become a detective (see below).

The Master Crook

1913 British film (British & Colonial/3 reels). The Master Crook returns stolen gems after a blind girl frees him from a sewer in which a gang has tied him upside down. Arthur Finn played the crook, Mary Pickering was the blind girl and Harry Lorraine, Bert Berry and Jack Jarman were the gang members. Charles Weston directed.

The Master Crook Outwitted by a Child

1914 British film (British & Colonial/3 reels). The Master Crook plants stolen diamonds on an orphan fruit-seller but the child outwits him with the help of a detective. Ernest G. Batley directed and played the crook, Dorothy Batley was the child and Ethel Bracewell was the girl.

The Master Crook Turns Detective

1914 British film (British & Colonial/3 reels). The Master Crook is framed for stealing a necklace but he wins it back at a game of roulette. Ernest G. Batley, who also directed the film, played the crook with Ethel Bracewell as the girl.

Master Cupid, Detective

1911 film (Essanay/1 reel). Presumably a romantic comedy but details not available.

The Master Key

1914 American thrill-a-minute serial (Universal/fifteen 2-reel chapters) based on a novel by John Fleming Wilson. The master key is a poor gold mine and a clue to the location of a rich gold mine. Ruth (Ella Hall) has to battle villainous Harry Wilkerson (Harry Carter)

Villains attempt to abduct Ruth (Ella Hall) in the serial *The Master Key*.

for both with the help of boyfriend John Dore (Robert Leonard). The ultimate clue is buried in a sunken ship. Calder Johnson wrote the screenplay and Robert Leonard directed. The episodes are titled *Gold Madness, A Shipwreck and Wrecked Hopes, The Ghost Appears, Over the Divide, The Lost Vein, Wilkerson Strikes, The Battle in the Dark, The Struggle on the Roof, Arrested for Murder, The Fight for the Mine, The Secret of the Chest, The Quest for the Idol, A Queer Alliance, The God Takes Toll* and *Fate Unlocks the Doors*.

The Master Mystery

1919 American serial (Rolfe Photoplays/fifteen 2-reel episodes) based on a story by Arthur B. Reeve who wrote the screenplay with Charles Logue. Justice Department detective Quentin Locke (Harry Houdini) investigates a cartel protected by a dangerous giant robot wielding a gas weapon that creates the "Madagascar Madness." He has to escape (miraculously) from some fiendish traps involving barbed wire, electric chairs, torture chambers, runaway elevators and underwater confinement. He does it with panache. Floyd Buckley played Q the Automaton (the robot), Marguerite Marsh was Eva Brent, Ruth Stonehouse was Zita Dane and Edna Britton was De Luxe Dora. Harry Grossman and Burton L. King directed. The serial episodes are titled *Living Death, The Iron Terror, The Water Peril, The Test, The Chemist's Shop, The Mad Genius,*

Detective Quentin Locke (Harry Houdini) has to cope with a killer robot in the serial *The Master Mystery*.

Barbed Wire, The Challenge, The Madagascar Madness, The Binding Ring, The Net, The Death Noose, The Flash of Death, The Tangled Web and *Bound at Last or The Unmasking of the Automaton*. The UCLA Film and Television Archive has preserved the serial which is on DVD.

The Master Rogue

1914 American film (Kalem/2 reels) with George Melford, Marin Sais, James H. Horne, Edward Clisbee and William West. George Melford directed.

The Master Rogues of Europe

1915 American film (Universal/3 reels). The rogues in this film are a man and woman planning to rob the safe of the woman's husband. Their plan is overheard by an inventor passing by their house so they grab him and dump him into a nearby lake. As he is wearing his latest invention, a "swimming vest," he survives handily and gets the police to arrest the roguish duo. The *Variety* critic panned the films saying it "drops with a sickenen thud."

Max, Gaston

Gaston Max of the Paris Police, Sax Rohmer's dapper French detective reputed to be "the greatest criminal investigator in Europe," appeared in four novels and six radio plays. He made his first appearance in 1915 in the serial *The Yellow Claw* in *Lippincott's Magazine* where he was introduced in a chapter titled "Presenting M. Gaston Max." The other Max novels were *The Golden Scorpion* (1919). *The Day the World Ended* (1930) and *Seven Sins* (1944). *The Yellow Claw* was filmed in England in 1921.

The Mazarin Stone

1923 British film (Stoll/2 reels), an episode in the *Last Adventures of Sherlock Holmes* series based on a story by Sir Arthur Conan Doyle. Sherlock Holmes solves the mystery of the theft of the Mazarin stone. Eille Norwood portrays Holmes with Hubert Willis as Dr. Watson. Alfred Moise was the cinematographer and George Ridgewell wrote the adaptation and directed. Print survives at BFI archive.

McGuirk, the Sleuth

1912 American comedy (Crystal Film-Universal/1 reel) starring Pearl White and

Chester Barnett plays an incompetent detective in the comedy *McGuirk the Sleuth.*

Chester Barnett. McGuirk joins a fake detective agency and sets out to detect a crime. When he hears Percy swearing vengeance, he thinks he has found a criminal but Percy is merely upset because he loves Birdie and her father won't let them marry. McGuirk follows Percy and is soon in deep trouble. Phillips Smalley directed. White and Barnett starred in a series of Crystal comedies.

Medicine Bend

1916 American film (Mutual Star /5 reels) based on the second half of Frank Spearman's novel *Whispering Smith*. J. P. McGowan played railroad detective Smith and directed. Smith is reluctant to arrest Sinclair (Paul C. Hurst) for robbing trains because of his love for Sinclair's wife Marian (Helen Holmes). Sinclair is shot by a posse member when he attempts to kill Smith who is now able to marry Marian.

Melody of Death

1922 British film (Stoll/5 reels) based on the 1915 novel *Melody of Death* by Edgar Wallace. A husband sets out to rescued his kidnapped wife and retrieve a valuable jewel. Philip Anthony starred with support from Enid R. Reed, Dick Sutherd and H Agar Lyons. Leslie Howard Gordon wrote the screenplay and F. Martin Thornton directed.

Melting Millions

1917 American serial (Pathé/ten 2-reel chapters). Heiress Allene Ray attempt to gain possession of her inheritance but the villainous E. H. Calvert plots to get the loot himself. She gets help from an heroic lieutenant (Walter Miller) and a mysterious stranger for ten not-very-exciting episodes titled *A Shot in the Dark, Perilous Waters, The Fatal Attack, The Heiress of Craghaven, The Hidden Harbor, A Strange Voyage, The Mysterious Prisoner, The Imposter, The Spy* and *Exposed*.

The Menace of the Mute

1915 American film (5 reels) based on the story "The Menace of the Mute" by John Thomas McIntyre in *Ashton-Kirk: Investigator*. Ashton-Kirk is asked by Edyth Vail (Louise Rutter) to investigate the murder of David Hume (Sheldon Lewis). She fears her fiancé Allen Morris (William Harrigan) may have done it as he visited the deceased on the night of the murder. He didn't, of course, and Ashton-Kirk traps the real killers, one of whom is a mute. See Ashton-Kirk for other films.

The Metzer Murder Mystery

1917 American film (Monmouth/2 reels), an episode in the serial *Jimmy Dale Alias the Grey Seal*) based on stories by Frank L Packard. Socialite Jimmy Dale, secretly the crime fighter known as The Grey Seal, is an urban Robin Hood. In this episode he solves the mystery of the Metzer murder. Mildred Considine wrote the screenplay and McRae Webster directed.

Mickey the Detective

1928 American comedy (Larry Darmour Productions/2 reels) starring Mickey McGuire (Mickey Rooney) as the detective. Billy Barty played Mickey's brother and Delia Bogard was tomboy Taylor. Joseph Basil, E.V. Durling and Fontaine Fox wrote the screenplay and Albert Herman directed.

The Microscope Mystery

1916 American film (Triangle/5 reels). A scientific detective, actually a doctor, uses a microscope to solve a murder mystery. Wealthy hypochondriac Ira Dayton (F. A. Turner) is tricked into signing a $10,000 check by a quack doctor (Pomeroy Cannon). Dayton's daughter Jessie (Constance Talmadge) goes to the quack to demand the return of money and while they argue he is shot. She is tried for his murder but the local doctor (Wilfred Lucas) analyzes the gun with a microscope and proves the shooter was a consumptive. Ira's consumptive assistant Jud (Monte Blue) confesses and Jessie is freed. William E. Wing wrote the screenplay and Paul Powell directed.

A Midget Sherlock Holmes

1912 American comedy (Pathé Frères/1 reel), a parody of the Sherlock Holmes films.

The Midnight Ace

1928 American black cast film (Dunbar Film/7 reels) based on a story by Jack Harrison who also wrote the screenplay. A master criminal known as The Midnight Ace (A. B. De Comathiere) leaves ace of spades playing cards as signatures at the scenes of his crimes. He is loved by a young girl who does not know that he is married. When a detective gives her this information, she goes to the Ace's house just in time to save his wife's life. The Ace is captured and killed while trying to escape. The cast included Mabel Kelly, Susie Sutton, Oscar Roy Dugas, Walter Cornick, Roberta Brown and Bessie Givens. This was the first production of a Pittsburgh company founded by Swan Micheaux, the brother of pioneer African-American filmmaker Oscar Micheaux. Director John H Wade was black but most of the company executives were white.

A Midnight Adventure

1928 American film (Rayart Pictures/6 reels) based on a story by Arthur Hoerl. Guests as a country mansion suspect each other when a man is murdered at midnight. The women are the chief suspects as several had affairs with him before they were married and had been blackmailed. Jeanne Wentworth (Edna Murphy) is engaged to the district attorney, who thinks she may be guilty, but another admirer proves her innocence and uncovers the real killer. Duke Worne directed and Arthur Hoerl wrote the screenplay.

Midnight Faces

1926 American film (Goodwill Pictures/5 reels) takes place in one of those old houses full of mystery that pop up in many films of the silent era. This one is in the Florida Everglades and can only be reached by boat. It has been inherited by a young man (Francis X Bushman, Jr.) who is taken there by a suave attorney (Jack Perrin) who is actually a crooked swindler. The house is supposed to be empty but it quickly fills up with people including a suspicious crippled guy in a wheelchair (Charles Belcher) and a terrified woman (Kathryn McGuire) who gets kidnapped. One of them turns out to be an undercover detective who eventually arrests the bad guys. Bennett Cohn wrote and directed the film. On DVD.

Danger is everywhere in a mysterious Florida mansion in *Midnight Faces*.

Midnight Life

1928 American film (Gotham Productions/5 reels) based on the 1913 novel *The Spider's Web* by Reginald Wright Kauffman. New York police detective Jim Logan (Francis X. Bushman), seeking the man who killed a friend, discovers it is gangleader Harlan Phillips (Cosmo Kyrle Bellew). Phillips sets a trap for Logan but it backfires and it is the gangster who is shot. Adele Buffington wrote the screenplay and Scott R. Dunlap directed.

Midnight Madness

1918 American film (Bluebird Photoplays/5 reels). While robbing jewels from a case in a museum, a thief cuts his hand. Prentice Tiller (Kenneth Harlan) is dressing a cut in his hand in his hotel room when overhears Gertrude (Ruth Clifford) in the next room telephoning Molitor to whom she is to deliver some jewels. He goes to her room pretending to be Molitor but flees when the real Molitor (Harry Van Meter) arrives, also wounded in the hand. Prentice follows Molitor and Gertrude to Paris where they meet master crook Chevat (Louis Willoughby). Gertrude is almost killed but Prentice rescues her and captures the jewel gang after revealing that he is really a detective. Rupert Julian directed and Elliott J. Clawson wrote the screenplay.

The Midnight Man

1919 American serial (Universal/eighteen 2-reel chapters) starring James J. Corbett as the bane of the criminal class. As Corbett was heavyweight boxing champion at this time, the crooks really had something to fear. Kathleen O'Connor and Joseph W. Girard gave support, Harvey Gates wrote the screenplay and James W. Horne directed. The episodes, in order of release, were: *Cast Adrift, Deadly Enemies, Ten Thousand Dollars Reward, At Bay, Unmasked, The Elevator Mystery, The Electric Foe, Shadow of Fear, The Society Hold-Up, The Blazing Torch, The Death Ride, The Tunnel of Terror, A Fight to the Finish, The Jaws of Death, The Wheel of Terror, Hurled from the Heights, The Cave of Destruction* and *A Wild Finish*.

Midnight Shadows

1924 American film (Arrow Film-Dearhold/5 reels). Several people named Smith turn up for the reopening of a hotel near a goldmine where there have been robberies. Bill Smith and his woman friend are actually detectives and they eventually arrest fake mineowner J. B Smith and fake detective Harry Smith. Edmund Cobb and Florence Gilbert head the cast and Francis Ford wrote the screenplay and directed.

The Midnight Summons

1924 British film (Stoll/2 reels), an episode in *The Further Mysteries of Fu Manchu* series based on a story by Sax Rohmer Harry Agar Lyons plays Dr. Fu Manchu, Fred Paul is Nayland Smith and Humberston Wright is Dr. Petrie. Fred Paul directed and wrote the screenplay and Frank Canham was the cinematographer.

Midnight Thieves

1926 American film (Kerman Films–A. G. Steen/5 reels). English actor Herbert Rawlinson and former serial queen Grace Darmond play the thieves in this mystery film directed by John Ince. It was made by one of the lesser-known Poverty Row studios and barely noticed by critics.

Grace Darmond and Herbert Rawlinson as maid and butler watch a safe being opened in *Midnight Thieves*.

The Midnight Trail

1918 American film (Mutual Film/5 reels). Mystery loving millionaire Jack Woodford (William Russell) decides to try his hand at real-life detecting when he hears Alice Moreland (Francelia Billington), the daughter of the Rev. Robert Moreland (Sydney Deane), talking about a jewel robbery at her home. Pretending to be the investigating detective, he goes there with his valet Jasper (Harvey Clark) and becomes suspicious of Moreland's secretary Harvey Faxon (Carl Stockdale) and Alice's brother Harry (Jerome Sheler). He discovers that Alice takes jewels from the safe while sleepwalking and Faxon takes them off her when she returns to her room. He arranges for Faxon's arrest. Charles Turner Dazey wrote the screenplay and Edward Sloman directed.

The Midnight Watch

1927 American film (Rayart Pictures/6 reels). Bob Breemer (Roy Stewart), college student and part-time detective, sets out to prove that his sweetheart Rose (Mary McAllister) did not steal a pearl necklace from her employers. Chief Callahan (David Torrence) assigns him the boring midnight watch but Bob uses it to discover the real thief, an underworld friend of Callahan's. Trem Carr wrote the screenplay and Charles Hunt directed.

The Million Dollar Mystery

1914 American serial (Thanouser/twenty-three 2-reel chapters) based on a novel by Harold MacGrath. The Black Hundred Society, headed by villain Braine (Frank Farrington), and evil Countess Olga (Marguerite Snow), attempt to steal one million dollars from heroine Florence (Florence La Badie). She gets help from newspaperman Jim (James Cruze) and survives several attempts to murder her. Lloyd Lonergan wrote the screenplay and Howell Hansel directed. The chapter titles, which outline the plot, were *The Airship in the Night, The False Friend, A Leap in the Dark, The Top Floor Flat, The Battle at the Bottom of the Sea, The Coaching Party of the Countess, The Doom of the Auto Bandits, The Wiles of a Woman, The Leap from an Ocean Liner, Unknown, In the Path of the Fast Express, The Elusive Treasure Box, The Secret Agent from Russia, Tracked by the Secret Service, The Borrowed Hydroplane, Drawn into the Quicksand, A Battle of Wits, Trapped by Flames, The Underground River, The Secret Warning, the Document out of the Treasure Box, The Waterloo of the Conspirators* and *The Mystery Solved.*

Million Dollar Mystery

1927 American film (Rayart/5 reels). A Secret Service detective (James Kirkwood) goes undercover so he can infiltrate a gang of thieves. He foils the robbery of a wealthy man and wins the love of the man's daughter (Lila Lee) after he confesses his secret identity. Arthur Hoerl wrote the screenplay and Charles Hunt directed.

Million Dollar Robbery

1914 American film (Solax/4 reels). A detective (J.W. Conway) investigates the robbery of a million dollars from the home of a banker (Harrish Ingraham). It turns out not to be the result of the banker's encounter with a hypnotist (Edwin Brandt). Pell (James O'Neil) is blamed at first but the real burglar is the butler. Claire Whitney played Daphne Pell, Fraunie Fraunholz was Roger, Vinnie Burns was the Maid, Jack Burns was the police captain and Harris Gordon was Pell's secretary. Herbert Blaché directed.

The Millionaire Baby

1915 American film (Selig/6 reels) based on the 1905 mystery novel *The Millionaire Baby* by Anna Katharine Green. The "millionaire

Florence La Badie has $1 million that others want in the popular Thanhouser serial *The Million Dollar Mystery*.

baby," a child who is heir to three fortunes, disappears. A reward of $50,000 is offered for her return, no questions asked. Investigators learn that the child's real mother is actress Valerie Carew (Grace Darmond) who gave her up for adoption as a baby. Marion (Mrs. A. C. Marston) had used the baby to win back errant husband Philo (Frederick Hand) pretending it was her child. Now that Valerie has retired from the stage she wants the child back After investigations it is discovered that Marian herself took the girl and hid her to avoid giving her up. Lawrence Marston directed and Gilson Willets wrote the screenplay.

The Miracle

1923 British film (Stoll/2 reels), an episode in the *Mystery of Fu Manchu* series based on a story by Sax Rohmer. Nayland Smith (Fred Paul) solves the case of the mysterious death of Lord Southery. A. E. Colby directed, Frank Wilson wrote the screenplay with Colby and D. P. Cooper was the cinematographer. Print survives at BFI film archive.

The Miracle Man

1919 American film (Paramount/8 reels) based on Frank L. Packard's novel *The Miracle Man* published in *Munsey's Magazine* in 1914 and the play derived from it by George M. Cohan. Con man Tom Burke (Thomas Meighan) reads about a deaf, dumb and nearly blind faith healer called the Patriarch (Joseph J. Dowling) living in a small town. He makes plans for a foolproof scam with his talented gang. Rose (Betty Compson) poses as the patriarch's long-lost niece, the Frog (Lon Chaney) pretends to have his twisted limbs healed so that he can walk again and drug addict Dope (J. M. Dumont) promotes the swindle. When a real crippled boy, inspired by the Frog's fake cure, walks for the first time, the money starts to roll in. But the atmosphere around the Patriarch affects the crooks and they begin to change for the better. George Loane Tucker wrote the screenplay and directed the film which made stars of Chaney and Compson.

Les Misérables

The most hated detective in all fiction was created by Victor Hugo in his 1862 novel *Les Misérables*. Inspector Javert was based on Vidocq, a one-time criminal who became director of the French civil police. Javert, who says "the law doesn't allow me to be merciful," devotes much of his time to tracking down Jean Valjean, a reformed convict who spent 14 years in prison for stealing a loaf of bread. Javert is eventually defeated in spirit by the goodness of Valjean. The novel was filmed eight times in the silent era. See descriptions below plus *Aa mujô— Dai ippen: Hôrô no maki* and *The Bishop's Candlesticks*.

Les Misérables

1909 American film (Edison/3 reels), the first film based on Victor Hugo's novel *Les Misérables*. It was distributed in three episodes beginning with *The Price of a Soul* in August 1909 followed by *The Ordeal* in September and *A New Life* in October.

Les Misérables

1909 American film (Vitagraph/4 reels) film based on Victor Hugo's novel *Les Misérables*. William V. Ranvous played Javert, Maurice Costello was Valjean, Helen Costello was the child Cosette and the cast included Charles Kent, Edith Storey and William Humphrey. J. Stuart Blackton directed and Eugene Mullin wrote the screenplay. The film was released in four episodes: Part I, *The Galley Slave* on September 4, 1909; Part II, *Fantine* on September 25; Part III, *Cosette* on October 23 and Part IV on November 27.

Les Misérables

1913 French film (SCAGL/4 reels) film based on Victor Hugo's novel *Les Misérables* and distributed in America by Pathé Frères. Henri Étiévant played Inspector Javert, Henri Krauss was Valjean, Maria Fromet was Cosette, Maria Ventura was Fantine, Mistinguett was Éponine, Gabriel de Gravone was Marius, Émile Mylo was Thénardier and Eugénie Nau was Madame Thénardier. Albert Capellani directed and Paul Capellani wrote the screenplay.

Convict Jean Valjean (Henri Krauss) gets ready to escape in the 1913 French version of *Les Misérables.*

Les Misérables

1917 American film (Fox/6 reels) based on Victor Hugo's novel *Les Misérables*. Hardee Kirkland played Javert, William Farnum was Valjean, George Moss was the Bishop, Gretchen Hartman was Fantine, Kittens Reichert played Cosette as a child and Jewel Carmen played her as a young woman, Harry Spingler was Marius, Dorothy Bernard was Eponine, Anthony Phillips was Gavroche, Edward Elkas was Thenardier and Mina Ross was Madame Thenardier. Frank Lloyd wrote the screenplay and directed.

Les Misérables

1922 British film (Master Films/1 reel) based on Victor Hugo's novel *Les Misérables*. This was a condensation of the novel created for the *Tense Moments with Great Authors* series. Lyn Harding played Valjean, H. B. Parkinson directed and W. C. Rowden wrote the screenplay.

Les Misérables

1925 French film (Société des Cinéromans/4 hours) based on Victor Hugo's novel *Les Misérables*. This epic version of the classic was filmed on the actual locations specified in the novel and shown in two parts over two days. Jean Toulout played Inspector Javert, Gabriel Gabrio was Valjean, Paul Jorge was Monsignor Myriel, Sandra Milovanoff was Fantine and the grown-up Cosette, Andrée Rolane was Cosette as a child, François Rozet was Marius, Charles Badiole was Gavroche, Georges Saillard was Thénardier, Renée Carl was Madame Thénardier and Suzanne Nivette was Eponine. Henri Fescourt directed from a screenplay he wrote with Arthur Bernède.

Miss Clever

Miss Clever was an "American" woman detective portrayed by Norwegian actress Ada Egede-Nissen (as "Ada Van Ehlers") in a series of German feature films produced in 1917/1918/1919 by the Egede Nissen Film Company. The four 1917 films, written by Rudolf Baron and Else Cressin and directed by Georg Alexander (who took leading roles in them), were *Ein Detektiv-Duell, Das Geheimnis der Breifmarke, Der Kampf met dem Sturmvogel* and *Der Haisschmuck*. The series resumed in 1918 with four more films and ended in 1919 with two more (titles unknown). Ada and her two sisters starred in over thirty films for the Egede Nissen Film Company.

Miss Nobody

Miss Nobody was an "American" woman detective portrayed by Senta Eichstaedt in a series of 1913 German films produced by Karl Werner for his company. They were popular with audiences who enjoyed the deductive abilities of Miss Nobody and their exciting chase sequences over rooftops and bridges. Supporting cast members included Josef Coenen, Hansi Dege, Karl Harbacher, Ernst Körner. Adele Reuter-Eichberg and Fred Selva-Goebel. The three films, directed by Willy Zeyn and written by Rudolf Del Zopp, were *Der Schwarze Diamant* (The Black Diamond), *Das Geheimnis von Chateau Richmond* (The Mystery of Castle Richmond) released in America without nationality or credits and *Die Jagd nach der Hundertpfundnote oder Die Reise um die Welt* (The Hunt for the Hundred Pound Note or Travels around the World).

Miss Raffles

1914 American film (Vitagraph/2 reels). Dorothy Kelly stars as a gentlewoman crook similar to gentleman thief Raffles in this comedy. The supporting cast included James Morrison, Denton Vane, Harry Scarborough and Mrs. E.M. Kimball. Mrs. Tom Coleman wrote the screenplay and Theodore Marston directed.

Miss Sherlock Holmes

1908 American film (Edison/625 feet). Florence Turner plays a woman detective who models herself on Sherlock Holmes. Bannister Merwyn wrote the screenplay and Edwin S. Porter directed.

Missing Daughters

1924 American film (Choice Productions/7 reels). Secret Service detective Rogers (Rockcliffe Fellowes) investigates Roche (Chester Bishop), the owner of the Golden Calf Restaurant whom he suspects of criminal activities. Eva (Eva Novak), who works for Rogers, lives with Pauline (Pauline Starke) and Eileen (Eileen Percy), Roche's secretary. All three of the girls get involved and kidnapped and have to be rescued by Rogers. William H. Clifford wrote the screenplay and directed.

The Missing Links

1916 American film (Triangle/5 reels). Detective Chris Tompkins (Robert Lawler) is hired to investigate the murder of Justice of the Peace Jasper Starr (William Higby). Henry Gaylord (Robert Harron), who recently eloped with Starr's daughter, is the chief suspect but his brother Horace (Elmer Clifton) thinks he is innocent. Tomkins finds a pair of cuff links at the crime scene and gets the real criminal to confess. Norma and Constance Talmadge also had roles in the film. Bernard McConville wrote the screenplay, Lloyd Ingraham directed and D. W. Griffith supervised the production.

Missing Millions

1922 American film (Paramount/6 reels) based on Jack Boyle's Boston Blackie stories "A Problem in Grand Larceny" and "An Answer in Grand Larceny." Boston Blackie (David Powell) and Mary Dawson (Alice Brady) steal gold being shipped to Jim Franklin (Frank Losee) because Mary wants revenge on Franklin who sent her father to prison. When the ship's purser is accused of the crime, Mary and Blackie return the gold to prove him innocent. It arrives too late to help Franklin clear his debts so he commits suicide. Joseph Henabery directed and Albert Shelby Le Vino wrote the screenplay. See also Blackie, Boston.

The Missing Three Quarter

1923 British film (Stoll/2 reels), an episode in the *Last Adventures of Sherlock Holmes* series based on a story by Sir Arthur Conan Doyle. Sherlock Holmes solves the mystery of the disappearance of a rugby player before a big game. Eille Norwood portrays Holmes with Hubert Willis as Dr. Watson. Alfred Moise was the cinematographer and George Ridgewell wrote the adaptation and directed. Print survives at BFI archive.

Mr. Bumptious, Detective

1911 American comedy (Edison/1 reel) starring John R. Cumpson as incompetent Detective Bumptious. He is hired for a case by Alice Washburn but it does not go well. Bannister Merwin wrote the screenplay and directed the film.

Mr. Hoops, the Detective

1912 American film (Comet/1 reel). No information available.

Mr. Justice Raffles

1921 British film (Hepworth/6 reels) based on Barry Perowne's 1909 novel *Mr. Justice Raffles*. The story revolves around the gentleman cracksman Raffles who is trying to help a friend foil a crooked insurer. Gerald Ames played Raffles and Lyonel Watts was Bunny. Blanche MacIntosh wrote the screenplay while Ames and Gaston Quiribet directed. See *Raffles* for other films.

Gerald Ames is Raffles in the British film *Mr. Justice Raffles*.

Mr. Wise, Investigator

1911 American film (Essanay/560 feet) staring Sidney Aisworth, Ruth Stonehouse and Victor Potel. E. Masson Hopper wrote the screenplay and directed.

A Modern Jekyll and Hyde

1913 American film (Kalem/2 reels) loosely based on Robert Louis Stevenson's 1886 novella *The Strange Case of Dr. Jekyll and Mr. Hyde*. Robert Broderick stars as the modern equivalent of Jekyll-Hyde with Irene Boyle as his sweetheart. See *Dr. Jekyll and Mr. Hyde* for other films based on the novel.

A Modern Sherlock

1917 American comedy (Triangle/1 reel), a Sherlock Holmes parody starring Eve Southern and Eddie Sutherland.

The Money Corral

1919 American film (Artcraft-Willliam S Hart Productions/5 reels) based on a story by Charles Alden Seltzer. Montana cowboy Lem Beason (William S. Hart) turns detective to help Chicago railroad magnate Gregory Collins (Winter Hall) whose vault (the 'money corral" of the title) has been robbed twice. He goes to Chicago to investigate, outwits the local gangsters and discovers that the thefts were arranged by Collins' secretary (Hershel Mayall). After being rewarded with a ranch he goes back to Montana with Rose (Jane Novak). Lambert Hillyer co-wrote the screenplay William S. Hart and directed.

Money Madness

1917 American film (Universal/5 reels) based on Frank Spearman's novel *Whispering Smith* with Charles H. Mailes playing railroad detective Whispering Smith. The detective's nephew Tom (Alfred Vosburg) asks him to investigate a bank conspiracy. He arrests the employees involved and saves the bank from ruin. The cast also included Don Bailey, M. Everett, Mary MacLaren and Eddie Polo. William Parker wrote the screenplay and Henry McRae directed.

Money to Burn

1926 mystery film (Lumas-Gotham Productions/6 reels) based on Reginald Wright Kauffman's novel *Money to Burn*. Ship doctor Dan Stone (Malcolm McGregor) knocks down a man bothering Dolores (Dorothy Devore) and mistakenly believes he killed him. He flees the ship with Dolores who is returning to the villa of her uncle Don Diego (Eric Mayne). Diego's partner Ortego (George Chesebro) offer him refuge if he will cure a mysterious patient. He discovers that the patient is an engraver held against his will, the key element in a counterfeiting ring run by Diego. Dan gets the U.S. Marine to raid the villa and arrest the crooks. James Bell Smith wrote the screenplay and Walter Lang directed.

The Monogrammed Cigarette

1910 American film (Yankee Film Company/1 reel). After her detective father is killed, a young woman takes over his agency and solves the case he was working on. A monogrammed cigarette is the main clue. Harry C. Mathews directed.

Monsieur

1911 American film (Edison/1 reel) based on a story by mystery writer Thomas Hanshew, the creator of master criminal Hamilton Cleek. Marc McDermott and Miriam Nesbitt star with support from Robert Conness and Nancy Avril.

Monsieur Lecoq

1913 French film (Éclair/3 reels) based on Émile Gaboriau's novel *Monsieur Lecoq*. Detective Lecoq investigates a case of multiple murders but thinks it was justified so he lets the killer go free. Maurice Tourneur wrote and directed the film starring George Treville, Harry Baur, Jules Mondos, Maurice de Féraudy, Charles Krauss, Fernande Petit, Pauline Polaire and Henry Roussel. The film was shown in America in 1914 and led to a 1915 American remake (see below).

Monsieur Lecoq

1915 American film (Thanhouser/4 reels) based on Émile Gaboriau's novel *Monsieur Lecoq*. It was written and directed by Maurice Tourneur who filmed the same story in France in 1913. Detective Lecoq finds a man with a revolver standing over dead bodies in an inn and has him arrested. He deduces that a woman and a lame man were there earlier and gets the suspect released so he can follow him. He learns that he is a duke who followed his wife to the inn where he learned she was being blackmailed. When the blackmailers grabbed her, the duke shot them. To save the duke from further disgrace for what Lecoq considers a justified crime, he destroys the evidence. William Morris played Lecoq, Alphonse Ethier was the Duke, Florence LaBadie was the Duchess and Julia Blanc was Mother Chupin.

The Monster

1925 American film (MGM/7 reels) based on the 1922 play *The Monster* by Crane Wilbur. Johnny (Johnny Arthur), who's just received a detective diploma from a correspondence school, investigates the disappearance of his boss Watson. He learns that he was kidnapped by mad Dr. Ziska (Lon Chaney) who plans to use him in a weird experiment in his sanitarium. Ziska captures Johnny and Watson's daughter Betty (Gertrude Olmsted) but Johnny escapes and brings the police in time to save Betty. Willard Mack and Albert Kenyon wrote the screenplay and Roland West directed.

The Moon Diamond

1926 British film (FHC Productions/2 reels), an episode in the series *Inscrutable Drew, Investigator* featuring Henry Ainley as private detective Victor Drew. In this episode Drew and his assistant Dracos investigate the theft of the jewel known as the Moon Diamond. Elliot Stannard wrote the screenplay and A. E. Coleby directed.

The Moonstone

Wilkie Collins' novel *The Moonstone* (1868) features one of the first important detectives in English literature, Sergeant Cuff. He is called to investigate the theft of a giant yellow diamond that has disappeared from the room of Rachel Verinder who has just inherited it. The diamond, which had been stolen from the Temple of the Moon in India, is reputed to bring bad luck to all who possess it. Three priests from the Temple of the Moon have come to England. They kill the man who stole it and they now seek the gem itself. The novel was filmed four times in the silent era. See below and *The Quest of the Sacred Jewel*.

The Moonstone

1909 American film (Selig Polyscope/1 reel) based on Wilkie Collins' novel *The Moonstone*. A police detective investigates the theft of a valuable diamond.

The Moonstone

1911 American film (Urban Production/1 reel) based on Wilkie Collins' novel *The Moonstone*. A priceless diamond is stolen and a police detective is asked to investigate.

The Moonstone

1915 American film (World Film/5 reels). based on Wilkie Collins' novel *The Moonstone*. A valuable diamond mysteriously disappears. Sergeant Cuff was eliminated from the plot and *Variety* said the film was too mysterious to be understood. Elaine Hammerstein plays Rachel Verinder, Eugene O'Brien is Franklin Blake, William Rosell is Godfrey White and Ruth Findlay is Rosanna Spearman. Frank Crane directed from a screenplay by E. M. Ingleton.

Le Mort qui tue (The Dead Man Who Kills)

1913 French serial (Gaumont/90 minutes in six 1-reel chapters) written and directed by Louis Feuillade and based on the 1911 Fantômas novel *Le Mort qui Tue*. This is the third serial in the Fantômas series. Detective Juve and reporter Fandor survive Fantômas's attempt to dynamite them and are able to renew their chase after the master criminal. In this series he continues his robbing and killing ways and even creates fake fingerprints with a glove made of human skin. At the end Juve and Fandor think they have finally trapped the elusive crook but he vanishes through a secret wall panel. René Navarre plays Fantômas, Bréon is Detective Juve, George Melchior is Fandor and Renée Carl is Fantômas's lover Lady Beltham. Guérin was the cinematographer. On DVD. See also *Fantômas*.

Mortmain

1915 American film (Vitagraph/5 reel) based on the novel *Mortmain* by Arthur Cheyney Train serialized in *The Saturday Evening Post* in 1906 and published in book form in 1907. Musician Mortmain (Robert Edeson) is accused of murdering banker Russell who has made him bankrupt. After seeing a doctor friend graft a new paw on a cat, he is etherized by the doctor and has a new hand attached. He chokes the real murderer with his new hand and then awakes to find it was an ether dream. The murderer, who is still alive and was also bankrupted, confesses to the crime and Mortmain is free to marry Bella Forsythe (Muriel Ostriche). Marguerite Bertsch wrote the screenplay and Theodore Marston directed.

Moscow After Dark

1914–1916 Russian mystery crime series directed by Alexander Drankov. It was famous for its thrill-filled episodes and somewhat lurid titles like *The Bloody Fortnight* and *In the Claws of the Yellow Devil*. The series, strongly imitative of French crime series like *Fantômas*, was hugely popular with Russians in its time but does not seem to have traveled abroad.

Mrs. Balfame

1917 American film (Frank Powell Productions/5 reels) based on Gertrude Atherton's novel *Mrs. Balfame*. Mrs. Balfame (Nance O'Neil), married to a brutal drunk, learns about an untraceable poison from her friend Anna Steur (Anna Raines). She decides to kill her husband with it and laces his lemonade with poison just before he is to come home. She leaves the house with a revolver when she sees a man outside. The maid sees her go out with the gun so when Balfame is shot and killed, she thinks Mrs. Balfame did it. She is about to be convicted when Steur confesses on her deathbed to the killing. Frank Powell directed and wrote the screenplay.

Mrs. Plum's Pudding

1915 American comedy (Universal/5 reels). Bungling detective Lee Potts (Lee Moran) investigates the theft of the deed to a ranch belonging to Mrs. Plum (Marie Tempest) and her son Eddie (Eddie Lyons). They now have no proof of their ownership of oil found on the ranch. Mrs. Plum was to have wed Lord Burlington (W. Grahame Browne) but he asks for a postponement and leaves. Despite this development Eddie and socialite Betty Van Zant (Violet MacMillan) marry anyway. Lord Burlington returns and says he still wants to marry Mrs. Plum. She tells him the stolen documents were fakes; her oil millions are safe. Al Christie directed. First film in the *Detective Potts* series.

A Murder in Limehouse

1919 British film (Life Dramas/2 reels), an episode in the series *The Adventures of Dorcas Dene, Detective*. Dene is an actress who become a detective to earn money after her husband is blinded. Winifred Rose plays Dene and Tom Radford is her husband. George Sims wrote the screenplay and Frank Carlton directed.

Murder Scene from "King of the Detectives"

1903 American film (Biograph/75 feet) photographed by G. W. Bitzer. This is a film of a scene from Theodore Kremer's Broadway play *The King of Detectives* staged at the Star Theater in 1902 and 1903. Kremer (1871–1923) was known for melodramatic mystery plays with titles like *The Great Automobile Mystery* and *Secret Service Sam*. His 1906 play *Bertha, the Sewing Machine Girl* was filmed by Fox in 1926.

The Murders in the Rue Morgue

1914 American film (Paragon Photo Plays/4 reels) based on Edgar Allan Poe's classic tale "The Murders in the Rue Morgue" published in 1841. The arrogantly intellectual C. Austin Dupin, the first significant detective in fiction, solves a baffling locked room mystery with his powers of ratiocination. He discovers who carried out the mysterious murders in the Rue Morgue in Paris after visiting the crime scene and noticing a high window. Robert Goodman wrote the screenplay with Sol A. Rosenberg and directed. Dupin is not called a detective in the story; the word didn't exist at the time.

The Musgrave Ritual

1912 Anglo-French film (Franco British Film Company–Éclair/2 reels), an episode in the *Sherlock Holmes* series based on a story by Sir Arthur Conan Doyle. Sherlock Holmes solves a mystery revolving around the Musgrave Ritual. George Treville played Sherlock Holmes with M. Moyse as Dr. Watson and British actors in the supporting roles. Treville also directed in collaboration with Conan Doyle. See Holmes, Sherlock for other films.

The Musgrave Ritual

1922 British film (Stoll/2 reels), an episode in the *Further Adventures of Sherlock Holmes* series based on a story by Sir Arthur Conan Doyle. Sherlock Holmes solves the secret of the Musgrave Ritual. Eille Norwood portrays Holmes with Hubert Willis as Dr. Watson. George Ridgewell wrote the adaptation and directed. A print survives at the BFI archive.

My Lady Incog

1916 American film (Paramount/5 reels). Nell Carroll (Hazel Dawn) goes to work for a detective agency and gets sent to a Palm Beach hotel to pretend to be Baroness Du Passey. A gang of swindlers are cheating wealthy hotel guests and she is asked to get evidence of this. She falls in love with businessman Teddy De Veaux (Robert Cain) but faces a problem when a man claiming to be Baron Du Passy turns up. He is actually just another imposter but she doesn't know this so she flees the hotel. After giving up detective work, she decides to reconnect with Teddy as herself. William Clifford wrote the screenplay and Sidney Olcott directed.

My Lady Raffles

1914–1916 American series (Universal/eight 3-reel episodes) starring Grace Cunard as society crook Lady Raffles and Francis Ford as Phil Kelly. The series began in March 1914 with *The

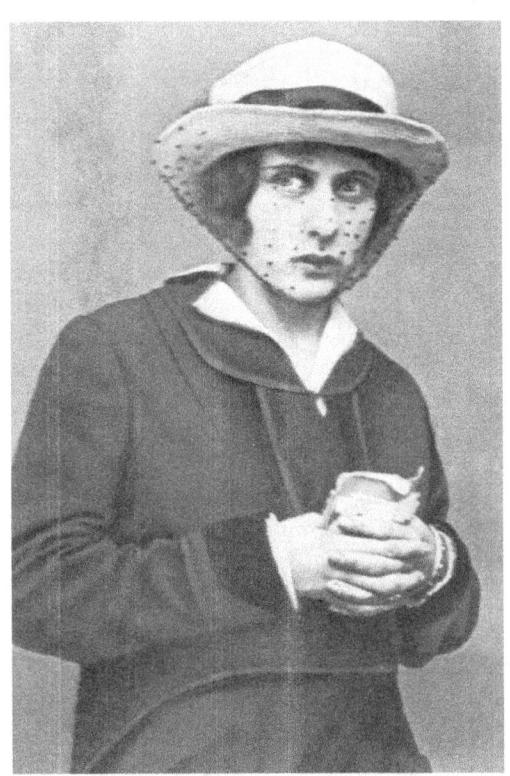

Grace Cunard is society crook Lady Raffles in *My Lady Raffles.*

Twins' Double in which Cunard played a triple role using double exposure. The other episodes were *The Return of the Twins' Double, The Mysterious Leopard Lady, The Mystery of the White Car, The Mysterious Rose, The Mystery of the Throne Room* and *Lady Raffles Returns*. Cunard wrote the screenplays and Ford directed.

My Lady's Garter

1920 American film (Paramount/5 reels) based on the 1912 novel *My Lady's Garter* by Jacques Futrelle. The famous jeweled garter of the Countess of Salisbury is stolen from the British Museum and a famous thief known as the Hawk is suspected. Secret Service detective Bruce Calhoun (Wyndham Standing) is assigned to find him and pays a visit to a country estate where he believes the Hawk may strike next. He stays on a yacht in the harbor and become involved with Helen Hamilton (Sylvia Breamer), daughter of the estate owner. Henry Van Derp (Holmes E. Herbert), also interested in Helen, accuses Calhoun of being the Hawk after some jewels are stolen. Calhoun is tracked by local detectives and besieged by the Hawk but is able to escape when his yacht is blown up and a train wrecked. He finally discovers and arrests the real Hawk. Lloyd Lonergan wrote the screenplay and Maurice Tourneur directed.

My Lady's Latchkey

1921 American film (Katherine MacDonald Pictures/6 reels) based on the satiric 1920 novel *The Second Latchkey* by Charles N. and Alice M. Williamson. Annesley Grayle (Katherine MacDonald), a young woman in quest of romantic adventure and bored with life in the House of Gloom with her aunt, agrees to pose as the wife of American Nelson Smith (Edmund Lowe). He needs a fake wife for mysterious purposes. After they marry for real, she learns that he is a jewel thief. When he's accused of stealing a diamond, she saves him by hiding it but feels maybe she should report him to the police. After she has to save him from being shot by a jealous countess, she persuades him to reform. Finis Fox wrote the screenplay and Edwin Carewe directed.

Le Mystère de la chambre jaune
(The Mystery of the Yellow Room)

1913 French film (Éclair/3 reels) based on Gaston Leroux's classic locked room mystery *Le Mystère de la chambre jaune*. Mathilde has been assaulted in a locked room and valuable papers belonging to her scientist father stolen. There seems no possible solution but Marcel Simon as the amateur detective Rouletabille solves it even when Sûréte detective Larsan is baffled. Laurence Dulc played Mathilde and Paul Escoffier was Larsan. Maurice Tourneur and Emile Chautard directed. See also *The Mystery of the Yellow Room*.

Le Mystère de la tour Eiffel
(The Mystery of the Eiffel Tower)

1927 French film (Film d'Art/7 reels) written by Alfred Machard and directed by Julien Duvivier. The Mironton Brothers are major fairground attractions but one of them is heir to a fabulous fortune. The mysterious Companions of the Antenna, headquartered in the Eiffel Tower, does not want this inheritance to take place so it creates impossible traps for the pair. Felicient Tramel plays the dual role of the Mironton Brothers with Gaston Jacquet as Sir William Dewitt and Regine Bouet as Sylvanie.

Le Mystère de la villa Mortain
(The Mystery of the Mortain Villa)

1919 French film (Éclair/5 reels), Master detective Nick Carter (Pierre Bressol) investigates the assassination of the beautiful Madame Mortain, courted by the elegant Verzé and killed while criminals were robbing her villa. Nick suspects set-daughter Ginette (Jeanne Ambroise) but eventually discovers that her jealous husband (Jean Toulut) shot her. Verzé strangles him. Etienne Michel wrote the screenplay and Pierre Bressol directed.

Le Mystère du lit blanc
(The Mystery of the White Bed)

1909 French film (Éclair/1 reel), an episode in the *Les Nouveaux Exploits de Nick Carter* series featuring master detective Nick Carter In this episode Carter has to solve a mystery about a bed. killed himself. Pierre Bressol played Nick

Carter and Victorin Jassett wrote and directed the film. Distributed in America as *The Mystery of the White Bed*.

Le Mystère du phare d'Armor (The Mystery of the Armor Lighthouse)

1919 French film (Cinematographe Harry/ 4 reels). Yvonne, the daughter of the Armor Lighthouse keeper, is courted by sailor Yvon but she fancies an American painter. He returns home when the war begins and she discovers he was really a German spy. When he returns with a group of German soldiers disguised as French sailors to blow up the lighthouse, she and Yvon stop him. With Maud Richard, Lino Manzoni and Blanchard. G Laine directed.

Les Mystères de Paris (The Mysteries of Paris)

1922 French serial (Phocea Film/twelve 3-reel chapters) based on the famous novel by Eugene Sue. The complicated plot has many mysteries mostly revolves around Rodolph, the Grand Duke of Gerolstein. He is a good man roaming the slums of Paris in disguise while he learning about the life and problems of the poor and the crimes against them. His principal opponent is the evil Lady Sarah MacGregor, once his morganatic wife and the mother of a child he does not at first know about. She is beautiful orphan Fleur-de-Marie who he adopts without knowing she is his daughter. The episodes are *Le Tapis franc, La Ferme de bouqueval, Les Justiciers. Le Ménage Pipelet, Les Suites d'un bal à l'ambassades, Misère, Le Martyre de Louise Morel, L'Etude de Maître Ferrand, L'Ile du Ravaguer, Le Maître d'école et la chouette, Celle que venge, Son altesse fleur de Marie.* There is also an American film based on the novel called *The Secrets of Paris*.

The Mysteries of the Grand Hotel

1915 American series (Kalem/twelve 2-reel episodes.) Detective stories set in grand hotels revolving around investigations of thefts and other hotel crimes. They were directed by James W. Horne and written by Hamilton Smith and the casts included True Boardman, Marin Sais. Ollie Kirkby, Tom Lingham, Frank Jonasson, Paul Hurst, Charles Cummings and William H West. The first episode of the series, *The Strangler's Cord* was released on July 21 1915. The other episodes were *The Disappearing Necklace, A Double Identity, The False Clue, The Man in Irons, The Man on Watch, The Riddle of the Rings, The Secret Code, The Substitute Jewel, Out, Under Oath, When Thieves Fall Out, The Wolf's Prey.*

The Mysterious Airman

1928 American serial (Weiss Brothers Artclass Pictures/ten 2-reel episodes) based on a story by Arthur B. Reeve who also wrote the screenplay. Jack Baker (Walter Miller), head of Baker Airways, turns detective to find who is destroying his planes. He is aided in investigating by fiancée Shirley (Eugenia Gilbert). When he learns that a gang of air pirates headed by the mysterious Pilot X are responsible, he sets out to catch them. Harry Revier directed. The episodes were titled *The Winged Avenger, The Sky Writer, The Girl Who Flew Alone, The Smoke Screen, The Air Raid, The Vampire Pilot, The Faker Pilot, The Air Raft, The Hidden Hanger* and *Mystery Pilot X*.

The Mysterious Dr. Fu Manchu

1929 American film (Paramount/8 reels) loosely based on the story "The Mysterious Dr. Fu Manchu" by Sax Rohmer. Warner Oland stars as Fu Manchu in this film made in silent and sound versions. It explains why he became evil; he wants revenge because his family was killed by allied troops during the Boxer Rebellion while he was saving the life of little Lia. When Lia grows up and becomes a beautiful woman (Jean Arthur), he forces her to help get revenge. His next victim is to be General Petrie (Charles Stevenson) but Dennis Nayland Smith (O. P. Heggie) is on his trail. Lia falls in love with the general's grandson Jack (Neil Hamilton) and is saved but Fu Manchu escapes. Rowland V. Lee directed and Florence Ryerson and Lloyd Corrigan wrote the screenplay. See *Dr. Fu Manchu* for other films.

Mysterious Goods

1923 American film (Aywon Film/5 reels). George Larkin plays a detective out West tracking down a gang that stole the plans for a valuable invention. He catches them but is nearly killed in a final desperate battle with them that takes place in a wagon about to be hit by a train. Charles R. Seeling directed.

The Mysterious Mr. Browning

1918 American film (Arrow Film–H. N. Nelson Attractions/5 reels). Wealthy Mr. Browning (Walter Miller) joins the Detroit underworld disguised as the criminal Red Harrigan and soon creates his own gang. He is eventually tracked down by a famous detective (Paul Panzer) and has to escape by diving into the Detroit River. The detective then learns that Harrigan/Browning is his own long lost brother. Sidney M Goldin wrote the screenplay and directed.

The Mysterious Mr. Tiller

1917 American film (Bluebird Photoplays/5 reels) based on the story "The Face of Prentice Teller." Detective Clara Hawthorne (Ruth Clifford) pretends to be a rich woman to trap master thief Ramon Mordant (Frank Brownlee) who has stolen a priceless necklace. She becomes involved with a crook known as the Face (Rupert Julian) who gets hold of the necklace before she does. He then turns it over to her revealing that he is actually detective Prentice Tiller. Rupert Julian directed and Elliott J. Clawson wrote the screenplay.

The Mysterious Pearl

1921 American serial (Photoplay-Berwilla/fifteen 2-reel chapters). Ben Wilson stars as a Scotland Yard detective investigating pearl thefts in this complicated story about a secret system for making pearls that requires real pearls as an ingredient. Neva Gerba plays the thief who steals the pearls for the evil man who creates the pearls and becomes known as "The Pearl" for her misdeeds. Naturally they fall in love and she turns out to be quite innocent and the evil guy gets killed by her dead father who wasn't dead at all and gave back all the pearls she stole. J. Grubb Alexander and Harvey Gates wrote the really complex screenplay and Ben Wilson co-directed with Duke Worne. The episodes are titled *The Pearl Web, The Brass Spectre, The Hand in the Fog, Four Black Pennies, Through the Door, The Bride of Hate, The Getaway, Broken Fetters, Leering Faces, The Graven Image, The Phantom Husband, The Door Between, The Living Death, The Sting of the Lash* and *The Pearl*.

The Mystery Club

1926 American film (Universal/7 reels) based on the 1920 novel *The Crimes of the Armchair Club* by Arthur Somers Roche serialized in *Hearst's* magazine. Four millionaires bet they can commit crimes without being caught by the police and form The Mystery Club for this purpose. Inspector Burke (Alfred Allen) is to be judge. After a jewel robbery, Burke is reported murdered and a note is found implicating the club. Member Dick Bernard (Matt Moore) is told by his girlfriend Nancy (Edith Roberts) that the jewels will be returned for a fee. Eventually he learns that it was all just a hoax to get the millionaires interested in supporting criminal reform. Helen Broderick and Edward J. Montagne wrote the screenplay and Herbert Blaché directed.

The Mystery Mind

1920 American serial (Supreme Pictures/fifteen 2-reel episodes) based on a story by Arthur B. Reeve who wrote the screenplay with John Grey. Dr. Dupont (J. Robert Pauline) and Dr. Sutton (Paul Panzer) head a dangerous expedition up the Orinoco River seeking mysterious poisons and possible gold. Vera (Peggy Shanon) and Violet (Violet Macmillan) are also involved as people begin to get murdered and hypnotism is employed. The episodes were *The Hypnotic Club, The Fires of Fury, The War of Wills, The Fumes of Fear, Thought Waves, A Halo of Help, The Nether World, The Mystery Mind, Dual Personality, Hounds of Hate, The Sleepwalker, The Temple of the Occult, The Blinding Ray, The Water Cure* and *The Gold of the Gods*.

The Mystery of a Hanson Cab

Fergus Hume's 1886 novel was the top selling detective novel of the nineteenth century and inspired four silent films. It revolves around the investigation of a man's murder by chloroform in a hansom cab in Melbourne,

Australia. Detective Gorby arrests Irishman Brian Fitzgerald who had been courting the same woman as the murdered man. Fitzgerald's lawyer, who believes him innocent, turns detective to discover the real killer. See three of the films below and *The Great Hansom Cab Mystery*.

The Mystery of a Hansom Cab

1911 Australian film (Amalgamated Pictures/2 reels) based on the novel by Fergus Hume. This pioneering film version of the novel was shot on location in the center of Melbourne and was given a major premiere in that city. It was directed by W.J. Lincoln.

The Mystery of a Hansom Cab

1915 British film (B & C/5 reels) based on the novel by Fergus Hume. James Dales played Brian Fitzgerald, Fay Temple was Madge Frettleby, Milton Rosmer was Mark Frettleby, A.V. Bramble was Moreland and Arthur Walcott was Oliver White. Eliot Stannard wrote the screenplay and Harold Weston directed.

The Mystery of a Hansom Cab

1925 Australian film (Pyramid Pictures/10 reels) based on the novel by Fergus Hume Arthur Shirley played the leading role of Brian Fitzgerald with Grace Glover as his fiancée Madge, Godfrey Cass, Isa Crossley, Vera Remée, Roland Stavely and Cora Warner. Shirley also wrote the screenplay and directed.

The Mystery of a Taxicab

1914 American film (Universal-Joker /2 reels) starring Louise Fazenda, Bobby Vernon, Max Asher and Harry McCoy. Allen Curtis directed.

A Mystery of Boscombe Vale

1912 Anglo-French film (Franco British Film Company–Éclair/2 reels), an episode in the *Sherlock Holmes* series based on a story by Sir Arthur Conan Doyle. Sherlock Holmes solves the mystery of the Boscombe Valley tragedy. George Treville played Sherlock Holmes with M. Moyse as Dr. Watson and British actors in the supporting roles. Treville also directed in collaboration with Conan Doyle. See Holmes, Sherlock for other films.

The Mystery of Brayton Court

1914 American film (Vitagraph/1 reel) based on a story by W.A. Tremayne. Maurice Costello stars in this mystery with co-director Robert Gaillard. The supporting cast includes Jack Brawn, Estelle Mardo, Enid Hunt and George Stevens.

The Mystery of Brudenell Court

1924 British film (Stoll/2 reels), an episode in the *Old Man in the Corner* series based on a story by Baroness Orczy. An armchair detective known as the Old Man in the Corner solves a crime while sitting in a tea shop and tells the solution to a young woman journalist. Rolf Leslie played the Old Man and Renée Wakefield was journalist Mary Hatley with supporting cast of John Hamilton and Molly Johnson. D. P. Cooper was the cinematographer and Hugh Croise wrote the adaptation and directed.

The Mystery of Carter Breene

1915 American film (Centaur Star/3 reels) starring Crane Wilbur as an undercover detective pretending to be a drug addict so he can investigate a gang that is marketing drugs. The supporting cast includes J. H. Lynch as Carter Breene, Celia Stanton as Margery Breene and Carl von Schillere as Arthur Breene. Crane Wilbur wrote the screenplay and Robert Broadwell directed. *Variety* said it was "an old school melo with the finale showing the man of mystery to be a detective."

The Mystery of Dead Man's Isle

1915 American film (Selig/2 reels) based on a story by James Oliver Curwood. Clyde Benson and Edith Johnson had the leading roles and Giles Warren directed.

The Mystery of Dr. Fu Manchu

1923 British series (Stoll/fifteen 2-reel episodes) starring Harry Agar Lyons as Fu Manchu, Fred Paul as Nayland Smith and Humberston Wright as Dr. Petrie. The supporting cast included Joan Clarkson, Frank Wilson and Pat Royale. A. E. Colby directed the films, Frank Wilson wrote the screenplays with Colby and D. P. Cooper was the cinematographer. The films in the series, most of which survive at the BFI Film Archive, are based on the original stories. They are *The Clue of the Pigtail, The Cry of the Night Hawk, The Fiery Hand, The Fungi Cellars, The Miracle, The Queen of Hearts, The Sacred Order, The Shrine of Seven, The Silver Buddha* and *The West Case*. See *Dr. Fu Manchu* for other films.

The Mystery of Dogstooth Cliff

1924 British film (Stoll/2 reels), an episode in the *Old Man in the Corner* series based on a story by Baroness Orczy. An armchair detective known as the Old Man in the Corner solves a crime while sitting in a tea shop and tells the solution to a young woman journalist. Rolf Leslie played the Old Man and Renée Wakefield was journalist Mary Hatley. D. P. Cooper was the cinematographer and Hugh Croise wrote the adaptation and directed.

The Mystery of Eagle's Cliff

1915 American film (Thanhouser/1 reel). A murder mystery solved by an infant as played by Thanhouser's child star Helen Badgely. She and her mother are ostracized by villagers who believe her father killed a man from whom he borrowed money because his locket with her picture is found in the dead man's hand at the bottom of a cliff. The mystery is solved by Helen who finds the dead man's wallet with a paper proving his innocence. With Wayne Arey as her father and Lorraine Hulin as her mother.

The Mystery of Edwin Drood

The most famous murder mystery without a solution. Charles Dickens's had completed only the first six chapters of *The Mystery of Edwin Drood* when he died in 1870 but critics think it could have been one of the great mystery novels. Many authors have tried to complete it since but no version has been judged a complete success. Edwin Drood, who was engaged to Rosa Budd, disappears. His rivals are suspected. Was Drood murdered by his uncle Jasper or is he still alive? Who is the disguised detective-like Datchery? Can the uncompleted novel be filmed? Three silent filmmakers tried (see below).

The Mystery of Edwin Drood

1909 British film (Gaumont/1 reel) based on the novel by Charles Dickens. This relatively short film features thirteen scenes set in Jasper's study, an opium den, a river bank, a country church and Bow Street. Cooper Willis played Edwin Drood, Nancy Bevington was Rosa Budd and James Annand was Neville Landless. Arthur Gilbert directed.

The Mystery of Edwin Drood

1911 American film (Urban Production/1 reel) based on the novel by Charles Dickens. Edwin Drood has disappeared Was he murdered by a rival for the hand of Rosa Budd or is he still alive?

The Mystery of Edwin Drood

1914 American film (World Film/5 reels) based on the novel by Charles Dickens. Opium addict John Jasper lusts after Rosa Budd who is engaged to his nephew Edwin Drood. Jasper throws his nephew into a lake after knocking him out but Drood is rescued by fishermen. Neville Landless is arrested for the supposed murder after being accused by Jasper. A mystery man named Datchery, who has been watching Jasper, is revealed to be Landless' sister Helena. She brings Drood out of hiding and frees her brother. Rodney Hickok played Drood, Tom Terriss was Jasper, Vinnie Burns was Rosa Budd, Paul Sterling was Neville Landless and Margaret Prussing was Helena Landless. Tom Terriss wrote the screenplay and Herbert Blaché directed.

The Mystery of Grandfather's Clock

1914 American film (Kalem/1 reel) starring Alice Joyce, George Moss, Stuart Holmes, Tom Moore and Jon E. Brennan.

The Mystery of Green Park

1914 American (?) film (Eclipse-Urban/2 reels) based on a novel by Arnodl Galopin.

The Mystery of Grayson Hall

1914 American film (Universal Éclair/2 reels) starring Fred Hearn, Edna Payne, Lindsay J. Hall and Hal Wilson.

The Mystery of Henri Villard

1915 American film (Biograph/2 reels) starring Isabel Rea, Helen Bray, William J.

Buter and Hector Sarno. George Morgan directed.

The Mystery of Mr. Bernard Brown

1920 British film (Stoll/5 reels) based on a story by E. Phillips Oppenheim. A novelist is accused of stabbing a woman's fiancé and has to turn detective to prove his innocence. With Edward Arundel, Pardoe Woodman, Clifford Heatherley, Norma Whalley and Frank E. Petley. Sinclair Hill directed and Mrs. Sydney Groome wrote the screenplay.

The Mystery of Orcival

1916 American film (Biograph/3 reels). based on Émile Gaboriau's 1867 novel *Le Crime d'Orcival*. Monsieur Lecoq investigates the murder of a countess in the village of Orcival. J. Farrell MacDonald directed the cast headed by Jack Drumier, Gretchen Hartman, Charles Hill Mailes, Jack Mulhall, G. Raymond Nye and Charles Perley. *L'Affaire d'Orcival* is based on the same book.

The Mystery of Richmond Castle (Das Geheimnis von Chateau Richmond)

1913 German film (Midgar Features–Karl Werner Film /4 reels). This film in the German *Miss Nobody* detective series was released in America in1914 without indication of nationality so it was reviewed as an American picture. Senta Eichstaedt, who played Miss Nobody, was renamed Grace Carter in the American titles. She is hired to investigate a man who has inherited Richmond Castle and discovers that he is being threatened by a secret society. She helps him outwit them by dressing in his clothes and leading the gang on a wild goose chase. The police capture the gang and all ends well. Rudolf Del Zopp wrote the German screenplay and Willy Zeyn directed.

The Mystery of Room 13

1915 American film (Edison/4 reels). June Baxter (Lillian Herbert) goes to Room 13 at a hotel to see her husband Count Rizzo (Guido Colucci) from whom she is separated. He demands money for a divorce and they struggle. June's lover Clay Foster (Marc McDermott) rescues her. The count is found dead the next morning and June is arrested but Clay claims he did it. After investigation by a newspaper reporter, the real killer is found. George Ridgwell directed and Lee Arthur wrote the screenplay.

The Mystery of Room 422

1917 American film (Kalem/1 reel), an episode in the series *Grant, Police Reporter*. Grant (George Larkin) investigates the mystery of Room 422 and gets help from Ollie Kirby and Robert Ellis. Robert Welles Ritchie wrote the screenplay and Robert Ellis directed.

The Mystery of Room 643

1914 American film (Essanay/2 reels) starring Francis X. Bushman, Gerda Holmes, Bryant Washburn and Rapley Holmes.

The Mystery of the Amsterdam Diamonds

1914 American film (Edison/1 reel), an episode involving stolen diamonds in *the Chronicles of Cleek* series written by Thomas W. Hanshew. Ben Wilson plays master criminal Hamilton Cleek, known as the "man of forty faces," and Robert Brower is his nemesis Detective Narko. Harry Beaumont and Gertrude McCoy give support and George Lessey directed.

The Mystery of the Brass Bound Chest

1917 American film (Kalem/2 reels), an episode in the serial *The Girl from Frisco* starring Marin Sais and True Boardman.

The Mystery of the Bride in White

1908 American film (Kalem/1 reel) written by Kalem star Gene Gautier, who plays the mysterious bride, and directed by Sidney Olcott.

The Mystery of the Burning Freight

1917 American film (Kalem/1 reel), an episode in the railroad series *A Daughter of Daring* in which Helen Gibson solved mysteries, fought villains, demonstrated derring-do and worked with detectives. The supporting cast included Lloyd Whitlock, George

Routh and George A. Williams. Herman A. Blackman wrote the screenplay and Scott Sidney directed.

The Mystery of the Counterfeit Tickets

1917 American film (Signal Films-Mutual/2 reels), the final episode of the series *The Railroad Raiders*. Helen Holmes and Leo Maloney solve the mystery of how her father was unjustly convicted of stealing money from the railroad. J. P. McGowand directed and Ford Beebe wrote the screenplay.

The Mystery of the Diamond Belt

1914 British film (Davidson/3 reels), one of a seven film series featuring master detective Sexton Blake written and directed by Charles Raymond. A diamond belt is stolen by the use of a trick table in a hotel after a young woman is forced to provide information by her criminal father. Sexton Blake is called to investigate and succeeds in catching the crooks with the help of his dog Pedro but not before getting thrown into a dungeon for awhile. Philip Kay played Blake with Lewis Carlton as his assistant Tinker, Eve Balfour as Kitty the Moth and Percy Moran as Flash Harry. See Blake, Sexton for the other films.

The Mystery of the Double Cross

1917 American serial (Astra-Pathé/fifteen 2-reel chapters) based on a story by mystery writer Jacque Futrelle. Mollie King is the heroine and Leon Bary the hero of this unusual tale about a man who must marry a girl bearing the mark of the "double cross" to inherit a fortune. Villain Ralph Stuart keeps trying to kill him to prevent this but he is rescued every time by the mysterious Masked Stranger. Gilson Willets wrote the screenplay and William Parke directed. The chapters are *The Lady in Number 7, The Masked Stranger, An Hour to Live, Kidnapped, The Life Current, The Dead Come Back, Into Thin Air, The Stranger Disposes, When Jail Birds Fly, The Hole-in-the-wall, Love's Sacrifice, The Riddle of the Cross, The Face of the Stranger, The Hidden Brand* and *Mystery of the Double Cross*. On DVD.

Hero Peter Hale (Leon Bary) dives off a transatlantic liner in the Pathé serial *The Mystery of the Double Cross*.

The Mystery of the Dover Express

1914 American film (Edison/1 reel), an episode concerning a train in *the Chronicles of Cleek* series written by Thomas W. Hanshew. Ben Wilson plays master criminal Hamilton Cleek, known as the "man of forty faces," and Robert Brower is his nemesis Detective Narko. Harry Beaumont and Gertrude McCoy give support and George Lessey directed.

The Mystery of the Dutch Cheese Maker

1914 American film (2 reels), an episode in the serial *Zudora* written by Harold MacGrath and Daniel Carson. Marguerite Snow attempts to unravel a series of mysteries, acquire a fortune and avoid getting killed by evil villains. She gets help from James Cruze. Howell Hansel directed.

The Mystery of the Empty Room

1915 American film (Vitagraph/2 reels) starring Alice Lake, William Dangman, Ethel Corcoran and John Costello. Courtlandt Van Deusen directed.

The Mystery of the Fadeless Tints

1914 American film (Edison/1 reel), an episode in *the Chronicles of Cleek* series written by Thomas W. Hanshew. Ben Wilson plays "man of forty faces" Hamilton Cleek and Robert Brower is Detective Narko. George Lessey directed.

The Mystery of the Glass Tubes

1914 American film (Edison/1 reel), an in *the Chronicles of Cleek* series written by Thomas W. Hanshew. Ben Wilson plays master criminal Hamilton Cleek and Robert Brower is Detective Narko. George Lessey directed.

The Mystery of the Haunted House

1914 American film (2 reels), an episode in the serial *Zudora* written by Harold MacGrath and Daniel Carson. Marguerite Snow attempts to unravel a series of mysteries, acquire a fortune and avoid getting killed by evil villains. She gets help from James Cruze. Howell Hansen directed.

The Mystery of the Haunted Hotel

1913 American film (Thanhouser/1 reel). A visiting doctor solves the mystery of a haunted hotel in Cape May, New Jersey. After the owner's wife drowns at sea, her ghost returns to haunt the place and drives away customers. The doctor shows that the "haunting" is actually being done by the woman's daughter who had become deranged by the death of her mother. With Harry Benham, Florence LaBadie and William Russell. Lloyd F. Lornegan wrote the screenplay and Carl Gregory directed.

The Mystery of the Hidden House

1914 American film (Vitagraph/2 reels) based on a story by Amelia Rives. The cast included Margaret Gibson, Karl Formes, Alfred Vosburgh and Anne Schaefer. Ulysses Davis directed.

The Mystery of the Hindu Image

1914 American film (Majestic-Mutual/1 reel). Raoul Walsh stars with support from Nick Cage, Dark Cloud, Eagle Eye and Richard Cummings.

The Mystery of the House

1915 American film (Universal/2 reels), an episode in the serial *The Black Box* based on a story by E. Phillips Oppenheim. Herbert Rawlinson stars as detective Herbert Quest who battles a master criminal while he tries to discover the secret of the black box with the help of Anna Little. Quest is a kind of scientific Sherlock Holmes.

The Mystery of the Jewel Casket

1905 American film (Biograph/1 reel) made by cinematographer G. W. Bitzer.

The Mystery of the Khaki Tunic

1924 British film (Stoll/2 reels), an episode in the *Old Man in the Corner* series based on a story by Baroness Orczy. An armchair detective known as the Old Man in the Corner solves a crime while sitting in a tea shop and tells the solution to a young woman journalist. Rolf Leslie played the Old Man and Renée Wakefield was journalist Mary Hatley. D. P. Cooper was the cinematographer and Hugh Croise wrote the adaptation and directed.

The Mystery of the Ladder of Light

1914 American film (Edison/1 reel), an episode in *the Chronicles of Cleek* series written by Thomas W. Hanshew. Ben Wilson plays master criminal Hamilton Cleek, known as the "man of forty faces," and Robert Brower is his nemesis Detective Narko. Yale Boss and John Sturgeon give support and George Lessey directed.

The Mystery of the Laughing Death

1914 American film (Edison/1 reel), an episode in *The Chronicles of Cleek* series written by Thomas W. Hanshew. Ben Wilson plays the "man of forty faces" Hamilton Cleek with Robert Brower as his enemy Detective Narko. Cora Williams and Hughie Mack gave support, Ashley Miller wrote the screen play and George Lessey directed.

The Mystery of the Leaping Fish

1916 American comedy (Triangle/2 reels) starring Douglas Fairbanks Sr. as a cocaine-addicted comic detective named Coke Enyday.

He is asked to investigate an opium smuggler and becomes involves with Bessie Love and Alma Rubens in this bizarre movie written by D. W. Griffith and Tod Browning and directed by John Emerson. On DVD.

The Mystery of the Locked Room

1915 American film (Universal-Rex/3 reels) based on a story by William Addison Lathrop. After the murder of a man in a supposedly locked room, his daughter's boy friend is suspected. Actually it is the butler who was behind the crime. Ben Wilson and Dorothy Phillips star with a supporting cast included Ned Rearson and Bert Busby, Wilson directed. *Variety* termed it "an ordinary murder mystery."

The Mystery of the Lost Cat

1913 American comedy (Solax/2 reels) starring comic Billy Quirk Quirk as detective Burstup Holmes. He is really awful as an investigator but he thinks of himself as the equivalent of Sherlock Holmes. He plays a bumbling detective who models himself on Sherlock Holmes. The supporting cast included Blanche Cornwall and Darwin Karr. Alice Guy Blaché directed.

The Mystery of the Lost Ships

1914 American film (2 reels), an episode in the serial *Zudora* written by Harold McGrath and Daniel Carson. Marguerite Snow attempts to unravel mysteries, gain a fortune and avoid getting killed. She gets help from James Cruze. Howell Hansen directed.

The Mystery of the Lost Stradivarius

1914 American film (Edison/1 reel), an episode in *the Chronicles of Cleek* series written by Thomas W. Hanshew. Ben Wilson plays the "man of forty faces" Hamilton Cleek and Robert Brower is his enemy Detective Narko. Jerome Storm and Richard Neil give support and George A Lessey directed.

The Mystery of the Man Who Slept

1915 American film (Universal-Rex/3 reels) starring Ben Wilson and Dorothy Phillips with supporting cast of Joseph Girard, Curtis Benton and Hal de Forrest.

The Mystery of the McWinter Family

1914 American film (2 reels), an episode in the serial *Zudora* written by Harold Mac-Grath and Daniel Carson (a.k.a. as *The Case of the McWinter Family*). Marguerite Snow unravels mysteries, gain a fortune and avoids getting killed. She gets help from James Cruze. Howell Hansen directed.

The Mystery of the Milk

1914 American comedy (Biograph/1 reel) based on a story by William E. Wing and directed by Mack Sennett. The film featured Eddie Dillon, Charles Avery, Kate Bruce and Clara Bracey.

A Mystery of the Mountains

1915 American film (Biograph/2 reels) with Ivan Christy, Mary Maltesta, Jack Drumier, Kate Bruce and James Furey.

The Mystery of the Octagonal Room

1914 American film (Edison/1 reel), an episode in *the Chronicles of Cleek* series written by Thomas W. Hanshew. Ben Wilson plays master criminal Hamilton Cleek, known as the "man of forty faces," and Robert Brower is his nemesis Detective Narko. Sally Crute and Joe Manning give support and George Lessey directed.

The Mystery of the Old Mill

1914 British film (Big Ben Films-Pathé/3 reels). Detective Dick Steel (H. O. Martinek) uncovers a blackmail scheme involving Kate (Ivy Montford) and Daphne (Irene Vernon). L.C. MacBean wrote the screenplay and H. O. Martinek directed.

The Mystery of the Poison Pool

1914 American film (Picture Playhouse/5 reels). African adventurer Cameron, missionary Dorothy and British police detective Walton are the main character in this murder mystery. Cameron saves Walton from a giant python in an early scene and is later rewarded when Walton saves his life even though he suspects him of murdering a visitor to a village. Dorothy finds the real killer. James Gordon, F. A. Turner and Betty Harte are the stars. *Vari-*

ety thought the early snake episode the best part of the film.

A Mystery of the Rails

1916 American film, (Kalem/1 reels), an episode in the series *The Hazards of Helen* starring Helen Gibson as the heroic railroad telegrapher who has to investigates criminal activity and fight every kind of railroad villain while leaping to and from moving trains. James Davis directed.

The Mystery of the Sea View Hotel

1914 American film Universal-Rex/2 reels) starring Ben Wilson as a detective.

The Mystery of the Sealed Art Gallery

1914 American film (Edison/1 reel), an episode in *the Chronicles of Cleek* series written by Thomas W. Hanshew. Ben Wilson plays master criminal Hamilton Cleek, known as the "man of forty faces," and Robert Brower is Detective Narko. Gertrude McCoy give support and George Lessey directed.

The Mystery of the Seven Chests

1914 American film (Selig/2 reels) based on a story by James Oliver Curwood and directed by E.A. Martin. The cast included William Stowell, Lillian Hayward and Ada Gleason.

The Mystery of the Silent Death

1915 American film (Essanay/2 reels). A villainous husband works out an evil scheme to get hold of his wife's fortune. Beverly Bayne starred as the wife in danger opposite Lester Cuneo and Albert Roscoe. Edward T. Lowe directed. *The Moving Picture World* thought it was worthy of comparison to Edgar Allan Poe.

The Mystery of the Silent Death

1928 British film (British Filmcraft/2 reels), one of a six-film series featuring master detective Sexton Blake as played by Langhorne Burton with Mickey Brantford as his assistant Tinker. The supporting cast included Roy Travers, Thelma Murray, Ray Raymond and Mrs. Fred Emney. George J. Banfield produced, Leslie Eveleigh directed and Lewis Jackson wrote the screenplay. (See Blake, Sexton for other films.)

The Mystery of the Silver Skull

1913 American film (Vitagraph/2 reels) based on a story by James Oliver Curwood. Maurice Costello stars as a detective similar to those he played in the 1-reel Lambert Chase series. Mary Charleson and L. Roger Lytton provided support while Costello and Wilfred North directed.

The Mystery of the Silver Snare

1914 American film (Edison/1 reel), an episode in *the Chronicles of Cleek* series written by Thomas W. Hanshew. Ben Wilson played master criminal Hamilton Cleek and Robert Brower was Detective Narkom. May Abbey and Gertrude McCoy gave support and George Lessey directed.

The Mystery of the "Sleeper" Trunk

1909 American film (Kalem/1 reel).

The Mystery of the Sleeping Death

1914 American film (Kalem/2 reels) Alice Joyce plays a safe cracker who get caught by millionaire Tom Moore and this causes them to fall into a deep sleep. It seems they are reincarnations of ancient Indian lovers who were cursed by a priest with the "sleeping death" as their love was forbidden. Their story is told by a modern mystic who says they can now wake up and live happily ever after. Robert Walker plays the mystic and Benjamin Ross is the priest. C. Doty Hobart wrote the script and Kenean Buel directed. A print survives at an archive.

The Mystery of the Sleeping House

1914 American film (2 reels), an episode in the serial *Zudora* written by Harold MacGrath and Daniel Carson. Marguerite Snow has to solve the mystery of the sleeping house while trying to win a fortune and avoid getting killed. She succeeds with help from James Cruze. Howell Hansen directed.

The Mystery of the Spotted Collar

1914 American film (2 reels), an episode in the serial *Zudora* written by Harold McGrath and Daniel Carson. Marguerite Snow has to solve the mystery of the spotted collar (and many others) as she tries to a fortune and avoid getting killed. She does so with help from James Cruze. Howell Hansen directed.

The Mystery of the Stolen Child

1912 American film (Vitagraph/1 reel), one of eight films featuring the Sherlock Holmes–like detective Lambert Chase. He was created for the Vitagraph Studio by writer B. R. Brooker and actor Maurice Costello who portrayed him. In this story about a stolen child, Helene Costello played the child, Clara Kimball Young was the nurse and George Cooper was the kidnapper Hazel Neason wrote the screenplay and Costello co-directed with William V. Ranous. See Chase, Lambert for other films.

The Mystery of the Stolen Jewels

1912 American film (Vitagraph/1 reel), one of eight films featuring detective Lambert Chase created for the Vitagraph Studio by writer B. R. Brooker and actor Maurice Costello. In this case Chase (Costello) finds stolen jewels hidden in a ventilator on a boat and rigs a device to tell him when the crooks come for them. Clara Kimball Young and James Young played the thieves and the cast included Kate Price and Georgia Maurice. Hazel Neason wrote the screenplay and Costello and William V. Ranous directed. A print of this film survives at the BFI film archive. See Chase, Lambert for other films.

The Mystery of the Talking Wire

1914 American film (Edison/1 reel), an episode in *the Chronicles of Cleek* series written by Thomas W. Hanshew. Ben Wilson played master criminal Hamilton Cleek, known as the "man of forty faces," and Robert Brower was his nemesis Detective Narkom. Charles Sutton and Charles Ogle gave support and George Lessey directed.

The Mystery of the Tapestry Room

1915 American film (Universal/3 reels) based on a story by George Edwardes–Hall Murdock MacQuarrie directed and played the lead role with support from Marjorie Beardsley, Kingsley Benedict and Bob Chandler. H.G. Stafford wrote the screenplay.

The Mystery of the Tea Dansant

1915 American film (Kalem/2 reels), an episode of the serial *The Girl Detective.* Ruth Roland stars as a society girl who works with the police and is able to help them solve crimes because of her society connections The supporting cast includes Cleo Ridgeley and Thomas Lilngham. Hamilton Smith wrote the screenplay, Knute Olaf Rahmn was cinematographer and James W. Horne directed.

The Mystery of the Thoroughbred

1913 French film (Pathé/1 reel), an episode in a popular tongue-in-cheek comedy series about an "American" detective named Nick Winter. In this episode Nick has a problem with a horse. Gérard Bourgeois wrote the screenplay and directed.

The Mystery of the Throne Room

1915 American film (Universal/3 reels), an episode in the *My Lady Raffles* series. Grace Cunard stars as society crook Lady Raffles with Francis Ford as Phil Kelly. Cunard wrote the screenplay and Ford directed.

The Mystery of the Torn Note

1910 American film (Lubin/1 reel). No other information available.

The Mystery of the White Car

1914 American film (Universal/3 reels), an episode in the *My Lady Raffles* series. Grace Cunard stars as society crook Lady Raffles with Francis Ford as Phil Kelly and Ernest Shields giving support. Cunard wrote the screenplay and Ford directed.

The Mystery of the Yellow Room
(Le Mystère de la chambre jaune)

Gaston Leroux's classic locked room mystery *Le Mystère de la chambre jaune*, published in English in America as *The Mystery of the Yellow Room*, has been filmed twice. It introduced the great amateur detective Joseph Rouletabille who outwits the famous professional detective Fréderic Larsan of the Sûréte. A young woman named Mathilde has been assaulted in a locked room and valuable papers belonging to her scientist father stolen. There seems no possible solution to the crime but Rouletabille, an investigative reporter for a Paris newspaper, finds a surprising one. See also *Le Mystère de la chambre jaune*.

The Mystery of the Yellow Room

1919 American film (Realart-Mayflower/6 reels) based on Gaston Leroux's classic locked room mystery *Le Mystère de la chambre jaune*. Mathilde has been assaulted in a locked room and valuable papers belonging to her scientist father stolen. There seems no possible solution but Lorin Raker as amateur detective Rouletabille solves it. Ethel Grey Terry played Mathilde, George Cowl was Larsan, William S. Walcott was Mathilde's father and Edmund Elton was her fiancé. Emile Chautard directed.

The Mystery of 13

1919 American serial (Burston/fifteen 2-reel chapters) starring Francis Ford who also wrote and directed. A secret society of thirteen hooded villains oppose hero Ford (he also plays his brother) and heroine Rosemary Theby as they seek a lost pirate treasure. The chapter titles tell the story: *Bitter Bondage, Lights Out, The Submarine Gardens, The Lone Rider, Blown to Atoms, Single Handed, Fire and Water, Pirate Loot, The Phantom House, The Raid, Bare Handed, The Death Ride, Brother Against Brother, The Man Hunt* and *The 13th Card*.

The Mystery of 13 Hill Street

1914 European film (Film Release of America/3 reels). This film, reviewed by *Variety* in April 1914, is probably a German picture but remains unidentified. A tin box containing $25,000 is stolen from a messenger by a man wearing fake whiskers (we see him put them on). A young gypsy is arrested for the crime but his intrepid sweetheart tracks down the real thief on horseback. She is captured by the thieves and locked in a room but is able to see where the box of money is hidden and tell the detectives who have followed her. The man with the whiskers escapes by leaping off a high bridge but is caught in the water. *Variety* thought the bridge stunt was the best thing in the film but the rest was "pure melodrama."

The Mystery of Thor Bridge

1923 British film (Stoll/2 reels), an episode in the *Last Adventures of Sherlock Holmes* series based on a story by Sir Arthur Conan Doyle. Sherlock Holmes solves a "murder" case that turns out to be suicide. Eille Norwood portrays Holmes with Hubert Willis as Dr. Watson. Alfred Moise was the cinematographer and George Ridgewell wrote the adaptation and directed. Print survives at BFI archive.

A Mystery of Wall Street

1913 American film (Thanhouser/1 reel). The mystery is why a revengeful Wall Street broker was absent all day while his evil machinations were reverses. He had tried to ruin the father of a girl who had rejected him but her sweetheart arranged for him to be trapped in a steel cab while the financial situation was sorted out. With Mignon Anderson, Eugene Moore and Harry Benham.

The Mystery of West Sedgwick

1913 American film (Edison/2 reels) based Carolyn Well's short story "The Gold Bag." The cast included Gertrude McCoy, Augustus Phillips, May Abbey and Charles Sutton.

The Mystery of Wickham Hall

1914 American film (Powers/3 reels) based on a story by Bess Meredyth. Cleo Madison stars with support from Edwin Alexander, Ray Gallagher and Ray Hanford.

The Mystery Road

1921 British film (Famous Players–Lasky British/7 reels) based on a novel by E. Phillips Oppenheim. An English girl dies after having an affair with an aristocrat in Nice and detectives investigate what happened. With Mary Glynn, David Powell, Ruby Miller, Irene Tripod and Percy Standing. Mary O'Connor and Margaret Turnbull wrote the screenplay and Paul Powell directed.

The Mystery Solved

1914 American film (Thanhouser/2 reels), the final episode of the serial *The Million Dollar Mystery* based on a novel by Harold MacGrath. The Black Hundred Society fails in its final attempt to steal one million dollars from heroine Florence (Florence La Badie) as she solves the last mystery the help of newspaperman James Cruze. Lloyd Lonergan wrote the screenplay and Howell Hansel directed.

The Mystic Hour

1917 American film (Apollo Pictures/5 reels) based on a story by Agnes Fletcher Bain. The painter Guido (Charles Hutchison) is obsessed with the idea of killing wealthy Clavering (John Sainpolis) who more or less forced Margaret (Alma Hanlon), whom Guido loves, to marry him. One night Guido dreams he murders Clavering and the next morning Clavering is found dead. Guido is sure he is the murderer but Margaret persuades him paint a picture of the dream. When Clavering's butler see the painting, he is terrified and confesses that he murdered his employer. Richard Ridgely directed and Frederick Rath wrote the screenplay.

Nameless Men

1928 American film (Tiffany-Stahl Productions/6 reels) based on a story by E. Morton Hough. Detective Robert Strong (Antonio Moreno) pretends to be a convict to gain the trust of inmate Hughie (Ray Hallor) who knows where money from a robbery is hidden. Hughie arranges for Strong to meet his partner Blackie (Eddie Gribbon) who was not caught. In the meantime Strong becomes involved with Hughie's sister Mary (Claire Windsor). The meeting with Blackie goes wrong and Strong is nearly killed but he eventually recovers the loot. John Francis Natteford wrote the screenplay and Christy Cabanne directed.

Nat Pinkerton

Film series featuring "Nat Pinkerton of the Pinkerton Detective Agency" were made in Denmark, France and Germany from 1909 to 1921. Nat was a German creation, an amalgam of Pinkerton agency detectives and pulp detective Nick Carter who made his first appearance in a German magazine in 1907. The name had international appeal, however, and there were soon Nat Pinkerton stories published in many countries as well as three series of films (see below).

Detective Nat Pinkerton became popular in French and German magazines and was soon appearing in films in both countries.

Nat Pinkerton

1909 Danish series (Nordisk/two 1-reel film) featuring "Nat Pinkerton of the Pinkerton Detective Agency" and distributed in America by the Great Northern company. In *Nat Pinkerton or the Lost Child*, the detective investigates the crimes of a bigamist who is attempting to kill a boy to keep him from revealing the bigamist's past. *In Nat Pinkerton II* he has to battle a gang of anarchists who plan to assassinate a governor.

Nat Pinkerton

1910–1914 French series (Eclipse-Urban-Minerva/forty 1- and 2-reel films) featuring "Nat Pinkerton of the Pinkerton Detective Agency." They were directed by Pierre Bressol who played Pinkerton. Representative titles of the forty films in the series include *Les Rats d'Hôtel* (1910), *L'Auberge Sanglante* (1911), *L'Affaire d'Excelsior Park* (1911) *Nat Pinkerton contre tous* (1912), *Les Cent Mille Dollars de la Banque Norton* (1912), *L'Armoire secrète* (1913), *Les Diamants du Hollandais* (1913), *Nat Pinkerton contre Pégomas* (1914) and even *Nat Pinkerton contre Nat Pinkerton* (1914). The only surviving print seems to be *Le Cheveu d'or* (1912) in which Pinkerton investigates the theft of an invention. See also Pinkerton, Nat.

Nat Pinkerton

1920–1921 German series (Dua Film/two 5-reel films) featuring "Nat Pinkerton of the Pinkerton Detective Agency." They were directed by Wolfgang Neff and written by Jane Bess. They were *Nat Pinkerton im Kampf 1—Das Ende des Artisten Bartolini* (1920) with Sybill de Brée and Bela Lugosi and *Nat Pinkerton im Kampf 2—Diebesfallen* (1921) with Sybill de Brée, Curt Cappi, Fritz Falkenberg and Hilde Piscator. See also Pinkerton, Nat.

The Naval Treaty

1922 British film (Stoll/2 reels), an episode in the *Further Adventures of Sherlock Holmes* series based on a story by Sir Arthur Conan Doyle. Sherlock Holmes solves the mystery of a missing naval treaty. Eille Norwood portrays Holmes with Hubert Willis as Dr. Watson. George Ridgewell wrote the adaptation and directed. A print survives at the BFI archive.

Neal of the Navy

1915 American serial (Balboa/fourteen 2-reel episodes) based on a story by mystery writer William Hamilton Osborne. Annapolis cadet Neal Hardin (William Courtleigh, Jr.) is framed and thrown out of the Academy for cheating. It seem to have something to do with the mystery surrounding a buried treasure that he and sweetheart Annette (Lillian Lorraine) are searching for. There are certainly villains trying to kill them. Douglas Bronston wrote the screenplay and William Bertram and William M. Harvey directed. The episodes were *The Survivors, The Yellow Packet, The Failure, The Tattered Parchment, A Message from the Past, The Cavern of Death, The Gun Runners, The Yellow Peril, The Rolling Terror, The Sun Worshippers, The Dreadful Pit, The Worm Turns, White Gods* and *The Final Goal.*

Lillian Lorraine is Neal's sweetheart in the Balboa serial *Neal of the Navy.*

The Net

1916 American film (Thanhauser-Mutal/5 reels). A detective (Morgan Jones) with few scruples and less morality runs away with a woman (Ethel Jewett) who is about to marry a fisherman (Bert Delaney). He had been pursuing her for a robbery when she fell in the sea and was rescued by the fisherman. When the fisherman rescues a second woman (Marion Swayne), the detective scares her away and sends the first woman back to try to obtain a fortune the fisherman has inherited. Lloyd Lonergan wrote the screenplay and George Foster Platt directed.

The New Adventures of J. Rufus Wallingford

1915 American serial (Wharton/fourteen 2-reel episodes) based on stories by George Randolph Chester. Con man J. Rufus Wallingford and his partner Blackie Daw arrived in a small town where Violet and Fanny Warden convince them to swindle the clique that ruined Fanny's father Burr McIntosh played Wallingford, Max Figman was Blackie Daw, Lolita Robertson was Violet, Frances White was Fanny and Edward O'Connor was Onion Jones. James Gordon and Leopold Wharton directed the serial from a screenplay by Charles W. Goddard. The episode titles are *The Bungalow Bungle, Three Rings and a Goat, A Rheumatic Joint, The Master Stroke, The Lilac Splash, A Trap for Trapp, The Bang Sun Engine, A Transaction in Summer Boarders, Detective Blackie, Apples and Eggbeaters, A Stony Deal, Buying a Bank with Bunk, The Missing Heir* and *Lord Southpaugh*. See also Wallingford, J. Rufus.

The New Adventures of Terence O'Rourke

1914 American series (Universal/three 2-reel episodes) based on mystery writer Louis Joseph Vance's stories about the roguish Irish adventurer Terence O'Rourke. The episodes are titled *The Palace of Dust, When a Queen Loved O'Rourke* and *The Road to Paradise*. See Terence O'Rourke, Gentleman Adventurer for further information and other films.

The New Exploits of Elaine

1915 American serial (Star-Pathé/ten 2-reel chapters) based on *The Triumph of Elaine* by Arthur B. Reeve The Clutching Hand has been defeated by Craig Kennedy (Arnold Daly) and Elaine (Pearl White) but there is a new villain to fight, the Oriental crime lord Wu Fang (Edwin Arden). He is trying to get hold of a torpedo invented by Kennedy but Elaine, now in love with Kennedy, gets in the way. Journalist Walter Jameson (Creighton Hale) keeps us abreast of what's happening. George B. Seitz directed, Charles L. Goddard. Bertram Millhauser and Seitz wrote the screenplay and Joseph Dubray was cinematographer. The chapters are titled *The Serpent Sign, The Cryptic Ring, The Watching Eyes, The Vengeance of Wu Fang, The Saving Circles, Spontaneous Combustion, The Ear in the Wall, The Opium Smugglers, The Tell-Tale Heart* and *Shadows of War*. See also *The Exploits of Elaine*.

Nick Carter

1921/1922 German series (Althoff Film/four films) with Bruno Eichgrün playing master detective Nick Carter. The four films feature Carter fighting different villains but always, of course, defeating them. The films, with their English release titles, are *Erzgauner* (The Cunning Rogue), *Das Gasthaus von Chicago* (The Chicago Inn), *Frauen, die Ehe brechen* (Women and the Marriage Break) and *Der Passagier in der Zwangsjacke* (The Passenger in a Straitjacket). Eichgrün directed the first three and Rudolf Walther-Fein directed the last one.

Nick Carter

1922 American series (Murray W. Garsson Productions/four 2-reel films) featuring master detective Nick Carter. Edmund Lowe played Nick Carter under the direction of Alexander Hall and the supporting casts include Diana Allen and Henry Sedley. The films were *A Game of Graft, The Last Call, The Spirit of Evil* and *Unseen Foes*.

Nick Carter acrobate (Nick Carter Acrobat)

1909 French film (Éclair/1 reel), an episode in the *Les Nouveaux Exploits de Nick Carter* series about the master detective Nick Carter. In this episode Carter shows off his acrobatic abilities. Pierre Bressol played Nick Carter and Victorin Jassett wrote and directed the film. Distributed in America as *Nick Carter as Acrobat*.

Nick Carter, le roi des détectives
(Nick Carter, the King of Detectives)

1908 French series (Éclair/each 1 reel) featuring the master detective Nick Carter. They written and directed by Victorin Jassett and starred Pierre Bressol as Nick Carter. The first series of six films about Carter were distributed as *Nick Carter, le roi des détectives*. They were so successful that a further six were distributed in a series titled *Les Nouveaux Exploits de Nick Carter*. The films were popular in England and America as well as France and seem to have created a Nick Carter vogue. In each episode Carter solved a new case and conquered evil-doers. The first film in the series was *Le Guet-apens*, released in America as *Nick Carter the King of Detectives and the Kidnappers' Plot*. The other episodes in the first series were *L'Affaire des bijoux* (The Great Jewel Affair), *Les Bandits en noirs* (Nick Carter and the Black-Coated Thieves, *Les Dévaliseurs de banque* (The Bankers), *Les Empreintes* (The Fingerprints) and *Les Faux-Monnayeurs* (The False Coiners).

Nick Winter et le courrier diplomatique
(Nick Winter and the Dispatch)

1911 French film (Pathé/1 reel), an episode in a popular tongue-in-cheek comedy series about an "American" detective named Nick Winter. In this episode Nick proves to be a clever detective despite his failings. Georges Vinter played Nick and Paul Garbagni wrote the screenplay and directed. (A print of this film survives in an archive.) See Winter, Nick for other films.

Nick Winter et le rapt de Mlle Werner
(Nick Winter and the Kidnapping of Miss Werner)

1911 French film (Pathé/1 reel), an episode in a popular tongue-in-cheek comedy series about an "American" detective named Nick Winter. In this episode sets out to rescue a kidnapped woman but gets captured himself. He is saved because the kidnap gang decides to smoke his drugged cigars and knock themselves out. Georges Vinter played Nick and Gérard Bourgeois wrote the screenplay and directed. (A print of this film survives in an archive.) See Winter, Nick for other films.

Nick Winter et ses aventures
(Nick Winter and His Adventures)

1921 French serial (Nick Winter Films/ten 2-reel episodes) featuring Nick Winter, an "American" detective in Paris whose adventures are tongue-in-cheek parodies of Nick Carter films. In this serial Nick (Georges Vintner) is involved in three adventures: the first involves a crooked inheritance scheme, the second a man unjustly accused of a crime and the third a famous singer and her husband. The episodes are *Les Oiseaux de nuit*, *L'Introuvable*, *Un Héritage difficile*, *La Villa mystérieuse*, *La Mort que rôde*, *L'Étau se desserre*, *Le Drame de l'Alhambra*, *L'Audacieuse Filature*, *La Malle vivante* and *A la Jean Bart*. See Winter, Nick for other films.

Nick Winter l'adroit détective
(Nick Winter, Detective)

1911 French film (Pathé/1 reel), an episode in a popular tongue-in-cheek comedy series about an "American" detective named Nick Winter. In this episode Nick proves to be a clever detective despite his failings. Georges Vinter played Nick and Paul Garbagni wrote the screenplay and directed. (A print of this film survives in an archive.) See Winter, Nick for other films.

Nick Winter, la voleuse et la somnambule (Nick Winter, the Thief and the Sonmambulist)

1911 French film (Pathé/1 reel), an episode in a popular tongue-in-cheek comedy series about an "American" detective named Nick Winter. In this episode Nick has to cope with two strange contacts. Georges Vinter played Nick and Gorieux wrote the screenplay and directed. (A print of this film survives in an archive.) See Winter, Nick for other films.

Nick Winter plus fort que Sherlock Holmes (Nick Winter Stronger than Sherlock Holmes)

1913 French film (Pathé/1 reel), an episode in a popular tongue-in-cheek comedy series about an "American" detective named Nick Winter. In this episode Nick shows he is stronger than Sherlock Holmes. Georges Vinter played Nick and Paul Garbagni wrote the screenplay and directed. See Winter, Nick for other films.

Nikola, Dr.

Australian author Guy Boothby's evil genius Dr. Nikola made his debut in 1895 in *A Bid for Fortune* and was featured in four more novels. The villainous doctor had hypnotic powers and no scruples in his attempts to gain a fortune. He was first discovered by filmmakers in Denmark, where a popular serial about him was filmed in 1909, and then in England, where he was featured in a 1917 film. See *Dr. Nikola* and *A Bid for Fortune*.

The Noble Bachelor

1921 British film (Stoll/2 reels), an episode in the *Adventures of Sherlock Holmes* series based on a story by Sir Arthur Conan Doyle. Sherlock Holmes solves the mystery of a missing bride. Eille Norwood portrays Holmes with Hubert Willis as Dr. Watson. William J. Elliot wrote the script and Maurice Elvey directed. A print of this film survives at the BFI archive.

Nobody

1921 American film (First National/7 reels). Jewel Carmen stars at Mrs. Smith in this unusual mystery set in a jury room during a murder trial. Wealthy businessman John Rossmore was found murdered in library and his butler is accused of killing him. Jury member Tom Smith (Kenneth Harlan) reveals the story behind the murder to the jurors. While he and his wife were on holiday in Palm Beach, Rossmore drugged Mrs. Smith and raped her and then blackmailed her into silence. Her mind broke under the pressure and she went to his house and shot him. The jurors agree never to tell what they have been told and acquit the butler. Charles H. Smith and Roland West wrote the screenplay and West directed.

Jewel Carmen stars as Mrs. Smith in the courtroom drama *Nobody*.

The No-Good Guy

1916 American film (Triangle/5 reels). The no-good guy is Jimmy Coghlan (William Collier) who reluctantly opens a detective agency when his political boss uncle "Big' Malone (Charles K. French) insists he gets a job. He tries to avoid working but finally has to take a case that involves going undercover and joining a criminal band. He falls in love with one of the gang members (Enid Markey) and discovers that his uncle is the gang boss. He denounces his uncle and decides to get married. C. Gardner Sullivan wrote the screenplay and Walter Edwards directed.

The Northern Mystery

1924 British film (Stoll/2 reels), an episode in the *Old Man in the Corner* series based on a story by Baroness Orczy. An armchair detective known as the Old Man in the Corner solves a crime while sitting in a tea shop and tells the solution to a young woman journalist. Rolf Leslie played the Old Man and Renée Wakefield was journalist Mary Hatley. D. P. Cooper was the cinematographer and Hugh Croise wrote the adaptation and directed.

The Norwood Builder

1922 British film (Stoll/2 reels), an episode in the *Further Adventures of Sherlock Holmes* series based on a story by Sir Arthur Conan Doyle. Sherlock Holmes solves the supposed murder of a builder at Norwood. Eille Norwood portrays Holmes with Hubert Willis as Dr. Watson. George Ridgewell wrote the adaptation and directed. A print survives at the BFI archive.

Not Guilty

1921 American film (Whitman Bennett Productions/7 reels) based on the 1913 novel *Parrot and Company* by Harold MacGrath. Paul Ellison (Richard Dix) exchanges identities with his twin brother Arthur (Dix again) and confesses to a murder he thinks his brother committed. This causes a lot of problems for his girlfriend Elsa (Sylvia Breamer) who never seems to know which one she is engaged to. It is all sorted out in Rangoon where gambler Newell Craig (Herbert Prior) confesses he was the real killer and Elsa has to decide which twin she prefers. J. Grubb Alexander and Edwin Bower Hesser wrote the screenplay and Sidney A. Franklin directed.

Les Nouveaux Exploits de Nick Carter (The New Exploits of Nick Carter)

1909 French series (Éclair/each 1 reel) featuring the master detective Nick Carter. It was written and directed by Victorin Jassett and starred Pierre Bressol as Nick Carter. The first series of six films about Carter, *Nick Carter, le roi des détectives,* were so successful that a further six were distributed in a series titled *Les Nouveaux Exploits de Nick Carter* (The New Exploits of Nick Carter). The films were popular in England and America as well as France and seem to have created a Nick Carter vogue. In each episode Carter solved a new case and conquered evil-doers. The episodes in the second series were *Le club des suicides* (The Suicide Club), *Les Dragées soporifiques* (The Sleeping Pills), *En danger* (In Danger), *Le Mystère du lit blanc* (The Mystery of the White Bed), *Nick Carter acrobate* (Nick Carter as Acrobat) and *Le Sosie* (The Double).

La Nouvelle Aurore (The New Dawn)

1919 French serial (Eclipse/sixteen 2-reel episodes) featuring the anti-hero convict Chéri-Bibi with an original screenplay by French mystery writer Gaston Leroux. Chéri-Bibi escapes for the second time from Devil's Island, this time in company with Palas, another innocent convict. They live the good life under assumed identities until the man who framed Palas turns up and creates problems. José Davert played Chéri-Bibi and René Navarre was Palas. Emile-Edouard Violet directed. See *Chéri-Bibi* for other films.

La Nouvelle Mission de Judex

1917 French serial (Gaumont/twelve 2-reel episodes) directed by Louis Feuillade and starring René Cresté as the righteous crime fighting hero Judex. The character of Judex was created by Feuillade with co-writer Arthur Bernède and featured in two serials. Louis Leubas played the evil banker Favraux and Musidora was Favraux's equally evil mistress Diana. Judex eventually spares the life of Favraux because of his love for the banker's innocent daughter Jacqueline (Yvette Andreyor). See also *Judex*.

Number 99

1920 American film (Robert Brunton Productions/5 reels) based on the 1919 novel *One Week-End* by Wyndham Martyn. Arthur Penryn (J. Warren Kerrigan), framed for a crime he did not commit, escapes from jail and hides out at nearby estate where a party is in progress. He makes friends with Cynthia (Fritzi Brunette), the daughter of the house, who lets him to impersonate a friend at the party. It goes wrong and the police are soon after him but luckily the man who framed him turns up a the party and is forced to confess his guilt. Jack

Cunningham wrote the screenplay and Ernest C. Warde directed.

The Oakdale Affair

1919 American film (World/6 reels) based on the novelette *The Oakdale Affair* by Edgar Rice Burroughs published in *Blue Book Magazine* in 1918. Gail Prim (Evelyn Greeley) disguises herself as a man and runs away from home to avoid an unwanted marriage. She gets involved with a gang of thieves and tells them she is the Oskaloosa Kid, a known criminal. Meanwhile the real Kid kills a man and Gail becomes involved with tramp Arthur (Reginald Denny). After many adventures Gail and Arthur are arrested as the suspected killers of the missing Gail. They are about to lynched when Gail's father arrives and identifies her. Arthur, of course, is not really a tramp but a famous writer doing undercover research. Wallace C. Clifton wrote the screenplay and Oscar Apfel directed.

Oathbound

1922 American film (Fox/5 reels). *Variety* felt this mystery film was too mysterious for its own good: "There is much mystery. The audience wonders what it is all about." A ship owner (Dustin Farnum) sends his brother (Fred Thomson) to investigate thefts from his ships but the brother is secretly part of the gang doing the robberies. The real investigation is carried out by Secret Service detective (Maurice Flynn) and an incompetent private eye (Norman Selby). Ethel Grey Terry adds glamour. Jack Strumwasser wrote the screenplay and Bernard Durning directed.

Octavius, Amateur Detective

1914 American comedy series (Edison/ten 1-reel films) about an ambitious amateur detective who bumbles his way through various adventures. He always solves his cases but it is by pure luck and wild coincidences. These are quite entertaining films (a number have survived), especially because the personality of Octavius. The screenplays were written by the mystery author Frederic Arnold Kummer. Herbert Yost, using the name Barry O'Moore, played the amateur detective under the direction of Charles M. Seay. The supporting casts included Edward Earle, Marjorie Ellison, Gladys Hulette, Augustus Phillips, Julian Reed and Jessie Stevens. The films in the series were *The Adventure of the Actress's Jewels, The Adventure of the Alarm Clock, The Adventure of the Counterfeit Money, The Adventure of the Extra Baby, The Adventure of the Hasty Elopement, The Adventure of the Lost Wife, The Adventure of the Missing Legacy, The Adventure of the Smuggled Diamonds, The Adventure of the Stolen Slipper* and *The Adventure of the Wrong Santa Claus*. Some of these films survive and two are on DVD.

Officer 174

1912 American film (Imp-Universal/1 reel). Officer 174 (King Baggott) turns detective to track down a major criminal and earn a much needed reward. Earlier he had been dismissed from the force for sleeping on duty because he had sat up all night with his sick wife (Jane Fearnley). He captures the criminal and his accomplice after a fight and is restored to the force.

Officer 444

1926 American serial (Davis Distributing-Goodwill/ten 2-reel chapters). Officer 444 (Ben Wilson) investigates the evil activities of a master criminal known only as The Frog. It turns out he is seeking a secret formula that will allow him to rule the world. Gloria Grey (Neva Gerber) gets kidnapped and has to be rescued from the Frog's home in the sewers. Francis Ford wrote the screenplay and directed. It must have been an off day for him. This serial, which survives and can be viewed, is considered the worst serial ever made.

The Old Man in the Corner

1924 British series (Stoll/twelve 2-reel episodes). The Old Man in the Corner, the first armchair detective, was the creation of Baroness Orczy. He was truly sedentary as he does his deducting while sitting in a London tea shop creating knots in a piece of string. He describes his solutions to crimes to a young woman journalist who acts as narrator. The first Old Man story, "The Fenchurch Street Mystery" was printed in *The Royal Magazine* in May 1901 and the stories were published in four collections beginning in 1909. The film series starred Rolf Leslie as the Old Man and Renée Wakefield as the reporter who hears how he solves crimes. Hugh Croise directed and wrote the screenplays with John J. Cox and D. P. Cooper as the cinematographers. The episodes, taken more or less directly from the stories, were *The Affair at the Novelty Theatre, The Brighton Mystery, The Hocussing of Cigarette, The Kensington Mystery, The Mystery of Brudenell Court, The Mystery of Dogstooth Cliff, The Mystery of the Khaki Tunic, The Northern Mystery, The Regent's Park Mystery, The Tragedy of Barnsdale Manor, The Tremarne Case* and *The York Mystery*. Several episodes survive at the BFI film archive.

Old Sleuth, the Detective

1908 American film (Kalem/1 reel). Old Sleuth was a famous nineteenth century American dime novel detective, the hero of hundreds of paperback adventures. The creation of Harlan Halsey, he made his first appearance in print in 1872 and by 1880 had his own magazine titled *The Old Sleuth Library*. He is not actually old but he liked to disguise himself as a bearded old man so no one would know who he really was. He barely made it into the twentieth century and seems to have aroused little interest in filmmakers This was his only film.

On Her Wedding Night

1915 American film (Vitagraph/4 reels). Amateur detective Henry Hallam (Antonio Moreno) investigates the murder of his friend John Klendon (Denton Vane) killed on the eve of his wedding to Helen Carter (Edith Storey). He left a note saying "It was I...." Hallam links up with an injured amnesiac man found near Klendon's house and they follow Helen to her settlement work. She is lured into a building by a Spanish woman (Carolyn Birch) named Inez who tries to kill her saying Klendon was her lover and betrayed her. Helen is rescued by Hallam and Inez kills herself. William Humphrey and Eugene Mullin wrote the screenplay and J. Stuart Blackton directed.

On the Pupil of His Eye

1912 American film (Vitagraph/1 reel), the first of eight films featuring detective Lambert

Old Sleuth set the standard for dime novel detectives as this thrill-filled cover shows.

Maurice Costello stars in the 1912 Lambert Chase detective series.

Chase. Modeled on Sherlock Holmes, Chase was created for the Vitagraph Studio by writer B. R. Brooker and actor Maurice Costello who portrayed him in all the films. Van Dyke Brooke played the butler, Rose Tapley was the housekeeper, James R. Waite was Senator Walker, James Morrison was Walker's nephew and Dorothy Kelly was the Senator's Ward. B. R. Brooker wrote the screenplay and Van Dyke Brooke and Maurice Costello directed. See Chase, Lambert for the other films.

One Chance in a Million

1927 American film (Gotham Productions-Lumas/5 reels). A Secret Service detective (William Fairbanks) goes undercover to capture jewel thieves. As his secret identity is not revealed until the end of the film, he is suspected of stealing the diamond himself. They belong to the beautiful Viora Daniels who forgives him when she learns the truth. L. V. Jefferson wrote the screenplay and Noel Mason Smith directed.

One Exciting Night

1922 American film (United Artists/11 reels) A detective (Frank Sheridan) has to solve two murders at a remote mansion where orphan Agnes (Carol Dempster) is being manipulated by her foster mother (Margaret Dale) in a marriage inheritance scheme. Meanwhile a gang of bootleggers are searching for money hidden in the house. D. W. Griffith directed this complicated mystery and Irene Sinclair wrote the screenplay.

One Hour Before Dawn

1920 American film (Pathé-Hampton Productions/6 reels) based on the 1919 mystery novel *Behind Red Curtains* by Mansfield Scott. Hypnotist Norman Osgood (Frank Leigh) suggests that George Clayton (H. B. Warner) should kill Harrison Kirke (Howard Davies) "one hour before dawn." When Kirke is found murdered, Clayton thinks he may have done it while he was asleep. Detective Inspector Malcolm Steele (Wilton Taylor) investigates and reveals the real killer. Anna Q. Nilsson provides the love interest, Fred Myton wrote the screenplay and Henry King directed.

One Hour Past Midnight

1924 American film (Jupiter Film /5 reels). Dorothy Brent finds her father missing and a dead stranger in the library. She asks her sweetheart Niles Whitney to protect her but he is deceived by a man pretending to be a detective and she is knocked out by an intruder. The police commissioner finds her father and proves that old "friend" Stephen Ellis was the villain. Beverly C. Rule wrote and directed the film.

One Million Dollars see The Honeymooning Detectives

One Million in Jewels

1923 American film (William R. Brush-American Releasing/5 reels). Secret Service detective Burke (J. P. McGowan) sets out to stop a gang from smuggling valuable jewels into America from Cuba. Gang leader Helen (Helen Holmes falls in love with him but when things go wrong she is killed. Burke foils the smuggling attempt with the help of Sylvia (Elinor Fair). J. P. McGowan wrote the screenplay and directed.

The $1,000,000 Reward

1920 American mystery serial (Grossman/fifteen 2-reel chapters) based on a story by Arthur B. Reeve. South African diamond mine heiress Betty (Lillian Walker) has been secretly reared in California but when her father dies stockholders need to find her to divide up the mine. They offer a million dollar reward which entices a gang of crooks to join forces with an evil stockbroker (William Russell) who wants her dead. Her sweetheart (Coit Albertson) helps her survive and defeat the baddies. Saul Harrison wrote the screenplay and George Lessey directed. Most of the episode titles are unknown but the first five were *The Diamond Robbery, The Escape, The Rescue, Elixir of Death* and *A Dynamite Plot*.

Der Onyxknopf

1917 German film (May Film/4 reels) featuring the "American" detective Joe Deebs as played by Max Landa. This was an early film in the long-running Deeb series created by producer Joe May who wrote the screenplay with

Max Landa in *Der Onyxknopf*.

E.A. Dupont. The supporting cast included Hugo Flink, Bruno Kastner, Leopoldine Konstantin and Eva Maria. See Deebs, Joe for other films.

The Open Door

1919 American film (Art Class Pictures/6 reels). Joe Moore (John P. Wade) serves a prison term for embezzlement and then asks his former partners to pay him what they owe for a secret agreement. Owens (Frank Evans) refuses but Horton (Robert Broderick), who raised Moore's daughter while he was in prison, promises to pay. When Horton is found murdered, Moore is suspected. When the agreement is found it reveals that Moore took the blame for the embezzlement for $25,000 and a promise to care for his daughter. Owens was the real embezzler and the killer. Garfield Thompson wrote the screenplay and Dallas M. Fitzgerald directed.

Die Ophir, die Stadt der Vergangenheit (The Lost City of Ophir)

1919 German film (May Film/9 reels), the fifth episode in the big budget German series *Herrin der Welt* (Mistress of the World) based on a novel by Karl Figdor. Mia May stars as Maud Gregaards who finally reaches the lost city of Ophir where the treasure of the Queen of Sheba is hidden. The supporting cast includes Michael Bohnen, Hans Mierendorff and Henry Sze. Ruth Goets wrote the screenplay and Uwe Jens Krafft directed.

The Other Half of the Note

1914 American film (Kalem/3 reels). Detective Tom Cole (Robert Ellis) investigates a jewel smuggling scheme on a trans–Atlantic passenger ship. He finds half a note telling where the gems are hidden while the smuggler's confederates get the other half. The detective is engaged to the niece (Irene Boyle) of a senator (Richard Purden) and this causes problems when he has to pretend to arrest her brother (Winthrop Chamberlain). This is one of those rare mysteries where the butler actually did do it.

Otto, the Sleuth

1916 American comedy short (Lubin/2 reels) based on a story by Marie Foster. Davy Don starred as detective Otto with supporting cast of Florence Williams, Bernard Siegel and Patsy De Forest. Edwin McKim directed and wrote the screenplay.

La Oubliette (The Dungeon)

1912 French film (Gaumon/3 reels) directed by Louis Feuillade. Detective Jean Dervieux (René Navarre) is called to investigate the disappearance of a man's wife from an ancient chateau they have just bought. He discovers that she had, as a lark, hidden in an old chest that had a false bottom and fallen into an underground dungeon. The detective follows her down and then fires a pistol to attract the attention of the husband who throws down a rope ladder.

Out of the Shadow

1919 American film (Paramount/5 reels) based on the 1902 mystery novel *The Shadow of the Rope* by E. W. Hornung. Ruth Minchin (Pauline Frederick) is accused of murdering her husband but acquitted. Richard Steel (Wyndham Standing), who loves Ruth, sends her to his aunt's country home to rest. Reporter Edward Langholm (Ronald Byram) follows her and learns Richard paid a tramp (Harry Kosher) to keep quiet. The tramp says Ruth's husband tried to blackmail Richard over an

Australian crime so Richard is arrested by the investigating detective (W. Harcourt). Ruth remembers that her husband hit her when she helped a poor pianist named Severino (Syn De Conde) who confesses that he killed her husband. Emile Chautard directed the film and Eve Unsell wrote the screenplay.

The Outsider

1917 Metro film (6 reels) based on mystery writer Louis Joseph Vance's 1915 novel *Nobody*. Bored shopgirl Sally (Emmy Wehlen) gets involved with society folk who plan to steal their own jewels to collect insurance money. They agree to take her to Newport with them if she keeps quiet. When a detective turns up, they try to kidnap her to keep her quiet but it goes wrong and the scheme unravels at masquerade ball. Sally decides to give up society life and marry a Western millionaire (Herbert Heyes). Charles A. Taylor wrote the screenplay and William C. Dowlan directed.

Die Pagode (The Pagoda)

1917 German film (Stuart Webbs Film Company /4 reels) featuring the "American" detective Stuart Webbs played by Ernst Reicher. The supporting cast included Lupu Pick and Olga Engl. Ernst Reicher wrote the screenplay and Max Fassbender was the cinematographer.

The Page Mystery

1917 American film (World Film/5 reels). Millionaire Ralph Cornwell (Arthur Ashley), who calls himself Col. Page, is murdered during a party at his hunting lodge. The chief suspects are his runaway wife Edith (June Elvidge), lodge caretaker Alan Winthrop (Carlyle Blackwell) and disgruntled former employee Saul Potter (Albert Hart) whose wife was ruined by Page. Investigators discover that Potter did shoot at Page but he missed; the bullet that killed the millionaire was fired by his cast-off mistress Laura (Pinna Nesbit). Frank R. Adams wrote the screenplay and Harley Knoles directed.

The Paliser Case

1920 American film (Goldwyn/5 reel) based on a story by Edgar Saltus. Cassy Cara (Pauline Frederick) marries rich scoundrel Monty Paliser (Warburton Gamble) to help her father (James Neil) out of financial difficulties but the ceremony is a fake. Cassy leaves Paliser and goes to Lennox (Albert Roscoe), the man she really loves. They separately make plans to kill Paliser who is found stabbed to death the next day. Lennox is arrested but Cassy says she did it. Before either is prosecuted, Cassy's father confesses he killed Paliser for dishonoring his daughter. William Parke directed and Edfrid Bingham wrote the screenplay.

Panama n'est pas Paris
(Panama Is Not Paris)

1927 French film (ACE/7 reels) based on Francis Carco's novel *Les Innocents* and distributed in America as *The Apaches of Paris*. Parisian apache Mylord (Jaque Catelain) decides to reform after meeting an American woman (Lia Eibenschutz). He opposes a robbery arranged by gang leader Bécot (Charles Vanel) but finds reforming is not easy. Meanwhile his môme Savonnette (Ruth Weyher) has her own ideas. Nikolai Malikoff directed.

Parisian apache Jaque Catelain and his môme Ruth Weyher in *Panama n'est pas Paris*.

Das Panzergewölbe
(The Armored Vault)

1914 German film (Stuart Webbs Film Company/4 reels) featuring the "American" detective Stuart Webbs played by Ernst Reicher. This was the last Webbs film to be created by the team of director Joe May and screenwriter-star Reicher. After it May went off to create the similar Joe Deebs detective series.

Das Panzergewölbe
(The Armored Vault)

1926 German film (Rex-Film/6 reels) featuring the "American" detective Stuart Webbs played by Ernst Reicher. This was the last Webbs film and seemed to have been produced by Lupu Pick as a kind of coda or swan song to the longest-running German detective series. It was a remake of a 1914 Webbs film with Webbs looking looking old and tired. The film ends with Webbs disappearing behind a secret door in his library as the camera zooms in on a row of books featuring the adventures of famous detectives including Stuart Webbs, Sherlock Holmes, Nick Carter and Nat Pinkerton. (A print of this film survives in an archive.)

Le Parfum de la dame en noir
(The Perfume of the Lady in Black)

1914 French film (Éclair/4 reels) based on a novel by Gaston Leroux published in America as *The Perfume of the Lady in Black*. Maurice de Féraudy stars as the French newspaperman detective Rouletabille who is called upon a second time to solve a mystery involving beautiful Mathilde, the victim in *Le Mystère de la chambre jaune*. And once again he has to outwit the ultra-clever Fréderic Larsan, formerly of the Sûreté. Maurice Tourneur directed. See *The Mystery of the Yellow Room*.

Partners in Crime

1928 American film (Paramount/7 reels) based on a story by Grover Jones and Gilbert Pratt who also wrote the screenplay. Detective Mike Doolan (Wallace Beery) and reporter "Scoop" McGee (Raymond Hatton) are asked by cigarette girl Marie (Mary Brian) to investigate the kidnapping of her sweetheart Richard (Jack Luden). He had witnessed a robbery and was taken prisoner by the criminals but the police chief (Joseph W. Girard) thinks he was the robber. The bumbling investigators locate the gang's hideout, start a gang war, set off tear gas bombs and attract the attention of the police who arrest everybody. Frank Strayer directed.

Partners of the Night

1920 American film (Goldwyn/6 reels) based on the story "Partners of the Night" by LeRoy Scott published in *Metropolitan* in October 1916. Chief of detectives Mathew Bradley (Emmett Corrigan) frames detective Clifford (William B. Davidson) and dismisses him from the force. He is angry because Clifford arranged for Mary Regan (Pinna Nesbit) to make restitution rather than arresting her for embezzlement. Police Commissioner Thorne (William Ingerson) sympathizes with Clifford so Bradley sets out to frame him as well. He tells Mary to give an envelope to Thorne containing a bribe but she substitute a blank paper and puts the bribe in the chief's cigar. The chief is exposed and Clifford is reinstated. LeRoy Scott and Charles Whittaker wrote the screenplay and Paul Scardon directed.

Der Passagier in der Zwangsjacke
(The Passenger in a Straitjacket)

1921 German film (Althoff Film/2 reels), an episode in the four-film *Nick Carter* series featuring master detective Nick Carter. It was released in English-speaking countries as *The Passenger in a Straitjacket*. Bruno Eichgrün played Nick Carter and wrote and directed the film.

The Passing of Mr. Quinn

1928 British film (Strand/6 reels) based on Agatha Christie's 1924 novel *The Passing of Mr. Quin*. The story revolves around the mystery of Quinn's death (the film's screenwriter added an "n" to his name). and whether he was killed by a tramp. Leslie Hiscott wrote the adaptation and directed the film for Julius Hagen Productions. The cast was headed by Stewart Rome as Quinn, Clifford Heatherley as Prof. Appleby, Vivian Baron as Derek Cappel, Ursula Jeans as the Maid, Kate Gurney as the Landlady, Mary

Stewart Rome is the mysterious Quinn in *The Passing of Mr. Quinn.*

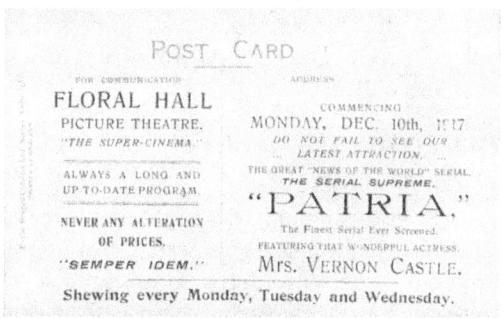

Mrs. Vernon Castle as Patria in the serial *Patria* and a card advertising the serial.

Brough as the Cook and Trilby Clark as Mrs. Appleby.

Paths to Paradise

1925 American film (Paramount/7 reels) based on the 1914 play *The Heart of a Thief* by Paul Armstrong. Molly (Betty Compson), the queen of crooks, is fleeced by a conman (Raymond Griffith) pretending to be a gullible tourist. After he allows himself to be cheated, he shows his detective badge and hints he can be bribed. She gives him all her earnings. They meet again at a mansion where she is posing as a maid and he is pretending to be detective guarding a valuable necklace. They team up to steal the necklace and head for Mexico with motorcycle cops in hot pursuit. Keene Thompson wrote the screenplay and Clarence Badger directed.

Patria

1917 American serial (Pathé/fifteen 2-reel chapters) based on Louis Joseph Vance's novel *The Last of the Fighting Channings*. Munitions factory owner Patria Channing (Mrs. Vernon Castle) joins forces with secret service agent Donald Parr (Milton Sills) to battle thrill-a-minute plots by Japanese and Mexican government villains to get her $100 million trust fund and overthrow the American government. This jingoist serial was such blatant propaganda that President Wilson ordered flags and names that identified the nationality of the villains cut from the film. The chapters were titled *Last of the Fighting Channings, The Treasure, Winged Millions, Double Crossed, The Island God Forgot, Alias Nemesis, Red Dawn, Red Night, Cat's Paw and Scapegoat, War in the Dooryard, Sunset Falls, Peace on the Border, Wings of Death, Border Peril* and *For the Flag.*

Paul Sleuth and the Mystic Seven

1914 British film (Cricks & Martin/3 reels), an episode in the *Paul Sleuth* series released in America as *The Secret Seven*. Paul Sleuth is able to locate and rescue a kidnapped heiress by hiding a movie camera in the headlights of the ransom car. Stanhope Sprigg wrote the script and Dave Alylott directed The most exciting part of the film was supposed to be Sleuth's big fight with the chief villain in a balloon but the *Variety* reviewer was not impressed. See also Sleuth, Paul.

Paul Sleuth Crime Investigator: The Burglary Syndicate

1912 British film (Cricks & Martin/1 reel), an episode in the *Paul Sleuth* series. Paul Sleuth captures a killer and then pretends to be him so he can capture his whole gang. Stanhope Sprigg wrote the script and Dave Alylott directed. See also Sleuth, Paul.

Paul Sleuth: The Murder of Squire Jeffrey

1913 British film (Cricks & Martin/1 reel), an episode in the *Paul Sleuth* series. Paul Sleuth pretends to be a murdered squire so he can trap a burglar. Stanhope Sprigg wrote the script and Dave Alylott directed. See also Sleuth, Paul.

Paul Sleuth: The Mystery of the Astorian Crown Prince

1912 British film (Cricks & Martin/1 reel), an episode in the *Paul Sleuth* series. Paul Sleuth takes the place of the Astorian king so he can protect the crown prince from would-be kidnappers. Stanhope Sprigg wrote the script and Dave Alylott directed. See also Sleuth, Paul.

Pawned

1922 American film (Selznick-Select/5 reels) based on the 1921 novel *Pawned* by mystery writer Frank L. Packard who also wrote the screenplay. John Bruce (Tom Moore) goes to New York to investigate goings-on at a nightclub owned by Gilbert Larmond (Eric Mayne). He becomes involved with Claire Veniza (Edith Roberts) and when he is badly hurt she has to compromise herself with drug addict Dr. Crang (Charles Gerard) to save him. Claire's father rescues her by driving his taxi off a ferryboat with Crang as passenger. Irvin V. Willat directed.

The Peacock Fan

1929 American film (Chesterfield/6 reels). Chinese detective Chang Dorfman (Lucien Prival) solves the mystery of the murder of an American antiques collector. A peacock fan in his collection, which had earlier figured in a double murder, provides the clue. Arthur Hoerl wrote the screenplay and Phil Rosen directed.

Pearl as a Detective

1913 American film (Crystal Film Company/split reel). Pearl White play a detective who is hired to see if a man (Chester Barnett) is cheating on his wife. There are comic complications, of course, as in all Pearl's early comedies with Barnett. Phillips Smalley directed.

Pearl White in her early days as a comedy star for Crystal in *Pearl as a Detective*.

The Peddler of Lies

1920 American film (Universal/5 reels) based on the novel *The Peddler* by Henry C. Rowland published in *The Saturday Evening Post* in 1919. A famous diamond belonging to the Marquise D'Irancy (Bonnie Hill) is stolen during a blackout at a party at the Metcalf estate and James Kirkland (Harold. Miller) is accused. His sister Diana (Ora Carew) defends him and is aided by a mysterious peddler named Clamp (Frank Mayo). Clamp, who is actually a detective on the trail of the de Vallignac gang, investigates and proves that the gem was stolen by Leontine de Vallignac (Ora Devereaux). Philip J. Hurn wrote the screenplay and William C. Dowlan directed.

Peggy Does Her Darndest

1919 American comedy (Metro/5 reels) based on the story "Peggy Does Her Darndest" by Royal Brown published in *Red Book Magazine* in 1918. Tomboy Peggy Ensloe (May Allison) takes a correspondence course so she can become a detective. When Hugh Wentworth (Robert Ellis) brings a valuable diamond to her father, a real detective is hired to pose as a butler protect the gem. Not to be outdone Peggy disguises herself as a maid and captures jewel thief "Lonesome Larry" Doyle (Augustus Phillips) by the use of judo. George D. Baker wrote the screenplay and directed.

The Pell Street Mystery

1924 American film (Robert J. Horner Productions–Realart/6 reels). A newspaper reporter (George Larkin) goes undercover to investigate the murder of a wealthy man in Chinatown. He infiltrates a gang but barely survives when his cover is blown. Along the way he meets Florence Stone, Ollie Kirkby and Frank Whitson. Jeanne Poe and George Larkin wrote the screenplay and Joseph Franz directed. *Variety* said it was "filled with glaring directorial errors and cheap sets" but had "impressive audience punch."

Pellie, Dr. Brian

1910–1913 British series (Clarendon/seven 1-reel films). Master criminal Dr. Brian Pellie hypnotizes an heiress, robs a bank, kidnaps a millionaire's bride and impersonates people for his nefarious purposes. Wilfred Noy directed the seven films relating his villainous adventures. See *Dr. Brian Pellie and the Bank Robbery*, *Dr. Brian Pellie and the Baronet's Bride*, *Dr. Brian Pellie and the Secret Despatch*, *Dr. Brian Pellie and the Spanish Grandee*, *Dr. Brian Pellie and the Wedding Gifts*, *Dr. Brian Pellie Escapes from Prison* and *Dr. Brian Pellie, Thief and Coiner*.

The People vs. Nancy Preston

1925 American film (PDC/7 reels). based on Frank A. Moroso's novel *The People Against Nancy Preston*. Gloomy Gus (Ed Kennedy), a detective working for the Tierney Detective Agency, continues to harass Bill Preston (David Butler) after his release from prison. When Bill is killed during a bank robbery, Mike Horgan (John Bowers) offers Bill's wife Nancy (Marguerite De La Motte) and son (Frankie Darro) protection. Mike is arrested and sent to prison for a robbery and Nancy is falsely accused of a murder. They both escape and flee to a small town where Mike begins to practice medicine. The ever-persistent detective James Tierney (Alphonse Ethier) locates them but falls ill and his life is saved by Mike and Nancy. When Gloomy Gus arrives with a warrant, Tierney sends him away and lets the couple go free. Marion Orth wrote the screenplay and Tom Forman directed. The novel was previously filmed as *Dice of Destiny*.

Le Père Goriot

French novelist Honoré de Balzac (1799–1850) did not write detective fiction but his novels often featured detectives and criminals. *Le Père Goriot* introduced the master criminal Vautrin, the Napoleon of crime. He was loosely based on French criminal-turned-detective Vidocq and he soon became one of the dominating characters in Balzac's "Human Comedy" series. Like his role model, Vautrin eventually turns detective and becomes head of the French Sûreté. *Le Père Goriot* was filmed four times in the silent era: by Armand Numès in France in 1910, by Travers Vale in America in 1915, by

Jacques de Baroncelli in France in 1921 and by E. Mason Hoppe in America in 1926 with Vautrin transformed into a righter of wrongs.

The Perfect Crime

1925 British film (Stoll/2 reels) based on a story by "Seamark," an episode in the second series of *Thrilling Stories from the Strand*. J. Fisher White played the Bank Manager and Walter Summers wrote the screenplay and directed.

The Perfect Crime

1928 American film (FBO/7 reels) based on Israel Zangwill's 1896 novel *The Big Bow Mystery*. Criminologist Benson (Clive Brook), who is obsessed with the idea of the "perfect crime," decides to prove his theory. He murders Frisbie (Tully Marshall), leaves no clues and is not suspected When Stella (Irene Rich) agrees to marry him, he thinks he has found happiness. Unfortunately Trevor (Carroll Nye), who once lived with Frisbie, is accused of the murder and sentenced to die. Benson will have to confess to the crime to free Trevor. Then he wakes up and finds it was only a bad dream. Bert Glennon directed and Ewart Adamson wrote the screenplay.

The Perfect Sap

1927 American film (Ray Rockett Productions/6 reels) based on the 1926 play *Not Herbert* by Howard Irving Young who wrote the screenplay. Wealthy would-be detective Herbert Alden (Ben Lyon) is practicing housebreaking with his valet when he meets thieves Polly (Pauline Starke) and George (Tammany Young) who think he's a master thief. George arranges with a thief called Tony-the-Lizard (Lloyd Whitlock) to rob the guests at a masked ball given by Herbert's father. Tony asks Herbert for advice and Herbert reveals the robbery plot. Femme fatale Ruth Webster (Virginia Lee Corbin) accuses Polly of being in on the robbery but Polly, a newspaper reporter in disguise, reveals that Ruth is the real thief. Howard Higgin directed.

The Perils of Pauline

1914 American serial (Pathé-Eclectic/twenty 2-reel episodes) based on a story by

The serial that made the cliffhanger ending famous was *The Perils of Pauline.*

playwright Charles W. Goddard and starring Pearl White as a daredevil heroine always in jeopardy. She plays a woman menaced by a villain (Paul Panzer) who wants her inheritance and somewhat protected by a boyfriend (Crane Wilbur) but she is no helpless damsel. To avoid being killed she climbs up fire escapes, races over rooftops, leaps off trains and performs dangerous stunts. This was the serial that originated the term "cliffhanger" and each chapter has its own mystery to be solved. George B Seitz wrote the screenplay and Louis J. Gasnier and Donald McKenzie directed. The chapters did not have titles when the serial was first released but were added afterwards by distributors so the titles vary. On DVD.

The Perils of Our Girl Reporters

1916 American serial (Niagara-Mutual/fifteen 2-reel episodes) in which girl reporters investigate crimes and mysteries and help police arrest evildoers. Helen Green played the heroine Jessie in the first three episodes and Zena Keefe portrayed her in the rest. The supporting cast included Mildred Bailey, Ethel Sinclair, Mabel Montgomery and Earl Metcalfe. Edith Sessions Tupper wrote the screenplays (each episode was a different story) and George Terwilliger directed. The episodes were *The Jade Necklace, The Black Door, Ace High, The White Trail, Many a Slip, The Long Lane, Smite of Conscience, Birds of Prey, Misjudged, Taking Changes, The Meeting, Outwitted, The Schemers, The Counterfeiters* and *Kidnapped*.

Perils of the Rail

1926 American film (Anchor Film/5 reels), the last of the railroad adventures mysteries starring Helen Holmes with many a nod back to *The Hazards of Helen*. She has to investigate the disappearance of valuable ore from railroad cars and perform her splendid stunts for the last time leaping from speeding cars to runaway explosives-laden railroad trucks. Her longtime partner J. P. McGowan produced and directed from a screenplay by William E. Wing. On DVD.

Helen Holmes returns for the last time to the railroad mystery genre in *Perils of the Rail*.

A Petticoat Detective

1912 American film (Powers/1 reel) about a female detective.

The Phantom Buccaneer

1916 American film (Essanay/5 reels) based on Victor Bridges' mystery novel *Another Man's Shoes*. Stuart Northcote (Richard C. Travers) shoots a man in South America and escapes to London pursued by a gang led by the dead man's daughter Mercia (Gertrude Glover). Stuart persuades Jack Burton, who looks like him (and is played by the same actor), to take his place while he goes underground. Mercia catches Jack and learns of the switch so she helps him trick the gang which thinks she has betrayed them. The gang kill the real Stuart and blame the murder on her and Jack who are arrested. H. Tipton Steck wrote the screenplay and J. Charles Haydon directed. Remade in 1922 as *Another Man's Shoes*.

Das Phantom der Oper

1916 German film (Greenbaum-Film/7 reels) based on Gaston Leroux's novel *Fantôme de l'opéra*. Nils Olaf Chrisander stars as Erik the Phantom with Aud Egede Nissen as Christine Daaé. Greta Schröder wrote the screenplay and Ernst Matray directed.

The Phantom of the Opera

The Phantom, one of the most famous villains of fiction and the movies, made his debut in 1910 in Gaston Leroux's novel *Fantôme de l'opéra* (The Phantom of the Opera) but did not become a iconic figure until 1925 when Lon Chaney impersonated him on screen. The phantom is a real person, a disfigured mad composer named Erik who lives in the cellars of the Paris Opera House and advances the career of young soprano Christine Daaé through acts of terror. The novel and films feature a police inspector who investigates the mystery of the Phantom in the company of Christine's lover Raoul. Leroux wrote only one novel about the Phantom but there have been many sequels, prequels and imitations by other authors. For the films see above and below.

The Phantom of the Opera

1925 American film (Universal/8 reels) based on Gaston Leroux's novel *Fantôme de l'opéra*. Lon Chaney stars as the Phantom. Mary Philbin is the soprano Christine Daaé, Virginia Pearson is the victimized diva Carlotta, Norman Kerry is Raoul and Arthur Edmund Carewe is the police inspector. Elliot J. Clawson wrote the screenplay, Charles van Enger was the cinematographer and Rupert Julian directed. This film survives and is on DVD.

Lon Chaney as the terrifying Phantom with the soprano he loves (Mary Philbin) in the 1925 version of *The Phantom of the Opera*.

The Phantom Shotgun

1917 American film (Falcon Featuresl/4 reels) based on a story by Stanley Clisby Arthur. Van Buren Courtland (R. Henry Grey) is framed for forgery by his partner Hamilton Forbes (Frank Brownlee) because of their rivalry for the hand of Elizabeth Kennedy (Kathleen Kirkham). When Courtland leaves to find a witness to clear his name, Forbes convinces her Courtland has died so she will agree to marry him. Courtland returns and goes to the ship on which they are honeymooning. When Forbes is killed, he is the principal suspect but then a deck steward who may have witnessed the murder is killed with the same mysterious shotgun. Reporter Larkins (William Marshall) investigates, finds the shotgun and proves that the killer was passenger Frank Marshall (Barney Furey) whose sister had been seduced by Forbes. Frances E. Guihan wrote the screenplay and Harry Harvey directed.

Phantomas

1916–1920 German series (Greenbaum Film/twelve 2-reel episodes) produced by Julius Greenbaum. This obscure series was a German imitation of the French *Fantômas* series with Erich Kaiser-Titz playing the title role in six

Erich Kaiser-Titz was a *Fantômas* clone in the German film series *Phantomas*.

films and Rolf Loer taking the part in the others. The films have screenplays by different writers including Richard Wilde, Herman Gellner, Paul Rosenhayn, Victor Alt, Carl Boese and O. Schubert-Stevens. The titles were *Ramara, Am Hochzeitsabend, Das Nachtgespräch, Der Erbe von Het Steen, Ein Schärfer Schuss, Ein Tropfen Gift, Das Nachtgespräch, Das Gestohlene Hotel, Der Teilhaber, Die Glocken der Katharinenkirche, Der Gelbe Schatten* and *Um Diamanten und Frauen.*

Le Pickpocket mystifié
(The Mystified Pickpocket)

1911 French film (Pathé/1 reel), an episode in a popular tongue-in-cheek comedy series about an "American" detective named Nick Winter. In this episode Nick is in disguise for a case and gets arrested instead of the pickpocket he is watching. He is embarrassed to have to prove his identity. Georges Vinter played Nick and Paul Garbagni wrote the screenplay and directed. (A print of this film survives in an archive.) See Winter, Nick for other films.

Pidgin Island

1916 American film (Metro/5 reels) based on the 1914 novel *Pidgin Island* by Harold MacGrath. Customs agent John Cranford (Harold Lockwood) takes a holiday on Pidgin Island in the Saint Lawrence River soon after arresting smuggler Michael Smead (Doc Pomeroy Cannon). When Cranford meets Smead's daughter (May Allison) on the island, he is immediately suspicious even after he learns that she is also a customs agent. When Cranford discovers that Smead has escaped from jail and is planning to smuggle pearls onto the island, she proves her honestly by helping him arrest her father. Fred J. Balshofer directed and wrote the screenplay with Richard V. Spencer.

Pilgrims of the Night

1921 film (Associated Producers/6 reels) based on the 1910 novel *Passers-By* by E. Phillips Oppenheim. Amateur detective Gilbert Hannaway (Walter McGrail) advises Christine (Rubye De Remer) that the man she is seeking to kill is Lord Ellingham (Lewis S. Stone). She thinks he betrayed her father Marcel (Frank Leigh). She fails in her murder attempt, discovers that he is her true father and that the real betrayer was the hunchback Ambrose (William V. Mong). Meanwhile Marcel escapes from prison and is killed by Ambrose. Edward Sloman wrote and directed the film.

Pimple, Detective

1913 British comedy (Folly Films/each 1 reel) starring Fred Evans as Pimple, a comic character he portrayed in dozens of movies between 1912 and 1918. In this film he plays a detective searching for a stolen baby. He finally finds it — in a dog kennel. Evans wrote and directed the film.

Pimple's Crime

1913 British comedy (Folly Films/each 1 reel) starring Fred Evans as Pimple, a comic character he portrayed in a series of short films. In this film his friends pretend to be detective when he thinks he has accidentally killed a man. Evans wrote and directed the film.

The Pinkerton Man

1911 American film (Powers/1 reel) about a Pinkerton detective.

Pinkerton, Nat

Detective Nat Pinkerton was a German creation, a combination of Pinkerton agency detectives and pulp detectives like Nick Carter. Most of his early adventures were simply rewrites of Nick Carter adventures. The name had such international appeal, however, that there were soon Nat Pinkerton stories published in other countries. The movie moguls liked the name so film series featuring "Nat Pinkerton of the Pinkerton Detective Agency" were produced in Denmark, France and Germany. See Nat Pinkerton for his films.

Pirates of the Sky

1927 American film (Pathé-Hurricane Film Corp/5 reels). The Secret Service asks amateur criminologist Bob Manning (Charles Hutchison) to investigate the disappearance of a mail plane and his reporter girl friend Doris (Wanda Hawley) wants in on the action. They are kidnapped by the gang behind the plane's disappearance but he is able to escape with some fancy stunt work and capture the crooks. Hutchison was known for his acrobatic stunts and this films featured him leaping between planes in mid-air. Elaine Wilmont wrote the screenplay and Charles Andrews directed.

A Plain Clothes Man

1908 American film (Essanay/1 reel). The "plain clothes man" is a detective called upon to investigate a crime using a satin slipper as a clue. It leads him a palatial mansion and several disguises as well as battles with baddies on sea and on land. Critic Frank Wiesberg of *Variety* commented wryly that "The film gives a fairly accurate idea of how the modern detective is popularly supposed to effect a capture; which differs considerably from his actual methods, but the ethics of modern "dramatics" seek not truth."

The Pleasure Buyers

1925 American film (Warner Bros./7 reels) based on the 1925 novel *The Pleasure Buyers* by Arthur Somers Roche. Socialite Joan Wiswell (Irene Rich) is a prime suspect in a murder case; she is innocent but is afraid her brother Tommy (Don Alvarado) could be the real murderer. Police commissioner Tad Workman (Clive Brook) investigates, finds four more suspects and eventually proves that the victim's valet did it by rigging a clock to fire a gun at the appropriate time. Hope Loring wrote the screenplay and Chet Withey directed.

Plunder

1923 American serial (Pathé/fifteen 2-reel chapters) starring serial queen Pearl White battling a master criminal for possession of skyscraper that hides an enormous secret treasure. She gets help from a mysterious Mr. Jones (Warren Williams). George B. Seitz directed and co-wrote the screenplay with Bertram Millhauser. The episodes are titled *The Bandaged Man, Held by the Enemy, The Hidden Thing, Ruin, To Beat a Knave, Heights of Hazard, Mocked from the Grave, The Human Target, Games Clear Through, Against Time, Spunk, Under the Floor, Swamp of Lost Souls,* *The Madman* and *A King's Ransom*. This was Pearl's last serial.

The Pointing Finger

1919 American film (Universal/5 reels) based on the story "No Experience Required" by Frank R. Adams first published in *Munsey's Magazine* in 1917. Mary Murphy (Mary MacLaren) steals $3.00 and escapes from an orphanage. Orphanage superintendent Grosset (Carl Stockdale) takes advantage of her running away to steal $10,000 and claim Mary took it. Mary changes her name and gets a job working for Professor Saxton (Johnnie Cook) but Grosset finds her and threatens her when she catches him robbing the professor's safe. Fortunately for Mary, the professor was behind a curtain at the time and heard everything. Grosset is arrested and Mary is marries the professor's nephew. Violet Clark wrote the screenplay and Edward Kull directed.

Poison

1924 American film (William Steiner Productions–New Cal Film/5 reels). Charles Hutchison plays an amateur detective asked to investigate liquor smuggling in San Francisco by the city's real police chief Dan O'Brien (the problem seems to be that it is bad liquor, not the good stuff). As Hutchinson was noted for his daredevil acrobatics there is a good deal of thrilling derring-do and impressive stunts. He also has to rescue pretty Edith Thornton. James Chapin directed and Hutchison wrote the screenplay himself.

The Poison Pen

1919 American film (World/5 reels) based on a story by Edwin August. Allayne (June Elvidge), the daughter of Bishop Filbert (Joseph Smiley), faints at the altar when she opens an anonymous poison pen letter. It is the latest in a series of nasty anonymous letters received in the village. When detectives try to find the writer, an infant is kidnapped. They trail a robed figure to the Filbert house and find Allayne writing a poison pen letter. It seems she has a split personality and wrote the letters in a somnambulistic state. A doctor cures her through hypnosis while the detectives find the kidnappers and rescue the infant. J. Clarkson Miller wrote the screenplay and Edwin August directed.

The Poisoned Light (Otrávené světlo)

1921 Czechoslovakian film (Kalos-American/5 reels). Engineer Bell (Karel Lamač) shows detective Hall (Jindřich Edl) how a light bulb filled with poison gas killed Dr. Selín (Jindřich Lhoták). Selín was about to buy an invention by Prof. Grant (Karel Fiala) but escaped convict Durk (Emil Artur Longen) learned about it and decided to steal the plans. Bell teams up with Grant's daughter (Anny Ondráková) to solve the murder. Jan S. Kolár and Karel Lamač wrote and directed the film photographed by Otto Heller. Anny Ondráková (as Anny Ondra) starred in Alfred Hitchcock's films *Blackmail* and *The Manxman*.

Anny Ondra, who was featured in the Czech film *The Poisoned Light*, went on to star in two features for Hitchcock in England.

Der Pokal der Fürstin
(The Prince's Cup)

1920 German film (Kassandra Film/5 reels), one of the episodes in the *Joe Jenkins, Detektiv* series. Kurt Brenkendorf plays Joe Jenkins and the supporting cast included Oskar Fuchs, Fred Selva-Goebel and Fritz Spira. Hans Felix wrote the screenplay and Bruno Ziener directed.

Police Reporter

1928 American serial (Weiss Brothers–Artclass/ten 2-reel chapters) based on a story by Arthur B. Reeve. Police reporter Walter Miller investigates a crime wave created by a mysterious master criminal known as The Phantom. His girlfriend Eugenia Gilbert also gets sucked into the traps set by the evil crook. Jack Nelson directed. The episodes are titled *The Phantom*, *Code of the Underworld*, *The Secret Tube*, *The Flaming Idol*, *The Phantom's Trap*, *The Girl Who Dared*, *The Wharf Rats*, *The Mystery Room*, *In the Phantom's Den* and *The Law Wins*.

La poliziotta (The Policewoman)

1912 Italian film (Ambrosia Film/1 reel) about a woman police detective starring Gigetta Morano. It was released in France as *La Détective* (The Woman Detective).

Polly the Girl Scout

1911 and 1913 British series of 1-reel films about a girl scout detective who catches crooks, foils crimes and rescues victims. May Morton played Polly and Rowland Talbot wrote the screenplays. The 1911 film was produced by Cricks and Martin with A. E. Holby directing, the 1913 ones were produced by Barker with Bert Haldane directing. See below for films.

Polly the Girl Scout

1911 British film (Cricks and Martin/1 reel). Polly and her fellow scouts trail a gypsy woman who has kidnapped a baby and are able to rescue it. A.E. Holby directed.

Polly the Girl Scout and Grandpa's Medals

1913 British film (Barker/1 reel). A newsboy steals an old man's medals but is chased by

Polly and gets run over. May Morton played Polly, J Hastings Batson was Grandpa and Kenneth Barker was the newsboy. Rowland Talbot wrote the screenplay and Bert Haldane directed.

Polly the Girl Scout and the Jewel Thieves

1913 British film (Barker/1 reel). Polly (May Morton) observes a robbery, chases the thieves, captures the crook's van and drives it to the police station. Rowland Talbot wrote the screenplay and Bert Haldane directed.

Polly the Girl Scout's Timely Aid

1913 British film (Barker/1 reel). Polly (May Morton) helps put a workman put in jail for stealing but later comes to the aid of his needy wife. Rowland Talbot wrote the screenplay and Bert Haldane directed.

The Pool of Flame

1916 American film (Universal/5 reels) based on mystery writer Louis Joseph Vance's novel *The Pool of Flame* about the Irish adventurer Terence O'Rourke. O'Rourke wants to marry Princess Beatrix but needs money so he accepts an offer of a $500,000 reward if he can find a giant ruby known as the Pool of Flame. It means competing with long-time enemies Chambret, Princess Karan and Duke Victor and involves much derring-do. See *Terence O'Rourke, Gentleman Adventurer* for other films.

The Poppy Girl's Husband

1919 American film (Famous-Players Lasky/5 reels) based on Jack Boyle's story "The Poppy Girl's Husband" in *Red Book Magazine*. Cracksman Boston Blackie (Walter Long) gives his old friend Hairpin Harry (William S. Hart). bad news when he is released from prison after ten years. Harry's wife Polly the Poppy Girl (Juanita Hansen) has divorced him and married Big Mike McCafferty (Fred Starr), the detective who put Harry in jail. When he learns they're planning to frame him again, he plots revenge but decides against it after meeting his son (Georgie Stone). William S. Hart; and Lambert Hillyer directed and C. Gardner Sullivan wrote the screenplay. See also Blackie, Boston.

The Port of Doom

1913 American film (Famous Players/4 reels). Kate Kirby (Laura Sawyer), daughter of crippled detective Kirby (House Peters), has become a detective herself. She is asked by a shipowner to investigate the disappearance of his daughter Vera who is in love with the captain of one of his ships. Kate discovers that the captain had been sent on a doomed voyage arranged by a rival for the shipowner's daughter. She charters a small boat and is able to rescue them in the nick of time. J. Searle Dawley wrote and directed the film, third in the *Kate Kirby* series.

Potts Bungles Again

1916 American comedy (Nestor/2 reels) starring Lee Moran as bungling Detective Potts Eddie Lyons plays his friend while Betty Compson and Ed Burns provide support. Louis J. Hubene wrote the script and al Christie directed. Third film in the *Detective Potts* series.

Poucette ou le plus jeune détective du monde (Poucette, or, the Youngest Detective in the World)

1920 French film (Visio Films/two 4-reel episodes) based on a novel by Alfred Machard. Poucette (Maurice Touzé) is a precocious 12-year-old, the adopted son of detective Radium (Guy Fauren). He imitates his father by investigating the disappearance of the son of the lady of the local castle The culprit turns out to be the child's real mother. Years before she had revenged herself on the lady by substituting her son for the lady's son and placing the lady's son in an orphanage. Now that she wants her true son back, she can reveal that the lady's son is actually Poucette. Simone Genevois played Anaïk, Paul Duc was Jean Martin-Chupart, Corinne was Sylviane Martin-Chupart and Jules Mondo was the grand Chacuhe. Adrien Caillard directed. The film was released in two parts titled *En plein mystère* and *Jusqu'au bout, j'attendrai*.

The Power God

1926 American serial (Davis Distributing–Goodwell/fifteen 2-reel chapters). Ben Wilson has to battle an evil syndicate to protect Neva Gerber. She is the daughter of a deceased inventor who invented a machine that produces power without fuel, and it threatens their monopoly. The daughter knows the secret of the invention but has lost her memory. Rex Taylor and Harry Haven wrote the screenplay and Francis Ford co-directed with Ben Wilson. The episodes are titled *The Ring of Fate, Trapped, The Living Dead, Black Shadows, The Death Chamber, House of Peril, Hands in the Dark, 59th Second, Perilous Water, Bridge of Doom, Treasury, The Storm's Lash, The Purloined Papers, The Flaming Menace* and *Wages of Sin*.

Les Premières Armes de Rocambole

1923 French film (SEC/6 reels) featuring the villainous anti-hero Rocambole created by Pierre Alexis Ponson Du Terrail. Gang leaders Sir William (Albert Decoeur) and Rocambole (Maurice Thorèze) create a scheme to get hold of the Count de Chambery's fortune by having Rocambole impersonate the rightful heir Jean Robert (Pierre Fresnay). It goes wrong on the day Rocambole is to marry a rich heiress. Charles Maudru wrote the screenplay and directed. See also *Rocambole*.

The Price of a Party

1924 American film (Howard Estabrook/6 reels) based on the story "The Price of a Party" by William Briggs MacHarg published in *Cosmopolitan* magazine. Cabaret dancer Grace Barrows (Hope Hampton) is paid by crooked broker Kenneth Bellwood (Arthur Carew) to vamp rival Robert Casson (Harrison Ford). (She says she needs the money to help her sick mother.) Grace's innocent younger sister Alice (Mary Astor) comes to town and enticed to visit Bellwood at his apartment. Grace goes there first with Bellwood's former mistress Evelyn and confronts him. After she leaves and Alice arrives, Bellwood is killed and Alice is accused of the murder. Luckily for her Evelyn decides to commit suicide and leave a note saying she did the killing. Alice is sent home. Charles F. Roebuck wrote the screenplay and Charles Giblyn directed.

The Price of Fear

1928 American film (Universal/5 reels) based on a story by William Lester (pseudonym of William A. Berke) who also wrote the screenplay. Amateur detective Grant Somers (Bill Cody) takes a job as a waiter at the Red Rooster Café so he can learn about a gang leader known as The Professor and makes friends with Satin Sadie (Grace Cunard). When a stool pigeon is murdered by the Professor's gang, Grant is the chief suspect. Mary (Duane Thompson), a professional detective working as a maid in the Professor's house, hears of a plot to kill Grant and advises him to flee. When the Professor discovers that Mary is a detective he orders her killed but Grant returns with police in time to rescue her and get the Professor and his gang arrested. Leigh Jason directed.

Grace Cunard played Satin Sadie in *The Price of Fear*.

The Price of Silence see At the Mercy of Tiberius

The Priory School

1921 British film (Stoll/2 reels), an episode in the *Adventures of Sherlock Holmes* series based on a story by Sir Arthur Conan Doyle. Sherlock Holmes solves a mystery involving a kidnapped schoolboy. Eille Norwood portrays Holmes with Hubert Willis as Dr. Watson. William J. Elliot wrote the script and Maurice Elvey directed. A print of this film survives at the BFI archive.

Proxies

1921 American film (Cosmopolitan/7 reels) based on the short story "Proxies," by Frank R. Adams first published in *Cosmopolitan* magazine in 1920. Reformed criminals Clare (Zena Keefe) and Peter (Norman Kerry) are working as maid and butler in the home of Christopher Darley (William Tooker). Business partner John Stover (Paul Everton) tries to get Darley involved in a crooked stock scheme but Darley refuses. Stover then gets a bunch of proxies that will allow him to outvote Darley and initiate the fraud but Clare and Peter learn about it. They arrange a holdup at a party, steal the proxy and burn it. Afterwards they tell Darley why they did it. He gives them a house as a wedding present. George D. Baker wrote and directed the film.

Pudd'nhead Wilson

1916 American film (Paramount/5 reels) based on the 1894 novel *The Tragedy of Pudd'nhead Wilson* by Mark Twain. Lawyer Pudd'nhead Wilson (Theodore Roberts) is an amateur detective with an obsession about fingerprints. In the pre–Civil War South this is considered ridiculous and he is mocked. However, sample prints made of two infants help solve a murder many years later. The children had been switched soon after their birth. The false Driscoll heir (Alan Hale) murders his uncle and blames his valet Chambers (Thomas Meighan) for the crime. But the valet is actually the real heir and Wilson proves this to a jury through their fingerprints. Margaret Turnbull wrote the screenplay and Frank Reicher directed.

The Purple Cipher

1920 American film (Vitagraph/5 reels) based on the story "The Purple Hieroglyph" by Will F. Jenkins published in *Snappy Stories* in 1920. Millionaire Leonard Staunton (Earle Williams) is touring Chinatown with Jack Baldwin (Ernest Shields), Alan Fitzhugh (Allen Forrest) and Jeanne Baldwin (Vola Vale) when Jeanne is abducted. She is rescued with the help of detective Frank Condon (Henry A. Barrows). Some time later Baldwin and Fitzhugh go missing, reportedly abducted by Chinese gangsters. When Jeanne is threatened, Staunton agrees to meet the blackmailers but turns up in a submarine. He captures the blackmailers who turn out to be Condon, Fitzhugh and Baldwin who planned the scheme. J. Grubb Alexander wrote the screenplay and Chester Bennett directed. The 1930 film *Murder Will Out* was based on the same story.

The Purple Mask

1916 American serial (Universal/fifteen 2-reel episodes) Rich socialite Patricia Montez (Grace Cunard) is secretly the Queen of the Apaches, a female Robin Hood who steals from the rich to give to the poor. Her trademark is a purple mask which she leaves at the crime scene.

Francis Ford is detective Phil Kelly in *The Purple Mask*.

Her nemesis is detective Phil Kelly (Francis Ford), known as the Sphinx for his stone face, who is always in hot pursuit. The supporting cast included Jean Hathaway, Peter Gerald, Jerry Ash, John Featherstone, John Duffy and Mario Bianchi. Cunard and Ford wrote the screenplay and Ford directed. The episodes are *The Vanished Jewels, Suspected, The Capture, Facing Death, The Demon of the Sky, The Silent Feud, The Race for Freedom, Secret Adventure, A Strange Discovery, House of Mystery, Garden of Surprise, The Vault of Mystery, The Leap, The Sky Monsters, Floating Signal* and *Prisoner of Love.*

The Quarry

1915 American film (Selig/3 reels) based on John A. Moroso's 1913 novel *The Quarry*. A man who has been framed for murder escapes but is pursued by a persistent detective. He is the quarry. Gilson Willets wrote the screenplay and Lawrence Marston directed. The novel was filmed a second time in 1921 as *City of Silent Men.*

Queen o' Diamonds

1926 American film (FBO/6 reels) based on a story by Fred Myton, who wrote the screenplay. Chorus girl Jerry Lyon (Evelyn Brent) pretends to be look-alike Broadway star Jeanette Durant (Brent again) who has been kidnapped. What she doesn't know is that the kidnapping was arranged by a gang of jewel thieves who were double-crossed by Jeanette's jewel thief lover (William Bailey). Soon she is in deep trouble and suspected of murdering one of the crooks. Brent demonstrated real effectiveness as a screen criminal; *Variety* called her the perfect "crookess." Chet Withey directed.

The Queen of Hearts

1918 American film (Fox/5 reels) based on a story by Harry O. Hoyt. Pauline Cheraud (Virginia Pearson) finds her father murdered in his library after he promises to close his gambling house. She takes control of the casino to find the killer. There are three suspects: one who owed her father a lot of money, one who said he would kill to win her affections and one whose coat button was found in library. It belongs Jimmie (Victor Sutherland) whom she loves but luckily servant Pierre confesses he killed his employer upon learning he was about to lose his job. Adrian Johnson wrote the screenplay and Edmund Lawrence directed.

The Queen of Hearts

1923 British film (Stoll/2 reels), an episode in the *Mystery of Fu Manchu* series based on a story by Sax Rohmer. Dr. Fu Manchu (Harry Agar Lyons) kidnaps Dr. Petrie (Humberston Wright) and a famous surgeon and forces them perform an operation he requires. A. E. Colby directed, Frank Wilson wrote the screenplay with Colby and D. P. Cooper was the cinematographer. Print survives at BFI film archive.

Queen of the London Counterfeiters

1914 British film (B&C/3 reels) shown in America as *Queen of the Counterfeiters*. A detective (Fred Morgan), on the trail of a female counterfeiter (Lillian Wiggns), gets tricked and thrown into the Thames in a sack.

The Quest of the Sacred Jewel

1914 American film (Eclectic-Pathé/4 reels) loosely based on Wilkie Collins' novel

Evelyn Brent is trying to get away with the loot in *Queen o' Diamonds.*

The Moonstone. A valuable jewel is stolen and a police inspector is asked to investigate. George Fitzmaurice directed and the cast included Charles Arling, Edna Mayo, William Roselle and Ernest Truex. See *The Moonstone* for other films based on the novel.

Quincy Adams Sawyer

Suave Boston lawyer Quincy Adams Sawyer, the creation of American author Charles Felton Pidgin, was featured in *Quincy Adams Sawyer, Detective* (1912) and other tales of Mason Corner folks in Massachusetts. Sawyer appeared in two silent films, both based on a play about the character (see below).

Quincy Adams Sawyer

1912 American film (Puritan Special Features/4 reels) based on the 1902 play *Quincy Adams Sawyer* by Justin Adams. Boston lawyer Quincy Adams Sawyer goes to rural Mason's Corner to help a friend persuade Mrs. Putnam to let him marry her adopted daughter Lindy. Mrs. Putnam want the girl to marry lawyer Obadiah Strout instead and threatens to conceal the secret of her birth unless she cooperates. Sawyer does some detective work and discovers that the girl's father is Lord Fernborough of England and that the proof is in a letter held by Mrs. Putnam's blind niece Alice Pettingill Alice gives Lindy the letter, Quincy falls in love with Alice and a doctor restores her sight.

Quincy Adams Sawyer

1922 American film (Sawyer-Lubin Pictures/8 reels) based on the 1902 play *Quincy Adams Sawyer* by Justin Adams. Boston lawyer Quincy Adams Sawyer (John Bowers) goes to the small town of Mason's Corner to look into the affairs of Mrs. Putnam (Claire McDowell) after the death of her husband. Lindy Putnam (Barbara La Marr) sets her sights on him but Quincy prefers the beautiful blind Alice Pettingill (Blanche Sweet). Mrs. Putnam's lawyer Obadiah Strout (Lon Chaney) causes trouble until Quincy uncovers Strout's efforts to swindle Mrs. Putnam. The starry cast also included Elmo Lincoln, Louise Fazenda, June Elvidge, Gale Henry and Hank Mann. Clarence G. Badger directed.

Der Rabbi von Kuan-Fu
(The Monk of Kuan Fu)

1919 German film (May Film/9 reels), the third episode in the big budget and German series *Herrin der Welt* (Mistress of the World) based on a novel by Karl Figdor. Mia May stars as Maud Gregaards who has gone to China to get the key to the location of the lost treasure of the Queen of Sheba. It is contained in a jewel in the possession of the Kuan Fu monk. The supporting cast includes Michael Bohnen, Hans Mierendorff and Henry Sze. Richard Hutter wrote the screenplay and Joe May directed.

A Race with Rogues

1921 American film (Universal/2 reels), one of the episodes in the serial *The Diamond Queen*. Detective Bruce Weston (George Chesebro) helps Doris (Eileen Sedgewich) fight villains who want to steal her father's invention, a machine that turns dust into diamonds. George W. Pyper wrote the screenplay and Ed Kull directed.

Die Rache der Maud Fergusson
(Maude Fergusson's Revenge)

1920 German film (May Film/9 reels), the final episode in the big budget German series *Herrin der Welt* (Mistress of the World) based on a novel by Karl Figdor. Mia May plays Maud Gregaards-Fergusson who has become the richest woman in the world and is now able to exact revenge on her enemies, especially Baron Murphy (Hans Mierendorff). The cast includes Michael Bohnen and Henry Sze. Fritz Land wrote the screenplay and Joe May directed.

The Radio Detective

1926 American serial (Universal/ten 2-reel chapters) based on the 1925 story "The Radio Detective" by Arthur B. Reeve published in the collection *The Boy Scout's Craig Kennedy* (Reeve later turned the screenplay by Karl Krusada into a novel). Detective Craig Kennedy (John T. Prince) and a group of boy scouts come to the aid of scoutmaster Easton Evans (Jack Dougherty) who has invented a new radio system. A bunch of crooks are trying to steal it. William Craft and William Crinley directed.

Easton Evans (Jack Dougherty) rescues Ruth Adams (Margaret Quimby) in *The Radio Detective*.

Raffles

A. J. Raffles, the most famous gentleman cracksman in detective fiction, was the creation of E.W. Hornung. He made his first appearance in *Cassell's* magazine in 1898 and his popularity boomed after the publication of *The Amateur Cracksman* in 1899. The character was very popular with filmmakers and was featured in a dozen silent movies in America, Denmark, Italy and England. Raffles was not a member of society but he was accepted into it because he was a notable cricket player. His Watson-like chronicler is Bunny Manders, a devoted friend despite his dislike of the criminal life. See below and *Mr. Justice Raffles, La redenzione di Raffles* and *Sherlock Holmes vs. Raffles*.

Raffles, the Amateur Cracksman

1905 American film (Vitagraph/1 reel). Raffles, the gentleman cracksman created by E.W. Hornung, mixes with criminals and society and seems able to steal with impunity. J. Barney Sherry played Raffles and G. M. Anderson directed.

Raffles, the Amateur Cracksman

1917 American film (Hyclass/7 reels) based on E.W. Hornung's 1899 novel and the 1906 play *Raffles, the Amateur Cracksman* by Hornung and Eugene Presbrey. John Barrymore plays Raffles and Frank Morgan is Bunny. Raffles foils Scotland Yard detective Bedford (Frederick Perry) and succeeds in several jewel thefts while wooing beautiful Gwendolyn (Evelyn Brent). George Irving directed, Anthony P. Kelly wrote the screenplay and Harry B. Harris was the cinematographer. This film survives and is DVD.

Raffles, the Amateur Cracksman

1925 American film (Universal/6 reels) based on E.W. Hornung's novel and a 1906 play by Hornung and Eugene Presbrey. House Peters plays Raffles and Freeman Wood is Bunny. Detective Bedford (Frederick Esmelton) attempts to trap Raffles using a pearl necklace as bait but Lady Gwendolyn (Miss Du Pont) learns about it and gives Raffles a warning. He escapes with

House Peters was Raffles in *Raffles, the Amateur Cracksman*.

her and the pearls but later returns the pearls with a promise to reform. King Baggot directed, Harvey Thew wrote the screenplay and Charles Stumar was the cinematographer.

Ragan in Ruins

1925 British film (Stoll/2 reels) based on a story by "Seamark," an episode in the second series of *Thrilling Stories From The Strand*. Fred Paul and Prudence Ponsonby starred, Hugh Croise wrote the screenplay and Fred Paul directed.

A Railroad Conspiracy

1913 American film (Kalem/1 reel), one of the films in *The Railroad Detective* series. This one featured Miriam Cooper and Mrs. James Ross.

The Railroad Detective

1908–1913 American series (Kalem/1 reel films). The Kalem studio specialized in railroad movies including the long-running *The Hazards of Helen* series. One of its earliest ventures in the genre was an occasional series built around a railroad detective. The titles included *The Railroad Detective* (1908), *A Railroad Lochinvar* (1912), *The Railroad Detective's Dilemma* (1913), *The Railroad Inspector's Peril* and *A Railroad Conspiracy* (1913).

The Railroad Detective

1908 American film (Kalem/1 reel), the first film in *The Railroad Detective* series.

The Railroad Detective's Dilemma

1913 American film (Kalem/1 reel), the third film in *The Railroad Detective* series. This one featured Miriam Cooper, James B. Ross, Robert Walker and Harland Moore.

The Railroad Inspector's Peril

1913 American film (Kalem/1 reel), one of the films in *The Railroad Detective* series. This one featured Miriam Cooper and Robert Walker.

A Railroad Lochinvar

1912 American film (Kalem/1 reel), the second film in *The Railroad Detective* series. This one featured Henry Hallam, Miriam Cooper, Guys Coombs and William H. West.

The Railroad Raiders

1917 American serial (Signal Films-Mutual/2 reels). Helen Holmes joins railroad detective Leo Maloney in investigating the mystery of how her innocent father was convicted on circumstantial evidence of stealing money from the railroad. It turns out the criminals hired a look-alike to accept the money when it was delivered to the station. The duo go after the crooks to get the proof. J. P. McGowan directed and Ford Beebe wrote the screenplay. The episodes are *Circumstantial Evidence, A Double Steal, Inside Treachery, A Race for a Fortune, A Woman's Wit, The Overland Disaster, Mistaken Identity, A Knotted Cord, A Leap for Life, A Watery Grave, A Desperate Deed, A Fight for a Franchise, The Road Wrecker, The Trap* and *Mystery of the Counterfeit Tickets*.

A Rank Outsider

1920 British film (Broadwest/5 reels). based on the 1900 novel *A Rank Outsider* by Nat Gould. The story revolves around a murder and a frame-up at a racetrack. The cast included Gwen Stratford as Myra Wynchmore, Cameron Stratford as Captain Ferndale, Lewis Dayton as Guy Selby, John Gliddon as Ralph Wynchmore, Miles Mander and Martita Hunt. Patrick L. Mannock wrote the screenplay and Richard Garrick directed.

Raskolnikov

1916 Hungarian film (3 reels). based on Fyodor Dostoevsky's 1866 novel *Crime and Punishment* which features the detective Porfiry who extracts a confession of murder from the student Raskolnik. With Károly Lajthay. See also *Crime and Punishment*.

Raskolnikov

1923 German film (Leonardi film/9 reels) based on Fyodor Dostoevsky's 1866 novel *Crime and Punishment*. Grigori Chmara played the student Raskolnikov with Maria Krishanowskaja as Sonia in this highly stylized expressionistic version of the novel created by writer-director Robert Wiene. Inspector Porfiry investigates the crime. See also *Crime and Punishment*.

Das Rätselhafte Inserat
(The Puzzling Advertisement)

1915 German film (May Film/4 reels) featuring the "American" detective Joe Deebs as played by Harry Liedtke. This was a film in the long-running Deebs series created by producer Joe May in 1914 who also wrote and directed it. The supporting cast included Leopold Bauer, Kurt Busch, Hugo Flink and Else Roscher. See Deebs, Joe for other films.

Das Recht auf das Dasein
(The Right to Exist)

1913 German film (Delmont/2 reels). Writer/director/star Joseph Delmont plays a German detective who solves crime while performing daredevil stunts.

Red Aces

1929 British film (British Lion/7 reels) based on the title story of Edgar Wallace's 1929 collection *Red Aces* about former Scotland Yard detective J. G. Reeder. A gambler frames a banker for the murder of a man and Reeder has to uncover the truth. The film was written and directed by Wallace himself and he presumably selected George Bellamy to portray Reeder. The supporting cast included Janice Adair as Margot Lynn, Muriel Angelus as Ena Burslem, Douglas Payne as Inspector Gaylor, Nigel Bruce as T. B. Kinsfeather and Geoffrey Gwyther as Kenneth McKay. See also Reeder, J. G.

The Red Circle

1915 American serial (Balboa-Pathé/fourteen 2-reel episodes). Ruth Roland plays a Jekyll-and-Hyde heroine cursed with a mysterious red circle birthmark that causes her to commit crimes. Frank Mayo plays a detective who chases after and discovers the secret of her double-sided personality. After many thrilling adventures he catches and cures her. Will M. Ritchey and H. M Horkeimer wrote the screenplay and D. Sherwood MacDonald directed. The episodes were titled *Nevermore, Pity the Poor, Twenty Years Ago, In Strange Attire, Weapons of War, False Colors, Two Captives,*

Ruth Roland commits crimes because of her birthmark in *The Red Circle* (sheet music cover).

Peace at Any Price, Dodging the Law, Excess Baggage, Seeds of Suspicion, Like a Rat in a Trap, Branded as a Thief and *Judgment Day*.

The Red Circle

1922 British film (Stoll/2 reels), an episode in the *Further Adventures of Sherlock Holmes* series based on a story by Sir Arthur Conan Doyle. Sherlock Holmes uncovers the secrets of Italian secret society. Eille Norwood portrays Holmes with Hubert Willis as Dr. Watson. George Ridgewell wrote the adaptation and directed. Print survives at the BFI archive.

The Red Glove

1918 American serial (Universal/eighteen 2-reel chapters) based on Douglas Grant's novel *The Fifth Ace*. The masked criminal known as the Vulture (Leon De La Mothe) and his gang terrify rancher Billie (Marie Walcamp) as they try to solve the mystery of the treasure hidden in the Pool of Lost Souls. Hope Loring wrote the screenplay and J. P. McGowan directed. The episodes are titled *The Pool of Mystery, The Claws of the Vulture, The Vulture's Vengeance, The Passing of Gentleman Geoff, At the Mercy of a Monster, The Flames of Death, A Desperate Chance, Facing Death, A Leap for Life,*

Out of Death's Shadow, Through Fire and Water, In Death's Grip, Trapped, The Lost Millions, The Mysterious Message, In Search of a Name, The Rope of Death and *Run to Earth*.

Red Lights

1923 American film (Goldwyn/7 reels) based on *The Rear Car: A Mystery Play* by Edward E. Rose. Sheridan Scott (Raymond Griffith) is a different kind of detective. He calls himself a "crime deflector" who prevents rather than solves crimes. His latest case involves Ruth Carson (Marie Prevost), the daughter of a railroad president. She had been kidnapped as a child and just found in Los Angeles but she seems to be in great danger. Detective Scott deflects the danger and discovers the reasons behind it. Carey Wilson wrote the screenplay and Clarence Badger directed. The play was filmed again in 1934 as *Murder in the Private Car*.

The Red Mouse see The Half Million Bribe

La Redenzione di Raffles

(The Redemption of Raffles)

1914 Italian film (Pasquali/3 reels) starring Ubaldo Maria Del Colle as the gentleman cracksman Raffles. He is hired by Nilde Bruno to retrieve a stolen manuscript that will reveal the hiding place of a treasure. Luigi Mele directed. The film was shown in America (confusingly) as *Lupin, the Gentleman Burglar*. See also *Raffles*.

The Red-Headed League

1921 British film (Stoll/2 reels), an episode in the *Adventures of Sherlock Holmes* series based on a story by Sir Arthur Conan Doyle. Sherlock Holmes solves a mystery involving red-headed men and a raid on a bank vault. Eille Norwood portrays Holmes with Hubert Willis as Dr. Watson. William J. Elliot wrote the script and Maurice Elvey directed. A print of this film survives at the BFI archive.

The Reed Case

1917 American film (Universal/5 reels) based on a story by Allen Holubar who also wrote the screenplay, directed the film and starred in it. Detective Jerry Brennon. (Holubar) takes a vacation at a mountain cabin owned by his friend Senator Reed (George Pearce). After being shot at, he finds a secret room where Reed's daughter Helen (Louise Lovely) has been imprisoned by kidnappers. It all turns out to be a plot by a rejected suitor who had hoped to win her love by rescuing her. She prefers the detective.

Reeder, Mr. J. G.

J. G. Reeder, the creation of Edgar Wallace, is a former Scotland Yard detective with mutton chop whiskers and pince-nez glasses who always carries an umbrella. He may not look impressive but he has an enviable memory for faces and the ability to solve cases by the use of what he calls his "criminal mind." His cases are described in *The Mind of Mr. J. G. Reeder* (1925), *Red Aces* (1929) and other Wallace collections. Reeder appeared in only one silent film, *Red Aces*.

The Regent's Park Mystery

1924 British film (Stoll/2 reels), an episode in the *Old Man in the Corner* series based on a story by Baroness Orczy. An armchair detective known as the Old Man in the Corner solves crimes while sitting in a tea shop and tells the solutions to a young woman journalist. Rolf Leslie played the Old Man and Renée Wakefield was journalist Mary Hatley. D. P. Cooper was the cinematographer and Hugh Croise wrote the adaptation and directed.

The Reigate Squires

1912 Anglo-French film (Franco British Film Company–Éclair/2 reels), an episode in the *Sherlock Holmes* series based on a story by Sir Arthur Conan Doyle. Sherlock Holmes solves a mystery involving evil deeds at Reigate. George Treville played Sherlock Holmes with M. Moyse as Dr. Watson and British actors in the supporting roles. Treville also directed in collaboration with Conan Doyle. See Holmes, Sherlock for other films.

The Reigate Squires

1922 British film (Stoll/2 reels), an episode in the *Further Adventures of Sherlock Holmes* series based on a story by Sir Arthur Conan Doyle. Sherlock Holmes solves the mystery of murders and burglaries at Reigate. Eille Norwood portrays Holmes with Hubert Willis as Dr. Watson. George Ridgewell wrote the adaptation and directed. A print survives at the BFI archive. See Holmes, Sherlock for other films.

Rescued by Rover

1905 British film (Hepworth/1 reel). Dog detective Rover follows the trail of a gypsy who has kidnapped a baby and leads the father to her lair. This famous film was a family production with Rover played by Hepworth's collie Blair, the father played by Cecil Hepworth who directed with Lewin Fitzhamon, the mother played by Mrs. Hepworth who wrote the screenplay and the baby by Barbara Hepworth who carried out her part with panache. This film survives and is on DVD.

The Resident Patient

1921 British film (Stoll/2 reels), an episode in the *Adventures of Sherlock Holmes* series based on a story by Sir Arthur Conan Doyle. Sherlock Holmes solves a mystery about a frightened man who hanged himself. Eille Norwood portrays Holmes with Hubert Willis as Dr. Watson. William J. Elliot wrote the script and Maurice Elvey directed. A print of this film survives at the BFI archive.

The Return of Boston Blackie

1927 American film (Chadwick/6 reels) based on a story by Jack Boyle. Cracksman Boston Blackie (Raymond Glenn) decides he will attempt to reform a pretty blonde (Corliss Palmer) who stole a necklace from a cabaret dancer (Rosemary Cooper). The necklace, it turns out, was given to the dancer by the blonde's womanizing father so Blackie replaces it in his safe as a warning. Harry O. Hoyt directed and Leah Baird wrote the screenplay. See also Blackie, Boston.

Rickshaw, the Detective

1911 American film (Reliance/1 reel). No other information available. Rickshaw is one of the detectives in the British series *Three-Fingered Kate*.

The Riddle of the Green Umbrella

1914 American film (Kalem/2 reels) based on a story by Hugh C. Weir. Detective Madelyn Mack (Alice Joyce) solves a murder mystery in a college town while helping a friend (Marguerite Courtot). Professor Helmar (James B Ross) owns a green umbrella which contains a death-dealing needle once used by the Borgias. He is poisoned by Professor Reynolds (Jere Austin) who says Professor Lloyd (Guy Coombs) did the dastardly deed using the umbrella. Mack, who has other ideas, gets a job as a maid in Reynolds home and uses a vocophone, a detectophone and a recordophone to trap him into a confession. "All the newest appliances of use to detectives have a place in this up-to-date tale of mystery," commented *Moving Picture World*. Sydney Raymond wrote the screenplay and Kenean Buel directed.

The Riddle of the Tin Soldier

1913 American film (Kalem/2 reels) based on a story by Hugh C. Weir. Detective Madelyn Mack (Alice Joyce) is hired by Andrews to find his five-year-old son Archie who has been kidnapped. Mack suspects Andrews' daughter Ethel of being involved and discovers the kidnapping was a fake arranged by Ethel to teach her father a lesson after he refused to help with her settlement work. When Ethel tries to bring Archie home, gangsters capture them both and send a note demanding ransom. Madelyn discovers that the note paper contains a drug used in certain cigarettes and finds a man smoking one. She follows him, discovers where Ethel and Archie have been taken and summons police who capture the kidnappers. The cast included Harry F. Millarde, Mary Clowes, Marguerite Courtot and George Hollister, Jr. Sydney Raymond wrote the screenplay and Kenean Buel directed.

The Ringer

1928 British film (British Lion/7 reels) based on the play *The Ringer* by Edgar Wallace, an adaptation of his novel *The Gaunt Stranger*. Wallace also wrote the screenplay. The Ringer is a criminal master of disguise. The police have no idea what he looks like without his disguise and are unable to prevent his killing a solicitor who caused the death of his sister. Leslie Faber played Dr. Lomond, Lawson Butt was solicitor Maurice Meister, Annette Benson was Cora Ann Milton, Nigel Barrie was Inspector Wembury and Hayford Hobbs was Inspector Bliss. Arthur Maude directed.

Rinty of the Desert

1928 American film (Warner Bros./5 reels). German shepherd Rin Tin Tin played a dog detective in this film assisting police detective Pat (Carroll Nye) in finding kidnapped Pop Marlow (Otto Hoffman). Rinty leads Pat to the underworld hideout where Pop is held prisoner by the evil Doyle (Paul Panzer). Harvey Gates wrote the screenplay and D. Ross Lederman directed.

Rin Tin Tin is the dog detective in *Tracked by the Police.*

A Rival Sherlock Holmes (Un rivale di Sherlock Holmes)

1907 Italian film (Ambrosio/584 feet) distributed in the U.S. in 1908 as *A Rival Sherlock Holmes.* Arrigo Frusta wrote and directed it. *The Motion Picture World* called it "A pictorial detective story of merit with many lightning changes of disguise by the detective in his pursuit of the lawbreakers. Exciting scenes and physical encounters are numerous. A sensational subject of superb dramatic effect."

The River House Mystery

1926 British film (FHC Productions/2 reels), an episode in the series *Inscrutable Drew, Investigator* featuring Henry Ainley as private detective Victor Drew. In this episode Drew and his assistant Dracos investigate the mystery of the river house. Frank Stuart plays Dracos, Warren Hastings is Dr. Humphries, Doris Nicholls is Violet Humphries and Ivor James is Martin Howard. Elliot Stannard wrote the screenplay and A. E. Coleby directed.

The Road of Strife

1915 American serial (Lubin/fifteen 2-reel chapters). Mysteries abound in this serial about a woman (Mary Charleson) who has lived an isolated life with an old professor. When she finally does get out and meets Crane Wilbur, he thinks she's a bit balmy and send her back home where she finds the professor dead. Or maybe not, as there is no body around when she gets help from Wilbur. Did she really see a mysterious hand clutching a curtain or has she gone mad? It takes fifteen chapters to find out. Emmett Campbell Hall wrote the screenplay and John Ince co-directed with Howell Hansell. The episodes are titled *The House of Secrets, The Face of Fear, The Silver Cup, The Ring of Death, No Other Way, The Strength of Love, Into the Night, In the Wolf's Den, The Iron Hand of the Law, The Unsparing Sword, The Valley of Shadow, The Sacrifice, The Man Who Did Not Die, A Story of the Past* and *The Coming of the Kingdom.*

Rocambole

Rocambole was the creation of French *feuilleton* novelist Pierre Alexis Ponson Du Terrail. Like Raffles and Arsène Lupin, he began as a villainous anti-hero and ends up as a righteous superhero. His adventures, which featured mysteries, began in 1857 in *L'Héritage Mys-*

térieux and continued through 1870. Ponson Du Terrail's died during the German invasion of France in 1871 but other writers then took up the task of recording Rocambole's adventures. Five Rocambole films were made in the silent era and dozens more after the coming of sound. See below and *Les Amours de Rocambole* and *Les Premières Armes de Rocambole*.

Rocambole

1914 French series (SCAGL/three 2-reel films) starring Gaston Silvestre as the villainous anti-hero Rocambole created by Pierre Alexis Ponson Du Terrail. The series was written and directed by Georges Denola and. the films were titled *Jeunesse de Rocambole*, *Exploits de Rocambole* and *Rocambole et l'héritage du marquis de Morfontaine*.

The Rogue

1918 American film (King Bee/2 reels) starring Oliver Hardy, Billy West, Leatrice Joy and Ethel Burton. Arvid Gillstrom directed.

A Rogue in Love

1916 British film (London-Jury/4 reels) based on a novel by Tom Gallon. Ex-convict Badgery (James Reardon) is asked to tell a poor man that his legacy does not exist but is unable to do it. It works out in the end, however.

A Rogue in Love

1923 British film (Diamond Super/6 reels) based on a novel by Tom Gallon. Ex-convict Badgery (Frank Stanmore) is asked to tell a poor man that money he is expecting from a rich uncle in New Zealand will not come because the man died. He goes to see the man (Fred Rains) at his boarding house but cannot bring himself to pass on the bad news, especially after meeting the man's daughter (Betty Farqhar) and falling in love with a woman working at the boarding house (Ann Trevor). It all works out in the end as the uncle is not dead. Harry Hughes wrote the screenplay and Albert Brouett directed.

The Rogue Syndicate

1915 American film (Kalem/1reel), an episode in the serial *The Ventures of Marguerite* starring Marguerite Courtot. She plays a rich heiress threatened by various villains who want to kidnap her and prevent her from getting married so she can inherit a fortune. The supporting cast include Richard Purdom, E. G. Roseman and Phil Hardy.

The Rogue Unmasked

1920 British film (Torquay & Paignton Photoplay Productons/2 reels), an episode in the serial *The Great London Mystery*. The Master Magician (illusionist David Devant) exposes a supernatural fraud Charles Raymond directed and co-wrote the screenplay with Hope Loring.

A Rogue with a Heart

1916 American film (Universal/1 reel) based on a story by Harry Ditmar. Hobart Henley, Sydney Bracey and Sydell Dowing are the stars and Robert F. Hill directed.

Rogues and Romance

1920 American film (Pathé/2 reels) based on the play *The Golden Senorita* by George B. Seitz who wrote the screenplay and directed. An American girl in Spain falls in love with a Spanish revolutionary and has to be rescued by her American fiancé. With June Caprice, Harry Semels, Marguerite Courtot and William P. Burt. *Variety* described the film as "inadequate."

The Rogues of London

1915 British film (Barker/4 reels). A minister's son stops a maid from killing herself and she prevents him from being framed for the murder of a crook's mistress. With Blanche Forsythe, Fred Paul, Maud Yates and Roy Travers. Rowland Talbot wrote the screenplay and Bert Haldane directed.

The Rogues of Paris

1913 American film (Solax/4 reels). Detective Henriette (Claire Whitney) and her detective father Lecoq set out to stop villainous Fauvel and his adventuress cohort Cora (Fraunie Franholz) from swindling his wealthy ward Margaret (Vinnie Burns). Director Alice Guy Blaché filmed this tale on location at Lake Hopaway and a Russell Sage castle.

Rogues of the Turf

1910 British film (Walterdaw/1 reel) The rogues are a racetrack tout and his bookie partner who attempt to bribe a jockey but are exposed by a stable boy.

Rogues of the Turf

1923 British film (Carlton-Butcher/6 reels) based on a play by John F. Preston. A racehorse owner's wife hatches a plan to steal a horse trained by her ex-husband. With Olive Stone, Fred Groves, James Lindsay, James Reardon and Mavis Clare. Wilfred Noy wrote the screenplay and directed.

A Rogue's Defeat

1917 American film (Monmouth/2 reels), an episode in the serial *Jimmy Dale Alias the Grey Seal* based on stories by Frank L Packard. Socialite Jimmy Dale, secretly the crime fighter known as The Grey Seal, is an urban Robin Hood. In this episode he battles and defeats a fellow rogue. Mildred Considine wrote the screenplay and McRae Webster directed.

The Rogue's Heart

1909 American film (Biograph/1 reel) written and directed by D. W. Griffith. With Marion Leonard, Florence Lawrence, Owen Moore, Linda Arvidson, Mack Sennett.

A Rogue's Nemesis

1916 American film (Kalem/2 reels), an episode in the progressive series *Social Pirates*. The "social pirates" are Marin Sais and Ollie Kirby, who work to bring justice to the poor while exposing criminals. James W. Horne directed.

The Rogue's Nest

1917 American film (Universal-IMP/2 reels) starring Edith Roberts, Lee Hill, Harry Mack and Nellie Allen. Constance Crawley and Arthur Maude wrote the screenplay and Donald McDonald directed.

The Rogue's Pawn

1917 American film (Kalem/1 reel), an episode in the series *Grant, Police Reporter*. Grant (George Larkin) investigates the mystery of Room 422 and gets some help from Ollie Kirby and Robert Ellis. Robert Welles Ritchie wrote the screenplay and Robert Ellis directed.

A Rogue's Romance

1919 American film (Vitagraph/5 reels) based on a story by H. H. Van Loan. Monsieur Picaard (Earle Williams) lives a double life in Paris as master thief and socialite but the police are suspicious. He falls in love with Helen Deprenay (Katherine Adams) but she has been warned against him. To prove himself he pretends to be a Scotland Yard detective and catches a jewel thief who was attempting to swindle the community. He then tells the police that Picard no longer exists and leaves with Helen. James Young wrote the screenplay and directed.

A Rogue's Wife

1915 British film (Neptune-Walterdaw/4 reels). A thief steals a lord's diamond and marries a vicar's daughter but gets betrayed by his ex-mistress. With Gregory Scott, Daisy Cordell, Joan Ritz, Frank Tennant.

Romance of a Rogue

1928 American film (Quality Distributing/6 reels) based on a novel by Ruby Mildred Ayres. H. B. Warner is sent to prison on the eve of his wedding to Anita Stewart because of lies by a villain in a wheelchair. When he gets out he seeks revenge. With Al Fisher and Charles Gerrard. Adrian Johnson wrote the screenplay and King Baggot directed.

The Romance of Elaine

1915 American serial (Wharton-Pathé/twelve 2-reel chapters) Villainous foreign agent Marcus Del Mar/Doctor X (Lionel Barrymore) attempts to steal plans for a super-torpedo invented by scientific detective Craig Kennedy (Arnold Daly) but Elaine Dodge (Pearl White) and Walter Jameson (Creighton Hale) keep getting in the way. A mysterious masked man rescued Elaine when she gets into danger. George B. Seitz, Joseph A Golden and Louis Gasnier directed while Seitz, Charles Goddard and Bertram Millhauser wrote the screenplay. The chapters are titled *The Last Torpedo, The Gray*

Friar, The Vanishing Man, The Submarine Harbor, The Conspirators, The Wireless Detective, The Death Cloud, The Search Light Gun, The Life Chain, The Flash, The Disappearing Helmet and *The Triumph of Elaine*. See *The Exploits of Elaine*.

Romance of the Underworld

1927 American film (Fox/7 reels) based on the 1911 play *A Romance of the Underworld* by Paul Armstrong. Detective Edwin Burke (Robert Elliott) discovers that pimp Derby Dan Manning (Ben Bard) is blackmailing former dance hall hooker Judith (Mary Astor) and investigates. It seems she married a guy who knew nothing of her past and Dan is threatening to tell all unless he gets compensation. With Judith's cooperation Burke gets enough evidence to put Dan in prison but not before her husband learns about her past. It works out all the same. Douglas Doty wrote the screenplay and Irving Cummings directed.

Rouletabille chez les bohémiens

(Rouletabille and the Bohemians)

1922 French serial (Société des Cinéromans/ten 2-reel episodes) starring Gabriel de Gavrone as Rouletabille under the direction of Henri Fescourt. Rouletabille, the clever detective who solved *The Mystery of the Yellow Room*, becomes involved in a complicated series of crimes. They include the theft of a precious book from the Bohemians by adventurer Hubert (Joe Hamman), the kidnapping of Odette (Edith Jehanne) by the Bohemians who believes she should be their queen and the revenge schemes of Bohemian leader Callixte (Suzanne Talba). Rouletabille sorts it out. This was an original screenplay by Gaston Leroux which he later turned into a novel.

Rouletabille, Joseph

Joseph Rouletabille, an amateur detective created by French author Gaston Leroux, made his debut in 1907 in the classic locked room mystery *Le Mystère de la chambre jaune* (The Mystery of the Yellow Room) and returned in its sequel *Le Parfum de la dame en noir* (The Perfume of the Lady in Black). Both have been filmed. Rouletabille is an investigative reporter for the Paris newspaper *L'Époque* but he is also a brilliant detective as he demonstrates in eight novels using logic and intuition to solve crimes. In *Le Mystère de la chambre jaune* Mathilde is assaulted in a locked room and valuable papers belonging to her scientist father are stolen. The famous detective Fréderic Larsan of the Sûréte investigates but young Rouletabille surprises everyone by proving that Larsan himself is the thief. Larsan returns in *Le Parfum de la dame en noir* and terrifies Mathilde until Rouletabille once again intervenes. Rouletabille was also featured in a silent French serial. See *The Mystery of the Yellow Room*, *Le Parfum de la dame en noir* and *Rouletabille chez les bohémiens*.

Rubber Heels

1927 comedy (Paramount/7 reels). Hawks (Chester Conklin) heads a gang of crooks who pretend to be private detectives for hire so they can steal jewels and return them for large rewards. Homer (Ed Wynn), who has taken a mail order course in detection but is still clueless, is hired by Hawks as a joke but fired when he asks for a salary. When Princess Aline (Thelma Todd) comes New York to sell the royal jewels, Hawks and Homer attend a reception in her honor. Despite everything Homer is able to retrieve the jewels when they are stolen and get the crooks arrested. J. Clarkson Miller wrote the screenplay and Victor Heerman directed.

The Rube Detective

1912 American comedy (Kalem/1 reel) starring comic John E. Brennan and William R. McKay. A rural detective played (Brennan) investigates a case.

The Running Fight

1915 American film (Pre-Eminent Films/5 reels) based on the 1910 novel *The Running Fight* by mystery writer William Hamilton Osborne. The plot of this overly-complicated murder mystery defies explication (and logic) but essentially goes like this. Banker Peter Wilkinson (Robert Cummings) bankrupts his firm and puts the money in an account belonging to his daughter Leslie (Violet Heming). His former mistress Madeline (Clarissa Selwynne) tries to kill him but misses and shoots his secretary. Bank vice president Illingsworth (George Pauncefort) is mistakenly sentenced to death for the killing. Wilkinson tries to sort it out with bribes but when that doesn't work out he helps his daughter's fiancé get elected governor so he can arrange pardons all round. This doesn't work out either so he stages a fake suicide. Louis Albion wrote the screenplay and James Durkin directed. *Variety* thought it was an excellent film. So it goes.

Running Water

1922 British film (Stoll/6 reels) based on the 1907 novel *Running Water* by A.E.W Mason. Garrett Skinner (Julian Royce) plans to arrange for the "accidental" death of young Wallie Hine (George Turner) after he has been persuaded to ensure his life for a large amount. Skinner's daughter Sylvia (Madge Stuart) arrives at the Alpine resort where they are staying and discovers the plot. Her sweetheart Capt. Hilary Cheyne (Lawford Davidson) helps her foil the plot. Kinchen Wood wrote the screenplay and Maurice Elvey directed.

The Sacred Order

1923 British film (Stoll/2 reels), an episode in the *Mystery of Fu Manchu* series based on a story by Sax Rohmer. Nayland Smith (Fred Paul) is lured into a trap by Dr. Fu Manchu (Harry Agar Lyons) using the Sacred Order of the White Peacock as bait. A. E. Colby directed, Frank Wilson wrote the screenplay with Colby and D. P. Cooper was the cinematographer. Print survives at BFI film archive.

The Sacred Ruby

1920 American Film (Arrow Film/5 reels) starring Glen White as Tex, a famous criminologist. Tex investigates the theft of a sacred East Indian ruby by a Hindu priest (David Wall) and the framing of am innocent man (Willard Cooley) with a false ruby. He is captured and almost killed by the thieves before the police intervene. Alexander Frank wrote the screenplay Glen White directed the film for the *Tex, Elucidator of Mysteries* series.

Sam Simpkins, Sleuth

1912 American comedy (Essanay/1 reel). Howard Missimer plays a comic detective in this send-up of sleuth films.

Say It with Sables

1928 American film (Columbia/6 reels) based on a story by Peter Milne and Frank Capra who wrote the screenplay and directed. Police detective Mitchell (Alphonse Ethier) investigates the gunshot death of golddigger Irene Gordon (Margaret Livingston) and suspects it is not the suicide it has been made to appear. He finds an earring clutched in her hand and a new sable coat. He learns that the coat came from Doug Caswell (Arthur Rankin) who had planned to marry her. Doug confesses he killed her after learning that she was the former mistress of his father John (Francis X. Bushman). His father contradicts him and says he was the killer. Mitchell searches the house and finds a earring that matches the one found at Irene's. Doug's mother Helen (Helene Chadwick) suggests that the murderer might have been a woman who went to Irene's apartment to get back love letters and struggled with her over a gun that went off accidentally. The detective says this was unlikely as he knows Irene committed suicide. He gives her back her earrings.

A Scandal in Bohemia

1921 British film (Stoll/2 reels), an episode in the *Adventures of Sherlock Holmes* series based on a story by Sir Arthur Conan Doyle. Sherlock Holmes is hired by a king to recover and incriminating photograph and meets a woman just as clever as he is. Eille Norwood portrays Holmes with Hubert Willis as Dr. Watson. William J. Elliot wrote the script and Maurice Elvey directed. A print of this film survives at the BFI archive.

The Scarab Ring

1921 American film (Vitagraph/6 reels) based on the short story "The Desperate Heritage" by Harriet Gaylord. Constance (Alice Joyce) learns from her dying father that he has been blackmailed by a cashier in his bank who had knowledge of his part in a crime, and she swears to keep the secret from her younger sister Muriel (Maude Malcolm). Hugh (Claude King) learns of the crime and threatens to reveal it unless Constance persuades Muriel to marry him. Martin is found dead and a scarab ring, like one owned by Constance, is found near the body. She is acquitted because of insufficient evidence but tells her fiancé (Joe King), that she killed him in defense of her honor. He forgives her and they decide to marry. C. Graham Baker wrote the screenplay and Edward José directed.

The Schemers

1922 American black cast film (Reol Productions/5 reels). A detective comes to the aid of a research chemist harassed by two men who want him to reveal a formula for a gasoline substitute. The chemist's sweetheart is kidnapped and he is framed for theft. The detective sorts it all out and proves that the men are notorious criminals. Heading the African-American cast were Lawrence Chenault, Edna Morton, G. Edward Brown, Walter Thomas, Bob Slater and Orma Crosby. Wallace Johnson wrote the screenplay and directed.

Der Schwarze Diamant
(The Black Diamond)

1913 German film (Werner/4 reels) featuring a woman detective known as *Miss Nobody*, part of a three-film series produced by Karl Werner for his company. Miss Nobody, who was portrayed by Senta Eichstaedt, was famous for her deductive abilities and the films were known for their exciting car chases. Rudolf Del Zopp wrote the screenplay and Willy Zeyn directed.

The Scrap of Paper

1920 American Film (Arrow Film/5 reels) starring Glen White as Tex, a famous criminologist. Milk producers sign a secret agreement to keep prices high but then milk trust boss Jacob Strauss (William Fredericks) is murdered and the document stolen. The other milk producers are the chief suspects but Tex has other ideas; he finds the real killer in an opium den. With supporting cast including Jane McAlpine Joseph Striker Leo Delaney and David Wall. Tom Collins directed the film for the *Tex, Elucidator of Mysteries* series.

A Search for Evidence

1903 American film (Biograph/217 feet). A detective and a wife peer through a series of keyholes at hotel rooms until they find one containing her husband and his cutie. It's the grounds for divorce she is seeking. G. M. Bitzer photographed it inventively in keeping with the story by using keyhole-shaped masks for the camera.

Search, the Scientific Detective

1914 American film (Biograph/half reel). Eddie Dillon directed and portrayed Search in this comedy parodying the work of Arthur Reeve's popular "scientific detective" Craig Kennedy.

The Second Stain

1922 British film (Stoll/2 reels), an episode in the *Further Adventures of Sherlock Holmes* series based on a story by Sir Arthur Conan Doyle. Sherlock Holmes solves the mystery of a missing government document and the murder of a crook. Eille Norwood portrays Holmes with Hubert Willis as Dr. Watson. George Ridgewell wrote the adaptation and directed. A print survives at the BFI archive.

Le Secret d'Argeville
(The Secret of Argeville)

1920 French film (Pathé-/3 reels), a late episode in a popular tongue-in-cheek comedy series about an "American" detective named Nick Winter. In this episode Nick (Georges Vinter) investigates the disappearance of valuable jewels at the Argeville Chateau and his chief suspect is Jeanne Brindeau. Paul Garbagi wrote the screenplay and directed. See also Winter, Nick.

The Secret of the Hills

1921 American film (Vitagraph/5 reels) based on William Garrett's novel The Secret of the Hills. American newspaperman Guy Fenton (Antonio Moreno) accidentally switches overcoats with the guardian of Marion Overton's (Lillian Hall) and is found murdered soon afterwards. Fenton is accused of the crime but is helped to escape by his friend Drew (Kingsley Benedict). Papers in the coat gives the location of a lost treasure which they eventually locate but not before Fenton and Marion are kidnapped by villainous Miltimore (Walter Rodgers) who also seeks the treasure. Drew rescues them and Miltimore is killed in a struggle after confessing to the murder. Chester Bennett directed and E. Magnus Ingleton wrote the screenplay.

The Secret Seven see Paul Sleuth and the Mystic Seven

The Secrets of Paris

1922 American film (Mastadon Films–Whitman Bennett/7 reels) based on the French novel *Les Mystères de Paris* by Eugène Sue. Rudolph is promoted from duke to king in the American adaptation of this famous novel. Rudolph (Lew Cody) is roaming the slums of Paris in disguise looking for his daughter by a peasant sweetheart. He becomes interested in Mayflower (Gladys Hulette) who lives with a band of thieves but does not at first realize she is his lost daughter. When she is kidnapped he joins forces with her friend François (William Collier, Jr.) to rescue her. They succeed but François is killed while helping them escape from a flooded dungeon. Dorothy Farnum wrote the screenplay adaptation and Kenneth Webb directed. There is also a French serial version of the novel, *Les Mystères de Paris*.

Secrets of the Night

1925 American film (Universal/7 reels) based on the 1929 play *The Nightcap, a Mystery Comedy* by Guy Bolton and Max Marcin (New York, 1929). Andrews (James Kirkwood) fakes his own murder at a party to stop a bank examiner from examining his records. The chief suspects are Hammond (Tom Ricketts), who loves Andrews' daughter Anne (Madge Bellamy), and Knowles (Arthur Stuart Hull) who thought Andrews had been flirting with his wife (Rosemary Theby). Detective Reardon (Arthur Thalasso) "solves" the case when the supposedly deceased Andrews reappears and announces that a large doubtful loan has been repaid to his bank. Edward J. Montagne wrote the screenplay and Herbert Blaché directed.

Sein bester Freund (His Best Friend)

1915 German film (May Film/4 reels) featuring the "American" detective Joe Deebs as played by Max Landa. This was an early film in the long-running Deeb series created by producer Joe May There were over thirty Deebs films with the detective portrayed by six different actors. See Deebs, Joe for other films.

Sergeant Lightning and the Gorgonzola Gang

1915 British comedy (Phoenix/1 reel). Detective Lightning catches houseboat thieves who use poison gas made from Gorgonzola cheese. James Read play Sgt. Lightning with Little Chrysia as Arabella. Read also wrote and directed the film.

Seven Keys to Baldpate

Earl Derr Biggers' 1912 mystery novel *Seven Keys to Baldpate* tells the story of a writer who makes a bet that he can finish a novel in twenty-four hours in the closed and deserted Baldpate Inn. It turns out to be not very deserted as people keep arriving with keys, seven in all. The novel was turned into a popular Broadway play in 1913 by George M. Cohan and the novel/play was filmed three times in the silent era, once with Cohan (see below).

Seven Keys to Baldpate

1916 Australian film (J.C. Williamson/5 reels) based on the novel and the play *Seven Keys to Baldpate*. A writer bets he can finish a novel in twenty-four hours in the deserted Baldpate Inn. Alex C. Butler played Jim Cargan, Dorothy Brunton was Mary Norton, J. Plumpton Wilson was Peters Agnes Keogh was Myra Thornhill and Gerald Harcourt was Lou Max. Alex C. Butler wrote the screenplay and Monte Luke directed.

Seven Keys to Baldpate

1917 American film (Artcraft/5 reels) based on the novel and the play *Seven Keys to Baldpate*. Magee (George M. Cohan) goes to Baldpate Inn to win a bet from its owner by be-

Magee offers to complete it in 24 hours at the deserted mountain resort Baldpate Inn owned by a friend. The caretaker gives him a key, which he says is the only one, and Magee begins writing. Then a man unlocks the door with a duplicate key and hides $200,000 in the safe. Five more people enter with their own keys, including crooks after the money. Magee thinks it's a frame-up to prevent his finishing the novel but then a policeman arrives with the seventh key and arrests them. Magee finishes the book and we discover that everything we saw was actually the plot of the novel. Fred Newmeyer directed from a screenplay by Frank Griffin, Wade Boteler and Jack MacKenzie.

The Seven Pearls

1916 American serial (Astra-Pathé/fifteen 1-reel chapters) revolves around seven pearls which need to be recovered by Creighton Hale or his girlfriend Mollie King will end up in a harem. Hale stole the pearls when he got involved with a gang of thieves but has reformed for love. Unfortunately the pearls are now scat-

Magee (George M. Cohan, right) makes a bet with his boss (John C. King) in *Seven Keys to Baldpate* that he can write a novel in 24 hours.

ginning a novel at midnight and finishing it in 24 hours. He is interrupted by a man who comes to the inn to bribe a mayor. Then newspaper reporter Mary Norton (Anna Q. Nilsson) arrives sniffing a bribe story. After more interruptions, gunplay, thefts and a visit from the police, Magee is about to quit when the Baldpate owner arrives and says he staged everything to keep the writer from winning the bet. But as the clock strikes twelve, Magee finishes the novel anyway and we learn that what we saw was the fantasy told in his novel. Hugh Ford wrote the screenplay and directed the film photographed by Ned Van Buren and Lewis W. Physioc. This film survives and is on DVD.

Seven Keys to Baldpate

1925 American film (Paramount/7 reels) based on the novel and the play *Seven Keys to Baldpate*. Writer William Magee (Douglas MacLean) is engaged to his publisher's daughter Mary (Edith Roberts) but the father is angry because he has not delivered a promised novel.

Creighton Hale has to locate the pearls in *The Seven Pearls* or his girlfriend will end up in a harem.

tered around the world and need a lot of detective work to find, especially as villain Leon Bary is also seeking them. The chapters were titled *The Sultan's Necklace, The Bowstring, The Air Peril, Amid the Clouds, Between Fire and Water, The Abandoned Mine, The False Pearl, The Man Trap, The Message on the Wire, The Hold-Up, Gems of Jeopardy, Buried Alive, Over the Falls, The Tower of Death* and *The Seventh Pearl*. Charles W. Goddard and George B. Seitz were the writers and Burton L. King and Donald McKenzie directed.

Sexton Blake

1909–1910 series (London Cinematograph/three 1-reel films) featuring master detective Sexton Blake. It was written and directed by S. Wormald with C. Douglas Carlile starring Sexton Blake. In *The Council of Three* he poses as a messenger boy to catch crooks, in *Lady Candale's Diamonds* he trails jewel thieves and in *The Jewel Thieves Run to Earth* he rescues a man tied to a clock-operated gun.

Sexton Blake

1909 British film (Melodrama/1 reel) directed by C. Douglas Carlile who played master detective Sexton Blake. The detective disguises himself as a minister to prevent a woman from marrying a murderer. The film was based on Carlile's stage play *Sexton Blake Detective* derived from the story *Five Years After* by W. Murray Graydon. See Blake, Sexton for other films.

Sexton Blake

1914–1915 British series (Davidson/seven 3-reel films) about master detective Sexton Blake written and directed by Charles Raymond. Phillip Kay played Blake in the first three films with Lewis Carlton as Tinker while Harry Lorraine played Blake in the last four with Bert Rex as Tinker. The films, which tell complete stories, were also distributed in America. They were *Britain's Secret Treaty, The Counterfeiters, The Great Cheque Fraud, The Kaiser's Spy, The Mystery of the Diamond Belt, The Stolen Heirlooms* and *The Thornton Jewel Mystery*.

Sexton Blake

1928 British series (British Filmcraft/six 2-reel films). about master detective Sexton Blake produced by George J. Banfield. Langhorne Burton played Sexton Blake with Mickey Brantford as Tinker. Blake solved a crime in each episode. See *Blake the Lawbreaker, The Clue of the Second Goblet, The Great Office Mystery, The Mystery of the Silent Death, Sexton Blake Gambler* and *Silken Threads*.

Sexton Blake, Gambler

1928 British film (British Filmcraft/2 reels), part of a six-film series featuring master detective *Sexton Blake* as played by Langhorne Burton with Mickey Brantford as his assistant Tinker. The supporting cast included Marjorie Hume, Frank Atherley, Adeline Hayden Coffin and Oscar Rosander. George J. Banfield produced and directed and G. H Teed wrote the screenplay.

Langhorne Burton was the famous detective in the 1928 British series *Sexton Blake*.

Sexton Blake vs. Baron Kettler

1912 British film (Humanity Story/645 feet) directed by Hugh Moss who played master detective Sexton Blake. The story, which involves the theft of secret defense plans, was based on a Blake tale in the periodical *Union Jack Weekly*.

Sexton Pimple

1913 British film (Folly/1 reel). Detective Sexton Pimple (Fred Evans) takes over a train to protect the King of Cork from spies in this parody of the Sexton Blake detective films. Part of the long-running Pimple series, it was distributed in America with the title *Pimple, Detective*.

British comic Fred Evans (Pimple) parodies the Sexton Blake films in *Sexton Pimple*.

Shadowed into the Underworld

1915 European detective film (4 reels) distributed in America by Lewis Pennant Pictures and panned by *Variety* as "palpably thin and far-fetched." It features a buxom woman detective with a male partner (he has "glued-on whiskers') investigating a murder in a nightclub. After a shoot-out, the villain is killed. The original film was probably German, possibly one of the *Miss Nobody* series.

Shadows of Night

1928 American film (MGM/7 reels). Flash the dog joins forces with reporter Jimmy (Lawrence Gray) to solve the murder of a policeman in this gangster tale. Flash tears off the license plate of the killer's car as he flees allowing Jimmy to identify him and track him down. When the cop-killer tries to escape in a coffin in a fake funeral, dog and human are not fooled. Warner Richmond plays the bad guy with Louise Lorraine and Polly Moran enlivening the plot. D. Ross Lederman directed. And co-wrote the screenplay with Ted Shane.

Sherlock Ambrose

1918 American comedy (L-KO Kompany/2 reels) starring Mack Swain as Ambrose the detective. The supporting cast included Lily Butler, Rae Godfrey, Hughie Mack, Jack Pearson and Bill Smithens Walter S. Fredericks directed.

Sherlock Bonehead

1914 American comedy (Kalem/2 reels) starring comic Lloyd Hamilton as a bonehead detective emulating Sherlock Holmes with support from Ruth Roland and Marshall Neilan. Neilan directed.

The Sherlock Boob

1914 American comedy (Rex/1 reel) starring Robert Z. Leonard as a boobish emulator of detective Sherlock Holmes. Leonard also wrote the screenplay and directed. Ella Hall lends support.

Sherlock Boob, Detective

1915 American comedy (Crown City–Mica/1 reel) about a boob who tries to be a detective in the Sherlock Holmes manner. Written by Bruce M. Mitchell.

Sherlock Brown

1922 American comedy (Bayard Veillier Productions–Metro/5 reels). Bert Lytell stars as would-be detective William Brown. He buys a detective badge for $5 and offers his help when a secret formula for explosives is stolen. Barbara (Ora Carew) discovers that villainous J. J. Wallace (DeWitt Jennings) has the formula and Brown helps her get hold of it. It is lost again (she was actually a crook as well) but after many misadventures Brown regains it and the baddies are caught. Bayard Veiller directed and Lenore J. Coffee wrote the screenplay. *Variety* thought it was skillful and amusing.

Sherlock Hawkshaw and Company

1921 American animated film (Bud Fisher Film Corp./1 reel) satirizing the Sherlock Holmes films. It was written and directed by Bud Fisher and based on his comic strip *Mutt and Jeff*.

Sherlock Holmes

1909 Danish series (Nordisk/ six 2-reel films). The success of the 1908 series *Sherlock Holmes vs. Raffles* starring writer-director Viggo Larsen as Holmes led Nordisk to make six more non-canonical Holmes films in 1909 which were also released in America. Larsen starred in the first three and Forrest Holger-Madsen took over the role of Holmes for the final three. Alwin Neuss played Dr. Watson in all six The English titles of three of the films were *The Theft of the Diamonds*, *The Murder in Baker Street* and *The Hotel Mystery*. See Holmes, Sherlock for list of other Holmes films.

Sherlock Holmes

1912 Anglo-French series (Éclair/eight 2-reel films) with Frenchman George Treville playing the great detective Sherlock Holmes and M Boyce as Dr. Watson. They were filmed at Bexhill-on-Sea under the direction of Treville with Arthur Conan Doyle's cooperation. The supporting roles were played by British actors. The films were *The Adventures of the Copper Beeches*, *The Beryl Coronet*, *The Reigate Squires*, *The Musgrave Ritual*, *A Mystery of Boscombe Vale*, *Silver Blaze*, *The Speckled Band* and *The Stolen Papers*. *Copper Beeches* is on video. See Holmes, Sherlock for list of other Holmes films.

Sherlock Holmes

1916 American film (Essanay/7 reels) based on the 1899 play *Sherlock Holmes* by

Viggo Larsen played Holmes in 1908 and 1909 Danish films.

William Gillette played Holmes in a 1916 American film.

William Gillette and starring Gillette as Holmes, Edward Fielding as Watson and Ernest Maupain as Moriarty. Holmes is hired by an aristocratic family to recover embarrassing papers held by Alice Faulkner (Marjorie Kay). Her sister was mistreated by the family and she has vowed revenge. Holmes gets the papers but gives them back when he realizes he has fallen in love with Alice. He says he will wait until she gives them to him herself. Holmes tells the family he failed but Alice, now in love with Holmes, rushes in and hands over the papers. Arthur Berthelet directed and H. S. Sheldon wrote the screenplay. See Holmes, Sherlock for list of other Holmes films.

Sherlock Holmes

1922 American film (Goldwyn/9 reels) based on the 1899 play *Sherlock Holmes* by William Gillette and starring John Barrymore as Holmes. Holmes is asked by Watson (Roland Young) to help Prince Alexis (Reginald Denny) clear himself of false theft charges. He does so, traps the real culprit, Professor Moriarty (Gustav von Seyffertitz), and winds the hand of Alice Faulkner (Carol Dempster). Albert Parker directed and Marion Fairfax and Earle Browne wrote the screenplay. See Holmes, Sherlock for list of other Holmes films.

Sherlock Holmes and the Great Murder Mystery

1908 American film (Crescent/1 reel) in which Sherlock Holmes is involved in a case involving a murder by a gorilla. It seems to have been based on Edgar Allan Poe's 1841 story "The Murders in the Rue Morgue" rather than a story by Sir Arthur Conan Doyle.

Sherlock Holmes Baffled

1903 American film (Biograph/284 feet). Filmed in 1900 and copyrighted in 1903, this was the first film about a detective. Sherlock Holmes is in his library reading when a burglar comes in and put his silver in a bag. When Holmes tries to catch him, he vanishes leaving the bag behind. Holmes picks up the bag, but the bag vanishes and the thief reappears and vanishes with the bag. Holmes sits down, baffled by the wonders of early trick photography. Arthur Marvin was the cameraman. This film survives and is on video. See Holmes, Sherlock for list of other Holmes films.

The Sherlock Holmes Girl

1914 American comedy (Edison/500 feet) starring Bliss Milford as the Sherlock Holmes girl. Milford wrote the script and Charles H. France directed.

Sherlock Holmes, Jr.

1911 American comedy (Rex/1 reel) directed by Edwin S. Porter. A parody of the Sherlock Holmes films.

Sherlock Holmes Solves the Sign of the Four

1913 American film (Thanhouser/2 reels) based on a story by Arthur Conan Doyle adapted for the screen by Lloyd Lonergan. Sherlock Holmes solves the mystery of the murder of a man and the theft of a box of valuable

John Barrymore played Holmes in a 1922 American film.

jewels. The only clue is a torn paper with the words "The Sign of the Four." Harry Benham played Sherlock Holmes, Charles Gunn was Dr. Watson and Mignon Anderson was the woman who should have inherited the jewels.

Sherlock Holmes vs. Raffles

1908 Danish series (Nordisk/three 2-reel episodes) starring writer-director Viggo Larsen as Sherlock Holmes and. Forrest Holger-Madson as Raffles. These non-canonical films, which describes Holmes' battle against master criminal Raffles, were distributed in America in 1909 by the Great Northern film company. The titles in English and Danish are: *Sherlock Holmes* (Sherlock Holmes I: Livsfare), *Sherlock Holmes II: Raffles Escapes from Prison* (Sherlock Holmes II: Raffles Flugt fra Faengslet) and *Sherlock Holmes III: The Detective's Adventure in the Gas Cellar* (Sherlock Holmes III: Det hemmelige Dokument). The Great Northern brochure called it "The season's biggest feature film. Sherlock Holmes captures the king of criminals. An absorbing subject, the interest of which is enhanced by novel stage effects. The fight in the moving train is the perfection of realism." The films won praise from American critics.

Sherlock, Jr.

1924 American comedy (Metro/5 reels). Buster Keaton stars as Sherlock Jr., a projectionist who takes a correspondence course in detecting. When he falls asleep, he dreams of his success as a detective, foiling a rival and rescuing his girl. The rival had accused him of stealing a watch from his girl's father but his girl solves that crime while he's asleep. Kathryn McGuire is the Girl, Ward Crane is the Rival and Joseph Keaton is the Father. Keaton directed from a screenplay by Clyde Bruckman. On DVD.

Sherlock Sleuth

1925 American comedy (Hal Roach/2 reels). Cyril Fromage (Arthur Stone), house detective at the Hotel Omigosh, is trying to catch a thief known as the Weasel. The hotel switchboard operator (Martha Sleeper) and the hotel manager (Noah Young) get involved in the action and a series of gags.

The Shielding Shadow

1916 American serial (Astra-Pathé/fifteen 2-reel chapters) based on a story by Randall Parrish. Serial queen Grace Darmond and partner Ralph Kellard starred in this suspenseful but confusing mystery about the theft of a cloak by a gang of thieves and their attempt to recover it. The cloak, when linked with a box

Buster Keaton dreams of his success as a detective in *Sherlock Jr.*

Grace Darmond (above) and Ralph Kellard (opposite) star in a serial about invisibility, *The Shielding Shadow.*

of black pellets (don't ask), gives the wearer invisibility. The chapter titles tell the story: *The Treasure Trove, Into the Depths, The Mystic Defender, The Earthquake, Through Bolted Doors, The Disappearing Shadow, The Awakening, The Haunted Hand, The Incorrigible Captive, The Vanishing Mantle, The Great Sacrifice, The Stolen Shadow, The Hidden Menace, Absolute Black* and *The Final Chapter*. George B. Seitz wrote the screenplay and Louis J. Gasnier and Donald MacKenzie directed.

The Shoes That Danced

1918 American film (Triangle/5 reels) based on mystery writer John A. Moroso's story "The Shoes That Danced" published in Metropolitan Magazine in 1917. Shopgirl Rhoda (Pauline Starke) loves Harmony Lad (Wallace MacDonald) who heads the New York Street gang Hudson Dusters. After two gang murders, she persuades him to give up crime for a singing career at the Pepper Box cabaret. Stumpy (Dick Rosson), the new leader of the Dusters, shoots a rival and Harmony is blamed and sought by the police. Rhoda tricks Stumpy into following her home and police arrest him thinking he is Harmony. Frank Borzage directed and Jack Cunningham wrote the screenplay.

Shorty and Sherlock Holmes

1914 American comedy (Broncho/2 reels), a parody of the Sherlock Holmes films starring Shorty Hamilton as Shorty with Sylvia Ashton and Betty Burbridge. Jay Hunt directed.

The Shrine of Seven Lamps

1923 British film (Stoll/2 reels), an episode in the *Mystery of Fu Manchu* series based on a story by Sax Rohmer. Nayland Smith (Fred Paul) shoots by Dr. Fu Manchu (Harry Agar Lyons), captures the Si-Fan gang and rescues the slave Karamanch. A. E. Colby directed, Frank Wilson wrote the screenplay with Colby and D. P. Cooper was the cinematographer. Print survives at BFI film archive.

The Sign of the Claw

1926 American film (Gotham/6 reels) starring German shepherd Peter the Great who was promoted as a dog detective. It was advertised as starring "Peter the Great in The Great Dog Detective Drama." In the film he helps his master, patrolman Robert Conway (Edward

Peter the Great is the dog detective in *The Sign of the Claw.*

Hearn) solve a bank robbery and frees a man who is tied up. James Bell Smith wrote the screenplay and B. Reeves Eason directed. Peter made six films in the 1920s and got top billing in most of them though this was the only one in which he was advertised as a detective. In *The Silent Accuser* (1924/MGM/6 reels) directed by Chester M. Franklin, he is witness to a murder and helps a wrongfully accused man wring a confession out of the real killer. In *Wild Justice* (1925/UA/6 reels) directed by Chester Franklin, he helps convict the man who killed his master. In *King of the Pack* (1926/ Gotham/ 6 reels) directed by Frank Richardson, he confronts a nasty widow and forces her to jump off a cliff. This film survives and is on DVD.

The Sign of the Four

1923 British film (Stoll/7 reels), an episode in the *Further Adventures of Sherlock Holmes* series based on a story by Sir Arthur Conan Doyle. Sherlock Holmes investigates a murder that leads back to criminal events in India. Eille Norwood plays Sherlock Holmes with Arthur Cullin as Dr. Watson, Madame d'Esterre as Mrs. Hudson, Isobel Elsom and Mary Morstan. Maurice Elvey directed and wrote the screenplay. Print survives at BFI film archive.

The Silent Command

1915 American film (Universal/4 reels). A father (Robert Leonard) promises to give his daughter (Ella Hall) to a doctor to pay for the operation that saved her life but reneges on the deal. The enraged doctor (Harry Carter), who is also a hypnotist, hypnotize the girl and she is seen approaching her sleeping father with a dagger. When he is found dead, she is arrested but her lawyer (Alan Forrest) thinks she is innocent. He finds a button that belonged to the doctor's butler and has the butler hypnotized. The butler confesses he was the murderer. Robert Leonard wrote the screenplay and directed.

The Silent Master

1917 American film (Selznick-Robert Warwick Film/6 reels). based on E. Phillips Oppenhem's novel *The Court of St. Simon*. Monsieur Simon (Robert Warwick), the Master, leads a band of Parisian Apaches who have their own code of justice. He involves a young American (Donald Galaher) is his schemes and the boy ends up in prison. Simon disbands his group and marries a woman (Olive Tell) who turns out to be the sister of the boy he ruined. French crime film master Léonce Perret made his American debut writing and directing this film.

The Silk Lined Burglar

1919 American film (Universal/6 reels) based on Jack Boyle's story "Miss Doris, Safecracker" in *Red Book Magazine*. Boston Blackie (Sam De Grasse) is hired by Doris Macon (Priscilla Dean) to open a safe in the home of Hoffmeier (Fred Kelsey). Doris takes papers and Blackie takes phonograph records which prove Hoffmeier is a German spy. Doris, it turns out, is in the secret service and Blackie wins praise from the government for his help. Jack Dillon directed and Fred Myton wrote the screenplay. See also Blackie, Boston.

Silken Threads

1928 British film (British Filmcraft/2 reels), one of a six-film series featuring master detective Sexton Blake played by Langhorne Burton with Mickey Brantford as his assistant Tinker. The supporting cast included Marjorie Hume, Leslie Perrins, Frank Atherley and Mrs. Fred Emney. George J. Banfield produced. Leslie Eveleigh directed and G. H. Teed wrote the screenplay. (See Blake, Sexton for background on detective and list of other films in which he appears.)

Silver Blaze

1912 Anglo-French film (Franco British Film Company–Éclair/2 reels), an episode in the *Sherlock Holmes* series based on a story by Sir Arthur Conan Doyle. Sherlock Holmes solves mystery revolving around a murder and a vanishing racehorse. George Treville played Sherlock Holmes with M. Moyse as Dr. Watson and British actors in the supporting roles. Treville also directed in collaboration with Conan Doyle. See Holmes, Sherlock for other films.

Silver Blaze

1923 British film (Stoll/2 reels), an episode in the *Last Adventures of Sherlock Holmes* series based on a story by Sir Arthur Conan Doyle. Sherlock Holmes solves the mystery of a famous racehorse that has vanished. Eille Norwood portrays Holmes with Hubert Willis as Dr. Watson. Alfred Moise was the cinematographer and George Ridgewell wrote the adaptation and directed. Print survives at BFI archive.

The Silver Buddha

1923 British film (Stoll/2 reels), an episode in the *Mystery of Fu Manchu* series based on a story by Sax Rohmer. Dr. Petrie (Humberston Wright) is captured by Dr. Fu Manchu (Harry Agar Lyons) while visiting an antique shop he suspects of harboring the evil doctor. A. E. Colby directed, Frank Wilson wrote the screenplay with Colby and D. P. Cooper was the cinematographer. Print survives at BFI film archive.

The Silver Car

1921 American film (Vitagraph/6 reels) based on a story by Wynham Martyn who wrote the screenplay and turned it into the novel *The Secret of the Silver Car*. Master criminal and sometimes detective Anthony Trent recognizes "William Smith" as a former war comrade he believed dead. When Colonel Langley refuses to divulge the man's real name, Trent breaks into his safe and finds that "Smith" is Arthur Grenvil and was falsely incriminated in a fraud aimed at his uncle. Trent helps Grenvil's sister Daphne destroys the fake evidence. When Trent then learns that the uncle is being blackmailed by Count Temesvar of Croatia, who threatens to expose a treaty, he gets the treaty and wins the hand of Daphne. Earle Williams played Trent, Kathryn Adams was Daphne, Geoffrey Webb was Grenvil and Eric Mayne was the nasty Count. David Smith directed.

Silver Fingers

1926 American film (Capitol Productions/5 reels) starring George Larkin. He plays a detective who pretends to be a master criminal so he can protect a diamond collection from being stolen by a gang of thieves. He not only succeeds, he wins the love of the daughter (Charlotte Morgan). of the owner of the diamonds. J. P. McGowan directed.

The Sin That Was His

1920 American film (Select-Selznick/6 reels) based on the 1917 novel *The Sin That Was His* by mystery writer Frank L. Packard. Gambler Raymond Chapelle (William) Faversham agrees to deliver money to the mother of a friend and gets into an argument with the friend's criminal brother who demands the money. Their fight wakes the mother who fires a gun in the darkness killing her son. Raymond flees and takes on the identity of a priest who is then mistaken for Raymond and arrested. Raymond decides to confess to clear him when the mother reveals that she shot her son. Edmund Goulding wrote the screenplay and Hobart Henley directed.

Sis the Detective

1916 American comedy (Kalem/2 reels) starring Rose Melville. Melville played an unsophisticated country bumpkin who is a lot smarter that she appears in her country bump-

Earle Williams plays master criminal and sometimes detective Anthony Trent in *The Silver Car.*

kin pigtails and gingham dress. Melville made twenty-one films as Sis and in this one she becomes a clever detective. Melville, who created the character on stage, became so famous in the role that she could not play anyone else. The film series was shot in Jacksonville, Florida, by Robert Ellis with scripts by Frank Howard Clark and Edwin F. Coffin.

The Six Napoleons

1922 British film (Still/2 reels), an episode in the *Further Adventures of Sherlock Holmes* series based on a story by Sir Arthur Conan Doyle. Sherlock Holmes solves the mystery revolving around the breaking of six busts of Napoleon. Eille Norwood portrays Holmes with Hubert Willis as Dr. Watson. George Ridgewell wrote the adaptation and directed. A print survives at the BFI archive.

Das Skelett des Herrn Markutius (The Skeleton of Mr. Markutius)

1920 German film (PAGU/5 reels) featuring the "American" detective Joe Deebs played by Curt Goetz. This was a late film in the long-running Deeb series created by producer Joe May in 1914. After May stopped making Deebs films, the mantle was picked up by Projektions-AG Union (PAGU). Curt Goetz wrote the screenplay and Victor Janson directed. The supporting cast included Franz von Egenieff, Hadrian Paul, Otto von Netto and Karl Rückert. See Deebs, Joe for other films.

The Sleuth

1911 French comedy (Eclipse/500 feet) about an inept detective.

The Sleuth

1921 American comedy (Reelcraft/1 reel) starring Billy Franey as a bumbling detective.

The Sleuth

1922 American comedy (Hal Roach-Pathé/2 reels) starring James Parrott as a comic detective. Raymond Grey directed.

The Sleuth

1922 American comedy (Vitagraph/2 reels) about an incompetent detective starring Larry Semon and Oliver Hardy. Semon wrote and directed the film with Tom Buckingham.

The Sleuth

1925 American comedy (Standard Cinema Corp/2 reels) starring Stan Laurel as an ineffective detective.

Sleuth, Paul

1912–1914 British series of 1-reel films revolving around detective Paul Sleuth portrayed by Charles Vane. Sleuth's primary gimmick was to disguise himself as someone else so he could trap criminals. The films were based on stories by Stanhope Sprigg, directed by Dave Alylott and produced by Cricks and Martin. See *Paul Sleuth* for the films.

Sleuthing

1913 American film (Vitagraph/2 reels) starring Norma Talmadge with supporting cast of Florence Radinoff, Wally Van, Kate Price, Hughie Mack and Joseph J. Dowling. Bert Angeles directed and Beta Breuil wrote the screenplay.

Sleuths

1919 American film (Mack Sennett Comedies/2 reels). Comedy about starring Ben Turpin, Chester Conklin, Heinie Conklin, Tom Kennedy and Marie Prevost. Richard Jones directed.

Sleuths and Slickers

1918 American film (Vitagraph/2 reels). Comedy about incompetent detectives written by and starring Joe Rock and Earl Montgomery. J. A. Howe directed.

Sleuths and Surprises

1918 American film (Vitagraph/1 reel). Comedy about ineffective detectives written and directed by Henry Kernan.

The Sleuths at the Floral Parade

1913 American comedy (Keystone/1 reel), a film in the *Two Sleuths* series produced and directed by Mack Sennett and starring Sennett and Fred Mace.

The Sleuths Last Stand

1913 American comedy (Keystone/1 reel), a film in the *Two Sleuths* series produced and directed by Mack Sennett and starring Sennett and Fred Mace.

Sleuths Unawares

1913 American film (Vitagraph/1 reel). Comedy about detectives directed by and starring Robert Thornby. The cast included George Stanley, Loyola O'Connor, George Cooper and Otto Lederer.

Slim Becomes a Detective

1913 American comedy (Universal Frontier/1 reel), a film in the *Slim* series of comedies starring Walter L. Rogers. In this one he becomes an incompetent detective. Elizabeth Burbridge adds support.

Smith, Dennis Nayland

Sir Denis Nayland Smith, the Scotland Yard detective nemesis of Dr. Fu Manchu in the stories by Sax Rohmer, was first seen on the screen in a 1923 British series titled *Mystery of Dr. Fu Manchu*. Smith was portrayed by Fred Paul with Harry Agar Lyons as Fu Manchu. The series was so popular a second series was made in 1924, *Further Mysteries of Dr. Fu Manchu*, with Smith reprising the role. See also *Dr. Fu Manchu*.

Smith, Whispering

Whispering Smith is a railroad detective created by Frank Hamilton Spearman for his 1906 novel *Whispering Smith*. Spearman traveled to Wyoming to get background for his novel and supposedly based him on a real person. The novel follows Whispering, so called because he lost his voice through a bad cold, through four years of adventures The character was so popular he inspired five silent films. See *Whispering Smith* for the films.

Sniffkins Detective and the Missing Cigarette Cards

1914 British comedy (Cricks/1 reel) directed by Edwin J. Collins. A comic detective tracks down thieves who stole cigarette cards.

The Social Code

1923 American film (Metro/5 reels) based on Rita Weiman's story "To Whom It May Concern." Viola Dana plays Babs, a debutante flapper who has to comes to the rescue of her boyfriend (Malcolm McGregor) who is on trial for murder. He refuses to give an alibi that would ruin a woman's reputation but she finds a solution. Oscar Apfel directed and Rex Taylor wrote the screenplay.

The Society Raffles

1905 American film (Biograph/59 feet). A man in evening dress seats a lady by an open window after conferring with his burglar accomplice outside. While talking to her he removes her diamond tiara from her head and passes it to his accomplice without her noticing F. A. Dobson wrote, directed and photographed this one-minute film about a Raffles-like crook.

A Society Sherlock

1916 American comedy (Victor/2 reels), a parody of the Sherlock Holmes films starring Irma Dawkins and William Garwood. Garwood directed and Norbert Lusk wrote the screenplay.

The Solitary Cyclist

1921 British film (Stoll/2 reels), an episode in the *Adventures of Sherlock Holmes* series based on a story by Sir Arthur Conan Doyle. Sherlock Holmes solves a mystery involving a woman who is being followed by a mysterious cyclist. Eille Norwood portrays Holmes with Hubert Willis as Dr. Watson. William J. Elliot wrote the script and Maurice Elvey directed. A print of this film survives at the BFI archive.

The Son of Wallingford

1921 American film (Vitagraph/8 reels) George Randolph Chester and his wife wrote the screenplay and directed this sequel to his famous novel *Get-Rich-Quick-Wallington*. Wallingford's son Jimmy (Tom Gallery) goes to a small town and discovers oil on a farm belonging to the family of his girl Mary (Priscilla Bonner) but problems arise. J. Rufus Wallington (Wilfrid North) comes to town disguised as a rich East Indian, "discovers" oil using fake pumps and sells stock to the townspeople. Landowner Henry Beegoode (Van Dyke Brooke) denies having sold the land to Wallingford and wants it back but the conman then exposes the well as a fake, part of a scheme to expose Beegoode. The bill of sale is returned and oil is discovered for real. See also Wallingford, J. Rufus.

Le Songe de Nick Winter
(Nick Winter's Dream)

1911 French film (Pathé/1 reel), an episode in a popular tongue-in-cheek comedy series about an "American" detective named Nick Winter. In this episode Nick has a troubling dream. Gérard Bourgeois wrote the screenplay and directed. (A print of this film survives in an archive). See Winter, Nick for other films.

Sonka the Golden Hand
(Sonka Zolotaya Ruchka)

1915 Russian serial (six episodes) also known as *Sonka the Golden Hand or Adventures of the Famous Swindler Sonia*. Sonka was a serial character featured in Russian crime films of the 1910s. She was based on an actual pickpocket who ended up on a prison island in real life but her true progenitors were the daredevil heroines of American serials like Pearl White. This was Sonka's most famous serial; she was portrayed by V. Hoffman under the direction of Alexander Drankov. The character also appeared in Yevgeni Bauer's *The Adventures of Shpeier and His Gang the Jack of Hearts* where she battles a rival swindler.

The Sons of Satan

1916 British film (London Film/5 reels) based on the 1914 novel *Sons of Satan* by William Le Queux. A detective leads a double life as a law enforcer and as the secret head of a gang of jewel thieves known as the Sons of Satan. Problems arrive when he falls in love with an actress. Gerald Ames played the detective criminal with Blanche Bryan as the actress. The supporting cast included Hayford Hobbs, Charles Rock, Wyndham Guise and Lewis Gilbert.

Gerald Ames is both detective and criminal in *The Sons of Satan*.

Le Sosie (The Double)

1909 French film (Éclair/1 reel), an episode in the *Les Nouveaux Exploits de Nick Carter* series about the master detective Nick Carter In this episode Carter meets a man who appears to be his double. Pierre Bressol played Nick Carter and Victorin Jassett wrote and directed the film. Distributed in America as *Nick Carter's Double*.

The Speckled Band

1912 Anglo-French film (Franco British Film Company–Éclair/2 reels), an episode in the *Sherlock Holmes* series based on a story by Sir Arthur Conan Doyle. Sherlock Holmes solves the mystery of the deadly speckled band. George Treville played Sherlock Holmes with M. Moyse as Dr. Watson and British actors in the supporting roles. Treville also directed in collaboration with Conan Doyle. See Holmes, Sherlock for other films.

The Speckled Band

1923 British film (Stoll/2 reels), an episode in the *Last Adventures of Sherlock Holmes* series based on a story by Sir Arthur Conan Doyle. Sherlock Holmes solves the mystery of how a woman was killed and saves her sister's life. Eille Norwood portrays Holmes with Hubert Willis as Dr. Watson. Alfred Moise was the cinematographer and George Ridgewell wrote the adaptation and directed. Print survives at BFI archive.

The Spirit of Evil

1922 American film (Garsson Productions/2 reels), one of four films in a *Nick Carter* series featuring detective Nick Carter. In this one he has to fight the spirit of evil itself. Carter was played by Edmund Lowe under the direction of Alexander Hall. With Diana Allen and Henry Sedley.

A Squeedunk Sherlock Holmes

1909 American comedy (Edison/half reel). The adventures of an amateur detective in a small town "Squeedunk" is American slang for a very small town.

The Star Reporter

1921 film (Berwilla–Arrow Film/6 reels). based on Wynham Martyn's novel *The Mysterious Mr. Garland*. Nan Lambert (Billie Rhodes) gets help from Anthony Trent (Truman Van Dyke) while investigating why her father has been confined to a sanitarium. They discover that Conington Warren (William Horne) schemed with associates to kidnap Nan's father and place him in the sanitarium. They give the evidence to the district attorney and Trent then reveals his real identity as a newspaper reporter. Duke Worne directed.

Stepping Lively

1924 American film (Carlos Productions/ 6 reels) based on a story by Frank Howard Clark who also wrote the screenplay. Dave Allen (Richard Talmadge) is the secretary of a bank president in this mystery about the disappearance of valuable bonds. Mostly he demonstrates super-athletic skills by jumping onto trains, diving into lakes, scaling fences and beating up thugs. He outwits villain Mario (Josef Le Barion) and underworld gangleader Black Mike (William Clifford), gets the bonds back and wins the hand of the banker's daughter (Mildred Harris). *Variety* said it was "about as original as a pancake recipe." James W. Horne directed.

Stingaree

Stingaree is a Robin Hood–like Australian bandit created by novelist E. W. Hornung, the creator of Raffles. He is actually an Englishman named Irving Randolph who was cheated out of his fortune by a villainous brother. He is portrayed in two Kalem serials by True Boardman with Marin Sais as the woman who loves him, Paul Hurst as his friend and partner Howie and William Brunton as his nasty brother Robert.

Stingaree

1915 American serial (Kalem/twelve 2-reel chapters). Stingaree is a Robin Hood–like Australian bandit created by E. W. Hornung. He is actually an Englishman named Irving Randolph who was cheated out of his fortune by a villainous brother. He was portrayed in two Kalem serials (this is the first) by True Boardman with Marin Sais as the woman who loves him, Paul Hurst as his friend and partner Howie and William Brunton as his nasty brother Robert. James W. Horne directed. The episodes were *An Enemy of Mankind, A Voice in the Wilderness, The Black Hole of Glenrenald, To the Vile Dust, A Bushranger at Bay, The Taking of Stingaree, The Honor of the Road, The Purification of Mulfers, The Duel in the Desert, The Villain Worshipper, The Moth and the Star* and *The Darkest Hour*. See also *The Further Adventures of Stingaree*.

The Stockbroker's Clerk

1922 British film (Still/2 reels), an episode in the *Further Adventures of Sherlock Holmes* series based on a story by Sir Arthur Conan Doyle. Sherlock Holmes solves the mystery surround the changing of jobs by a stockbroker's clerk. Eille Norwood portrays Holmes with Hubert Willis as Dr. Watson. George Ridgewell wrote the adaptation and directed. A print survives at the BFI archive.

The Stolen Heirlooms

1915 British film (Davidson/3 reels), one of seven films featuring the famous detective Sexton Blake in a series written and directed by Charles Raymond. Blake is drugged and tied to a sawmill while trying to save a man from jewel theft charges. Harry Lorraine played Blake with Bert Rex as his assistant Tinker. (See Blake, Sexton for other films and background.)

The Stolen Jewels

1908 film (Biograph/1 reel). Detectives search a home for valuable jewels that went missing while a stockbroker and his wife were at the opera. The stockbroker has a run of bad luck, goes bankrupt and is about to sell everything he owns to clear his debts. A friend visits them, falls over a chair and crushes their child's toy dog which had originally contained candy. The jewels spill out.

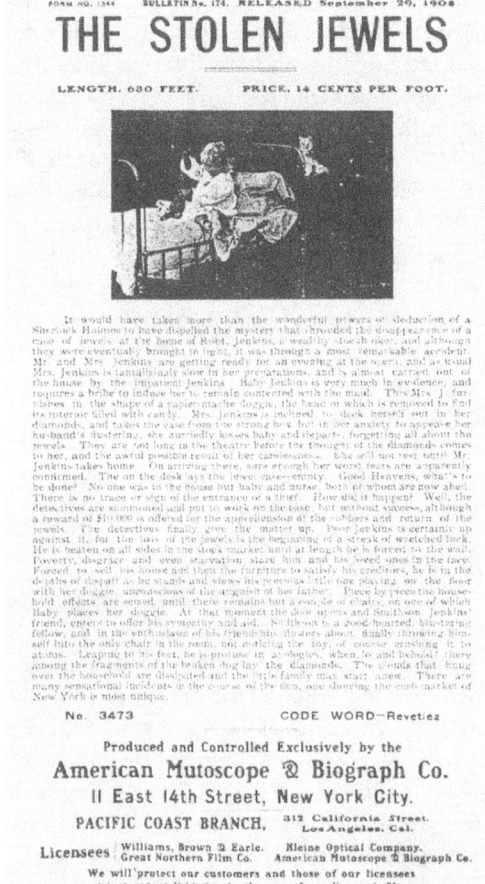

The 1908 *Biograph Bulletin* describing the mystery *The Stolen Jewels*.

The Stolen Papers

1912 Anglo-French film (Franco British Film Company–Éclair/2 reels), an episode in the *Sherlock Holmes* series based on a story by Sir Arthur Conan Doyle. Sherlock Holmes solves a mystery involving stolen government papers George Treville played Sherlock Holmes with M. Moyse as Dr. Watson and British actors in the supporting roles. Treville also directed in collaboration with Conan Doyle. See Holmes, Sherlock for other films.

The Stolen Plans; or, The Boy Detective

1908 American film (Vitagraph/half reel). A boy detective foils a group of villains and recovers plans that were stolen.

The Stolen Purse

1913 American comedy (Keystone/1 reel), a film in the *Two Sleuths* series produced and directed by Mack Sennett and starring Sennett and Fred Mace. They play comic detectives.

Stolen Secrets

1924 American film (Universal/5 reels) based on a story by Richard Goodall. Criminologist Miles Manning (Herbert Rawlinson) rids a city of its criminals by posing as the villainous master criminal known as "The Eel." The mayor's daughter (Kathleen Myers), who thinks he really is a crook, had asked him to do it to help her father. Rex Taylor wrote the screenplay and Irving Cummings directed.

The Strange Case of Mary Page

1916 American serial (Essanany/fifteen 2-reel chapters). Mary Page (Edna Mayo) is accused of murdering theatrical mogul David Pollock (Sydney Ainsworth) and is defended by her attorney lover Phil Langdon (Henry B. Walthall). This is a courtroom drama told in flashback with a different key event explored in each chapter. Frederick Lewis and H. H. Sheldon wrote the screenplay and J. Charles Haydon directed. The chapters are titled *The Tragedy World, The Trail, The Web, The Mark, The Alienist, The Depths, A Confession, The Perjury, The Accusing Eye, The Clue, The Raid, The Slums, Dawning Hope, Recrimination* and *The Verdict*.

Henry Walthall and Edna Mayo star in the courtroom mystery *The Strange Case of Mary Page.*

A Strange Disappearance

1915 American film (IMP/3 reels) based on the 1880 mystery novel *A Strange Disappearance* by Anna Katherine Green. This was the second novel featuring Green's famous detective Ebenezer Gryce but, as with the 1923 film version of *The Leavenworth Case*, his character is not featured in the film. King Baggot stars as the investigator Andrew Blake with Edna Hunter as his sweetheart Evelyn, Ned Reardon as the scoundrel Hoenmaker, Jane Gail as Hoenmaker's daughter Luthia and Frank Smith as John Blake. George Lessey directed and Raymond L. Schrock wrote the screenplay.

Stronger Than Sherlock Holmes (Più forte che Sherlock Holmes)

1913 Italian comedy (Itala Film/1 reel), a parody of the Sherlock Holmes films starring Domenico Gambino as Saltarelli and Emilio Vardannes as Totò Travetti. Giovanni Pastrone directed.

A Study in Scarlet

1914 British film (Samuelson/6 reels) based on the Arthur Conan Doyle novel *A Study in Scarlet*. Sherlock Holmes investigates a murder and finds a Mormon connection. This was the first feature film based on a Holmes story. James Bragington plays Sherlock Holmes with support from Fred Paul, Agnes Glynne, Harry Paulo and James Le Free. George Pearson directed and Harry Engholm wrote the screenplay. See Holmes, Sherlock for other films.

A Study in Scarlet

1914 American film (Universal/2 reels) based on the Arthur Conan Doyle novel *A Study in Scarlet*. Sherlock Holmes investigates a murder and finds a Mormon connection. Francis Ford plays Sherlock Holmes with John Ford as Dr. Watson. Francis Ford directed and Grace Cunard wrote the screenplay. See Holmes, Sherlock for other films.

The Studio Murder Mystery

1929 American film (Paramount/8 reels) based on the novel *The Studio Murder Mystery* by A. C. and C. Edington published in *Photo-*

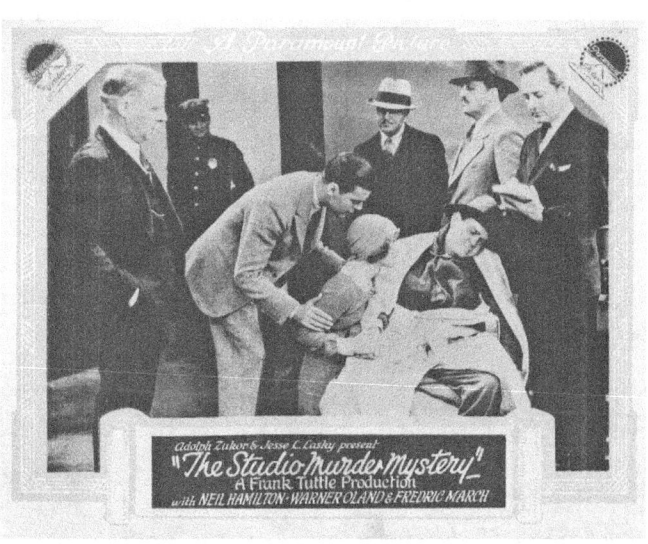
Lobby card publicizing *The Studio Murder Mystery.*

play in 1928. Detective Dirk (Eugene Pallette) investigates a murder at the Superior Films studio. Womanizing star Richard Hardell (Fredric March) has been found dead on a deserted sound stage and there are five suspects: his jealous wife Blanche (Florence Eldridge), his cuckolded director Rupert Borka (Warner Oland), his deceived girlfriend Helen (Doris Hill), Helen's brother (Gardner James) and Helen's father (Guy Oliver). Helen is convicted but writer Tony White (Neil Hamilton) investigates further and proves Borka was the real killer. Frank Tuttle directed and Ethel Doherty wrote the screenplay. Released in silent and sound versions. On video as a silent film.

The Suicide Club

At least five silent films were based on the Robert Louis Stevenson mystery story *The Suicide Club* published in *London Magazine* in 1878. The films have many variations on the original plot but keep the central concept. The original is set in Victorian London where Prince Florizel and Major Geraldine infiltrate a secret society of people intent on killing themselves. One member learns he has inherited a lot of money after he draws a fatal lot and is expected to kill himself. The club won't let him change his mind. The president of the club turns out to be a criminal. See below and *Le Club Des Suicides, Der Geheimnisvolle Klub* and *Unheimliche Geschichten*.

The Suicide Club

1909 American film (Biograph/1 reel) directed by D.W. Griffith and loosely based on the story by Robert Louis Stevenson. Herbert Yost plays a Suicide Club of America member who draws the fatal lot. He withdraws to kill himself but is interrupted by a woman (Violet Mersereau) who hands him a note. He decides he would rather live. The other members are Charles Avery, John R. Cumpson, Arthur V. Johnson, Owen Moore, Anthony O'Sullivan, Herbert Prior, David Miles and Mack Sennett. Frank E. Woods wrote the screenplay and G. W. Bitzer was the cinematographer.

The Suicide Club

1914 British film (British & Colonial/3 reels) loosely based on the story by Robert Louis Stevenson. Colonel Geraldine (F. Gray Murray) saves the life of Prince Florizel (Montagu Love) who has joined a suicide club as a lark and has been tricked in committing to kill himself. Elisabeth Risdon plays Zephyrine, Fred Groves is the evil president of the club and Compton Coutts is Silas O. Scuddermore. Maurice Elvey directed.

The Suitcase Mystery

1910 American film (Edison/1 reel) written and directed by Charles M. Seay.

The Sultana

1916 American film (Pathé/5 reels) Based on the 1914 novel *The Sultana* by Henry C. Rowland. Greg Kirkland (E. T. Peters) makes a bet he can steal the Sultana diamond tiara. He succeeds and then gives it to his friend Virginia (Ruth Roland) to return. She elopes with Count Strelitso (Edwin J. Brady) before she has time to do and he demands she give him the tiara. She flees from him and is eventually rescued by Kirkland's friend Thomas Miller (William Conklin) who helps her return the Sultana. Will M. Ritchey wrote the screenplay and Sherwood MacDonald directed.

Sureluck Jones

1912 American comedy (Thanhouser/1 reel). A parody of the Sherlock Holmes films. The "great detective" Surelock Jones thinks a young girl loves him because he can deduce it. She actually prefers a younger man and together they outwit the detective through fake cases he cannot solve.

Susie, the Sleuth

1916 American comedy (Vitagraph/2 reels) starring Edith Storey as Susie with supporting cast of Antonio Moreno, John Costello. Rose Tapley. George Stevens and Arthur Robinson. Kenneth S. Webb wrote the screenplay and George D. Baker directed.

Suspense

1919 American film (Screencraft Pictures/6 reels) based on the 1918 novel *Suspense* by mystery writer Isabel Ostrander. Secret plans are stolen from an admiral and his daughter Ruth (Mollie King) sets out to find them. She hears her father's secretary plotting with another man and follows them to the Fifth Avenue home of Mrs. Vanderhold (Isabel O'Madigan). She becomes her secretary using an assumed name and gets help from detective Herbert Ross (Harris Gordon). When she learns that the plans are hidden in a safe in Mrs. Vanderhold's Long Island villa she goes after them. There is a shootout but Ross gets the upper hand and the villains are arrested. Eve Unsell wrote the screenplay and Frank Reicher.

Suzanne Marwille, Detective
(Suzanne Marwille, detektivem)

1922 Czechoslovakian comedy (Iris Film/5 reels) based on a story by Vladimír Majer who also wrote the screenplay. An inventor (Alois Sedlacek) stages a fake robbery to attract attention to his new invention. His daughter (Suzanne Marwille) investigates the theft during a heavy snowfall and catches the supposed robber. Václav Binovec directed.

Syd, the Bum Detective

1915 American film (Mica/1 reel), one of the comedies in the *Syd* series starring Sydney De Gray. In others he plays an athlete, a sweetheart and a masher.

Sylvia of the Secret Service

1917 American film (Pathé/5 reels) based on a story by Joseph Trant. Scotland Yard detective Hemming (J. W. Percival) and American Secret Service agent Sylvia Carroll (Irene Castle) investigate the theft of a famous diamond from a ship. Curtis Prescott (Elliott Dexter), who had been hired by a diamond merchant to transport it, is accused of masterminding the theft. Sylvia thinks he is innocent and disguises herself as a millionairess and a slum girl to catch the real thieves. Philip Bartholomae wrote the screenplay and George Fitzmaurice directed.

Tamburin und Castagnetten
(Tambourine and Castanets)

1920 German film (PAGU/5 reels) featuring the "American" detective Joe Deebs played by Carl Augen. This was a late film in the long-running Deeb series created by producer Joe May in 1914. After May stopped making Deebs films, the mantle was picked up by Projektions-AG Union (PAGU). Martin Hartwig and Léo Lasko wrote the screenplay and directed. The supporting cast included Fred Immler, Mabel May-Yong and Hans Adalbert Schlettow. See Deebs, Joe for other films.

Tangled Lives

1917 American film (Fox/5 reels) loosely based on Wilkie Collins's novel *The Woman in White*. Genevieve Hamper plays Laura, Stuart Holmes is Roy Schuyler (a character replacing Sir Percival) Walter Miller is Walter and Claire Whitney is Marion. Gordon Edwards directed and Mary Murillo wrote the screenplay. See also *The Woman in White*.

The Taxi Mystery

1926 American film (Banner Productions/6 reels) based on a story by Tom J. Hopkins who wrote the screenplay. Edith Roberts plays a double role in this mystery. Millionaire Harry Canby (Robert Agnew) finds a taxi without a driver at the docks, helps a girl escape from thugs and discovers that the taxi driver was killed. He identifies the girl as musical comedy star Nancy Cornell (Roberts) but she denies ever meeting him. He investigates and discovers that look-alike Vera Norris (Roberts) has been plotting to take Nancy's place to get her money. Fred Windemere directed.

The Teeth of the Tiger

1919 American film (Paramount/6 reels) based on Maurice Leblanc's 1914 novel *The Teeth of the Tiger* about the French master thief Arsène Lupin. Lupin (David Powell), who has reformed and is living in New York under a false name, is asked for protection by his friend Henry Forbes (Joseph Herbert). When Forbes is murdered, French detective Jabot (Templar Saxe) and the New York police detectives suspect Lupin as well as Forbes' widow (Myrtle Stedman), her lover (Charles Gerard) and Forbes' secretary (Marguerite Courtot). After many chases, traps and arrests, Lupin reveals the murderer to be Forbes' doctor (Frederick

Burton). Chet Withey directed, Roy Somerville wrote the screenplay and Al Ligouri was the cinematographer. (See Lupin, Arsène for details about the character and a listing of the other films in which he appeared.)

Terence O'Rourke, Gentleman Adventurer

1914–1916 Universal films series based on mystery writer Louis Joseph Vance's stories about the roguish Irish adventurer Terence O'Rourke. They began appearing serially in *The Popular Magazine* in 1904 and were published in book form as *The Romance of Terence O'Rourke* (1905) and *The Pool of Flame* (1909). The stories tell of his adventures and the villains he battles in India, Egypt and Turkey while wooing Princess Beatrix. There were ten films in all, three 2-reel series and a feature. J. Warren Kerrigan played O'Rourke, Lois Wilson was his love Beatrix, Harry Carter was the villainous Duke Victor, Bertram Grassby was his arch-enemy Chambret and Maud George was his seductive enemy Princess Karan. Otis Turner directed and F. McGrew Willis wrote the screenplays. See below plus. *The Further Adventures of Terence O'Rourke, The New Adventures of Terence O'Rourke* and *The Pool of Flame*.

Terence O'Rourke, Gentleman Adventurer

1914 American serial (Universal/three 2-reel episodes) series based on mystery writer Louis Joseph Vance's stories about the roguish Irish adventurer Terence O'Rourke. The episodes are titled *His Heart, His Hand and His Sword, The Empire of Illusion* and *The Inn of the Winged Gods*.

The Terrible People

1928 American serial (Pathé/ten 2-reel chapters) based on a 1926 novel by Edgar Wallace. The "Terrible People" are villains seeking revenge against the detective, judge and others who arranged the capture and execution of a murderous forger. Serial queen Allene Ray is, as usual, in terrible trouble but, as always, gets aid from Walter Miller. George Arthur Gray wrote the screenplay and Spencer G. Bennet directed. The chapters are titled *The Penalty, Disaster, The Claws of Death, Hidden Enemies, The Disastrous Rescue, The House of Peril, In the Enemy's Hands, The Dread Professor, The Death Trap* and *The Capture*.

The Terror

1928 American film (Warner Bros./9 reels) based on the novel *The Terror* by Edgar Wallace. The maniac killer known as The Terror has taken up residence in an old English inn. The guests include Scotland Yard detective Ferdinand Fane (Edward Everett Horton), spiritualist Mrs. Elvery (Louise Fazenda), beautiful Olga Redmayne (May McAvoy) and revenge-minded criminals Joe Connors and Soapy Marks. There are mysterious goings-on and murders before the identity of The Terror is revealed. Harvey Gates wrote the screenplay and Roy Del Ruth directed.

Louise Fazenda plays a spiritualist in *The Terror*.

Terror Island

1920 American film (Paramount/7 reels) based on a story by mystery writer Arthur B. Reeve and John Grey. Harry Houdini gets a number of opportunities to show off his ability to make death-defying escapes in this South Sea islands film shot on Santa Catalina Island. He is hired to rescue Lila Lee's father from islanders who are holding him to ransom in order to get back a pearl stolen from their idol. He also had to battle bad guys Eugene Pallette and Wilton Taylor and spend a lot of time underwater saving Lila who keeps getting thrown in the sea. Walter Woods wrote the screenplay and James Cruze directed. The film has been preserved by the Library of Congress and is on DVD.

The Test of Honor

1919 film (Paramount/5 reels) based on the 1907 novel *The Malefactor* by mystery writer E. Phillips Oppenheim. Martin Wingrave (John Barrymore) gets in a fight with the husband of Ruth Curtis (Marcia Manon) and he dies from a heart attack though Ruth could have been saved him. Martin is convicted of manslaughter and sent to prison. When he gets out he seeks revenge but needs help from his friend Juliet (Constance Binney) who prevents him from being poisoned by Ruth. He gets his revenge. Eve Unsell wrote the screenplay and John S. Robertson directed.

Tex, Elucidator of Mysteries

American film series (Arrow/all 5 reels) produced by William Steiner in 1920 and starring Glen White as famous criminologist/detective Tex. These films do not seem to have been based on published stories though Sherlock Holmes was sometimes called an "elucidator of mysteries." Tom Collins directed six of them and wrote two but no credit is given for the creation of the series or the character of Tex. Jane McAlpine, Leo Delaney and David Wall had supporting roles in most of the films. As these were small budget pictures and not much written about at the time, they have been virtually forgotten though they seem to have had reasonable popularity. See *The Bromley Case, Circumstantial Evidence, The House of Mystery, The Sacred Ruby, The Scrap of Paper, The Trail of the Cigarette, The Triple Clue, The Wall Street Mystery*, and *The Unseen Witness*.

Glen White starred as detective Tex in a series of 1920 Arrow films including *The House of Mystery* (brochure cover).

Their First Divorce Case

1911 American comedy (Biograph/1 reel), a film in the *Two Sleuths* series produced and directed by Mack Sennett and starring Sennett and Fred Mace. They play comic detectives who badly bungle their first divorce case.

Their First Kidnapping Case

1911 American comedy (Biograph/1 reel), a film in the *Two Sleuths* series produced and directed by Mack Sennett and starring Sennett and Fred Mace. They play comic detectives on a kidnapping case who find the wrong baby; it has a contagious disease and they catch it.

There Are No Villains

1921 American film (Metro/5 reels) based on the story "There Are No Villains" by Frank R. Adams. Secret Service agent Rose Moreland (Viola Dana) needs evidence to convict opium smuggler George Sala (Edward Cecil) and thinks she can get it through ex-soldier John King (Gaston Glass). She persuades him to join Sala's gang but her boss, Detective Flint (De

Secret Service agent Rose (Viola Dana) gets herself all tied up in *There Are No Villains*.

Witt Jennings), becomes suspicious and has her followed. King says he will quit Sala's gang if she will marry him and she agrees as then she won't then have to testify against him. Flint arrives to arrest King who confounds him by revealing that he is also in the Secret Service. Mary O'Hara wrote the screenplay and Bayard Veiller directed.

A Thief in the Dark

1928 American film (Fox/6 reels) based on a story by Andrew Bennis. Phony spiritualists working with a carnival are also thieves. Professor Xeno (Michael Vavitch) kills an old woman so he can steal her case of jewels but young Ernest (George Meeker) falls in love with her granddaughter Elise (Doris Hill). Xeno is killed when he opens the jewel case which explodes in his face; it had been booby trapped by the old woman. Albert Ray directed and C. Graham Baker wrote the screenplay.

The Thirteenth Chair

1919 American film (Pathé/6 reels) based on Bayard Veiller's play *The Thirteenth Chair*. Crooked stockbroker Stephen Lee (Marc McDermott) is killed while attacking Helen Trent (Suzanne Colbert) whom he is blackmailing. Lee's friend Wales (George Deneubourg) tries to show that Helen was the killer by arranging a fake séance where he will pretend to be Lee's spirit while seated in the thirteenth chair. However he is killed before he can speak. Inspector Donohue (Walter Law) arranges another fake séance that tricks Philip Mason, whose wife committed suicide after an affair with Lee, into confessing to the murder. Leonce Perret directed and wrote the screenplay. The play was filmed twice more in the sound era.

The Thirteenth Hour

1927 American film (MGM/6 reels). Criminologist Professor Leroy (Lionel Barrymore) is actually a criminal wanted for murder. When Detective Matt Gray (Charles Delaney) learns this he goes to his and rescues a woman captive (Jacqueline Gadsdon) with the help of his dog Napoleon. The professor dies after falling from a roof while battling the dog. Chester Franklin and Douglas Furber wrote the screenplay and Franklin directed.

$30,000

1920 American film (Robert Brunton Productions/5 reels) based on a mystery story by H. B. Daniel filled with unbelievable coincidences. Attorney John Trask (J. Warren Kerrigan) is given $30,000 by Christine Lloyd (Nancy Chase) to buy a necklace. The necklace was stolen by her brother to pay gambling debts and she is getting it to protect him. Trask hides the money in his office but it's found by the janitor (Joseph J. Dowling) who steals it. By an amazing coincidence, it is the janitor's daughter Aline (Fritzi Brunette) who bring the necklace to his office. When Trask finds the money gone, he goes to the gambling casino and by another helpful coincidence wins

$30,000 and buys the necklace. When he discovers it's a fake he has to go back to the casino and get the real one. The repentant janitor returns the $30,000 and all ends well. Jack Cunningham wrote the screenplay and Ernest C. Warde directed.

The Thornton Jewel Mystery

1915 British film (Davidson/3 reels), one of seven films featuring detective Sexton Blake in a series written and directed by Charles Raymond. Flash Kate frames a drunkard for a theft she committed and Blake is saved by Tinker who makes a daring dive. Harry Lorraine played Blake with Bert Rex as his assistant Tinker and Miss Vere as Flash Kate. (See Blake, Sexton for other films and background.)

Thou Shalt Not Steal

1917 American film (Fox/5 reels) loosely based on Émile Gaboriau's novel *Le Dossier No. 113* but transferred to America with Monsieur Lecoq given an American name. Detective Farrel (Lem F. Kennedy) investigates a case of robbery and blackmail with lots of people wearing disguises. The villainous Lord Haverford (John Goldsworthy), who lusts after Mary (Virginia Pearson), turns out to be an imposter and is exposed by the real Lord Haverford who has disguised himself as a detective. The proof is a bitten wrist. William Nigh directed and Adrian Johnson wrote the screenplay. The novel was also filmed as *File No. 113*.

Three-Fingered Kate

1909–1912 British tongue-in-cheek series starring Ivy Martinek as master criminal Kate, Alice Moseley as her sister Mary, Charles Calvert as Detective Sheerluck and Edward Durrant as Detective Rickshaw. The films were written and directed by H. Oceano Martinek (Ivy's brother) for British & Colonial Kinematograph. See below and *Exploits of Three-Finger Kate*.

Three-Fingered Kate: Her Second Victim, the Art Dealer

1909 British film (British & Colonial/1 reel). Jewel thief Three-Fingered Kate and her sister Mary rob a baron's art gallery and escape by fleeing over the rooftops.

Ivy Martinek stars as master criminal Kate in the British *Three-Finger Kate* series.

Three-Fingered Kate: Her Victim the Banker

1910 British film (British & Colonial/1 reel). A clever detective tracks Kate through the fingerprints she left on forged note.

Three-Fingered Kate: The Case of the Chemical Fumes

1912 British film (British & Colonial/1 reel). Kate and her sister Mary rob the guests at party given by a lord after knocking them out by pumping sleeping gas into the room.

Three-Fingered Kate: The Episode of the Sacred Elephants

1910 British film (British & Colonial/1 reel). Kate robs a colonel and then escapes by disguising herself a curio dealer.

Three-Fingered Kate: The Pseudo-Quartette

1912 British film (British & Colonial/1 reel), the final episode in *the Three-Fingered Kate* series—Kate and her sister Mary kidnap musicians who are due to play at an aristocratic ball and take their places so they can rob the wealthy guests.

Three-Fingered Kate: The Wedding Presents

1912 British film (British & Colonial/1 reel). Kate and her sister Mary tunnel through a fireplace in order to rob wedding presents from the house next door.

Three Keys

1925 American film (Banner/6 reels) based on the 1909 novel *The Three Keys* by Frederick Ormand (pseudonym of mystery writer Frederic Van Rensselaer Dey). George Lathrop (Gaston Glass) steals $100,000 from Jack (Jack Mulhall) to help his fiancée Alice (Miss Du Pont). as her father John (Charles Clary) is about to go bankrupt. Jack finds out what happened and why and works it out so his friend won't go to jail. Alice breaks her engagement with George who decides to marry his ward Clarita (Edith Roberts), the long-lost daughter of Trevor. Robert Dillon wrote the complicated screenplay and Edward J. Le Saint directed.

The Three Students

1923 British film (Stoll/2 reels), an episode in the *Last Adventures of Sherlock Holmes* series based on a story by Sir Arthur Conan Doyle. Sherlock Holmes solves the mystery of the disappearance of examination papers at Cambridge. Eille Norwood portrays Holmes with Hubert Willis as Dr. Watson. Alfred Moise was the cinematographer and George Ridgewell wrote the adaptation and directed. Print survives at BFI archive.

A Thrilling Detective Story

1906 American comedy (Lubin/325 feet). A woman goes into a book store in Philadelphia where she buys and starts reading a novel titled *The Murderer of His Seventeen Wives: A Thrilling Detective Story*. She becomes so engrossed in the book as she walks along that she falls down, runs into people and falls into the river. She gets home battered and bandaged but still reading.

Thrilling Stories from The Strand

1924 British series (Stoll/six 2-reel films) based on criminous stories first published in *The Strand*, the British magazine famous for publishing the Sherlock Holmes stories and other mysteries. The films were *The Acid Test, After Dark, The Cavern Spider, The Drum, Holloway's Treasure* and *Fighting Snub Reilly*.

Thrilling Stories from the Strand

1925 British series (Stoll/six 2-reel films) and the second series based on crime stories first published in *The Strand*, the British magazine known for Sherlock Holmes and other mystery stories. The films in the second series were *A Dear Liar, The Honorable Member for Outside Left, A Madonna of the Cells, The Perfect Crime* and *Ragan in Ruins*.

Through the Dark

1924 American film (Cosmopolitan/8 reels) based on Jack Boyle's story "The Daughter of Mother McGinn." Boston Blackie (Forrest Stanley) is helped by schoolgirl Mary (Colleen Moore) after he escapes from prison but this gets her expelled from school. Her mother (Margaret Seddon) operates a refuge for criminals so Blackie decides to hide out there. Blackie decides to go straight and marry Mary. George Hill directed and Frances Marion wrote the screenplay. See also Blackie, Boston.

Through the Wall

1916 American film (Greater Vitagraph/6 reels) based on the 1909 novel *Through the Wall* by mystery writer Cleveland Moffett. Detective Paul Stanton also known as Paul Coquenil (William Duncan) uncovers the complicated schemes of master criminal Felix Heidelmann (George Holt). He had posed as a wealthy man and married rich widow Mrs. Kittredge (Anne Schaeffer). When she drowns on an ocean voyage, he pretends to be the father of Kittredge's daughter Anne (Nell Shipman) who he holds prisoner. When Alice's uncle Martinez recognizes him, Heidelman kills him and puts the blame on Alice's brother Lloyd (Webster Campbell). Detective Stanton sorts it all out and rescues Alice. Marguerite Bertsch wrote the screenplay and Rollin S. Sturgeon directed. The source novel was praised by Ellery Queen and by Peter Wimsey in Dorothy Sayers' novel *The Unpleasantness at the Bellona Club*.

The Ticket of Leave Man

The 1863 British play *The Ticket-of-Leave Man* by Tom Taylor featured a character known as Hawkshaw, the Detective. The popularity of the play made Hawkshaw the prototype for a detective and "Hawkshaw" became a synonym for "detective." A ticket-of-leave man is a former convict, a man who has been released from prison. The play remained popular in the early 20th century and inspired four silent films (see below). Taylor (1817–1880), who wrote over a hundred plays, is best known as the author of *Our American Cousin*, the play Abraham Lincoln was watching at the Ford Theater the night he was assassinated.

The Ticket of Leave Man

1912 Australian film (Australian Life Biograph/4 reels) based on the play by Tom Taylor and featuring detective Hawkshaw. Louise Lovely starred under the direction of Gaston Mervale.

The Ticket-of-Leave Man

1913 American film (Dragon/2 reels) based on the play by Tom Taylor featuring detective Hawkshaw.

The Ticket-of-Leave Man

1914 American film (Biograph/2 reels) based on the play by Tom Taylor. George Morgan, Louise Ducey, Charles Hill Mailes and Louise Vale have the leading roles under the direction of Travers Vale.

The Ticket-of-Leave Man

1918 British film (Barker/6 reels) based on the play by Tom Taylor. Aubrey Fitzmaurice played Detective Hawkshaw with Daphne Glenn as May, Edwards George Foley as Bob Brierley and Wilfred Benson as James Tiger Dalton Bert Haldane directed.

The Tiger of San Pedro

1921 British film (Stoll/2 reels), an episode in the *Adventures of Sherlock Holmes* series based on the story "Wisteria Lodge" by Sir Arthur Conan Doyle. Sherlock Holmes solves the murder of a man involved in tracking down an exiled dictator. Eille Norwood portrays Holmes with Hubert Willis as Dr. Watson. William J. Elliot wrote the script and Maurice Elvey directed. A print of this film survives at the BFI archive.

The Tiger's Trail

1919 American serial (Astra/fifteen 2-reel chapters) based on a story by Gilson Willets with screenplay by Arthur B. Reeve and Charles Logue. Outlaws and Hindu tiger worshippers try to cheat a young woman out of her rich mines. Ruth Roland plays the woman who gets help from George Larkin while facing danger from Tiger Face (Harry Moody). Robert Ellis and Louis J. Gasnier directed. The episodes are titled *The Tiger Worshippers, The Glowing Eyes, The Human Chain, Danger Signals, The Tiger Trap, The Secret Assassin, The Flaming Waters, Danger Ahead, The Raging Torrent, Bringing in the Law, In the Breakers, The Two Amazons, The False Idol, The Mountain Hermit* and *The Tiger Face*.

Ruth Roland has trouble with tiger worshippers in the serial *The Tiger's Trail*.

Tigris

1913 Italian film (Itala Film/four reels) about a cunning master criminal and his crafty detective nemesis. Detective Roland (Alessandro Bernard) spends much of the film putting on various disguises as he attempts to identify and catch criminal mastermind Tigris (Edoardo Davesnes) who is also a master of disguise; he can even disguise himself as the police commissioner (Dante Cappelli) and the respectable businessman Leblanc. At one point Tigris even challenges Roland to a duel of disguises (Tigris wins). Roland gets captured and thrown under a train by Tigris's gang (he survives) and drugged by an exotic dancer (he has surrealistic visions) but he wins out after a nasty trip down a sewer. He also wins the girl, Leblanc's sister Lidia (Lydia Quaranta), Vincenzo Denizot directed this farrago with Natale Chiusano as cinematographer. The film was a major success in America and England where it was advertised as "A veritable Niagara of sensation that will sweep your patrons off their feet." It even won praise from *The Moving Picture World* and *The Bioscope*. The film survives and is on video.

Tih Minh

1918 French serial (Gaumont/12 chapters/418 minutes) written and directed by French serial genius Louis Feuillade. Vampire queen Irma Vep was killed at the end of *Les vampires* but her gang has survived in Nice. In this sequel Tih Minh has taken over as their leader and plans to take over the world. Mary Harald plays Tih Minh with René Cresté as Jacques d'Athys, Georges Biscot as Placido and Édouard Mathé as Sir Francis Grey. The episodes are titled *Le Philtre d'oubli, Dramas dans la nuit, Les Mystères de la Villa Circé, L'Homme dan la malle, Chez les fous, Oiseaux de nuit, L'Evocation, Sous le voile, La Branche du salut, Mercredi, Le Document* and *Justice*. The film, released in America in 1919 *as In the Clutches of the Hindoos*, has survived and a restored version was shown at the New York Film Festival in 1980.

Criminal mastermind Tigris (Edoardo Davesnes) in one of his disguises in the 1913 Italian film *Tigris*.

Tih-Minh (Mary Harald) takes over the Vampire gang in the French serial *Tih-Minh*.

Tiller, Prentice

1917–1918 American film series (Bluebird/two 5-reel films) based on stories by Elliot J. Clawson about a detective named Prentice Tiller who specializes in jewel thefts. Clawson wrote the screenplays and Rupert Julian directed. See *Midnight Madness* and *The Mysterious Mr. Tiller*.

Times Have Changed

1923 American film (Fox/5 reels) based on the 1923 novel *Times Have Changed* by Elmer Holmes Davis. Mark O'Rell (William Russell) is sent to New York by his wife's aunt to recover a valuable quilt. He finds the quilt which he discovers conceals stolen jewels. He is pursued by police and thieves but after complications police arrest the thieves, and Mark takes the quilt home. Jack Strumwasser wrote the screenplay and James Flood directed.

Tipped Off

1923 American film (Playgoers Pictures/5 reels). Mildred (Arline Pretty), the secretary of playwright Anthony Moore (Harold Miller). desperately wants to star in his new crime play. Her brother and sister arrange a fake robbery so she demonstrate her acting ability. It goes wrong when real thieves The Fox (Tom Santschi) and Chang Wo (Noah Beery) arrive and kidnap her. The crooks get caught with the help of a detective (Si Wilcox) and Mildred explains what happened. Frederick Reel, Jr., wrote the screenplay and Finis Fox directed.

Too Much Married

1921 American film (5 reels) based on a story by Florence Bolles. Betty (Mary Anderson), a guest at a society wedding, is stopped by a detective (Ben Lewis) who wants to search her bag. A valuable necklace has been stolen from the bride. He does not find it and lets her go. Bystander Billy (Jack Connolly), then drops the necklace in her bag without being seen. The detective tries to question Billy but he escapes. Meanwhile Betty searches for her fiancé, Bob (Roscoe Karns), who was taken to a hospital after a car accident. Billy finds them and tries to get hold of the bag. After many complications he is caught and reveals what happened. John W. Grey wrote the screenplay and Scott Dunlap directed.

La Torre dell'espiazion
(The Tower of Atonement)

1913 Italian film (Aquila Films, Torino/4 reels) written and directed by Roberto Roberti and shown in America in 1914 as *Tower of Terror*. The complicated story revolves around an English duke who marries a woman in India. The evil banker Mayer sends a villain to kill the wife and kidnap her daughter Zazia and uses her to force the duke to marry Mayer's daughter Elda. Twenty years later the duke sends his secretary Folkestone to rescue Zazia when he learns she is alive. He succeeds but the jealous Elda arranges for Zazia to be kidnapped again and imprisoned in the Tower of Terror. Folkestone rescues her just before the tower blows up and buries the villains. *Variety* enjoyed it saying it "will please all lovers of the cheap form of literature." The main actors are Antonietta Calderari, Bice Waleran, Giovanni Pezzinga and Roberto Roberti.

The baby Zazia is about to be kidnapped in *The Tower of Terror.*

Die Toten Erwachen (The Dead Awake)

1915 German film (Stuart Webbs Film Company/4 reels) featuring the "American" detective Stuart Webbs played by Ernst Reicher in the longest running of all German detective series. In this adventure Webbs gets involved with the living dead as wax statues come alive when he confronts a murderer in gothic basement. Ernst Reicher wrote the screenplay. (Print survives in film archive). See Webbs, Stuart for other films.

Tracked by the Police Dog

1908 French film (Pathé/half reel) about a dog trained to be a detective in France. It was distributed in America with this title. Original title unknown.

Traffic in Souls

1913 American film (Universal/7 reels). A police officer and his sweetheart investigate a white slavery ring that has trapped the woman's sister and eventually find that a famous philanthropist is the leader of the gang. After recording evidence with a secret device, they are able to free the girls and destroy the gang and its leaders. Matt Moore played the police officer, Jane Gail was his girl, Ethel Grandin was the trapped sister and William Welsch was the villainous philanthropist. Walter MacNamara wrote the screenplay supposedly based on the *Rockefeller White Slavery Report* and an investigation by District Attorney Whitman. George Loane Tucker directed it in semi-documentary form. This film survives and is on DVD.

Matt Moore rescues Ethel Grandin in the white slave drama *Traffic in Souls*.

The Tragedy of Barnsdale Manor

1924 British film (Stoll/2 reels), an episode in the *Old Man in the Corner* series based on a story by Baroness Orczy. An armchair detective known as the Old Man in the Corner solves crimes while sitting in a tea shop and tells the solutions to a young woman journalist. In this episode he solves a mystery involving the death Lord Barnsdale's aunt. Rolf Leslie played the Old Man and Renée Wakefield was journalist Mary Hatley with supporting cast of Marion Benham, Arthur Lumley and Cecil Mannering. D. P. Cooper was the cinematographer and Hugh Croise wrote the adaptation and directed. Print survives at BFI archive.

The Trail of Graft

1917 American film (Kalem/1 reel), an episode in the series *Grant, Police Reporter*. Grant (George Larkin) investigates a politician who is taking graft. After he is imprisoned in the grafter's smoke-filled office with the grafter's stenographer (Ollie Kirby), whose notes constitute needed evidence, he climbs out on a rope with the girl on his back and swing across and down to safety. Robert Ellis directed and Robert Welles Ritchie wrote the screenplay.

The Trail of the Cigarette

1920 American Film (Arrow Film/5 reels) starring Glen White as Tex, a famous criminologist. Tex investigates the murder of a girl at a dance where the only clue is a crushed cigarette. Many people smoked that brand and the wrong person is arrested but Tex finally finds the guilty smoker. The supporting cast included Alexander F. Frank, Eugene Acker, Stanley Walpole and David Wall. Alexander F. Frank and Richard Goodall wrote the screenplay and Tom Collins directed the film for the *Tex, Elucidator of Mysteries* series.

The Trail of the Octopus

1919 American serial (Hallmark/fifteen 2-reel chapters) advertised as being "the mysterious adventures of a master criminologist." Ben Wilson plays the detective who teams with Neva Gerber to battle the villainous Octopus and his gang to get possession of nine daggers that will open a treasure fault. J. Grubb Alexander wrote the screenplay and Duke Worne directed. The episodes, in order of release, were *The Devils Trade-Mark, The Purple Dagger, Face to Face, The Hand of Wang, The Eye of Satan, Behind the Mask, The Dance of Death, Satan's Soulmate, The Chained Soul, The Ape Man, The Red Death, The Poisoned Talon, The Phantom Mandarin, The House of Shadows* and *The Yellow Octopus*.

Ben Wilson is the detective battling the criminals in the serial ***The Trail of the Octopus***.

Trailing the Counterfeiters

1911 American comedy (Biograph/1 reel), a film in the *Two Sleuths* series produced and directed by Mack Sennett and starring Sennett and Fred Mace. They play comic detectives.

Trapped by Camera see *Die geheimnisvolle Villa*

Trapped by Pinkertons

1906 American film (Selig/1 reel). The Pinkerton Detective Agency sent its agents west to chase down and capture outlaws, especially railroad thieves The success of its agents led to the use of name "Pinkerton" as a synonym for "detective." Dashiel Hammett was a Pinkerton detective before he started writing detective stories.

Trapped in the Great Metropolis

American film (Rolands Feature Film Co./5 reels). A woman reporter (Rose Austin) and her detective boyfriend investigate the white slave racket. She pretends to be Madame Dufrene, a South American slave buyer, and discover that the boss of the crooked "Social Employment Bureau" is a respectable local businessman honored as a philanthropist. He escapes but later dies of a heart attack.

The Tremarne Case

1924 British film (Stoll/2 reels), an episode in the *Old Man in the Corner* series based on a story by Baroness Orczy. An armchair detective known as the Old Man in the Corner solves a crime while sitting in a tea shop and tells the solution to a young woman journalist. Rolf Leslie played the Old Man and Renée Wakefield was journalist Mary Hatley. D. P. Cooper was the cinematographer and Hugh Croise wrote the adaptation and directed.

Trent, Anthony

Master criminal Anthony Trent was the creation of English mystery writer Wyndam Martyn and appeared in two silent features, *The Silver Car* and *The Star Reporter*. He was originally a Raffles-like thief whose specialty was stealing major jewels but he eventually reformed and turned detective and reporter. He was featured in 25 novels starting in 1918 with *Anthony Trent, Master Criminal.*

Trent's Last Case

Edmund C. Bentley's detective Philip Trent humanized detective fiction by coming up with the wrong solution in *Trent's Last Case* (1913) and falling in love with the chief suspect. Bentley said he had set out "to create a detective who was recognizable as a human being." Trent did not return until the 1930s when Bentley featured him in *Trent's Own Case* (1936) and *Trent Intervenes* (1938). *Trent's Last Case* was filmed twice in the silent era (see below).

Trent's Last Case

1920 British film (Broadwest/5 reels). Trent investigates the murder of an American millionaire and falls in love with his widow. His solution to the crime is absolutely brilliant — and totally wrong. Gregory Scott stars as Trent with George Foley as the millionaire, Pauline Peters as his wife, Clive Brook as John Marlow and Cameron Carr as Inspector Murch. P. L. Mannock wrote the screenplay and Richard Garrick directed.

Trent's Last Case

1929 American film (Fox/6 reels). Raymond Griffith stars as Philip Trent investigating the apparent murder of millionaire Sigsbee Manderson (Donald Crisp). Inspector Murch (Ed Kennedy) suspects everybody including Manderson's wife, secretary, uncle, butler and maid. Marceline Day played Mrs. Manderson, Lawrence Gray was Jack Marlowe, Raymond Hatton was Joshua Cupples, Nicholas Soussanin was Martin and Anita Garvin was Ottilie. Scott Darling wrote the screenplay and Howard Hawks directed.

The Trey o' Hearts

1914 American serial (Universal/fifteen 2-reel chapters) based on Louis Joseph Vance's mystery novel *The Trey o' Hearts.* An old crippled man and his daughter plot to kill a man because they believe the man's father was the cause of the man's injury. She has a twin sister which rather complicates things, especially when they both fall in love with the hero and

Cleo Madison holds up the "death sign" three of hearts card in the serial *Trey o' Hearts.*

one is struck by lightning. Cleo Madison plays the twin sisters and George Larkin is the lucky hero. The episodes are titled *Flower of the Flames, White Water, The Sea Venture, Dead Reckoning, The Sunset Tide, The Crack o' Doom, Stalemate, The Mock Rose, As the Crow Flies, Steel Ribbons, The Painted Hills, The Mirage, The Jaws of Death, The First Law* and *The Last Trump.*

The Triple Clue

1920 American Film (Arrow Film/5 reels) starring Glen White as Tex, a famous criminologist Tex has to work against deadline and prove that Jack Rogers (Stanley Walpole), about to be executed for murder, is innocent. He returns to the scene of the crime and finds a woman's shoe buckle that belonged to Jack's former sweetheart Rose (Clarice Young) He finds her at the last moment, gets a confession and stops the execution with minutes to spare Tom Collins wrote and directed the film for the *Tex, Elucidator of Mysteries* series.

Glen White as detective Tex in *The Triple Clue* (brochure cover).

The Troubles of an Amateur Detective

10909 American comedy (Vitagraph/half reel) about an amateur detective written by Roy L. Mcardell and directed by George D. Baker.

The Trunk Mystery

1927 American film (Pathé/5 reels) based on a story by Forrest Sheldon. Retired Secret Service agent Jim Manning (Charles Hutchison) buys a trunk at a police auction. That night his house is broken into by Margaret Hampton (Alice Calhoun) and criminals Fawcett and Turner. The crooks escape but Margaret stays and explains that her father was put in prison for stealing a pearl necklace from his jewel merchant employer Stevanov. She thinks her father was innocent and that Stevanov hid the necklace in the trunk for collection later. The crooks return the next night but can't find necklace which Manning had removed from the trunk. Stevanov and the two crooks are arrested. Frederic Chapin wrote the screenplay and Frank Hall Crane directed.

Le Trust, ou les batailles de l'argent
(The Trust, or the Money Battles)

1911 French film (Gaumont/2 reels) directed by Louis Feuillade. René Navarre stars as detective Julian Kieffer in this early Feuillade film. It was made for the pioneering realist series *La Vie telle qu'elle est* (Life as It Really Is).

The Truthful Liar

1922 American film (Paramount/6 reels) based on a story by Will J. Payne. Tess (Wanda Hawley, who is married to David (Edward Hearn) but feeling neglected, gets into trouble when she goes to a gambling house with old boyfriend Arthur (Casson Ferguson). He is wounded in a raid arranged by gangster Potts (George Siegmann) and her rings are stolen. Potts gets an incriminating letter written by Tess and attempts to blackmail her but is murdered. Tess is the chief suspect until Police Commissioner Rogers (Charles K. French) proves that the murderer was a gangland enemy of Potts. Thomas N. Heffron directed and Percy Heath wrote the screenplay.

A Turf Conspiracy

1918 British film (Granger/5 reels) based on the 1916 novel *A Turf Conspiracy* by Nat

Violet Hopson is a widow involved with a racetrack gang in *A Turf Conspiracy*.

Gould. In this race track crime thriller, a betting ring hires a widow to keep a stable under their control and a detective investigates. Violet Hopson played Madge Iman, W.R. Harrison was Detective Thawson, Gerald Ames was Gordon Chorley, Joan Legge was Olga Bell, Cameron Carr was Superintendent Ladson and Arthur Walcott was Jack Rook. Bannister Merwin wrote the screenplay and Frank Wilson directed.

The Turn of the Wheel

1918 American film (Goldwyn/5 reels). Opera diva Geraldine Farrar stars as Rosalie in this murder mystery set in Monte Carlo. She becomes involved with gambler Maxfield (Herbert Rawlinson) who is arrested for the murder of his ex-wife. He won't defend himself but she believes him innocent and sets out to find the truth. The killer turns out to be a philanderer named Wally (Hassard Short) who was having an affair with Maxfield's sister-in-law and shot the ex-wife while struggling with Maxfield. Reginald Barker directed and Tex Charwate wrote the screenplay.

Twin Pawns

1919 American film (Pathé/5 reels) "suggested" by Wilkie Collins's *The Woman in White* with plot and characters greatly altered. Mae Murray plays twins Daisy and Violet White who were separated at birth, Warner Oland is the evil John Bent who manipulates the twins like pawns, J. W. Johnston is their father Harry White and Henry G. Sell is Bob Anderson, the friend who sorts it all out. See also *The Woman in White*.

The Two Sleuths

1911–1912 comedy series (Biograph/five 1-reel films) produced and directed by Mack Sennett and starring Fred Mace and Mack Sennett. They place comic detectives. The films in the first series, in order of their release, *were $500 Reward, Trailing the Counterfeiters, Their First Divorce Case, Caught with the Goods* and *Their First Kidnapping Case.*

The Two Sleuths

1912–1913 comedy series (Keystone/five 1-reel films) produced and directed by Mack Sennett and starring Fred Mace and Mack Sennett. They play comic detectives. The films of the second series, in order of their release, were *At It Again, A Bear Escape, The Stolen Purse, The Sleuth's Last Stand* and *The Sleuths at the Floral Parade.*

Ultus

Ultus, a daring avenger and "master of a thousand disguises," was featured in a series of British films produced in 1916 and 1917. Writer-producer George Pearson modeled *Ultus* on the French *Fantômas* series and cast Aurele Sydney (an Australian with French parents) in the title role. J. L.V. Leigh played master detective Conway Bass who pursues Ultus throughout the series with Mons Goujet as his spy assistant Eugene Lester. Emile Lauste was the impressive cinematographer for the Gaumont series which was popular in France and America as well as in England.

Ultus: The Man from the Dead

1916 British series (Gaumont-Victory/six episodes). Diamond miner Dick Morgan (Aurele Sydney) survives an attempt by his treacherous partner Gilbert Townsend (A. Caton Woodville) to kill him in the Australian desert

Aurele Sydney plays a superhero in the British series *Ultus.*

but is badly wounded. He returns to England five years later as "Ultus the Avenger" to take elaborate revenge on Townsend (now Sir Gilbert) and proves himself to be a master of disguise. Detective Conway Bass (J. L.V. Leigh) is soon on his trail, however, with the help of his spy Eugene Lester (Mons Goujet). Lady Townsend (Marjorie Dunbar) knows nothing of the evil deeds of her husband.

Ultus 1: The Townsend Mystery

1916 British film (Gaumont-Victory/4 reels). Diamond miner Dick Morgan (Aurele Sydney) has struck it rich in the Australian desert but his treacherous partner Gilbert Townsend (A. Caton Woodville) plans to kill him so he can have the diamonds himself. Morgan survives and decides to take an elaborate revenge on Townsend in the guise of Ultus the Avenger.

Ultus 2: The Ambassador's Diamond

1916 British film (Gaumont-Victory/4 reels). "Ultus the Avenger" (Aurele Sydney) arrives in England and discovers that his wealthy ex-partner Townsend (A. Caton Woodville) is now Sir Gilbert Townsend and married to the beautiful Lady Townsend (Marjorie Dunbar). He plans his revenge.

Ultus 3: The Grey Lady

1916 British film (Gaumont-Victory/4 reels). Ultus (Aurele Sydney) is using the Grey Lady (Mary Dibley) and her gang to exact revenge on his evil ex-partner (A. Caton Woodville). Detective Conway Bass (J. L.V. Leigh) is in hot pursuit.

Ultus 4: The Traitor's Fate

1916 British film (Gaumont-Victory/4 reels). Ultus (Aurele Sydney) and the Grey Lady Mary Ferris (Mary Dibley) plot revenge on Townsend (A. Caton Woodville) who betrayed Mary's father as well. Detective Conway Bass (J. L.V. Leigh) has a plan to catch Ultus.

Ultus 5: The Secret of the Night

1917 British film (Gaumont-Victory/4 reels). Ultus (Aurele Sydney) hides out in Devon with the Grey Lady and rescues a child heiress from a pair of villains who were hired to kill her. This venture leads to his being captured by Detective Conway Bass (J. L.V. Leigh) and put in prison.

Ultus 6: The Three Button Mystery

1917 British film (Gaumont-Victory/5 reels) originally known as *Ultus and the Cabinet Minister's Overcoat*. Ultus (Aurele Sydney) escapes from prison and rescues a government minister kidnapped by the evil Derwent (Charles Rock), Elsie (Manora Thew) creates problem but finally Ultus defeats Derwent and then disappears.

Under Suspicion

1918 American film (Metro/5 reels) based on the story "The Woolworth Diamonds" by Hugh C. Weir published in *The Saturday Evening Post*. Millionaire Gerry Simpson (Francis X. Bushman) meets newspaperwoman Virginia Blake (Beverly Bayne) at a party where jewels are stolen from hostess Alice Woolworth. The chief of detectives (Franklyn Hanna) investigates but it is Virginia who finds a clue in the form of a button torn from the thief's coat. When she discovers it is identical to buttons on

Virginia (Beverly Bayne) finds the important clue in *Under Suspicion*.

Simpson's coat, she searches his apartment and finds a cache of jewels. She is discovered by the real thief and almost killed but rescued by Simpson. Albert Shelby Le Vino wrote the screenplay and Will S. Davis directed.

Unexpected Places

1918 American film (Metro/5 reels) based on the novelette *Unexpected Places* by Frank R. Adams first published in *Blue Book Magazine*. Newspaperman Dick Holloway (Bert Lytell) investigates the murder of a valet employed by Lord Varden (Colin Kenny). Varden drinks poisoned coffee but is saved by Holloway who takes his place when the aristocrat is hospitalized. He accepts an invitation to visit relative Ruth Penfield (Rhea Mitchell) who is kidnapped by a gang who offer to exchange her for secret papers held by Varden. Holloway rescues her and the police arrest the gang. Albert Shelby Le Vino and George D. Baker wrote the screenplay and E. Mason Hopper directed.

Unheimliche Geschichten (Eerie Tales)

1919 German anthology film (Richard Oswald–Produktion/5 reels). with episode loosely based on the Robert Louis Stevenson story *The Suicide Club*. in an old bookstore At night, portraits of Death, the Devil and the Strumpet come to life and amuse themselves by reading stories about themselves in various guises. *The Suicide Club* is the fourth story with Conrad Veidt playing the club president, Anita Berber as his sister and Reinhold Schünzel as detective Arthur Silas. Richard Oswald directed. See also *The Suicide Club*.

The U.S. Revenue Detective

1920 American film (Yankee/1 reel). No further information.

Unknown Treasures

1926 American film (Sterling Pictures/6 reels) based on Mary Spain Vigus's story "The House Behind the Hedge." Bob Ramsey (Robert Agnew) searches his late uncle's deserted house for securities he believes are hidden there. Mary (Gladys Hulette), who loves him, plants securities there with the hope that he will marry her when he finds them. His cousin Ralph (John Miljan) also goes looking for the securities and ends up getting strangled. Bob follows an ape to the hideout of the caretaker Simmons (Gustav von Seyffertitz) who stole the securities from Ralph. The angry ape kills Simmons, Bob gets the securities back and Mary get Bob. Archie Mayo directed and Charles A. Logue wrote the screenplay.

An Unpaid Ransom

1915 American film (Edison/1 reel), based on the story "The Case of the Under Secretary" by Scott Campbell. This was one of five films in the *Felix Boyd* series, about a detective who is a combination of Nick Carter and Sherlock Holmes. The cast included Augustus Phillips, Bessie Learn, Carlton King and Frank Trenor. Langdon West directed. (See Boyd, Felix for other films.)

Unseen Foes

1922 American film (Garsson Productions/2 reels), one of four films in a *Nick Carter* series featuring the famous detective Nick Carter. In this one he has to do battle without knowing who he is fighting. Carter was played by Edmund Lowe under the direction of Alexander Hall. With Diana Allen and Henry Sedley.

The Unseen Witness

1920 American Film (Arrow Film/5 reels) starring Glen White as Tex, a famous criminologist. Tex investigates the murder of a man found dead in his library His secretary Harry Gray (Joseph Striker), who had been fired the day before, is the chief suspect but he claims he saw the killer escape through a window. This is considered impossible as the window is on the 16th floor of the building but Tex proves it is not. A rival, who lived on the floor above, had made his escape with a rope after the murder. The supporting cast including William Fredericks, Jan McAlpin, David Wall and Leo Delaney. Tom Collins wrote and directed the film for the *Tex, Elucidator of Mysteries* series.

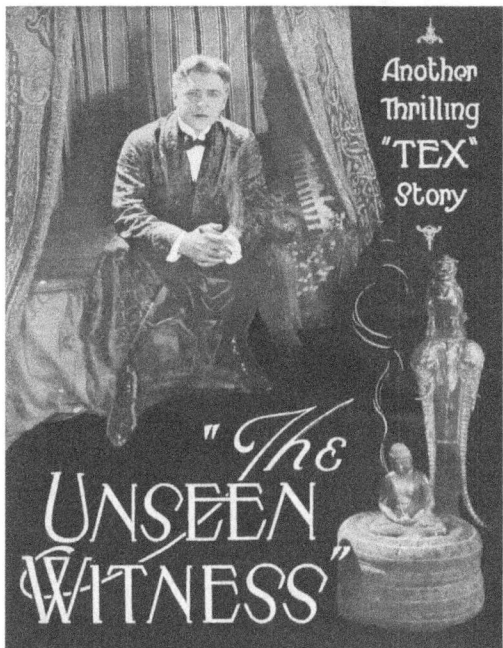

Detective Tex solves an impossible case in *The Unseen Witness* (brochure cover).

An Unwilling Burglar

1915 comedy (Lubin/2 reels) starring Billie Reeves with Carrie Reynolds and Ferdinand O'Beck. Mark Swan wrote the screen play and Earl Metcalfe directed.

Up and At 'Em

1922 American film (RC Pictures/5 reels) starring Doris May who was promoted as a "flapper detective." She disguises herself as her father's chauffeur and accompanies a gang of crooks when they rob the home of an art collector, then tracks them to a waxworks. Lewis Milestone and William A Seiter wrote the screenplay and Seiter directed.

Valentine, Jimmy

Jimmy Valentine, the creation of O Henry, first appeared in the 1909 story *A Retrieved Reformation*. The story was transformed by Paul Armstrong into the 1910 Broadway play *Alias Jimmy Valentine* and the play made the character famous. Valentine, a master safecracker, has reformed after falling in love and now lives quietly in a small town. A detective, who has been chasing him for a year, arrives on the day that Valentine may be forced to reveal his safecracking prowess. His sweetheart's little sister has been locked in a bank vault which only he can open before the air in the vault is exhausted. If he does it the detective will know who he is, arrest him and send him back to prison. He opens the safe anyway but the detective tells him he could not possibly be the Jimmy Valentine he is seeking. The play was the basis of silent films in 1915, 1920 and 1928. For the films see *Alias Jimmy Valentine*.

The Valley of Fear

1916 British film (Samuelson/5 reels) based on the novel *The Valley of Fear* by Arthur Conan Doyle. Sherlock Holmes investigates the murder of a man who had once been a Pinkerton agent in the Pennsylvania coal fields. H. A. Saintsbury plays Holmes with Arthur M. Cullin as Watson and Booth Conway as Moriarty. Alexander Butler directed and Harry Engholm wrote the screenplay. See Holmes, Sherlock for other films.

Les Vampires

1915 French serial (Gaumont/7 hours in

Irma Vep (Musidora) is the memorable star of the French serial *Les Vampires*.

ten episodes) written and directed by Louis Feuillade. Musidora stars as Irma Vep in this legendary crime serial, one of the glories of the French cinema banned by Paris police for glorifying crime. It revolves around the activities of a group of super-criminals led by a Grand Vampire (Jean Aymé) and involves countless secret passageways, hidden trapdoors, rooftop chases and amazing disguises. Investigative reporter Phillipe Guérande (Édouard Mathé) and his assistant Mazamette (Marcel Lévesque) relentlessly pursue the gang but audiences were most fascinated by Musidora in her skintight black costume, a truly liberated woman who quickly became a cinematic icon. The chapter titles, in English as on the DVD, are *The Severed Head, The Ring That Kills, The Red Codebook, The Spectre, Dead Man's Escape, Hypnotic Eyes, Satunsus, The Thunder Master, The Poisoner* and *The Terrible Wedding.*

The Vanderhoff Affair

1915 American film (Kalem /4 reels). Mystery film in which a villainous uncle drugs his niece with "loco weed" so she will be declare insane and he can take over her fortune. She communicates with the hero by writing notes with milk that seem blank but reveal messages when scorched. Marguerite Courtot played the heiress, Hal Forde was the man who rescues her, Robert G. Vignola was the good doctor who helped Henry Hallam was the villainous uncle and Helen Lindroth and T J. Dow were the evil Mexican servants. Robert G. Vignola directed.

The Vanishing Cracksman

1914 American film (Edison/1 reel), an episode in *the Chronicles of Cleek* series written by Thomas W. Hanshew. Ben Wilson plays master criminal Hamilton Cleek, known as the "man of forty faces," and Robert Brower is his nemesis Detective Narko. Harry Beaumont and Gertrude McCoy give support and George Lessey directed.

Vanity

1916 American film (Metro/5 reels) based on a story by Aaron Hoffman. Crooked detective James Burke (Tom O'Keefe) forces fashion model Phyllis Lord (Emmy Wehlen) to obtain evidence against Robert Armstrong (Edward Martindell) for use in a murder trial. She records Armstrong talking about the murder but it turns out the killing was done by his father and was in self-defense. Phyllis, now in love with Robert, blackmails the detective into dropping the charges. Wallace C. Clifton wrote the screenplay and John B. O'Brien directed.

Velvet Fingers

1920 American serial (Pathé/fifteen 2-reel chapter) described as "a dashing serial replete with mystery, daring and thrilling incident." A Raffles-like thief battles a Sherlock Holmes–like detective in his quest for valuable jewels. Producer/director George B. Seitz played the gentleman crook Velvet Fingers with Harry Semels as his detecting opponent Professor Robin and Marguerite Courtot as the woman in the case. Bertram Millhauser wrote the story and James Shelley Hamilton wrote the screenplay. The episodes, in order of release, were: *To Catch a Thief, The Face Behind the Curtain, The Hand from Behind the Door, The Man in the Blue Spectacles, The Deserted Pavilion, Unmasked, The House of 1000 Veils, Aiming Straight, The Broken Necklace, Shots in the Dark, The Other Woman, Into Ambush, The Hidden Room, The Trap* and *Out of the Web.*

Vengeance Is Mine

1917 American film (Pathé/5 reels) based on the novel *Vengeance Is Mine* by John A. Moroso. Paula Farrington vows to revenge her father who was ruined by a secret financial ring. With the help of a reformed burglar she obtains papers proved the ring is headed by — the father of the man she loves. She decides that love is more important that vengeance and her decision results in the villain's reformation. Irene Castle played Paula with support from Frank Sheridan, Helene Chadwick, Ethel Grey Terry and Elliot Dexter. Howard Irving Young wrote the screenplay and Frank Crane directed.

The Ventures of Marguerite

1915 American serial (Kalem/sixteen 1-reel chapters) starring Marguerite Courtot as a rich heiress threatened by various villains who want to kidnap her and prevent her from getting married so she can inherit a fortune. A mystic even offers her uncle money if she will become a priestess in his religion. She gets help from Richare Purdom. The others in the cast included E.T. Roseman, Paul Sherman, Bradley Barker, Edwin Brandt and Phil Hardy. Hamilton Smith co-directed with John E. Mackin and Robert Ellis. The episodes are titled *When Appearances Deceive, The Rogue Syndicate, The Kidnapped Heiress, The Veiled Priestess, A Society Schemer, The Key to a Fortune, The Ancient Coin, The Secret Message, The Oriental's Plot, The Spy's Ruse, The Crossed Clues, The Tricksters, The Sealskin Coat, The Lurking Peril, The Fate of America* and *The Trail's End*.

Venus of Venice

1927 American film (First National/7 reels) based on a story by Wallace Smith who wrote the screenplay. Beautiful Venetian thief Carlotta (Constance Talmadge) is nicknamed the Water Rat by the police as she always escapes capture by diving into a canal. After she and her "blind beggar" partner Marco (Michael Vavitch) rob the guests at a wedding, she ends up in a gondola with wealthy artist Kenneth (Antonio Moreno). She and Marco make plans to rob him but he catches them out so instead they plan to steal pearls from his fiancée during the Venetian Carnival. Carlotta falls in love with Kenneth and things work out differently. Marshall Neilan directed.

The Verdict

1925 American film (Truart Film Corp./7 reels). Fashion house mogul Pierre Ronsard (Lou Tellegen) wants to break up the marriage of Jimmy (William Collier, Jr.) and Carol (Louise Lorraine), who work for him. He tells Carol he has papers proving Jimmy is embezzling company funds and will give them to her if she agrees to have dinner with him. Ronsard is shot by an unknown person at the dinner. As Jimmy was in the area he is tried for the murder. Carol tries to sacrifice herself by saying she is the killer but then Ronsard's butler tells the jury he killed Ronsard in self defense. Fred Windemere directed and John F. Natteford wrote the screenplay.

Vidocq

1911 French film (SCAGL/2 reels) based on the *Memoirs* of François-Eugène Vidocq, the French criminal who reformed and became the first official police detective. Harry Baur portrays Vidocq. Louis Launay and Marc Mario wrote the screenplay and Gérard Bourgeois directed.

Vidocq

1922 French film (Société des Cinéromans/8 reels) based on a novelized version of Vidocq's *Memoirs* written by *Judex* author Arthur Bernède. *Fantômas* star René Navarre plays Vidocq and Elmire Vautier plays his wife Manon-la-Blonde. The film follows Vidocq as he rises from being a petty criminal to an influential police detective. Jean Kemm directed.

Vidocq, François-Eugène

François-Eugène Vidocq (1775–1857), the French criminal who reformed and became the first official police detective, was not a fiction writer but most critics consider his *Memoirs* to be pretty fictional. They certainly read like fiction and they set the pattern for detective fiction influencing writers from Edgar Allan Poe to Sir Arthur Conan Doyle. The *Memoirs* were filmed by the French, beginning in 1909 with *La Jeunesse de Vidocq* and 1910 with *L'Évasion de Vidocq*. The other films about him are listed below.

Violet Dare, Detective

1913 American film (Lubin/2 reels). Isabel Lamon starred as detective Violet Dare opposite Richard Travers in this early woman sleuth film.

The Village Sleuth

1920 American film (Paramount/5 reels) based on a story by Agnes Christine Johnston who wrote the screenplay. Farm boy William Wells (Charles Ray) dreams of becoming a detective though he is unable even to solve the mystery of his father's missing melons. He wants to get a job as a detective at a sanitarium but gets a job as a hired man. He becomes involved with chorus girl Pinky (Winifred Westover) who is accused of murdering the husband of another inmate. He investigates and captures a thief. The missing husband reappears and Wells is praised for his detective work. Jerome Storm directed.

A Voice in the Dark

1921 American film (Goldwyn/5 reels) based on the 1919 play *A Voice in the Dark* by Ralph E. Dyar. District Attorney Day (Ramsey Wallace) investigates the murder of a doctor in which two sisters are the main suspects. Adele (Ora Carew) was engaged to the doctor and Blanche (Irene Rich), who is Day's fiancée, had nearly been dishonored by him. Blind and deaf witnesses at the sanitarium where Sainsbury worked help him solve the crime. Arthur F. Statter wrote the screenplay and Frank Lloyd directed.

The Voice in the Fog

1915 American film (Paramount/5 reels) based on the 1915 novel *The Voice in the Fog* by Harold MacGrath. Thomas Webb (Donald Brian) inherits the Moncton peerage and the valuable Moncton pendant loses his right to the title for three months to Mason (Frank A. Connor) in a crooked poker game. Mason poses as Lord Moncton on a transatlantic liner so he can rob rich families while Webb works as a secretary. American heiress Kitty Killigrew (Adda Gleason) is robbed of her copy of the pendant but can identify the voice she heard in the fog. It turns out to belong to Webb who confesses his real identity. Kitty figures out a way to expose Mason and get her jewelry back. Hector Turnbull wrote the screenplay and J. P. McGowan directed.

The Voice on the Wire

1917 American serial (Universal/fifteen 2-reel chapters) based on a novel by Eustace Hale Ball. Detective John Shirley and his partner Polly investigate a crime wave started by Dr. Reynolds. Reynold's wife had been mummified by fellow scientist Laroux as part of a test of his theory about the "Living Death" and Reynolds is out for revenge. J. Grubb Alexander wrote the screenplay and Stuart Paton directed. The chapters are *The Oriental Death Punch*, *The

Neva Gerber and Ben Wilson on promotional cards for the serial *The Voice on the Wire*.

Mysterious Man in Black, *The Spiders' Web*, *The Next Victim*, *The Spectral Hand*, *The Death Warrant*, *The Marked Room*, *High Finance*, *A Stern Chase*, *The Guarded Heart*, *The Thought Machine*, *The Sign of the Thumb*, *Twixt Death and Dawn*, *The Light Dawn* and *The Living Death*.

Le Voleur mondain (The Worldly Thief)

1909 French comedy (Pathé Frères/1 reel) starring French comic Max Linder as Arsène Lupin. Linder also directed the film written by Georges Fagot. See also Lupin, Arsène.

The Wakefield Case

1921 American film (World Film/6 reels) based on a story by Mrs. L. Case Russell Wakefield (Herbert Rawlinson) turns investigator after his detective father is killed while pursuing men who stole rubies from the British Museum. It appears the mysterious "Breen girl" was the cause of his father's death so he follows her to America. He falls in love with Ruth Gregg (Florence Billings) who turns out to be the Breen girl but she is actually an undercover agent for the Secret Service. Nothing and no one is as first assumed but the case is solved and the murdering thieves arrested. Shannon Fife wrote the screenplay and George Irving directed.

The Wall Street Mystery

1920 American Film (Arrow Film/5 reels) starring Glen White as Tex, a famous criminologist. Tex investigates the murder of Wall Street broker Norman Temple (David Wall). The chief suspects are James Borden (Alexander Frank), who had threatened Temple over an unpaid bill, and Temple's Japanese valet who had quarreled with the broker the day before. Tex clears both of them and proves that the murderer was a clerk (Leo Delaney) who Temple caught robbing his safe. Pierce Kingsley wrote the screenplay and Tom Collins directed the film for the *Tex, Elucidator of Mysteries* series.

Wallingford, J. Rufus

J. Rufus Wallingford, a character created by George Randolph Chester, is one of the great confidence men of mystery fiction and his exploits were quite popular with filmmakers in the silent era His printed adventures began in 1908 in the novel *Get-Rich-Quick Wallingford* in which he arrives in a town with no money and gets rich by inventing an imaginary tack company. His swindles continued in four more story collections. Wallingford's exploits inspired George M. Cohan to write a Broadway play about him and the play was the basis of the 1915 film series *Get-Rich-Quick Wallingford*. For his other films see *The New Adventures of J. Rufus Wallingford* and *The Son of Wallingford*.

Walter the Sleuth

1926 British comedy short (British Super Comedies/2 reels). A woman asks Walter to pretend to be a detective to protect her father's diamond. This was one of the films in the "Walter" series written by and starring Walter Forde and directed by James B. Sloan. The supporting cast included Pauline Peters and George Foley.

Wanted at Headquarters

1920 American film (Universal/5 reels) based on the story "Kate Plus Ten" by Edgar Wallace. Kate Westhanger (Eva Novak), the secret leader of a gang of thieves, gets a job at a gold syndicate while preparing to rob a gold shipment. She becomes involved with detective Michael Pretherson (Leonard C. Shumway) and dares him to stop the robbery. The theft is a success but the suspicious gang captures Kate and her detective friend and are about to kill

Tex (Glen White) investigates the murder of a broker in *The Wall Street Mystery*.

them when the police arrive. After a ferocious firefight in which everyone in the gang is killed, she decides to reform, return the gold and marry the detective. Wallace Clifton wrote the screenplay and Stuart Paton directed.

The Ware Case

1917 British film (Broadwest/6 reels) based on a play by George Pleydell Bancroft. Sir Hubert Ware is accused of drowning his wife's brother to get his money. He is acquitted but then repents, admits his guilt and kills himself. Matheson Lang played Sir Hubert Ware in this first film version of the play with Violet Hopson as Lady Magdalene Ware and Ivy Close as Marian Scales. J. Bertram Brown wrote the screenplay and Walter West directed.

Matheson Lang as Ware in the 1917 film of *The Ware Case*.

The Ware Case

1928 British film (FMP/7 reels). based on a play by George Pleydell Bancroft. Sir Hubert Ware is accused of drowning his wife's brother. He is acquitted but later admits his guilt and kills himself. Stewart Rome played Sir Hubert Ware in this second film version of the play with Betty Carter as Lady Magda Ware and Cameron Carr as Inspector Watkins. Lydia Hayward wrote the screenplay and Manning Hayes directed.

Warning Shadows (Schatten — Eine nächtliche Halluzination)

1923 German film (Friedrich Wilhelm Murnau-Stiftung/8 reels). This mystery thriller, which Siegfried Kracauer called one of the "masterpieces of German cinema," has no dialogue (i.e., no intertitles) but plenty of plot. Cinematographer Fritz Arno Wagner and writer/director Arthur Morrison tell its somewhat horrific story visually. A puppeteer illusionist hired to entertain the guests of a baron and his wife at a nineteenth century dinner party reveals what might happen if the jealous baron and the guests who fancy his wife don't tone down their emotions. Fritz Kortner plays the baron, Ruth Weyher is his wife, Gustav von Wangenheim is her lover, Alexander Granach is the magician who creates the prophetic shadows, Rudolf Klein-Rogge is an admirer of the

A sinister puppeteer entertains guests of a baron at a nineteenth century dinner party in *Warning Shadows*.

wife and Fritz Rasp plays a spooky servant. On DVD.

The Wasp

1914 American film (Selig/2 reels) film based on a story by J. A. Lacey and featuring "Dick Little, Secret Service Operative" in a detective drama. The cast included Guy Oliver as Dick Little, Stella Razetto as Stella LeSaint, George Hernandez as John Ward, Pauline Sain as Marie Collins and Fred Huntly as Joe Collins. Edward J. LeSaint directed.

The poster for *The Wasp*, a lost 1914 Selig detective film.

The Waterwheel of Death
(Het Waterrad des doods)

1921 Dutch film (Zwarte Pilj Films/4 reels) featuring "American" detective Nick Carter. Dick Laan, who plays Nick Carter, also wrote and directed the film in which Carter's son is captured by villains and tied to a waterwheel. The movies was meant to be parody of the clichés of detective films. Only fragments of the film survive.

The Way Women Love

1920 American film (Arrow-Lyric films/5 reels) based on the story "Behind the Green Portieres" by Herman Landon in *Detective Story Magazine*. Judith (Rubye De Remer) has faith that her fiancé Ralph (Walter Miller) did not kill Trent (Henry Pemberton) though he threatened to when Trent insulted her. At first it looks like Trent committed suicide and made it appear that Barr killed him. After more revelations, it looks like Barr really did kill him. Then another person is killed and it gets more complicated. Judith's loyalty saves Barr in the end. Marcel Perez wrote the screenplay and Marcel Perez directed.

The Web of Chance

1919 American comedy (Fox/5 reels) based on the story "Right After Brown" by Edgar Franklin (pseudonym of Edgar Franklin Stearns). Dorothy Hale (Peggy Hyland), niece of detective John Harrison (E. B. Tilton), falls in love with Arthur Brown (Harry Hamm), the leading suspect in a robbery her uncle is investigating. Dorothy turns amateur detective to

Peggy Hyland turns amateur detective in *The Web of Chance*.

follow Brown by using multiple disguises. Eventually she finds that Brown is actually the boss of the company that was robbed and the man who hired her uncle. However, the real criminal is caught through Dorothy's efforts. Douglas Bronston wrote the screenplay and Alfred E. Green directed.

Webbs, Stuart

Stuart Webbs was an "American" detective featured in a German film series created by producer Joe May. Ernst Reicher played Webbs in over fifty films from 1914 to 1926, the longest running and most influential detective series in Germany. Like all German film detectives of the time he was given an Anglo-Saxon name, presumably for authenticity. The first Webbs film was the 1914 *Die geheimnisvolle Villa* (The Mysterious Villa) which was distributed in America with the title *Trapped by Camera*. It was followed by the popular *Der Mann im Keller* (The Man in the Cellar), a print of which survives in an archive. The third was *Der Geisterspuk im Hause des Professors*. It was followed by *Das Panzergewölbe* and *Die Toten Erwachen*. Another film that has survived is *Der Gestreifte Domino*.

Ernst Reicher played detective Stuart Webbs in a German film series.

The last film in the series was a remake of *Das Panzergewölbe* in 1926, a kind of fond farewell to the famous detective Reicher wrote the screenplays for all the films and the supporting casts included Max Landa, Sabine Impekoven, Julius Falkenstein, Olga Engl, Lulu Pick, Alice Hechy, Eduard Rothauser and Josef Schelepa.

Der weibliche Detektiv
(The Female Detective)

1912 Austrian film (Wiener Kunstfilm/3 reels) featuring Viennese theater actors in a story about a woman detective. It was filmed on location in Vienna and its environs.

A Weighty Matter for a Detective

1915 American film (Edison/1 reel) starring Jessie Stevens and Arthur Housman. Charles M. Seay wrote the screenplay and directed.

A Well-Planned West End Jewel Robbery

1919 British film (Life Dramas/2 reels), an episode in the series *The Adventures of Dorcas Dene, Detective*. Dene is an actress who become a detective to earn money after her husband is blinded. Winifred Rose plays Dene and Tom Radford is her husband. George Sims wrote the screenplay and Frank Carlton directed.

The West Case

1923 British film (Stoll/2 reels), an episode in the *Mystery of Fu Manchu* series based on a story by Sax Rohmer. Harry Agar Lyons plays Dr. Fu Manchu, Fred Paul is Nayland Smith and Humberston Wright is Dr. Petrie. A. E. Colby directed, Frank Wilson wrote the screenplay with Colby and D. P. Cooper was the cinematographer.

What Happened to Mary?

1912 American serial (Edison/twelve 1-reel episodes). based on stories published in *The Ladies World*. The first American serial though it is not a cliffhanger. Mary (Mary Fuller) is a foundling who has to run away from her foster father and cope with villains as she battles to get her just inheritance. A friend asks her to turn detective ("I'd like to do that" she says) to get evidence to put evil uncle Craig (Charles

Mary (Marry Fuller) tries her hand at detective work in (with Charles Ogle) *What Happened to Mary?*

Ogle). in jail. Bannister Merwin, James Oppenheim and Horace G. Plympton wrote the screenplay and J. Searle Dawley and Walter Edwin directed. The episodes are titled *The Escape from Bondage, Alone in New York, Mary in Stage Land, The Affair at Raynor's, A Letter to the Princess, A Clue to her Parentage, False to their Trust, A Will and A Way, A Way to the Underworld, The High Tide of Misfortune, A Race to New York* and *Fortune Smiles*.

What Women Will Do

1921 American film (Associated Exhibitors/6 reels) based on a story by Charles A. Logue. Lily Gibbs (Anna Q. Nilsson) is persuaded by criminals Jim (Earl Metcalfe) and Joe (George Majeroni) to pretend to be the wife of the dead son of wealthy Mrs. Wade (Jane Jennings).They use a fake séance to convince the mother and she takes Lily under her protection. Lily is reformed by the treatment she receives and falls in love with a man (Allan Forrest) who treats her with respect. When she learns that Joe killed Mrs. Wade's son, she turns against him and both Joe and Jim are killed. Mrs. Wade forgives Lily for what she did. Charles E. Whittaker wrote the screenplay and Edward José directed.

What's Bred ... Comes Out in the Flesh

1916 British film (Master/4 reels) based on the novel *What's Bred in the Bone* by Grant Allen published in the magazine *Tit Bits* in 1891. Judge Gildersleeve (Lauderdale Maitland) tries a man (Frank Tennant) in court for a crime that he himself had committed. A woman friend (Janet Alexander) suspects the truth and finally gets the judge to confesses. Sidney Morgan wrote the screenplay and directed the film.

Wheels of Justice

1915 American film (Vitagraph/4 reels). Broker's wife Rita Reynolds (Eulalie Jensen) shoots her husband (Charles Eldridge) when he catches her opening his safe and then pins the murder on Ralph Brooks (James Morrison). He is convicted and sent to prison. Burglar "Red" Hall (George Cooper), who witnessed the murder, blackmails Rita and plans to rob her friends. Ralph escapes from prison and contrives a scheme to get Rita to confess to the murder. Edward J. Montagne wrote the screenplay and Theodore Marston directed.

Whispering Smith

Railroad detective Whispering Smith was so popular that he inspired five silent films and a new genre of stories about railroad detectives. He was created by Frank Hamilton Spearman in his 1906 novel *Whispering Smith* which portrays Smith's life during four years of detective work. Spearman went to Wyoming to get background for his novel and supposedly based him on a real person. For the films featuring him see below plus *Medicine Bend* and *Money Madness*.

Whispering Smith

1916 American film (Mutual Star/5 reels) directed by J. P. McGowan who played railroad detective Whispering Smith. The detective is sent to investigate a series of train wrecks and robberies and finds his old sweetheart Marian (Helen Holmes) married to the wrecking crew foreman Murray Sinclair (Paul C. Hurst). He leans that Sinclair is responsible for the wrecks but lets him go free for the sake of Marian. This film, based on the first half of Frank Spearman's novel Whispering Smith, was the first feature for Helen Holmes, the star of the railroad serial *The Hazards of Helen*.

Whispering Smith

1926 American film (PDC–Metropolitan/7 reels). based on Frank Spearman's novel *Whispering Smith* starring H. B. Warner as railroad detective Smith. He investigates the looting of train wrecks and finds Murray Sinclair (Eugene Pallette) responsible but hesitates to act when he falls in love with Sinclair's wife Marian (Lilyan Tashman). He is aided by McCloud (John Bowers) and his girl Dicksie (Lillian Rich). Elliott J. Clawson wrote the screenplay and George Melford directed.

Whispering Smith Rides

1927 American serial (Universal/ten 2-reel chapters) based on Frank Spearman's novel *Whispering Smith*. Wallace MacDonald plays railroad detective Smith with J. P. McGowan in a supporting role. Smith investigates the case of a woman (Rose Blossom) whose guardian is trying to stop a railroad from being built. Arthur Henry Gooden wrote the screenplay and Ray Taylor directed. The ten episodes were titled *Lawless Men, Caught in the Crash, Trapped, The Ambush, Railroad Gold, The Interrupted Wedding, A Coward of Conscience, The Bandit's Bargain, The Trail of Sacrifice* and *A Call of the Heart*.

Whispering Wires

1926 American film (Fox/6 reels) based on the play *Whispering Wires* by Kate L. McLaurin and Henry Leverage. Comedy murder mystery

John Bowers and Lillian Rich is a scene from the 1926 film *Whispering Smith*.

Anita Stewart is in great danger from a telephone in *Whispering Wires*.

featuring two incompetent detectives (Mack Swain and Arthur Housman) who look and act like Laurel and Hardy clones. A stockbroker and his lawyer are killed by the use of a nasty trick telephone and the stockbroker's niece (Anita Stewart) is threatened. She is saved at the last moment by her boyfriend (Edmund Burns) no thanks to the detectives or their equally incompetent bloodhound who thinks the butler is the bad guy. L. G. Rigby wrote the screenplay and Albert Ray directed. On video.

While London Sleeps

1926 American film (Warner Bros./6 reels) based on a story by Walter Moroso who also wrote the screenplay. Inspector Burke of Scotland Yard (De Witt Jennings) is determined to capture Limehouse criminal boss London Letter (Otto Matieson) but is foiled by the cleverness of the criminal's dog Rinty (Rin-Tin-Tin). Burke's daughter (Helene Costello) rescues Rinty from the abusive crook and he becomes devoted to her. When she is kidnapped by Letter, Rinty comes to her rescue and kills the monstrous ape-man who is holding her prisoner. H. P. Bretherton directed. *Variety* said the only convincing actor in the film was Rin-Tin-Tin.

The White Circle

1920 American film (Paramount/5 reels) based on the 1882 story "The Pavilion on the Links" by Robert Louis Stevenson published in *The New Arabian Nights*. The Carbonari, an Italian secret society, are the villains of this story as they relentlessly pursue a banker (Spottiswoode Aitken) who gambled away their investments. He hides out in a castle in Scotland with his daughter (Janice Wilson) and an adventurer (Harry S. Northrup) who agrees to protect him but finally realizes that the Carbonari will not be satisfied with anything less than his death. He sacrifices himself for the sake of his daughter. Jack Gilbert and Jules Furthman wrote the screenplay and Maurice Tourneur directed.

The White Moll

1920 American film (Fox/6 reels) based on the 1920 novel *The White Moll* by Frank L. Packard serialized in *Blue Book Magazine*. Serial queen Pearl White plays Rhoda, The White Moll, in this underworld story where everyone seems to have a sobriquet instead of a name. The Moll is hired by a repentant Rich Man (John P. Wade) to return his stolen wealth to those he stole it from. It ain't easy. She has to battle the evil gangleader The Dangler (J. Thornton Baston) and save people like The Sparrow (Walter Lewis) before winning the love of The Adventurer (Richard C. Travers). Detective Henry (Charles J. Slattery) seems sympathetic to this economic angel of mercy. E. Lloyd Sheldon wrote the screenplay and Harry Millarde directed.

Who Is Number One?

1917 American serial (Paramount/fifteen 2-reel chapters) based on a mystery novel by Anna Katharine Green. The mysterious criminal known only as Number One is seeking revenge on the Hale family but no one knows why. The father is a famous inventor and the revenge seems aimed at him. Aimee Villon (Kathleen Clifford) agrees to protect the family because of her love for Tommy Hale (Cullen Landis) but relationships are more complicated than first appears. After many tricky plot turns we learn that Aimee herself is Number One. The other cast members included Gordon Sackville, Neil Hardin, Ruth Smith, Ethel Ritchie and Corinne Grant. William Bertram directed. The chapter titles are *The Flaming Cross, The Flying Fortress, The Sea Crawler, A Marine Miracle, Halls of Hazard, The Flight of the Fury, Hearts in Torment, Walls of Gas, Struck Down, Wires of Wrath, The Rail Raiders, The Show Down, Cornered, No Surrender* and *The Round Up*.

Who Killed Walton?

1918 American film (Triangle/5 reels) based on the story "The Veil" by Norman Sherbrooke. Marian (Mary Mersch) wakes up next to the dead body of Walton (Frank Bonn), an artist who had been hired to illustrate her new book. He had tried to seduce her earlier that night in a restaurant and she had fainted. Marian's fiancé, self-righteous anti-vice crusader

Austin (Edwin J. Brady), denounces her a murderer but her friend George (J. Barney Sherry) agrees to help. He calls on Elsa (Dora Rodgers), a woman who had been involved with Walton and had quarreled with him on the night of his death. When Walton dropped dead of a heart failure, the jealous Elsa had Marian carried to his apartment to implicate her. Marian is declared innocent and switches fiancés. Frank Condon wrote the screenplay and Thomas N. Heffron directed.

Wild, Wild Susan

1925 American movie (Paramount/6 reels) based on the story "The Wild, Wild Child" by Stuart M. Emery published in *Liberty Magazine* in 1925. Wealthy Susan (Bebe Daniels), seeking wild thrills, takes a job with a private detective agency. She meets Tod (Rod La Rocque) who is working as a cab driver under a false name to get material for a novel and they fall in love. Tod hires the detective agency to find him and gets Susan assigned to the job. When she can't find him, she gets assigned to another case. She follows a gang of crooks to an old dark house where frightening things happen to her. Eventually she realizes it is a set-up arranged by Tod and her family to cure her of her seeking thrills. Tom J. Geraghty wrote the screenplay and Edward Sutherland directed.

William Baluchet, roi des détectives

(William Baluchet, King of Detectives)

1921 French serial (Monat Films/five 2-reel episodes) based on André Bencey's novel *William Baluchet, roi des détectives* and directed by Gaston Leprieur. The orphan Marthe (Yvonne Desvignes), who has been raised by a countess and made her heir, is murdered. Detective William Baluchet (Georges Mauloy) investigates The primary suspect is the countess's son Jean but there are plenty of others. The cast included Armand Numes as Castal, Suzanne Talba as Señora Leona and Maria Fromet as Roberte Castal. The episodes were titled *Le Testament de la comtesse de Pressac*, *Les Mystères de Passy*, *Jours d'angoisse*, *L'Homme aux trois visages* and *Le Voile se déchire*. See also Baluchet, William.

Willy Walrus, Detective

1914 American comedy (Universal/1 reel) starring William Wolbert (as Willy Walrus) and Bess Meredyth. Allen Curtis directed and Wolbert wrote the screenplay. This was the second film in the four made for the Willy Walrus series but the only one in which he played a detective.

Winter, Nick

Nick Winter is an "American" detective in Paris who starred in a series of French films for Pathé and other companies between 1910 and 1921. They were tongue-in-cheek parodies of the Nick Carter films and were so popular that at least eight of them survive in film archives. Georges Vinter portrayed Nick in most of the films under the direction of writer/directors Paul Garbagni and Gérard Bourgeois. The surviving films, all early and 1-reel, include *La Banque ténébreuse*, *Comment Nick Winter connut les courses*, *Encore Nick Winter*, *Le Pickpocket mystifié*, *Nick Winter, la voleuse et la somnambule*, *Nick Winter et le courrier diplomatiqu*, *Nick Winter et le rapt de Mlle Werner* and *Le Songe de Nick Winter*.

The other early Nick Winter films were *Le Flair de Nick Winter* and *Nick Winter et le perroquet de Mademoiselle Durand* in 1910; *Un Élève de Nick Winter*, *Nick Winter contre Nick Winter*, *Nick Winter et l'affaire du Celebric Hotel*, *Nick Winter et les faux monnayeurs*, *Nick Winter et le vol de la Joconde*, *Nick Winter et les vols de Primrose*, *Nick Winter et le parfum révélateur*, *Dick Johnson le voleur gentleman contre Nick Winter*, *Le Parfum revelateur*, *Le Roman d'une pauvre fille*, *Le ruses de Nick Winter* in 1911; *Max Linder contre Nick Winter*, *Nick Winter contre le banquier Werb*, *Nick Winter et la mariage de Miss Woodman*, *Nick Winter plus fort que Sherlock Holmes*, *La Resurrection de Nick Winter* in 1912; *Nick Winter et l'énigme du lac Némi*, *Nick Winter et les as de trèfle*, *Nick Winter et le mystère de la Tamise*, *Le professeur Mystere*, *Ténébres* in 1913; *Nick Winter et l'homme au masque*, *Nick Winter et la grotte mystérieuse*, *Nick Winter et la parure d'opale* in 1914.

Nick's final films were made in the '20s

and included three 3-reel features (*La Boucle énigmatique*, *Le Dossier 33* and *Le Secret d'Argeville*) and a serial (*Nick Winter et ses aventures*).

The Wise Detectives

1914 American comedy film (Lubin/2 reels) starring Harry Lorraine and Mae Hotely E.W. Sargent wrote the screenplay and C.W. Ritchey directed.

The Witness for the Defense

1919 American film (Paramount/5 reels) based on A. E. W. Mason's play and novel *The Witness for the Defense*. Stella Derrick (Elsie Ferguson), on trial for the murder in India of her brutal husband Captain Ballantyne, is saved by the testimony of big game hunter Henry Thresk (Wyndham Standing). But his testimony was false and he wants "payment" for his lie. Ouida Bergère wrote the screenplay and George Fitzmaurice directed.

Wits vs. Wits

1920 American film (Hallmark Pictures/5 reels). Marguerite Marsh plays an undercover detective who pretends to be a pickpocket so she can avenge her father. She tricks a crooked bank teller to gets her a job with the leader of a band of thieves.(Charles Middleton). Working with a police detective (Joseph Marba) and using a hidden dictaphone, she gets evidence about the gang and has them arrested. Harry Grossman wrote the screenplay and directed. *Variety* called it "monotonous" and "unconvincing."

The Wizard

1927 American film (Fox/6 reels) based on Gaston Leroux's 1912 novel *Balaoo*. A mad doctor trains an ape to kill people so he can avenge the death of his son. A newspaper reporter investigates and discovers the secret in time to save the life of a judge and his daughter. Gustav von Seyffertitz played mad Dr. Coriolos, Edmund Lowe was newspaperman Stanley Gordon, Norman Trevor was Judge Webster, Leila Hyams was his daughter Anne, E. H. Calvert was murder victim Edwin Palmer and George Kotsonaros was the Ape. Richard Rosson directed while Harry O. Hoyt and Andrew Bennison wrote the adaptation. (The novel was filmed in France in 1913 as *Balaoo*.)

Wo ist Coletti? (Where Is Coletti?)

1912 German film (Vitascop/2 reels). Berlin detective Jean Coletti (Hans Junkermann) insists that a criminal can hide in the city of Berlin without being recognized even if his photo is widely circulated. To prove this he publishes his own photo and then disappears after offering a large reward to anyone who can find him in 24 hours. A lot of people try. Madge Lessing plays the dancer Lolotte, Heinrich Peer is Anton the barber, Anna Müller-Lincke is the resolute lady, Hans Stock is Count Edgar and Max Laurence is the old count. Max Mack directed and Franz von Schoenthan wrote the screenplay.

Die Wohltäterin der Menschheit (The Benefactress of Mankind)

1920 German film (May Film/9 reels), the seventh episode in the big budget German series *Herrin der Welt* (Mistress of the World) based on a novel by Karl Figdor. Mia May stars as Maud Gregaards-Fergusson who has found the lost treasure of the Queen of Sheba and become the richest woman in the world. She decides to use the money to become the benefactress of mankind. The supporting cast includes Michael Bohnen, Hans Mierendorff and Henry Sze. Richard Hutter wrote the screenplay and Joe May directed.

Wolf's Clothing

1927 American film (Warner Bros./8 reels) based on the serial *Wolf's Clothing* by Arthur Somers Roche published in *Cosmopolitan* in 1926. Douglas Gerrard plays a somewhat silly English society detective involved with a New York subway guard (Monte Blue) who is pretending to be millionaire playboy. Blue was hit by a car driven by the millionaire and they switched identities but he then gets kidnapped along with Patsy Ruth Miller. After many adventures, including saving the passengers on a runaway subway train, Blue wakes up in hospital with Miller as his nurse. It was all a dream.

Darryl Zanuck wrote the screenplay and Roy Del Ruth directed.

A Woman in Grey

1920 American serial (Serico Producing Company/fifteen 2reel chapters) based on the novel *A Woman in Grey* by Charles N. and Alice M. Williamson. The old Armory house, once the scene of a murder, could conceal a treasure but it certainly has numerous secret passageways, hidden staircases and sliding walls. A coded message found in a bible may provide an answer. Wilfred Amory, son of the late owner, is looking for the treasure along with more mysterious folk. Arline Pretty star as Ruth Hope, the Woman in Grey, with Henry G. Sell as Amory's Attorney, Fred C. Jones as a Man of Mystery, John Heenan as Wilfred Armory, Margaret Fielding as Amory's niece, Ann Brody as Miss Traill and Jane Mair as Grace Carleton. Walter R. Hall wrote the screenplay and James Vincent directed. The chapters were titled *The House of Mystery, The Dagger of Death, The Trap of Steel, The Strangle Knot, The Chasm of Fear, The Grip of Fate, At the Mercy of Flames, The Drop to Death, Burning Strands, House of Horrors, Fight for Life, Circumstantial Evidence, The Secret Chamber, Pages of the Past* and *Exonerated*. On DVD.

Arline Pretty stars as Ruth Hope, the Woman in Grey, in the serial *The Woman in Grey*.

The Woman in White

Wilkie Collins's novel *The Woman in White* (1860) features amateur detective Walter Hartwright who helps to unravel the complicated plot surrounding the mysterious woman in white. The story revolves around Laura who has been defrauded of her estate by evil husband Sir Percival Glyde and his villainous partner Count Fosco. She gets it back with help from her half sister Marion and Hartwright who has turned detective out of love for Marion. *The Woman in White* was filmed seven times in the silent era. See below, and *Tangled Lives* and *Twin Pawns*.

The Woman in White

1912 American film (Gem-Universal/2 reels) based on Wilkie Collins's novel *The Woman in White*. Count Fosco (Alexander Frank) and his wife (Viola Alberti) take charge of heiress Laura (Janet Salisbury) and force her to marry impecunious Sir Percival (Charles Craig) after getting rid of drawing teacher Walter (Charles Perley). When she won't pay his debts, they put her in a lunatic asylum and replace her with a lookalike. After Walter sees the mysterious Woman in White, things start to go wrong for the evil duo. George Nickolls wrote and directed the film.

The Woman in White

1912 American film (Thanhouser/2 reels) based on Wilkie Collins's novel *The Woman in White* about a scheme to defraud a woman of heir inheritance. Marguerite Snow plays Laura and Anne with James Cruze as the evil Sir Percival and William Garwood as the amateur detective Walter. Lloyd Lonergan wrote the screenplay.

The Woman in White

1917 American film (Thanhauser/6 reels) based on Wilkie Collins's novel *The Woman in White*, about a scheme to defraud a woman of

Florence La Badie plays the endangered heroine Laura in the 1917 film version of Wilkie Collins' thriller *The Woman in White*.

heir inheritance. Florence La Badie plays the double role of Laura and Ann with Richard Neill as Sir Percival, Arthur Bower as Count Fosco, Wayne Arey as Walter and Gertrude Dallas as Marian. Lloyd Lonergan wrote the screenplay and Ernest Warde directed.

The Woman in White

1929 British film (British and Dominion/6 reels) based on Wilkie Collins's novel *The Woman in White* about a scheme to defraud a woman of heir inheritance Blanche Sweet stars as Laura, Cecil Humphreys is Sir Percival, Frank Perfitt is Count Fosco, Haddon Mason is Walter and Louise Prussing is Marion. Herbert Wilcox directed.

The Woman of Mystery

1914 American film (Solax/4 reels). Woman detective Nelson (Fraunie Fraunholz) is hired by actress Norma (Claire Whitney) to find out who is trying to kill her. There is also a robbery scheme involving a woman of mystery (Vinnie Burns). Alice Guy Blaché wrote and directed this early woman detective film.

A Woman Redeemed

1927 British film (Stoll/8 reels) based on the mystery novel *The Fining Pot Is for Silver* by F. Britten Austin. "The fining pot is for silver, and the. furnace for gold: but the Lord trieth the hearts. A wicked doer giveth heed to false lips" is from Proverbs 17:3. An evil count forces a young woman to marry an inventor so she can steal his plans for a radio-controlled torpedo. James Carew played the Count, Joan Lockton was Felice, Brian Aherne was Geoffrey, Stella Arbenina was Marta, Gordon Hopkirk was Angelo, Frank Denton was Courtney and Robert English was Mather. Sinclair Hill directed and Mary Murillo wrote the screenplay.

The Woman Under Oath

1919 American film (Tribune Production/6 reels). Grace Norton (Florence Reed), the first woman juror in a New York trial, is the lone voice against conviction of Jim O'Neil who was found holding a revolver over his dead employer Edward Knox. He admits he meant to kill him because he had raped his sweetheart but found him already dead. After an all-night session Grace learns that her sister Edith has died. She tells the jury members that she was the one who killed Knox because he had seduced her sister and then refused to marry her. The foreman reminds the jury of their oath to keep their discussions secret; they vote to acquit O'Neill but not to reveal Grace's story. John M. Stahl directed.

The Woman Who Dared

1911 American film (Yankee/1 reel). A woman takes over a detective agency after her detective father is murdered. Her first case is investigating his murder.

The Woman Who Dared

1916 American film (California Motion Picture Corp/7 reels) based on the 1903 novel *The Woman Who Dared* by Alice Muriel Williamson. Leslie T. Peacocke wrote the screenplay and George Middleton directed. Opera diva Princess Beatrix de Rohan (Beatriz Michelena) becomes involved in the theft of a secret document through a request from her brother Henri (Clarence Arper). Italian diplomat Count D'Olli (Albert Morrison), who is courting her, has the document which she steals and gives it to Henri's messenger. After he is killed by Duke Grozzi

(Andrew Robson), who plans to blackmail her. American Noel Brent (William Pike) saves the day and wins Beatriz.

The Woman Who Touched the Legs see Ashi ni sawatta onna

The World's Great Snare

1916 American film (Paramount/5 reels) based on the 1896 novel *The World's Great Snare* by E. Phillips Oppenheim and directed by Joseph Kaufman. Bryan (Irving Cummings) learns he is heir to an English title and goes to San Francisco to find Huntley (Ferdinand Tidmarsh) who has the papers proving his inheritance. But Huntley has given the papers to gambler Rutten (Riley Hatch) to pay debts. Bryan goes to a dance hall to see Rutten and meets Huntley's former mistress Myra (Pauline Frederick) who he defends from Rutten. When Myra learns about the missing papers, she steals them back when Huntley is murdered by a criminal cohort. She is accused of the murder but Bryan helps her prove her innocence. After more complications Bryan decides to give up his title and stay with Myra.

The Would-Be Detective

1913 American film (Gem Motion Pictures/1 reel). No details available.

The Would-Be Detectives

1913 British comedy (Sun-Cosmo/1 reel). Incompetent sleuth Bexton Slake searches for a kidnapped baby in this parody of the Sexton Blake detective films.

The Yellow Claw

1921 British film (Stoll/6 reels) based on the 1915 novel *The Yellow Claw* by Sax Rohmer. French detective Gaston Max (Harvey Braban) and English detective Inspector Dunbar (Sydney Seeward) track down the mysterious "Mr. King" who heads an organization named the "Sublime Order." King, the prototype for Dr. Fu Manchu, employs opium smugglers who murder the wife of a novelist. Kitty Fielder played the Lady of Poppies and June was Mrs. Verson. Rene Plaisetty directed and Gerard Fort Buckle wrote the screenplay.

The Yellow Face

1921 British film (Stoll/2 reels), an episode in the *Adventures of Sherlock Holmes* series based on a story by Sir Arthur Conan Doyle. Sherlock Holmes solves a mystery involving a man with a yellow face living alone in a cottage. Eille Norwood portrays Holmes with Hubert Willis as Dr. Watson. William J. Elliot wrote the script and Maurice Elvey directed. A print of this film survives at the BFI archive.

The Yellow Pawn

1916 American film (Paramount/5 reels) based on the story "A Close Call" by Frederic Arnold Kummer published in *All-Story Magazine* in 1914. Kate Turner (Cleo Ridgeley) loves artist James Weldon (Wallace Reid.) but circumstances cause her to marry district attorney Allen Perry (William Conklin). Years later detectives arrest Weldon for the murder of his brother Tom (George Webb). Perry tries to force him to confess and gets so angry he threatens to shoot him. Weldon's servant Sen Yat (Mr. Kuwa) leaps to his aid, stabs Perry and confesses that he killed Tom when he caught him stealing from his brother. George H. Melford directed and Margaret Turnbull wrote the screenplay.

The York Mystery

1924 British film (Stoll/2 reels), an episode in the *Old Man in the Corner* series based on a story by Baroness Orczy. An armchair detective known as the Old Man in the Corner solves crimes while sitting in a tea shop and tells the solutions to a young woman journalist. In this episode he solves a mystery involving the death of a bookmaker. Rolf Leslie played the Old Man and Renée Wakefield was journalist Mary Hatley with supporting cast of Dallas Cairns, Jak Denton and Minna Grey. D. P. Cooper was the cinematographer and Hugh Croise wrote the adaptation and directed. Print survives at BFI archive.

You'd Be Surprised

1926 American film (Paramount/6 reels) based on a story by Jules Furthman who wrote the screenplay. A district attorney (Edward

Martindel) is murdered at his houseparty after the lights are shut off and diamond is stolen and. The coroner (Raymond Griffith) finds the DA's ward Ruth (Dorothy Sebastian) hidden in a large clock with the jewel but she still claims she's innocent. The coroner is attacked by the DA's valet when the lights go out again but then the valet is murdered. The coroner finally discovers the real killer — by accident. Arthur Rosson directed.

Za La Mort

Za la Mort is an Italian Apache-style criminal who turns into a crime fighter. He was created by writer-director Emilio Ghione who played the role in a series of Italian films in the 1910s and 1920s. Za was first seen in *Nelly la gigolette* in 1915 in company with Francesca Bertini but came into his own in the serial *Za la Mort* (1915/four episodes). It revealed that he was formerly the Viscount De Ghion who faked his own death after being crookedly disinherited and then went underground to take his revenge. He is reformed by Za la Vie (played by Kally Sambucini) and stays on the side of righteousness after that. Za's other films include the serials *Il triangola giallo* (1917/four episodes) and *I topi grigi* (1918/eight episodes) and the features *L'ultima impresa* (1917) *Il numero 121*(1918), *Dollari e Fraks* (1919), *S.E. la Morte* (1919). *Il Castello di bronzo* (1920), *Za la Mort contro Za la Mort* (1922), *Un frak e un apache* (1923) *and Ultimissime della notte* (1924). The early films were produced by Tiber Film of Rome, the later ones by Ghione himself.

Zigomar

Zigomar, a mysterious masked French master criminal created by Léon Sazie in 1909 for *Le Matin*, seems to have been the role model for *Fantômas*. He was featured in an early 1910s French film series directed by Victorin-Hippolyte Jasset with Nick Carter and Paulin Broquet as his detective opponents. The films, all three reels, were *Zigomar* (1910), *Zigomar, roi des voleurs* (1911), *Zigomar contre Nick Carter* (1912) which seems to be the only surviving film in the series, and *Zigomar peau d'anguille* (1913). Alexandre Arquillière played Zigomar, Charles Krauss was Nick Carter, André Liebel was Paulin Broquet and the supporting cast including Attilo Maffie as the Aviator and Josette Andriot as La Rosaria. These films apparently had a world wide audience as Japanese criminals began to emulate Zigomar soon after the series opened in Japan in 1911.

Zigomar contre Nick Carter

1912 French film (3 reels), the second episode in the *Zigomar* series directed by Victorin Hippolyte Jasset. In this episode master criminal Zigomar (Alexandre Arquillière) battles master detective Nick Carter (Charles Krauss) in a titanic matching of pulp heroes. A print of this film survives and a new score was composed for it by François Servenier in 2004.

Emilio Ghione created the popular criminal Za La Mort and played him in a series of Italian films of the 1910s and 1920s.

Zudora or The Twenty Million Dollar Mystery

1914 American serial (Thanhouser/twenty 2-reel chapters). This was the sequel *to The Million Dollar Mystery* with the ante upped by $19 million. Marguerite Snow attempts to unravel a series of mysteries, acquire a fortune and avoid getting killed by some evil villains. She gets help from James Cruze. The story was by Harold MacGrath and Daniel Carson Goodman with Lloyd Lonergan and F. W. Doughty as the scriptwriters and Howell Hansel as director. The chapters, which more less tell the story, are titled *The Mystic Message of the Spotted Collar, The Mystery of the Sleeping House, The Mystery of the Dutch Cheese Maker, The Secret of the Haunted Hills, The Case of the Perpetual Glare, The Mystery of the McWinter Family, The Mystery of the Lost Ships, The Foiled Elopement or The Mystery of The Chang Case, Kidnapped or The Mystery of the Missing Heiress, The Gentlemen Crooks and the Lady, A Message from the Heart, A Bag of Diamonds, The Secret of Dr. Munn's Sanatorium, The Missing Million, The Robbery of the Ruby Coronet, The Battle of the Bridge, The Island of Mystery, The Cipher Code, The Prisoner in the House* and *The Richest Woman of the World*.

Appendix

Authors Whose Stories Were Filmed in the Silent Era

Adams, Frank R.

American playwright and short story writer Frank R Adams (1883–1963) wrote all types of genre fiction, including detective and mystery stories (even a Craig Kennedy tale), but created no continuing characters His mystery/detective stories filmed in the silent era include *Unexpected Places* (1918), *The Brass Bullet* (1918), *The Pointing Finger* (1919), *There Are No Villains* (1921), *Proxies* (1921) and *The Last Hour* (1923) Other notable films based on his stories include *Enchantment* (1921) with Marion Davies, *Stage Struck* (1925) with Gloria Swanson and *Almost a Lady* (1926) with Marie Prevost.

Aldrich, Thomas Bailey

American author Thomas Bailey Aldrich (1836–1906) wrote several murder mystery stories, including a notable tale about eccentric detective Paul Lynde (*Out of His Head*) and an under-rated novel (*The Stillwater Tragedy*). The only one of his stories filmed in the silent era concerns a murder but it is rarely classified as a crime story. *Judith of Bethulia* (1904) tells the story of the killing of Assyrian General Holofernes by Jewish vamp Judith. It was made into a classic film by D. W. Griffith in 1913. Aldrich borrowed the plot from *The Bible*.

Allain, Marcel *and* Souvestre, Pierre

French authors Marcel Allain (1885–1970) and Pierre Souvestre (1874–1914) were the creators of the super-villain *Fantômas* and his arch-enemy Detective Juve. The first adventures of this "emperor of crime" were published in 1911 and were translated into 44 languages. The character attracted the attention of French filmmaker Louis Feuillade who began to make serials about him with René Navarre as Fantômas and Bréon as Juve: they were titled *Fantômas* (1913), *Juve contre Fantômas* (1913), *Le Mort qui tue* (1913), *Fantômas contre Fantômas* (1914) and *Le Faux Magistrat* (1914). The films, close adaptations of the novels, survive and are on DVD while the books remain in print.

Allen, Grant

Canadian author Grant Allen (1848–1899) created the first criminal in mystery fiction who was the hero of his adventures. Colonel Clay is a rogue, a swindler and a delight as he outwits his rich victim in *An African Millionaire*, a series of stories published in *The Strand* in 1896–1897. Unfortunately he never attracted the attention of filmmakers. Allen also created two of the earliest female detectives, Miss Cayley of *Miss Cayley's Adventures* (1899) and *Hilda Wade* (1900), for *The Strand* but they didn't make it to the screen either. The silent movies based on Allen stories were *What's Bred ... Comes Out in the Flesh* and *Scallywag*.

Anderson, Frederick Irving

American author Frederick Irving Anderson (1877–1947), who published most of his stories in *The Saturday Evening Post*, was the creator of the ingenious master criminal Godahl the Infallible and the sophisticated jewel thief Sophie Lang. Godahl never made it to the screen (more's the pity) but Lang was featured in several 1930s movies. One of Anderson's lesser known detective tales, *The Golden Fleece*, was the basis of a 1918 film, and his remarkable *Book of Murder* remains in print.

Applin, Arthur

English writer Arthur Applin (1873–1949/pseudonym of Gustav Trugard) published over fifty mystery and romance novels between 1908 and 1939 but only one was filmed. *Wicked* (1920), the story of a blackmail scheme, was the basis of 1920 British film *All the Winners* starring Owen Nares.

Atwood, Bertram

British author Bertram Atwood (1880–1952) was the creator of Smiler Bunn, one of the most original of the gentleman thieves. He is quite different from Raffles being fat, middle-aged and somewhat comical and he steals mainly from other crooks. His story was told in five collections beginning with *The*

Amazing Mr. Bunn (1911) where he is picked up and trained by suffragettes. Atwood also created amateur detective Prosper Fair and female rogue Winnie O'Wynn. These three characters did not make it to the screen but two criminous stories by Atwood did: *After Dark* was included in the series *Thrilling Stories From The Strand Magazine* (1924) and *The Secret Kingdom* (1925) was based on his novel *Hidden Fires*.

Austin, F. Britten

The popular British author Frederick Britten Austin (1885–1943) had three of his crime stories made into films in England in the silent era. *The Drum* was featured in the 1924 series *Thrilling Stories From The Strand*, *The Last Witness* was made into a feature in 1925 and *A Woman Redeemed* was made into a feature in 1927.

Balzac, Honoré de

French novelist Honoré de Balzac (1799–1850) did not write detective fiction but his novels often featured detectives and criminals. *Le Père Goriot* introduces the master criminal Vautrin, the Napoleon of crime, loosely based on French criminal-turned-detective Vidocq, and he is one of the dominating characters in the Human Comedy series. Like his role model, Vautrin eventually turns detective and becomes head of the French Sûreté. *Le Père Goriot* was filmed four times in the silent era: by Armand Numès in France in 1910, by Travers Vale in America in 1915, by Jacques de Baroncelli in France in 1921 and by E. Mason Hoppe in America in 1926 with Vautrin transformed into a righter of wrongs.

Barr, Robert

British author Robert Barr (1850–1912) is best known for creating Eugène Valmont, the first French detective in English literature. His adventures were collected in *The Triumphs of Eugène Valmont* (1906) but did not attract the attention of filmmakers. Barr wrote many other criminous stories and two of them were the basis of silent films, *The Premature Compromise* (1914/Edison) and *An Invasion and an Attack* (1915/Edison).

Bentley, E. C.

British author Edmund Clerihew Bentley (1876–1956), who is as famous for creating the poetic format known as the clerihew as for writing detective novels, is sometimes called the father of the modern detective novel. His detective Philip Trent humanized detective fiction by coming up with the wrong solution in *Trent's Last Case* (1913) and falling in love with the chief suspect. *Trent's Last Case* was filmed twice in the silent era. Bentley featured Trent in two other books, *Trent's Own Case* (1936) and the story collection *Trent Intervenes* (1938). His only non-Trent mystery was *Elephant Work* (1950) about an amnesiac detective.

Bernède, Arthur

French author Arthur Bernède (1871–1937) created two of the most memorable characters of the French silent serials, the righteous avenger Judex (with Louis Feuillade) and the mysterious Belphégor, the Ghost of the Louvre. He wrote the novels featuring the characters and the screenplays for both serials. He also created a famous fictional detective, Chantecoq, known as the King of Detectives, who appeared in several books including *Belphégor*. His novelized version of the *Memoirs* of the first real detective was filmed as *Vidocq* with *Fantômas* star René Navarre in the leading role.

Biggers, Earl Derr

American author Earl Derr Biggers (1884–1933) was the creator of Charlie Chan, the most famous Chinese detective in fiction and the movies. Chan made his first appearance in print in 1925 in the novel *The House Without a Key* and his first appearance on screen in the 1926 Pathé serial based on it. Biggers' first best-selling mystery novel was *Seven Keys to Baldpate* (1913) which George M. Cohan turned into a Broadway play in 1913; it was filmed three times in the silent era. Twelve other Biggers stories were made into silent films including *The Blind Adventure* (1918), *Fifty Candles* (1921) and *Inside the Lines* (1918).

Blyth, Harry

Scottish journalist Harry Blyth (1852–1898), who created the famous British detective Sexton Blake in 1893, has been more or less forgotten but his Blake stories continue to be reprinted. The first, "The Missing Millionaire" published in *The Halfpenny Marvel* on December 20, 1893, is in various collections including David Stuart Davies' *Vintage Mystery and Detective Stories*. Although Blyth created Blake, he cannot be credited for the character's immense popularity as he died five years after writing the first story; more than 150 other writers have penned Blake stories and films since. The character didn't make Blyth rich either; he sold the rights to his publisher for a pittance. Sexton Blake films began to be made in England in 1909 and still continued. Blyth's other stories include "The Black Pirate," the probable inspiration for the 1926 Douglas Fairbanks film.

Boothby, Guy

Australian author Guy Boothby 1867–1905) wrote a large number of thrillers and mysteries but is best known as the creator of the evil genius Dr. Nikola. The villainous doctor was featured in five novels beginning with *A Bid for Fortune* in 1895. Nikola was quickly discovered by filmmakers in Denmark,

Harry Blyth created British detective Sexton Blake in 1893, and his stories were being turned into films by 1909.

Dr. Nikola began his evil career in a novel by Guy Boothby and was featured in films in Denmark and England.

where a serial about him was filmed in 1909, and in England, where he was featured in a 1917 film. Boothby's other great creation was the gentleman crook Simon Carne who was suavely stealing stuff for two years before Raffles got around to it but he never made it into the movies.

Boyle, Jack

American author Jack Boyle (1890–1928), the creator of the famous safecracker Boston Blackie, had a life as interesting as his literary crook. He became an opium addict while working as a newspaper reporter in San Francisco's Chinatown and ended up going to prison for forgery and armed robbery. He wrote his first Boston Blackie story while serving time in San Quentin and sold it to *The American Magazine* which published it in 1914. He attracted the attention of Hollywood in 1918 when his *Red Book Magazine* story "Boston Blackie's Little Pal" was filmed with Bert Lytell as Blackie. In 1919 he published his only book, the collection *Boston Blackie*, and in 1922 he worked on the screenplay of the Blackie film *The Face in the Fog*. He continued working in the cinema industry until his death and was involved with ten Blackie films and eight other pictures: *Boomerang Bill* (1922), *The Last Moment* (1923), *The Silent Accuser* (1924), *The Whipping Boss* (1924), *Soiled* (1924), *The Sporting Chance* (1925), *Satan Town* (1926) and *Burning Bridges* (1928). Boyle died in 1928 but his creation Boston Blackie lived on in later films and radio shows, most famously in a 1940s series starring Chester Morris.

Braddon, Mary Elizabeth

English author Mary Elizabeth Braddon (1835–1915) did not write detective fiction (her books were described as "sensation novels") but she did feature detectives in her novels and mystery critics Barzun and Taylor have pointed out that her novel *Lady Audley's Secret* (1862) has "more detection than is found in many a modern thriller." Most of her books have crime and mystery elements and they often feature amateur detectives like the barrister stepson in *Lady Audley's Secret*. Braddon also wrote series featuring detectives including the Detective Faunce novels (*Rough Justice* and *His Darling Sin*) and the Valentine Hawkehurst books (*Birds of Prey* and *Charlotte's Inheritance*). Braddon is a major novelist but she was ignored by the literary establishment until fairly recently. Many of her books are now coming back into print as she has been taken up feminist critics. *Lady Audley's Secret* was filmed five times in the silent era and the somewhat similar *Aurora Floyd* was filmed thrice. Daniel Frederick Whitcomb wrote the screenplay and Henry King directed.

Bridges, Victor

Victor Bridges (1878–1972), pseudonym of George DeFreyne, was a popular mystery/ genre novelist in the early years of the 20th century and several of his books were filmed. *Another Man's Shoes* was filmed by Essanay in 1916 as *The Phantom Buccaneer* and by Universal in 1922 as *Another Man's Shoes*. *The Man from Nowhere* was filmed by Universal in 1916. *Mr. Lyndon at Liberty* was filmed in England in 1915, *The Lady from Long Acre* was filmed by Fox in 1921 and 1925 and *Greensea Island* was filmed in England in 1923 as *Through Fire and Water*.

Campbell, Scott

American dime novelist and pulp writer Scott Campbell (pseudonym of Frederick W. Davis) wrote hundreds of detective and mystery stories in the early years of the twentieth century for pulps like *The Popular Magazine* and *Detective Story Magazine*. He created the private detective Felix Boyd in *The Popular Magazine* in 1904 and featured him in more than sixty stories. Boyd was a mixture of Nick Carter and Sherlock Holmes, a brilliant thinker and a mean street fighter. Five Felix Boyd cases taken from the 1906 collection *Below the Dead-Line* were filmed by Edison in 1914 and 1915.

Chester, George Randolph

American author George Randolph Chester (1869–1924) created one of the great confidence men of mystery fiction, James Rufus Wallingford. His adventures began in 1908 in *Get-Rich-Quick Wallingford* in which he arrives in a small town with no money and gets rich quick by inventing an imaginary tack company His swindles continued in four more short story collections. Wallingford's exploits inspired George M. Cohan to write a Broadway play in 1910 and the play became the basis of a 1915 film series. Chester wrote many other stories and novels that were filmed including *The Making of Bobby Burnit* (1914), *The Enemy* (1915), *Five Thousand an Hour* (1918), *My Man* (1924), *Quarantined Rivals* (1927) and *The Head of the Family* (1928). He was also a prolific screenwriter with credits on twenty-four silent movies including *The Lavender Bath Lady* (1922).

Christie, Agatha

British mystery writer Agatha Christie (1890–1976) began her hugely successful career in 1920 with the publication of *The Mysterious Affair at Styles* featuring Hercule Poirot and was soon one of the most popular authors in the world. Film producers were a bit slow in noticing this, however, as there were only two silent films based on her work — and one of them was in Germany. Christie's married detectives Tommy and Tuppence Beresford were the stars of the German film and the strange Harley Quinn was featured in the earliest British film based on her mystery fiction.

Cohen, Octavus Roy

American writer Octavus Roy Cohen (1891–1959) is best known for his "humorous" dialect stories about African-Americans, including a series about a private detective named Florian Sappey. While the stories were considered funny in their time, they now appear blatantly racist. None were filmed. Cohen also wrote mainstream mystery and detective fiction and stories in other genres. Sixteen were filmed in the silent era and four are criminous. Tod Browning's *The Eyes of Mystery* (1918) stars Bradley Barker as a detective sent to investigate a kidnapping. Thomas H. Ince's *The Kaiser's Shadow* (1918) features Dorothy Dalton in a story about the abduction of an inventor by German agents. William K. Howard's *Red Dice* (1926) features Rod La Roque getting money from a bootlegger by insuring his life in the bootlegger's favor. Scott Pembroke's *The Law and the Man* (1928) stars Tom Santschi as a corrupt political boss who plans to reform. Cohen's white detective Jim Hanvey was featured in a 1937 film.

Collins, Wilkie

English author Wilkie Collin (1824–1889) created two of the most popular and influential mystery novels of the nineteen century, *The Woman in White* (1860) and *The Moonstone* (1868). He is considered one of the originators of the detective novel as both books feature a memorable detective, an amateur (Walter Hartwright) in *The Woman in White* and a professional (Sergeant Cuff) in *The Moonstone*. The popularity of these novels is reflected in the proliferation of silent films based on them. The other silent films based on mystery novels by Collins are *The Dead Secret* (1913) and *Armadale* (1916). Three non-mystery works by Collins were filmed: *The New Magdalen* in 1910, 1912 and 1914; *Dream Woman* in 1914 and *She Loves and Lies* in 1920.

Conan Doyle, Arthur

Scottish doctor Arthur Conan Doyle (1859–1930) wrote a good deal of enjoyable fiction, like the great historical novel *The White Company*, but he is known primarily for his creation of the most famous detective in fiction. He grew tired of Sherlock Holmes after two dozen stories and tried to kill him off but the detective wouldn't stay dead so Conan Doyle had to start writing about him again. The first Sherlock Holmes film, made in 1903, was also the first film about a named detective. There are now more than

Sherlock Holmes, the most famous detective in fiction and film, is shown battling with arch-enemy Moriarty at Reichenbach Falls in Switzerland in this illustration from *The Strand*.

200 Holmes films and 75 of them are silent. See Holmes, Sherlock for titles and descriptions. Some of Conan Doyle's other stories were also filmed in the silent era, most notably *The Lost World* (1925).

Coryell, John Russell

American dime novelist John Russell Coryell (1848–1942) was the creator of Nick Carter, the most popular of all American pulp detectives and the star of many movies. Coryell, who lived an adventurous life in the far East before settling down to a writing career in New York, published the first Carter story in Street and Smith's *New York Weekly* in 1886. It was called *The Old Detective's Pupil; or, the Mysterious Crime of Madison Square* and was published anonymously like all the Nick Carter stories. Coryell wrote two more Nick Carter serials for the *Weekly* and then left to write Bertha M. Clay serials. Nick Carter, however, remained with Street and Smith where other authors took up his story. His popularity was such that by 1896 had his own magazine. See Carter, Nick for his films.

Davis, Frederick W.

American author Frederick W. Davis (1858–1933), who wrote mystery and detective stories using the pseudonym Scott Campbell, was an amazingly prolific writer. He churned out stories from 1893 into the 1930s for Street and Smith magazines, especially *Magnet* and *The Popular Magazine*. His most important creation was private detective Felix Boyd whose adventures began in *The Popular Magazine* in 1904 and were filmed by Edison in 1914.

Davis, Richard Harding

The intrepid Richard Harding Davis (1864–1916) was an adventure-seeking American journalist who covered several wars but still found time to write fiction, including mysteries and detective stories. One has become a much-anthologized classic, the surprise-laden novelette *In The Fog* (1901). More than forty of his stories were filmed in the silent era including *In The Fog* as *How Sir Andrew Lost His Vote* (1911), *The Amateur* as *The Amateur Detective* (1914), *The Lost House (1915), Vera, the Medium* (1917), *The Men of Zanzibar (1922), The Exiles* (1923) and *Let 'Er Go Gallegher (1928)*.

Dey, Frederic Van Rensselaer

American dime novelist Frederic Van Rensselaer Dey (1861–1922), a.k.a. Nick Carter, a.k.a. Varick Vanardy, a.k.a. Frederic Ormond, a.k.a. Marmaduke Dey, is one of the great overlooked detective writers. He is reputed to have written over one thousand Nick Carter novels and many other detective stories under other pseudonyms. Three silent films were based on his Varick Vanardy novels: *The Girl by the Roadside* (1918/ Bluebird) and *The Girl in the Rain* (1920/Universal) were based on his 1917 novel *The Girl by the Roadside,* and *Alias the Night Wind* (1923/Fox) was based on his 1913 novel *Alias the Night Wind*. A novel he wrote as Frederic Ormond, *The Three Keys* (1909). was filmed by Banner in 1925 as *Three Keys*. Dey was the author of the first novel every written about the movies, a 1910 Nick Carter adventure titled *Shown on the Screen or The Moving Picture Mystery*. He died a penniless suicide in 1922 when he could no longer sell his stories.

Dickens, Charles

Charles Dickens (1812–1870) did not write detective fiction but he created some notable detectives in his novels. Inspector Bucket, the first important detective in English literature, is introduced in the novel *Bleak House*. The plot is really too complex to put on film but attempts were made in the silent cinema era by concentrating on Bucket's investigation of a murder. Dickens' last work, *The Mystery of Edwin Drood*, which he died before completing, would probably have been one of the great mystery novels; many authors have tried to finish it sense but

Dostoevsky, Fyodor

Russian novelist Fyodor Dostoevsky (1821–1881) (the English tend to spell his name as Dostoyevsky) did not write detective stories but he did create one of the most memorable detectives in literary fiction. In his novel *Crime and Punishment* (1866), Inspector Petrovich relentlessly interrogates university student Raskolnikov whom he suspects of killing a pawnbroker and her sister. He not only gets a confession, he gets repentance. *Crime and Punishment* was filmed four times in the silent film era, in Russia in 1913 by Ivan Vronsky, in America in 1917 by Lawrence B. McGill, in Germany in 1923 by Robert Wiene and in India in 1924.

Edington, A. C., *and* C.

Mystery writers Arlo Channing Edington (1890–1953) and Carmen Ballen Edington 1894–1972) had two of their criminous books made into silent movies. *The Studio Murder Mystery* has all the clichés and characters one expects to find in a movie mystery: an arrogant star, a monocled German director, a Jewish studio head, a sweet ingénue and a detective with little knowledge of moviemaking. It was made into a silent film by Paramount in 1929. The other silent film based on a criminous Edington novel is *Bare Knuckles*, a 1921 Fox movie about an underworld tough guy who decides to go straight but then runs into problems.

England, George Allan

Nebraska-born writer George Allan England (1877–1936) published a large number of genre stories in pulp magazines in the early years of the 20th century. He was particularly popular for his science-fiction tales but he was also a prolific contributor to detective magazines. Two of his detective stories were filmed in the silent era, *The Alibi* (1916) and *The Brass Check* (1918).

Fredericks, Arnold *see* Kummer, Frederic Arnold

Froest, Frank

English mystery writer Frank Froest, best known for his "Crime Club" stories with George Dilnot, was a real detective and superintendent of the Criminal Investigation Department of New Scotland Yard for a time. Two of his novels were turned into films by Vitagraph in 1917, *The Grell Mystery* and *The Maelstrom*.

Futrelle, Jacques

American author Jacques Futrelle (1875–1912) went down with the Titanic (heroically) but his mystery detective fiction survived and it is still quite popular. His stories about Professor Augustus S.F.X. Van Dusen, the man known as The Thinking Machine, never go out of print and "The Problem of Cell 13" has become one of the classics of the locked room genre. Two of Futrelle's mystery novels were filmed in the silent era, *The Diamond Master* and *My Lady's Garter* and he wrote the story that was the basis of serial *The Mystery of the Double Cross*. His espionage novel *Elusive Isobel* was filmed in 1914 as *Adventures in Diplomacy*.

Gaboriau, Émile

French novelist Émile Gaboriau (1835–1973) has been described as the father of the detective novel. His fictional detective, *Monsieur Lecoq* is a precursor of Sherlock Holmes and Holmes seemed to be a bit jealous of him. Lecoq's introductory case *L'Affaire Lerouge* (1886) is considered the first genuine detective novel; it was filmed by Metro in 1917, one of seven silent movies based on Lecoq stories. Gaboriau wrote other kinds of novels as well and several were filmed in the silent era including *La Clique dorée* (as *The Evil Women Do*), *La Maison du passeur* and *Le*

Emile Gaboriau's Monsieur Lecoq, a precursor of Sherlock Holmes, was featured in seven silent films.

Capitaine noir. They are criminous and entertaining but they are not detective/ mystery novels.

Ghione, Emilio

Italian writer/director/actor Emilio Ghione (1879–1930) created the hugely popular *Za la Mort*, a kind of apache Arséne Lupin, and starred in a series of films about this Robin Hood of the slums in the 1910s and 1920s. He also wrote, directed and starred in detective films like *La banda delle cifre* (1915) in which he portrayed a detective who tracks down and captures a gang of thieves,

Gollomb, Joseph

American mystery writer Joseph Gollomb (1881–1950) wrote three novels featuring criminal psychologist Francis Galt, nicknamed Goldfish. Galt was featured in the 1919 Vitagraph film *A Girl at Bay* based on a short story Gollomb also wrote the screenplay for the 1916 Vitagraph film *The Man Hunt*.

Gould, Nat

English author Nat Gould (1857–1919) was the early twentieth century equivalent of Dick Francis, hugely popular for his horse racing mysteries. He is almost forgotten today but in his time there were better known writers. He began his career in Australia as a sportswriter specializing in horse racing and then returned to England to write fiction about the turf. Novels like *The Exploits of A Race-Course Detective* featuring detective Valentine Martyn sold in the millions He published 130 racing novels with sales estimated at more than 24 million. Seven of his criminous racetrack stories were turned into English films by Broadwest: *The Chance of a Lifetime* (1916), *A Gamble for Love* (1917*)*, *A Fortune at Stake* (1918), *A Turf Conspiracy* (1918), *A Great Coup* (1919), *A Dead Certainty* (1920) and *The Rank Outsider* (1920).

Gowing, Sidney

British author Sidney Gowing (1878-?) wrote mysteries and other genre fiction under his own name and the pseudonyms David Goodwin, John Goodwin and John Tregallis. Three of his novels as David Goodwin were filmed, two in the silent era. The 1921 novel *Paid in Full* (US title: *The Man With the Brooding Eyes*) was filmed in America in 1926 as *Brooding Eyes* and *The House of Marney* was filmed in England the same year

Green, Anna Katharine

American author Anna Katharine Green (1846–1835) is considered the godmother of the American detective story because of her success with *The Leavenworth Case* (1878), one of the earliest American detective novels. Ebenezer Gryce, the detective who

Anna Katharine Green's *The Leavenworth Case*, one of the earliest American detective novels, was filmed in 1923.

solved the case, went on to star in *A Strange Disappearance* (1880) and other detective stories. *A Strange Disappearance* was made into a film in 1915 followed by *The Leavenworth Case* in 1923 but neither made Ebenezer Gryce into a movie star as he was cut out of the plot of both films. Green wrote many other mysteries and several were the basis of silent films including *The Millionaire Baby* (1915), *Who Is Number One?* (1917), *Graft* (1915) and *His Wife's Husband* (1922).

Hanshew, Thomas W.

English author Thomas W. Hanshew (1857–1914) wrote many types of mysteries, including even Nick Carter stories, but is best known for creating Hamilton Cleek, the man of forty faces. Cleek has such a mobile face that he can change his appearance in an instant without makeup. Hanshew began Cleek's adventures with *The Man of Forty Faces* series in *People's Ideal Fiction Magazine* in 1910 and followed with the *Cleek of Scotland Yard* series in *Cassell's Saturday Journal* in 1912. *The Chronicles of Cleek* were filmed by Edison in 1913 with Ben Wilson as Cleek. Three other Hanshew stories were filmed by Edison in 1911: *Monsieur, A Case of High Treason* (based on "The Under Man") and *His Misjudgment* (based on "Purple and Fine Linen"). Some of Hanshew's stories were written in collaboration with his wife Mary and she continued writing stories about Cleek after her husband's death.

Henry, O.

O. Henry (1862–1910), pseudonym of William Henry Porter, is not usually thought of as a writer of detective tales but many of his 600 stories feature mysteries and detectives. The most famous is his 1909 story about a detective and a safecracker, "A Retrieved Reformation," which became the popular play *Alias Jimmy Valentine* filmed three times in the silent era. His satirical tale "The Detective Detector" is a send-up of the deductive methods of famous detectives. Over a hundred O. Henry stories were turned into silent films including criminous tales like *Trying to Get Arrested* (1909), *A Double Dyed Deceiver* (1920) and *Roads of Destiny* (1921).

Hoffman, E.T.A

German author/composer E. T. A Hoffman (1776–1822) is not usually thought of a writer of detective tales but he wrote one of the first and most intriguing. The 1819 novella *Das Fräulein von Scudéry* (*Mademoiselle De Scudery*) features a clever woman who acts as a detective to solve a murder mystery that baffles the police of 17th century Paris. A goldsmith obsessed with jewelry kills people who have commissioned works from him so he can reclaim them. She discovers he has a split personality. The novella was turned into the 1923 Japanese film *Blood and Soul* (*Chi to rei*) by filmmaker Kenji Mizoguchi and into the 1926 German opera *Cardillac* by composer Paul Hindemith.

Hornung, E. W.

British author Ernest William Hornung (1866–1921) is best known as the creator of A J. *Raffles*, gentleman cracksman and outstanding cricket player. Raffles, who became the model for a gentleman thief, made his first appearance in stories in *Cassell's* magazine in 1898 that were published as *The Amateur Cracksman* in 1899. He had a great appeal to early filmmakers and was on screen by 1905. Hornung, who was married to Arthur Conan Doyle's sister Constance, wrote many other mystery/detective novels that were filmed including a series about an Australian bushranger (Stingaree) and a feature film about a murder (*Out of the Shadow*). His pirate novel *Dead Men Tell No Tales* was filmed by Vitagraph in 1920 but his admired *Crime Doctor* series never made it to the screen.

Hugo, Victor

French novelist Victor Hugo (1802–1885) did not write detective novels but he did create the most hated detective in all fiction. Inspector Javert, whom we meet in Hugo's novel *Les Misérables* (1862), spends much of his time mercilessly tracking down Jean Valjean, a reformed convict who spent 14 years in prison for stealing a loaf of bread. The novel was filmed eight times in the silent era.

Hume, Fergus

English author Fergus Hume (1859–1932) wrote the top selling detective novel of the nineteenth century, *The Mystery of a Hansom Cab* (1886). It was his first book and by far his most successful. Set in Melbourne, Australia, it revolves around the murder, by chloroform, of a man in an hansom cab. Hume wrote another hundred mysteries but never again had such success. It didn't make him rich either; he sold all rights to a group of investors. *The Mystery of a Hansom Cab* was filmed three times in the silent era.

The Mystery of the Hansom Cab was the top-selling detective novel of the nineteenth century and was filmed three times in the silent era.

Jackson, Frederick

American author Frederick Jackson (1886–1953), who was also a film and stage producer, wrote all types of fiction, including mystery and detective stories, screenplays and plays. Most of his stories appeared in pulp magazines like *Detective Story Weekly* and *Argosy* but they provided the basis for more than thirty silent films. They include *A Detective's Strategy* (1912) based on his story *Thistledown*, the Pearl White serial *The Fatal Ring* (1917), *Ladies Beware* based on his story "Jack of Diamonds" and *The Jade Box* (1930).

Jacques, Norbert

German author Norbert Jacques (1880–1954) is mostly remembered for his three novels about the master criminal Dr. Mabuse and the German films based on them directed by Fritz Lang. The 1920 novel *Dr. Mabuse, der Spieler* was the basis of Lang's silent film masterpiece *Dr. Mabuse the Gambler* (1922) and was published in English in 1923 as *Dr. Mabuse, Master of Mystery*. Lang made two Mabuse films in the sound era and films by other directors featuring Mabuse continued to be made in Germany into the 1990s. Two other silent films were based on novels by Jacques, *Mensch gegen Mensch* (1924) and *Das Frauenhaus von Rio* (1927), both directed by Hans Steinhoff.

Kummer, Frederic Arnold

Frederic Arnold Kummer (1873–1943), who also wrote as Arnold Fredericks, was a popular author with filmmakers in the silent era when seventeen of his stories were filmed. He also wrote for the stage, including librettos for musicals by Victor Herbert and Sigmund Romberg. His comic detective *Octavius, Amateur Detective* sparked a 1913 Edison series and his "Honeymoon Detectives" Richard and Grace Duvall were featured in two 1915 movies, *One Million Dollars* and *The Ivory Snuff Box*. Two other Kummer mysteries were filmed, *The Yellow Pawn* (1916) and *The Green God* (1918). Despite his popularity, Kummer is virtually forgotten today and there are no entries on him in the guides to mystery writers.

Landon, Herman

American mystery writer Herman Landon (1892–1960) wrote dozens of stories and serials in the 1920s for *Detective Story Magazine*, many of them featuring Martin Dale, The Picaroon, and Cuthbert Vanardy, The Grey Phantom. Landon also published mystery novels under the pseudonym of Harry Coverdale. The 1920 film *The Way Women Love* was based on his story "Behind the Green Portieres" first published in *Detective Story Magazine*.

Leblanc, Maurice

French author Maurice Leblanc (1864–1941) was the creator of Arsène Lupin, the gentleman thief who became the rage of the world after his appearance in the French magazine *Je Sais Tout* in 1905 and the publication of his collected adventures in *Arsène Lupin, Gentleman-Cambrioleur* (1907). He was soon being featured in silent movies in France Germany, America, England, Hungary and Japan. Leblanc wrote other notable books, including the science-fiction classic *The Three Eyes*, but his fame rests on Lupin whose adventures remain in print and are still as stylish as anything in detective fiction.

Le Queux, William

English author William Le Queux (1864–1927), one of the great pioneers of espionage fiction, also wrote detective and mystery tales. His more than one hundred books include several about detectives and criminals including *The Mystery of a Motor-Car, Mysteries of a Great City* and *The Crimes Club*. His 1914 detective novel *The Sons of Satan* was the basis of a 1916 British film. Also filmed were *The White Lie* (1914/Gaumont) and *No Greater Love* (1915/Selig).

Leroux, Gaston

French author Gaston Leroux (1869–1927) was the creator of three icons of crime fiction, detective Joseph Rouletabille (eight novels), heroic criminal Chéri-Bibi (three novels) and the operatic villain known as the *Phantom of the Opera*. Rouletabille made his debut in 1907 in one of the most famous locked room mysteries, *Le Mystère de la chambre jaune* (The Mystery of the Yellow Room) and was

The Mystery of the Yellow Room, of the most famous locked room mysteries, was on screen by 1913.

on screen by 1913. Chéri-Bibi made his debut in the novel *Chéri-Bibi* serialized in *Le Matin* in 1913 and filmed the same year. The Phantom made his debut in 1910 in the novel *Fantôme de l'opéra* (The Phantom of the Opera) but did not become iconic until 1925 when Lon Chaney impersonated him on screen. Leroux's lesser known crime novel *Balaoo* (1912) was filmed twice in the silent era.

Lowndes, Marie Belloc

English author Marie Belloc Lowndes (1869–1947) is best known for her novel *The Lodger* (1913), a variation on the Jack the Ripper case, which Alfred Hitchcock's used as the basis of one of his best films. She was a prolific writer of mystery and detective fiction having publishing her first crime novel, *When No Man Pursueth*, in 1910 and even creating a series around an elderly French detective named Hercules Popeau before Agatha Christie created Hercules Poirot. Two other Lowndes stories were turned into silent films, the murder mystery *The House of Peril* (1922), based on her novel *The Chink in the Armour*, and the romantic comedy *Shameful Behavior?* (1926). Lowndes also wrote a popular non-fiction book about a famous murder, *Lizzie Borden: A Study in Conjecture*.

MacGrath, Harold

Harold MacGrath (1871–1932) was one of the most popular genre writers of the early twentieth century and many of his stories were filmed. His greatest contribution to popular culture was the creation of the mystery/suspense serial through Selig's *The Adventures of Kathlyn* (1913). Another novel was the basis of the Thanhouser serial *The Million Dollar Mystery* (1914) with Florence La Badie. More than twenty silent films were based on his stories including mysteries like *The Voice in the Fog* (1915), *Pidgin Island* (1916) and *Not Guilty* (1921). Among the other films based on MacGrath stories and novels, some criminous, are *The Man on the Box* (1914 and 1925), *The Carpet from Bagdad* (1915), *The Goose Girl* (1915), *Half a Rogue* (1916), *A Splendid Hazard* (1920), *The Yellow Typhoon* (1920), *The Drums of Jeopardy* (1923) and *Danger Street* (1928).

MacHarg, William

American mystery writer William MacHarg (1872–1951) had two of his novels turned into films in the silent era, *Blind Man's Eyes* (1919) and *The Price of a Party* (1924). There were also films made of his novels *Wine* (1914) and *Roulette* (1924) which are criminous but not mysteries.

Martyn, Wyndham

English mystery writer Wyndam Martyn (1875-?) is best known for his novels featuring the Raffles-like thief Anthony Trent who only steals really big jewels. Trent was featured in 25 novels starting in 1918 with *Anthony Trent, Master Criminal* and appeared in two films in the silent era. The Trent films are the 1921 Vitagraph picture *The Silver Car* and the 1921 Berwilla picture *The Star Reporter*. Other novels by Martyn that were filmed include *Number 99* in 1920 and *All the World to Nothing* in 1916.

Mason, A. E. W.

British author Alfred Edward Woodley Mason (1865–1948) wrote popular mystery novels, most notably *Murder at the Villa Rose* featuring Inspector Hanaud, but he also penned memorable adventure stories like *The Four Feathers*. Three other works were filmed in the silent era: a murder mystery play *The Witness for the Defense* (filmed by Paramount in 1919), a gambling novel titled *Running Water* (filmed by Stoll in England in 1922) and a French Foreign Legion novel titled *The Winding Stair* (filmed by Fox in America in 1926).

A. E. W. Mason's mystery novel *Murder at the Villa Rose* was filmed in England in 1920.

McIntyre, John Thomas

John Thomas McIntyre (1871–1951) created Ashton-Kirk, a Philadelphia detective in who specialized in mysteries involving old documents. His adventures were told in *Ashton-Kirk, Investigator* (1910), *Ashton-Kirk: Special Detective* (1912), *Ashton-Kirk: Secret Agent* (1912) and *Ashton-Kirk: Criminologist* (1918). Stories from these books were the basis of feature films produced by Gold Rooster-Pathé in 1915 starring Arnold Daly. McIntyre also wrote a series of 1940 detective novels featuring Jerry Mooney

Moffett, Cleveland

American author and playwright Cleveland Moffett (1863–1926) is best known as a mystery writer for his riddle story "The Mysterious Card" (1896), his anthology *True Detective Stories from the Archives of the Pinkertons* (1897) and his novels set in Paris featuring detective Paul Coquenil. The Coquenil novel *Through the Wall* (1909), praised by Ellery Queen as "a neglected high spot" and lauded by Peter Wimsey in *The Unpleasantness at the Bellona Club*, was filmed by Vitagraph in 1916.

Moroso, John A.

American author John Antonio Moroso (1874–1957) wrote a number of tales featuring the vindictive detective James Tierney including the novel *The People Against Nancy Preston* (1921) and the story collection *The Listening Man* (1924). His novels and stories were popular with filmmakers and eight silent films were based on them. *The People Against Nancy Preston* was filmed in 1920 and 1925, *The Quarry* was filmed in 1915 and 1921, *Vengeance Is Mine* was filmed in 1917, "In the Spring" was filmed in 1918 as *The Hand at the Window* and *The Shoes That Danced* was filmed in 1918. His influential non-mystery novel *The Stumbling Herd* (it portrays New York ghetto life) was filmed in 1926 as *Rose of the Tenements*.

Oppenheim, E. Phillips

English author E. Phillips Oppenheim (1866–1946), once promoted as the "Prince of Storytellers," is best known for spy and espionage novels like *The Great Impersonation* but he also wrote detective/mystery novels and many were filmed. His forte is plot, not character, but his books are entertaining and he was extremely popular with movie companies during the silent era. The first film based on an Oppenheim mystery was "The Tragedy of Charlecot Mansions" filmed in 1914 as *The Floor Above*. Oppenheim's scientific detective Herbert Quest was the protagonist of the 1915 Universal serial *The Black Box*. His *The Game of Liberty* was filmed in England in 1916. By 1919 Oppenheim's stories were attracting the interest of major actors: Marion Davies starred in *The Cinema Murder,* Sessue Hayakawa starred in *The Illustrious Prince*, John Barrymore starred in *The Test of Honor* based on *The Malefactor* and Pauline Frederick starred in *The World's Great Snare*. In 1920 Alma Taylor starred in *Anna the Adventuress*. In 1921 Dorothy Dalton starred in *Behind Masks* based on *Jeanne of the Marshes* and Lewis S. Stone starred in *Pilgrims of the Night* based on *Passers-By*. There were also films of *The Amazing Partnership, The Conspirators, Dangerous Lies, Expiation, The Golden Web, The Mystery of Mr. Bernard Brown* and *The Silent Master.*

Orczy, Emmuska

Baroness Emmuska Orczy (1865–1947) was born in Hungary but she wrote in English and created some of the most memorable characters in fiction. The most famous is the French Revolution hero known as the Scarlet Pimpernel but she also created notable sleuths. They include the armchair detective known as the Old Man in the Corner, the female police detective known as Lady Molly of Scotland Yard and the investigative lawyer Patrick Mulligan known as Skin o' My Teeth. The Old Man made it to the screen in the silent film era in a 1924 British series titled *The Old Man in the Corner.*

Baroness Orczy's *The Old Man in the Corner* was featured in a British film series in 1924.

Osborne, William Hamilton

American mystery writer William Hamilton Osborne (1873–1942) obviously appealed to silent filmmakers as twelve of his stories were made into movies. They include *The Boomerang* (1913 and 1919), *The Running Fight* (1915), *The Catspaw* (1916), *The Half Million Bribe* (1916) based on the novel *The Red Mouse*, *Neal of the Navy* (1915) and *Hearts or Diamonds?* (1918) based on the short story "Adrienne Gascoyne." Non-mystery films based on stories by Osborne include *The Scapegoat* (1913), *A Pitfall of the Installment Plan* (1913) *The Alarm of Angelon* (1915), *The Battle of Truth* (1916) and *Love and the Law* (1919).

Ostrander, Isabel

American author Isabel Ostrander (1883–1924), who co-authored a novel with the famous detective William J. Burns, also wrote as David Fox, Douglas Grant and Robert Orr Chipperfield. She published more than twenty mystery novels under various names between 1915 and 1928 and two were filmed in 1919, *Suspense* and *Island of Intrigue*.

Packard, Frank L.

Canadian writer Frank L. Packard, (1877–1942) created the super thief and sometime crime fighter Jimmie Dale known as the Gray Seal. He is also able to disguise himself as underworld denizen Larry the Bat and dope fiend Smarlinghue. Dale's adventures first appeared in *People's Magazine* in 1914 and were later published as novels. They were seen on screen in the 1917 sixteen-episode serial *Jimmy Dale, Alias the Grey Seal* with Elmo Lincoln playing the Grey Seal as Jimmy rather than Jimmie. Packard had his greatest screen success with his confidence crooks novel *The Miracle Man* which was made into a popular 1919 movie that made stars of Lon Chaney and Betty Compson. Other films based on Packard's criminous stories include *From Now On* (1920), *The White Moll* (1920), *The Sin That Was His* (1920) and *Pawned* (1922).

Pidgin, Charles Felton

American author Charles Felton Pidgin (1844–1923) wrote *Quincy Adams Sawyer;, or, Mason's Corner Folks* (1900), *Quincy Adams Sawyer, Detective* (1912) and other homespun tales about Mason Corner folks in rural Massachusetts. Most of them have elements of detection. Sawyer was featured in two silent films, both based on a play about the character written by Justin Adams titled *Quincy Adams Sawyer*.

Poe, Edgar Allan

Edgar Allan Poe (1809–1849) created C. Austin Dupin, the first notable detective in fiction and the role model for most later detectives. Dupin was featured in three stories, "The Murders in the Rue Morgue" (1841), "The Mystery of Marie Roget" (1842) and "The Purloined Letter" (1944). Only one Dupin adventure was filmed in the silent era, *The Murders in the Rue Morgue,* but Poe's other works inspired four films. D.W. Griffith's *The Avenging Conscience; Thou Shalt Not Kill* (1914), which features a detective, is based on the Poe story "The Tell-Tale Heart." D. W. Griffith's *Edgar Allan Poe* (1909) portrays Poe's wife on her deathbed while his poem "The Raven" sells for virtually nothing. Charles J. Brabin's feature *The Raven* (1915), based on Poe's poem "The Raven" and George Hazelton's play *The Raven: The Love Story of Edgar Allan Poe*, stars Henry B. Walthall as Poe. William J. Scully's feature *Annabel Lee* (1921) was inspired by the poem "Annabel Lee."

Ponson Du Terrail, Pierre Alexis

Pierre Alexis Ponson Du Terrail (1829–1871) was one of the most popular French pulp writers of the nineteenth century, churning out *roman feuilleton* for the daily newspapers. His most popular creation was Rocambole, the protagonist of a series of novels written from 1857 to 1870 beginning with *L'Héritage Mysterieux* (The Mysterious Inheritance). Like Raffles and Arsène Lupin, he begins as a villainous anti-hero and ends up as a good guy, the first modern superhero. Ponson Du Terrail died during the German invasion of France in 1871 but other writers took on the task of creating further adventures for Rocambole. Two films were made about Rocambole in the silent era and many more after the coming of sound.

Prichard, Hesketh

British author/explorer Hesketh Prichard (1876–1922), whose own life was as thrilling as anything in fiction, created a notable detective and a famous rogue. The detective, the protagonist of *November Joe, the Detective of the Woods* (1913), is a backwoods Sherlock Holmes who can read nature like Holmes can read clues. The rogue was Don Q, a hard-boiled Spanish Robin Hood he devised in collaboration with his mother Kate Prichard (1851–1935). Don Q's adventures began in *Badminton Magazine* in 1898 and were collected in several books. Don Q was impersonated on film by Douglas Fairbanks in *Don Q, Son of Zorro* (1925) but November Joe never made it to the screen. Aside from writing fiction, Prichard was an explorer, hunter, cricketer and World War I hero; his book *Sniping in France 1914–18: With Notes on the Scientific Training of Scouts, Observers, and Snipers* is a standard work. He also wrote books about his travels through Patagonia and Labrador. His full name was Hesketh Vernon Hesketh-Prichard.

Reeve, Arthur B.

American mystery writer Arthur B. Reeve (1880–1936) was the creator of the once famous "scientific detective" Craig Kennedy who employed the new inventions of his time including lie detectors, x-rays and sound analyzers. Hugely popular in the silent cinema era but little read today, Kennedy was featured in five serials beginning with the 1914 Pearl White cliffhanger *The Exploits of Elaine*. Reeve also wrote films starring master magician Harry Houdini (*The Master Mystery, The Grim Game, Terror Island*) and other chapter plays (*The Hidden Hand, The House of Hate, The Tiger's Trail, The Mystery Mind,* and *The Mysterious Airman*). The American serial would not have been what it was without him.

Rinehart, Mary Roberts

Mystery writer Mary Roberts Rinehart (1876–1958) is credited with having founded the had-I-but-known type of story in which the heroine unfailingly walks into danger despite being warned. Her creations include an inventive spinster known as Tish, who has entertaining adventures of all kinds, and Nurse Adams, known as Miss Pinkerton because of her tendency to get involved with crimes. She is probably best known today for her novel *The Circular Staircase* and her play *The Bat*, both filmed. More than thirty other Rinehart's stories were filmed in the silent era including two Tish stories and several with espionage plots. Those with a mystery element included *Acquitted* and *The Breaking Point*.

Roche, Arthur Somers

American mystery writer Arthur Somers Roche (1883–1935) was so popular with filmmakers in the silent era that fifteen movies were based on his tales. His 1916 novel *Loot* was filmed twice by Universal, first as the serial *The Gray Ghost* in 1917 and then as the feature film *Loot* in 1919. The other silent films based on his novels that can be considered mysteries are *Find the Woman* (1922), *Living Lies* (1922), *The Pleasure Buyers* (1925), *The Mystery Club* (1926), *The Girl from Chicago* (1927), *Finger Prints* (1927), *Come to My House* (1927) and *Wolf's Clothing* (1927).

Rohmer, Sax

Sax Rohmer, the pseudonym of British author Arthur Henry Sarsfield Ward (1883–1959), was the creator of. the most famous Oriental villain in fiction, Dr. Fu Manchu. He also created the dapper French detective Gaston Max of the Paris Police, the Dream Detective Moris Klaw and Fu Manchu's female counterpart Sumuru. The evil doctor made his first appearance in print in 1912 in *The Storyteller* magazine and in book form in 1913 in *The Mystery of Dr. Fu Manchu*. He was featured in two British film series and an American feature in the silent era and dozens more after the coming of sound. Gaston Max, who made his first appearance in print in

Sax Rohmer's famous villain Dr. Fu Manchu was featured in two British film series and an American feature in the silent era.

1915 in *The Yellow Claw*, was brought to the screen in 1920 in the film version of the novel. Sumuru had to wait for the coming of sound to get her stories onto the screen but the strange tales about the Dream Detective have not yet been filmed.

Rowland, Henry C.

American mystery writer Henry C Rowland (1874–1933) had eleven of his tales filmed in the silent era. Four were mysteries: *The Closing Net* (1915), *The Sultana* (1916), *Duds* (1920) and *The Peddler of Lies* (1920). The other films based on his stories were *The Return of Gentleman Joe* (1915), *Business Rivals* (1915), *Jabez's Conquest* (1915), *Bragga's Double* (1915), *Filling His Own Shoes* (1917), *Bonnie, Bonnie Lassie* (1919) and *Conquering the Woman* (1922).

Scott, Mansfield

American mystery writer Mansfield Scott created a Boston police detective named Inspector Malcome Steele for his 1919 novel *Behind Red Curtains* and featured him in two further novels, *The Black Circle*

(1928) and *The Spider's Web* (1929). *Behind Red Curtains* was filmed in 1920 as *One Hour Before Dawn* with Wilton Taylor as Steele. Scott's only other series detective was Kendall McArthur who was featured in three stories collected in *The Sportsman-Detective* (1930).

Sims, George R.

English author George R. Sims (1847–1922) was the creator of Dorcas Dene, one of the first and most interesting female detectives. She was an actress who became a detective to earn money after her husband was blinded. Her adventures, related in *Dorcas Dene, Detective* (1897) and its sequel, were featured in the 1919 British film series *The Adventures of Dorcas Dene*. Dene was also a noted poet and playwright and his 1902 book *Biographs of Babylon* was one of the first to used the motion pictures as subject matter.

Spearman, Frank H.

Frank H. Spearman (1859–1950) created the railroad detective Whispering Smith for his 1906 novel *Whispering Smith* basing him on a railroad detective he met in Cheyenne, Wyoming. The character was so popular that five silent films were based around him and railroad detective stories eventually became a genre. Spearman was so knowledgeable about railroads that he published a study called *The Strategy of Great Railroads* (1904). He had had earlier success with railroad fiction as well, notably the collection titled *The Nerve of Foley, and other Railroad Stories*. The title story of this collection was the basis of the 1926 film *The Runaway Express*. When Helen Holmes, the star of the railroad series *The Hazards of Helen*, left Kalem and needed a screenwriter for her Mutual railroad film *The Girl and the Game*, she hired Spearman. The following year she and her director husband J. P. McGowan turned Whispering Smith into a film with McGowan portraying Smith. There was only one Whispering Smith novel but Spearman wrote a sequel in the form of a screenplay for the 1927 Universal serial *Whispering Smith Rides*.

Sprigg, Stanhope

Stanhope Sprigg, a British newspaper editor and correspondent, created the detective Paul Sleuth whose adventures were filmed in 1912. He was also the creator of Dirk, the Dog Detective whose stories were told in *Harmsworth's Wonder Magazine* in1895. Dirk belonged to Paul Sleuth who taught him all he knew all about detection.

Stevenson, Robert Louis

Scottish author Robert Louis Stevenson (1850–1894) is one of fiction's great tale spinners with classic yarns like *Treasure Island* and *Kidnapped* but he also wrote a number of mystery-crime stories. The most famous is *The Strange Tale of Dr Jekyll and Mr. Hyde* (1886) which gave life to one of the most terrifying villains in literature; seven films about *Dr Jekyll and Mr. Hyde* were made in the silent era. Less well-known are the stories *The Suicide Club* and "The Pavilion on the Links" filmed as *The White Circle*. The collections *New Arabian Nights* (1882) and *More New Arabian Nights* (1885) contains other famous mystery stories like "The Dynamiter." *The Wrong Box* (1889), in which a lawyer detective tries to track down a corpse that keeps moving about, was not filmed until 1966.

Train, Arthur Cheyney

American mystery writer Arthur Cheyney Train (1875–1945), who began publishing stories in magazines in 1904, is best known for his creation of the Yankee lawyer Ephraim Tutt. Train was himself a lawyer and Tutt is one of the kindest lawyers in mystery fiction, usually portrayed defending a helpless victim. Tutt didn't make it to the screen but five other tales by Train were the basis of silent films: *Mortmain* (1915), *The Man Hunt* (1916), *Rose of the South* (1916), *His Children's Children* (1923), and *The Blind Goddess* (1926).

Twain, Mark

Mark Twain (1835–1910) is not usually thought of a detective story writer but he was and featured deduction and detective scenes in many of his books. Some are pure detective stories like *Tom Sawyer, Detective* and the parodies "The Stolen White Elephant" and "A Double-Barreled Detective Story." One of his most impressive amateur "detectives" is Judith Loftan, the woman who deduces that the disguised Huck Finn is not a girl and tells him how she deduced it. Twain was one of the first writers to feature fingerprint identification in his fiction and fingerprints are central to the story "A Thumb-Print and What Came of It" in *Life on the Mississippi* and the novel *The Tragedy of Pudd'nhead Wilson*. He was working on a novel titled *Jim Wheeler, Detective* when he died.

Vance, Louis Joseph

American mystery writer Louis Joseph Vance (1879–1933) was the creator of *The Lone Wolf*, a sophisticated thief named Michael Lanyard who eventually turned detective and good guy. He was featured in six silent films and a dozen more in the sound era. Vance became popular in the late 1900s when three of his "B" mystery novels became bestsellers: *The Brass Bowl* (1907), *The Black Bag* (1908) and *The Bronze Bell* (1909). All three were made into silent films and three others became the basis of thrill-a-minute serials, *The Trey o'Hearts*, *Terrance O'Rourke Gentleman Adventurer* and *Patria*. Other fast-paced Vance tales with criminous elements that were filmed include *The Bandbox, The Destroying*

Louis Joseph Vance's sophisticated thief The Lone Wolf was featured in six silent films.

Angel, The Outsider, Cynthia-of-the-Minute and *Lost at Sea*. Vance's influence on early mystery cinema deserves study.

Wallace, Edgar

Prolific English author Edgar Wallace (1875–1932) was the fastest mystery writer of all time (he once wrote a novel in a weekend). He was hugely popular in the 1920s and though his popularity has diminished, most of his books remain in print. His most famous creation was the vigilante group The Four Just Men featured in his first novel. Twenty-seven of his novels and stories were made into films in the silent era and they all have criminous and mystery elements. *Angel Esquire* (1919), *The Brotherhood* (1926), *Chick* (1928), *The Clue of the New Pin* (1929), *The Crimson Circle* (1922), *A Dear Liar* (1925), *The Diamond Man* (1924), *Down Under Donovan* (1922), *Fighting Snub Reilly* in the series *Thrilling Stories From The Strand* (1924), *The Flying Fifty-Five* (1924), *The Flying Squad* (1929), *The Forger* (1928), *The Green Archer* (1925), *The*

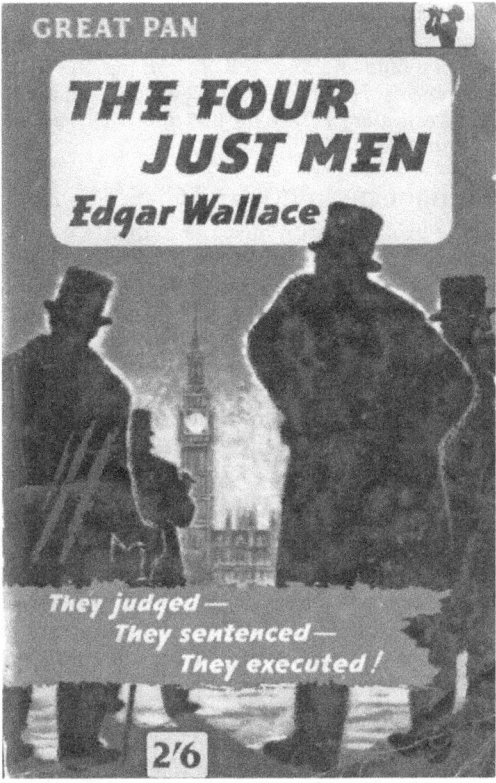

Edgar Wallace's first and most popular novel *The Four Just Men* was filmed in England in 1924.

Green Terror (1919), *The Man Who Bought London* (1916), *The Man Who Changed His Name* (1928), *The Mark of the Frog* (1928 serial), *Melody of Death* (1922), *Nurse and Martyr* (1915), *Pallard the Punter* (1919), *The Red Aces* (1929: see J. G. Reeder), *The Ringer* (1928), *The River of Stars* (1921), *The Terrible People* (1928), *The Terror* (1928), *The Valley of Ghosts* (1928) and *Wanted at Headquarters* (1920).

Weir, Hugh C.

American mystery writer/screenwriter Hugh C. Weir (1885–1934) created Madelyn Mack, one of the first notable woman detectives in crime fiction. Two of her adventures were filmed by Kalem with Alice Joyce as Madelyn Mack, *The Riddle of the Tin Soldier* (1913) and *The Riddle of the Green Umbrella* (1914). Weir's stories were published in 1914 as *Miss Madelyn Mack, Detective* in a book that featured photos of Joyce as Mack in the Kalem films. Two other stories were the basis of films, *The Adventure of the Yellow Curl Papers* (1915) and *Under Suspicion* (1918) based on his story "The Woolworth Diamonds." Weir was also a prolific screenwriter and wrote stories and scripts for at least a dozen movies including the 1915 films *Graft, The Circus Girl's Romance, Dr. Mason's Temptation, Extravagance, A Substitute Widow, The Test of a Man* and *The Wolf of Debt*; the 1916 films *Dolly's Scoop, Hypocrisy, The Lawyer's Secret* and *Why Mrs. Kentworth Lied*; and the 1919 film *What Shall We Do with Him?*

Williamson, A. M. *and* C. N.

The prolific British husband-and-wife writing team Alice Muriel Williamson (1869–1933) and Charles Norris Williams (1859–1920) wrote dozens of mysteries and other types of popular fiction and their stories about motoring adventurer Christopher Race were featured in most issues of *The Strand* in 1906/1907. Their work has mostly been ignored by the mystery establishment and Alice doesn't even get mentioned in the standard reference works on women mystery writers. All the same they were very popular in their heyday and more than a dozen films were based on their tales, most with elements of mystery and crime. Their stories about the aristocratic detective writer Lord John, who has to turn detective himself, were collected as *Lord John in New York* (1918) and filmed by Universal in 1915 as the serial *Lord John's Journal*. Their novel *A Woman in Grey* was filmed as a serial in 1920, *The Second Latchkey* was filmed in 1921 as *My Lady's Latchkey* and *The Lion's Mouse* was filmed in England in 1922. Alice's *The Woman Who Dared* was filmed in 1916, her *The Life Mask* was filmed in 1918 and one of her stories was included in the Universal serial *Graft* (1915). The other films based on the Williamson novels and stories are not mysteries but often have a criminous element. They include *The Lightning Conductor* filmed in 1914, *The House of the Lost Court* filmed in 1915. *The Scarlet Runner* filmed in 1916 as a serial, *The Shop-Girl* filmed in 1916 as *Winifred the Shop Girl*, *Lord Loveland Discovers America* filmed in 1916, *The Demon* filmed in 1918, *The Guests of Hercules* filmed in 1920 as *Passion's Playground*, *My Friend the Chauffeur* filmed in Germany in 1926 and "Honeymoon Hate" filmed in 1927.

Woodrow, Nancy Mann Waddel

American novelist Nancy Mann Waddel Woodrow (1870–1935) had four of her books made into movies in the silent era. The drama *The Piper's Price* was filmed by Blackbird in 1917, the mystery *The Hornet's Nest* by Vitagraph in 1919, the melodrama *Her Second Chance* by First National in 1926 and the mystery *The Black Pearl* by Trem Carr in 1928.

Zangwill, Israel

English author Israel Zangwill (1864–1926) wrote only one mystery novel but it was a humdinger and won him fame as the godfather of the locked room mystery. *The Big Bow Mystery*, first published in 1891 in the *London Star*, combines a tantalizing puzzle with a memorable portrait of working class life in Victorian London. Zangwill, who was born in London's East End, was once known as the Dickens of the ghetto; today he is mostly remembered for this mystery story. *The Big Bow* was filmed in 1928 as *The Perfect Crime*.

Bibliography

Abel, Richard. *Americanizing the Movies and "Movie-Mad" Audiences, 1910–1914.* Berkeley: University of California Press, 2006.

_____. *The Ciné Goes to Town: French Cinema 1896–1914.* Berkeley: University of California Press, 1994.

_____. *French Cinema: The First Wave, 1915–1929.* Princeton, NJ: Princeton University Press, 1984.

_____. *The Red Rooster Scare: Making Cinema American, 1900–1910.* Berkeley: University of Carlifornia Press, 1999.

_____. *Silent Film.* New Brunswick, NJ: Rutgers University Press, 1996.

_____, ed. *Encyclopedia of Early Cinema.* New York: Routledge, 2005.

Albert, Walter. *Detective and Mystery Fiction: An International Bibliography of Secondary Sources.* Madison, IN: Brownstone, 1985.

Allen, Dick, and David Chacko, eds. *Detective Fiction: Crime and Compromise.* New York: Harcourt Brace, 1974.

Ashley, Mike. *The Mammoth Encyclopedia of Modern Crime Fiction.* New York: Carroll & Graf, 2002.

Bachman, Gregg, and Thomas J. Slater, eds. *American Silent Film.* Carbondale: Southern Illinois University Press, 2002.

Baker, Robert A., and Michael T. Nietzel. *Private Eyes: One Hundred and One Knights, A Survey of American Detective Fiction, 1922–1984.* Bowling Green, OH: Bowling Green State University Popular Press, 1988.

Barnes, Melvin. *Murder in Print: A Guide to Two Centuries of Crime Fiction.* London: Barn Owl, 1986.

Barzun, Jacques, and Wendell Hertig Taylor. *A Catalogue of Crime: Being a Reader's Guide to the Literature of Mystery, Detection and Related Genres.* New York: Harper & Row, 1989.

Benvenuti, Stefano, and Gianni Rizzoni. *The Whodunit: An Informal History of Detective Fiction.* New York: Collier, 1981.

_____, _____, and Michel Lebrun. *Le Roman criminel: histoire, auteurs, personages.* Nantes, France: L'Atalante, 1982.

Bleiler, Richard J. *Reference Guide to Mystery and Detective Fiction.* Englewood, CO: Libraries Unlimited, 1999.

Boileau-Narcejac. *Le Roman policier.* (Que sais-je?) Paris: Press Universitaires de France, 1982.

Bondanella, Peter. *Hollywood Italians: Dagos, Palookas, Romeos, Wise Guys, and Sopranos.* New York: Continuum, 2004.

Bordwell, David, with Janet Staiger and Kristin Thompson. *The Classical Hollywood Cinema: Film Style and Mode of Production to 1960.* New York: Columbia University, 1985.

Bourgeau, Art. *The Mystery Lover's Companion.* New York: Crown, 1986.

Bowser, Eileen. *The Transformation of Cinema 1907–1915.* Berkeley: University of California Press, 1990.

Braff, Richard E. *The Braff Silent Short Film Working Papers: Over 25,000 Films, 1903–1929, Alphabetized and Indexed.* Jefferson, NC: McFarland, 2002.

Braham, Persephone. *Crimes Against the State, Crimes Against Persons: Detective Fiction in Cuba and Mexico.* Minneapolis: University of Minnesota Press, 2004.

Breen, Jon L. *Novel Verdicts: A Guide to Courtroom Fiction.* Metuchen, NJ: Scarecrow, 1984

_____. *What About Murder? A Guide to Books about Mystery and Detective Fiction.* Metuchen, NJ: Scarecrow, 1981.

Brownlow, Kevin. *Hollywood: The Pioneers.* London: Collins, 1979.

_____. *The Parade's Gone By.* London: Paladin, 1968.

Brunsdale, Mitzi. *Gumshoes: A Dictionary of Fictional Detectives.* Westport, CT: Greenwood, 2006.

Butler, William. *The Durable Desperadoes: Critical Study of Enduring Heroes.* London: Macmillan, 1973.

Card, James. *Seductive Cinema: The Art of Silent Film.* New York: Knopf, 1994.

Cassiday, Bruce, ed. *Modern Mystery, Fantasy and Science Fiction Writers.* New York: Continuum, 1993.

_____. *Roots of Detection: The Art of Deduction before Sherlock Holmes.* New York: Ungar, 1983.

Chirat, Raymond. *Catalogue des films français de fiction de 1908 à 1918.* Paris: Cinémathèque française, 1995.

_____. *Catalogue des films français de long métrage: Films de fiction 1919–1929.* Toulouse, France: Cinémathèque de Toulouse, 1984.

Clurman, Robert, ed. *Nick Carter, Detective: Six Astonishing Adventures.* New York: Macmillan, 1963.

Conquest, John. *Trouble Is Their Business: Private Eyes in Fiction, Film and Television, 1927–1988.* New York: Garland, 1990.

Cook, Michael L. *Monthly Murders: A Checklist and Chronological Listing of Fiction in the Digest-Size Mystery Magazines in the United States and England.* Westport, CT: Greenwood, 1982.

_____. *Mystery, Detective and Espionage Magazines.* Westport, CT: Greenwood, 1983.

Cox, J. Randolph. *The Dime Novel Companion: A Source Book.* Westport, CT: Greenwood, 2000.

Craig, Patricia, and Mary Cadogan. *The Lady Investigates: Women Detectives and Spies in Fiction.* New York: St. Martin's, 1981.

Czech National Film Archive. *Czech Feature Film I, 1890–1930.* Prague: Narodni Filmovy Archiv, 1995.

Czitrom, Daniel J. "American Motion Pictures and the New Popular Culture, 1893–1918" in *Popular Culture in American History*, Jim Cullen, ed. Malden, MA: Blackwell, 2001.

D'Agostino, Annette M. *Filmmakers in the Moving Picture World: An Index of Articles, 1907–1927.* Jefferson, NC: McFarland, 1997.

Davies, David Stuart. *Holmes at the Movies.* London: New English Library, 1976.

DeAndrea, William L. *Encyclopedia Mysteriosa: A Comprehensive Guide to the Art of Detection in Print, Film, Radio, and Television.* New York: Prentice Hall, 1994.

Deleuse, Robert. *Les maîtres du roman policier.* Paris: Bordas, 1991.

Disher, M. Willson. *Melodrama: Plots That Thrilled.* London: Macmillan, 1954.

Dove, George N., and Earl F. Bargainnier, eds. *Cops and Constables: American and British Fictional Policeman.* Bowling Green, OH: Bowling Green State University Popular Press, 1986.

Dumaux, Sally A. *King Baggot: A Biography and Filmography of the First King of the Movies.* Jefferson, NC: McFarland, 2002.

Edmonds, I.G. *Big U: Universal in the Silent Days.* London: A.S. Barnes, 1977.

Elsaesser, Thomas. *A Second Life: German Cinema's First Decades.* Amsterdam: Amsterdam University Press, 1996.

Enstad, Nan. *Ladies of Labor, Girls of Adventure: Working Women, Popular Culture and Labor Politics at the Turn of the Twentieth Century.* New York: Columbia University Press, 1999.

Everson, William K. *The Detective in Film: A Pictorial Treasury of the Screen Sleuth from 1903 to the Present.* Secaucus, NJ: Citadel Press, 1972.

Forshaw, Barry. *The Rough Guide to Crime Fiction.* London: Rough Guides, 2007.

Fossati, Franco, and Roberto Di Vanni. *Guida al "giallo."* Milan, Italy: Gammalibri, 1980.

Geherin, David. *The American Private Eye: The Image in Fiction.* New York: Frederick Ungar, 1985.

Gifford, Denis. *Books and Plays in Films 1896–1915.* Jefferson, NC: McFarland, 1991.

_____. *The British Film Catalogue: 1895–1985.* Oxford, UK: Facts on File, 1986.

Gow, Gordon. *Suspense in the Cinema.* London: Tantivy, 1968.

Guérif, François. *Le Cinéma policier français.* Paris: Editions Henri Veyrier, 1981.

Hagen, Ordean A. *Who Done It? Guide to Detective, Mystery and Suspense Fiction.* New York: Bowker, 1969.

Hansen, Miriam. *Babel and Babylon: Spectatorship in American Silent Film.* Cambridge, MA: Harvard University Press, 1991.

Hanson, Patricia King, ed. *American Film Institute Catalog of Motion Pictures: Feature Films, 1911–1920.* 2 vols. Berkeley: University of California Press, 1988.

Harding, Colin, and Simon Popple, eds. *In the Kingdom of Shadows: A Companion to Early Cinema.* London: Cygnus Arts, 1996.

Hardy, Phil, ed. *The BFI Companion to Crime.* London: Cassell, 1997.

Harrison, Dick, ed. *Best Mounted Police Stories.* Edmonton: University of Alberta Press, 1978.

Hartman, Donald K. *Fairground Fiction: Detective Stories of the Columbia Exposition.* Kenmore, NY: Motif, 1992.

Haycraft, Howard. *The Art of the Mystery Story.* New York: Carrol & Graf, 1974.

Heising, Willetta. *Detecting Men: Reader's Guide for Mystery Series by Men.* Dearborn, MI: Purple Moon, 1998.

_____. *Detecting Women: Reader's Guide for Mystery Series by Women.* Dearborn, MI: Purple Moon, 1995.

Holman, Roger, et al. *National Film Archive Catalogue: Silent Fiction Films 1895–1930.* London: British Film Institute, 1960.

Hoppenstand, Gary, ed. *The Dime Novel Detective.* Bowling Green, OH: Bowling Green University Popular Press, 1982.

Horvilleur, Gilles. *Dictionnaire des personnages du cinéma.* Paris: Bordas, 1975.

Hubin, Allen J. *Crime Fiction 1749–1980: A Comprehensive Bibliography.* New York: Garland, 1984.

Hughes, Howard. *Crime Wave: The Filmgoer's Guide to the Great Crime Movies.* New York: Tauris, 2006.

Jacob, Livio, and Piera Pata. *Mack Sennett, King of Comedy.* Pordenone, Italy: Grafiche Editoriali Artistiche Pordenonesi, 1983.

Jakubowski, Maxim. *Great TV and Film Detectives: A Collection of Crime Masterpieces Featuring Your Favorite Screen Sleuths.* Pleasantville, NY: Reader's Digest, 2005.

Kalbus, Oskar. "Detektive auf der Leinwand" in *Vom*

Werden deutscher Filmkunst, 1. Teil: Der stumme Film. Altona-Bahrenfeld: Cigarette Bilderdienst, 1935.

Kinnard, Roy. *Horror in Silent Films: A Filmography, 1896–1929.* Jefferson, NC: McFarland, 1995.

Klein, Kathleen, ed. *Great Women Mystery Writers, Classic to Contemporary.* Westport, CT: Greenwood, 1994.

_____. *The Woman Detective: Gender and Genre.* Urbana: University of Illinois Press, 1988.

Kline, Jim. *The Complete Films of Buster Keaton.* Secaucus, NJ: Citadel, 1993.

Knight, Stephen. *Continent of Mystery: A Thematic History of Australian Crime Fiction.* Victoria: Melbourne University Press, 1997.

Koszarski, Richard. *An Evening's Entertainment: The Age of the Silent Feature Picture, 1915–1928.* New York: Scribner, 1990.

Lacassin, Francis. *Mythologies du roman policier 1 & 2.* Paris: Union General, 1974.

Lahue, Kalton C. *Continued Next Week: History of the Moving Picture Serial.* Norman: University of Oklahoma Press, 1964.

_____. *World of Laughter: The Motion Picture Comedy Short, 1910–1930.* Norman: University of Oklahoma Press, 1966.

Langman, Larry, and Daniel Finn. *A Guide to American Silent Crime Films.* Westport, CT: Greenwood, 1994.

Lauritzen, Einar, and Gunnar Lundquist. *American Film-Index 1908–1915 and 1916–1920.* 2 vols. Stockholm: Film-Index, 1976/1984.

Lofficier, Jean-Marc, and Randy Lofficier. *Shadowmen: Heroes and Villains of French Pulp Fiction.* Encino, CA: Black Coat, 2003.

Lowe, Denise. *An Encyclopedic Dictionary of Women in Early American Films 1895–1930.* New York: Haworth, 2005.

Magill, Frank N. *Critical Survey of Mystery and Detective Fiction.* 4 vols. Pasadena, CA: Salem, 1988.

Magliozzi, Ron, ed. *Treasures from the Film Archives: A catalog of Short Silent Fiction Films Held by the FIAF Archives.* Metuchen, NJ: Scarecrow, 1988.

Mason, Bobbie Ann. *The Girl Sleuth: A Feminist Guide.* Old Westbury, NY: Feminist, 1975.

McDonnell, Patricia. *On the Edge of Your Seat: Popular Theater and Film in Early Twentieth-Century Art.* New Haven, CT: Yale University Press, 2002.

McFarlane, Brian. *The Encyclopedia of British Film.* London: Methuen, 2003.

McReynolds, Louise. *Russia at Play: Leisure Activities at the End of the Tsarist Era.* Ithaca, NY: Cornell University Press, 2002.

Mellot, Philippe. *Les Maîtres du mystère de Nick Carter à Sherlock Holmes, 1907–1914.* Paris: Trinckvel, 1997.

Melvin, David, and Ann Skene. *Crime, Detective, Espionage, Mystery and Thriller Fiction and Film: A Comprehensive Bibliography of Critical Writing Through 1979.* Westport, CT: Greenwood, 1980.

Miller, Blair. *American Silent Film Comedies: An Illustrated Encyclopedia of Persons, Studios and Terminology.* Jefferson, NC: McFarland, 1995.

Miller, Rick. *Photoplay Editions: A Collector's Guide.* Jefferson, NC: McFarland, 2002.

Mitchell, Glenn. *A-Z of Silent Film Comedy: An Illustrated Companion.* London: Batsford, 1998.

Morris, Peter. *Embattled Shadows: Canadian Cinema, 1895–1939.* Montreal: McGill–Queen's University Press, 1978.

Munden, Kenneth W., ed. *American Film Institute Catalog of Motion Pictures: Feature Films, 1921–1930.* 2 vols. New York: Bowker, 1971.

Murphy, Bruce F. *The Encyclopedia of Murder and Mystery.* Basingstoke, UK: Palgrave, 1999.

Musser, Charles. *Before the Nickelodeon: Edwin S. Porter and the Edison Manufacturing Company.* Berkeley: University of California Press, 1991.

_____. *The Emergence of Cinema: The American Screen to 1907.* Berkeley: University of California Press, 1990.

Nickerson, Catherine Ross. *The Web of Iniquity: Early Detective Fiction by American Women.* Durham, NC: Duke University Press, 1998.

North, Joseph H. *The Early Development of the Motion Picture (1887–1909).* New York: Arno, 1973.

Olderr, Steven. *Mystery Index: Subjects, Settings and Sleuths of 10,000 titles.* Chicago: American Library Association, 1987.

Ousby, Ian. *Guilty Parties: A Mystery Lover's Companion.* New York: Thames & Hudson, 1997.

Panek, LeRoy. *Watteau's Shepherds: The Detective Novel in Britain, 1914–1940.* Bowling Green, OH: Bowling Green University Popular Press, 1979.

Pearson, Edmund. *Dime Novels; or, Following an Old Trail.* Boston: Little, Brown, 1929.

Penzler, Otto, Chris Steinbrunner and Marvin Lachman. *Detectionary.* New York: Ballantine, 1980.

Peterson, Audrey. *Victorian Masters of Mystery: Wilkie Collins to Conan Doyle.* New York: Ungar, 1990.

Pitts, Michael R. *Famous Movie Detectives.* 3 vols. Metuchen, NJ: Scarecrow, 1979.

Prager, Arthur. *Rascals at Large, or, The Clue in the Old Nostalgia.* Garden City, NY: Doubleday, 1971.

Priestman, Martin. *The Cambridge Companion to Crime Fiction.* Cambridge, UK: Cambridge University Press, 2003.

Pronzini, Bill, and Marcia Muller. *1001 Midnights: The Aficionado's Guide to Mystery and Detective Fiction.* New York: Arbor House, 1986

Queen, Ellery. *The Detective Short Story: A Bibliography.* New York: Biblo & Tannen, 1969.

Rainey, Buck. *Serials and Series: A World Filmography, 1912–1956.* Jefferson, NC: McFarland, 1999.

_____. *Those Fabulous Serial Heroines: Their Lives and Films.* Metuchen, NJ: Scarecrow, 1990.

Raymond, Lee. *Pearl White, the Peerless Fearless Girl.* New York: A. S. Barnes, 1969.
Read, Eric. *Australian Silent Films: A Pictorial History, 1896–1929.* Melbourne, Australia: Lansdowne, 1970.
_____. *History and Heartburn: The Saga of Australian Film, 1896–1978.* Sydney, Australia: Harper, 1979.
Reilly, John M., ed. *Twentieth-Century Crime and Mystery Writers.* New York: St Martin's, 1985.
Reynolds, Quentin. *The Fiction Factory: From Pulp Row to Quality Street.* New York: Random House, 1955.
Ringgold, Gene, and DeWitt Bodeen. *The Films of Cecil B. DeMille.* New York: Citadel, 1969.
Roberts, Garyn G., Gary Hoppenstand and Ray Browne. *Old Sleuth's Freaky Female Detectives.* Bowling Green, OH: Bowling Green State University Popular Press, 1990.
Robinson, David. *From Peep Show to Palace: The Birth of the American Film.* New York: Columbia University Press, 1996.
Sampson, Robert. *Yesterday's Faces: A Study of Series Characters in the Early Pulp Magazines.* 5 vols. Bowling Green, OH: Bowling Green State University Popular Press, 1987.
Sandburg, Carl. *"The Movies Are": Carl Sandburg's Film Reviews and Essays, 1920–1928.* Chicago: Lake Claremont, 2000.
Savada, Elias, comp. *American Film Institute Catalog of Motion Pictures Film Beginnings, 1893–1910.* 2 vols. Metuchen, NJ: Scarecrow, 1995.
Sherk, Warren M., ed. *The Films of Mack Sennett: Credit Documentation from the Mack Sennett Collection at the Margaret Herrick Library.* Lanham, MD: Scarecrow, 1998.
Shibuk, Charles. "Dramatizations of the Great Literary Detectives and Criminals, Part IV: Films." *The Armchair Detective*, vol. 2, no. 1, October 1968, and no. 3, April 1969.
Singer, Ben. *Melodrama and Modernity: Early Sensational Cinema.* New York: Columbia University Press, 2006.
Slide, Anthony. *The American Film Industry: A Historical Dictionary.* Westport, CT: Greenwood, 1986.
_____. *Aspects of American Film History Prior to 1920.* Metuchen, NJ: Scarecrow, 1978.
_____. *The Big V: A History of the Vitagraph Company.* Metuchen, NJ: Scarecrow, 1976.
_____. *Early American Cinema.* Metuchen, NJ: Scarecrow, 1994.
_____. *Silent Players: A Biographical and Autobiographical Study of 100 Silent Film Actors and Actresses.* Lexington: University Press of Kentucky, 2002.
_____. *Silent Topics: Essays on Undocumented Areas of Silent Film.* Metuchen, NJ: Scarecrow, 2004.
Slung, Michele B. *Crime on Her Mind: Fifteen Stories of Female Sleuths from the Victorian Era to the Forties.* New York: Pantheon, 1975.
Spehr, Paul C., with Gunnar Lundquist. *American Film Personnel and Company Credits 1908–1920: Filmographies Reordered by Authoritative Organizational and Personal Names from Lauritzen and Lundquist's American Film-Index.* Jefferson, NC: McFarland, 1996.
Steinbrunner, Chris, and Otto Penzler. *Encyclopedia of Mystery and Detection.* London: Routledge & Kegan Paul, 1976.
Swanson, Jean, and Dean James. *By a Woman's Hand: Mystery Fiction by Women.* New York; Berkley, 1994.
Symons, Julian. *Mortal Consequences: A History from the Detective Story to the Crime Novel.* New York: Schocken, 1973.
Tannert, Mary W., and Henry Kratz, trans. and eds. *Early German and Austrian Detective Fiction.* Jefferson, NC: McFarland, 1999.
Tasker, Yvonne, ed. *Action and Adventure Cinema.* New York: Routledge, 2004.
Thomson, H. Douglas. *Masters of Mystery: A Study of the Detective Story.* New York: Dover, 1978.
Toulet, Emmanuelle. *Domitor Bibliographie internationale du cinéma des premier temps.* Laval, Quebec: Domitor, 1987.
Tuska, Jon. *In Manors and Alleys: Casebook on the American Detective Film.* Westport, CT: Greenwood, 1988.
Usai, Paolo Cherchi, ed. *Vitagraph Co. of America.* Pordenone, Italy: Edizione Studio Tesi, 1987.
Variety Reviewers. *Variety Film Reviews, 1907–1929.* 3 vols. New York: Garland, 1983.
Wagenknecht, Edward. *The Movies in the Age of Innocence.* Norman: University of Oklahoma Press, 1962.
Walker, John, ed. *Halliwell's Film and Video Guide.* London: HarperCollins, 2002.
_____. *Halliwell's Who's Who in the Movies.* London: HarperCollins, 2001.
Watt, Peter Ridgway, and Joseph Green. *The Alternative Sherlock Holmes: Pastiches, Parodies and Copies.* Burlington, VT: Ashgate, 2003.
Weltman, Manuel, and Raymond Lee. *Pearl White: The Peerless Fearless Girl.* New York: A.S. Barnes, 1969.
Winn, Dilys, ed. *Murder Ink: The Mystery Reader's Companion.* New York: Workman, 1977.
_____. *Murderess Ink: The Better Half of the Mystery.* New York: Workman, 1979.

Index

Aa mujo-Dai ippen: Horo no maki 3, 142
The Abandoned Room 130
The Abbey Grange 3, 90
Abe, Yutaka 19
Abel, Alfred 72
Die Abenteurer G.m.b.H. 3
Ace High 177
The Ace of Hearts 3
The Ace of Scotland Yard 4, 32
The Ace of Spades 4
The Acid Test 4, 220
Acker, Eugene 225
The Acquittal 4
Acquitted 4
The Active Life of Dolly of the Dailies 4–5
Adair, Belle 67
Adams, Claire 37
Adams, Frank R. 37, 104, 123, 171, 180, 184, 217, 230, 249
Adams, Justin 186, 260
"Adrienne Gascoyne" 105
The Adventure of the Actress's Jewels 5, 167
The Adventure of the Alarm Clock 5, 167
The Adventure of the Ambassador's Disappearance 5, 46
The Adventure of the Copper Beeches 6, 52, 202
The Adventure of the Counterfeit Bills 6, 46, 53
The Adventure of the Counterfeit Money 6, 38, 167
The Adventure of the Extra Baby 6, 167
The Adventure of the Hasty Elopement 6, 167
The Adventure of the Italian Model 6, 46
The Adventure of the Lost Wife 6, 167
The Adventure of the Missing Legacy 6, 167
The Adventure of the Retired Army Colonel 6–7, 46
The Adventure of the Smuggled Diamonds 7, 167
The Adventure of the Stolen Slipper 7, 167
The Adventure of the Thumb Print 7, 46, 94
The Adventure of the Wrong Santa Claus 7, 167

The Adventure of the Yellow Curl Papers 7, 263
Adventurers, Inc. 3
The Adventures of Dorcas Dene 7, 32, 60, 116, 147, 238, 262
The Adventures of Joe Fock 7
The Adventures of Kathlyn 7–8, 258
The Adventures of Lieutenant Petrosino 8
The Adventures of P.C. Sharpe 8
The Adventures of Ruth 8–9
The Adventures of Sherlock Holmes 9
Adventures of Sherlock Holmes or Held for a Ransom 9
Adventures of Shpeier and His Gang the Jack of Hearts 210
Adventures of Van Bibber 14
The Affair at the Novelty Theatre 9
An Affair of Nations 9010
Affaire des bijoux 10
Affaire d'Orcival 10
Affaire du train 10
Affaire Lerouge 81, 125, 254
After Dark 10
Aherne, Brian 245
Ainley, Henry 51–52, 56, 116, 127, 146, 192
Albertson, Arthur 16, 98
Albertson, Coit 169
Aldini, Carlo 3, 17
Aldrich, Thomas Bailey 249
Alexander, Georg 61, 92, 103, 120, 143
Alexander, J. Grubb 48, 128, 151, 166, 184, 225, 234
Alias Jimmy Valentine 10–11, 231, 256
Alias Ladyfingers 11
Alias Mary Brown 11
Alias Nemesis 173
Alias the Lone Wolf 11–12
Alias the Night Wind 12, 203, 253
The Alibi 12, 13
All the Winners 13
All the World's a Stage 13
Allain, Marcel 249
Allen, Alfred 151
Allen, Diana 14, 91, 123, 163, 211, 230
Allen, Florence 4
Allen, Grant 239, 249
Allen, Nellie 194
Allen, Paul H. 130

Allen, Ricca 126
Allison, May 117, 175, 179
Alone in London 13
The Alster Case 13–14
Altar of Sacrifice 83
Alylott, Dave 174, 208
Amann, Betty 19
The Amateur Detective 14
The Amazing Impostor 14
Amazing Lovers 14–15
The Amazing Partnership 15
The Ambassador's Diamond 229
Ames, Gerald 15, 17, 91, 144–145, 210, 228
Les Amours de Rocambole 15
Anderson, Frederick Irving 249
Anderson, Mary 81, 223
Anderson, Mignon 160, 204
Andrews, Ann 94
Andrews, Charles 180
Andrews, Frank 80
Andreyor, Yvette 119, 133, 166
Andriot, Josette 47, 247
Angel Esquire 15, 263
Anna the Adventuress 15, 259
Another Man's Shoes 15–16, 177, 252
Apartment 29 16
The Ape 16
Apfel, Oscar 35, 40, 126, 167, 209
Applin, Arthur 13, 249
The Arabia Equine Detective 16
Arden, Edwin 98, 163
The Argyle Case 16 41
Arling, Charles 58, 62, 186
Armadale 17, 252
Armoire Secrète 162
The Armored Car 17
Armored Vault 172
Armstrong, Paul 10, 49, 173, 195, 231
Arnheim, Valy 61, 108
Arquillière, Alexandre 247
Arsène Lupin 17–18, 45, 77, 93, 131, 216, 235, 257
Arsène Lupin 17
Arsène Lupin contra Sherlock Holmes 18, 110, 131
Arsène Lupin contre Herelock Sholmes 18
Arsène Lupin's Last Adventure 18
Arthur, Jean 150
Arundell, Teddy 3, 15, 20, 88
Arvidson, Linda 194
Ashi ni sawatta onna 18–19, 246

Ashton-Kirk 9, 10, 19, 112, 138, 259
Asphalt 19
Asquith, Anthony 53
Astor, Gertrude 98, 129
Astor, Mary 74, 183, 195
At Bay 19
At Death's Door 83
At It Again 19
At the Mercy of Tiberius 20, 96, 183
At the Villa Rose 20
Atherley, Frank 200, 206
Atherton, Gertrude 147
Atkey, Bertram 10
Atkinson, Harold M. 4
Atwood, Bertram 249–250
Das Auge des Gotzen 20, 59
Augen, Carl 59–60, 215
Aurele, Sydney 15, 102, 228–9
Aurora Floyd 20, 106, 252
Austin, F. Britten 75, 124, 245, 250
The Avenging Arrow 20–21
The Avenging Conscience: Thou Shalt Not Kill 21, 260
The Avenging Shadow 21, 73
The Awakening 205

Babette 21–22
Baby Sherlock 22, 110
Bachelor Brides 22
Back to Liberty 22, 36, 252
Badger, Clarence 123, 173, 186, 190
Baffles, Gentleman Burglar 22
The Bag of Diamonds 248
Baggot, King 71, 105, 120–122, 124, 131, 133, 188, 194, 213
Bailey, Ernest G. 46, 136
Baird, Leah 6, 57, 60, 67, 126
Baker, George D. 49, 109, 175, 184, 214, 227, 230
Baker, Graham 86, 95, 102, 197, 218
Balaoo 22, 243
Balfour, Eve 13, 82, 155
Baluchet, William 10, 22, 242
Balzac, Honoré de 175, 250
The Bandaged Man 180
The Bandbox 22, 262
Les Bandits en noirs 23
Bandit's Bargain 240
Banfield, George J. 32, 51, 100, 158, 200, 206
The Bank Burglars 65
The Bank Mystery 98
The Bankers Double 23
La Banque ténébreuse 23
Der Bär von Baskerville 23
Bara, Theda 122
Barcelona and Its Mysteries 23, 80
Bare Knuckles 254
Baring, Nora 53
Barker, Bradley 16, 80, 125, 233
The Barnes Murder Case 23, 52
Barnett, Charles 15
Barnett, Chester 111, 137–138, 174
Barr, Robert 237, 250
Barrabas 23
Barrymore, Ethel 126
Barrymore, John 25, 71, 187, 203, 217, 259

Barrymore, Lionel 11, 40, 80, 109, 126, 194, 218
Barty, Billy 138
The Baskerville Bear 23
The Bat 23
Batley, Ernest G. 46, 136
Battle of Wits 4, 141
Bauer, Yevgeni 210
Baur, Harry 17, 78, 118, 146, 233
Bayley, Hilda 3
Bayne, Beverly 37, 158, 229
A Bear Escape 24, 228
Beaumont, Harry 106, 154–5, 232
Beauty and the Rogue 24
Bedford, Barbara 4, 24, 45
The Bedroom Window 24, 126
Beebe, Ford 155, 188
Beery, Noah 60, 223
Beery, Wallace 77, 172
Before Midnight 24
Behind Masks 24–25
Behind the Curtain 25
Bell, Arthur 9, 90
Bell, Temple 15
Bellamy, George 75, 88, 189
Bellamy, Madge 30, 198
Bellew, H. Kyrle 9, 139
The Beloved Rogue 25
Below the Deadline 25
Belphégor 25, 250
Benham, Harry 20, 70, 156, 160, 204
Bennet, Spencer G. 29, 86, 191, 114, 216
Bennett, Charles 9
Bennett, Chester 46, 184, 198
Bennett, Enid 93
Bennett, Frank 117
Bennett, Frederick 100
Bennett, Joe 58, 96
Bennett, Whitman 125, 166, 198
Benson, Clyde 49, 152
Bentley, E.C. 226, 250
Beranger, Clara 24, 71, 103
Berber, Anita 230
Beresford, Tuppence and Tommy 3, 25, 252
Bergère, Ouida 19, 53, 243
Beringer, Esme 13
Bernède, Arthur 25, 143, 250
Bernstein, Isadore 4
Berry, Bert 62, 136
Bertini, Francesca 247
The Beryl Coronet 9, 25–26, 202
Bess, Jane 3
Bess the Detectress 26
Bess the Detectress in Tick, Tick, Tick 26
Bess the Detectress or the Dog Watch 26
Bess the Detectress or the Old Mill at Midnight 26
Besserer, Eugenie 49
The Betrayal 31, 67, 116
Betsy's Burglar 26
Beware of Blondes 26–27
A Bid for Fortune 27, 72, 165, 250
The Big Bow 264
The Big Bow Mystery 176, 264

The Big City 27
Big Town Ideas 27
Biggers, Earl Derr 46, 48, 114, 198, 250
Billings, Florence 34, 235
Billington, Francelia 31, 140
The Billionaire Lord 27
Billy the Detective 27
Bingham, Edfrid 38, 171
Binks the Hawkshaw 28
Binney, Constance 217
Binovec, Vaclav 7
Birds of Prey 177, 251
The Bishop's Candlesticks 28, 142
Bitter Bondage 160
The Black Bag 28, 262
The Black Beach 130
The Black Bird 28–29
The Black Book 29
The Black Box 29, 156, 259
The Black Cap 58
The Black Circle 98, 261
The Black Dam 29
The Black Diamond 143, 197
The Black Door 177
The Black Gate 30
Black Hand 8, 14, 64, 124
Black Paradise 30
The Black Pearl 30, 264
Black Peter 30, 90
Black Roses 30
The Black Secret 30–31
Black Shadows 183
The Black Sheep of the Family 31
A Black Sherlock Holmes 31, 110
The Black Triangle 31
Blackbirds 28, 31, 264
Blackie, Boston 31–32, 35–36, 56, 80, 144, 161, 182, 191, 206, 220, 251
Blackie's Redemption 31–32
The Blackmailer 32
Blackton, J. Stuart 9
Blackwell, Carlyle 40, 65, 112, 171
Blake, Sexton 32, 39, 51, 54, 90, 98, 100, 119, 155, 158, 200, 206, 212, 219
Blake of Scotland Yard, 32
Blake the Lawbreaker 32
Blau-weisse Steine 32, 68
Bleak House 32–33, 40
The Blind Adventure 33, 250
The Blind Detective 33
The Blind Goddess 33, 262
Blind Man's Eyes 33–34, 258
Blood and Soul 34
The Blue Carbuncle 34, 123
The Blue Diamond 18
Blue Mountains Mystery 34
The Blue Pearl 34
Blue-White Stone 32
Blyth, Harry 32, 250–2511
Blythe, Betty 101, 109
Boardman, True 90, 150, 211
Bobby als Detective 34
Bobby Bumps and the Detective Story 34
Bobby the Boy Scout or the Boy Detective 34, 186

The Boomerang 34–35
Boone, John 11
Boothby, Guy 27, 72, 250–251
Boots 35
Borden, Olive 51
Borgnine, Ernest 8
Borodin, Elfriede 3
Borrowed Finery 35
Borzage, Frank 88, 93, 205
The Boscombe Valley Mystery 35, 90
Boss, Yale 37, 44, 73, 156
Boston Blackie 31–32, 35–36, 56, 80, 144, 161, 182, 191, 206, 220, 251
Boston Blackie 35
Boston Blackie's Little Pal 251
La Boucle énigmatique 36
Bound and Gagged 36
Bourgeois, Gérard 10, 47, 159, 164, 210, 233, 242
Bow, Clara 124
Bowers, John 3, 58, 60, 175, 186, 240
The Boy Detective 34
Boyd, Felix 23, 36–37, 44, 68, 134, 230, 252
Boyle, Irene 65, 145, 170
Boyle, Jack 31, 35–36, 56, 80, 182, 191, 206, 220, 251
Brabin, Charles J. 22, 260
Bracken, Bertram 35, 116
Braddon, Mary Elizabeth 20, 106, 122, 251–252
Brady, Alice 115, 144
Brady, Edwin J. 214, 242
Brand of Satan 56
The Branded Four 37
Brandt, Edwin 141, 233
Brantford, Mickey 32, 51, 100, 158, 200, 206
The Brass Bowl 37, 262
The Brass Bullet 37, 104–5, 249
The Brass Check 37–38, 254
The Brass Spectre 151
The Breaker 38
The Breaking Point 38, 261
Breamer, Sylvia 43, 149, 166
Breese, Edmund 22, 45, 104
Brent, Evelyn 75, 185, 187
Bréon 81, 83, 84, 119, 147, 249
Bressol, Pierre 10, 23, 48, 50, 65, 75, 77–8, 84, 103, 149, 162–3, 210
Brett, Harold 62, 73–74
A Bride for a Knight 38
The Bride's Silence 38
The Bridge of Doom 183
Bridges, Victor 15–16, 133, 177, 252
The Brighton Mystery 38, 168
Brindeau, Jeanne 10, 197
Britain's Secret Treaty 38–39, 200
The Broken Coin 39
Broken Fetters 151
Broken Jade 48
The Broken Necklace 232
Broken Spell 56
The Bromley Case 39, 217
Bronston, Douglas 116, 162, 238
The Bronze Bell 40, 262

Brooding Eyes 40, 255
Brook, Clive 176, 180, 226
Brooke, Van Dyke 6, 7, 169, 210
Brooker, B.R. 5–7, 46, 159, 169
Brower, Robert 48, 106, 154–9, 232
Brown, Clarence 4
Browning, Tod 27–29, 80, 127, 157, 252
Brownlee, Frank 35, 69, 116, 151, 178
The Bruce Partington Plans 40, 90
Brunette, Fritzi 101, 166, 218
Brunton, William 90, 211
Buchanan, Donald 88
Buchanan, Jack 40
Buchanan, Robert 13
Bucket, Inspector 33, 40, 253
Buel, Kenean 80, 158, 191
Buffington, Adele 124, 139
Bulldog Drummond 40, 60, 76, 95
Bulldog Drummond 40
Bulldog Drummond's Third Round 40
A Bundle of Trouble 40, 63
Bungalow Bungle 163
Bungling Bill, Detective 40–41
Burbridge, Elizabeth 91, 209
Burgess, Gelett 135
The Burglar and the Lady 41
The Burglary Syndicate 174
Buried Alive 37, 104, 200
Burleigh, Bertram 51
Burning Up Broadway 41
Burns, Edmund 241
Burns, Edward 84, 124
Burns, Vinnie 141, 153, 193, 245
Burns, William J. 41, 80, 87, 145, 182, 184
Burnt Fingers 41
Burroughs, Edgar Rice 167
Burstup Holmes 27, 41–42, 110
Burstup Holmes, Detective 41–42
Burstup Holmes Murder Case 42
Burton, Charlotte 66, 105
Burton, Langhorne 32, 51, 100, 158, 200, 206
Bushman, Francis X. 37–38, 58, 85, 139, 196, 229
By Whose Hand? 42

Cabanne, Christy 161
Cabaret 27, 42
Cadell, Jean 15
The Café L'Egypte 42, 90
Cafe of Destruction 140
Cairns, Dallas 85, 110, 246
Calamity Ann, Detective 42
Calhoun, Alice 227
Calínez and Gedeón Detectives 42
Calthrop, Donald 51, 88
Calvert, E.H. 78
Calvert's Valley 42–43
Camillo Emulates Sherlock Holmes 43, 110
Camp, Charles Wadsworth 98, 130
Campbell, Colin 30, 114
Campbell, Scott 23, 36, 44, 68, 134, 230, 252

Canham, Frank 42, 53–54, 90, 96, 102, 120, 140
Capra, Frank 196
Caprice, June 193
Captain of His Soul 43, 182
Captain of Villainy 90
The Cardboard Box 43, 123
Carew, James 15, 75, 113, 245
Carew, Ora 11, 129, 175, 202, 234
Carewe, Edwin 149
Carey, Harry 97, 135
Carl, Renée 81, 83, 84, 119, 143, 147
Carlile, C. Douglas 53, 118, 123, 200
Carlton, Frank 7, 32, 116, 147, 238
Carlton, Lewis 39, 98, 119, 155, 200
Carlyle, Francis 61–62
Carmen, Jewel 23–24, 143, 165
Carr, Cameron 51, 59, 226, 228, 236
Carrington, Elaine S. 13
Carson, Daniel 155–158
Carter, Harry 98, 136, 206, 216
Carter, Nick 43, 163–165
The Carter Case 43–44
Case, Helen 9
A Case of High Treason 44, 256
A Case of Identity 44
The Case of the German Admiral 39
The Case of the Missing Girl 41, 44
The Case of the Vanished Bonds 37, 44
Cassinelli, Dolores 108
Castle, Florence 87
Castle, Irene (Mrs.Vernon Castle) 52, 86, 135, 173, 215, 232
Castle, John 55
Castleton, Barbara 78
The Cat and the Canary 44–45, 104
Catelain, Jaque 171
The Catspaw 45, 260
Caught, a Detective Story 45
Caught in the Fog 45
Caught with the Goods 45
Cave of Despair 116
Cavern of Death 162
The Cavern Spider 45, 220
Cecil, Edward 60, 217
Chains of Evidence 45
Chairo no-Onna 45
Champion of Lost Causes 4546
Chan, Charlie 46, 48, 250
Chaney, Lon 3, 4, 27–28, 81, 87, 127, 142, 146, 177–178, 186, 258, 260
Chapin, Frederic 16, 227
Chapman, Edythe 11
Charles Augustus Milverton 46, 90
Charles Peace, King of Criminals 46, 125
The Charlotte Street Mystery 64
Chase, Lambert 5–7, 46, 159, 169
Chasm of Fear 244
Chauncey Proves a Good Detective 46
Chautard, Emile 127, 149, 160, 171
Cheating Cheaters 46–47
Chelsea 7750 47

Index

Chéri-Bibi 47, 166, 258
Chéri-Bibi 47
Chesebro, George 67, 145, 186
Chester, George Randolph 93, 163, 209, 235, 252
Cheveu d'or 48, 162
The Chicago May Modern Adventuress 48
The Chinatown Mystery 48
The Chinese Parrot 46, 48
Christie, Agatha 3, 25, 172, 252, 258
The Chronicles of Cleek 48, 50, 106, 154–159, 232, 255
The Cinema Murder 49, 259
The Circular Staircase 23, 49, 261
Circumstantial Evidence 25, 49, 188, 217, 244
The City Gone Wild 50
City of Silent Men 49, 185
Clark, Frank Howard 14, 208, 211
Clark, Harvey 96, 108, 140
Clark, Violet 129, 131, 180
Clary, Charles 8, 25, 65, 106, 114, 123, 220
Clawson, Elliott J. 140, 151, 178, 223, 240
Cleek, Hamilton 48, 50, 255–256
Clifford, Ruth 30, 40, 139, 151
Clifton, Elmer 4, 35, 144
Clifton, Walter 52, 167, 232
Cline, Edward F. 108
Clisbee, Edward 94, 137
Close, Ivy 236
The Closed Door 50, 94
The Closing Net 50, 261
Le Club des suicides 50
The Clue 50
The Clue of the Cigar Band 50
The Clue of the New Pin 50–51, 263
The Clue of the Oak Leaf 51, 116
The Clue of the Pigtail 51, 153
The Clue of the Second Goblet 51, 200
Cobb, Edmund 88, 140
Coffee, Leonore J. 11, 202
Cohan, George M. 93, 142, 198–199, 250
Cohen, Bennett 21, 75
Cohen, Octavus Roy 80, 252
Colby, A.E. 8, 51, 57, 84, 90, 142, 152, 185, 196, 205, 207, 238
Collana dei quattro millione 51
The College Boys Special 51, 58
Collier, Constance 33
Collier, William 99, 165, 198, 233
Collins, Edwin J. 209
Collins, Tom 49, 113, 197, 217, 225, 230, 235
Collins, Wilkie 17, 56, 59, 146, 215, 228, 244–245, 252
Colman, Ronald 15, 76
Colwell, Goldie 8, 127
Come to My House 51
Comment Nick Winter connut les courses 51, 242
Compson, Betty 27, 47, 142, 173, 182, 260

Compton, Fay 114
Conan Doyle, Arthur 252–253
Condon, Frank 49, 242
The Confidence Man 51–52
Conklin, Chester 22, 104, 195, 208
Conklin, William 130, 214, 246
Conness, Robert 23, 37, 44, 68, 134, 146
Considine, Mildred 12, 118, 138, 194
The Conspiracy 52
The Conspirators 23, 52, 141, 195, 259
Convict 993 52
Conway, Booth 231
Conway, J.W. 141
Conway, Jack 11, 16, 58,
Cooper, Bigelow 23, 44, 134
Cooper, D.P. 9, 38, 51, 84, 90, 110, 142, 152, 153, 156, 166, 168, 185, 190, 196, 205, 207, 224, 225, 238, 246
Cooper, George 6, 7, 32, 51, 57, 159, 209, 239
Cooper, Miriam 80, 188
Cooper, Rosemary 191
The Copper Beaches 9, 52
The Copper Cylinder 52, 116
Corbett, James J. 140
A Corn-Fed Sleuth 53
Cornwall, Blanche 42, 44, 64, 157
Coryell, John Russell 253
Cossar, John 14, 86, 99
Costello, Helen 41, 86, 142, 159, 241
Costello, Maurice 5–7, 9, 46, 56, 142, 152, 158–159, 168–169
A Cottage on Dartmoor 53
The Coughing Horror 53, 90
The Council of Three 53, 200
Counterfeit 53
The Counterfeiters 53–54
Courtot, Marguerite 36, 54, 104, 191, 193, 215, 232
Cousins of Sherlock Holmes 54
The Cowboy Cavalier 54
Cragmire Tower 54
Crane, Frank 98, 125, 147, 232
Crane, Ward 35, 55, 204
Crime and Punishment 54, 188–189, 254
The Criminal Path 54–5
The Crimson Circle 55, 263
The Crimson Flash 55
The Crimson Runner 55–56
The Crimson Stain Mystery 56
Crisp, Donald 74, 226
Croise, Hugh 9, 38, 59, 110, 111, 120, 132, 152, 153, 156, 166, 168, 188, 190, 224, 225, 246
Crolius, Louie 14
Crooked Alley 31, 56
The Crooked Man 56, 123
A Crooked Romance 56
Crooked Streets 56
Crosland, Alan 25, 80
Cruze, James 50, 70, 141, 155–159, 217, 241, 248
The Cry of the Night Hawk 56–57

Cuff, Sergeant 56
Cummings, Irving 66, 195, 212, 246
Cummings, Robert 11, 54, 195
Cunard, Grace 4, 32, 39, 73, 104, 131, 148–149, 159, 183–5, 213
Cunning Rogue 78, 163
Cunningham, Jack 20, 65, 101, 114, 205, 219
Currier, Frank 33, 109
The Curse of Ravenscroft 56, 116
Curtis, Allen 26, 123, 152, 242
Cynthia-of-the-Minute 57, 263
The Cypher Message 57

Dagger of Death 244
Dale, Jimmy 57, 118
Dalton, Dorothy 24–25, 109, 128, 130, 259
Daly, Arnold 19, 79, 163, 194
Die Dame in Koffer 57, 172, 195
Dana, Viola 209, 217–218
Dane, Karl 11, 64
Dane, Zina 136
The Dancing Men 34, 57, 123
The Danger Girl 58
Dangerous Lies 58
Dangerous Traffic 58
Daniels, Bebe 89, 242
Dare-Devil Detective 63
Dark Stairways 58
Darmond, Grace 99, 105, 111, 140, 142, 204
A Daughter of Daring 58, 154
A Daughter of the Law 58
Davesnes, Edoardo 222
Davidson, Lawford 3, 55, 97, 196
Davies, Acton 5
Davies, Howard 105, 169
Davies, Marion 49, 249
Davis, Frederick W. 36, 252
Davis, James 58, 64, 105, 146
Davis, Owen 42, 101, 104
Davis, Richard Harding 253
Davo, Harry 51
Dawley, Searle 47, 112, 122, 182, 239
Day, Alice 97
Day, Marceline 25, 27, 64, 127, 226
The Dazzling Miss Davison 58–59
A Dead Certainty 59
Dead Man's Escape 232
The Dead Secret 59, 252
Dean, Priscilla 55, 58, 80, 98, 206
Dear Liar 59, 220, 263
Death Cloud 195
Death Noose 137
Death Rail 29
Death Ray 80
Death Ride 140, 160
Death Studio 31
Death Switch 113
Death Trap 67, 100, 216
Death Warrant 234
Decoeur, Albert 15, 183
Deebs, Joe 20, 59–60, 68, 92–93, 169–70, 189, 198, 208, 215
De Grasse, Joseph 109
De Grasse, Sam 4, 61, 206

Delaney, Leo 49, 217, 230, 235
D'Elba, H. 11
De Mille, Cecil B. 65, 268
De Mille, William 24, 103
Dempster, Carol 130, 169, 203
Dene, Dorcas 7, 32, 60, 116, 147, 238, 262
The Desert of the Lost 60
The Deserted Engine 58, 60
Desmond, William 4, 43, 87, 114
D'Esterre, Madame 3, 9, 90, 112, 123, 206
The Destroying Angel 60
Le Détective 61
The Detective 61
Détective Amateur 61
Detective and Matchmaker 61
The Detective and the Jewel Trick 61
Detective Barock Holmes and His Hound 61
Detective Blinn 61
Detective Bonzo and the Black Hand Gang 61
Detective Burton's Triumph 61
Detective Craig's Coup 61–62
Detective Dan Cupid 62
Detective Daring and the Thames Coiners 62
Detective Dervieux 62
Detective Dorothy 62
Detective Dot 62
Le Détective Féminin 62
Detective Ferris 62
Detective Finn 62
Detective Finn and the Foreign Spies 62
Detective Finn or in the Heart of London 62
Détective Flegmatique 62
A Detective for a Day 62
Le Detective Gallows contre la band des XXX 63
Detective Hayes 63
Detective Henry and the Paris Apaches 63, 241
Detective in Peril 63
Il Detective innamorato 63
Detective Potts 40, 63, 75, 147, 182
The Detective Queen 63
Detective Robert's Peril 63
Detective Sharp and the Stolen Miniatures 63–64
Detective Short 64
Detective Swift 64
Detective Yuri 64, 122
Detectives 64
The Detective's Conscience 64
The Detective's Daughter 64
The Detective's Desperate Chance 64
The Detective's Dog 64, 73
The Detective's Nursemaid 64
The Detectives of the Italian Bureau 64
The Detective's Peril 64,
The Detective's Ruse 64
The Detective's Santa Claus 64
The Detective's Sister 64–65

The Detective's Stratagem 65
A Detective's Strategy 65
The Detective's Trap 65
A Detective's Trip Around the World 65
The Detectress 26, 65
Ein Detektiv-Duell 60
Das Detecktiveduell—Harry Hill contra Sherlock Holmes 61
Les Dévaliseurs de banque 65
De Vaul, William P. 4
The Devil Stone 65
The Devil to Pay 65
The Devil's Foot 9, 65–66
Dey, Frederic Van Rensselaer 12, 87, 94, 253
The Diamond from the Sky 66
The Diamond Man 66–67, 263
The Diamond Master 67, 254
The Diamond Mystery 67, 111
The Diamond Queen 67, 186
The Diamond Runners 67–68
Diamonds of Destiny 32, 68
Dice of Destiny 68, 175
Dickens, Charles 32, 40, 153, 253–254
Dickson's Diamonds 37, 68
Dillon, Jack 26, 43, 131, 206
A Dime Novel Detective 68, 168, 266
Diplomaten 59, 68
The Disappearance of Lady Frances Carfax 68, 123
Dix, Beulah Marie 88, 125
Dixey, Henry E. 47, 122
Dixon, Thomas, Jr. 37, 46, 99
Do Detectives Think? 68–69
Dr. Brian Pellie 69, 175
Dr. Brian Pellie and the Bank Robbery 69
Dr. Brian Pellie and the Baronet's Bride 69
Dr. Brian Pellie and the Secret Despatch 69
Dr. Brian Pellie and the Spanish Grandee 69
Dr. Brian Pellie and the Wedding Gifts 69
Dr. Brian Pellie Escapes from Prison 69
Dr. Brian Pellie, Thief and Coiner 69
Dr. Fu Manchu 42, 51, 53–4, 57, 69, 84, 90, 102, 120, 140, 150, 152–3, 185, 196, 209, 261
Dr. Gar el Hama 69–70
Dr. Gar el Hama 69–70
Dr. Gar el Hama II 70
Dr. Gar el Hama III 70
Dr. Gar el Hama IV 70
Dr. Gar el Hama V 70
Dr. Jekyll and Mr. Hyde 70–72, 117, 145, 262
Dr. Jekyll and Mr. Hyde 70–71
Dr. Jekyll and Mr. Hyde or a Strange Case 70
Dr. Mabuse 72, 131–2, 257
Dr. Mabuse, der Spieler 72
Dr. Nikola 27, 72, 165, 250–1

Dr. Nikola 72
Dr. Sin Fang 72
The Dog Detective 72
Dog Detective 73
Dog Detectives 73
Dog Justice 73
Dolly Plays Detective 5, 73
Don Q 73
Don Q and the Artist 73
Don Q—How He Outwitted Don Luis 73
Don Q—How He Treated the Parole of Gevil Hay 73
Don Q, Son of Zorro 74
Donaldson, Arthur 85, 101, 108
Dope 74
The Dorrington Diamonds 75
Le Dossier 3 75
Dostoevsky, Fyodor 54, 188, 254
A Double Identity 75, 150
Doubling with Danger 75
Dougherty, George S. 126
Dougherty, Jack 186–187
Dove, Billie 93, 128
Dowland William 129, 171, 175
Dowling, Joseph J. 65, 142, 208, 218
The Downfall of Potts 75
Les Dragées soporifiques 75
The Dragnet 75
Une Drame en express 75
Drumier, Jack 20, 85, 154, 157
The Drum 75, 220, 250
Drummond, Bulldog 40, 60, 76, 95
Duds 76, 261
Dull Care 76
The Dummy 76
Dunbar, Marjorie 229
Dunbar, Robert 11
Dunham, Maudie 13
Dunham, Phil 26
Dupin, C. Auguste 76, 148, 260
Du Pont, Miss 187, 220
Duvall, Grace 76–77
Duvall, Richard 76–77
Dwan, Allan 42, 47, 52
The Dying Detective 77
Dynamite 73, 88

Earle, Edward 33, 98
Eason, B. Reeves 205–206
Easton, Clem 7, 37
Easy Pickings 77
Edington, A.C. 254
Edington, C. 254
Edwin, Walter 5, 73, 101, 239
Eichgrün, Bruno 79, 89, 91, 163, 171
Eichstaedt, Senta 92, 117, 143, 154, 197
Eldridge, Charles 5, 6, 109, 239
Elkas, Edward 45, 143
Elliot, William J. 26, 33, 44, 52, 66, 77, 135, 165, 184, 190–1, 196, 209, 221, 246
Ellis, Robert 98, 154, 170, 175, 194, 208, 221, 224, 233
Ellwanger, W.T. 15

Elvey, Maurice 9, 20, 26, 33, 44, 52, 66, 77, 112, 135, 165, 184, 190–1, 196, 206, 209
Elvidge, June 171, 180, 186
Emerson, John 52, 157
Emney, Fred 158, 206
Les Empreintes 77
The Empty House 9, 63, 77
Empty Pockets 77
En danger 78
Encore Nick Winter 78, 242
Engholm, Harry 213, 231
The Engineer's Thumb 78, 123
England, George Allan 12, 37, 254
Erzgauner 78, 163
The Eternal Law 78
Ethier, Alphonse 128, 146, 175, 196
Evans, Ena 85, 110
Evans, Fred 201
Évasion de forçat de Croze 78
Évasion de Vidocq 78
Eveleigh, Leslie 100, 158, 206
Everton, Paul 49, 126, 184
Every Thief Leaves a Clue 78
The Evidence of the Film 79
The Exiles 79, 253
Expiation 79, 119, 259
Exploits of a Race-Course Detective 255
The Exploits of Elaine 79- 80, 120, 163, 194–5, 261
The Exploits of Three-Fingered Kate 80, 191, 219–20
Exposure of the Land Swindlers 80
The Exquisite Thief 80
The Eyes of Mystery 80, 252

The Face in the Dark 80
The Face in the Fog 80
Face to Face 80
Fairbanks, Douglas 73–74, 134, 250, 260
The False Faces 81, 116, 127
The False Magistrate 84
The Family Stain 81, 125
Fangs of Vengeance 73, 81
Fantômas 81–84, 119, 147, 249
Fantômas 82–83
Fantômas à l'ombre de la guillotine 83
Fantômas contre Fantômas 83
Fare, Betty 4
Farley, Dot 126
Farley, James 11, 38
Farnum, Dorothy 110, 198
Farnum, Dustin 167
Farnum, Franklyn 87
Farrar, Geraldine 65
Farrington, Adele 95
Fassbender, Max 92–93, 135, 171
The Fatal Ring 83–84, 257
Le Faux Magistrat 84
Les Faux-Monnayeurs 84
Fazenda, Louise 23, 85–86, 101, 126, 186, 216
Fearless 73, 81
Fearnley, Jane 115, 121, 122, 167
Feet of Clay 84, 154
The Female Detective 62

The Female Sleuth 84,
Ferguson, Casson 11, 227
Ferguson, Elsie 53, 243
Feuillade, Louis 23, 62, 81, 83, 84, 119, 147, 166, 170, 227, 232, 250
Field, George 61
Field, Gladys 71
Fielder, Kitty 246
Fielding, Edward 203
Fielding, Harry 116
Fielding, Margaret 244
Fielding, Pete 129
Fielding, Romaine 64
The Fiery Hand 84, 153
Fife, Shannon 99, 124, 130, 235
Fifty Candles 84, 250
Figdor, Karl 89, 93, 107, 122, 170, 186, 243
The Fight for Millions 84
Fighting Snub Reilly 85, 220, 263
File No. 113 85, 219, 266
The Film Detective 85
The Final Problem 85, 123
Finch, Flora 104
Find the Woman 85
Finger Prints 85–86, 261
The Fire Detective 86
The First Law 86, 226
Fisher, Bud 202
Fitzgerald, Aubrey 124
Fitzgerald, Dallas M. 45, 170
Fitzhamon, Lewis 61, 64, 191
Fitzmaurice, George 19, 53, 186, 215, 243
$500 Reward 86
$5,000,000 Counterfeiting Plot 87
$5,000 Reward 87
Flame 73, 124
The Flaming Clue 87
Flanagan, D.J. 34
Flanagan, David 11
The Flashlight 87
Fleming, Carroll 14
Fleming, Victor 33
The Floor Above 87
Flugrath, Edna 109
Flying Colors 87–88
Flying Squad 88, 263
Foley, George 226, 235
Fontanals, Alfredo 42
Fontanes, Germaine 15
Foolish Monte Carlo 88
Foote, Courtenay 40, 67
For the Defense 88
Ford, Francis 39, 48, 88, 117, 131, 140, 148, 159, 167, 183–185, 213
Ford, Harriet 16, 76
Ford, Harrison 183
The Forger 88, 263
Forman, Tom 49, 56, 175
Forrest, Allan 14, 110, 239
Four Black Pennies 151
The Four-Footed Ranger 73, 88
The Four Just Men 88
Four Thirteen 88
The Fourteenth Man 88
Fox, David 260
Fox, Earle 14, 84
Fox, Finis 11, 32, 58, 149, 223

Fox, Fontaine 138
Fox, Lucy 87, 119
Fox, Reginald 67, 120, 134
Foxe, Earle 14
The Frame Up 89
Francis, Alec 11, 45, 67, 80, 123, 126
Franju, Georges 119
Frank, Alexander 113, 196, 235, 244
Franklin, Chester 25, 64, 206, 218
Franz, Joseph 12, 175
Die Frau mit den Millionarden 89
Frauen, die Ehe brechen 89, 163
Fraunholz, Fraunie 41, 245
Frederick, Pauline 170–1, 246, 259
Fredericks, Arnold 254
Free Lips 89
French, Charles K. 165, 227
Fresnay, Pierre 183
Die Freundin des gelben Mannes 89
Fritzchen als Sherlock Holmes in Germany 89
Froest, Frank 254
Fröhlich, Gustav 19
From Now On 89
Fu Manchu 42, 51, 53–4, 57, 69, 84, 90, 102, 120, 140, 150, 152–3, 185, 196, 209, 261
Fuller, Mary 4, 5, 73, 238
The Fungi Cellars 89, 153
The Further Adventures of Sherlock Holmes 90
The Further Adventures of Stingaree 90
The Further Adventures of Terence O'Rourke 90
The Further Exploits of Sexton Blake 90
The Further Mysteries of Dr. Fu Manchu 90
Furthman, Jules 4, 24, 43, 75, 124, 241, 246
Futrelle, Jacques 77., 149, 155, 254

Gaboriau, Emile 10, 81, 85, 125, 146, 154, 219, 254–255
Gail, Jane 71, 213, 224
Gaillard, Robert 5, 7, 102, 152
A Game of Graft 90, 163
The Game of Liberty 91, 259
The Game of Three 87, 91
The Gangsters and the Girl 91
Gar El Hama 69–70
Garbagni, Paul 51, 164–155, 179
Garrick, Richard 17, 188, 226
Garwood, William 7, 79, 129, 209, 244
Gas, Oil and Water 91
Gasnier, Louis 64, 80, 130, 176, 194, 205, 221
Das Gasthaus von Chicago 91, 163
The Gate Crasher 91
Gates, Harvey 25, 55, 58, 80, 129, 140, 151, 192, 216
Das Geheimnis der Breifmarke 92, 143
Das Geheimnis der Mumie 92
Das Geheimnis von Chateau Richmond 92, 143, 154

Der Geheimnisvolle Klub 92
Die Geheimnisvolle Villa 92
Der Geheimsekretär 92
Der Geisterspuk im House des Professors 92, 238
The Gentleman Burglar 93, 131, 190
Gerard, Charles 45, 194
Gerber, Neva 37, 65, 167, 183, 225, 234
Gerrard, Douglas 87, 243
Die Geschichte der Maud Gregaards 93
Das Gesetz der Mine 59, 93
Der Gestreifte Domino 93, 238
Get-Rich-Quick Wallingford 93
Getting Evidence Showing the Trials and Tribulations of a Private Detective 93–94
Ghione, Emilio 247, 255
Giblyn, Charles 119, 122, 125
Gibson, Helen 64, 105, 154, 158
Gilbert, Eugenia 42, 150
Gillette, William 202–203
Gilmore, Barney 84, 91
Girard, Joseph W. 37, 140, 172
A Girl at Bay 94, 255
The Girl by the Roadside 94, 95, 253
The Girl Detective 94–95
The Girl Detective's Ruse 95
The Girl from Chicago 95, 261
The Girl from Havana 95
The Girl in the Rain 95
The Girl in the Web 95–96
The Girl on the Stairs 96
Gish, Dorothy 35, 87
Glass, Gaston 97, 118, 217, 220
Glaum, Louise 34, 128–129
Gleason, Ada 158
The Gloria Scott 96, 123
Goddard, Charles 111, 80, 107,163, 194, 200
God's Witness 20, 96
Goetz, Curt 59, 208
The Golden Fleece 96, 249
The Golden Pince-Nez 96
The Golden Pomegranates 90, 96
The Golden Web 96–97, 259
Goldin, Sidney M. 8, 124, 151
Goldwyn 3, 76, 80, 119, 171–2, 190, 203, 228, 234
Gollomb, Joseph 94, 255
Gone 50
Gooden, Arthur Henry 25, 116, 240
Goodwin, John 40, 113, 255
The Goose Girl 258
Gordon, Bruce 73, 86
Gordon, Harris 14, 141, 215, 141, 215
Gordon, Huntly 97, 110, 130
Gordon, James 44, 157, 163
Gordon, Julia Swayne 17, 25, 133
Gordon, Leslie Howard 13, 138
Gordon, Maude Turner 47
The Gorilla 97
Gouget, Henry 10
Gould, Nat 228, 255
Goulding, Edmund 207

Gowing, Sidney 255
Graft 97, 255
Grandin, Ethel 56, 120–121, 224
Grandon, Francis J. 57, 76
Grant, Police Reporter 97–98, 154, 194, 224
Grassby, Bertram 84, 88, 96, 115, 128, 216
Gray, Arthur 86, 94
Gray, Clifford 16
Gray, Eve 3
Gray, George Arthur 216, 226
Gray, Gilda 42
Gray, Lawrence 201
The Gray Ghost 98, 129, 261
The Gray Mask 98
Graydon, W. Murray 200
The Great Bradley Mystery 98
The Great Cheque Fraud 98, 200
The Great Diamond Mystery 99
The Great Diamond Robbery 99
The Great Hansom Cab Mystery 99, 152
The Great Jewel Affair 10, 164
The Great Jewel Robbery 99
The Great K & A Train Robbery 99–100
The Great London Mystery 100, 193
The Great Mail Robbery 100
The Great Office Mystery 100, 200
The Great Radium Mystery 100
The Great Ruby 100
The Great Ruby Mystery 100
The Great Universal Mystery 100–101
The Great Vacuum Robbery 101
The Greek Interpreter 90, 101
Greeley, Evelyn 40, 167
Green, Alfred E. 51, 238
Green, Anna Katharine 103, 109, 124,109, 141, 241, 255
Green, Judd 13
The Green Archer 101, 263
The Green Cloak 101
The Green Flame 101
The Green God 101–102, 257
The Green Mist 90, 102
The Green Terror 102, 263
Greenwood, Winifred 61, 114
Gregory, Jackson 11
The Grell Mystery 102, 254
Grey, Clifford 58
Grey, Gloria 32
Grey, John 43, 102,151, 216, 223
Grey, Minna 58, 246
Grey, R. Henry 178
Grey, Raymond 208
Grey Boy 21, 73
The Grey Glove 102
Grey Seal 12, 57, 118, 138, 194, 260
Greywater Park 90, 102
Gribbon, Eddie 23, 161
Griffith, Corinne 94
Griffith, D.W. 21,87, 109, 130, 144, 157, 169, 194, 214, 249, 260
Griffith, Edward H. 12
Griffith, Raymond 109, 173, 190, 226, 247
Griffiths, Eleanor 13

The Grim Game 102, 111, 261
Grossman, Harry 81, 136, 243
Groves, Fred 55, 194, 214
Grumpy 102–103
Gryce, Ebenezer 103, 125
Le Guet-apens 103, 164
Gunn, Charles 43, 204
The Gunsaulus Mystery 103
Gurney, Kate 20, 120, 172
Guy Blaché, Alice 41–42, 44, 157, 245

Haines, William 11
Der Haisschmuck 103
Haldane, Bert 181–2, 193
Haldane of the Secret Service 103, 111
Hale, Alan 20, 56, 85, 125–126, 184
Hale, Creighton 80, 116, 163, 194, 199
The Half Million Bribe 103, 260
Hall, Alexander 91, 123, 163, 211, 230
Hall, Ella 136, 201, 206
Hall, George Edwards 78, 128
Hall, Winter 11
Hallor, Edith 34, 54
Ham the Detective 103
Hamilton, Gilbert P. 43, 96
Hamilton Cleek 48, 50, 255
Hammerstein, Elaine 16–17, 147
Hanaud, Inspector 20, 103–104
The Hand at the Window 104
The Hand Print Mystery 104
The Handsome Brute 104
Hansen, Howell 155–9, 248
Hansen, Juanita 37, 182
Hanshew, Thomas W. 48, 106, 146, 154–159, 232, 255–256
Harald, Mary 222
Hardin, Eric 4
Hardin, Neal 162, 241
Hardrock Dome, the Great Detective 104, 110
Hardy, Oliver 68–69, 76, 208
Harlan, Kenneth 26, 47, 77, 139, 165
Harris, Mildred 58, 211
Hart, Albert 32, 171
Hart, William S. 145, 182
Harte, Betty 70, 157
Hartman, Gretchen 22, 85, 143, 154
Hastings, Carey L. 14
Hatch, Riley 122, 246
Hatton, Raymond 31, 172, 226
The Haunted House 104
The Haunted Island 104–105
The Hawk's Trail 105
Hawkshaw 28, 221
Hawley, Wanda 179, 227
Hayakawa, Sessue 30, 50, 115, 259
Hayden, Katheleen 51, 88, 134
Haydon, Charles 14, 177, 212
The Hazards of Helen 64, 68, 105, 158, 177, 188, 240–241, 262
Hearn, Edward 20, 73, 227
Hearts or Diamonds? 105–106
Heatherley, Clifford 33, 154, 172

Heffron, Thomas 132, 227, 242
Hemlock Hoax, the Detective 106, 110
Henabery, Joseph 89, 134, 144
Henley, Hobart 80, 97, 193, 207
Henning, Ugo 53
Henry, Gale 65, 123, 186
Henry, O. 10, 231, 256
Hepworth, Barbara 191
Hepworth, Cecil 15, 113, 191
Her Bitter Lesson 20, 106
Her One Mistake 106
Herdman, John 4
The Heritage of Hamilton Cleek 48, 106
Herman, Albert 53, 138
Herrin der Welt 89, 93, 106–107, 122, 170, 186, 243
Hertel, Aage 69
Hey Hey Cowboy 107
Heyes, Herbert 9, 171
The Hidden Hand 29, 107, 261
The Hidden Light 108
Hide and Seek Detectives 108
Higgs, Harry 108
High Stakes 108
Hill, Bonnie 175
Hill, Doris 214, 218
Hill, Harry 61, 108–1099
Hill, Robert F. 32, 56, 58, 94, 100, 104, 193
Hill, Sinclair 4, 20, 52, 75, 79, 110–111, 154, 245
Hilliard, Ernest 41, 123
Hines, John 11
Hiram Green, Detective 109
His Darker Self 109
His Father's Son 109
His Hidden Talent 109
His Last Bow 109, 123
His Wife's Friend 109
His Wife's Husband 109–110, 255
Hitchcock, Alfred 58, 127, 181, 258
Hively, George 28, 131
Hobart, Doty 85, 158
The Hocussing of Cigarette 110, 168
Hoerl, Arthur 22, 30, 139, 141, 174
Hoffman, Aaron 232
Hoffman, E.T.A. 34, 256
Hoffman, Otto 192
Hoffman, Ruby 84
Hoffman, V. 210
Hofman, Luigi 7
The Hole in the Wall 110
Holger-Madsen, Forrest 202, 204
Holland, Edna 6
Holloway's Treasure 110, 220
Holmes, Gerda 85, 154
Holmes, Helen 67, 105, 138, 155, 169, 177, 188, 240, 261
Holmes, Sherlock 9, 18, 26, 34–35, 43–44, 56–57, 68, 77–78, 89, 90, 96, 109–12, 148–9, 189–92, 202–4, 206–213, 253–254; parodies and imitations 110–111
Holmes, Stuart 54–55, 80, 153, 215
Holt, George 61, 220
Holt, Jack 31, 33, 56, 128
Homlock Shermes 111

The Honeymooning Detective 111
The Honorable Member for Outside Life 111
The Hope Diamond Mystery 111
Hopson, Violet 227–228, 236
Hopwood, Avery 23
Horler, Sidney 111
Horne, James W. 50, 75, 90, 94, 134, 150, 159, 194, 211
The Hornet's Nest 111
Hornung, E.W. 22, 90, 170, 187, 211, 256
Horton, Edward Everett 216
Houdini, Harry 102, 111, 133, 136–137, 216
The Hound of the Baskervilles 9, 23, 111–112
An Hour Before Dawn 112
The House of Fear 19, 105, 112
The House of Hate 112–113, 261
The House of Marney 113, 255
The House of Mystery 113
House of Peril 114
The House of Whispers 114
The House on the Marsh 114
The House Without a Key 114
Housman, Arthur 238, 241
How Sir Andrew Lost His Vote 114, 253
Howe, Betty 12, 33
Howell, Dorothy 12
Howell, Hazel 27
Hoyt, Arthur 58, 108
Hoyt, Harry O. 103, 185, 191, 243
Hugo, Victor 3, 28, 118, 142–143, 256
Hulette, Gladys 5, 56, 167, 198, 230
Hume, Benita 50
Hume, Fergus 99, 151–152, 256
Hume, Marjorie 200, 206
Humphrey, Willliam 88, 103, 142, 168
Humphreys, Cecil 88, 114, 245
Hunt, Jay 31, 97, 205
Hunter, Edna 118, 213
Huntly, Fred 49, 237
Hurst, Paul 50, 68, 90, 94, 150, 211
Hutchison, Charles 161, 179–180, 227
Hutter, Richard 89, 93, 107, 122, 186, 243
Hyams, Leila 11, 243
Hyland, Peggy 20, 22, 237
The Hypnotic Detective 114

I Will 114
The Iced Bullet 114–115
The Illustrious Prince 115, 259
In Old Tennessee 115
In the Grip of Spies 115
In the Hollow of Her Hand 115
In the Phantom's Den 181
Ince, John 32, 34, 99, 140, 192
Ince, Thomas H. 34, 114, 120, 252
Ingleton, E. Magnus 11, 131, 198
Ingraham, Harrish 141
Ingraham, Lloyd 14, 144
Inscrutable Drew 51–52, 56, 116, 127, 146, 192

Inscrutable Drew, Investigator 116
The Inspirations of Harry Larrabee 116
An Insurance Fraud 7, 116
An Invincible Sleuth 116
The Invisible Web 116
Irma Vep 231–232
The Iron Claw 116
The Iron Man 116
Irving, George 34, 187, 235
The Island of Intrigue 116–117, 260
Isono, Akio 3
The Italian Sherlock Holmes 110, 117
Ito, Daisuke 3
The Ivory Snuff Box 77, 117, 257
Iwata Yukichi 3
Izzy the Detective 117

Jackson, Frederick 65, 83, 117, 122, 256–257
Jacques, Norbert 72, 131, 257
The Jade Box 117, 257
Die Jagd nach der Hundertpfund-note 117
Jalovec, Alois 7
Jane's Sleuth 117
Der Januskopf 70, 117
Jasset, Victorin 10, 22–23, 50, 65, 75, 77–78, 84, 103, 150, 164, 166, 210, 247
Javert, Inspector 118, 142
The Jazz Girl 118
Jeaves, Allan 40
Jencikova, Hana 7
Jennings, DeWitt 10, 202, 218, 241
Le Jeunesse de Vidocq 118
The Jewel Thieves Run to Earth by Sexton Blake 118, 200
Jimmy Dale Alias the Grey Seal 118
Joe Jenkins, Detektiv 57, 118, 181
Johnson, Adrian 56, 185, 194, 219
Johnson, Arthur V. 214
Johnson, Calder 136
Johnson, Edith 152
Johnson, Emory 98
Johnson, Molly 75, 152
Johnson, Teft 6
Johnson, Wallace 197
Jonasson, Frank 94, 150
Jones, Dick 101
Jones, Edgar 103, 127
Jones, Fred C. 244
Jones, Grover 75, 172
Jones, Marc Edmund 56
Jones, Morgan 162
Jones, Richard 208
Jose, Edward 50, 116, 197, 239
Joy, Leatrice 3, 193
Joyce, Alice 104, 132, 158, 191, 196, 263
Judex 118–119, 166
Julian, Rupert 125, 140, 151, 178, 223
Just for Tonight 119
Juve 119, 249
Juve contre Fantômas 119, 249

Index

Kaiser-Heyl, Willy 112
Kaiser-Titz, Erich 178
The Kaiser's Spy 119, 200
Der Kampf mit dem Sturmvogel 120
Karamaneh 90, 120
Karloff, Boris 69, 97, 111
Karr, Darwin 42, 44, 64, 85, 157
Katchem Kate 120
Kaufman, Joseph 127, 246
Kay, Philip 39, 98, 119, 155
Keaton, Buster 204, 267
Keefe, Zena 176, 184
Kellard, Ralph 204–205
Keller, Gertrude 50
Kellino, W.P. 14, 102
Kelly, Anthony P. 187
Kelly, Dorothy 133, 144, 169
Kelly, Jack 89
Kelly, Mabel 139
Kelly, Phil 148, 159
Kelsey, Fred 75, 97, 121, 206
Kennedy, Craig 120, 163, 249, 261
The Kensington Mystery 120, 168
Kent, Charles 67, 142
Kent, Cranford 4
Kent, Cromwell 88
Kent, Henry 114
Kent, Larry 104
Kent, Stuart 53
Kenyon, Doris 22, 93, 107
Keppens, Emile 47, 133
Kerr, Robert P. 14
Kerrigan, Warren 42, 101, 114, 166, 216, 218
Kerry, Norman 4, 93, 178, 184
The Kid and the Sleuth 120
King, Burton 133, 136, 200
King, Henry 24, 68, 106, 169, 252
King, Joe 104, 131, 197
King, Mollie 155, 215
The King of Detectives 120
King, the Detective 120–121
King, the Detective 120–121
King, the Detective and the Opium Smugglers 121
King, the Detective in Formula 879 121
King, the Detective in the Jarvis Case 121
King, the Detective in the Marine Mystery 121
Kinkaid, Gambler 121
Kirby, Kate 47, 112, 122, 182
Kirby, Ollie 50, 150, 154, 175, 194, 224
Kirkwood, James 87, 141, 198
Kishin Yuri keiji 122
Klein-Rogge, Rudolf 72, 236
Die König Macombe 122
Kortner, Fritz 236
Krauss, Charles 47, 146, 247
Kri Kri 51, 116
Kühne, Friedrich 108, 112
Kummer, Frederick Arnold 5–7, 77, 101, 111, 117, 167, 246, 257

La Badie, Florence 20, 70, 79, 96, 141, 146, 156, 161, 245, 258
Lackteen, Frank 29, 86, 101
Ladies Beware 122, 257
Lady Audley's Secret 122–123, 251-2
Lady Baffles and Detective Duck 65, 123
Lady Candale's Diamonds 123, 200
Lady Raffles 123
Lake, Alice 32, 110
La Marr, Barbara 186
Landa, Max 59, 92–93, 169–170, 198, 238
Landon, Herman 237, 257
Lane, Adele 57, 64
Lang, Fritz 72, 107, 131, 257
Lang, Walter 42, 97, 145
La Plante, Laura 44–45, 56, 77
Larkin, George 150, 154, 175, 194, 221, 224, 226
Larsen, Viggo 18, 202, 204
The Last Adventures of Sherlock Holmes 123
The Last Call 123, 163
The Last Hour 123, 249
The Last of the Mafia 124
The Last Witness 124, 250
Laurel, Stan 68–69, 208
The Lavender Bath Lady 124, 252
Lawful Cheaters 124
Lawrence, Edmund 126, 185
Lawrence, Florence 194
The Law's Lash 73, 124
Leave It to Me 124
The Leavenworth Case 124–125
Leblanc, Maurice 17–18, 257
Lecoq, Monsieur 10, 81, 125, 146, 254
Lee, Carey 81
Lee, Catherine 124
Lee, Christopher 69
Lee, Lila 30, 141, 217
Lee, Robert N. 12
Lee, Roland V. 150
Leigh, Frank 126, 169, 179
Leithoff, Eberhard 3
Leonard, Marion 37, 59, 194
Leonard, Robert 136, 206
The Leopard Lady 125
Le Queux, William 210, 257
Leroux, Gaston 22, 47, 149, 159–160, 172, 177–178, 195, 243, 257–258
Le Saint, Edward J. 40, 49, 106, 129, 220, 237
Leslie, Gladys 103
Leslie, Rolf 9, 38, 110, 120, 152-3, 156, 166, 190, 224-5, 246
Lessey, George 48, 97, 106, 154–9, 169, 213, 232
Levering, George 85, 126, 131
Le Vino, Albert S. 36, 144, 230
Lewis, Ben 223
Lewis, Frederick 112
Lewis, Ralph 21, 77
Lewis, Sheldon 9, 71, 79, 107, 112, 116, 138
Lewis, Walter 39, 241
Lewis, Willard 106
Liebel, André 247
Liedtke, Harry 59, 189
Life Mask 125, 264
Life of Charles Peace 46, 125–126
Life or Honor? 126
Life's Whirlpool 126
Lincoln, Abraham 221
Lincoln, Elmo 118, 186, 260
Linder, Max 242
Lindsay, James 13, 194
The Line-Up at Police Headquarters 126
Lingham, Anna 94
Lingham, Thomas 9, 150
The Lion Man 126
The Lion's Mouse 126, 264
Listen Lester 126
Little, Anna 29, 100, 156
The Little Detective 127
Living Lies 127
The Livingston Case 127
Lloyd, Frank 143, 234
The Locked Door 116, 127
Lockwood, Harold 179
The Lodger 127, 258
Logue, Charles 14, 47, 112, 119, 136, 221, 230, 239
London After Midnight 127
The Lone Wolf 11–12, 81, 127–129, 262–263
The Lone Wolf 128
The Lone Wolf Returns 128
The Lone Wolf's Daughter 128
Lonergan, Lloyd 141, 149, 161, 163, 203, 244, 248
Loot 129
Lord John's Journal 129
Lorraine, Harry 54, 62, 90, 105, 136, 200, 212, 219
Lorraine, Lillian 162
Lorraine, Louise 35, 67, 117, 201, 233
Losee, Frank 76, 144
Lost at Sea 129–130
Love, Bessie 4, 5, 157
The Love Flower 130
Love Letters 41, 124, 130, 196
Love Without Question 130–131
Lovely, Louise 190, 221
Love's Prisoner 131
Lowe, Edmund 30, 37, 45, 91, 123, 127, 149, 163, 211, 230, 243
Lowndes, Marie Belloc 114, 127, 258
Lucas, Wilfred 4, 41, 138
Lucille Love, Girl of Mystery 131
Lugosi, Bela 117
Lupin, Arsène 17–18, 77, 131, 190, 215–216, 235, 257
Lupin the Gentleman Burglar 131
Luring Lips 131
Luring Shadows 131
Lyon, Ben 176
Lyons, Eddie 40, 63, 75, 147
Lyons, Harry Agar 51, 53, 57, 69, 84, 90, 120, 185, 196, 205, 207, 209, 238
Lyson, H. Agary 51
Lytell, Bert 11, 32–33, 36, 78, 128, 201, 230, 251
Lyton, Phyllis 9

Index

Mabuse, Dr. 72, 131–132, 257
A Macaroni Sleuth 132
MacDonald, Donald 12
MacDonald, J. Farrell 154
MacDonald, Katherine 149
MacDonald, Sherwood 189, 214
MacDonald, Wallace 89, 205, 240
Mace, Fred 19, 24, 45, 86, 208–9, 212, 217, 225
MacGrath, Harold 7, 8, 141, 155–158, 160, 166, 179, 234, 248, 258
MacHarg, William 33, 183, 258
Mack, Hughie 156, 201, 208
Mack, Madelyn 132, 191, 263
MacKenzie, Donald 44, 62, 64, 176, 200, 205
MacQuarrie, George 49, 85, 130
The Mad Doctor 132
Madame Sphinx 132
Madison, Cleo 100, 160, 226
A Madonna of the Cells 132, 220
The Maelstrom 132–133, 254
Maffie, Attilo 247
Mailes, Charles Hill 154, 221
Main de fer 133
Main de fer contre la Bande aux Gant Blancs 133
Majeroni, George 101, 239
Maloney, Leo J. 67, 86, 94
The Man Behind the Curtain 133
The Man from Beyond 133
The Man from Nowhere 133–134
The Man from Painted Post 134
The Man Hunt 134
The Man in the Blue Spectacles 232
The Man on Watch 134
The Man Who Bought London 134
The Man Who Changed His Name 134
The Man Who Vanished 134
The Man with the Twisted Lip 9, 134–135
A Manhattan Knight 135
Der Mann im Keller 135
Mannock, Patrick 59, 123, 188
Marion, Frances 49, 220
Marion, Frank 14
The Mark of Cain 135
The Mark of the Frog 135
Markey, Enid 165
Marriott, Moore 9, 52
Marsh, Mae 80
Marsh, Marguerite 43, 81, 126, 136, 243
Marshall, George 9
Marshall, Tully 11, 47, 65, 176
Marshall, William 178
Marston, Lawrence 79, 142, 185
Marston, Theodore 20, 30, 94, 144, 147, 239
Martin, E.A. 158
Martin, Hal 4
Martindell, Edward 247
Martinek, H.O. 50, 73–4, 115, 157, 219
Martinek, Ivy 73, 219
Martini, Elsa 120
Martyn, Wyndam 166, 207, 211, 225, 258

Masakuni, Hiroshi 3
La Maschera che sanguina 135
Mason, A.E.W. 20, 103, 196, 243, 258
Mason, Gladys 15
Mason, Haddon 245
Mason, Julia 31
Mason, LeRoy 21
Mason, Noel 124, 169
Mason, Shirley 99
The Master Cracksman 135
The Master Crook 136
The Master Crook Outwitted by a Child 136
The Master Crook Turns Detective 136
Master Cupid, Detective 136
The Mastery Key 136
The Master Mystery 111, 136–137, 261
The Master Rogue 137
The Master Rogues of Europe 137
Mathews, Harry C. 22, 145
Mathis, June 37, 80, 109
Maude, Arthur 51, 88, 192, 194
Maudru, Charles 15, 183
Maupain, Ernest 38, 203
Max, Gaston 137, 261
May, Doris 40
May, Joe 19, 59, 68, 92–3, 107, 122, 135, 186, 243
May, Mia 89, 93, 106–107, 122, 170, 186, 243
Mayne, Eric 25, 145, 174, 207
Mayo, Edna 186, 212–213
The Mazarin Stone 123, 137
McAllister, Mary 4, 141
McAllister, Ruth 101
McAvoy, May 24, 45, 102, 216
McCoy, Gertrude 15, 37, 67, 106, 154–5, 158, 160, 232
McCullough, Philo 42, 77, 99
McDermott, Marc 15, 21, 45, 60, 114, 146, 154, 218
McDowell, Claire 43, 65, 186
McGlynn, Frank 16, 64
McGrail, Walter 31, 45, 179
McGuirk, the Sleuth 137–138
McIntosh, Blanche 15
McIntosh, Burr 101, 163
McIntyre, John Thomas 9, 19, 112, 138, 259
McRae, Duncan 73
McRae, Henry 4, 145
Medicine Bend 138
Meighan, Thomas 31, 49, 50, 52, 142, 184
Melchior, George 81, 83, 84, 119, 147
Melford, George 64, 137, 240
Melody of Death 138, 263
Melting Millions 138
The Menace of the Mute 19, 138
Meredyth, Bess 160, 242
Mereille, Claude 15
Mersereau, Violet 7, 94, 214
Metcalfe, Earl 177, 231, 239
The Metzer Murder Mystery 118, 138
Michelena, Beatriz 245

Mickey the Detective 138
The Microscope Mystery 138
A Midget Sherlock Holmes 110, 138
The Midnight Ace 138–139
A Midnight Adventure 139
Midnight Faces 139
Midnight Life 139
Midnight Madness 139–140, 223
The Midnight Man 140
Midnight Shadows 140
The Midnight Summons 90, 140
Midnight Thieves 140
Midnight Trail 140–141
Midnight Watch 141
Mierendorff, Hans 3, 17, 89, 93, 107–8, 122, 170, 186, 243
Mike Donegal's Escape 94
Milestone, Lewis 231
Millarde, Harry 104, 191, 241
Miller, Ashley 19, 156
Miller, J. Clarkson 45, 119, 181, 195
Miller, Patsy Ruth 38, 92, 96, 243
Miller, Walter 29, 81, 94, 101, 114, 138, 150–1, 215–6, 237
Millhauser, Bertram 31, 84, 112, 163, 180, 194, 232
The Million Dollar Mystery 141, 160, 248, 258
Million Dollar Robbery 141
Millionaire Baby 141–142, 255
Mills, Evelyn 11
Mills, Martin 59
Mills, Thomas 76, 94
Minter, Mary Miles 14, 24
The Miracle 142, 153
The Miracle Man 142, 260
Les Misérables 3, 28, 118, 142–143
Miss Cayley's Adventures 249
Miss Clever 60–1, 92, 103, 120, 143
Miss Nobody 143–144
Miss Raffles 144
Miss Sherlock Holmes 110, 144
Missing Daughters 144
The Missing Links 144
Missing Millions 144
The Missing Three Quarter 144
Mr. Bumptious, Detective 144
Mr. Hoops, the Detective 144
Mr. Justice Raffles 144–145, 187
Mr. Wise, Investigator 145
Mitchell, Rhea 36, 105, 230
Mizoguchi, Kenji 34, 77
A Modern Jekyll and Hyde 70, 145
A Modern Sherlock 110, 145
Moffett, Cleveland 220, 259
Moise, Alfred (aka Alfred Moses) 3, 34, 43, 56–57, 68, 78, 85, 96, 109, 123, 137, 144, 160, 207, 211, 220
Mondos, Joseph 10, 117, 146
The Money Corral 145
Money Madness 145
Money to Burn 145
Mong, William V. 131, 179
The Monogrammed Cigarette 145
Monsieur Lecoq 125, 146, 154, 219, 254
Monsieur Lecoq 146
The Monster 146

Montagne, Edward J. 16, 133, 151, 198, 239
Montford, Ivy 50, 115, 157
Moody, Harry 89, 221
The Moon Diamond 116, 146
The Moonstone 17, 30, 56, 146–147, 186, 252
Moore, Colleen 220
Moore, Matt 26–27, 38, 151, 224
Moore, Owen 28, 194, 214
Moore, Tom 42, 76, 104, 119, 153, 174
Moran, Lee 63, 132, 147
Moreno, Antonio 51, 86, 112, 135, 161, 168, 197, 214, 233
Morey, Harry 88
Morgan, George 154, 221
Morgan, Sidney 27, 40, 239
Moroso, John A. 49, 104, 131, 185, 232, 259
Morris, Chester 13, 31, 251
Morris, Gouverneur 3
Morris, Margaret 116, 135
Morris, Reggie 65, 109
Morris, William 146
Morrison, Albert 245
Morrison, Arthur 111, 236
Morrison, James 6, 12, 126, 134, 144, 169, 239
Le Mort qui tue 82, 147, 249
Mortimer, Edmund 11, 79
Mortmain 147, 262
Moscow After Dark 147
Moyse, M. 6, 26, 148, 152, 190, 206, 210, 212
Mrs. Balfame 147
Mrs. Plum's Pudding 63, 147
Mulhall, Jack 37, 154, 220
Mullin, Eugene 142, 168
A Murder in Limehouse 7, 147
Murder Scene from King of the Detectives 148
The Murders in the Rue Morgue 76, 148, 203, 260
Murphy, Edna 82, 139
Murray, Charles 101, 108
Murray, Mae 228
The Musgrave Ritual 90, 148, 202
Musidora 119, 166, 231–232
My Lady Incog 148
My Lady Raffles 123, 148–149, 159
My Lady's Garter 149, 254
My Lady's Latchneur 149, 264
Myers, Carmel 58, 123
Le Mystère de la chambre jaune 149, 159–60, 172, 195, 257
Le Mystère de la tour Eiffel 149
Le Mystère de la villa Mortain 149
Le Mystère du lit blanc 149–150, 166
Le Mystère du phare d'Armor 150
Les Mystères de Paris 150, 198
Mysteries of Fu Manchu 42, 53–4, 96, 102, 120, 140
The Mysteries of the Grand Hotel 75, 134, 150
The Mysterious Airman 150, 261
The Mysterious Dr. Fu Manchu 150
Mysterious Goods 150–151

The Mysterious Mr. Browning 151
The Mysterious Mr. Tiller 151, 223
The Mysterious Pearl 151
The Mystery Club 151, 261
The Mystery Mind 151, 261
The Mystery of a Hansom Cab 99, 151–1522, 256
The Mystery of a Taxicab 152
A Mystery of Boscombe Vale 152
The Mystery of Brayton Court 152
The Mystery of Brudenell Court 152, 168
The Mystery of Carter Breene 152
The Mystery of Castle Richmond 92, 143
The Mystery of Dead Man's Isle 152
The Mystery of Dr. Fu Manchu 152–153
The Mystery of Dogstooth Cliff 153, 168
The Mystery of Eagle's Cliff 153
The Mystery of Edwin Drood 153, 253
The Mystery of Grandfather's Clock 153
The Mystery of Grayson Hall 153
The Mystery of Green Park 153
The Mystery of Henri Villard 153–154
The Mystery of Hill Street 160
The Mystery of Mr. Bernard Brown 154, 259
The Mystery of Orcival 10, 125, 154
The Mystery of Richmond Castle 154
The Mystery of Room 13 154
The Mystery of Room 422 154
The Mystery of Room 643 154
The Mystery of the Amsterdam Diamonds 48, 154
The Mystery of the Brass Bound Chest 154
The Mystery of the Bride in White 154
The Mystery of the Burning Freight 58, 154–155
The Mystery of the Counterfeit Tickets 155, 188
The Mystery of the Diamond Belt 155, 200
The Mystery of the Double Cross 66, 155, 254
The Mystery of the Dover Express 48, 155
The Mystery of the Dutch Cheese Maker 155, 248
The Mystery of the Empty Room 155
The Mystery of the Fadeless Tints 48, 156
The Mystery of the Glass Tubes 48, 156
The Mystery of the Haunted Hotel 83, 156
The Mystery of the Haunted House 156
The Mystery of the Hidden House 156
The Mystery of the Hindu Image 156

The Mystery of the House 156
The Mystery of the Jewel Casket 156
The Mystery of the Khaki Tunic 156, 168
The Mystery of the Ladder of Light 48, 156
The Mystery of the Laughing Death 48, 156
The Mystery of the Leaping Fish 111, 156–157
The Mystery of the Locked Room 157
The Mystery of the Lost Cat 41, 157
The Mystery of the Lost Ships 157, 248
The Mystery of the Lost Stradivarius 48, 157
The Mystery of the Man Who Slept 157
The Mystery of the McWinter Family 157, 248
The Mystery of the Milk 157
A Mystery of the Mountains 157
The Mystery of the Octagonal Room 48, 157
The Mystery of the Old Mill 157
The Mystery of the Poison Pool 157–159
A Mystery of the Rails 158
The Mystery of the Sea View Hotel 158
The Mystery of the Sealed Art Gallery 48, 158
The Mystery of the Seven Chests 158
The Mystery of the Silent Death 158, 200
Mystery of the Silver Skull 158
The Mystery of the Silver Snare 48, 158
The Mystery of the Sleeper Trunk 158
The Mystery of the Sleeping Death 158
The Mystery of the Sleeping House 158
The Mystery of the Spotted Collar 158–159
The Mystery of the Stolen Child 159
The Mystery of the Stolen Jewels 159
The Mystery of the Talking Wire 48, 159
The Mystery of the Tapestry Room 159
The Mystery of the Tea Dansant 94, 159
The Mystery of the Thoroughbred 159
The Mystery of the Throne Room 159
The Mystery of the Torn Note 159
The Mystery of the White Car 149, 159
The Mystery of the Yellow Room 149, 159–60, 172, 195, 257
The Mystery of 13 160
The Mystery of 13 Hill Street 160
The Mystery of Thor Bridge 123, 160

A Mystery of Wall Street 160
The Mystery of West Sedgwick 160
The Mystery of Wickham Hall 160
The Mystery Road 160
The Mystery Solved 141, 160–161
The Mystic Hour 161
Myton, Fred 68, 121, 169, 185, 206

Nagel, Conrad 45, 95, 102, 127
Naldi, Nita 38, 71, 133
Nameless Men 161
Nares, Owen 13, 249
Nat Pinkerton 1, 48, 161–1622, 172, 179
The Naval Treaty 90, 162
Navarre, René 47, 62, 81, 83, 84, 119, 147, 166, 170, 227, 249
Neal of the Navy 162, 260
Neil, Richard 44, 68, 109, 157
Neill, R. William 22, 30, 130
Ne Moyer, Frances 84
Nesbitt, Miriam 5, 45, 146
The Net 162–163
Neuss, Alwin 70, 111, 202
The New Adventures of J. Rufus Wallingford 163, 216, 235
The New Adventures of Terence O'Rourke 163
The New Exploits of Elaine 163
Nick Carter 1, 10, 23, 43–44, 50, 68, 77–78, 103, 163–4, 166, 179, 210–1, 230, 247, 252–3, 266–7
Nick Carter 163
Nick Carter acrobat 163–164
Nick Carter, le roi des détectives 164
Nick Winter 23, 36, 51, 75, 78, 159, 164–5, 179, 197, 210, 242–3
Nick Winter et le courrier diplomatique 164
Nick Winter et le rapt de Mlle Werner 164, 242
Nick Winter et ses aventures 164
Nick Winter la voleuse et la sonnambule 164, 242
Nick Winter l'adroit détective 164
Nick Winter plus fort que Sherlock Holmes 165, 242
Nikola, Dr. 27, 72, 165, 250–251
Nilsson, Anna Q. 47, 77, 169, 199, 239
The No-Good Guy 165
The Noble Bachelor 9, 165
Nobody 165
North, Harry J. 15
North, Wilfred 158, 209
Northcote, Sydney 62
The Northern Mystery 165–166, 168
Northrup, Harry S. 80, 241
Norwood, Eille 3, 26, 34–35, 40, 43–44, 46, 56–57, 77–78, 96, 109–110, 165–166, 189–191, 196–197, 206–209, 211, 220–221
The Norwood Builder 90, 166
Not Guilty 166
Les Nouveaux Exploits de Nick Carter 166
La Nouvelle Aurore 47, 166
La Nouvelle Mission de Judex 166
Novak, Eva 35, 126, 144, 235

Novak, Jane 61, 89, 97, 130, 145
Novello, Ivor 127
Novotny, Joe 7
Novotny, Vladimir 7
Nugent, J.C. 13
Number 99 166
Nye, Carroll 95, 176, 192

O. Henry 256
The Oakdale Affair 167
Oathbound 167
Octavius, Amateur Detective 167
Odette, Mary 55, 67, 126
Officer 174 167
Officer 444 167
Ogle, Charles 5, 114, 159, 239
Oland, Warner 52, 74, 84, 150, 214, 228
Olcott, Sidney 14, 148, 154
The Old Man in the Corner 9, 38, 110, 120, 152–153, 156, 165–168, 190, 224–5, 246, 259
Old Sleuth, the Detective 168
O'Moore, Barry 6, 7
On Her Wedding Night 168
On the Pupil of His Eye 46, 168–169
Ondra, Anny 181
One Chance in a Million 169
One Exciting Night 169
One Hour Before Dawn 169
One Hour Past Midnight 169
The $1,000,000 Reward 169
One Million Dollars 169
One Million in Jewels 169
Der Onyxknopf 59, 169–170
The Open Door 170
Die Ophir, die Stadt der Vergangenheit 122, 170
Oppenheim, E. Phillips 15, 29, 49, 52, 58, 79, 87, 91, 96–97, 115, 154, 156, 160, 179, 217, 246
Orczy, Baroness 9, 38, 110, 120, 152–153, 156, 166–167, 190, 224–225, 246, 259
O'Rourke, Terence 90, 163, 182, 216
Orth, Marion 42, 51, 58, 175
Osborne, Jefferson 127
Osborne, Marjorie 34
Osborne, William Hamilton 34, 45, 103, 105, 162, 195, 260
Ostrander, Isabel 117, 214, 260
Ostriche, Muriel 14, 42, 147
Oswald, Richard 112, 230
The Other Half of the Note 170
Otto, the Sleuth 170
La Oubliette 62, 170
Out of the Shadow 170
The Outsider 171, 263
Owen, Cecil 94
Owen, Louise 41
Owen, Seena 80, 125
Owens, Raymond 80

Packard, Frank L. 12, 57, 89, 118, 138, 142, 194, 260
The Page Mystery 171
Die Pagode 171
The Paliser Case 171

Pallette, Eugene 11, 214, 217, 240
Panama n'est pas Paris 171
Pangborn, Franklin 86
Panzer, Paul 112–113, 151, 176, 192
Das Panzergewölbe 172, 238
Le Parfum de la dame en noir 172, 195
Parke, William 52, 56, 155, 171
Parker, William 106, 145
Partners in Crime 172
Partners of the Night 172
Der Passagier in der Zwangsjacke 163, 172
The Passing of Mr. Quinn 172–1733
Pastrone, Giovanni 213
Paths of Paradise 173
Paton, Stuart 28, 88, 98, 111, 234, 236
Patria 173
Paul, Fred 42, 51, 53–4, 57, 72, 84, 90, 96, 102, 114, 120, 124, 132, 140, 142, 188
Paul Sleuth 174, 198, 208, 262
Paul Sleuth and the Mystic Seven 174
Paul Sleuth Crime Investigator: The Burglary Syndicate 174
Paul Sleuth: The Murder of Squire Jeffrey 174
Paul Sleuth: The Mystery of the Astorian Crown Prince 174
Pawned 174, 260
Payne, Douglas 75, 90, 189
The Peacock Fan 174
Pearl as a Detective 174
Pearson, Virginia 27, 178, 185, 219
The Peddler of Lies 175, 261
Peggy Does Her Darndest 175
Pelisek, Frantisek 7
The Pell Street Mystery 175
Pellie, Dr. Brian 69, 175
The People vs. Nancy Preston 68, 175, 259
Percy, Eileen 27, 41, 124, 134, 144
Le Père Goriot 175–176, 250
The Perfect Crime 176, 264
The Perfect Sap 176
Perfitt, Frank 110, 245
The Perils of Our Girl Reporters 176–177
The Perils of Pauline 176
Perils of the Rail 177
Perley, Charles 154, 244
Perret, Leonce 78, 133
Perrin, Jack 58, 117, 126, 139
Perrins, Leslie 3251, 206
Perry, Frederick 81, 187
Peter the Great 73, 205
Peters, House 47, 112, 122, 182, 187
Petrosino, Joseph 8
Petrova, Olga 125
A Petticoat Detective 177
The Phantom Buccaneer 16, 177, 252
Das Phantom der Opera 177
Phantom House 160
Phantom Husband 151
Phantom Image 56
Phantom Mandarin 225

Phantom Melody 105
The Phantom of the Opera 177–178, 181, 257–258
Phantom Rider 104
Phantom Shadow 83
The Phantom Shotgun 178
The Phantom Sword 83
Phantomas 178–179
Philips, Austin 4
Phillips, Augustus 160, 167, 175, 230
Phillips, Dorothy 87, 157
Pickford, Jack 23, 76
Pickford, Lottie 66
Le Pickpocket mystifié 179
Pidgeon, Walter 76, 97
Pidgin, Charles Felton 186, 260
Pidgin Island 179, 258
Piel, Harry 23, 59, 68
Pike, William 44, 246
Pilgrims of the Night 179, 259
Pimple 179, 201
Pimple, Detective 179
Pimple's Crime 179
Pinkerton, Nat 1, 48, 161–162, 172, 179
The Pinkerton Man 179
Pirates of the Sky 179–180
Pitts, ZaSu 88
A Plain Clothes Man 180
The Pleasure Buyers 180, 261
Plunder 98, 180
Plympton, George H. 12, 33
Poe, Edgar Allan 21, 76, 148, 158, 203, 233, 260
The Pointing Finger 180, 249
Poison 180
The Poison Pen 180–181
The Poisoned Light 181
Der Pokal der Fürstein 118, 181
Poland, Joseph Franklin 14, 90
Police Reporter 181
Polito, Sol 11
La Poliziotta 181
The Polly Girl Scout 181–182
Polly the Girl Scout 181
Polly the Girl Scout and Grandpa's Medals 181–182
Polly the Girl Scout and the Jewel Thieves 182
Polly the Girl Scout's Timely Aid 182
Polo, Eddie 39, 97–98, 145
Ponson Du Terrail, Pierre Alexis 183, 192–193, 260
Ponsonby, Prudence 188
The Pool of Flame 182, 216
The Poppy Girl's Husband 31, 182
The Port of Doom 122, 182
Porter, Edwin S. 93, 127, 144, 203
Potts Bungles Again 63, 182
Poucette ou le plus jeune détective du monde 182
Powell, David 53, 58, 144, 160, 215
Powell, Paul 4, 26, 56, 58, 88, 138, 160
The Power God 182–183
Les Premières Armes de Rocambole 183

Pretty, Arline 107, 223, 244
Prevost, Marie 108, 190, 208, 249
Price, Herbert C. 53
Price, Kate 62, 99, 159, 208
The Price of a Party 183
The Price of Fear 183
The Price of Silence 20, 183
Prichard, Hesketh 73–74, 260
Prichard, Kate 74
Prior, Herbert 4, 32, 44, 166, 214
The Priory School 9, 183–184
Prisco, Albert 4
Proxies 184, 249
Pudd'nhead Wilson 184
The Purple Cipher 184
The Purple Mask 184

The Quarry 49, 185, 259
Queen o' Diamonds 185
The Queen of Hearts 185
Queen of the London Counterfeiters 185
The Quest of the Sacred Jewel 146, 185–186
Quincy Adams Sawyer 186
Quincy Adams Sawyer 186, 260
Quirk, Billy 27–28, 41–42, 44, 157

Der Rabbi von Kuan-Fu 107, 186
A Race with Rogues 186
Die Rache der Maud Fergusson 186
Radford, Tom 7, 32, 116, 147, 238
The Radio Detective 120, 186–187
Raffles 131, 144–145, 187, 190, 192, 204, 211, 249, 251, 256
Raffles 187
Raffles, the Amateur Cracksman 187–188, 256
Ragan in Ruins 188, 220
A Railroad Conspiracy 188
The Railroad Detective 58, 188, 239
The Railroad Detective's Dilemma 188
The Railroad Inspector's Peril 188
A Railroad Lochinvar 188
The Railroad Raiders 155, 188
Ralson, Esther 33
Ranger 73
A Rank Outsider 188, 255
Raskolnikov 188–189
Rasp, Fritz 112, 237
Ratcliffe, E.J. 15
Das Rätselhafte Inserat 59, 189
Rawlinson, Herbert 15, 28–29, 43, 58, 99–100, 140, 156, 212, 228, 235
Ray, Albert 218, 241
Ray, Allene 101, 114
Ray, Charles 34, 91, 233
Raymond, Charles 39, 54, 73–4, 98, 100, 119, 155, 200, 212, 219
Raynham, Fred 32, 51, 79, 85, 100
Das Recht auf das Dasein 189
Red Aces 189–190, 263
The Red Circle 90, 189
The Red Glove 189–190
The Red-Headed League 9, 190
Red Lights 190
The Red Mouse 103, 190, 260

La redenzione di Raffles 131, 187, 190
Reed, Barney 6
Reed, Donald 135
Reed, Enid R. 138
Reed, Florence 19, 245
Reed, Julian 167
Reed, Katherine S. 94
Reed, Luther 93
The Reed Case 190
Reeder, Mr. J.G. 189–90, 263
Reeve, Arthur B. 43, 79, 107, 112, 120, 136, 150–151, 169, 181, 186, 221, 260–261
The Regent's Park Mystery 168, 190
Reicher, Ernst 25, 92–93, 135, 171–172, 184, 215, 224, 238
Reicher, Frank 25, 184, 215
Reid, Wallace 65, 246
The Reigate Squires 90, 190–191, 202
Rescued by Rover 73, 191
The Resident Patient 9, 191
The Return of Boston Blackie 31, 191
Rex, Bert 54, 200, 212, 219
Rhodes, Billie 211
Rice, Elmer 88
Rich, Lillian 68, 88, 97, 240
Rickshaw, the Detective 191
The Riddle of the Green Umbrella 132, 191, 263
The Riddle of the Tin Soldier 132, 191, 263
Ridgeley, Cleo 94, 159, 246
Ridgely, Richard 44, 60, 161
Ridgewell, George 3, 15, 30, 34–5, 40, 43, 46, 55–6, 58, 68, 78, 85, 90, 96, 207–8, 211
Rin-Tin-Tin 192, 241
Rinehart, Mary Roberts 4, 23, 38, 49, 261
The Ringer 191–192, 263
Rinty of the Desert 192, 241
Ritchie, Franklin 20, 85
Ritchie, Robert Welles 98, 154, 194, 224
A Rival Sherlock Holmes 111, 192
The River House Mystery 116, 192
Roach, Hal 68–69, 204, 208
The Road of Strife 192
Robbins, Marc 11
Roberts, Edith 40, 118, 131, 151, 174, 199, 215, 220
Robson, Andrew 246
Robson, Victor 96
Rocambole 15, 183, 192–193, 260
Roche, Arthur Somers 51, 85, 95, 98, 127, 129, 151, 180, 243, 261
Rock, Charles 210, 229
Rodwell, Stanley 53
The Rogue 193
A Rogue in Love 193
The Rogue Syndicate 193
Rogue Unmasked 100, 193
A Rogue with a Heart 193
Rogues and Romance 193
A Rogue's Defeat 118, 194
The Rogue's Heart 194

A Rogue's Nemesis 194
The Rogue's Nest 194
The Rogues of London 193
The Rogues of Paris 193
Rogues of the Turf 194
The Rogue's Pawn 98, 194
A Rogue's Romance 194
A Rogue's Wife 194
Rohmer, Sax 51, 53–54, 57, 69, 84, 90, 96, 120, 137, 142, 150, 185, 196, 205, 207, 261
Roland, Henry C. 261
Roland, Ruth 8, 9, 20–21, 94, 159, 189, 201, 214, 221
Rolfe, B.A. 15, 131
Romance of a Rogue 194
The Romance of Elaine 194–195
Romance of the Underworld 195
Rome, Stewart 55, 134, 172–173, 236
Roscoe, Albert 158, 171
Rose, Winifred 7, 32, 116, 147, 238
Rosenhayn, Paul 58, 92, 179
Rosmer, Milton 15, 96, 152
Ross, James B. 65, 104, 188
Rosson, Arthur 99, 247
Rouletabille, Joseph 160, 195, 257
Rouletabille chez les bohémiens 195
Rowland, Henry C. 50, 76, 175, 214, 261
Rubber Heels 195
The Rube Detective 195
Rubens, Alma 85, 132, 157
Rule, Beverly C. 116, 169
The Running Fight 195–196, 260
Running Water 196
Russell, William 12, 24, 35, 66, 95, 105–6, 124, 140, 156, 169, 223
Rutter, Louise 9, 138

The Sacred Order 84, 153, 196
The Sacred Ruby 196, 217
Sais, Marin 50, 90, 94, 137, 150, 194, 211
Sam Simpkins, Sleuth 196
Sambucini, Kally 247
Sauer, Fred 3, 92
Sawyer, Laura 44, 47, 112, 122, 182
Say It with Sables 196
Sazie, Leon 247
A Scandal in Bohemia 9, 110, 196
The Scarab Ring 196–197
Scardon, Paul 12, 16–17, 102, 133–134, 172
The Schemers 177, 197
Schlettow, Hans Adalbert 53, 215
Schrock, Raymond L. 4, 16, 132, 213
Schroth, Heinrich 20, 59, 68
Der Schwarze Diamant 143, 197
Scott, Betty 14
Scott, Gregory 59, 194, 226
Scott, LeRoy 172
Scott, Mansfield 252, 261–22
Scott, William 42, 106
The Scrap of Paper 197, 217
A Search for Evidence 197
Search, the Scientific Detective 197
Seay, Charles M. 5–7, 109, 167, 214, 238

Sebastian, Dorothy 247
The Second Stain 197
Le Secret d'Argeville 197
The Secret of the Hills 197–198
The Secret Seven 198
The Secrets of Paris 198
Secrets of the Night 198
Sedgewich, Eileen 67, 100, 186
Sedley, Henry 85, 91, 108, 123, 163, 211, 230
Sein beste Freund 198
Seitz, George B. 27, 31, 50, 62, 80, 84, 100, 112, 116, 163, 180, 193–4, 200, 205
Selva-Goebel, Fred 57, 143, 181
Semels, Harry 36, 193, 232
Sennett, Mack 19, 24, 45, 86, 108, 157, 194, 208–9, 212, 214, 217, 225, 228, 266, 268
Sergeant Lightning and the Gorgonzola Gang 198
Servenier, François 247
Seven Keys to Baldpate 198–199, 250
The Seven Pearls 199–200
Sexton Blake 32, 39, 90, 114, 118, 155, 200–201, 246, 250
Sexton Blake 200
Sexton Blake, Gambler 200
Sexton Pimple 201
Seymour, Madeleine 3, 114
Shadowed into the Underworld 201
Shadows of the Night 201
Shelby, Margaret 14
Shepley, Ruth 11
Sheridan, Frank 169, 232
Sherlock Ambrose 201
Sherlock Bonehead 201
The Sherlock Boob 201
Sherlock Boob, Detective 201
Sherlock Brown 201–202
Sherlock Hawkshaw and Company 202
Sherlock Holmes 5–7, 18, 25–26, 34–6, 40–4, 46, 77–78, 109–112, 144–45, 148, 165–66, 189–192, 196–197, 201–214, 220–21, 252–54
Sherlock Holmes 202–203
Sherlock Holmes and the Great Murder Mystery 203
Sherlock Holmes Baffled 110, 203
The Sherlock Holmes Girl 203
Sherlock Holmes Jr. 203
Sherlock Holmes Solves the Sign of the Four 203–204
Sherlock Holmes vs. Raffles 204
Sherlock, Jr. 204
Sherlock Sleuth 204
Sherry, J. Barney 87, 108, 115, 126, 187, 242
The Shielding Shadow 204–205
Shields, Ernest 39, 159, 184
Shirley, Dorinea 90, 120
The Shoes That Danced 205
Shorty and Sherlock Holmes 205
The Shrine of Seven Lamps 205
Sidney, Scott 51, 58, 60, 77, 91, 155
Siegmann, George 105, 227

The Sign of the Claw 205–206
The Sign of the Four 206
The Silent Command 206
The Silent Master 206
The Silk Lined Burglar 206
Silken Threads 206
Silver Blaze 206–207
The Silver Buddha 207
The Silver Car 207
Silver Fingers 207
Sims, George 32, 116, 147, 238, 262
The Sin That Was His 207
Sis the Detective 207–208
The Six Napoleons 208
Das Skelett des Hern Markutius 208
The Sleuth 208
Sleuth, Paul 208
Sleuthing 208
Sleuths 208
Sleuths and Slickers 208
Sleuths and Surprises 208
The Sleuths at the Floral Parade 208, 228
The Sleuths Last Stand 209
Sleuths Unawares 209
Slim Becomes a Detective 209
Sloman, Edward 123, 141, 179
Smalley, Phillips 111, 138, 174
Smetana, Josef 7
Smith, Charles H. 165
Smith, David 207
Smith, Dennis Nayland 42, 51, 53, 54, 57, 69, 84, 96, 102, 120, 140, 142, 150, 152, 196, 205, 209, 238
Smith, Frank 28, 213
Smith, Frank Berkeley 21
Smith, Frank Leon 36, 86, 101, 114
Smith, Frank W. 121
Smith, Hamilton 50, 65, 75, 94, 134, 150, 159, 233
Smith, Harry 31
Smith, James Bell 97, 145, 206
Smith, John P. 61
Smith, Noel Mason 124, 169
Smith, R. Cecil 87, 109
Smith, Ruth 241
Smith, Sebastian 34
Smith, Wallace 233
Smith, Whispering 138, 145, 209, 239–240, 262
Smithens, Bill 201
Sniffkins Detective and the Missing Cigarette Cards 209
Snow, Marguerite 70, 103, 141, 155–8, 244, 248
The Social Code 209
The Society Raffles 209
A Society Sherlock 209
The Solitary Cylist 209
Somerville, Roy 4, 22, 216
The Son of Wallingford 209–210
Le Songe de Nick Winter 210
Sonka the Golden Hand 210
The Sons of Satan 210
Le Sosie 210
Souvestre, Pierre 249
Spearman, Frank H. 138, 209, 239, 262

The Speckled Band 210–211
The Spirit of Evil 211
Sprigg, Stanhope 174, 208, 262
A Squeedunk Sherlock Holmes 211
Standing, Wyndham 126, 149, 170, 243
Stanley, George 61, 209
Stannard, Elliot 51, 53, 56, 67, 116, 123, 146, 152, 192
The Star Reporters 211
Starke, Pauline 11, 144, 176, 205
Stedman, Myrtle 30, 115, 215
Stepping Lively 210
Sterling, Ford 60
Stevens, George 152, 214
Stevenson, Robert Louis 50, 70–1, 92, 117, 145, 214, 230, 241, 262
Stewart, Anita 88, 194, 240–241
Stiles, Leslie 3
Stingaree 90, 211, 256
The Stockbroker's Clerk 211
Stockdale, Carl 140, 180
The Stolen Heirlooms 211–212
The Stolen Jewels 212
The Stolen Papers 212
The Stolen Plans or the Boy Detective 212
The Stolen Purse 212
Stolen Secrets 212
Stonehouse, Ruth 14, 16, 121, 136, 145
Storey, Edith 80, 142, 168
Storm, Jerome 37, 73, 157, 234
The Strange Case of Mary Page 212–213
Strong, Eugene 15
Stronger Than Sherlock 213
The Studio Murder Mystery 213–214, 254
A Study in Scarlet 213
The Substitute Jewel 150
Sue, Eugene 150, 198
The Suicide Club 50, 92, 166, 214, 230, 262
The Suitcase Mystery 214
Sullivan, C. Gardner 13, 22, 34, 115, 165, 182
The Sultana 214
Sureluck Jones 214
Susie the Sleuth 214
Suspense 214–215
Sutherland, Eddie 145
Sutton, Charles 37, 44, 159–160
Suzanne Marwille, Detective 215
Swayne, Marian 84, 126
Sweet, Blanche 21, 50, 95, 186
Syd, the Bum Detective 215
Sydney, Aurele 15, 102, 228–229
Sylvia of the Secret Service 215
Sze, Henry 89, 93, 122, 170, 186, 243

Talbot, Rowland 181–182, 193
Talmadge, Constance 26, 138, 144, 233
Tamburin und Castagnetten 215
Tangled Lives 215
Tashman, Lilyan 123, 240
The Taxi Mystery 215

Taylor, Alma 15, 112–113, 259
Taylor, Ray 4, 21, 117, 240
Taylor, Rex 183, 209, 212
Taylor, Tom 28, 61, 221
Taylor, Wilton 11, 169, 217, 262
The Teeth of the Tiger 215–216
Tellegen, Lou 35, 233
Tempest, Marie 147
Tennant, Frank 194, 239
Tennyson, Walter 9
Terence O'Rourke, Gentleman Adventurer 216
Terhune, Albert Payson 56
The Terrible People 216
Terriss, Tom 85, 153
The Terror 216
Terror Island 216–217
Terry, Ethel Grey 16–17, 44, 119, 160, 167, 232
The Test of Honor 216
Tex, Elucidator of Mysteries 39, 49, 113, 196–197, 217, 224–226, 230, 235
Tex, Elucidator of Mysteries 217
Theby, Rosemary 5, 198
Their First Divorce Case 217, 228
Their First Kidnapping Case 217, 228
There Are No Villains 217–218
Thew, Harry 27, 76, 188
Thew, Manora 17, 20, 229
A Thief in the Dark 218
The Thirteenth Chair 218
The Thirteenth Hour 48, 218
$30,000 218–219
Thomas, Olive 131
Thompson, Garfield 17, 102, 133, 170
Thorèze, Maurice 15, 183
The Thornton Jewel Mystery 200, 219
Thou Shalt Not Steal 219
Three Bags of Silver 8
Three-Fingered Kate 80, 191, 219–220
Three-Fingered Kate 219
Three-Fingered Kate: Her Second Victim, the Art Dealer 219
Three-Fingered Kate: Her Victim the Banker 219
Three-Fingered Kate: The Case of the Chemical Fumes 219
Three-Fingered Kate: The Episode of the Sacred Elephants 219
Three-Fingered Kate: The Pseudo-Quartette 219–220
Three-Fingered Kate: The Wedding Presents 220
Three Keys 220, 253
The Three Students 220
A Thrilling Detective Story 220
Thrilling Stories from the Strand 4, 10, 45, 75, 85, 110, 220, 250, 263
Through the Dark 220
Through the Wall 220–221
The Ticket of Leave Man 28, 221
Tidmarsh, Ferdinand 246
The Tiger of San Pedro 9, 221
The Tiger's Trail 221, 261

Tigris 222
Tih Minh 222
Tiller, Prentice 140, 223
Times Have Changed 223
Tipped Off 223
Too Much Married 223
La torre dell'espiazion 223
Torrence, Ernest 33
Die Toten Erwachen 224
Tourneur, Maurice 11, 117, 146, 149, 172, 241
The Tower of Terror 223
Tracked by the Police Dog 73, 224
Traffic in Souls 224
The Tragedy of Barnsdale Manor 168, 224
The Trail of Graft 98, 224
The Trail of the Cigarette 217, 224–225
The Trail of the Octopus 225
Trailing the Counterfeiters 225, 228
Train, Arthur Cheyney 134, 147, 262
Trapped by Camera 225
Trapped by Pinkertons 225
Trapped in the Great Metropolis 225
Travers, Richard 4
Travers, Roy 110, 114, 134, 158, 193
Tree, Madge 3, 114
The Tremarne Case 168, 225
Trent, Anthony 225–226
Trent's Last Case 226
Treville, George 6, 17, 26, 148, 152, 190, 206, 210
The Trey o' Hearts 226, 262
Trimble, Lawrence 13
The Triple Clue 217, 226–227
Troubles of an Amateur Detective 227
Truesdell, Fred 11
The Trunk Mystery 98, 227
Trust, ou les batailles de l'argent 227
The Truthful Liar 227
Tucker, George Loane 17, 91, 142, 224
A Turf Conspiracy 227–228, 255
The Turn of the Wheel 228
Turnbull, Margaret 31, 50, 160, 184, 246
Turner, F.A. 4, 134, 138, 157
Turner, Florence 13, 144
Turner, George 196
Turner, Otis 29, 70, 100, 115, 122, 216
Tuttle, Frank 214
Twain, Mark 184, 262
Twin Pawns 228, 244
The Two Sleuths 228

Ultus 228
Ultus: The Man from the Dead 228–229
Ultus 1: The Townsend Mystery 229
Ultus 2: The Ambassador's Diamond 229
Ultus 3: The Grey Lady 229
Ultus 4: The Traitor's Fate 229

Ultus 5: The Secret of the Night 229
Ultus 6: The Three Button Mystery 229
Under Suspicion 229–230
Unexpected Places 230, 249
Unheimliche Geschichten 230
Unknown Treasures 230
An Unpaid Ransom 37, 230
Unseen Foes 163, 230
The Unseen Witness 217, 230–1
Unsell, Eve 76, 171, 215, 217
An Unwilling Burglar 231
Up and At 'Em 231
The U.S. Revenue Detective 230
Usihara, Kiyohiko 3

Vale, Louise 20, 85, 221
Vale, Travers 175, 221
Vale, Vola 11, 111, 184
Valentine, Jimmy 10–11, 231, 256
Valentine, Philip 53
The Valley of Fear 110, 231
Valli, Virginia 28, 52
Vallis, Robert 88
Les Vampires 118, 231–232
Vanardy, Varick 12, 94–5, 253
Vance, Louis Joseph 11, 22, 28, 37, 40, 57, 60, 81, 97, 127–9, 173, 226, 262–263
The Vanderhoff Affair 232
Van Doren, Fernande 10
Vane, Charles 9, 208
Vane, Denton 16, 94, 102, 133, 144, 168
Van Ehlers, Ada 61, 92, 103, 120, 143
The Vanishing Cracksman 48, 232
Vanity 232
Van Rensselaer, Frederic 95, 253
Veidt, Conrad 25, 117, 230
Veiller, Bayard 11, 202, 218
Velvet Fingers 232
Vengeance Is Mine 232
The Ventures of Marguerite 193, 232–233
Venus of Venice 233
Vep, Irma 231–232
The Verdict 233
Vernon, Bobby 152
Vidocq 78, 118, 142, 233, 250
Vidocq, François-Eugène 233
Vignola, Robert G. 42, 104, 232
The Village Sleuth 233–234
Vincent, James 65, 107, 244
Vintner, Georges 23, 36, 51, 75, 164–5, 179, 197, 242
Violet Dare, Detective 233
A Voice in the Dark 234
The Voice in the Fog 234
The Voice on the Wire 234
Le Voleur mondain 235

Wakefield, Renée 8, 38, 110, 120, 152, 153, 156, 166, 168, 190, 224, 225, 246
The Wakefield Case 235
Walcamp, Marie 189
Walcott, Arthur 15, 152, 228
Waleran, Rice 223

Walker, Lillian 133, 169
Wall, David 39, 49, 196–197, 217, 225, 230, 235
The Wall Street Mystery 160, 217, 235
Wallace, Edgar 3, 15, 50, 55, 59, 67, 85, 88, 101–102, 134–135, 138, 189–191, 216, 235, 263
Wallingford, J. Rufus 235
Walsh, George 22, 89, 135
Walter the Sleuth 235
Walthall, Henry 21, 35, 81, 87, 127, 212–213, 260
Walton, Gladys 16, 124
Wanted at Headquarters 235–236
Warde, Ernest C. 14, 65, 101, 114, 167, 219
Warden, Fanny 163
The Ware Case 236
Warning Shadows 236–237
Warwick, Robert 10, 16, 89, 206
Washburn, Bryant 13–14, 38, 62, 154
The Wasp 237
The Waterwheel of Death 237
The Way Women Love 237, 257
Wayne, Maude 12
The Web of Chance 237–238
Webb, Dick 15
Webb, Dunstan 74, 102
Webbs, Stuart 34, 59, 92–3, 135, 171–2, 224, 234, 238
Webster, McRae 12, 118, 138, 194
Wehlen, Emmy 171, 232
Der Weibliche Detektiv 238
A Weighty Matter for a Detective 238
Weiman, Rita 4
Weir, Hugh C. 7, 97, 132, 191, 229, 263–264
A Well-Planned West End Jewel Robbery 7, 238
Wells, Raymond 89, 104, 121
Werner, Karl 117, 143, 197
West, Billie 61, 117, 193
West, Charles 62, 65
West, Langdon 23, 37, 44, 68, 134, 230
West, Roland 13, 23, 146, 165
West, Walter 236
West, William 94, 114, 137, 150, 188
The West Case 153, 238
Westlake, Dorothy 112
Westlake, Eva 20
Weston, Charles 62, 136
Weston, Harold 13, 152
Westover, Winifred 233
Weyher, Ruth 171
What Happened to Mary? 238–239
What Women Will Do 239
What's Bred … Comes Out in the Flesh 239
Wheels of Justice 239
While London Sleeps 241
Whispering Smith 138, 145, 209, 239–240, 262
Whispering Smith 239–240
Whispering Smith Rides 240

Whispering Wires 240
White, Glen 39, 49, 87, 113, 196–7, 217, 224, 226–227, 230, 235
White, Pearl 30–31, 79, 83, 108, 112, 163, 174, 194, 210, 257, 261, 268
The White Circle 241, 262
The White Moll 241, 260
Whitney, Claire 41, 141, 193, 215, 245
Who Is Coletti? 243
Who Is Number One? 241
Who Killed Walton? 241–242
Wightman, Ruth 4
Wilbur, Crane 146, 152, 176, 192
Wild, Wild Susan 242
Willets, Gilson 9, 86, 142, 155, 185, 221
William Baluchet, roi des détectives 22, 242
Williams, Earle 5, 16–18, 30, 67, 102, 111, 132, 184, 194, 207
Williams, Eric Bransby 4, 10, 111
Williams, Kathlyn 8
Williamson, A.M. 126, 129, 149, 244, 264
Williamson, Alice M. 125, 129, 149, 244–245, 264
Williamson, C.N. 126, 129, 149, 244, 264
Williamson, J.C. 93, 102, 198
Willis, Hubert 3, 9, 26, 30, 34–35, 43–44, 56–57, 77–78, 96, 123, 165–16, 189–191, 196–197, 207–209, 211, 220–221
Willy Walrus, Detective 242
Wilson, Ben 37, 48, 106, 151, 154–9, 167, 182–183, 225, 232, 234, 255
Wilson, Frank 51, 57, 62, 84, 90, 96, 142, 152, 185, 196, 205, 207, 228, 238
Wilson, Lois 11
Windemere, Fred 105, 215, 233
Windsor, Claire 4, 161
Wing, William 138, 157, 177
Winter, Nick 23, 36, 51, 75, 78, 159, 164–165, 179, 197, 210, 242–243
The Wise Detectives 243
Withey, Chet 180, 185, 216
The Witness for the Defense 243
Wits vs. Wits 243
The Wizard 22, 243
Wo ist Coletti? 243
Die Wohltäterin der Menschheit 243
Wolf Pack 67
Wolf's Clothing 243–244
A Woman in Grey 244, 264
The Woman in White 244–245
Woman of Mystery 245
A Woman Redeemed 245, 250
The Woman Under Oath 245
The Woman Who Dared 245
The Woman Who Touched the Legs 18, 246
A Woman's Perfidy 112
A Woman's Wit 188
Wontner, Arthur 67

Wood, Freeman 96, 187
Woodrow, Nancy Mann Waddel 30, 111, 264
Woods, Frank E. 26, 214
Woods, Walter 37, 89, 97, 217
Woodville, A. Caton 228–229
Worldly Thief 235
The World's Great Snare 246, 259
Worne, Duke 37, 139, 151, 211, 225
Worsley, Wallace 4
Worthington, William 29, 96, 100, 115
The Would-Be Detective 246
The Would-Be Detectives 246
Wright, Fred E. 38
Wright, George A. 45
Wright, Helen 29
Wright, Humberston 42, 51, 54, 90, 96, 102, 120, 140, 152, 185, 207, 238,
Wright, Mack 126
Wright, Nanine 97
Wright, William Lord 4, 32
The Wrong Box 262
The Wrong Countess 9
Wynn, Ed 195
Wynn, Molly 51
Wynne, Bert 91

The Yellow Claw 137, 246, 261
The Yellow Face 246
The Yellow Pawn 246, 257
The York Mystery 168, 246
Yoshida, Hosaku 3
Yost, Herbert 5–7, 109, 167, 214
You'd Be Surprised 246–247
Young, Clara Kimball 46–47, 159
Young, Clarice 226
Young, Howard Irving 176, 232
Young, James 111, 194

Young, Lucille 120
Young, Noah 69, 204
Young, Roland 203
Young, Tammany 176
Young, Waldemar 27, 29, 96, 127
Younger, A.P. 11

Za la Mort 247
Zangwill, Israel 176, 264
Zeyn, Willy 92, 112, 117, 143, 154, 197
Zigomar 247
Zigomar 247
Zigomar contre Nick Carter 247
Zigomar, peau d'anguille 247
Zigomar, roi des voleurs 247
Zone of Death 72
Zorro 73–74, 260
Zudora or The Twenty Million Dollar Mystery 248

www.ingramcontent.com/pod-product-compliance
Lightning Source LLC
Chambersburg PA
CBHW081543300426
44116CB00015B/2740